EYEWITNESS COMPANIONS

Classical Music

GENERAL EDITOR
JOHN BURROWS
WITH CHARLES WIFFEN

and contributions from
Robert Ainsley, Duncan Barker, Karl Lutchmayer, Ivan Hewett,
Lisa Colton, Andrew Wilson, Nathanial Vallois, Ann Van Allen Russell,
Jenny Nex, Richard Langham-Smith, Sam Thompson, Simon Rees

780.9
CLA

"MUSIC EXPRESSES THAT WHICH CANNOT BE PUT INTO WORDS AND THAT WHICH CANNOT REMAIN SILENT." *Victor Hugo*

LONDON, NEW YORK,
MUNICH, MELBOURNE, AND DELHI

Senior Art Editor	Juliette Norsworthy
Project Art Editors	Victoria Clark, Maxine Lea
Designers	Liz Sephton, Francis Wong
Design Assistance	Paul Drislane, Kenny Grant, Vanessa Marr
Project Editors	Sam Atkinson, Catherine Day, Ferdie McDonald
Editors	Caroline Reed, Andrew Szudek, Belinda Wilkinson, Darren Henley (for Classic FM)
Picture Research	Maria Gibbs
Jacket Designer	Nathalie Goodwin
Jacket Editor	Mariza O'Keeffe
DTP	John Goldsmid
Production	Joanna Bull
Managing Editor	Debra Wolter
Managing Art Editor	Phil Ormerod
Editorial Director	Andrew Heritage
Art Director	Bryn Walls

First published in 2005 by
Dorling Kindersley Limited
80 Strand, London WC2R ORL
Penguin Group

First American Edition, 2005

Published in the United States by

DK Publishing, Inc.

375 Hudson Street, New York, New York 10014

04 05 06 06 08 09 10 9 8 7 6 5 4 3 2 1

Copyright 2004 Dorling Kindesley Limited

Library of Congress Cataloging-in-Publication Data
Classical music / general editor, John Burrows.-- 1st American ed.
    p. cm. -- (Eyewitness companions)
Includes index.
ISBN 0-7566-0958-5 (flexi)
1. Music appreciation. I. Burrows, John, 1939- II. Series.
MT6.C564 2005
780'.9--dc22

                    2004024370

Colour reproduction GRB, Italy
Printed and bound in China by L Rex

Discover more at

www.dk.com

CONTENTS

FOREWORD

I was first introduced by my Mother to the live performance of Classical music when I was 10 years old, at the Albert Hall in Nottingham. Sir Malcolm Sargent was conducting the Halle Orchestra, with the soloist Moura Lympany playing the Rachmaninov Piano Concerto No 2. The moment the orchestra began tuning up I was hooked and determined that music would play a vital role in my life. I played piano but it became obvious I was not cut out to be a professional musician, and so I became a music promoter. My first Classical concert was in 1970 with the London Symphony Orchestra conducted by André Previn at the New Theatre, Oxford. Since then I have been privileged to work among many musicians of the highest international calibre.

For many years I had wanted to share my passion and commitment to Classical music in book form. I first approached DK when they were developing an illustrated handbook on Shakespeare. I instantly realised there was much scope for an imaginatively illustrated reference book which covered as much of the subject as would be usefully practical. The book should inform, excite, inspire and be very accessible to Classical music lovers of all ages and levels of knowledge. Two very busy years later, I am delighted to present this book to the public. Many people have been involved with the creation of this book and I am indebted to them – it would not have happened without them. A big thanks to my dear friend Richard Havers, the Music Guru and now a major author himself, whose encouragement was vital to me; to my good friend Lady Solti; and to Dr Charles Wiffen and the many writers and academics who have collaborated on the book.

JOHN BURROWS
OBE HonRCM.

INTRODUCTION

Music has played a vital role in my life and from being a child in Yorkshire I was taught to love music by my father who was passionate about the value of music in our lives. Music is in my opinion the missing link between the physical and the spirit; it is also a great educator. Like my late husband, Georg Solti, I have always believed in the value of education and the knowledge that it is the only true foundation for life.

Without education, in whatever form, a child is denied a proper chance. The arts have been an integral part of my life, the theatre in all its disciplines, the visual arts, architecture, the countryside – which after all is nature's art when you consider the music of a mountain stream or the song of a bird. Music has dominated life for me and my daughters through the great influence and accomplishments of my husband. How lucky we were to have learnt music from him. He had extraordinary dynamism, and sheer vitality. He believed that music was a vital part of human society and over-whelmingly the greatest language of communication the best possible ambassador of world peace.

He was a great inspiration to us all and he said on many occasions "My life is the greatest proof that if you have talent, determination and luck, you will make it in the end. Never give up!" Because of the Second World War his early career was interrupted and for many years without any work, life was difficult. How often he was tempted to give up. He always believed that he had a guardian angel who guided him through difficult times and with determination and hard work he really did "make it in the end".

Georg was considered to be one of the greatest orchestral conductors of modern times and he helped shape the finest orchestras in the world. His output was astonishingly prolific, with 33 Grammy Awards and over 300 recordings. But, throughout our life together he wanted to share his music-making and teaching. I have watched with close interest the way this book has developed from its early stages of planning. Although no book can convey the extraordinary and rich aural experience that lies at the heart of music's impact, the *Eyewitness Companion Guide to Classical Music* goes further than most in providing the reader with useful signposts and information as they begin their voyage or careers in the world of serious music.

Many books have been written for aficionados and experts, and speak only to them, in a rarified and esoteric language. Such books often alienate the beginner, the student, or those who have always wanted to enter that world, but are frightened off by the perceived elitism and old traditions. Some books merely provide the bare bones of composers biographies,

MUSIC AND POPULAR CULTURE
In recent years, the exposure to, and making of, serious music has been greatly broadened through recording, radio, culture, and television.

dates and recordings, and make no attempt to convey the magic and the majesty, the power and the passion, and the sheer excitement of the musical experience. We are lucky to have such a rich pool of talent around us, performers and composers, who wish to share their enthusiasm and love of music. Recording, broadcasting, and the myriad means of other musical reproduction available to us today have greatly increased everybody's access to great music. This book has been conceived for the lay person, and can be used as an authoritative ready reference, or as a beginner's guide. Its rich array of illustrations serves to build an impression not just of each composer's life and interests, but hopefully a glimpse of their creative aspirations, too. Over 300 pieces of music are examined in useful detail. I hope this book will provide a useful traveller's guide both for the initiated and for those just setting out on their voyage of musical discovery.

Lady Solti.

INTRODUCING
CLASSICAL
MUSIC

The elements of
CLASSICAL MUSIC

The basic materials of music are pitch and rhythm. Conventions in Western art music have arisen over the centuries by which composers and performers can organize and manipulate these materials. Some composers achieve memorable effects by breaking the "rules", others by working imaginatively within them.

Musical notes are assigned different pitches, and are put together to form melodies. These may contain phrases, which can be thought of as musical sentences. Often each phrase contains as many notes as can be sung comfortably in a single breath. The simultaneous sounding of a number of different notes creates harmony. The flavour of these melodies and harmonies often results from the types of scales (or collections of notes) that are used.

If the individual notes of a composition are bricks, then the rhythm is like mortar, holding them together. Rhythm, at its most basic, is the beat of a piece of music and the metre – or time signature – the way in which the beat is grouped.

An entire piece of music can be constructed from these simple materials. It is like a building, designed by the composer according to a "form" – as with an architect's plan. A symphony is like a castle (with its own grand structure or form), whereas a short song will have a different and less complex form (more like a modest cottage). The colour or texture of a piece of music depends on how the voices or instruments are used, and how they are combined or orchestrated.

PITCH

For a sound to be produced, a vibration must be set up in the air. This may result from the motion of a taut string, the skin of a drum, or the column of air within a cylinder. If the vibration is regular, it is heard as an identifiable note of a certain pitch. If the vibration is fast, the pitch is heard as high; if it is slow, it will sound low or deep. As a general rule, the longer the string or column of air, the lower the pitch. The low threshold of human hearing is about 16–20 vibrations per second, while the upper threshold is about 20,000 vibrations per second.

The lowest notes of a pipe organ range from about 20 vibrations per second (or "cycles per second"), while a piccolo can reach about 4,176 cycles. An adult choir can produce anything from 64 to 1,500 cycles.

STANDARDIZED PITCH

The letter-name "A" is given to the pitch of 440 cycles per second, which is produced by a key just to the right of the middle of the piano keyboard (known as the note or "tone" a"). This is a standard universal measure of pitch. Without it, players would experience great difficulty adapting their instruments as they moved round the world.

MUSICAL NOTATION

In Western music, seven letters of the alphabet are assigned to different pitches, ranging from A to G. If you play all the white keys on the piano keyboard from one A up to the next A (eight notes) you will have

HARPIST PLAYING
On the harp, the shorter strings produce the higher notes, demonstrating clearly the relationship between the length of a vibrating string and its pitch.

covered an "octave". This particular series of notes corresponds to a scale known as the natural minor scale. Once you reach the next A you can repeat the cycle, and will hear higher versions of the same notes. If you start from C and repeat the procedure, you will hear the scale of C major.

If the length of a string is halved, a pitch is produced which is exactly double the frequency of the original pitch and sounds eight notes (or an octave) higher. In other words, if you halve the length of a string vibrating at 440 frequencies, you will hear the pitch of 880 frequencies, which corresponds to the next (or higher) A on the keyboard.

Although there are only seven letter names, other notes (the black keys on a piano, known as sharps or flats) exist in between some of these to produce a total of 12 notes.

INTERVALS

The gaps between the notes are known as "intervals", and moving from one note on the piano keyboard to its nearest neighbour covers the interval of a "semitone". Of course, with other instruments (such as the violin) it is possible to play in between these notes;

PIPE ORGAN
The lengths of the many pipes on a traditional organ determine the notes the instrument can produce.

PITCH AND NOTATION

Western music uses horizontal lines and spaces against which to plot musical notes in graphic notation. Since the 17th century, five lines have been used, comprising a "staff" or "stave". A sign known as a "clef" is used at the beginning of each stave to indicate which line or space should be used to denote a particular note. The most common clefs are the treble (or G) and bass (or F) clefs, the former being used for higher pitches and the latter for lower pitches. Thus, a violinist would typically use the treble clef, while a double-bass player would usually use the bass clef. A pianist normally uses both, the treble clef being usually assigned to the upper half of the keyboard (played by the right hand) and the bass clef to the lower half. The diagram below shows the relationship of the piano keyboard to the treble and bass clefs.

SHARPS AND FLATS

These are used to raise (sharpen) and lower (flatten) a note by a semitone. The interval from, for example, G to A is known as a "tone", while the interval from a G to G♯ is a "semitone" (the smallest possible interval on the keyboard). Although the G♯ is a raised G, it is in fact the same note as an A♭ (in other words, a lowered A).

		FLAT
♯SHARP	♭	

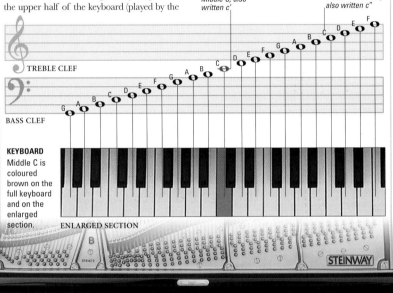

Middle C, also written c'

C above middle C, also written c"

TREBLE CLEF

BASS CLEF

KEYBOARD
Middle C is coloured brown on the full keyboard and on the enlarged section.

ENLARGED SECTION

STEINWAY

BASSOON

The range of the bassoon (the bass instrument of the woodwind family) is just over three octaves, similar to that of the male voice. Its lower notes correspond to the low notes of a bass singer, but its top notes are somewhat higher than a tenor. This range is similar to that of the cello and the trombone.

CLARINET

The range of the clarinet corresponds to the female voice. Its lowest notes are in the alto region while its high notes are close to those of a high soprano. It has a range of three and a half octaves and is most powerful in its upper register. The oboe, trumpet, and violin all have similar ranges to the clarinet.

PICCOLO

The piccolo (a small flute) is the smallest woodwind instrument and therefore produces the highest pitch of all the instruments of the family. Its range is nearly three octaves and it can reach higher pitches than the female voice. It often doubles lower instruments to provide brilliance and penetration in orchestral music.

SINGING IN HARMONY
The simultaneous production of musical tones in a complex interweaving of harmony and melody is one of the distinguishing features of Western music.

indeed, it is common for string instruments and voices to slide between notes for expressive effect.

HARMONY

Harmony is the result of combining musical notes, and when these are played simultaneously, they are said to form a "chord". Some chords sound dissonant, others harmonious or consonant. Harmony can be regarded as the resolution of tension. In conventional tonal music, certain phrases end in "cadences" (or closing progressions of chords). Common examples are the "perfect" cadence (which sounds conclusive), the "imperfect" (which sounds inconclusive and demands some kind of continuation), and the "plagal" (which sounds serious and final and is often used for the "Amen" of a hymn).

RHYTHM AND TEMPO

Many human activities, such as running, walking, or dancing produce distinctive rhythms, which are often reproduced in music. Rhythm involves not only the positioning or spacing of notes in time, but also their duration, and both of these can be notated in Western music (see p.22). Composers can show duration in terms of sound or silence: for sound, note shapes are used; "rests",

HARMONY AND INTERVALS

If two notes played together are separated by a consonant (harmonious) interval, the resulting sound will be pleasant or relaxing to our ears, whereas the notes of a dissonant interval clash with each other and demand to be resolved by a suitable consonance. The intervals considered dissonant have changed since the Middle Ages, but since the Classical and early Romantic eras the intervals illustrated below have been considered either consonant or dissonant.

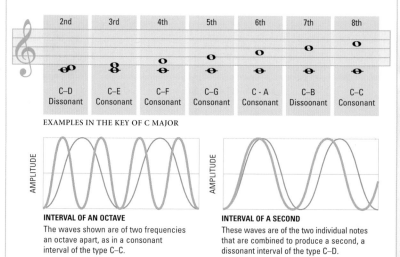

	2nd	3rd	4th	5th	6th	7th	8th
	C–D	C–E	C–F	C–G	C - A	C–B	C–C
	Dissonant	Consonant	Consonant	Consonant	Consonant	Dissoonant	Consonant

EXAMPLES IN THE KEY OF C MAJOR

INTERVAL OF AN OCTAVE
The waves shown are of two frequencies an octave apart, as in a consonant interval of the type C–C.

INTERVAL OF A SECOND
These waves are of the two individual notes that are combined to produce a second, a dissonant interval of the type C–D.

with corresponding values and names, are used to denote periods of silence.

The pulse (commonly known as the "beat") is a regular unit of time around which the rhythm of a piece is organized. In a march, this would be the position in time of each footstep. The composer will decide whether the pulse should be a crotchet or a minim, or any other note value.

The speed of the pulse is the "tempo" of the work. Most composers have used Italian terms to indicate tempo. Since the early 19th century, musicians have also used metronome settings. (A metronome is a device that can be set to "tick" at varying speeds and is calibrated according to divisions of the minute – for example, 60 or 120 beats to the minute.

METRE

The metre corresponds to the grouping of the pulse. Much classical music is grouped in twos or threes.

PULSE AND TEMPO	
ITALIAN	**ENGLISH**
Grave	Very slowly
Lento	Slowly
Largo	Broadly
Larghetto	Rather broadly
Adagio	Leisurely
Andante	At a walking pace
Moderato	Moderately
Allegretto	Fairly quickly
Allegro	Fast
Vivace	Lively
Presto	Very quickly
Prestissimo	As fast as possible

Each group is known as a "measure" or "bar" and in notation is separated by a "barline". The metre is indicated by a "time signature", such as 3/4. The top number shows the number of pulses or beats in a bar, while the lower number shows the value assigned to each beat. The time signature 3/4 indicates that there are three crotchet beats in a bar (typical of a dance such

NATURAL RHYTHMS
In nature, the sounds of horses cantering or of waves crashing on a beach create powerful, distinctive rhythms. Music owes much to such rhythmic sounds, not to mention more immediate rhythms, such as breathing and the beating of the human heart.

NOTES, TIME, RHYTHM, AND METRE

The chart below shows the time values of the notes used in Western music. For example, two minims are equal in length to a semibreve and two quavers are equal to a crotchet. All values are relative, however; a crotchet is not an absolute length, such as a second, but varies according to the composer's instructions or the performer's instinct. In slow music, a crotchet could be over two seconds in length; in quick music, less than half a second. The USA uses different names for these values, such as "whole note", and these are given below the English names.

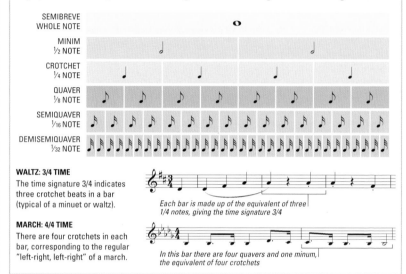

SEMIBREVE WHOLE NOTE	𝅝
MINIM ½ NOTE	𝅗𝅥
CROTCHET ¼ NOTE	♩
QUAVER ⅛ NOTE	♪
SEMIQUAVER ¹⁄₁₆ NOTE	♬
DEMISEMIQUAVER ¹⁄₃₂ NOTE	

WALTZ: 3/4 TIME
The time signature 3/4 indicates three crotchet beats in a bar (typical of a minuet or waltz).

Each bar is made up of the equivalent of three 1/4 notes, giving the time signature 3/4

MARCH: 4/4 TIME
There are four crotchets in each bar, corresponding to the regular "left-right, left-right" of a march.

In this bar there are four quavers and one minum, the equivalent of four crotchets

as a minuet or waltz). A march rhythm could be given the time signature 2/4, in which there would be two crotchet beats in every bar.

SCALES AND TONALITY

A scale (from the Latin *scala*, meaning steps) is a step-wise series of notes, usually between one note and the next note of that name an octave higher. In the West, scales may be traced back to medieval "modes", which were based on the musical ideas of the Ancient Greeks. These eventually came to be accepted as the principal scales for all music in the 16th century: the Ionian became the "major" scale, and the Aeolian the "natural minor" scale. Traditionally the associations of the major scale are positive – sometimes joyful, sometimes triumphant; Beethoven's "Eroica" Symphony, for example, is in the heroic key of E flat major. The minor scale is generally recognized as more sombre in mood – sometimes plaintive and sometimes tragic. The Funeral March from Chopin's Piano Sonata No. 2 is in the key of B flat minor.

MUSICAL FORM

All musical works – however short or long – are organized within a kind of frame, known a "form". The two

WALTZ TIME
One of the most familiar time signatures to dancers, the basic waltz metre (one-two-three, one-two-three) is three beats to each bar of music.

basic forms are "binary" (two sections, stated one after the other and sometimes repeated) and "ternary" (three sections, perhaps comprising section A, followed by section B, then section A again – musical sections or paragraphs are often identified by letters of the alphabet). Variants of these are to be found in more complex forms such as the "rondo", "variation", and "sonata" forms (see glossary).

DYNAMICS

Just as the pitch or rhythm of musical sound can be varied, so can the volume or intensity of that sound. In Western music, this variability

INDIAN MUSICIANS
Across the world, most cultures have their own scales, consisting not only of different notes from those used in the west, but of different numbers of notes.

has become known as "dynamics". As with tempo, it is common to use Italian terms to describe different dynamics, all of which are relative rather than absolute.

DYNAMICS	
Pianissimo (pp)	Very quietly
Piano (p)	Quietly
Mezzo piano (mp)	Moderately quietly
Mezzo forte (mf)	Moderately loudly
Forte (f)	Loudly
Fortissimo (ff)	Very loudly

KEY TO THE "WAVEFORMS" USED IN THE BOOK

Twenty-two of the "focus" works that appear in the book feature a "waveform" (a computerized image of the music) which shows the acoustic properties of a particular recording of the work. The information shown in the waveform relates *only* to that specific recording; another performer or ensemble could have performed the same work faster or slower, or placed climaxes at different points. See p. 512 for a list of the recordings used to make the waveforms.

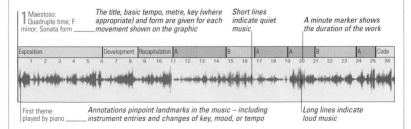

1 Maestoso:
Quadruple time; F minor; Sonata form _____ *The title, basic tempo, metre, key (where appropriate) and form are given for each movement shown on the graphic*

Short lines indicate quiet music

A minute marker shows the duration of the work

| Exposition | | | | | | Development | Recapitulation | A | | B | A | | A | | B | | A | Coda |
| 1 | 2 | 3 | 4 | 5 | 6 | 7 | 8 | 9 | 10 | 11 | 12 | 13 | 14 | 15 | 16 | 17 | 18 | 19 | 20 | 21 | 22 | 23 | 24 | 25 | 26 |

First theme played by piano _____

Annotations pinpoint landmarks in the music – including instrument entries and changes of key, mood, or tempo

Long lines indicate loud music

Classical Music
INSTRUMENTS

The design, construction, and acoustics of instruments change as musicians explore different ways of achieving what composers ask of them, and as instrument makers experiment with new materials and technologies. In the process, some instruments become obsolete, while those that fit in with new trends become popular.

Today's symphony orchestra has its roots in 16th-century instrumental consorts (p.27) and 17th-century bands. The earliest orchestras, usually attached to a court, a church, or a theatre, varied in structure from place to place. They were often directed from the keyboard or by the principal violinist.

During the 18th century, as popular works (such as those by Haydn and Mozart) began to be played all over Europe, some standardization of the orchestra became necessary. A string section comprising violins, violas, cellos, and double basses was usually joined by two oboes and two bassoons, with the occasional addition of two horns, a flute, two trumpets, and timpani. The clarinet became a standard member of the orchestra only at the end of the 18th century.

The 19th century saw the rise of public concerts in large halls, which necessitated louder instruments and larger orchestras. As a result, instruments changed: woodwind key systems were redesigned; the brass acquired valves; stringed instruments were adapted to enable them to project further. Larger and smaller versions of woodwind instruments, such as the piccolo, cor anglais, and bass clarinet, featured more frequently. Instruments were also added to the lower end of the brass section, with trombones and, later, tubas becoming standard members of the orchestra.

THE ORCHESTRA TODAY

The orchestra had by now more or less attained its present form, though in the 20th century a whole new range of percussion instruments became available. The Early Music revival has seen the recreation of historic styles of orchestra, but the dominant orchestral line-up remains the symphony orchestra under the direction of a conductor, with orchestras resident in most major cities throughout the world.

Early instruments

Many instruments from the past have disappeared from mainstream usage or have been replaced by modern equivalents. Over the last 50 years, however, makers and musicians have revived these instruments in an attempt to create historically informed performances. The ancestors of modern woodwinds usually have no keys, while those of the brass section include trumpets and horns without valves. Early stringed instruments, which have gut strings and lower tensions, tend to be softer in tone than their modern equivalents.

STRINGS

Viols have six or seven strings, with frets across the fingerboard. The outward-curving bow is held underhand. Some smaller viols, such as the **viola d'amore**, have additional sympathetic strings that run through the bridge and under the fingerboard. **Lutes** are plucked with the right hand and are often used as continuo instruments or to accompany singing. Some have additional bass strings known as diapasons. The **hurdy-gurdy** uses a wheel operated by a crank handle to "bow" the strings, and a small keyboard to stop the strings.

Peg box

Tuning pegs

Keyboard

Cover over rosined wheel

Handle

HURDY-GURDY

Decorative carved head

Sympathetic strings

Bridge

Tailpiece

VIOLA D'AMORE (1774)

Second peg box for bass diapason strings

Fretted fingerboard

Diapasons

Rose hole

18TH-CENTURY GERMAN BASS LUTE

Tuning pegs

Fingerboard

ENGLISH-MADE BASS VIOL (1713)

KEYBOARDS

The **harpsichord** is used in Early-Music ensembles as a continuo instrument, to add brilliance and rhythm to the texture. The strings, made of iron or brass, are plucked by small pieces of quill. The **virginal** and **spinet** are plucked in a similar way, while the **clavichord** uses small brass flags – tangents – to strike the strings. Clavichords are perfect domestic instruments as they are very quiet. In the **organ**, different sounds are produced by making pipes of different materials with a variety of cross-sections, and by exciting the air in the pipes in various ways, such as blowing air across a fipple (as in the recorder) or by using reeds.

Decorated keyboard

18TH-CENTURY CLAVICHORD

BRASS

The **cornett** was a treble instrument with open finger holes, made from a single piece of ivory or two carved pieces of wood glued together. The **serpent** was used as a bass instrument in military and church bands in the 18th and 19th centuries. The earliest **trumpets** were "natural" instruments (without valves or keys) which played a single harmonic series. Various devices were added in the 18th and 19th centuries to enable them to play more notes. **Horns** were also originally natural instruments, sometimes equipped with crooks to enable them to be played in different keys.

"Acorn cup" mouthpiece

Two carved pieces of walnut, bound with string and leather

Finger holes, placed for the convenience of the player's hands, were not acoustically correct

Keys used to change notes

Crooks attached to extend length of horn

19TH-CENTURY SERPENT

Open finger holes

LATE-18TH-CENTURY KEYED TRUMPET

18TH-CENTURY NATURAL HORN

CORNETT

WOODWIND

The earliest wind instruments were pipes made from wood or bone, with finger holes to change the sounding length and hence the pitch of the note produced. The **shawm** family are sounded by a double reed on a metal staple fitted into a "pirouette". Shawms were popular from the 13th to the 17th century and ranged from high soprano to a low bass called a pommer. Also a double-reed instrument, the **crumhorn** hides its reed within a cap. Its heyday was in the 16th and 17th centuries, when it was used to accompany religious ceremonies as well as secular dances. **Recorders** have a fipple or whistle-style mouthpiece and holes for one thumb and seven fingers. They were widely used as solo and consort instruments before the 19th century and have re-emerged in the 20th century for teaching music in schools. Many early woodwinds were made of close-grained woods such as boxwood, but makers have also experimented with ivory, glass, and various metals.

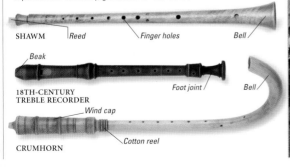

SHAWM   Reed   Finger holes   Bell

Beak

18TH-CENTURY TREBLE RECORDER

Foot joint   Bell

Wind cap

Cotton reel

CRUMHORN

A WIND CONSORT

Consorts were small groups of mixed instruments. The instruments played in a wind consort included the hautbois (ancestor of the oboe), cornett, and sackbut (ancestor of the trombone). In the 17th century, wind consorts would usually have been heard outside, often at gatherings of important people, with quieter string consorts used indoors.

Strings

The string section is the largest group in the orchestra and forms its core, and the leading voice among the strings is the violin, an instrument of extraordinary range and versatility. Orchestral violins are divided into two sections: "firsts" and "seconds". Violins, violas, cellos, and double basses are primarily played with a bow but, like the harp, can also be plucked. The left hand is used to stop the strings in order to change their vibrating length and hence the pitch of the notes. A variety of tonal effects can be achieved by placing the bow closer to or further away from the bridge, by damping the vibrations of the bridge using a mute, or by applying different bowing techniques. Since the early 19th century, many earlier stringed instruments have been altered to increase their volume and projection.

Orchestra

- First violins
- Second violins
- Violas
- Cellos
- Double basses
- Harp

Scroll

Screw for adjusting tension of hair

Tuning pegs

Rosined horsehair

Fingerboard, usually made of ebony

Ribs, made of maple

Table, made of pine

Carved wood, usually pernambuco

Bridge

Supporting spike

VIOLIN

Characteristics: With four strings tuned in fifths, violins are agile and versatile, and can play two or three notes simultaneously.
History: Early violins were in use in Italy from the early 16th century. Cremona and Brescia became important centres of violin-making from 1550.

VIOLA

Characteristics: The alto of the family, the viola is tuned a fifth below the violin. It has a darker, richer sound than the violin.
History: Larger and smaller viola-type instruments were used for both tenor and alto lines from the early 16th century. Its modern role developed in the 18th century.

CELLO

Characteristics: Tuned an octave below the viola, the cello (violoncello) is the bass of the violin family. It is also capable of playing virtuoso passages.
History: Appearing in the early 16th century, cellos were made by many of the famous Cremona violin makers.

Peg box. The tuning pegs jut out at the back and a cogwheel mechanism is used for tuning

Heavy, short bow

The double bass normally has four strings, but some are made with five

The double bass often retains the sloping shoulders of the medieval viol

Upper bouts

French-style frog

F-holes

Soundboard

Lower bouts

Bag for carrying bow

HARP

Characteristics: The modern orchestral harp has 47 strings stretched between the neck and soundboard, together with seven pedals for altering the pitches of the strings. As well as playing plucked chords, the harpist can use techniques such as glissandos and harmonics to create special effects. Harps are often associated with heavenly or ethereal music.

History: Small harps existed in ancient times and are still important in many folk traditions. The modern double-action pedal harp was developed in the 18th and 19th centuries by makers such as Cousineau and Erard in Paris and London.

The strings on a harp are attached at one end to the resonator; in the violin family they run above its surface

Pillar

Pedals for altering pitches of strings

DOUBLE BASS

Characteristics: Although properly a member of the viols, the double bass has been adopted as the lowest-pitched voice of the violin family. There are two main styles of bow: the French, held like a violin bow, and the German, held with the hand upside-down like a viol bow.

History: Early double basses often had six strings, while many 18th-century examples had only three. Modern ones have four or five.

ANTONIO STRADIVARI (c.1644–1737)

Stradivari emerged from a long tradition of violin makers in Cremona. Taught by Nicolo Amati, he educated his sons in the trade, and his family workshop produced violins, violas, cellos, pochettes, and guitars. Many consider his instruments the finest ever made. Debates continue concerning the woods and varnishes he used.

Woodwind

Woodwind instruments are derived from basic blown pipes and can be made from a wide variety of materials. Many produce their sound by means of a vibrating "reed". They come in families, with larger and smaller versions of the main orchestral instrument, and are used to add a variety of colours to the orchestral sound. The standard woodwind section of the modern orchestra comprises two flutes, piccolo, two oboes, cor anglais, two clarinets, bass clarinet, two bassoons, and contrabassoon. In some works, composers may call for additional woodwind instruments, such as saxophones and smaller high-pitched clarinets.

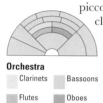

Orchestra
- Clarinets
- Flutes
- Bassoons
- Oboes

SINGLE REEDS

Characteristics: Single reeds use a cane reed, held over a slot in the mouthpiece by a ligature and placed against the player's lower lip. The clarinet can produce a wide variety of tone colours. The saxophone appears occasionally in the orchestra but is more common in wind and jazz bands.

History: Johann Christopher Denner of Nuremberg is reputed to have invented the clarinet at the beginning of the 18th century. More keys were gradually added in the 19th century.

CLARINET REED

Feathered edge

THEOBALD BOEHM (1794–1881)

Born in Munich, Boehm was a professional flautist who also worked in the jewellery and steel industries. He spent over 30 years remodelling the keywork and bores of flutes, and his 1847 cylindrical flute is the pattern for most modern instruments. Boehm's successors have applied his principles to other woodwind instruments.

Crook

Mouthpiece

All tone holes controlled by keys

Ligature holding reed

Barrel

Keys for left hand

Levers to extend range

Bell

Wide, conical bore, ending in bell

Upper octave key

Bell

CLARINET

ALTO CLARINET

BASS CLARINET

DOUBLE REEDS

Characteristics: The oboe and bassoon families have conical bores and a double reed, consisting of two pieces of shaped cane strapped together, which is held gently between the lips. The treble oboe is often given prominent melodies and requires a significant amount of air pressure to sound properly. The tenor voice of the cor anglais is popular as a solo instrument as it has a rich and sonorous quality. Forming the tenor and bass of the woodwind, the versatile bassoon has a bore which doubles back on itself. The large contrabassoon adds a deep bass to the woodwind section.

History: Both the oboe and the early bassoon first appeared in 17th-century France. While the oboe (from hautbois, meaning "high" or "loud wood") developed from the shawm, the bassoon's precursors were the dulcian ("sweet sounding") and fagot ("bundle of sticks").

Reed attached to bent crook

The tubing of the contrabassoon is twice the length of the bassoon's

Bell

Slender double reed

Long levers to reach widely spaced finger holes

Crook (metal tube that holds reed)

Staple (cork-covered tube)

Staple

Bore of oboe is conical

Distinctive bulbous bell

Hand support

BASSOON REED **OBOE REED** **OBOE** **COR ANGLAIS**

FLUTES

Characteristics: The air in a flute is set in motion by blowing across the edge of the embouchure hole. Usually providing the top woodwind voice, the flute also has a mellow low register. The smaller piccolo can cut through the entire orchestral texture to great effect.

History: Early flutes were usually made of boxwood or ivory and had open finger holes. The keywork of the modern flute (usually made of silver) is based on a 19th-century design.

Long wooden tube doubles back on itself

PICCOLO

Embouchure

Butt

CONTRA-BASSOON

FLUTE **BASSOON**

Brass

Brass instruments consist of a length of metal tubing ending in a flared bell. They use a slide mechanism or valves, which engage additional lengths of tubing to extend their range. The air column is set in motion by vibrating the lips against a cupped mouthpiece. Sound characteristics are partly a result of the width of the bore, as well as the shape and size of the mouthpiece and the bell. While they can be played subtly, brass instruments are often used for power and dramatic effect.

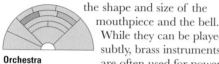

Orchestra

Horns   Trumpets

Trombones and tubas

Mouthpiece

Keys controlling rotary valves

Rotary valves

Tuning slide

FRENCH HORN

Characteristics: The tubing of the modern horn is mostly conical. It usually has three or four rotary valves, operated by the left hand, while the right hand is inserted into the bell to shape the sound. Most horns are pitched in F (single) or a combination of F and B flat (double or "compensating"). Horn players sometimes specialize in playing either high or low parts.
History: The natural horn was used as a signalling instrument on the hunting field. Before the advent of valves, some players used hand stopping (partly closing the bell with the right hand) to play notes outside the harmonic series, a technique that also changes the timbre of the note.

Bell

Small-cupped mouthpiece

FRENCH HORN MOUTHPIECE

TRUMPET

Valves

Mouth-piece

Bell

Cylindrical tubing

Characteristics: The bore of the orchestral trumpet is partly cylindrical and partly conical. It has three valves, which lower the pitch by a semi-tone, tone, or minor third. Different-sized trumpets (C, D, and B flat are most common) are used to make higher or lower parts easier to play. Inserting various mutes into the bell alters the timbre produced.
History: The early trumpet – a single length of tubing with a shallow flared bell – traditionally had a military or ceremonial function. From the late 18th century, various methods were developed to make more notes available, including the addition of crooks, slides, keys, or valves.

Cup

Shank

TRUMPET MOUTHPIECE

Water key

Slide to extend length of tubing

TUBA

Characteristics: Instruments of the tuba family (including euphoniums, sousaphones, and bombardons) have wide, conical bores and provide the bass of the brass section. Different shapes and sizes are used but the typical orchestral instrument has an upward-pointing bell, with three to six valves. The player uses a great deal of breath but less wind pressure than for smaller instruments.

History: First developed in Germany in the 1830s, the tuba was embraced enthusiastically by composers such as Berlioz. It had replaced its predecessor, the ophicleide (an early 19th-century invention) in most bands and orchestras by the 1870s.

Bell

Mouthpiece

Valves

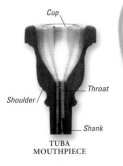

Cup

Throat

Shoulder

Shank

TUBA MOUTHPIECE

TROMBONE

Characteristics: The cylindrical bored trombone has a telescoping slide rather than valves to change the tube length. Seven slide positions are used, each changing the pitch by a semitone. Sizes range from soprano to contrabass trombones, with the tenor and bass being the typical orchestral instruments.

History: When trombones, or sackbuts, first appeared in the late 15th century, they lacked the flaring bell of modern instruments. Valves were added in the 1820s, but it is the slide version that now predominates.

Large-cupped mouthpiece

TROMBONE MOUTHPIECE

The bore of the trombone varies from country to country

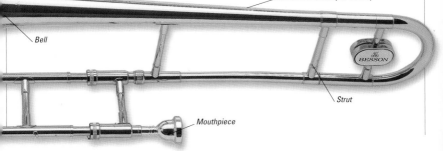

Bell

BESSON

Strut

Mouthpiece

Percussion and keyboards

The percussion section adds rhythmic vitality and drive to the orchestra. Percussion instruments are divided into two main categories: membranophones (where a stretched membrane is struck, as with a drum) and idiophones (where an object made of resonant material is struck). Some idiophones, such as the xylophone and tubular bells, are tuned and capable of producing melody as well as rhythm. Other idiophones used frequently in orchestral works range from cymbals, triangles, and tambourines to the more exotic tam-tam (a large oriental gong), wood block, castanets, and maracas. Special sound-effect instruments, such as the whip (two wooden slats that are slapped together), sleigh bells, rattles, or sirens, can also be employed. To these, keyboard instruments, such as the piano and celesta, are often added.

Orchestra

☐ Drums　　■ Other percussion instruments

DRUMS

Characteristics: Timpani (or kettledrums) are used in groups of two to five instruments and can be tuned by altering the skin tension using turning screws or a pedal. The snare drum is smaller and has a set of gut or metal springs stretched across its lower drum head which vibrate when the upper head is struck. The large bass drum is also double-headed and is struck using a stick with a large, soft head.

History: Drums came into the orchestra in the late 17th century, initially in combination with trumpets. Timpani arrived first, with other types gradually being added later.

Tensioned batter head

Tuning gauge

Tensioning screws

Copper or fibreglass shell

Batter head

Tuning pedal

Metal frame

SNARE DRUM

BASS DRUM

TIMPANUM AND DRUM STICK

IDIOPHONES

Characteristics: Cymbals are made from metal and are sounded either with a stick or by clashing a pair together. Tambourines consist of "jingles" fitted in a ring of wood, over which a membrane is sometimes fitted. They can be shaken, hit, or used to play a roll. The triangle – a steel bar bent to form an equilateral triangle – is hung from a string and may be hit with one or two metal beaters. Trills are played using quick strokes inside the top corner.

History: Many percussion instruments originate in China or Turkey and became regular members of the orchestra in the 19th and 20th centuries.

CYMBALS

Jingles

TAMBOURINE

TRIANGLE

TUNED IDIOPHONES

Characteristics: The glockenspiel consists of a series of metal bars tuned to a chromatic scale, laid out like a piano keyboard. Sticks with heads of wood, metal, rubber, or fabric can be used to create different tone qualities. A wooden equivalent, the xylophone, can have resonators fitted beneath its rosewood bars. Tubular bells, which are hit with a small mallet, are commonly used to evoke the sound of church bells.
History: Xylophones are found in many cultures, and, like tubular bells, were adopted by European composers in the 19th century. The first orchestral use of the glockenspiel is thought to be in Handel's *Saul* (1739).

Wooden bars

Resonators

Tuned steel pipes

XYLOPHONE

Metal plates

TUBULAR BELLS AND MALLET

GLOCKENSPIEL

KEYBOARDS

Characteristics: The piano, developed from the harpsichord in early-18th-century Florence by Bartolomeo Cristofori, is sometimes defined as a percussion instrument since its strings are struck by hammers. While early pianos are largely made of wood and have a delicate sound, modern grand pianos have metal frames, larger hammers, and heavier strings, and can be played much more loudly. The celesta, invented in 1886 by Auguste Mustel, is a keyboard instrument in which tuned metal plates are struck by hammers.

Metal frame supports tension of the strings

The left pedal ("una corda") moves the hammers so they strike only one of the two strings for each note in the treble and two of the three in the bass

Keyboard

Some pianos have a third central pedal which raises the dampers of those notes being played when depressed

Right pedal lifts all the dampers, allowing the strings to vibrate freely

GRAND PIANO

Classical music in
PERFORMANCE

A common perception of classical music is that it is performed in the formal surroundings of a concert hall and usually involves a large symphony orchestra and world-famous soloists and conductors. However, classical music can just as easily be brought to life in the home or out of doors.

The professional composer whose works are performed by professional musicians for a paying audience is a relatively recent phenomenon. The idea of attending an event specifically to listen to music – rather than to hear music in the course of a church service or an entertainment at court – would have been very unusual before the 17th century. In medieval times, most sacred music was performed by monks within the Church and secular music was played and sung by wandering minstrels. Just as many early composers were anonymous, so too were most early performers.

During the Renaissance and Baroque periods, performers began to emerge from obscurity. Some of the first to achieve fame in northern Europe were organists; during his lifetime, J S Bach may have been better known as an organist than as a composer. Another group of "celebrity" performers to emerge during the Baroque period were opera singers. Some of Handel's sopranos were notorious for their capricious demands. Once, during a particularly fraught rehearsal, the composer threatened to throw the soprano Francesca Cuzzoni from an upstairs window.

THE CONCERT

The word "concert" is probably derived from the Italian *concertare* ("to arrange", or "to get together"). In the 17th century, musicians would come together to perform both privately and publicly. An early example was in Lübeck, Germany, where it became fashionable in the 1620s for a performance of secular music to follow Evensong in a public building (such as the town hall). This came to be known as *Abendmusik*.

Concerts were enthusiastically taken up in England at the time of the Civil War, when hardly any music was performed in churches. Musicians responded to public demand by giving

MEDIEVAL MUSICIANS
A group of 14th-century musicians performs on a range of instruments, including drum, pipe, shawm, vielle with a curved bow, and psaltery.

concerts for which listeners paid an admission fee. Many were held in taverns such as London's Mitre Inn.

A MUSICAL HERITAGE

Until well into the 19th century, the composer and performer were often one and the same. The performance of "old" music (music composed by earlier generations) was rare until the 19th century. Until that time, almost all music heard was contemporary, often composed for specific events, whether sacred (as in the case of Bach's Cantatas) or secular (as in that of Handel's *Music for the Royal Fireworks*). It was in England that performers began to take an interest in music of the past: the Academy of

Ancient Music (established in 1726) performed music by such composers as Byrd and Purcell, whereas the rival Concerts of Ancient Music (founded in 1776) performed Baroque music, including that of Handel and Corelli.

Concert life was less developed in Vienna in the 18th century than in London, and there was no hall specially intended for concerts, so musical events took place in a variety of venues there including palaces, theatres, Masonic lodges, restaurants, and public gardens.

PROFESSIONAL MUSICIANS

The music societies formed during the 18th century organized concerts in which amateur musicians could perform under the direction of professionals. The composer Telemann founded such a society in Hamburg in 1713, and another was to be found in Leipzig, directed by the Kantor of the Thomaskirche – the position held by J S Bach at the time

MUSIC FOR THE ROYAL FIREWORKS (1749)
To celebrate the Peace of Aix-la-Chapelle, Handel was commissioned by King George II to write a suite to accompany a magnificent firework display in London

TIMELINE: CLASSICAL MUSIC IN PERFORMANCE

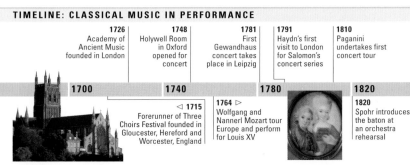

1726
Academy of Ancient Music founded in London

1748
Holywell Room in Oxford opened for concert

1781
First Gewandhaus concert takes place in Leipzig

1791
Haydn's first visit to London for Salomon's concert series

1810
Paganini undertakes first concert tour

1700　　**1740**　　**1780**　　**1820**

◁ **1715**
Forerunner of Three Choirs Festival founded in Gloucester, Hereford and Worcester, England

1764 ▷
Wolfgang and Nannerl Mozart tour Europe and perform for Louis XV

1820
Spohr introduces the baton at an orchestra rehearsal

BAROQUE ORCHESTRA
A chamber orchestra gathers around a harpsichord during rehearsals for an opera in Venice, c.1710.

of his death. The Leipzig society was named the Grosses Konzert in 1743, and by the middle of the 19th century, all its players were professionals. The organization – now the Leipzig Gewandhaus Orchestra – still exists today.

Many local music societies (as well as a few performers) began to sell admission to a series of concerts to the public, demanding payment prior to the first of the concerts. This became known as the "subscription concert". One of the first successful examples was that of J C Bach in London in 1765.

During the 18th and 19th centuries, concerts were long and diverse. The Gewandhaus subscription concerts would frequently contain an overture, an opera aria, an instrumental solo and a choral finale in each half, and might last for three or four hours in total. Where vocal music had been at the centre of 18th-century programmes, during the 19th century it became more accepted to perform movements from concertos and symphonies, although concerts solely of instrumental music were still rare.

The orchestra had emerged during the Renaissance period as a group of players brought together for important occasions. During the 18th century,

CONCERT HALLS

Initially concert halls were limited in size, but London's Hanover Square Rooms (1775) held in excess of 600 people. The audience was free to move around during the performance and talk, or to sit on sofas around the hall. With the increased projection capabilities of new instruments, concert halls could become larger. In 1826, Berlin's Singakademie was built for an audience of 1200. During the 19th century, cultural centres competed with each other to build larger, more elaborate halls, such as the Musikvereinsaal in Vienna (1870) and the Royal Albert Hall in London (1871).

PALAU DE LA MÚSICA CATALANA CONCERT HALL
This richly decorated auditorium was built in Barcelona in 1908 as a symbol of Catalan pride.

1840 ▷
Liszt uses the term "recital" for a solo concert

1880s
Foundation of Berlin Philharmonic, Boston Symphony, and Amsterdam Concertgebouw Orchestras

1940
Tanglewood Music Center founded by Serge Koussevitsky

◁ **2003**
Walt Disney Hall opens in Los Angeles

1860

1900

1940

1980

1870
Musikvereinsaal opened in Vienna

1877
Phonograph invented by Thomas Edison

1891 ▷
Carnegie Hall opens in New York; Paderewski tours USA for first time

1947
Amadeus Quartet founded

1976
Ensemble intercontemporain founded by Pierre Boulez

the modern string family replaced viols in this group and an important member was the keyboard player or "continuo" – a harpsichord, organ, or, later, piano that would play from the bass-line of the score.

By the 19th century, the continuo had disappeared and a standard layout had emerged. Violins were grouped into two sections and there were smaller groups of violas, cellos, and basses, while there was normally a pair each of flutes, oboes, clarinets, bassoons, trumpets, and horns ("double wind"), and timpani. During the 19th century, this group became extended so that piccolos, cor anglais, trombones, tubas, and further percussion were added.

The layout of orchestras has changed considerably over the years. Perhaps the most radical alteration in the course of the 20th century was the moving of the second violins next to the first violins and the cellos to the conductor's right.

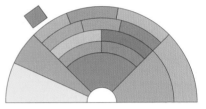

ORCHESTRA AT THE TIME OF HAYDN
The strings – not just the violins – were divided into two sections, one on either side of the leader, who sat at the piano and directed the orchestra.

MODERN SYMPHONY ORCHESTRA
Since roughly the time of the Second World War, both the first and second violins have sat on the conductor's left, facing the cellos and double basses on the right.

THE SYMPHONY ORCHESTRA
The personnel and seating arrangement of the modern orchestra is now effectively standardized around the world. The picture below shows the Bournemouth Symphony Orchestra with its principal conductor, Marin Alsop.

KEY

First violins	Second violins	Violas	Cellos	Double basses
Drums	Other percussion	Harp	Piano	Organ
Oboes	Flutes	Clarinets	Bassoons	
Horns	Trumpets	Trombones and tubas		

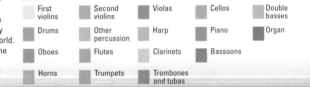

THE CONDUCTOR

The conductor became a focal point of interest through the efforts of Hector Berlioz in the 1830s. The conductor's job is about far more than keeping time. In performance, he or she may give cues to the players to indicate their entries, and may need to control the balance between sections. However, much of the work – on issues such as phrasing, bowing, breathing, or the respective attack and decay of sound – is done before the performance. Some conductors (Leonard Bernstein, Valery Gergiev) have been known for their extrovert use of gestures on stage, while others (Pierre Boulez, Bernard Haitink) are far more restrained. The one thing that all great conductors have in common is a natural sense of authority.

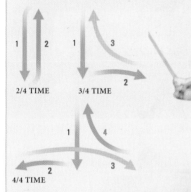

2/4 TIME

3/4 TIME

4/4 TIME

KEEPING TIME
Whatever the time signature, the first beat of each bar is shown by a downward gesture (the downbeat) and the last by an upward gesture (the upbeat).

THE CONDUCTOR'S ROLE
The conductor is responsible for overall interpretation and encourages the orchestra to perform as a unit.

As orchestras became established, a "canon" or core repertoire emerged – largely works by the Viennese composers (i.e. Mozart and Beethoven) as well as opera music by composers such as Gluck and Cherubini. By the end of the 19th century, concert activity had divided into solo recitals, chamber music performances, and orchestral performances. The crossover with opera had largely disappeared, which resulted in the shorter programme lengths we have today.

THE SOLO RECITAL

Liszt was responsible for introducing the solo recital in the late 1830s. He toured Europe extensively, performing in towns and cities from Scotland to Russia. One of his innovations was that of playing from memory. In the 21st century this has become the norm for soloists, but in Liszt's time it was considered dangerously radical.

At the same time that Liszt was establishing his reputation across Europe, a market was developing for the celebrity performer in the United States. The singer Jenny Lind, for example, drew an audience of over 7,000 at Castle Garden in New York in 1850, proving the commercial potential of America for performers

MUSIC FESTIVALS

Festivals date back to about 1715 with the first meeting of the cathedral choirs of Gloucester, Hereford, and Worcester (the Three Choirs Festival). Many great composers have inspired festivals in their memory, notably Handel (1784) and Beethoven (1845). The 20th century saw the establishment of festivals such as the Maggio Musicale Fiorentino (from 1933) and the Lucerne Festival (1938). The composers Benjamin Britten and Sir Peter Maxwell Davies established their own festivals in Aldeburgh and Orkney, respectively. American festivals include those at Aspen, Ravinia, and Tanglewood.

TANGLEWOOD FESTIVAL
The Boston Symphony Orchestra has staged its summer festival at Tanglewood since 1940.

and promoters. Pianists such as Thalberg and Anton Rubinstein toured the United States from the mid-19th century onwards, and Paderewski created a sensation with his tours there in the 1890s.

NEW ORCHESTRAS

The Berlin Philharmonic Orchestra, founded in 1882, has set what many consider the finest standards in orchestral playing. Brahms's friend Joseph Joachim was appointed its first conductor and was

succeeded by Liszt's pupil von Bülow in 1887. Prestigious orchestras were established on the other side of the Atlantic by wealthy industrialists: the Philharmonic Symphony Society

CLASSICAL MUSIC WITH A NEW FACE
Today's promoters are always on the lookout for talented, attractive soloists like Vanessa Mae (born 1978).

of New York (later the New York Philharmonic) in 1842 and the Boston Symphony Orchestra in 1881.

WIDER AUDIENCES

In the 19th century, concert series were founded to make music available to people who could not afford to attend subscription concerts. London's Crystal Palace concerts were a typical venture of this kind. Two free concerts were given daily throughout the 1850s.

Military bands also brought music to wider audiences. Under J P Sousa in the 1880s, the Marine Corps Band would give free weekly concerts at the White House and the Capitol in Washington. At the same time there was a great increase in the number of choral societies, especially in industrial regions such as northern England, Wales, and Germany's Ruhr Valley.

MODERN PERFORMERS

Few 20th- or 21st-century composers have been known as performers, but Richard Strauss, Bernstein, Boulez, and others have combined the roles of conductor and composer. Non-composing performers, however, have influenced the repertoire of their instruments profoundly. The cellist Mstislav Rostropovich worked closely with Prokofiev, Shostakovich, Schnittke, and Britten; the singer Kathy Berberian inspired Berio to compose vocal music; and the pianist David Tudor worked with John Cage and other avant-garde composers. Many performers have chosen to specialize in certain repertoires; Artur Schnabel, for example, was known for his renditions of the Beethoven piano sonatas. Some artists, such as the cellist Pablo Casals, are celebrated for the spirituality of their playing, while performers like violinist Jascha Heifetz and pianist Evgeny Kissin are noted for their technical prowess. Others, such as the pianist Alfred Brendel, seem to combine all these qualities with an intellectual integrity. Others still – violinists Maxim Vengerov and Nigel Kennedy, for example – are noted for their panache and conviction. Flamboyant artists who have raised the public profile of their instruments include the flautist James Galway, the percussionist Evelyn Glennie, the trumpeter Håken Hardenberger, and the viola player Yuri Bashmet. Some performers have looked to the east for inspiration; the violinist Yehudi Menuhin worked with sitar player Ravi Shankar, and more recently the cellist Yo-Yo Ma has initiated an East-West collaboration through his Silk Road Ensemble.

RECORDING

Recording made music available to all. The first wax recordings, at the end of the 19th century, were dominated by opera arias by singers such as Caruso, as the voice could be reproduced much better than instrumental music.

Electric recordings began in 1925, allowing longer excerpts of works to be recorded, and the arrival of LPs in 1948 allowed many works to be presented in their entirety. Stereo was introduced in 1958 and the CD in 1983.

Some commentators, such as Canadian pianist Glenn Gould, predicted that live concerts would be superseded by recorded music, but there is now more emphasis on live performance than there has been for half a century.

A RECORDING STUDIO
The availability of so many high-quality recordings means that new recordings of standard repertoire cannot be justified by the major record labels.

THE HISTORY OF
CLASSICAL
MUSIC

EARLY MUSIC
1000–1600

"Early Music" refers to the repertoire from historical periods less familiar to classically trained musicians and their audiences than that of the Classical and Romantic eras. This section covers the music of the Middle Ages and the Renaissance – a vast sweep of centuries of musical ideas, developments and performance styles.

I n terms of architecture, painting, and sculpture, the Renaissance can be said to have begun in 15th-century Florence. The transition between the music of the Middle Ages and the Renaissance is more difficult to identify, because musical styles developed gradually and in different ways across Europe. It is clear, however, that there were differences in the approach to musical composition as practised by the French composer Machaut in the 14th century and the Italian Palestrina in the 16th century. Works by influential composers such as Dufay and Josquin changed musical style considerably in the late 15th and early 16th centuries, so 1450 is a convenient date to separate medieval from Renaissance music. What is usually referred to as Renaissance music may be seen to end at the point where Monteverdi and his contemporaries experimented with the new "Baroque" genres of opera, sonata, and concerto at the beginning of the 17th century, although countries such as England were still in a rich period of "Renaissance" music until perhaps two or three decades later.

CHURCH MUSIC

The music that has survived is heavily weighted in favour of the sacred. Plainchant was by far the most common sort of sacred music during this entire period, and was sung in every church, monastery, cathedral, and chapel. It was monophonic music – it had just a single line of melody – and could be sung by one voice or many. Most church musicians would have been expected to commit hundreds of chants to memory as part of their musical training, even after Guido d'Arezzo developed the music stave in the 11th century.

MINSTREL PLAYING A VIELLE
This illustration is from a 13th-century illuminated manuscript, the *Cantigas de Santa Maria*, a collection of songs made for Alfonso X of Castile and León.

Secular monophonic music was created throughout this period, but only from the 12th century was it considered worthy of preservation in written collections. The most famous secular composers were the troubadours, trobairitz (female troubadours), and trouvères of medieval France, whose music and poetry usually expressed the ideals of courtly love. Little is known about how their music was performed, but it is possible that their songs were accompanied by the vielle, a forerunner of the violin with five strings, one of which could produce a regular drone like that of a hurdy-gurdy or bagpipe. The vielle may thus have provided just a steady drone or more complex accompaniments to a solo singer.

POLYPHONY

The rise of polyphonic (literally "many-voiced") forms of composition from approximately the 12th century took place within the Church, as singers elaborated on the basic plainchant by the addition of other vocal parts on special occasions, such as Christmas or Easter. In the Cathedral of Notre-Dame in Paris, Léonin and Pérotin are credited with having written the first body of two-, three-, and four-part music to be circulated in manuscript form. By the 13th century, a large repertory of polyphony was found in major churches across Europe, and secular forms of music were also being written in more than one part. By the 15th century, polyphonic music was widespread and had become a necessary part of important religious and courtly celebrations.

THE MOTET

The motet was one of the most popular sacred forms during the later Middle Ages, gradually making way for polyphonic settings of the Ordinary of the Mass (the parts of the Mass that remain the same every day). The motet was developed in the 13th century in northern France. The plainchant was placed into a strict rhythmic pattern, above which between one and three other lines

PLAINCHANT

Plainchant was the musical part of the liturgy in the Christian Church. Plainchant was monophonic, a single melodic line set in one of the eight church modes (scales based on a specific combination of intervals). These melodies might be short, regular and simple, or more extensive, elaborate, and complex. The texts used for chants were religious, and in Latin or Greek. Melodies were written down only from the 9th century, and there were regional variations in the chants used. Attempts were made to bring European churches into line so that all performed the same chants in the same way, but none were particularly successful.

MANUSCRIPT SCORE
This Flemish score of 1522 is illuminated with a painting of clerics playing music in a garden.

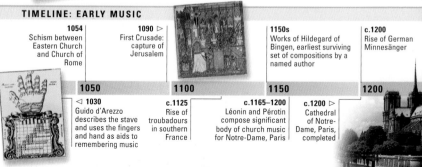

1054
Schism between Eastern Church and Church of Rome

1090 ▷
First Crusade: capture of Jerusalem

1150s
Works of Hildegard of Bingen, earliest surviving set of compositions by a named author

c.1200
Rise of German Minnesänger

1050　　**1100**　　**1150**　　**1200**

◁ **1030**
Guido d'Arezzo describes the stave and uses the fingers and hand as aids to remembering music

c.1125
Rise of troubadours in southern France

c.1165–1200
Léonin and Pérotin compose significant body of church music for Notre-Dame, Paris

c.1200 ▷
Cathedral of Notre-Dame, Paris, completed

MEDIEVAL NOBLES DANCING IN A GARDEN
This scene illustrates the great French medieval poem of courtly love, *Le Roman de la Rose*.

were placed; these upper parts were each given a new text, resulting in a complex texture in which many different words sounded together.

INSTRUMENTAL MUSIC

Along with new secular forms of song in the 16th century, such as the madrigal, instrumental music rose to such a status that it was more frequently copied down than it had been in the Middle Ages. The Renaissance saw a rise in the involvement of the merchant classes in the performance of music; the invention of music printing by Petrucci in 1501 meant that music could be sold and distributed more easily, cheaply, and reliably than ever before, though much was still written down in manuscript (literally "handwritten") form.

MONKS SINGING
French composers produced the first complex polyphonic settings of the liturgy. This illumination appears in a 13th-century French psalter.

Wealthy patrons of the 16th century demanded vocal and instrumental music for all sorts of musical combinations. In particular, "families" of instruments that comprised various sizes of one type of instrument (a consort of recorders, viols, or voices) flourished during the Renaissance period, though mixed or "broken" consorts of string, wind and voice were also cultivated. Dances such as the stately pavan and the galliard, a lively dance involving leaps, became enormously popular.

1338
Start of Hundred Years' War between England and France

◁ **c.1307**
Dante starts work on *La divina commedia*

1347 ▷
Black Death reaches Europe

1250

1300

1350

c.1250
Spanish *Cantigas de Santa Maria* written

c.1320
Publication of *Ars Nova*, musical treatise attributed to Philippe de Vitry

1327 ▽
Papacy transfers to Avignon in southern France. The vast papal palace dominates the town

c.1363
Machaut composes *Messe de Nostre Dame*

Secular vocal music was written in vernacular languages, and very often had an amorous subject. The madrigal rose to prominence in the 16th century and was notable for its use of subtle musical descriptions that matched the text, known as "word-painting". Composers delighted in devising ways to set the most expressive poetic phrases to music.

COMPOSERS AND PLAYERS

During the Middle Ages and the Renaissance, those who composed music were usually employed to do something else, such as work as a priest. To compose and write down music,

FUNERAL MASS
Monks in Gothic choir stalls sing a funeral mass for the Holy Roman Emperor Maximilian I, who died in 1519.

one had to be musically literate to some degree, especially for the composition of polyphony. People who received an education were usually either employed by the Church, living within a religious foundation such as a monastery or nunnery, or part of the nobility. During the Renaissance, the merchant classes valued an education for their sons and, to some extent, daughters. There were relatively few female composers during this period, although many anonymous pieces may in fact have been written by women, and women certainly performed music by men.

RELIGIOUS DIVISION

The Protestant Reformation of the 16th century had inevitable musical consequences, largely because the Protestant reformers destroyed as much Catholic music as possible and replaced it with new, more direct styles, particularly in England. This made extraordinary demands of English composers of the period. Thomas Tallis, for example, wrote music for four different monarchs,

THREE YOUNG WOMEN MAKING MUSIC
In this early 16th-century Flemish painting, the young women are performing "Jouissance vous donnerai" (I Will Give You Happiness), a popular song of the time.

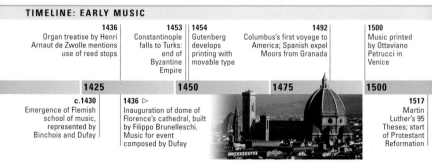

TIMELINE: EARLY MUSIC

1425	1436	1450	1453	1454	1475	1492	1500	1500
	Organ treatise by Henri Arnaut de Zwolle mentions use of reed stops		Constantinople falls to Turks: end of Byzantine Empire	Gutenberg develops printing with movable type		Columbus's first voyage to America; Spanish expel Moors from Granada	Music printed by Ottaviano Petrucci in Venice	

c.1430
Emergence of Flemish school of music, represented by Binchois and Dufay

1436 ▷
Inauguration of dome of Florence's cathedral, built by Filippo Brunelleschi. Music for event composed by Dufay

1517
Martin Luther's 95 Theses; start of Protestant Reformation

Today, few musicians perform Early Music unless they use authentic reproductions of the instruments for which it was written. The quest for authenticity is supported by the exploration of early written and pictorial sources in search of clues as to how instruments were played, indications of pitch, tempo, phrasing, ornamentation, and accompaniment style, and what sort of improvization might be appropriate. "Historically informed" performance gives a vibrant account of the possible sounds produced by early performers.

THE DUFAY COLLECTIVE
This British ensemble, seen here playing on harp and two vielles, performs all kinds of medieval and Renaissance music, both instrumental and vocal.

each of whom required music with a different religious emphasis: from the direct, Protestant settings of English texts favoured by Elizabeth I to the elaborate, Latin-texted polyphony composed for her half-sister, Mary.

The simplest post-Reformation religious polyphony involved straightforward chanting in harmony, all voices moving together in the same rhythm as one another (homophony). Other polyphonic musical forms were contrapuntal. The idea of a musical texture where voices imitated one another in counterpoint became a distinguishing feature of sacred and secular music of the late Middle Ages and Renaissance, and is perhaps most recognizable in the choral music of Palestrina and the instrumental fantasies of English consort music at the end of the period.

Although musicians found new ways to compose, using an increasingly subtle palette of rhythmic, harmonic and notational ideas, Early Music cannot be seen as a straightforward evolution from "primitive" plainchant to "sophisticated" polyphony. Fifteenth-century motets were often incredibly complex pieces of artistry, both notationally and in performance; instrumental dances in the 16th century were often delightfully simple.

THE MUSICAL LEGACY

In appreciating Early Music, we are limited by our ignorance of how it sounded in its original context and just what the music meant to those who sang, played, or listened to it. On the other hand, the great variety of interpretations available is testament to how much there remains to discover in this seemingly distant repertoire and the myriad ways in which we might enjoy getting to know it better.

LUTE
One of the most popular instruments of the Renaissance, the lute was probably introduced to Europe from Moorish Spain.

1524
Protestant hymnal by Luther and Johann Walther

1532
Henry VIII declares himself head of the Church of England

1551 ▷
Palestrina appointed choirmaster by Pope Julius III

c.1555
Amati family of violin-makers established in Cremona, Italy

1525　　**1550**　　**1575**　　**1600**

1540
Viol players from Venice, Cremona and Milan employed by Henry VIII in England

1545 ▷
Council of Trent meets to determine Catholic response to the Reformation

1591
William Byrd's *My Lady Nevelle's Booke*, a compilation of music for the virginals

Hildegard of Bingen

● 1098–1179   ♙ German   ♫ 77

Hildegard experienced intense visions (probably due to migraine), which she recorded in her books; she became known for her prophecies and miracles.

Writer, poet, religious leader, diplomat, and composer, Hildegard's achievements were remarkable – and unique for a woman of her time. Promised to the Church by her noble family, she spent years living in religious contemplation. Through correspondence with popes and emperors, she became a significant political and diplomatic figure and wrote extensively on medicine, science, and theology. Her contemplative and ecstatic music is comprised of single-line settings of religious texts: not plainchant, but specially composed, using frequently repeated and varied short patterns.

MILESTONES	
1112	Takes the veil at age 15
1136	Abbess of Disibodenberg Monastery
c.1147	Establishes religious house near Bingen
1150s	Lyrical poems and music, *Symphonia armonie celestium revelationum*, collected
1151	Writes *Ordo virtutum*, a morality play

Léonin (Leoninus)

● Died c.1201   ♙ French   ♫ Unknown

The only written reference to a musician named Léonin was penned more than a century after his death by an anonymous English monk, who wrote that he was "the best composer of organum for the amplification of divine service". Léonin was a teacher, administrator, and poet who became a canon at the new cathedral of Notre-Dame de Paris.
No music by him survives, but he is credited with the creation of the *Magnus liber*, the "Great Book" of chants used at Notre-Dame in the late 1100s. The book, later edited by Pérotin, laid the foundations for the idea of harmony and written-down composition.

MILESTONES	
1150s	Cathedral administrator in Paris
1163	Construction of Notre-Dame begins
c.1192	Ordained as a priest
c.1200	Compilation of *Magnus liber*, a book of plainchant

Philippe de Vitry

● 1291–1361   ♙ French   ♫ 30

From 1340, Vitry was one of France's leading intellectual figures – poet, philosopher, singer, composer, author, critic, bishop, and scholar. He travelled widely and was often involved in international relations. His motets – probably settings of his own Latin poems – enjoyed wide circulation and critical success, as did his poetry. The book of his teachings, *Ars nova*, established innovations such as the use of the minim and other short notes. Vitry may have invented the ballade, though no examples by him survive.

MILESTONES	
1310s	Motets enjoy success
c.1320	Collection of his musical theories, *Ars nova*, published
1331	Accompanies the Duke of Bourbon to London
1342	Composes motet *Petre clemens*
1351	Created Bishop of Meaux

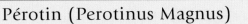

Pérotin (Perotinus Magnus)

● Active c.1200 ♙ French ⚏ Unknown

Pérotin, the first known composer of music in more than two independent parts, is a frustratingly shadowy figure. He is mentioned in late-13th-century documents as the man who edited and improved Léonin's *Magnus liber*, the book of music at Notre-Dame. He probably worked with the poet Philip the

MILESTONES	
c.1198	Writes quadruple (four-voice) organum
c.1199	Setting of sacred text *Viderunt omnes*
c.1200	Working at Notre-Dame; setting of sacred text *Sederunt principes*
c.1207	Deputy choirmaster at Notre-Dame
c.1210	Revises Léonin's *Magnus liber*

Chancellor, whose texts he set (in works such as *Beata viscera*), and he may have composed in the emerging genre of the motet, but very little is known about him for certain. However, Pérotin was certainly a pioneer: his two four-part settings of Latin texts have some startlingly modern-sounding touches.

The composer known as Pérotin may have actuallly been Petrus, a member of the hierarchy at the cathedral of Notre-Dame de Paris from about 1207 to 1238.

John Dunstable

● 1390–1453 ♙ English ⚏ c.52

So great was Dunstable's international reputation, both during his lifetime and for a long time afterwards, that he was credited with many innovations for which other English composers had been responsible. A century after his death, some writers were even erroneously labelling him the "inventor of counterpoint". Nevertheless, Dunstable was a leading exponent of the mellifluous new English style, exploiting the smooth intervals of a third and a sixth, and his influence on continental composers was enormous. Many vocal works possibly written by

him – including Mass movements, sacred Latin settings, dazzling motets, and English carols – survive, but their attribution and dating is very difficult, as little is certain about Dunstable's career. However, it is known that he enjoyed great financial success, owning a series of properties around southern England and in London.

Dunstable's epitaph in St Stephen Walbrook Church in London celebrates his skills as both musician and astronomer.

MILESTONES	
c.1422	May have travelled to France with the Duke of Bedford
1436	Large income from property
1438	Working for the Duke of Gloucester
c.1440	Enjoys reputation as the leading English composer of his time
c.1449	Possibly purchased Broadfield Manor, in Hertfordshire

Guillaume de Machaut

● c.1300–1377   🏳 French   ✍ 143

Because he was a priest, it is perhaps surprising that Machaut's music contains so many songs on the theme of unrequited love. His ill-fated love for a young girl – the noble Péronne – was expressed in his secular music and poetry, including *Le voir dit*, and his distinctive musical style includes intricate melodies and bold dissonance. However, it is his four-part Mass that has defined his reputation as a significant composer.

LIFE AND MUSIC

Guillaume de Machaut's career was based in the Church, but he also worked for several secular patrons. Remarkably, his entire compositional output has been preserved. He was a great entrepreneur, passing on reliable copies of his music and poetry to noblemen and -women across Europe. Aside from his Mass, Machaut also produced an impressive collection of motets and songs, many of which take the theme of courtly love. The strict poetic structures used by authors of this period – rondeau, virelai, ballade, and lai – are all represented in his work.

MILESTONES	
1323	Joins service of Jean de Luxembourg, King of Bohemia
c.1323	Possibly meets theorist and composer Philippe de Vitry
1327	Travels to Lithuania
1330	Recommended for position as canon of Verdun Cathedral
1340	Becomes canon of Reims Cathedral
1359	Reims besieged by the English
c.1363	Composes *Messe de Nostre Dame*
c.1363	Writes a collection of music, letters, and poetry, *Le voir dit*

KEY WORKS

DE TOUTES FLOURS
BALLADE

Machaut was one of the first to compose polyphonic settings of poetry in fixed forms; the song structures that were to dominate music for the next 150 years or more were established in his work. This four-part ballade is one of his finest pieces. The melody is sometimes quite chromatic, and the effect is one that Machaut seems to have enjoyed. In his verse, he compares the admired lady with beautiful flowers.

In recognition of his service to the King of Bohemia, Machaut was appointed canon of Reims Cathedral.

LE LAY DE BONNE ESPERANCE
LAI

This lai is one of the pivotal lyrical interludes in Machaut's *Le Voir Dit*, which describes the relationship between the aging poet and his beloved Péronne d'Armentieres. Here he acknowledges his debt to Hope. The 12 verses are monophonic, but they are highly sophisticated examples of this form. Machaut plays with features such as pitch, rhythm, and melody, to display a level of musical craftsmanship worthy of the piece's intricately formed poetry.

DOUCE DAME JOLIE
SONG

"Douce dame jolie" is a deceptively simple, monophonic (one-part) song, with verse that describes an unnamed, unattainable woman to whom the poet pledges to dedicate his life. It is written in the poetic form of the virelai, one of the "formes fixes" (the others being the rondeau and ballade) that had become popular over the preceding century. The first two notes use the same pitch, creating a feeling of insistence, before the melody dips downwards and back up again and the next two lines vary the first musical idea to new poetry. The second section of musical material raises the pitch higher than that a the opening, adding contrast.

MESSE DE NOSTRE DAME
CHORAL

Machaut wrote only one setting of the Mass Ordinary, from which he selected the Kyrie, Gloria, Credo, Sanctus, Agnus Dei, and "Ite missa est" for polyphonic treatment. This music may have been designed for singing at Lady Mass – a Saturday Mass in honour of the Virgin Mary at the Cathedral of Reims. It may have been performed regularly after its initial composition, as later copies contain some amendments to the music. Machaut's Mass is important in the history of music because it is the earliest cyclic Mass to have survived with movements that are known to be by the same composer, and may have been the first of its kind. The idea of writing a complete set of polyphonic movements that are musically related to one another did not catch on until half a century later, in the works of Dufay and his early Renaissance contemporaries.

The first and last three movements are set in a style usually associated with the isorhythmic motet, which involves the repetition of a plainchant in long, slow notes in the tenor part, in a strict rhythmic pattern. The central movements use a more direct, chordal manner, all four voices moving more or less together. Several aspects of the *ars nova*, the musical style typical of Machaut's period, are detectable. These include the use of "hocket", where a pair of voices alternates notes of a single melody, causing a disjointed effect. The harmony sounds distinctive because of the frequent use of dissonance, when notes that clash are used to drive the music forward toward the end of a phrase.

INFLUENCES

Machaut's surviving output dwarfs that of any of his French contemporaries, such as the doubtlessly influential Philippe de Vitry, making fair comparison problematic. His music has been used as the source material for contemporary works, such as Olivier Messiaen's orchestral work *Machaut à la manière*.

Guillaume Dufay

⬤ 1397–1474   🏴 Belgian   ✍ c.200

Guillaume Dufay was a musician whose talents were greatly admired across Europe during his own lifetime. His compositions include examples of nearly every genre available at the time, including some of the finest early cyclic Masses, motets, and secular songs. Though he was a medieval composer, Dufay's works anticipate the more expressive style and greater harmonic range of the Renaissance.

LIFE AND MUSIC

Precious little is known about Dufay's life, and writers continue to speculate about many details of his career. However, it is known that his parents were Marie Du Fayt and an unnamed priest, and his birth was thus illegitimate. In his youth he was known as William Du Fayt, and he went on to become the most acclaimed composer of the 15th century.

MILESTONES

1424	Perhaps moves to Laon, France
c.1426	Moves to Bologna, Italy; composes "Adieu ces bons vins de Lannoys"
1428	Works in Rome
1435	Works at papal chapel in Florence
1436	Composes motet *Nuper rosarum flores*
1450s	Composes *Missa "L'Homme armé"*

Around 200 of his works have survived, including eight Masses and more than 80 songs. Like many of his contemporaries, Dufay seems to have been aware not only of French compositional styles from the period (such as the works of Machaut) but also of English and Italian music.

Dufay's early years were spent as a chorister at Cambrai Cathedral, France, where he later went on to hold higher positions of authority.

KEY WORKS

MISSA "L'HOMME ARMÉ"
MASS SETTING

This is probably the earliest surviving Mass based on the famous secular song "L'homme armé" (The Armed Man), and it may have inspired later examples. The cantus firmus appears in the tenor part; singers who knew the original tune would certainly have spotted it, though to modern ears it can seem carefully hidden.

ADIEU CES BONS VINS DE LANNOYS
RONDEAU

The lyrics of this melancholy rondeau, as well as dating evidence within its manuscript source, help to build a biographical picture of Dufay's early career. The title tells a story in itself: "Farewell to the Fine Wines of the Laonnais". The song was written when Dufay left the town of Laon in France to take up an appointment in Bologna, Italy.

NUPER ROSARUM FLORES
MOTET

The first performance of this motet has been chronologically linked with the dedication of Brunelleschi's dome at the Florentine cathedral of Santa Maria del Fiore in 1436. The piece is written in four parts, but with one of the upper lines dividing to produce a five-part texture at certain moments.

Gilles Binchois

🔵 1400–1460   🏴 Belgian   ♫ 120

Gilles de Bin – or simply "Binchois" – was one of the three great composers of the early 1400s, alongside Dufay and John Dunstable. From a middle-class Mons family, Binchois trained as a chorister and organist, served as a soldier, and possibly visited England before joining the court at Burgundy. Unlike Dufay and Dunstable, he is not known as an innovator, but he was a great melodist, and his sacred music, ballades, and rondeaus – which sometimes have an English influence – were clearly important in his lifetime. He held various church posts and retired in the early 1450s on a generous pension.

MILESTONES

c.1425	Joins Burgundy court
1428	Music begins to be copied in Italy
1449	Travels to Mons with Dufay
c.1450	"Comme femme", rondeau, composed
1450s	Ockeghem's *Missa "De plus en plus"*, a Mass based on a Binchois melody

Gilles Binchois and his contemporary Guillaume Dufay were the great masters of the early Flemish school. There is evidence that the two composers (and their works) were well known to each other.

Johannes Ockeghem

🔵 c.1414–1497   🏴 Belgian   ♫ 50

Ockeghem appears in 1443 as a fully-fledged composer of sublime, creative music. His year of birth is a mystery, though his close friendship with Binchois suggests Ockeghem wasn't much older.

Flemish by birth, most of his work was done at the French royal court, where he was a highly esteemed and well-rewarded employee of Charles VII. He held various ecclesiastical posts and even engaged in delicate diplomatic assignments abroad – something for which his likeable, wise, honest, and generous character suited him. Ockeghem was deeply mourned at his death (and long after) by his younger colleagues, such as Josquin Desprez.

According to a contemporary, Ockeghem (shown here wearing glasses) was well known as an outstanding singer and master composer of "subtle songs, artful Masses, and harmonious motets".

MILESTONES

1446	Joins court of Charles I, Duke of Bourbon
1450s	Composes *Missa "L'homme armé"*, possibly his first Mass setting
1460	Composes the motet-chanson *Déploration on the Death of Binchois*

Josquin Desprez

● 1450–1521   🏳 Unknown   ♙ c.240

Josquin was celebrated both during and after his lifetime as one of the greatest musicians of the Renaissance period. He contributed to many genres, including motets, Mass settings and French and Italian chansons. The widespread dissemination of his music was made possible by the invention of music printing at the beginning of the 16th century, and we now know more about Josquin's music than about his life.

LIFE AND MUSIC

Josquin Desprez was a composer and singer whose skills were highly prized by the wealthiest patrons in Europe, including the d'Este family in Ferrara. He was the first composer to have had printed volumes of music entirely devoted to his work. Many aspects of Josquin's biography are poorly documented, especially details of his early life and education. A significant

MILESTONES

1459	Becomes a singer at Milan cathedral
c.1475	Working for the King of Anjou
1480	May have visited Hungary
1484	Working in Milan
1495	Working at the Papal chapel in Rome
1503	Enters the service of Duke Ercole d'Este in Ferarra
1501	Petrucci publishes six chansons attributed to Josquin
1502	*First Book of Masses* published

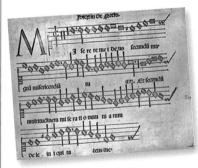

problem has been the frequent misattribution of pieces to Josquin that were not composed by him. His musical style displays great melodic invention and a keenness for such techniques as canon, as well as a fondness for popular songs.

Probably born in northern Europe, Josquin worked mostly in Italy. The recent invention of the printing press increased the influence of his music.

KEY WORKS

MASS "PANGE LINGUA"
CHORAL

This Mass is one of the composer's most sophisticated and beautiful works. Its cantus firmus – a hymn in the plaintive Phrygian mode – indicates that it was written for performance on the feast of Corpus Christi, celebrated on the Thursday after Trinity Sunday.

STABAT MATER DOLOROSA
CHORAL

Josquin's setting of the Crucifixion poem that describes Mary mourning at the foot of the Cross is written in five parts,

though only four carry the text. Perhaps in honour of the composer Gilles Binchois, this motet is based on the tenor line of *Comme femme desconfortée (A Woman in Distress)*.

PETITE CAMUSETTE
SONG

A playful vocal work, this chanson, which draws on a popular melody, shows a lighter side to Josquin's musical personality. Hidden in the six-part texture is a more formal device: the ingenious use of a canon performed by the alto and tenor parts.

Jacob Obrecht

● 1457–1505   ⚑ Dutch   ✍ c.100

Obrecht's music has been unfairly overshadowed by that of his contemporary Josquin Desprez. However, his talent for composition is evident in his substantial output of high quality sacred and secular music, lending some weight to the theory that he was able to compose an entire setting of the Mass Ordinary overnight. In a motet written in honour of his father, the composer referred to himself as "Orpheus Jacob".

LIFE AND MUSIC

Obrecht spent most of his career working in churches in Bruges, Antwerp, and Bergen op Zoom, though he was eventually encouraged to move to Italy. His writing – full of long sequences and parallel motion – was more traditional than some of his contemporaries', but was nonetheless adventurous in other ways, particularly in his treatment of cantus firmus (fixed song). Obrecht's approach to setting texts to music remained contrapuntal, however. His work did not contribute to the new trend that was emerging in Italy during the 16th century – that music should meticulously express the actual meaning of the words. His secular works included inventive canonic pieces for instruments, and he showed his national sentiment by arranging Dutch melodies.

MILESTONES	
1460s	Studies at University of Louvain
1484	Working at Cambrai Cathedral
1485	Leaves Cambrai to take up a position at Church of St Donatien in Bruges
1487	Visits Ferrara
1488	Composes the motet *Mille quingentis* in honour of his father, Guillermus.
1492	Working at the Church of Our Lady in Antwerp
1496	Working in Bergen op Zoom
1498	Working in Bruges
c.1500	Composes Mass "Super Maria zart"
1501	Working in Antwerp
1504	Returns to Ferrara to work for the d'Este ducal family
1505	Dies of plague in Ferrara

KEY WORKS

MISSA "SUB TUUM PRAESIDIUM"
CHORAL

The scoring of this Mass is unusual. After opening in only three parts, each new section of music adds another voice, until a seven-part texture is reached in the final portion of the Agnus Dei.

SALVE REGINA
CHORAL

This setting of the *Salve Regina* may have been performed both in Church and at popular, secular festivities, perhaps with instruments. Despite its modest scoring,

which allows references to the original antiphon to shine through, the texture is surprisingly rich and sonorous.

MISSA "SUPER MARIA ZART"
CHORAL

This four-part Marian Mass setting is something quite special. Lasting over an hour, its massive scale shows Obrecht's ingenuity when working on a large canvas. It is the longest Mass Ordinaries to survive.

Most of Obrecht's professional life was spent in religious employment; 27 of his surviving works are settings of the Mass.

Clément Janequin

● c.1485–c.1558   French   ♬ 250

Though he never held an important regular music post at a cathedral or court, Janequin's music enjoyed popular success – his chanson "La bataille" was one of the most-performed songs of the

16th century. Trained as a priest, he held a number of poorly paid Church posts, but in 1530 his song to celebrate Francois I's entry into Bordeaux, "Chantons, sonnons, trompettes", established his reputation as a composer. Though his music was published widely and known across Europe, Janequin suffered recurring money problems and split with his family over an unpaid loan.

MILESTONES	
1505	Junior clerk in Bordeaux
c.1515	Composes "La bataille", a chanson which imitates the noise of battle
1530	The chanson "Chantons, sonnons, trompettes" brings public fame
1530s	Most prolific period
1534	Choirmaster at Angers Cathedral
1549	Settles in Paris

Janequin's songs often use short melodic fragments which imitate natural or man-made sounds. "Les cris de Paris" evokes the sound of Parisian street life.

Alexander Agricola

● c1446–1506   Belgian   ♬ 120

Born Alexander Ackerman, the illegitimate son of a wealthy Dutch businesswoman, Agricola was an internationally popular composer in the 1490s. He worked in courts and churches in Italy, France, and the Low Countries, being in demand enough to name his own salary. Technically, his sacred Masses and motets, secular songs, and instrumental pieces – which show the influence of Okeghem – are typical of the time, but his music's intense and restless character was described by some contemporaries as "crazy and strange".

MILESTONES	
1470s	At court of Duke of Milan
1474	At court of Lorenzo de' Medici
1475	Working in Cambrai
1491	Leaves France for Florence
1490s	Songs gain international popularity
1499	Visits Ghent on mother's death
1500	Starts work for Burgundy court

Jacob Arcadelt

● c1507–1568   Belgian   ♬ 50

French by upbringing, Arcadelt – after a tentative start to his career in Italy – became a leading composer of secular works. From the 1530s until Lassus arrived in the 1550s, Arcadelt's simple, clear French chansons were highly popular. However, it was his 200-odd Italian madrigals, especially the four-part ones, which established his reputation in the 1530s: flexible, graceful, singable music that sensitively illustrated the text. The first of his five books of madrigals went through 58 editions, and was still being published in 1654.

MILESTONES	
1538	First book of madrigals
1540	Enters papal chapel in Rome
1544	Singing master at St Peter's Basilica
1551	Returns to France
1554	Enters service of Charles, Duke of Guise, later Archbishop of Rheims
1560s	Six books of chansons published

John Taverner

● 1490–1545 ▥ English ✍ c.70

Taverner was a man of great influence in England in the 16th century, both as a composer and through his work as an associate of Thomas Cromwell – Henry VIII's chief advisor who presided over the Dissolution of the monasteries. It is likely that Taverner empathized with the spirit of the Protestant reforms; one document records his shame at writing "popish ditties" – music that celebrated the Virgin Mary or Christian saints – in his earlier career.

LIFE AND MUSIC

As well as being a composer, Taverner worked as a singer, organist, and music teacher, and may have been politically active, too. In 1528, an investigation at Cardinal Wolsey's college, where Taverner was choirmaster, suspected him of circulating Lutheran literature and briefly imprisoned him. If the caricatures found in a copy of one of his works are accurate, his appearance was not as becoming as the beautiful choral works that form the major part of his output, which included motets, Masses, and secular items. He wrote eight Masses in all, and the tune for the "In nomine Domini" section of his *Missa "Gloria tibi Trinitas"* became one of the most popular cantus firmus melodies for instrumental music in England, in a genre known as the "In nomine" in honour of Taverner's vocal original. The opera *Taverner* by Peter Maxwell Davies depicts a popular account of the composer's life.

MILESTONES

c.1520	*Missa "Gloria tibi Trinitas"* composed
1525	Working at Tattershall Collegiate Church, Lincolnshire
1528	Imprisoned for heresy
1530s	Works as agent of Thomas Cromwell
1537	Joins the Guild of Corpus Christi in Boston, Lincolnshire
c.1540	Composes *Magnificat à 4*

KEY WORKS

MISSA "GLORIA TIBI TRINITAS"
MASS SETTING

The influence of the *Missa "Gloria tibi Trinitas"*, which dates to the mid-1520s, spread beyond sacred vocal music. At the "In nomine Domini" section of the Benedictus, the alto sings a freely composed melody in long, slow notes.

MAGNIFICAT À 4
CANTICLE

This Magnificat, for four adult male voices, may be the latest of Taverner's three settings. The text contains the words of the Virgin Mary at the Annunciation, and the piece may have been performed for the celebration of this feast in Boston, Lincolnshire.

Though he spent most of his time in Lincolnshire, Taverner was appointed to instruct the choristers at the newly founded Cardinal College in Oxford in 1528.

Thomas Tallis

● c.1505–1585   ⚑ English   ✍ 100+

Thomas Tallis's musical career spanned the reigns of four
English monarchs: Henry VIII, Edward VI, Mary (a Catholic)
and Elizabeth I (a Protestant). The period saw enormous shifts in
religious life and compositional style. Most of Tallis's output was for the church,
though he did write a handful of secular works. His flexibility as a composer
undoubtedly ensured his survival as a leading figure in English music.

LIFE AND MUSIC

Tallis trained as a musician in the pre-
Reformation Church. However, under
a succession of rulers, he was required
to write both Catholic and Anglican
service music, all of which was of first
quality. Brought up near Canterbury,
his appointments quickly drew him to
London. Tallis was a superb organist,
but few of his keyboard pieces have
survived. Dating his works is difficult,
especially as he occasionally reworked
old music for a new purpose. Well-
known for his florid Latin works, Tallis's
simpler, Anglican music is equally well
crafted and enjoyable to perform.

MILESTONES	
1531	Working at Dover Priory
1537	Working at St Mary-at-Hill in London
1538	Working at Waltham Abbey
1540	Waltham Abbey dissolved by Henry VIII; Tallis moves to Canterbury
1543	Employed by the Chapel Royal
1547	Accession of Edward VI
1552	Marries Joan
1553	Accession of Mary Tudor
1554	Composes Mass "Puer natus est nobis"
1558	Accession of Elizabeth I
1575	Byrd and Tallis awarded licence to print music; *Cantiones sacrae* published

KEY WORKS

O NATA LUX DE LUMINE
MOTET

Despite its Latin text, the lucid and
carefully-paced word setting of *O nata
lux de lumine* suggests it was composed
during the reign of Elizabeth I. It
appeared in *Cantiones sacrae,* a joint
publication between Thomas Tallis

and William
Byrd, and the
first collection
of motets
and hymns to
be published
in England.

In 1575 Elizabeth I
granted Tallis and
Byrd a 21-year
joint monopoly to
print music.

IF YE LOVE ME
ANTHEM

Compared with the rich and complex
Catholic works of the era, the style of
this anthem immediately transports the
listener to the heart of the Reformed
liturgy of the 1540s. In two sections,
the second of which is repeated, the
message to keep God's commandments
is communicated through carefully
paced phrasing and delicate imitation.

LAMENTATIONS OF JEREMIAH
CHORAL

Tallis wrote two settings of this emotive
text for Maundy Thursday. The first
uses the verses "Aleph" and "Beth",
the second "Gimel", "Daleth", and
"Heth". The music is rich, with gentle,
overlapping melodies.

FOCUS

SPEM IN ALIUM NUNQUAM HABUI
MOTET

Spem in alium is perhaps Tallis's best-known work. Some musicians have sought a numerically significant occasion for its composition, such as the 40th anniversary of the coronation of Elizabeth I, but no theory has been found that is wholly convincing. An earlier 40-part piece by Alessandro Striggio, *Ecce beatam lucem*, must have been an influence.

Tallis uses spatial elements by arranging the voices into eight five-part choirs, and the music can be heard to sweep around the full choir, or work with the sub-choirs singing across to one another. *Spem in alium* opens with a solo voice, but quickly builds as voices are layered on top of one another until the sound is rich and sonorous. The first voices gradually drop out of the texture at the same time, so the full choir does not sing together until the dramatic moment at bar 40, surely a reference to the number of parts. After this, the sound is passed, seamlessly, in reverse direction from the eighth sub-choir back to the first.

The co-ordination of 40 vocal parts, which might originally have been performed by soloists, is a major feat, particularly given the complex interplay of independent voices through much of the music. From bar 80, pairs or groups of choirs call and respond in a powerful and highly effective section, though the musical material is constantly varied. The full choir sings only four times; a dramatic rest in all parts precedes the final full-choir section that ends the work.

LAUDATE DOMINUM
MOTET

The five-part psalm-motet *Laudate dominum* was probably composed during the 1560s. Psalm-motets

had been developed by Tallis's contemporaries, including Christopher Tye and Robert White. The feeling of celebration is created with the opening idea, a rising phrase, in the contratenor for the word *laudate* (praise), imitated by the remaining voices as they enter one by one. The most important words and ideas are emphasized by repetition, such as the reiteration of the phrase *Et veritas Domini manet in aeternum (And the truth of the Lord endures forever)*, swung between upper and lower voices before performance by the full choir. The idea of the unchanging Christian Church may hint at Tallis's experiences of working through the troubled period of the Reformation, when many of the old Catholic traditions were erased from the new Anglican liturgy.

"The most frivolous and gallant words are set to exactly the same music as those of the Bible…"

HECTOR BERLIOZ ON THE MUSIC OF PALESTRINA

Giovanni Pierluigi da Palestrina

● c.1525–1594   ♙ Italian   ✍ 650+

Palestrina's is perhaps the most familiar name of all late Renaissance composers and his sacred music is widely regarded as a pinnacle of contrapuntal style, rich and flowing in its sound. Hundreds of his works survive and many of these were published during his lifetime. Although the majority of them were produced for use in religious worship, he also wrote over 100 madrigals, both secular and sacred.

Palestrina spent almost all his career working and composing for the Catholic Church in Rome, much of it for the Vatican.

LIFE

Apart from the fact that he was born in the town of Palestrina in Italy, practically nothing is known about Giovanni Pierluigi's early history. His later career centred mainly on Rome, where he was trained and where he worked for most of his life. As far as is known, Palestrina began his musical life as organist and choirmaster in 1544 in his native city. His reputation grew and he gained his first Roman post in 1550 as a choirmaster at the Cappella Giulia, a subsidiary of the Sistine Choir. It was soon after this that he published his first book of masses. A brief spell at the Sistine Chapel itself in 1555 ended in his dimissal by the new pope, ostensibly for being married. His rejection made Palestrina fall ill, but after recovering, he gained an appointment to the post of Maestro di cappella at the basilica of St John Lateran, although it did not not pay well. From 1561 to 1566 he worked at the more prestigious church of Santa Maria Maggiore, after which he enjoyed, until 1571, the patronage of the wealthy Cardinal Ippolito II d'Este. The remaining years of Palestrina's musical career were spent back at the Cappella Giulia and his intention to return to his native Palestrina in 1593 was never realized. After members of his close family died in the outbreaks of influenza in the early 1570s, and the death of his first wife, Lucrezia, in 1580, he considered pursuing a celibate way of life, but the following year he married a fur merchant, Virginia Dormoli. This marriage ensured him a steady income and Palestrina helped Virginia's business to flourish. Becoming a very wealthy man, he was financially able to publish 16 collections of his works.

MUSICAL OUTPUT	
MASSES	104
MOTETS	300+
OFFERTORIES	68
HYMNS	71+
OTHER SACRED VOCAL	46
MADRIGALS	61
Total:	650+

MUSIC

Given the sacred institutions that employed him, it is hardly surprising that most of Palestrina's output comprised music for the liturgy. His mastery of counterpoint resulted in subsequent generations using his works as a model for their own. His reputation was heightened by the composer Johann Joseph Fux's use of Palestrina's music in his treatise *Gradus ad Parnassum* (1725), and by 19th-century biographies that praised his music without reservation.

Palestrina's music is characterized by elegant melodic lines in all the vocal parts, by the careful treatment of dissonance, and by a sensitivity to text-setting that foreshadows the *seconda prattica* of the 17th century. While his music rarely contains overt word-painting, the meaning and accents of the Latin or Italian language are never lost. His most refined writing is to be found in his Masses, which are written in a variety of different ways; some were settings of borrowed musical material, while others were entirely freely composed. His madrigals include both secular and sacred songs.

MILESTONES	
1547	Marries Lucrezia Gori on 12 June
1554	Publication of first book of Masses
1555	Publication of first book of madrigals
1567	Publication of Masses, including *Missa "Papae Marcelli"*
1569	Publication of first book of motets for five voices
1581	Marries furrier Virginia Dormoli on 28 February
1588	Lamentations published
1589	Publication of hymns
1591	Settings for Magnificat published
1593	Publication of litanies and offertories

KEY WORKS

MISSA "L'HOMME ARMÉ"
MASS SETTING

Palestrina wrote two Mass settings based on the melody "L'homme armé", a popular song that provided the foundation for at least 40 Masses in the 15th and 16th centuries. The five-part setting dates from 1570, and the four-part Mass from 1582.

MISSA "PAPAE MARCELLI"
MASS SETTING

This Mass, published in 1567, takes its name from Pope Marcellus II, who held the Papacy for just three weeks in 1555. It used to be said that this Mass safeguarded the future of Catholic music, a myth that has proved difficult to dispel. The music's sense of balance and poise is evident from the opening Kyrie. Traces of the "L'homme armé" melody can be heard in this work.

IO SON FERITO, AHI LASSO
MADRIGAL

This five-part secular madrigal of 1561 ("Alas, I am wounded"), shows Palestrina's skilful but understated text setting, for example, in the use of long note values to evoke the agony of parting. The scoring is varied throughout this work, which ends with long held notes in the upper and middle parts, while the others parts work the cadence around them.

Palestrina presents his work to Pope Julius III on the title page of his *Missarum Liber Primus* (first book of masses), published in 1554.

FOCUS

MISSA BREVIS
MASS SETTING

The origin of the name *Missa brevis* (short Mass) for one of Palestrina's finest mass settings is unclear. It was published in 1570. After a contrapuntal Kyrie, the Gloria opens with all four parts in homophony before the parts begin to weave an imitative texture, sometimes working in pairs or trios. The new section at "Qui tollis peccata mundi" brings the parts together in a chordal texture. In the Benedictus, the three voices that open the movement are rejoined by the bass at "Osanna in excelsis".

The second part of the Agnus Dei divides the upper part, to give a five-part texture.

THE LAMENTATIONS OF JEREMIAH, LESSONS 1 TO 3
BIBLICAL SETTINGS

Palestrina's settings for three lessons from the Lamentations of Jeremiah were commissioned by Pope Sixtus V in 1587, and were published the following year. They replaced those of Carpentras, which had been sung by the papal choir for over 60 years during Holy Week. The opening of the first lesson of this serene setting for Maundy Thursday is chordal, but quickly moves to an imitative texture. The rhythm of the third lesson, from "Manum suam misit" is set in perfect complement to the stresses of the Latin text, briefly using a triple metre to achieve this.

MISSA "BENEDICTUS ES"
MASS SETTING

The probable model for this six-part Mass is a motet by Josquin Desprez (1520). The Kyrie opens with a rising scalic motive that passes from voice to voice. After the first words of the Gloria are intoned, the choir enters part by part, building a contrapuntal texture. At a new section, "Qui tollis peccata mundi",

the movement becomes more reserved and penitential and closes with a relatively simple Amen. The lengthy Credo text ends with a much more elaborate and boldly dissonant "Amen". In the Sanctus-Benedictus, the highest voice opens with long held notes, while the lower parts move in steady, but more active, lines. The concluding Agnus Dei is a gentle, lyrical prayer for atonement.

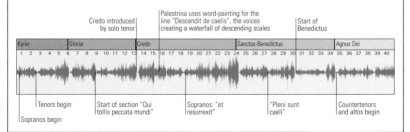

Credo introduced by solo tenor

Palestrina uses word-painting for the line "Descendit de caelis", the voices creating a waterfall of descending scales

Start of Benedictus

| Kyrie | Gloria | Credo | Sanctus-Benedictus | Agnus Dei |

1 2 3 4 5 6 7 8 9 10 11 12 13 14 15 16 17 18 19 20 21 22 23 24 25 26 27 28 29 30 31 32 33 34 35 36 37 38 39 40

Tenors begin

Sopranos begin

Start of section "Qui tollis peccata mundi"

Sopranos: "et resurrexit"

"Pleni sunt caeli"

Countertenors and altos begin

William Byrd

◐ c.1540–1623   ⚑ English   ✍ c.500

A Catholic in a Protestant land, William Byrd's reputation as a composer was such that he avoided the serious consequences of maintaining his faith under English law. Byrd's religious works show a polished contrapuntal technique, especially in their use of imitation. His verse anthems, motets, consort songs, and instrumental works are deeply expressive. His music rarely shows any influence of his teacher, Thomas Tallis.

LIFE AND MUSIC

Byrd is perhaps best known for his survival at the top of the establishment in Protestant England, despite his strong (and barely hidden) Catholic faith. His patrons, who included both wealthy Catholics and the "Virgin Queen", Elizabeth I, required a wide range of music from him for use in religious services and in the home. Apart from his Anglican music, Byrd composed and published many dangerously Catholic works that must have been performed only in a domestic context. He also produced much secular music, including some of the first notable repertoire for virginals.

MILESTONES	
1563	Appointed master of choristers and organist at Lincoln Cathedral
1572	Becomes Gentleman of Chapel Royal
1575	Elizabeth I grants Byrd and Tallis patent for publishing printed manuscript paper and music.
1575	Byrd and Tallis jointly publish *Cantiones*, comprising 17 pieces by each composer
1588	Publication of *Psalmes, sonets and songs*
1589	Publication of *Cantiones sacrae* and *Songs of Sundrie Natures*
1593	Buys Stondon Place near Stapleford-Abbott, Essex, his home for rest of life
1605	Publishes *Gradualia*, Vol 1 (Vol 2 appears in 1607)

KEY WORKS

AVE VERUM CORPUS
SEQUENCE

This sequence hymn, written for the feast of Corpus Christi, opens with all four voices in stately, reverential chords. In the second section, the upper part leads with new material, to be answered by the three lower voices, reinforcing the message, before an imitative section in which the mercy of Jesus is begged.

SUSANNA FAIR
SONG

The biblical story of Susanna revolves around the unwanted attention that the young virgin receives from two old men in the village as she is bathing. A popular story in this period, Byrd's setting is for voice and four viols.

MASS FOR FOUR VOICES
MASS SETTING

Byrd's Masses for three and five voices seem to have been based on this four-voice setting, and all would have been performed in secret Catholic services. The music is expressive, with a marked feeling of intensity, though the words are sung with great clarity.

Byrd wrote many madrigals and songs ideal for small social gatherings. Among them is "Ye Sacred Muses", a touching consort song in honour of his friend and colleague, Thomas Tallis.

FOCUS

GREAT SERVICE
LITURGICAL

Byrd was an innovator in form and technique in his liturgical works and contributed greatly to the developing genre of the English Anthem (including the newer "verse" style with organ accompaniment), composing his widely regarded *Great Service* in this format. The work its name from its massive scale; two choirs of five voices perform in different combinations across seven movements: Venite, Te Deum, Benedictus, Kyrie, Creed, Magnificat, and Nunc Dimittis. Most of Byrd's liturgical repertoire was written during his years at Lincoln, but this music was composed in London, probably sometime during the late 1580s. The earliest manuscript source calls it the "Long Service". Such is the variety of musical style, vocal scoring, and approach to word-setting in the *Great Service*, it seems likely that some or all movements existed independently before being conflated into one composite work in the manner of J S Bach's *Mass in B Minor*.

Unlike Byrd's three Mass settings in Latin, the *Great Service* is in English, for use in the Anglican liturgy. During the reign of Edward VI (1547–1553), Archbishop Thomas Cranmer's Lincoln Cathedral Injunctions (1548) had commanded that composers of Anglican music should seek clarity of textual expression, "a plain and distinct note for every syllable".

"QUI PASSE: FOR MY LADY NEVELL"
KEYBOARD

The virginals were much favoured by female musicians of the middle and upper classes throughout Europe. Most of Byrd's works for the instrument are collected in two books and the one dedicated to Lady Nevell contains this piece. "Qui passe: for my Lady Nevell" is a wonderful transformation of a piece published 34 years earlier by the Venetian composer Filippo Azzaiolo, "Chi passa per questa strada" ("Who Walks Along this Street"). Byrd re-worked the melody as a bass line, lacing the music with energetic rhythms and fast scales in both hands. The element of surprise is maintained throughout, through frequent changes between major and minor chords, and contrasting colours and textures. The effect is one of exuberant virtuosity.

> **INFLUENCES**
>
> William Byrd's main achievement was arguably his fusion of Renaissance counterpoint with the expressive elements of English music. Since his "rediscovery" in the 20th century, his works have become great favourites with performers, who consider them the peak of British music of the Renaissance era.

Orlande de Lassus

● 1532–1594   ▣ Belgian   ✍ 1,600

In his youth, Lassus travelled throughout Italy and Sicily in the service of various aristocrats. In the 1560s, when he was comfortably settled in Bavaria with a wife and children, he was the most celebrated musician in Europe. Various publishers spread his madrigals, chansons, and sacred music internationally, and he received several royal honours. His prolific and versatile output includes some of the most beautiful examples of 16th-century church choral music (alongside those of Palestrina and Victoria), such as his Mass for double choir, *Missa Osculetur me*, plus hundreds of motets, madrigals, chansons, and lieder – and even drinking ditties and comic songs – which reveal a likeable man of great humour and wit.

Lassus composed many celebrated works for the musicians of the Bavarian court. Here he is captured in miniature playing the spinet.

MILESTONES	
c.1544	In the service of the Viceroy of Sicily
1553	Becomes choirmaster in Rome
1556	Publication of first book of chansons
1556	Enters Bavarian court
1562	Promoted to chief Kapellmeister
1563	Begins work on *Seven Penitential Psalms*
1570	Rises to the nobility
1574	Receives order of the Golden Spur

Giulio Caccini

● c1550–1618   ▣ Italian   ✍ c.80

Like that of many of his contemporaries, Giulio Caccini's career involved the composition, performance, and teaching of music. Though linked with the significant new genre of opera, his major musical achievement was arguably the collection of accompanied songs *Le nuove musiche*. He was among the first generation of virtuoso singers who became successful composers, and developed the new genre of opera alongside the Florentine composer Jacopo Peri. After moving from Rome to the important cultural city of Florence, Caccini's career was financed by the wealthy Medici family. There, he became a member of the music patron Giovanni Bardi's Camerata, a group of intellectuals interested in Ancient Greek ideals. At a wedding between members of the Medici and d'Este families, Caccini was employed to sing, dressed as an angel, as part of an elaborate mechanized performance. In his songs, Caccini developed the monodic style that was to become a pillar of the Baroque era.

Caccini's opera *Eurydice*, which tells the story of Orpheus's journey to the Underworld, was first performed in Florence in 1602.

MILESTONES	
1566	Living in Florence
1570s	Joins Florentine Camerata and develops the recitative
1586	Performs at wedding of Virginia de' Medici and Cesare d'Este
1600	First performance of Caccini's opera *Il rapimento di Cefalo*
1602	Publication of *Le nuove musiche*

Andrea Gabrieli

● c.1510–1586 🏴 Italian 🎵 400

Though generally thought of as "uncle of the more accomplished Giovanni Gabrieli", one of his pupils, Andrea Gabrieli helped establish Venice's school of home-grown composers after domination by incomers from the Netherlands. An organist at St Mark's, he composed everything from large sacred and theatre works to songs and solo keyboard pieces, with popular success – many being republished decades after his death. Gabrieli's posthumous *Concerti* formed a collection of music for Venice's state functions.

MILESTONES	
1536	Gains fame as singer at St Mark's
1554	First published madrigal
1562	Friendship with Lassus begins
1566	Becomes organist at St Mark's
1578	Receives hardship payment to help maintain sister's family
1587	*Concerti* published posthumously

Hans Leo Hassler

● 1562–1612 🏴 German 🎵 50

The Hassler family included a number of accomplished musicians, but the multilingual, cosmopolitan Hans was one of the first Germans to study in Italy, and on his return he helped to establish Italian styles and idioms in the Protestant musical world. In Venice he studied with Giovanni Gabrieli, but spent his working life back in Germany: at Augsburg, his native Nuremberg, and finally Dresden. He was known mainly as an organist and organ designer, but also wrote many beautiful sacred choral works, such as *Sacrae cantiones* and *Sacri concentus*.

MILESTONES	
1586	Becomes organist at Augsburg
1607	Composes 52 Psalms and Christian songs for Lutheran rite

Tomás Luis de Victoria

● 1548–1611 🏴 Spanish 🎵 200

Victoria started composing in Italy and became the greatest Spanish composer of the Renaissance. His work – all sacred music in Latin, including 20 Masses, 52 motets, and many other liturgical pieces – shows the subtlety and beauty of Palestrina, with whom he may have studied in Rome. After working in Italian churches, Victoria returned to Spain in 1587 to serve Empress Maria, widow of the Holy Roman Emperor Maximilian II, as choirmaster and organist at a convent in Madrid. Supported by wealthy patrons throughout his life, he was able to publish his works in distinguished editions – and some were performed as far away as Mexico. Although many works are poignant and mystical, their prevailing mood – especially in his motets – is positive, as he was a cheerful man with strong family ties.

MILESTONES	
1560s	Serves as a chorister in Ávila
1565	Leaves for Rome to study for priesthood
1572	Writes first collection of motets
1575	Ordained as a priest
1583	Writes first Requiem Mass
1594	Attends Palestrina's funeral
1603	Writes *Officium defunctorum* for funeral of Empress Maria

Victoria sang as a chorister at the cathedral in his native Ávila, also the birthplace of Saint Teresa.

Giovanni Gabrieli

● c.1554–1612   ⚑ Italian   ✍ c.250

Giovanni Gabrieli and his uncle, Andrea, were prolific and innovative composers during the late Renaissance period. Giovanni's polychoral works for voices and instruments, particularly those intended for performance in religious services, make use of a wide variety of acoustic textures and effects. Although much of his output is sacred and vocal, he also wrote many keyboard works and madrigals.

LIFE AND MUSIC

Gabrieli was possibly born in Venice, a thriving centre of musical and religious activity. He may have been raised by his uncle, before travelling to study with Orlando Lassus in Munich. Aside from his compositional duties, Giovanni was employed as an organist and music teacher, and his published works reflect the diversity of the requirements of his patrons in Venice and northern Europe. His most famous publications,

the *Sacrae symphoniae* and *Symphoniae sacre*, include pieces for between six and 19 separate parts. Gabrieli was renowned for his technical abilities and his keyboard works include both improvisatory toccatas and more formally structured ricercari.

MILESTONES	
1564	Becomes organist at St Mark's, Venice
1575	Spends time at Bavarian court, Munich
1585	Becomes principal organist at St Mark's
1587	Composes *O magnum mysterium*, motet
1593	Publication of organ intonations on the 12 tones
1597	Publication of the *Sacrae symphoniae*
1593	Posthumous publication of the *Canzoni et sonate* and *Symphoniae sacrae*

Much of the sacred music written for St Mark's, Venice, in the polychoral style was by Giovanni Gabrieli. As many as five choirs were placed in different galleries around the high altar.

KEY WORKS

ANGELUS AD PASTORES
MOTET

The Christmas text relating to the angel and shepherds and the Nativity was set by Gabrieli as a 12-part work for two choirs of six voices.

CANZON DUODECIMI TONI
CANZONA

The instrumentation of this ten-part instrumental canzona is not specified in the original published score. However, its range and character suit

cornets and sackbuts very well, and often an organ is used to provide a basso continuo. It was written in the 12th mode, which was associated with victory and triumph.

O CHE FELICE GIORNO
MADRIGAL

This eight-part madrigal was written for performance before a noble patron in 1585, and was later revised as a Christmas motet with the new text *Hodie Christus natus est*.

FOCUS

SONATA PIAN' E FORTE, FROM SACRAE SYMPHONIAE

SONATA

Many of Gabrieli's works would have been performed by a rich combination of instruments, including strings, wind, organ, and plucked continuo. The antiphonal effects in the music were emphasized by the spatial arrangement of musicians in opposing organ lofts within the Church – a divided-choir technique known as cori spezzati. In the *Sonata pian' e forte*, one of three sonatas in the 1597 collection, the instrumental forces are divided into two choirs of four players each. As the title suggests, the dynamics are clearly marked by the composer, a relatively new practice at that time. The opening section consists of long, sustained homophony, but by the end of the piece the writing takes on a complex eight-part contrapuntal texture.

Gabrieli's sonatas and canzonas were written for instruments only, perhaps for the accompaniment of church processions. One may infer from their complex style that the musicians for whom they were written were highly accomplished, whether string, wind, brass, or keyboard players. Some parts, particularly those for higher-pitched instruments, are virtuosic. It is likely that even these pieces had a place in the most important celebrations of the Church calendar.

O MAGNUM MYSTERIUM

MOTET

A relatively early motet, *O magnum mysterium* is one of Gabrieli's finest pieces of music. The eight-part choir is divided into high and low voices. At the opening, the harmony is ambiguous, playing with major and minor chords, and the shifting between different tonal areas lends weight to the text, which focuses on the miracle of Christ's birth. The majority of the motet works steadily through the text, the phrases repeated by different combinations of voices. The two choirs sing antiphonally at the words "Beata virgo" ("Blessed virgin"), and the "Alleluia", which continues the use of cori spezzati, features a lively triple rhythm, apt for the celebration of the Christmas message. The text was set a number times during the Renaissance period, by other composers, including Tomás Luis de Victoria.

INFLUENCES

Gabrieli's successor at the Basilica of St Mark in Venice was Claudio Monteverdi, whose reputation dwarfed that of his predecessor. However, Gabrieli's innovative instrumental and choral music proved extremely popular with German composers, and was championed by German musicians writing about music in the 19th century.

Jacopo Peri

● 1561–1633   ▯ Italian   ✍ 50

As the composer of the first surviving opera – *Euridice* – Peri's place in music history is assured. A musician at the Medici court, he gained a reputation as an actor, singer, and dazzling chitarrone player. In collaboration with other Florentine musicians, poets, and philosophers throughout the 1590s, Peri helped devise the idea of opera. The result was *Dafne*, for which he set the text and sang Apollo. It was a small-scale affair, performed privately in a room. *Euridice* followed, first played before an intimate royal audience to celebrate the marriage of Maria de' Medici and Henri IV of France. Continuing to work for the Medicis, Peri became more in demand as a stage composer, and his songs were published by popular request. A slim, endearing man, he was nicknamed "Zazzerino" – a reference to his attractive, long blond hair.

Peri performed in many of his operas, and his singing received much praise.

MILESTONES	
1579	Organist in Florence
1588	Works at Medici court
1598	*Dafne*, opera, performed at Carnival
1600	*Euridice*, opera, premiered 6 October
1609	Song collection, *Le varie musiche*, first published
1620s	Writes three oratorios and two operas in collaboration with other composers

---

Jan Pieterszoon Sweelinck

● c.1562–1621   ▯ Dutch   ✍ 320

Sweelinck's life was virtually all spent in Amsterdam. A civil servant, his personal life was well regulated, comfortably rewarded, and uneventful. He was known across Europe as a teacher, drawing pupils from Germany in the 1600s, and his influence on north German organ playing culminated in the music of J S Bach. A perfecter of existing forms rather than a pioneer, he wrote around 70 keyboard works, such as fantasias – which led to the development of the fugue – and toccatas. None were published in his lifetime, but they were enthusiastically copied by pupils. In contrast, his 250 vocal works, which include chansons, madrigals, and motets, were all published.

Sweelinck served as an organist at Oude Kerk in Amsterdam for over 40 years, and was renowned for his brilliant improvisations.

MILESTONES	
c.1577	Starts as organist at Oude Kerk
1594	First published work: book of chansons
1597	First psalm settings published
1606	Portrait painted by brother Gerrit
1619	*Cantiones sacrae*, Catholic motets for five-part choir, published

John Dowland

● 1563–1626   🏳 English   ✎ 220

England's greatest composer of lute music and songs spent much of his career on the Continent, so he can have seen little of his family in London. Though he had patronage and enormous publishing success at home, and lasting influence abroad, he struggled for appointments in England. His involvement with scheming English Catholics in Italy didn't help his prospects, and he seems to have been a prickly, occasionally paranoid man. His *First Booke of Songs* was a bestseller and cemented his reputation. Its clever multi-directional layout, which enabled soloists or groups around a table to easily read parts singly or in combination, was a key to its success. Melancholy features strongly in his work: his bleak song "In darkness let me dwell" is remarkably dissonant and harmonically unstable.

Dowland's bittersweet melodies were greatly admired in his lifetime, and the poet Richard Banfield wrote that his "heavenly touch upon the lute doth ravish human sense".

MILESTONES	
1588	Listed among the major English composers
1594	Leaves England to work in Germany
1597	*First Booke of Songs* published
1598	Accepts position at Danish court
1604	*Lachrimae*, consort music, published
1612	Finally employed by the English court as one of the King's lutenists

Carlo Gesualdo

● c.1561–1613   🏳 Italian   ✎ 150

Prince of Venosa – and murderer? He found his wife, Maria d'Avalos, "in flagrante delicto" with the Duke of Andria – and both were assassinated. His vocal music is notorious for its remarkable dissonance. A gentleman amateur at first, he gained a professional reputation with his later madrigals. Gesualdo's last years were spent in morbid isolation at his castle, music-making his only pleasure.

MILESTONES	
1586	Marries Maria d'Avalos
1590	Wife and her lover murdered
1594	Marries noblewoman Leonora d'Este
1594	First book of madrigals published
1595	Retires to Gesualdo Castle, Avellino, outside Naples
1611	Three books of madrigals published

Thomas Campion

● 1567–1620   🏳 English   ✎ 100

Campion was born into an affluent family in Essex and became a dilettante theorist, poet, and musician. After John Dowland, he was the most prolific of lute-song composers, with over 100 to his name, the lyrics of which are of outstanding literary merit. He attended Cambridge University, studied law at Gray's Inn and medicine at Caen, but preferred socializing and cultural activities to studying. He wrote masques, poems, and five books of songs – some self-published with friends – and was much in demand to supply both texts and music for entertainments at the royal court of James I.

MILESTONES	
1586	Studies at Gray's Inn
1588	Works as an actor and singer
1601	*First Booke of Ayres* published
1605	Receives degree in medicine, Caen
1613	*Treatise on Counterpoint* published

The BAROQUE ERA *1600–1750*

The Baroque era saw the genesis of opera, the growth of the orchestra, and a flourishing of instrumental music, especially for the violin and keyboard. Most new fashions originated in Italy and Italian musicians dominated the field, but, by the end of the period, distinctive national styles had evolved.

T he word "baroque" was originally a pejorative term for a style of architecture and art produced between the end of the 16th and the mid-18th centuries, but by the time music scholars adopted the term it had lost most of its negative connotations.

The period was one of great creativity – from Shakespeare and Cervantes in literature to Newton and Galileo in science. Music, too, blossomed. By the 1590s a new musical style had emerged in contrast to the lush polyphony of Palestrina and his contemporaries. Instead of complex intertwining parts, the new style (dubbed *seconda prattica* or "second practice" to distinguish it from the *prima prattica* of earlier Renaissance compositions) placed a solo voice or instrument above

A YOUNG VIOLINIST
This painting by Dutch Baroque artist Hendrick Terbrugghen (1588–1629) shows a boy playing an early form of violin and singing.

a simple accompaniment consisting of a bass line with the chords lightly filled in above it (the basso continuo, a "continuous bass"). There were usually two instruments playing the continuo – a keyboard, lute, or guitar along with a low-ranged melodic instrument such as a cello, bass viol, or bassoon reinforcing the bass line.

The term "monody" (from the Greek meaning "one song") is used to describe this new combination of solo voice and basso continuo. Monody allowed the performer the freedom to embellish and ornament the melodic line at will, something unthinkable in the older polyphonic style.

THE BIRTH OF OPERA

This new style of singing allowed composers to convey the text clearly through a solo voice, while singers could interpret the words more dramatically. It was monody that made musical drama – opera – possible. The invention of opera

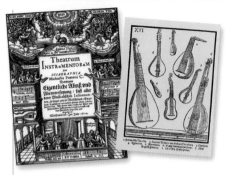

THE INSTRUMENTS OF THE EARLY BAROQUE
Michael Praetorius, a prolific German composer, published his *Syntagma Musicum* in 1619 . It includes an encyclopedic guide to the instruments of the day.

is credited to a group of Florentine musicians and poets known as the Camerata, particularly the composers Giulio Caccini and Jacopo Peri and the poet Ottavio Rinuccini, who were trying to recreate the singing style of Ancient Greek drama. This new style was first seen in *intermedi* – short musical dramas performed between the acts of spoken plays – but

in 1598 the three collaborated on *Dafne*, the first true opera. Two years later, both Peri and Caccini wrote operas on the Orpheus myth, *Euridice*, but it was Monteverdi's *Orfeo* (1607) that is seen as the true benchmark for early opera. The new art form would combine a variety of musical styles – speech-like recitative, moving arias, choral and instrumental interludes – into one large narrative structure.

The Catholic Church frowned on the "immoral" plots of some operas and banned their performance during Advent and Lent. The void was filled by another kind of dramatic vocal music: the oratorio. Operas and

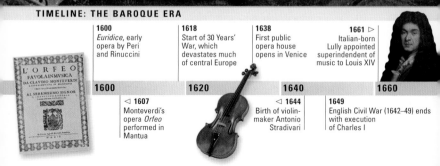

TIMELINE: THE BAROQUE ERA

1600	1618	1638	1661 ▷
Euridice, early opera by Peri and Rinuccini	Start of 30 Years' War, which devastates much of central Europe	First public opera house opens in Venice	Italian-born Lully appointed superintendent of music to Louis XIV

1600	**1620**	**1640**	**1660**
◁ 1607 Monteverdi's opera *Orfeo* performed in Mantua		◁ 1644 Birth of violin-maker Antonio Stradivari	1649 English Civil War (1642–49) ends with execution of Charles I

oratorios both employed recitative, arias, duets, and instrumental pieces, but oratorios were unstaged, with no costumes or sets, and naturally tended to be about biblical subjects. Comic opera was a later development, gaining ground in the 1730s. It deveoped from short comic pieces (*intermezzi*), such as Pergolesi's *La serva padrona* (1738), performed in the intervals between the acts of serious operas.

INSTRUMENTAL MUSIC

Opera was not the only musical form to flourish. Major and minor courts across Europe maintained chamber ensembles as a mark of prestige. This created a demand for instrumental sonatas and concertos to entertain the noble patrons and their guests. In the sonata, the violin (which could emulate certain qualities of the singing voice) gained a whole new repertoire and generated an increased interest in its potential. This was also the age of the great violin makers of Cremona – Amati, Stradivari, and Guarneri.

The 17th century also saw the birth of the orchestra, driven in large part by the growth in opera, the size of the ensemble growing along with the visual spectacle onstage. Keyboard music (mainly for harpsichord and organ) also flourished, and virtuosi such as Johann Pachelbel and the Couperins attracted much attention in court and church circles.

MUSICIANS AT THE COURT OF MODENA, c.1690
This painting by Anton Domenico Gabbiani shows a small chamber ensemble. A number of violinists and a cellist are gathered around the harpsichord player.

THE STAGING OF OPERA

Opera began as a court entertainment, usually for specific private occasions such as a marriage between two noble households. Venice opened a public opera house as early as 1638 and other cities, such as Hamburg (1678), gradually followed. The high ticket prices, however, restricted attendance to the merchant classes and above. Public demand ensured that performances grew more and more spectacular. Large amounts of money were spent on lavish costumes, lighting, and staging, with special effects including airborne chariots, gods descending from the heavens by means of complex systems of ropes and pulleys, and ornate group dances.

BAROQUE OPERA SET
The opera *Giunio Bruto* – the first act of which was by Cesarini, the second by Caldara, and the third by Alessandro Scarlatti – was first performed in 1707.

Although the innovations of the early Baroque came out of Italy, distinctive national styles began to emerge. The Italian style was one of melodic dominance, virtuosity, and a strong sense of metre; the French, developed by Lully at the court of Louis XIV, was strongly influenced by dance rhythms. The German style, taken to its greatest heights by J S Bach, was essentially a hybrid of the two, with the addition of a contrapuntal element.

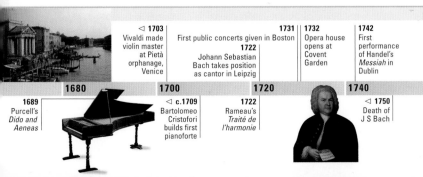

◁ **1703**
Vivaldi made violin master at Pietà orphanage, Venice

1731
First public concerts given in Boston

1722
Johann Sebastian Bach takes position as cantor in Leipzig

1732
Opera house opens at Covent Garden

1742
First performance of Handel's *Messiah* in Dublin

1680

1700

1720

1740

1689
Purcell's *Dido and Aeneas*

◁ **c.1709**
Bartolomeo Cristofori builds first pianoforte

1722
Rameau's *Traité de l'harmonie*

◁ **1750**
Death of J S Bach

*"The end of all good music
is to affect the soul."*

CLAUDIO MONTEVERDI

Claudio Monteverdi

◯ 1567–1643 Italian ✍ 254

More than any composer, Claudio Monteverdi defined the transition from the Renaissance style to the Baroque. Although his early madrigals reflect the lush chromatic style of the late Renaissance, Monteverdi not only embraced the simplified new style but was also its greatest advocate. His opera *L'Orfeo*, which explored the musical and dramatic possibilities of the new style, marked the beginning of a new era.

LIFE

A prolific songwriter, Monteverdi is best known for his secular madrigals on the theme of love.

Monteverdi began his musical career young, publishing his first book of madrigals at age 15 and his second eight years later. At this time he was making a living performing, eventually securing a position as a lowly court musician for the Duke of Mantua. It was here that he met his wife Claudia Cattaneo, the daughter of a colleague in the string band. Although his time in Mantua was productive, Monteverdi felt undervalued as a composer, eventually leaving for the more prestigious position of maestro di cappella at St Mark's Cathedral in Venice. In addition to his duties there he also continued to take on outside commissions, including several from his old employer, the Duke of Mantua. He often wrote music for the annual Venetian Carnival, most notably the stage work *Il combattimento de Tancredi e Clorinda* for a commedia troupe in 1624. Monteverdi cultivated his relationships with wealthy patrons and with other composers (Heinrich Schütz visited in 1628–29) and enjoyed a quiet middle age until 1630, when plague and a war in Mantua rocked Venice; subsequently Monteverdi entered the priesthood. His final years were spent revising his earlier works, completing his treatise on seconda pratica, and composing new music. His final book of madrigals was published posthumously in 1651.

MUSICAL OUTPUT							Total: 254
INSTRUMENTAL (1)							1
DRAMATIC (25)			1	5	8	4	7
SACRED VOCAL (20)	2			3	8	3	4
SECULAR VOCAL (208)	20	55	40	20	33	10	30
	1567	1585	1595	1605	1615	1625	1635	1643

MUSIC

Monteverdi's early madrigals may have been firmly in the traditional style, but by 1600 he had already begun to incorporate elements of the new, more austere style into his works, a practice which made him the target of criticism from conservative music critic Giovanni Artusi. Monteverdi responded by including a manifesto on the seconda pratica as a postface to his fifth book of madrigals in 1605. His published madrigals were already known as far as Copenhagen when he wrote his first opera, *L'Orfeo*, in 1607. A second opera, *Arianna*, followed the next year, fuelled by his grief over the loss of his wife. *Arianna* proved even more popular than *L'Orfeo*, particularly the Lament, which is the only surviving portion of the opera. Following his appointment to St Mark's in 1613, the focus of Monteverdi's writing shifted to sacred choral music, although he

MILESTONES	
1587	First of nine books of madrigals published
1590	Becomes string player for Duke of Mantua
1599	Marries singer Claudia Cattaneo
1600	Travels to Austria, Hungary, and Italy as part of Duke's entourage
1607	*L'Orfeo*; wife Claudia dies
1608	Writes *Arianna*
1610	Composes Mass and Vespers, dedicated to Pope Paul V
1613	Appointed maestro di cappella at St Mark's in Venice
1624	Writes Il combattimento de Tancredi e Clorinda

continued to write madrigals and dramatic music throughout his life, including *Il Ritorno d'Ulisse in Patria* (1640) and *L'Incoronazione di Poppea* (1642) for the new opera in Venice.

KEY WORKS

LUCI SERENE E CHIARE
MADRIGAL   3:30   1

This is a transitional madrigal, with elements of both the old and new styles. The five-part text setting is clear and uncomplicated; this may be in part to allow instruments to either replace or double vocal parts, as a later arrangement with basso continuo suggests. The poem ("Eyes serene and clear / You inflame me") by Ridolfo Arlotti is on the subject of suffering from the pangs of love.

SI, CH'IO VORREI MORIRE
MADRIGAL   3:00   1

Another five-part madrigal, *Si, ch'io vorrei morire* hides a much more earthy message. The

Cremona Cathedral, where Monteverdi began his musical career as a choirboy.

references to dying in the text are an allusion to a much more pleasant "ending", as supported by both other portions of the lyrics ("Ah mouth! Ah lips! Ah tongue!") and the rather unsubtle rising and falling of the music.

CRUDA AMARILLI
MADRIGAL   2:30   1

From the fifth book of madrigals, this five-part madrigal is more harmonically stable than *Luci serene*,

although elements of the older polyphonic style remain. This madrigal was specifically cited by Artusi as an example of the "Imperfections of Modern Music". The text ("Cruel Amaryllis") is taken from Giovanni Guarini's play *Il pastor fido*, a popular source for contemporary composers.

FOCUS

L'ORFEO

OPERA   108:00   5   🎼🎭🕯

Though not his first opera, Monteverdi's *L'Orfeo* was the first to gain broad acceptance and to popularize the elements of the *seconda pratica*. Based on the ancient Orpheus myth, the opera presents a variety of styles: "dry" and fully-accompanied recitative, florid arias, choruses and instrumental interludes. Also, in keeping with the traditions of Classical Greek drama, he makes use of deus ex machina ("god from a machine") in the final act.

PROLOGUE (16:30) Following the opening fanfare, the spirit of Music appears to introduce the tale.

ACT ONE (16:30) Nymphs and shepherds gather to celebrate the wedding of Orpheus and Euridice. They dance and offer up thanks to the gods.

ACT TWO (25:20) Orpheus is telling of his joy when a messenger arrives with bad tidings: Euridice has been killed by a snake. The assembled crowd bewail their grief, while Orpheus vows to descend to Hades to win Euridice back.

ACT THREE (27:00) Orpheus, guided by the spirit of Hope, arrives in the Underworld. He charms the boatman Charon to sleep with his song, and continues onward.

ACT FOUR (16:20) Won over by Orpheus's music, Persephone begs her husband Pluto to release Euridice; he agrees, on the condition that Orpheus not look upon her until he has returned to the living world. He sings first of his joy and then of his growing doubts that she is following him. Hearing a noise and fearing attack by the Furies, Orpheus turns, but as he sees Euridice she fades from view.

ACT FIVE (16:20) Orpheus returns to Thrace to mourn. His father, Apollo, chastises him and invites him to return to "where true virtue finds its due reward, joy and tranquillity". They rise to the heavens on the cloud, singing.

VESPRO DELLA BEATA VERGINE (VESPERS)

CHORAL   72:00   14   ⚓🎭🕯

Monteverdi's *Vespers for the Blessed Virgin* was written during his service for the Duke of Mantua, although his duties did not include composing sacred music. In fact, the work is dedicated to Pope Paul V and was published in a volume which also included his *Mass in illa tempore* as well as several Vespers psalm settings and motets. It is possible that he later used these as "audition pieces" to obtain the position at St Mark's in Venice. The work contains a mixture of both *prima* and *seconda pratica*, and a reworking of an instrumental toccata from *L'Orfeo*.

INFLUENCES

Monteverdi's writings on the *seconda pratica* and his madrigals, sacred music, and operas in that style make him the most influential composer of his time. His music also shows a slow movement from modal harmonies to the key-based tonal system we use today. He also played a vital role in the creation of secular music for the general public.

Gregorio Allegri

● 1582–1652　　♙ Italian　　✍ c.30

Although Allegri composed and published a steady stream of sacred works throughout his lifetime, he is remembered largely for his *Miserere*, an elaborate sacred motet sung by the papal choir during Holy Week every year until 1870. The details of the work were a closely guarded secret, although a fourteen-year-old Mozart reputedly reproduced the work from memory after one hearing.

LIFE AND MUSIC

Allegri's position as singer and maestro di cappella of the papal choir crowned a career which began as a boy chorister at age nine. He commenced his studies in composition with G M Nanino, the maestro di cappella at Rome's San Luigi dei Francesi. After appointments at cathedrals in Fermo and Tivoli, Allegri returned to Rome, eventually joining the papal choir. The music that he wrote for the Sistine Chapel, unlike his previous work, was old-fashioned for the time, following in the stile antico ("ancient style") of Palestrina, but, like that of Palestrina, demonstrating great subtlety and clarity of style. Allegri also published eight books of sacred motets in a more modern style between 1618 and 1639, which were intended for wider usage.

MILESTONES	
1607	Active as singer and composer at Fermo and Tivoli cathedrals
1618	Publishes first book of motets; *Concertini, libro I* published (now lost)
1619	*Concertini, libro II* published
1628	Appointed maestro di cappella of St Spirito in Sassia, Rome
1629	Joins papal choir in Rome
c.1638	Composes *Miserere Mei Deus*
c.1640	Publication of *Lamentationes Jeremiae prophetae I*, sacred vocal work
1650	Elected maestro di cappella of papal choir; composes *Sinfonia a 4*
c.1651	Publication of *Lamentationes Jeremiae prophetae II*, sacred vocal work

KEY WORKS

MISERERE MEI DEUS

PSALM SETTING　⏱ 12:10　📖 1　🎵

Allegri's famous *Miserere* and the shroud of secrecy surrounding it contain a larger story. The work itself is relatively simple, alternating between five-part and four-part choir sections separated by plainsong, and would have been performed with one singer on each part. What the Vatican did not wish to have copied were the added embellishments

Allegri joined the choir of the Sistine Chapel as composer and singer in 1629, and remained a member until his death.

above the basic chords; whereas with other similar compositions the singers would have added their own ornaments to the written music, often changing them with each performance, the embellishments for the *Miserere* (including the haunting high C) were also written down and had to be memorized by the choir, who would have been singing in the dark. The text is taken from Psalm 51 and begins "Have mercy upon me, O God". The psalm setting is traditionally sung as part of the Holy Week services leading up to Easter as a penitential song.

Thomas Weelkes

🌐 1575–1623 🏴 English ✒ 75

After establishing himself as a fine madrigal composer while still a teenager, the future looked bright for Thomas Weelkes. In 1603 he held a lucrative post at Chichester Cathedral, composed fine Church music, had a wealthy wife, and his recent book of madrigals – expressive, rich, and brilliantly constructed – was one of the most important of the English tradition. However, he began to spend more time in the tavern than the church, and his personal life and quality of work went into a long decline. He was eventually dismissed from his post at the cathedral for unruly, drunken behaviour.

MILESTONES

1597	First book of madrigals published
1598	Organist, Winchester College
1600	Composes madrigals for five and six voices
1617	Loses position at Chichester Cathedral

Johann Jacob Froberger

🌐 1616–1667 🏴 German ✒ 100

Froberger's keyboard music reflects his life: cosmopolitan and well-travelled, combining Italian, French, and German elements. He was court organist in Vienna, studied with Frescobaldi in Rome, and performed throughout Europe. Froberger was an early pioneer of the keyboard suite, some examples of which have personal programmes, with subtitles such as "Plainte, written in London to dispel melancholy", written after he had lost all his money to pirates.

MILESTONES

1634	Moves to Vienna
1637	Appointed court organist to Emperor Ferdinand III
1649	Publishes set of ricercares; starts three-year tour of Europe
1653	Starts work for Imperial Chapel at Regensburg
1656	Ricercares use new types of tuning
1662	Arrives penniless in London

Orlando Gibbons

🌐 1583–1625 🏴 English ✒ c.100

Born in Oxford and educated at Cambridge, where he sang with the King's College choir, Gibbons worked for the Chapel Royal from 1603 until his untimely death. He was recognised as one of the finest organists of his age; as a composer he mastered all the forms and styles of his time, including consort and keyboard music, but is remembered mainly for his fine church pieces and hymn tunes. What survives of the second of his two services, and his many verse anthems such as *This is the Record of John*, contain outstanding music, full of vitality and deft counterpoint that typifies the Baroque style. Most of his secular songs were written before he was 30, and the beautiful "Silver Swan", from the *First Set of Madrigals and Motetts*, has become well-known. So sudden was his death that he never made a will; his widow died before his estate was settled.

Along with his contemporary William Byrd, Orlando Gibbons contributed to the first book to be published containing music for the virginal.

MILESTONES

1598	Enters Cambridge University
1605	Becomes Gentleman of Chapel Royal
1612	*First Set of Madrigals and Motetts*
1619	Chamber musician to James I
1622	*O Clap Your Hands*, 8-part anthem
1623	Organist and chorus master at Westminster Abbey
1625	Dies suddenly from brain haemorrhage

PARTHENIA
or
THE MAYDENHEAD
of the first musicke that
 euer was printed for the VIRGINALLS
COMPOSED
By three famous Masters William Byrd D: John Bull & Orlando Gibbons
Gentlemen of his Maᵗⁱᵉˢ most Illustrious Chappell

Girolamo Frescobaldi

● 1583–1643　　♙ Italian　　✍ 35

As the child prodigy of a rich family, the young Frescobaldi had his musical skills displayed throughout Italy. A virtuoso keyboard player, he went on to enjoy prestigious court and church posts in Ferrara, Rome, and Mantua. After turning out some early madrigals, Frescobaldi focused on keyboard music, becoming the first major composer to face the challenges of developing a musical narrative. An outstanding improviser on harpsichord and organ, he produced an imaginative body of work covering every keyboard genre of the time, while also pioneering new techniques, especially in his capriccios and toccatas. Frescobaldi's influence was wide and long-lasting.

A virtuoso organist and imaginative improviser, Frescobaldi spent much of his musical career delighting court and Church with his keyboard skills.

MILESTONES	
1607	Makes only trip abroad, to Flanders
1608	Becomes organist at St Peter's, Rome
1613	Marries the mother of his illegitimate child
1627	Publishes his second *Libro di toccate*, (*Book of Toccatas*) for keyboard
1635	Publishes *Fiori musicali* (*Flowers of Music*), organ music for Mass

Francesco Cavalli

● 1602–1676　　♙ Italian　　✍ c.70

Cavalli was a close associate (and possibly pupil) of Monteverdi, on whose death he took over as the leading composer and performer in Venice. Born Francesco Caletto, he was an outstanding singer, and entered St Mark's choir under Monteverdi, eventually becoming the organist. Early on he composed Church music (much of it lost), but after marrying into money, he turned to stage projects. Public opera was booming, and he wrote 40 or so with great success, with *Equisto*, *Giasone*, *Xerxes*, and *Erismena* being staged throughout Italy. In contrast to early academic operas, Cavalli's were fast-paced and comic, and he developed the contrast between recitative and aria. His box-office appeal declined towards his death, but his reputation remained high.

MILESTONES	
1616	Joins the choir of St Mark's, Venice
1639	Stages his first opera, *Le nozze di Teti e di Peleo* (*The Marriage of Teti and Peleo*)
1643	Composes *Equisto*, opera
1662	Stages *Ercole amante* (*Hercules in Love*), opera, for Louis XIV in Paris
1665	Made principal organist at St Mark's

The daily round of religious ritual at St Mark's inspired much of the drama and vivacity in Cavalli's music.

Giacomo Carissimi

● 1605–1674   🏳 Italian   ✍ c.280

From the age of 23 until his death 46 years later, Carissimi was maestro di capella (chapel master) at Sant' Apollinare, the church of the Jesuit Collegio Germanico in Rome, renowned for its musical tradition. With his simple but effective style, he established the features of the Latin oratorio, using music as a kind of musical sermon, to vividly illustrate a religious point. He is famous, also, for having practically invented the cantata, whose text usually dealt with the pain of unrequited love. Carissimi was a prolific composer of motets and cantatas, though how prolific is hard to pinpoint, as many pieces were destroyed or lost. Though melancholy, Carissimi was a kind, well-respected man, and he supplemented his income by loaning money on generous repayment terms.

MILESTONES	
1628	Becomes maestro di capella at Assisi
1630	Appointed maestro di capella at Sant' Apollinare, Rome
c.1650	Composes *Jephtha*, oratorio
1654	Teaches Marc-Antoine Charpentier
1659	Funds two college sopranos from his own pocket

The Church of Santa Maria de Apollinare in Rome provided the inspirational setting for the first of Carissimi's oratorios, stimulating worship through the beauty of music.

Heinrich Schütz

● 1585–1672   🏳 German   ✍ 500

Spotted by a musician staying at the family inn, the young Schütz was encouraged to take up music, and went on to become the leading German composer of his time. After studying music in Venice, Schütz was appointed musical director at the Dresden court, where he composed for religious and political occasions. Although his huge output – mostly sacred – is strongly influenced by Italian styles, his dramatic choral works, inspired by the ideals of Martin Luther, put German music on the map. Schütz enjoyed a long and fruitful life, despite the early death of his wife and child.

At the family house in Weissenfels, Germany, the gifted young Schütz impressed a visiting musician with his precocious vocal and keyboard skills.

MILESTONES	
1609	Studies under Giovanni Gabrieli
1615	Starts work at the Dresden court
1627	Stages the first German opera, *Dafne*
1629	Publishes his first book of *Symphoniae sacrae* (Sacred Symphonies)
1633	Starts work at the Copenhagen court
1636	Publishes his first *Geistliche concerte* (concertos for voices and instruments)

Jean-Baptiste Lully

● 1632–1687 🏳 French ✒ 119

Jean-Baptiste Lully began life as the son of an Italian miller, but, after moving to France, his rapid ascension to a prestigious position in Louis XIV's (the Sun King) court made him the most influential composer in the history of French music. For about a quarter of a century he had almost total control over French musical life, including opera, ballet, and theatrical music, as well as music publishing.

LIFE AND MUSIC

Lully entered the French court at the age of 13 as a page and tutor, but soon joined the music establishment there. He became first a composer and then, Superintendent of the King's Chamber Music with responsibilities including direction of the King's prestigious string ensemble, the "24 violons du Roi". Much of his later career was devoted to composing ballets and grand operas for the court. Lully's death is famous: while conducting by pounding out the beat with a cane, he stabbed his toe; gangrene set in and he died soon after.

MILESTONES	
1646	Taken to Paris by Chevalier de Guise as tutor to his niece, Louis XIV's cousin
1652	Becomes ballet dancer at Louis' court
1661	Appointed Superintendent of Music; is naturalized as a French citizen
1662	Marries Madeleine Lambert, daughter of composer Michel Lambert
1670	Writes *Le bourgeois gentilhomme*
1672	Establishes Académie Royale de Musique for the performance of opera
1674	Composes *Alceste*, opera
1686	Composes *Armide*, opera

KEY WORKS

LE BOURGEOIS GENTILHOMME

COMEDY-BALLET ⏲ 103:00 📖 5 🎻🎭🎺🔔

This work came out of a renewed interest in Turkish culture in France following a rare visit to the French court by the Turkish envoy. Lully and the playwright Molière had already collaborated on other comedy-ballets – theatrical works that incorporated music and dance into the spoken drama – but it was with this work that they reached the pinnacle of the genre. The work features musical interludes between acts which, in effect, form part of the play itself. The first interlude, for example, consists of the story's dancing tutor demonstrating ballet steps. (He teaches the "middle-class gentleman" of the title how to behave in society.)

The inclusion of music and dancing tutors in the plot allows for further blending of music, dance, and drama in one work. The style of both text and music is light-hearted and satirical, with frequent tongue-in-cheek musical references to both the Turkish style and other modern musical fashions.

Most of Lully's operas included prologues that glorified the Sun King or the concept of kingship. Supernatural plots gave scope for lavish and ingenious stage effects.

ARMIDE

OPERA ⏱ 160:00 📖 5 🔱 ⚔ 🔔

Armide was the last of a series of lyric tragedies by Lully and his long-time librettist, Philippe Quinault. They had worked together since Lully's first opera, *Les fêtes de l'Amour et de Bacchus* in 1672. Quinault retired after *Armide*, which premiered in 1686, although Lully wrote two more operas before his death the following year.

Based on an epic poem by Italian poet, Torquato Tasso, and set during the First Crusade, the story is that of the sorceress Armide who falls in love with her sworn enemy Renaud. Unusually for the era, the opera centres almost entirely on the title character and her conflicting emotions. The work was an immediate success and became a staple of the French repertoire.

The opera opens with a Prologue in which the goddesses Glory and Wisdom summarize the plot and (obliquely) praise the king.

ACT ONE Armide has captured some crusaders in Damascus, but is obsessed with Renaud whom she cannot defeat. Her obsession worsens when Renaud frees the prisoners.

ACT TWO Renaud assures one of the rescued crusaders that his heart is safe from Armide's spells, but Armide send demons disguised as nymphs and shepherds to put Renaud to sleep. Armide approaches the sleeping warrior intending to kill him, but instead falls deeply in love.

ACT THREE Having won control over Renaud through sorcery, Armide finds herself controlled as well by her love, which cannot be returned. She implores the spirit of Hate to cure her, but when it attempts to do so she recants and sends Hate away. In spite, Hate condemns her to love eternally.

ACT FOUR Renaud's companions attempt to rescue him, only to be confounded by Armide's machinations.

ACT FIVE After a love scene in Armide's magical palace, she departs. Renaud's companions arrive and break her spell over him. Before they can leave she returns and, realizing she cannot keep Renaud, begs to be taken as a captive so that she may stay with him. Renaud, bound by Glory and Duty, refuses and leaves. Doomed by Hate's curse, Armide leaves in a flying chariot as demons destroy her castle.

INFLUENCES

As the sole composer of French opera for 15 years, Lully created a national style. His operas and opera-ballets were performed all over Europe, and inspired later composers such as Rameau and Gluck. Publication of his instrumental overtures and dance suites led to the development of the French suite genre used by Bach and Handel.

Barbara Strozzi

🜨 1619–1677 　📕 Italian 　✍ 8

The adopted, possibly illegitimate, daughter of Giulio Strozzi, the respected Venetian poet, Barbara Strozzi (alias Valle) was a singer much in demand at Venice's cultural events and meetings who became a composing professional. A student of Francesco Cavalli, she sang in many of his operas. She must also have performed her own compositions, many of which were for solo female voice on themes of love and emotional conflict. Strozzi published eight works, most after her father's death in 1652, suggesting she had to compose for her livelihood. She never married but had four children.

MILESTONES	
1637	Performing at Accademia degli Unisoni, Venice
1644	Begins composing
1651	Cantatas, Ariettas, and Duets, Op. 2
1654	Cantatas, Ariettas, and Duets, Op. 3

Giovanni Battista Vitali

🜨 1632–1692 　📕 Italian 　✍ 35

A composer, cellist, and singer, Vitali spent his life working in Italy's vibrant court, church, and institutional music scene. His relatively modest output includes some innovative instrumental music, and his ideas – such as linking themes and keys across movements, and the use of dance rhythms in all movements – laid the foundations of the Baroque trio sonata for successors such as Arcangelo Corelli and Henry Purcell. A pioneer in music publishing, Vitali also wrote important textbooks on musical composition, such as *Artifici musicali*, first published in 1689.

MILESTONES	
1674	Joint maestro di capella at Modena
1684	Sonata da chiesa, Op. 9
1684	Promoted to maestro di capella

Dietrich Buxtehude

🜨 c.1637–1707 　📕 Danish 　✍ 275

Buxtehude was effectively director of music for the city of Lübeck, Germany, and such was his reputation that J S Bach walked 300 km to hear him play. Only two major collections of his work (sets of ensemble sonatas) were published in his lifetime; his music was circulated mainly in manuscript copies. Though he wrote a wide range of vocal music, including the secular cantata "Alles, was ihr tut" (All That You Do), he is now remembered for his organ works – Lutheran chorales, wide-ranging improvisatory preludes, and the ostinato pieces which inspired Bach.

He had four daughters, and a condition of employment for his successor was to marry one; Johann Mattheson, a candidate in 1703, lost interest in the job when he realised this.

Buxtehude was organist at Lübeck's Marienkirche but also ran concert series in the church, at which sacred dramatic works were performed.

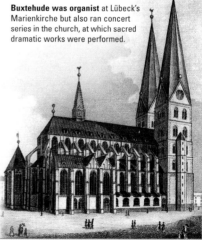

MILESTONES	
1668	Becomes organist at Lübeck; marries daughter of predecessor
1678	Introduces sacred dramatic works in *Abendmusiken* (evening concerts)
1680	Writes set of cantatas *Membra Jesu nostri*
1703	Handel and Mattheson visit
1705	J S Bach visits

Marc-Antoine Charpentier

● 1643–1704   ▶ French   ✍ 548

Unusually for a French composer of his time and talent, Charpentier never achieved a position at Louis XIV's court. Instead, he produced a wide variety of music for theatre and Church, collaborating with the dramatist Molière and producing several Masses, motets, and sacred dramas, including his "Christmas Oratorio". Seen as too "Italian" in his lifetime, his unique style is now coming to be fully appreciated.

LIFE AND MUSIC

Unlike his contemporary Lully, an Italian who came to epitomise French music, Charpentier was a Parisian who went to Italy to study composition, bringing back with him not only the works of Italian composers but also a unique hybrid writing style. He also enjoyed the patronage of Madamoiselle de Guise, a well-connected French noblewoman with a large private musical entourage, while his reputation as a composer of sacred music not only helped him to procure a position at the Jesuit church of Saint-Louis in Paris, followed by Sainte-Chapelle, but also won him commissions for the chapel of the Dauphin.

MILESTONES	
1662	Travels to Rome, possibly to study with Giacomo Carissimi
1673	Collaborates with Molière on his final play, *Le malade imaginaire*
1679	Begins composing for the Dauphin
1683	Misses auditions at the Chapelle Royale due to illness
1680s	Director of Music at Saint-Louis
1693	Première of *Médée* at the Académie Royale de Musique, Paris
1698	Appointed choirmaster of Sainte-Chapelle, Paris

KEY WORKS

THE CHRISTMAS ORATORIO
FRIGIDAE NOTIS UMBRA, H414

ORATORIO   ⏱ 29:20   📖 7   ♫ 🎻 🎵

Charpentier wrote four short Christmas oratorios in his lifetime; this one may have been composed for his patron, Madamoiselle de Guise, in the mid-1680s. Written for six voices, two violins, and basso continuo, the work comprises seven movements beginning with an introductory prelude for instruments alone. Throughout the oratorio one can hear elements of the older polyphonic style, particularly in the central chorus, reflecting Charpentier's Italian training.

MESSE DE MINUIT POUR NOËL, H9

MASS SETTING   ⏱ 29:20   📖 6   ♫ 🎻

Charpentier's *Midnight Mass for Christmas* is quintessentially a work of light to be performed at the darkest hour. Each of the six movements, set to the text of the

Charpentier's work with the playwright Molière led directly to his long-term involvement with the newly-formed Comédie-Française, which is currently the oldest national theatre company in the world.

traditional Latin liturgy, is based on popular French carol tunes of the period (some of which may still be known to audiences today). The Mass as a whole alternates between upbeat tunes and gentle lilting melodies, reflecting the contemplation of the Christ child.

Arcangelo Corelli

● 1653–1713   ⚑ Italian   ✍ c.82

Corelli, among his contemporaries, was the most famous violinist-composer of the Baroque period, and one of the most influential after Monteverdi. Although not a prolific composer – his entire output consisted of six collections – his instrumental writing was admired for its harmonic refinement and brilliance of style, and was highly influential to many composers, including Bach and Handel.

LIFE AND MUSIC

There is still very little is known about Corelli's background, although he did spend most of his working life in Rome. There he gained the patronage of several prominent aristocratic and royal supporters of the arts, including the exiled Queen of Sweden. He was regularly employed to direct performances of operas, oratorios, and other large works, including those by

From 1675 Corelli settled in Rome where he became one of the city's leading violinists. As a performer, he was admired for the exquisite tone of his playing.

Handel. Today, Corelli is primarily known for his 12 *Concerti grossi* that represented a new form of composition. As a violin virtuoso, he contributed to establishing modern bowing techniques and was one of the earliest performers to use double-stopping and chordal effects on the instrument. As a teacher of the violin his achievements were also outstanding, and his pupils included Francesco Geminiani and Antonio Vivaldi.

MILESTONES	
1679	Becomes chamber musician to the exiled Queen Christina of Sweden
1681	First set of 12 trio Church sonatas, *Sonate da chiesa*, Op.1 published
1687	Appointed music master to Cardinal Pamphili
1694	Composes *Sonate da camera*, Op. 4
1714	12 *Concerto grossi*, Op. 6, published

KEY WORKS

CONCERTO GROSSO, OP. 6, NO. 8
ORCHESTRAL   ⏱ 15:00   📖 4   ♫

Corelli's Op. 6 collection, published posthumously as a set of 12, are considered by many to be the epitome of the concerto grosso form. The first eight are set in "sonata da chiesa" or church sonata-style, the last of which has been dubbed the "Christmas Concerto", largely due to Corelli's label of "Pastorale" for the final movement, and would have been performed on Christmas Eve.

CONCERTO GROSSO, OP. 6, NO. 10
ORCHESTRAL   ⏱ 13:30   📖 4   ♫

The remaining four works in the Op. 6 set are in "sonata da camera" or chamber sonata-style. Unlike the more serious sacred works, the chamber sonatas are based on dances – in this instance, an Allemande, a Corrente, and a Minuetto – preceded by a stately Preludio movement. Corelli devoted much of his life to this fine collection, and both J S Bach and Handel drew upon his popular style.

FOCUS

SONATE A VIOLINO E VIOLONE O CIMBALO, OP. 5, NO. 12, "FOLLIA"

CHAMBER   12:00   4

Corelli's Op. 5 collection concludes with a movement of 24 variations on a simple melodic and harmonic sequence thought to have originated in Spain in the late 15th or early 16th century. However, this piece did not appear in print until 1672, in a version by Jean Baptiste Lully (*Air des hautbois Les folies d'Espagne*). Whether popularized by Lully, or simply a well-known tune, "La Folia" proved to be popular: between 1672 and Corelli's "Follia" Sonata of 1700, at least 28 other works used some version of the sequence.

The basic melody and harmony are elementary, comprising two short, virtually identical phrases. It is this simplicity, along with the compelling harmonic sequence, that is the likely source of its popularity, lending itself well to variation and improvisation. The variations themselves range in tempo from adagio to vivace, building in speed and intensity through subsequent variations and then subsiding again. The accompaniment is as important as the melody, and indeed the main melody occasionally appears in the bass line, while the violin plays arpeggiated chords in accompaniment. Occasionally the harmonic structure is also modified.

Corelli, virtuoso violinist that he was, incorporates numerous coloratura violin techniques throughout, ranging from florid passagework and arpeggiation to the messa di voce, a sustained note which swells from soft to loud and then fades slowly away again. In addition to the notated ornaments, the composer leaves ample room for improvisation on the part of the individual performer; in fact, several editions of the work, published by others after the 1700 edition, claim to incorporate ornaments used by Corelli himself in performance. However, it is likely that Corelli would have preferred each performance to show off the soloist's own inspirational flourishes, rather than slavishly mimic those of the original composer. Many editions of Corelli's "Follia" Sonata were published in his lifetime, including an arrangement for recorder and bass.

Johann Pachelbel

◉ 1653–1706   🏴 German   ✍ c.346

Pachelbel was one of the dominant figures of late 17th-century European keyboard and chamber music. Although chiefly known today for his Canon in D, he was well-known during his lifetime as both an organist and a prolific composer. His patron, the Duke of Saxe-Eisenach, once described him as a "perfect and rare virtuoso", while his development of the organ chorale as a form and his myriad *Magnificat Fugues for St Sebaldus* are particularly noteworthy.

LIFE AND MUSIC

Pachelbel's career is marked by a series of posts as organist at increasingly prestigious places, and by his growing influence as a teacher and composer. When work dried up at one position he moved on to the next, joining the courts at Eisenach and Stuttgart and then moving to Gotha as town organist. He was then invited by his home town, Nuremberg, to return to take up the prestigious post at St Sebaldus, where he remained until his death. Pachelbel's organ repertoire is particularly extensive, but it is in his cantus firmus organ chorales (which feature an ornamented imitative accompaniment to the main theme) and his later fugues that his influence is greatest.

MILESTONES	
1673	Becomes deputy organist of St Stephen's Cathedral in Vienna
1677	Becomes court organist at Eisenach
1678	Appointed organist at the Protestant Predigerkirche at Erfurt
c.1680	Composes Canon in D
1681	Marries Barbara Gabler
1683	Wife and infant son die of plague
1685	Marries Judith Drommer
1690	Joins Württemberg Court at Stuttgart
1692	Flees French invasion; becomes town organist at Gotha
1695	Invited to take up position at St Sebaldus in Nuremberg
1695	Starts writing *Magnificat Fugues*
1699	Writes *Hexachordum Apollinis*, harpsichord

KEY WORKS

CANON IN D

CHAMBER   ⏱ 04:00   📖 1   ⚐

In this now famous piece, three violins play the canon (each part entering with the exact same music two bars apart), while a basso continuo plays a ground, a short, simple passage of eight notes repeated over and over again: 54 times in this instance. The canon theme itself is also simple, starting with long, slow notes, then becoming quicker and more ornate as the work progresses. Although

Pachelbel's music was well-regarded in his lifetime, the little Canon in D remained relatively obscure until recently, gaining its current status as a staple of the classical repertoire only in the early 1970s. It has appeared in arrangements from full orchestra to string quartet, as a solo keyboard work, and in countless other versions including pop remixes.

Pachelbel's *Hexachordum Apollinis*, six sets of variations for harpsichord, had a title page engraved by composer and organist Nicolaus Schurtz.

MAGNIFICAT FUGUES

SOLO ORGAN   ⏳ 112:0   📖 95   🔊

The Magnificat plays an important role in the Protestant liturgy of the vespers services, and Pachelbel wrote several different settings of the text during his lifetime. Traditionally the organ was used in this context either to play alternate verses of the chant in some form, or to play a short prelude as a means of determining the opening pitch for the singers. Pachelbel's 95 Magnificat fugues had the latter, more utilitarian role in the daily services: to bring the singers in. He therefore produced several short fugues in each of the Church modes, so that the appropriate one could be used depending on the vocal music being sung on a given day, from the primus tonus (literally "first tone", based on C) through every note of the scale:

Magnificat Primi Toni – 23 fugues
Magnificat Secundi Toni – 10 fugues
Magnificat Tertii Toni – 11 fugues
Magnificat Quarti Toni – 8 fugues
Magnificat Quinti Toni – 12 fugues
Magnificat Sexti Toni – 10 fugues
Magnificat Septimi Toni – 8 fugues
Magnificat Octavi Toni –13 fugues

Pachelbel used original themes in most of the fugues, although some do incorporate the standard plainchant in part or in full. Like his previous fugues based on chorales, these settings are relatively uncomplicated and are closer to preludes than the more serious fugues other northern German composers were producing. Nearly all of Pachelbel's fugues need no use of pedals. Nevertheless, this large body of short fugues in different keys, styles, themes, and moods (from lilting and dance-like to bold with fanfare motifs) represents possibly the most impressive collection of organ music until J S Bach's a generation later.

These works also gave Pachelbel an opportunity to experiment with equal temperament, a tuning system of which he was a proponent. In the Baroque period the different tuning systems in use meant that intervals, particularly thirds and fifths, would sound different in different keys. The equal-temperament system, in which all semitones are equal and thus all keys equal, was gaining acceptance during Pachelbel's lifetime, and would be more dramatically showcased in Bach's *The Well-Tempered Clavier*.

Heinrich Ignaz Franz von Biber

● 1644–1704 ▶ Austrian ✎ 160

In 1670, Biber, a popular violin virtuoso, was sent by his employer in Bohemia to negotiate the purchase of new violins. He never returned. Instead he took a job with the Archbishop of Salzburg. His career flourished and he rose from servant to the nobility, having performed at, and composed for, royal occasions. Biber's picturesque and virtuosic violin sonatas include many special effects such as unusual tunings.

MILESTONES	
1669	Writes *Sonata representativa*
1674	Composes the "*Rosary*" *Sonatas*
1677	Performs for Emperor Leopold
1682	Composes for Imperial Jubilee
1690	Ennobled by Leopold
1704	Dies in Salzburg; his four surviving children become notable musicians

Alessandro Stradella

● 1639–1682 ▶ Italian ✎ 309

Of noble birth, Stradella was a singer, singing teacher, violinist, and composer. When an unknown assassin killed him in Genoa for reasons still unclear, it was the second attempt on his life. The first had been in 1677, after his reluctant marriage to Agnese, a pupil with whom he had run away. Her former lover had hired the attackers, and it caused an international incident. Through all the intrigue Stradella kept promoting his music, often receiving commissions from nobility. He composed his highly popular works quickly, including 170 cantatas, many operas, and the earliest known concerto-grosso-style work.

MILESTONES	
1674	Composes *Vola, vola*, concerto-grosso-style serenata
1678	Flees Rome for Genoa
1678	*La forza dell'amor paterno (The Power of a Father's Love)*, opera

Marin Marais

● 1656–1728 ▶ French ✎ 650

A shoemaker's son, Marais learned the viol so fast that he surpassed his teacher after six months. He soon joined the Paris  Opéra orchestra, moving on to a career as a pioneering viol virtuoso – known internationally for his wonderful technique and tone – and as a composer. He wrote four operas but is best known today for his imaginative instrumental music, which ranges from short, simple pieces to virtuoso experiments which use all the keys. From 1709, Marais withdrew from public life.

MILESTONES	
1679	Musician at French royal court
1686	Composes his first pieces for viol
1706	Writes *Alcyone*, opera

John Blow

● c.1648–1708 ▶ England ✎ c.400

Proud and statesmanlike, Blow rose from humble provincial origins to become the foremost musician in England by his mid-20s. He was a major figure in Restoration music and had royal posts created specially for him, including work at St Paul's Cathedral and Westminster Abbey. His secular works include ceremonial music, and *Venus and Adonis*, the first English opera. He wrote much religious music, notably over 100 strongly melodic anthems. Of his 12 Anglican services, the one in G major is masterly.

MILESTONES	
1668	Made organist of Westminster Abbey
1683	Writes masque *Venus and Adonis*
1685	Composes three anthems for the coronation of James II
1695	Writes *Ode on the Death of Purcell*

François Couperin

● 1668–1733   French   ✍ 126

François Couperin eclipsed the reputation of his famous composer uncle, Louis, from an early age, first as an organist and then as a composer of works for keyboard. His *Pièces de clavecin*, miniature character works for harpsichord, were described as "national treasures". They continue to be staples of the keyboard repertoire today as well as the epitome of French Baroque instrumental music.

LIFE AND MUSIC

Couperin was the most famous of a very distinguished family of musicians, and became known as "Couperin le Grand". He was only 11 when he inherited the prestigious organist's post at St Gervais in Paris on the death of his father, Charles. Church composer Michel-Richard Delalande took the post until Couperin could assume his duties at 18. From then on Couperin's star continued to rise. He won an appointments to the royal court at 25 and became one of the leading teachers of harpsichord and organ of his generation. He wrote a vast amount of sublime keyboard music, including his 27 famous suites *(ordres)* of harpsichord music, giving many of them evocative titles. He also produced several chamber and vocal works, and some key theoretical writings. His *L'art de toucher le clavecin (The Art of Playing the Harpsichord)*, published in 1716, was much admired by Bach, with whom he corresponded.

MILESTONES

1690	Obtains a *privilège du Roi* (printing licence) to publish his organ Masses.
1693	Louis XIV appoints him as one of the four court organist-composers
1694	Becomes tutor to king's children.
1702	Ennobled as *chevalier*
1703	Publishes psalm settings for the Chappelle du Roi (royal chapel)
1713	Publishes first book of *Pièces de clavecin*, harpsichord pieces.

KEY WORKS

VINGT-CINQUIÈME ORDRE

SOLO HARPSICHORD   ⏱ 17:00   ▥ 5   🎵

This multi-part suite for harpsichord first appeared in print in 1730 in Couperin's fourth book of the *Pièces de Clavecin*, his last published work. As with most of Couperin's harpsichord works, these are character pieces with descriptive (and sometimes enigmatic) titles evoking images and reminiscences.

The opening work, *La visionaire (The Visionary)*, describes a religious fanatic, and features the dotted rhythms and ornate elaborations

Couperin's treatise on harpsichord-playing technique was extremely influential.

common to French music of the period. (His embellishments are always written exactly into the music, excluding performer improvisation.) *La misterieuse (The Mysterious One)* is a contrasting piece, more elegant and lilting, while *La Monflambert* – named after the wife of a local councillor, whom it might describe – is more melancholy in mood. Another shift comes in the fourth piece, *La muse victorieuse (The Victorious Muse)*, with its triumphal flourishes in C major. Couperin finished the *Ordre* in a darker vein, perhaps because of his own declining health: both the title and the music of *Les ombres errantes (Wandering Shades)* have a pensive, almost funereal aspect.

Henry Purcell

◒ 1659–1695   ⚑ English   ✍ 515

Despite his relatively short life, Henry Purcell remains one of the most important English composers. His facility in writing for all genres and audiences, his popularity at court through the reigns of three different monarchs, and his vast output of court odes, theatrical music, sacred anthems, secular songs and catches, chamber music, and organ voluntaries are clear testament to his prodigious talent.

LIFE AND MUSIC

Henry Purcell moved in exalted Church and Court circles from an early age, becoming a chorister in the Chapel Royal at age ten, an (unpaid) member of Charles II's musical retinue at 14, a court composer at 18, and an organist at Westminster Abbey at 20. Considering this meteoric career, perhaps it is unsurprising that Purcell produced so much music for Church and Court services, including numerous sacred choral works and odes for courtly occasions (including several "welcome songs" for Charles II and James II). Purcell also composed secular songs throughout his lifetime, and wrote dramatic musical works for the stage from 1688 onwards.

MILESTONES

1669	Becomes chorister in the Chapel Royal
1677	Composes elegy *What Hope For Us Remains Now He Is Gone?* on the death of English composer, Matthew Locke
1679	Takes position as organist of Westminster Abbey
1680	Composes first music for the stage; marries Frances Peters
1683	Keeper of the King's Instruments; composes first *Ode for St Cecilia's Day*
1689	Opera *Dido and Aeneas* first performed
1691	Composes music for Dryden's play *King Arthur*
1692	Composes music for *The Fairy Queen*, an adaptation of Shakespeare's play, *A Midsummer Night's Dream*.

KEY WORKS

THE FAIRY QUEEN

SEMI-OPERA   ⏱ 130:00   📖 5   🎵🎻🎹

Written for a stage adaptation broadly based on William Shakespeare's play *A Midsummer Night's Dream*, Purcell's music for *The Fairy Queen* – with its vast amount of songs, dances, and other incidental music – raises the work from a play to a semi-opera. Dating from the prolific last few years of the composer's life, this five-act work contains a mixture of songs, masques, ballet, marches, and incidental music interspersed with spoken dialogue.

As court composer, Purcell was called upon to write music for royal celebrations, including the coronation of Queen Mary and William of Orange in 1685.

I GAVE HER CAKES

CATCH   ⏱ 1:00   📖 1   🎻

Purcell produced several secular catches (where the same music is sung by each singer in turn), some of which are quite ribald. This example, on a theme of drinking and flirting, dates from 1701.

DIDO AND AENEAS

OPERA   ⏱ 60:00   📖 3   🎵 🎭 🎼

Full opera was uncommon in 17th century England, so it is not surprising that Purcell composed only one, *Dido and Aeneas*, deciding to concentrate instead on incidental music for existing theatrical works. With a libretto by Nahum Tate, *Dido* owes much to the tradition of courtly masques, and in particular John Blow's *Venus and Adonis* of 1682. The opera consists of three short acts, each comprising several brief arias, recitatives, and dances; the whole work requires barely an hour to perform. The first known performance in 1689 was at Josiah Priest's Chelsea School for Girls, although it may have had an earlier premiere at the Royal Court; regardless, it was not performed again until 1700, five years after the composer's death. The opera's connection to the girls' school can be seen in the setting of the work: apart from Aeneas and some minor roles, the cast is almost entirely female.

ACT ONE Following the overture, the action begins with the arrival in Carthage of Prince Aeneas, who is fleeing the fall of Troy. Dido, Queen of Carthage, knows that Aeneas is fated to found Rome, but nevertheless falls for the prince, who in turn falls for her (with the active urging of the chorus and Dido's companion Belinda).

ACT TWO Dido's nemesis, the Sorceress, is introduced, along with her minions, who give voice to their hate. They plot to trick Aeneas into leaving Carthage by sending a witch disguised as Mercury to order him to leave the city and continue his journey onwards. Aeneas has vowed to stay with Dido but cannot disobey a divine command, and he is forced to leave.

ACT THREE The witches gloat over their triumph, while Aeneas's men prepare their ship for departure. Aeneas bids a difficult farewell to Dido, and then leaves. After a final broken-hearted lament, the well-known "When I am laid in earth", Dido kills herself. The opera concludes with a mournful chorus, "With drooping wings". From a structural viewpoint the lament is a fine example of Purcell's deft compositional touch; it follows the Venetian lament tradition – often seen in the work of Monteverdi – of using a simple repeated bass line with colourful variations above to great dramatic effect.

INFLUENCES

Purcell studied composition under John Blow (who he succeeded as organist at Westminster Abbey), Christopher Gibbons, and Matthew Locke (who he succeeded as court composer in 1677). Purcell also copied Continental styles; French dance rhythms are common in his works, and his trio sonatas are a conscious imitation of the Italian style.

Alessandro Scarlatti

🔵 1660–1725   🎵 Italian   ✍ 950

A maestro di cappella at 18, and with six successful operas performed in Rome's aristocratic circles by 23, Scarlatti's career had a remarkable start. He moved to Naples and by the 1690s was at the peak of his fame. By 1700 the city rivalled Venice as the leading operatic city, but Scarlatti was by then running into money problems – partly due to his large family – and, in looking for freelance work, he often ignored his contractual duties. After problematic spells in Rome and Venice, he returned to

Naples, but, despite his fine reputation, his later, more complex operas achieved only a lukewarm success. Routinely called the founder of Neapolitan opera, it seems his style was mostly pan-Italian; only one of his 110-plus operas, *Trionfo dell'onore*, is Neapolitan in music and text. He died in poverty, and is remembered as the father of the composer Domenico.

MILESTONES	
1670s	Studies in Rome
1679	Writes *Gli equivoci nel sembiante*, opera
1680	*L'honestà negli amori* performed for the Queen of Sweden
1685	Back in Naples. Domenico born
1706	Admitted to Arcadian Academy in Rome
1721	Composes the *St Cecilia Mass*

It was at the Teatro Capranica in Rome that Scarlatti produced some of his finest and most expressive operas, including *Telemaco* (1718), *Marco Attilio Regoló* (1719), and *Griselda* (1721).

Alessandro Marcello

🔵 1669–1747   🎵 Italian   ✍ c.45

Marcello led a rich and varied life and enjoyed a successful dilettante existence. He was a prominent member of Venetian cultural life, and his main contribution to music was as an academician. He composed occasionally, and his cantatas are more interesting for their lavish publication than their musical qualities. However, his instrumental music shows an accomplished knowledge of national styles and, thanks to his Oboe Concerto – so appealing to J S Bach that he transcribed it – he has a place in composing immortality.

MILESTONES	
1700	Diplomatic posts in Levant and the Peloponnese
1708	Cantatas published
1717	Writes Oboe Concerto
1719	Eight books of poetry published
1719	Becomes head of the Accademia degli Animosi, Cremona

As well as composing music for different venues, Marcello also collected valuable keyboard and wind instruments.

Tomaso Giovanni Albinoni

● 1671–c.1750   🏴 Italian   ♫ c.300

Due to his privileged background, Albinoni composed freelance, and knew more noble patrons than he did musicians. His prolific output includes 55 operas, and 59 concertos, in which he was probably the first to use the three-movement form consistently.

As the eldest son of a prosperous merchant in Venice, Albinoni didn't need to compose for a living and cultivated music more for pleasure than for profit.

He mass-produced his music but, thanks to his melodic gifts and individual style, he was as popular in his lifetime as Corelli and Vivaldi, and J S Bach used his Op. 1 as teaching material. But his popular fame rests on a piece he didn't write: "Albinoni's Adagio" was composed by Remo Giazotto around 1945; only the bass line was Albinoni's.

MILESTONES	
1694	Composes 12 Trio Sonatas, Op. 1
1705	Marries operatic soprano Margherita Raimondi
1715	Oboe Concerto, Op. 7, published
1722	Supervizes *I veri amici*, opera, Munich
1741	Writes last work, *Artamene*, opera

Jeremiah Clarke

● c.1674–1707   🏴 English   ♫ 60

The "Trumpet Voluntary" familiar from wedding ceremonies, once thought to be by Henry Purcell, in fact came from a harpsichord piece by Clarke, a prominent composer in the generation just after Purcell. Clarke served as organist at the cathedrals of Winchester and St Paul's, and at the Chapel Royal, and his output includes church music, odes, songs, and theatre music. He committed suicide in 1707, apparently after an unhappy love affair.

MILESTONES	
1685	Becomes chorister at Chapel Royal
1692	Organist at Winchester College
c.1697	Writes *Prince of Denmark's March* ("Trumpet Voluntary")
1699	"Vicar-choral" at St Paul's Cathedral
1700	Becomes "Gentleman-extraordinary" at the Chapel Royal
1702	Writes "Praise the Lord", anthem, for Queen Anne's coronation

Francesco Geminiani

● 1687–1762   🏴 Italian   ♫ 80

In the 1710s, the English were highly enamoured of Italian culture and inspired by the virtuosity of Italian violinists like Geminiani, who spent his working life in England.

He promoted himself as "Corelli's pupil" and enjoyed early success with his brilliant and expressive Corelli-like Op. 1 sonatas, and even more with his Op. 3 concerti grossi. Admired mainly as a player, Geminiani performed to nobility rather than the public, and was a prominent figure in London musical circles.

MILESTONES	
1714	Abandons Italy for London
1716	Composes Sonatas for Violin, Op. 1
c.1732	Writes concerti grossi, Opp. 2 and 3
1751	*The Art of Playing the Violin* published
1756	*The Enchanted Forest* performed, Paris

"I have heard him boast of composing a concerto faster than a copyist could write it down!"

CHARLES DE BROSSE, 1739

Antonio Vivaldi

● 1678–1741   ♙ Italian   ✍ 811+

Vivaldi was the most celebrated of all the Italian Baroque composers, and probably one of the most prolific. In addition to his more than 500 concertos, he produced several operas, sacred vocal works (including his famous Gloria) and numerous other instrumental works, while his virtuoso violin playing earned him international fame. Like his father, he had fiery red hair, earning him the nick-name "the Red Priest".

One of the most prolific composers of his day, Vivaldi is best known for his poetic work The Four Seasons.

LIFE

In many respects Antonio Vivaldi's life was as flamboyant as his music. The son of a violinist, he worked as a violinist himself while training to be a priest. In 1703 he obtained a post at the Pio Ospedale della Pietà, an institution for abandoned (though highly talented) girls where he taught and earned his students international fame. He rapidly made a name for himself as a composer as well, and publications of his music were widely praised and emulated. In 1713, the governors of the Ospedale commissioned several sacred works from him, and he began to write operas for the Venetian stage. He travelled a great deal, writing operas for Carnival in Mantua and Rome from 1723 onwards, while in Venice the governors requested two concertos a month from him. Vivaldi soon became associated with singer Anna Giraud, who appeared in many of his operas. In 1737, during a public contracts dispute, the rumours about their relationship, and his refusal to say Mass (due to asthma) caught up with him, and he was barred from Ferrara. After some opera performances fared badly he began to lose public favour, and as a final ignominy he fell ill and died on a trip to Vienna, only to be buried in a pauper's grave.

MUSICAL OUTPUT	1678	1710	1720	1730	1741	Total: 811+ UNDATED
CONCERTOS (529+)		38	38	1		452+
SONATAS (85)	11	18		6		50
SINFONIAS (19)						19
OPERAS (55)		20	16	19		
SACRED VOCAL (72)	3	1		68		
SECULAR VOCAL (51)	1	1	6			43

MUSIC

Arcangelo Corelli may have created the model for the Italian concerto but it was Antonio Vivaldi who showed what could be done with it. Vivaldi's skill as a violinist and orchestrator can be seen in the challenging roles he gives both to the solo instruments and ensembles, and having the talented performers of the Ospedale at hand meant that he could tailor his works to specific virtuosi and combinations of instruments. His vocal works also demonstrate a deft (and prolific) touch: his sacred solo and choral works range from the energetic to the sublime and show many of the same extravagances of his instrumental writing, and his operas were briefly the toast of Rome. Apart from the works published during Vivaldi's lifetime, the vast majority of his works are undated. Indeed, many have yet to be catalogued, although the current catalogue lists more than 800 works.

MILESTONES	
1693	Begins studies for the priesthood
1703	Following ordination, Vivaldi takes post teaching violin at the Ospedale della Pietà, an orphanage for girls
1705	Writes 12 Sonatas for Violin, Op. 1
1711	Publishes *L'estro armonico*, Op. 3, collection of concerti grossi
1716	Appointed maestro de'concerti at the Pietà
1718	Appointed music director to the court of Mantua
1725	*Le quattro staggioni* (*The Four Seasons*), Op. 8, Nos. 1–4, published
1740	Becomes music director to the court of Charles VI in Vienna

KEY WORKS

GLORIA, RV 589

GLORIA　　⏲ 60:00　　📖 12　　🎵 🥁 🎶

Written for the Ospedale, Vivaldi's Gloria contains a wealth of Baroque styles and contrasts. The opening choral annunciation is followed by a more contemplative "Et in terra pax" in B minor, which in turn is followed by a lively duet for women's voices. The work alternates choral sections and solos throughout; after a brief reprise of the opening music, an energetic choral fugue based on an earlier Gloria by Giovanni Maria Ruggieri brings the piece to a rousing conclusion.

NULLA IN MUNDO PAX SINCERA

MOTET　　⏲ 13:30　　📖 4　　🎵 🎶

The opening Larghetto may sound familiar to many listeners, having appeared in many soundtracks. The motet was written for less dramatic purposes, however; the text is a devotional prayer to Jesus and his peace. In the final Alleluia, the soprano demonstrates the type of florid virtuosity usually resolved for the strings, finishing with a flourish.

CONCERTO FOR FLUTE, OP. 10, NO. 3, RV 428, "THE GOLDFINCH"

ORCHESTRAL　　⏲ 10:00　　📖 3　　🎵 🎶

The "Goldfinch" Concerto is well known for its more overt representations of birdsong, the composer making use of an instrument for which he rarely wrote. The simple slow movement, set only for flute and continuo, is particularly fine.

The Ospedale della Pietà in Venice, with which Vivaldi was associated for much of his life, is still an orphanage today.

THE FOUR SEASONS, OP. 8, NOS. 1–4, RV 271

ORCHESTRAL   🕑 36:00   📖 4   ⚘ ☉

These four concertos for violin and orchestra are part of a set of 12 published in Amsterdam in 1725 titled *Il cimento dell'armonia e dell'inventione*, or *The Trial of Strength Between Harmony and Invention*. Unlike most of Vivaldi's concertos, these four have a clear programme: each concerto was accompanied by an illustrative sonnet printed in the principal violin's partbook, each on the theme of the respective season. The author of these poems is unknown, although there is some speculation that Vivaldi himself may have written them. The concertos remained popular long after Vivaldi's death, particularly in France (where "Spring" was a favourite of the French court), and today they are some of the most recorded and performed works ever.

CONCERTO NO. 1, "SPRING" (ALLEGRO – LARGO – ALLEGRO, 7:30) In the Largo of "Spring", the text tells how "the goatherd sleeps with his trusty dog beside him"; the languorous musical setting is interrupted only by the "barking" of a solo viola.

CONCERTO NO. 2, "SUMMER" (ALLEGRO NON MOLTO – ADAGIO/PRESTO – PRESTO, 9:15) Here the hot sun beats down on the farm labourers but a storm looms, finally breaking in the third movement in a furious hailstorm matched by an equally furious hail of rapid passagework in the orchestra and solo.

CONCERTO NO. 3, "AUTUMN" (ALLEGRO – ADAGIO MOLTO – ALLEGRO, 11:15) "Autumn" opens with a clomping peasant dance to celebrate the harvest and concludes with a hunt (complete with "horns, guns, and dogs") that eventually brings down a wild stag.

CONCERTO NO. 4, "WINTER" (ALLEGRO NON MOLTO – LARGO – ALLEGRO, 8:30) Finally, "Winter" describes first the shivering and chattering of teeth, then the calm moments by the fire, and lastly the fierce joy of sliding on the crackling ice and hearing the whistling of the winter winds.

INFLUENCES

The qualities of Vivaldi's music – concise themes, clarity of form, rhythmic vitality, homophonic texture, balanced phrases, dramatic dialogue between soloist and ensemble – directly influenced many composers including J S Bach, who transcribed several of Vivaldi's concertos for keyboard.

Georg Philipp Telemann

● 1681–1767   ♙ German   ✍ c.3,700

Telemann was one of the most prolific composers of the Baroque period. He gained an international reputation through both the quality of his music – which always reflected the current musical fashion – and the wide dissemination of his works: his innovative German periodical *Der getreue Music-Meister* provided amateur musicians with instrumental and vocal pieces for domestic music-making.

LIFE AND MUSIC

After holding several Church and Court positions in Poland and Germany, Telemann was appointed music director and cantor at Hamburg in 1723, a prestigious post that he held until his death. Today he is chiefly known for his solo and trio sonatas, but his instrumental works include many orchestral suites, concertos, quartets, trios, and compositions for keyboard, and his cantatas and larger Church works number over 1,000. There are also some 50 operas, including his delightful comedy *Der geduldige Socrates* (*The Patient Socrates*).

MILESTONES	
1701	Enrols as law student at the university in Leipzig; meets Handel
1702	Becomes director of the Leipzig Opera
1704	Appointed director of the New Church in Leipzig
1708	Appointed Konzertmeister in Eisenach; forms friendship with J S Bach
1721	Becomes music director of Hamburg; composes *Der geduldige Socrates*, opera
1728	*Der getreue Music-Meister* first published
1733	*Musique de table* published
1755	Composes several sacred oratorios; writes theoretical works

KEY WORKS

NOUVEAUX QUATUORS EN SIX SUITES

CHAMBER   ⏱ 78:00   📖 28   ♀

A collection of six multi-movement chamber works published in 1738 during Telemann's visit to Paris, this set contains two concertos, two sonatas, and two balletts. While these works reflect the French style, the structure is more Italian. Unlike the trio sonatas, which were scored for four instruments these are true quartets for three melody instruments (flute, violin, viola da gamba, or cello – and accompaniment (harpsichord).

MUSIQUE DE TABLE

CHAMBER   ⏱ 270.00   📖 68   ♫ ♀ ◐

This set of works, considered by scholars to be Telemann's *magnum opus*, was published in three separate anthologies, each containing an orchestral suite, trio, quartet, concerto for several solo instruments, a solo sonata, and a single movement piece the composer titled "Conclusion".

In 1722, Leipzig city council failed to secure Telemann as Cantor of the Thomaskirche; the post was offered to their third choice, J S Bach.

BOURLESQUE DE QUIXOTTE

ORCHESTRAL 🕐 18:50 📖 7 🎵

Telemann popularized the French orchestral suite in Germany, gaining much inspiration from the works of Lully whom he much admired. There is no standard organization for these multi-movement works, except that they open with the typical overture in French style: a Grave slow section dominated by dotted rhythms, followed by an Allegro fugal section which leads to a return to the slower opening section. This opening movement is followed by a selection of dance movements, with the only criteria being that they are arranged to contrast with one another. Telemann also modelled the French fashion of giving programmatic titles to the suites. With this suite Telemann provides six programmatic movements (following the French overture) based on Cervantes's "Knight of the Doleful Countenance" and his servant Sancho Panza.

OVERTURE (GRAVE-ALLEGRO-GRAVE, 5:33) The first movement follows the familiar French overture style, as described in more detail above.

LE REVEIL DE QUIXOTTE (ADAGIO, 2:50) *The Knight's Awakening* characterizes our hero Don Quixote's slow wakening through the use of long notes, pauses, and simple lyrical minuet rhythm.

SON ATTAQUE DES MOULINS À VENT (VIVACE, 1:46) In high relief is *Attack on the Windmills* with its quick semiquavers and repeated notes representing Don Quixote attacking his imagined enemies.

SES SOUPIRS AMOUREUX APRÈS LA PRINCESSE DULCINÉE (ANDANTE, 3:11) *Sighs of Love for the Princess Dulcinea* reflects Don Quixote's love, with the inclusion of sighing motifs and musical suspensions representing his yearning for Dulcinea.

SANCHE PANCHE BERNÉ (ALLEGRO, 1:50) This movement is an imaginative musical description of Quixote's servant Sancho Panza through the inclusion of octave jumps, with ornamented turns, within a strict rhythm.

LA GALOPE DE ROSINANTE / CELUI D'ANE DE SANCHE (ALLEGRO, 2:14) The penultimate movement, is a description of Don Quixote's horse Rosinante galloping along in 3/8 time contrasting with Panza's donkey whose stubbornness is reflected by pauses and dotted rhythms.

LE COUCHÉ DE QUIXOTTE (ANDANTE, 2:46) Telemann puts our hero to sleep in this final movement, *The Sleep of Quixote*, with a simple, lyrical melody – just the opposite of the previous movement, and returning full circle to the beginning of the story.

Jean-Philippe Rameau

● 1683–1764   ᛈ French   ✍ 76

Jean-Philippe Rameau was not only the most important French composer of the 18th century, but also an influential music theorist. His style of operatic writing ended the posthumous reign of Lully, whose model had been followed for half a century. Also a harpsichordist and organist, Rameau wrote many works for the keyboard. His highly ornamented compositions stand out as the epitome of Rococo style.

LIFE AND MUSIC

Rameau composed only a few small keyboard and sacred works prior to 1722, but the publication of his treatise on harmony that year marked the beginning of a productive period. His *Pièces de clavecin* were published in 1724, followed by a new theory book in 1726, and sets of keyboard works and cantatas in 1729. He wrote his first opera, *Hippolyte et Aricie*, at the age of 50. It drew the interest of Louis XV and Rameau later received several royal commissions as a result. His music is characterized by a musical dynamism that contrasts with the staider Lulliste style – Voltaire once dubbed Rameau "our hero of the semiquavers".

MILESTONES	
1702	Appointed organist of Clermont-Ferrand cathedral
1722	Publishes the highly influential *Traité de l'harmonie;* settles in Paris
1726	Marries Marie-Louise Mangot; publishes *Nouveau système de musique théorique*
1733	First opera, *Hippolyte et Aricie*, is produced
1739	Premiere of *Dardanus*, opera
1736	Completes *Les indes galantes*, opera
1741	Writes *Pièces de clavecin en concert*
1745	Comedy-ballet *Platée* is premiered at Versailles for dauphin's wedding
1754	*Observations sur notre instinct pour musique* is published
1764	Is ennobled; dies a few months later

KEY WORKS

PIÈCES DE CLAVECIN (1724)

KEYBOARD   ⏱ 24:00   🎵 9   🎵

In this, his second set of harpsichord works, Rameau first demonstrated his characteristic florid style, with dramatic runs of scales, and rapid and complex passages that fully exploit the harpsichord keyboard. The influence of Couperin is sometimes evident, but Rameau's athletic style takes these character pieces to a new level.

PIÈCES DE CLAVECIN EN CONCERT

INSTRUMENTAL   ⏱ 60:00   🎵 16   ♟

Rameau's final published collection of instrumental works comprises five suites of largely character pieces

named after either images or tableaux *(La pantomime, L'indiscrète)*, or after people such as society figures, students, or composers *(La Marais, La Forqueray* and even *La Rameau)*. Although these are ensemble pieces, the harpsichord is very much the featured instrument.

Rameau's satirical comedy-ballet *Platée*, featuring a grotesque swamp nymph, was written for the wedding of the dauphin to a reputedly plain Spanish princess.

FOCUS

HIPPOLYTE ET ARICIE

OPERA   165:00   5

Despite Rameau's characteristically frenetic compositional style, this, his first opera, (or properly, *tragédie en musique*), is very much in the French tradition: five acts in length, with a divertissement (a dance or other spectacle) in each act, and a plot based on figures from Classical mythology or history. Nonetheless, the style of music received both enthusiastic praise and critical dismissal. Many felt its vigorous passage work was too "Italian" and ornate. This opera may have been the first work to which the term "Baroque" was applied, though this would have been meant as an insult. Ironically, 20 years later, Parisian supporters of Italian opera would accuse Rameau of not being Italian enough.

The libretto by Abbé Simon-Joseph Pellegrin is based on Racine's play, *Phèdre*, of 1677, with elements of the tragedies of Euripides and Seneca. It concerns the incestuous love of Phèdre (Phaedra) for her stepson Hippolyte (Hippolytus). Despite the title, much of the action centres on Hippolyte's father, Thésée (Theseus), King of Athens.

PROLOGUE (27:30) Diana, goddess of the chaste, pledges to protect Hippolyte and Aricie, daughter of a rival family forced by Thésée to remain chaste. Phèdre lusts after Hippolyte.

ACT ONE (28:30) Aricie is preparing to take her vow of chastity to Diana when Hippolyte pledges his love to her. Phèdre jealously tries to force Aricie to continue her vows, but Diana offers the young lovers her help.

ACT TWO (27:30) This is devoted to Thésée's journey to Hell and confrontation with Pluto. As he leaves, the Fates prophesy that he will find hell in his own house.

ACT THREE (29:30) Hippolyte pledges loyalty to Phèdre, which she mistakes for a profession of love and declares hers for him. He rejects her. She seizes his sword in a suicide attempt, which Thésée, just returned, believes to be an attempted rape. He curses his son.

ACT FOUR (22:30) Hippolyte and Aricie plan to flee, but a monster summoned by Thésée's curse attacks Hippolyte, who disappears, engulfed in flames. Phèdre, full of remorse, kills herself.

ACT FIVE (31:30) Thésée also attempts suicide, but it is revealed that Hippolyte has been saved by the gods. He and Aricie are reunited in a happy ending.

Domenico Scarlatti

🔵 1685–1752   🇮🇹 Italian   ✍ c.717

Son of Alessandro Scarlatti, harpsichordist, and composer Domenico Scarlatti's greatest contribution were his single-movement keyboard sonatas, yet only a small number were published in his lifetime. Although born in the same year as Bach and Handel, Scarlatti's light, homophonic compositional style is more characteristic of the early Classical period, and also reveals his innovative approach to harmony.

LIFE AND MUSIC

Very little is known about Domenico Scarlatti's life, despite the vast amount that has been written about him. Much of his early life was spent travelling with his father, who managed his career closely. However, Scarlatti soon established his own name as a keyboard virtuoso and composer (one story – possibly apocryphal – tells of a performing competition between Domenico and Handel). His appointment to the household of the exiled Queen of Poland led to more prestigious positions: first at the Vatican, then at the Portuguese court, and finally at the Spanish court in Madrid, where the majority of his keyboard works were written.

MILESTONES	
1700	Becomes organist and composer of Capella Reale in Naples.
1708	Appointed maestro di cappella to Maria Casimir, exiled Queen of Poland, in Rome
1714	Employed as maestro di cappella at Cappella Giulia at the Vatican
1719	Becomes mestre of the Royal Chapel to King João of Portugal
1728	Composes *Festeggio armonico*
1729	Marries Maria Catalina Gentili in Rome; joins Spanish court
1738	*30 Essercizi per gravicembalo* published – bringing Scarlatti international recognition
1754	Composes *Missa quattuor vocum*

KEY WORKS

SONATAS IN A MAJOR, K181, K182

SOLO PIANO   📖 2   🎵

Scarlatti's keyboard sonatas have a distinctive style that is immediately recognizable, despite their extremely simple binary form. Despite the similarity of key and tempo (Allegro) and the use of repeated motives throughout, these two pieces are entirely different in character: K.181 is marked by the repetition of strikingly dissonant chords, while K.182 is more nimble and dance-like, with great leaping arpeggios.

SALVE REGINA

CHORAL   ⏱ 7:00   📖 6   🎭 🎻 🎵

The *Salve regina*, for soprano, strings, and basso continuo, is one of Scarlatti's earliest works, dating from the early 1700s. He presents a condensed version of the text in six short movements. Written in a variety of styles – from simple fugues to virtuosic displays of vocal dexterity – the effects range from joyous lyricism to mournful chromaticism.

Festeggio armonico celebrates the betrothal of Scarlatti's pupil Maria Barbara to the Spanish crown prince.

STABAT MATER

CHORAL   26:45   7

Scarlatti may be best known for his 500 or more essercizi, or keyboard sonatas, but in the years before his appointment to the Spanish court he composed a variety of music, including 13 operas (now largely forgotten) and several sacred works for the maestro di cappella positions he held. Of the latter, his Stabat Mater for ten voices and basso continuo stands out as a work of great grandeur, depth of expression, and harmonic colour.

Composed in Rome for the Cappella Giulia sometime between 1713 and 1719, it is thought that this work may have been intended for private devotions. The subject matter is full of pathos, describing the anguish of the Virgin Mary at the foot of the Cross; the name refers to the first line of the text, "Stabat Mater dolorosa" ("There stood the Mother grieving"). The second half of the text becomes a prayer to the Virgin herself, followed by a brief prayer to Christ in the final stanzas.

The composition is divided into seven sections in contrasting styles, each section comprising one to five stanzas of the text. Scarlatti eschews the double-choir writing, which was popular in Rome at the time, in favour of using all ten voices as independent forces – often bringing solo parts to the fore against the rich contrapuntal textures. The long vocal phrases, imitative passages, use of dissonance for ornamental effect, and chromatic melodies are in many ways reminiscent of the Renaissance style of Palestrina and the *prima prattica*, yet there are other, more contemporary influences evident as well. He achieves moments of strong emotional contrast when chromatic counterpoint gives way to bold choral scales ("Quis est homo, qui non fleret"), and austere solo dissonances ("Quis non posset contristari"). There are operatic influences as well, as in the ornate duet on "Inflammatus et accensus" and the upbeat fugal "Amen" which concludes the work.

Interestingly, it was about the same time, or perhaps a few years later, that Alessandro Scarlatti – also working in Rome – produced his own setting of the Stabat Mater text.

"Handel understands effect better than any of us; when he chooses, he strikes like a thunderbolt."

WOLFGANG AMADEUS MOZART

George Frideric Handel

● 1685–1759 ⚑ German/English ✍ 487

Handel was the consummate 18th-century artist, traveller, and
entrepreneur. In his lifetime he came to represent not only a unique
synthesis of German instrumental and Italian operatic writing, but also
an entire era of music in England. Although largely known today for his
Water Music, *Music for the Royal Fireworks* and *Messiah*, it is his dramatic
works that were the focus of much of
his career, and which made his name.

LIFE

Handel initially began studying law before
devoting his full attention to a career in
music. After a brief period at university
he moved to Hamburg and an orchestral
position at the opera house, where he
composed his first opera (*Almira*). From
Hamburg he travelled to Italy in 1706, and
then to Hanover, where he took the position
of Kapellmeister at the Electoral court. The
post allowed for extensive travel and so he
went to London, where Italian opera was gaining in
popularity. His opera *Rinaldo* was a great success; although
he returned briefly to Hanover he received permission to
travel again to London on the condition he return within a
reasonable time. He never did; instead, in 1714, his employer
the Elector of Hanover succeeded to the English throne
as George I, and Handel entered the service of the Royal
Court. The next decade saw his fortunes rise and fall as he
competed with the Italian opera and as opera itself gained
and lost the interest of the public. His oratorios and other
choral works, however, enjoyed more success. During the last
decade of his life he suffered from declining health. He had
had two strokes earlier, but in his 60s his sight began to fail
irreparably. Nevertheless, he continued to compose, arrange
earlier works and supervise productions until his death.

Handel became a
British citizen in 1727.
He wrote four anthems
for the coronation of
King George II that year,
including "Zadok the
Priest", which has been
sung at every British
coronation since.

MUSICAL OUTPUT Total: 487

	1685	1710	1720	1730	1740	1750	1759
CONCERTOS (57)	3	2	9	29	11	3	
KEYBOARD (64)	1	24	5	31		3	
OTHER INSTRUMENTAL (99)	2	3	15	30	18	31	
DRAMATIC (46)	6	6	15	15	4		
SACRED (63)	32	10	8	8	5		
SECULAR (158)	71	21	16	17	30	3	

MUSIC

Handel's operas owe much to the popular Italian style, with lyrical, virtuosic arias, dynamic string writing, and a simple, sturdy approach to harmonic progression that belies his Germanic roots. Even the most contrapuntal passages in his choral works contain a clarity not found in the works of his contemporary J S Bach.

Handel's versatility enabled him to write for all kinds of occasion. Despite his Lutheran upbringing, he produced a number of sacred works for the Catholic Church during his time in Italy, and likewise during a brief period spent in the service of James Brydges, Duke of Chandos, he composed the "Chandos Anthems" in the English style.

Handel's large-scale choral works are perhaps his most significant legacy. They were his most consistently successful works and enjoyed multiple revivals even in his lifetime.

MILESTONES	
1697	Appointed assistant organist at Halle Cathedral
1703	Moves to Hamburg
1706	Travels to Italy; composes operas and first oratorios
1708	In Italy performs with an orchestra led by Arcangelo Corelli
1710	Appointed Kapellmeister to the Elector of Hanover (later George I)
1711	First trip to London
1712	Settles in England
1717	Water Music suites, HWV348–50
1720	Appointed musical director of Royal Academy of Music
1723	Appointed composer of the Chapel Royal; composes *Giulio Cesare*, HWV17
1735	*Esther*, HWV50, first English oratorio
1742	*Messiah*, HWV56, premiered in Dublin
1749	*Music for the Royal Fireworks*, HWV351, performed in Green Park, London
1751	Suffers from failing sight, which leads to total blindness by 1753

KEY WORKS

GIULIO CESARE IN EGITTO, HWV17

OPERA　🔊 240:00　📖 3　🎵🎶🎼

Giulio Cesare in Egitto (Julius Caesar in Egypt) premiered on 20 February 1724 at the King's Theatre in London, at a time at which Handel's operatic career was at a peak. It starred many of the leading Italian singers of the day, including the soprano Francesca Cuzzoni as Cleopatra and the castrati Senesino and Gaetano Berenstadt as Caesar and Ptolemy respectively. The libretto by Nicolo Haym portrays the various characters as strong, complex individuals, giving Handel a wide emotional range to play with.

ORGAN CONCERTOS OP. 4, NO. 4 IN F, HWV292

ORCHESTRAL　🔊 14:45　📖 4　🎶🎼

Handel was a talented organist, and his organ concertos, originally intended to be performed between the sections of his oratorios, gave him a chance to demonstrate his virtuosity. The Op. 4, No. 4 concerto (1735) was intended for a performance of *Athalia*. Previous concertos had accompanied *Esther*, *Deborah*, and *Alexander's Feast*.

In this 19th-century engraving, Handel and King George I of England listen to the Water Music from the royal barge on the Thames.

FOCUS

WATER MUSIC, HWV348–50

INSTRUMENTAL   ⏱ 45:00   📖 3   ♒

On 17 July, 1717, a royal event of unusual splendour took place on the River Thames in London. King George I and a large number of nobles travelled up the Thames from the royal palace at Whitehall to Chelsea on open river barges, serenaded by 50 musicians playing three instrumental suites composed by Handel for the occasion. The guests feasted at Chelsea until the early morning, then returned to the barges and to Whitehall to the same music with which they had arrived.

These works were mere light entertainment, yet Handel employs his usual deft touch as a composer, presenting a happy juxtaposition of traditional minuets and English country dances. The *Water Music* also marks the first appearance of the French horn in an English orchestra, an instrument well-suited for outdoor performance.

SUITE 2 IN D MAJOR

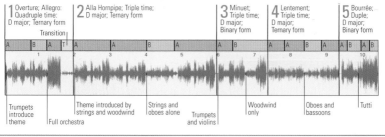

1 Overture; Allegro: Quadruple time; D major; Ternary form
Transition

2 Alla Hornpipe; Triple time; D major; Ternary form

3 Minuet; Triple time; D major; Binary form

4 Lentement; Triple time; D major; Ternary form

5 Bourrée; Duple; D major; Binary form

Trumpets introduce theme | Full orchestra | Theme introduced by strings and woodwind | Strings and oboes alone | Trumpets and violins | Woodwind only | Oboes and bassoons | Tutti

MESSIAH, HWV56

ORATORIO   ⏱ 142:00   📖 16   ⚔ ♫ ♫

In 1741 Handel received an invitation from the Lord Lieutenant of Ireland to help raise money for three major Dublin charities through performances of his music. Although Handel was in poor health at the time, he was determined to compose a new sacred oratorio for the occasion, and turned to Charles Jennens, his librettist for *Saul* and *Israel in Egypt*, for an appropriate subject. Jennens responded with a collection of Old and New Testament verses arranged into a three-part "argument" (as the librettist himself descibed it). The result was the best-known and best-loved of all Handel's oratorios.

The text was not without controversy, with newspapers weighing in with debates as to its "blasphemous" nature. The finished product, however, produced a very different reception, earning critical praise first in Dublin and then in London. Handel made several subsequent revisions to the work, including a version created for Thomas Coram's Foundling Hospital in 1754. Although the work remains a perennial favourite, nowadays most Christmas performances include only the first part plus the Hallelujah Chorus from Part Two.

"The aim and final end of all music should be none other than the glory of God and the refreshment of the soul."

JOHANN SEBASTIAN BACH

Johann Sebastian Bach

◗ 1685–1750   ♒ German   ✍ 972

During his lifetime, Johann Sebastian Bach was known mostly as an organist, and was outshone as a composer by his sons. By the end of the 18th century, however, his musical oeuvre of vocal, choral, keyboard, and instrumental works – both sacred and secular – had been rediscovered by a new and more appreciative audience who admired their unique quality and spirit. Since then his star has not stopped rising.

LIFE

Orphaned at age 10, Bach moved in with his brother, Johann Christoph, who taught him the organ. After studying briefly in Lüneburg, he was appointed organist at the Bonifaciuskirche at Arnstadt, though he proved quarrelsome; first he almost duelled with a student, then he angered the town consistory by overstaying his leave. Bach stayed until 1707, when he moved to Mühlhausen; in short order he married his cousin Maria, fought with his new students, and left for the ducal court in Weimar. The new post paid well and Bach thrived until internal court politics made his position untenable. He left to become Kapellmeister at the Cöthen court in 1717, although the duke had him imprisoned for a month for disloyalty. Bach's wife died in 1720 and he married singer Anna Wilcke the next year. In 1723 he became Kantor at the Thomasschule in Leipzig, and in 1729 he became Director of the Collegium Musicum at the university. In 1737, critic Johann Scheibe criticised Bach's music, accusing him of bombast and artificiality, but he continued to compose and perform until failing eyesight made writing difficult. Following two unsuccessful eye operations, his health deteriorated and he died three months later.

A master of counterpoint, J S Bach composed numerous orchestral pieces, plus seminal works for cello and harpsichord.

MUSICAL OUTPUT							Total: 972
ORCHESTRAL (29)		13	16				
CHAMBER (41)	1	9	8	10	13		
ORGAN MUSIC (260)	81	59	30	28	14		48
OTHER KEYBOARD (190)	25	60	59	27	2		17
SACRED VOCAL (416)	7	22	166	24	9		188
SACRED SECULAR (36)		5	17	12	2		
	1685	1710	1720	1730	1740	1750	UNDATED

MUSIC

Bach was ultimately a pragmatic man, and much of his output relates directly to the demands of his life at the time. His early tutelage on the organ sparked his interest in the works of other North German organ composers, such as Buxtehude and Reincken (both of whom he later met). He continued to develop his organ compositions at Arnstadt and Weimar, also producing cantatas on a regular basis for chapel. In Cöthen, his courtly duties demanded more secular fare, and many of his instrumental works date from this period, including the six *Brandenburg Concertos*, the *Clavierbüchlein* for his new wife Anna, and the *Orgel-Büchlein*.

It was as Kantor at Leipzig that Bach held the widest remit for composition. His duties included producing and directing music for civic events and for organising music for the four main town churches, plus whatever was required for his teaching duties at the Thomasschule. His Leipzig period saw a tremendous outpouring of sacred and secular cantatas and motets for all occasions and church feasts, including five complete cycles of cantatas for the entire church year.

In contrast his instrumental writing waned until he took on the directorship of the Collegium Musicum; Bach revised several of his earlier instrumental works for their weekly concerts and produced new music as well, most notably the comic *Coffee Cantata* (until 1741 the Collegium met in Gottfried Zimmermann's coffeehouse). Works from his final decade include the *Goldberg Variations*,

The town of Eisenach, where Bach was born in 1685. The hilltop castle (Wartburg) is where Martin Luther translated the New Testament into German in 1521.

The Art of Fugue, and *The Musical Offering* (the latter dedicated to Frederick the Great). His sacred writing continued as well; this period saw the composition of the Mass in B minor, the *Christmas Oratorio*, and the *St Mark Passion*.

Bach's compositional style demonstrates a profound understanding of both harmonic progression and the intricacies of Baroque counterpoint; indeed, he was regarded during his life as the greatest contrapuntalist ever. His early studies in organ and composition gave him a

The Thomasschule in Leipzig, where Bach was kantor from 1723 until 1729. For Bach this was a time of great productivity.

horough understanding of the fugue and the dense, cerebral North German style. The interest in the Italian concerto and the French overture and dance suites came later, and were synthesized into a cohesive style.

Bach was a craftsman in both good and bad senses; his formal and harmonic structures were intricate in detail (Friedrich Nietzsche said that Bach's music gave him a sense of 'the higher order of things"), but he was often accused of being overly formalistic as well, creating complex works at the expense of emotional expression. When the lighter, more 'natural" courtly style began to gain wider popularity in the 1730s, Bach was accused of being out of fashion. Ironically it was his composer sons Carl Philipp Emanuel and Johann

Prince Leopold of Anhalt-Cöthen was 23 years old when he hired Bach as his Kapellmeister in 1717.

Christian Bach who came to prominence as the leading representatives of the new style.

After Bach's death, his music remained synonymous with the old style. However, it had its proponents, most notably Baron Gottfried von Swieten, who organized concerts of Bach's music in Vienna. Beethoven is known to have played the "48"; one cannot hear the choral fugue in his Symphony No. 9 without speculating on Bach's influence.

MILESTONES

1692	Enters Eisenach's Lateinschule
1695	Father dies; lives with brother Johann Christoph, who teaches him the organ
1700	Becomes chorister at Lüneburg
1703	Appointed violinist in court orchestra of Duke of Weimar; leaves to become organist at Arnstadt
1705	Walks some 215 miles to Lübeck to meet Dietrich Buxtehude
1707	Appointed organist at Mühlhausen; marries his cousin Maria Barbara Bach
1708	Becomes court organist and chamber musician (later concertmaster) to the Duke of Weimar
1714	Son Carl Philipp Emanuel born
1717	Takes position of director of music (Kapellmeister) at the court of Cöthen; many of his instrumental works are written in this period, including the *Brandenburg Concertos*
1721	Wife dies; marries Anna Wilcke
1723	Prince Leopold of Anhalt-Cöthen dies, terminating Bach's position as Kapellmeister
1723	Appointed kantor of Thomasschule, Leipzig, after Georg Telemann (the most famous composer of the day) turns down the post; the majority of his cantatas are composed in this period; produces *Magnificat*
1724	First performance of *St John Passion*
1729	Becomes Director of Collegium Musicum; first performance of *St Matthew Passion*
1733	Writes a portion of the Mass in B minor
1735	Birth of his youngest son Johann Christian Bach (the "London Bach")
1746	Failing eyesight; composes *The Art of Fugue*
1747	Visits son (C P E Bach), in Potsdam and plays for the king, Frederick the Great; one of the works improvised during this visit becomes *A Musical Offering*
1749	Finishes Mass in B minor
1750	Ill health leads to fatal eye operations

A page from the second fugue of Bach's *Well-Tempered Clavier*

The Monteverdi Choir and the English Baroque Soloists sing Bach's Mass in B minor at the London Royal Albert Hall, 2004.

KEY WORKS

THE WELL-TEMPERED CLAVIER, BWV 846–893

SOLO HARPSICHORD   255:00   96

Also known as the *48 Preludes and Fugues*, the *Well-Tempered Clavier* represents a lifetime of work by Bach. The first collection of 24 preludes and fugues dates from 1722, while the second set of 24 was finished some twenty years later. Each prelude is a freely-composed work, exploring a particular musical idea without specified form. Conversely, fugues follow a stricter set of rules; the juxtaposition of the two adds both affective colour to the performance and a broader challenge to the performer. These may have been intended as technical exercises but if so they remain complex, elegant pieces, exploring all areas of the harpsichord keyboard.

Bach wrote a series of sonatas which explored the full range and character of the harpsichord.

MASS IN B MINOR, BWV 232

MASS   106:00   27

The Mass in B minor was an ongoing work; the Sanctus was written in 1724 while the Credo dates from near the end of his life. The Kyrie and Gloria are taken from a 1733 Mass dedicated to the Dresden court, and the last four movements are parody works, based on other music and added later.

SIX SUITES FOR SOLO CELLO, BWV 1007–1012

SOLO CELLO   140:00   36

Each of these cello suites has a prelude and five dance movements comprising a wide variety of styles. They are remarkably sophisticated and self-contained works, and form the foundation of the solo cello repertoire.

CHRISTMAS ORATORIO, BWV 248

ORATORIO   150:00   6

The *Christmas Oratorio* is properly a six-part cycle: six sacred cantatas to be performed on the three days of Christmas, New Year's Day, the Sunday after the New Year and the Feast of the Epiphany. Much of the music is reworked from earlier secular cantatas which were written for the Collegium Musicum in Leipzig.

FOCUS

ST MATTHEW PASSION, BWV 244

ORATORIO   160:00   68

INFLUENCES

Bach passed on a technical mastery of keyboard playing and musical form to his sons, but was seen as out of fashion by the end of his life. Later revivals of his music, most notably by Mendelssohn, brought new interest in his compositional style and in Baroque counterpoint in general.

The Lutheran oratorio passion, a sacred drama popular in Germany, already existed in the 17th century as a mixture of Lutheran chorales, strophic arias, and choruses. By the next century, composers (including Bach) had added the flare of operatic recitative and aria to the genre. Bach wrote three Passions during his career: the *St Matthew*, the *St John* and the *St Mark*, though of these the latter has largely been lost. The first two, however, remain favourites of the choral repertoire and are frequently performed in concert during the Easter season. The *St Matthew Passion*, for double chorus, double orchestra, two organs and soloists, is a grand work first performed on Good Friday 1727. The text is taken from the Gospel According to Matthew, chapters 26 and 27, with added recitative and aria texts by local poet Christian Friedrich Henrici. The narrative structure is thus: the Evangelist narrates the unfolding events as they occur in recitatives, with occasional lines of dialogue sung by soloists. Solos are also used for prayers and commentary on the story, as in the alto solo "Buss und Reu" ("Grief and Sin"). The chorus sometimes take a direct participatory role, presenting dialogue by the crowds in the drama for example, and sometimes offer detached commentary or prayer, including the interjected chorales. While Bach never wrote an opera, the Passions are very much in the same theatrical vein.

PART ONE (68:00) The work opens with a prologue in which the chorus lament the events to come. The narrative proper begins in Bethany with Christ prophesying his own imminent crucifixion. The story then follows the Biblical story of Judas's collusion with the Pharisees, Jesus's appeals to God, and finally the betrayal and arrest. After each section of narrative a commentary is inserted in the form of a recitative and aria or a chorale.

PART TWO (92:00) After another Prologue, which bemoans the arrest of Jesus, the second part begins with the interrogation before Caiaphas, Peter's denial, and the judgment by Pilate. Bach concludes the work with Jesus's crucifixion, death and entombment, and a final choral lament.

MUSICAL OFFERING, BWV 1079

CHAMBER   🎧 49:00   📖 16   ♯

On Sunday 7 May, 1747 (so the story goes) Bach arrived at the royal court in Potsdam and was immediately summoned to the King's presence. Frederick the Great was an avid musician himself and often played the flute alongside his court musicians (including Bach's son Carl Philipp Emanuel). Frederick sat at the keyboard and played Bach the "royal theme"; Bach listened and then freely improvised a three-part fugue on the same theme. The next night Bach was invited back, but was challenged to provide a six-part fugue on the same theme, a daunting task. Bach demurred, instead improvising a six-part fugue on another theme, but subsequently wrote out a similar fugue on the king's theme. He then elaborated a series of other pieces on the same theme including a full trio sonata for flute, violin and continuo, had the music bound and inscribed with an extended dedication, and presented to the delighted monarch.

A string ensemble, featuring violinists Itzhak Perlman and Pinchas Zukerman, perform the sixth of Bach's *Brandenburg Concertos*.

Canadian pianist Glenn Gould made a critically acclaimed recording of the *Goldberg Variations* in 1955 A second, equally brilliant, recording came in 1981.

GOLDBERG VARIATIONS, BWV 988

KEYBOARD   🎧 78:00   📖 32   🔊

As the story goes, during a trip to Dresden in 1741, Bach presented Count von Keyserlinck his *Aria mit verschiedenen Veränderungen (Aria with Sundry Variations)* for use by the resident harpsichordist in the Count's household, one Johann Gottlieb Goldberg. Goldberg had studied with Bach as well as with Bach's eldest son Wilhelm Friedemann (then resident in Dresden). As Goldberg was only 14 in 1741, the story may well be apocryphal; if not, that Bach would present such a difficult work to such

THE BRANDENBURG CONCERTOS, BWV 1046–1051

CHAMBER   🎧 95:00   📖 6   ♯ 🔊

This set of six varied concertos was dedicated to Margrave Christoph Ludwig of Brandenburg in 1721. The works were shelved in the Margrave's library and lay there unplayed.
CONCERTO NO. 1 (20:00) In the first concerto Bach borrowed from his earlier "Hunt" Cantata, hence the

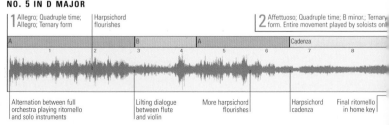

BRANDENBURG CONCERTO NO. 5 IN D MAJOR

1 Allegro; Quadruple time; Allegro; Ternary form	Harpsichord flourishes				**2** Affettuoso; Quadruple time; B minor; Ternary form. Entire movement played by soloists onl
A		B	A		Cadenza
1	2	3	4	5	6	7	8
Alternation between full orchestra playing ritornello and solo instruments		Lilting dialogue between flute and violin	More harpsichord flourishes		Harpsichord cadenza Final ritornello in home key

a young performer implies either great talent on Goldberg's part or great optimism on Bach's. The variations were published as Part IV of Bach's *Clavier-Übung (Keyboard Works)* collection the next year. The 30 so-called *Goldberg Variations* (plus the aria and final reprise) are one of the most complex sets of theme and variations ever written. The "aria", or main theme, is a sarabande in two sections; the theme, unusually, lies in the bass line. Each of the variations follows the same bass line and harmonic progression in some form, albeit often with additional notes interjected. Bach presents a surprising array of forms: gigue (No. 7), fugue (No. 10), French overture (No. 16), and of course a few flashy showpieces. As an added level of complexity, every third variation is a canon, written

at increasingly broad intervals: in No. 3 the second part enters one bar later at the unison, in No. 6 the second part enters a major second up from the first entry, and so forth to the interval of a ninth in No. 27. The final variation is a quodlibet – a contrapuntal combination of two popular tunes, set above the main theme in the bass.

prominent horn part. The last movement comprises a series of dances.

CONCERTO NO. 2 (11:15) The opening movement offers in quick succession the same solo phrase played by violin, oboe, recorder, and trumpet.

CONCERTO NO. 3 (11:00) The first and last movements are pure Italian-style string ensemble writing, while the second was notated by the composer as just a few unornamented chords.

CONCERTO NO. 4 (13:45) Bach combined a solo violin concerto with a concerto grosso, with the violin vying for attention with two recorders.

CONCERTO NO. 5 (19:35) The fifth concerto marks Bach's first use of the transverse flute. The harpsichord plays a prominent role throughout.

CONCERTO NO. 6 (15:00) The final work of the collection features a string ensemble throughout.

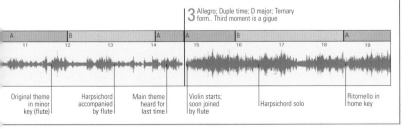

3 Allegro; Duple time; D major; Ternary form.. Third moment is a gigue

A	B		A	B		A
11	12	13	14	15	16	17	18	19

| Original theme in minor key (flute) | Harpsichord accompanied by flute | Main theme heard for last time | Violin starts; soon joined by flute | Harpsichord solo | Ritornello in home key |

Domenico Zipoli

● 1688–1726 ▶ Italian ✎ Unknown

From 1650 to 1750 the Jesuits recruited leading musicians to work in the South American colonies. Zipoli, who studied music in Rome and joined the Jesuits there, became the most celebrated of them. Decades after his death, his naturally flowing melodies and harmonies were still played in churches and Indian villages in his adoptive Argentina. As well as oratorios and Church music, such as his *South American Mass*, Zipoli wrote concise and charming keyboard pieces. He died shortly before he was due to receive priest's orders.

MILESTONES	
1716	*Sonate d'intavolatura*, collection of organ and harpsichord pieces
1717	Sails for South America
1724	Graduates from Jesuit college in Córdoba, Argentina
1732	Jesuit documents record the popularity of his music in Indian villages

Guiseppe Tartini

● 1692–1770 ▶ Italian ✎ c.350

Unusually for his time, Tartini composed almost solely for violin, writing concertos and sonatas – including his famous "Devil's Trill" Sonata – and resisting invitations to write operas. His early music is influenced by Corelli. Something of a mystic, he theorized about the relations between music and emotions. After gaining international fame as a violin virtuoso (his technique sharpened by three years' practice while hiding in a monastery), he set up a highly regarded violin school.

MILESTONES	
1710	Marriage disapproved of; flees Padua
1723	Performs in Prague for coronation
c.1727	Sets up violin school in Padua
1734	Violin Sonatas, Op. 1, published
1754	First music treatise published

Giovanni Battista Pergolesi

● 1710–1736 ▶ Italian ✎ 30–80

Pergolesi's early death from tuberculosis, and the huge posthumous popularity of his moving Stabat mater in the late 18th century, raised him to almost mythical status and resulted in many works being falsely attributed to him. He was nonetheless a successful and respected composer in Naples during the rise of Italian comic opera. He wrote regularly for the theatre, his comic works in minor theatres were very popular (*Lo frate 'nnamorato*, in Neapolitan dialect, contained local folk songs), and he enjoyed royal patronage.

MILESTONES	
1732	Enters employment at royal chapel
1732	Writes *Lo frate 'nnamorato*, opera
1736	Composes Stabat mater

Louis-Claude Daquin

● 1694–1772 ▶ French ✎ Unknown

At the age of six, Daquin played before Louis XIV, and at eight conducted his own choral work *Beatus Vir*. The child prodigy went on to a brilliant career in cultured Parisian society, known as a virtuoso improviser on the harpsichord and organ. Some of his improvisations went into his *Nouveau livre de noëls*, but his few surviving other published compositions only hint at his skills. Sometimes his music shows echoes of Couperin, but often it is highly original, such as the *Trois cadences*, which uses a triple trill. His best-known work is the sprightly *Le coucou (The Cuckoo)* from his 1735 harpsichord book.

MILESTONES	
1735	*Livre de pièces de clavecin* published
1739	Becomes organist at Chappelle Royale
1755	Made organist at cathedral of Notre-Dame in Paris
1757	*Nouveau livre de noëls* published

Thomas Augustine Arne

● 1710–1778 ▣ English ✍ Unknown

The British national anthem and "Rule, Britannia!" ensure Arne's immortality. He wrote mostly theatre music (operas, masques, and incidental music) and books of songs. His prolific output, much of it now lost, varies in quality.

Arne enjoyed huge popularity in London's theatre land during the 1740s; he was a stage man through and through: his sister was the finest tragic actress in the country and his wife a renowned singer. Arne's innovations included all-sung comic opera and the first use in England of the clarinet (in *Thomas and Sally*).

MILESTONES

1740	*Alfred*, masque, with "Rule, Britannia!"
1745	"God Bless our Noble King", song
1760	Writes *Thomas and Sally*, comic opera

Domenico Paradies

● 1707–1791 ▣ Italian ✍ Unknown

Critical and popular reaction to the operas of Paradies, from *Alessandro in Persia* staged in Lucca in Italy to *Fetonte* in London, was lukewarm: Charles Burney, the music historian, described his music as ill-phrased and graceless. Nevertheless, Paradies always found work, such as supplying individual arias to various productions, although he enjoyed more success as a teacher of harpsichord and composition. His fame rests on one progressive, sophisticated set of sonatas conceived for harpsichord, the *Sonate de gravicembalo*. Mozart's father admired these pieces, and they achieved rapid fame throughout Europe.

MILESTONES

1738	Writes *Alessandro in Persia*, opera
1746	Emigrates to London
1747	Writes *Fetonte*, opera
1754	Writes 12 *Sonate de gravicembalo*
1770	Returns to Venice

William Boyce

● 1711–1779 ▣ English ✍ c.180

A rival of Arne in London's 18th-century music theatres Boyce also enjoyed national popularity with his instrumental music, songs, and secular choral works, often written in an italianate, late-Baroque style. A mild, diligent man, his music varies in quality, but his best works, such as *Solomon* or his 12 Sonatas, show technical accomplishment and a gift for melody.

MILESTONES

1736	Appointed composer to Chapel Royal
1742	Composes *Solomon*, serenata
1747	Writes 12 Sonatas for Two Violins and Bass
1749	Boyce Festival held in Cambridge
1761	Composes for George III's coronation
1770s	Deafness forces him to give up work

John Stanley

● 1712–1786 ▣ English ✍ 50

Blinded at the age of two, Stanley began studying music five years later as a diversion, but progressed so fast that by age 12 he was a church organist and by 17 was Oxford's youngest music graduate. He was also a fine violinist, and directed concerts in London's booming subscription scene, as well as Handel's oratorios. Known today for his organ voluntaries, he also composed fine concertos and cantatas which move forwards from Handel to the newer, lighter "galant" sound.

MILESTONES

1742	Composes Six Concertos, Op. 2
1748	First set of organ voluntaries published
1779	Succeeds William Boyce as Master of the King's Band

The
CLASSICAL ERA
1750–1820

Between 1750 and 1820, composers such as Haydn, Mozart, and Beethoven developed a new, simpler musical style, whose maxims – clarity, restraint, and balance – mirrored contemporary intellectual and artistic values. Almost every subsequent development in Western art music can be traced back to this period.

Among the forerunners of the Classical era were composers such as C P E Bach, Johann Quantz, and Baldassare Galuppi. Their works were a reaction against the complexity of Baroque music – its intricate polyphony, counterpoint, and ornamented melody. Instead, composers aimed for a style where a simple melody was accompanied by harmonic progressions.

The Enlightenment, with its focus on rational, human ideals, played a major part in this shift in aesthetic values. So, too, did interest in the simple elegance of Greek and Roman art and architecture, inspired in part by the discovery of the ruins of Pompeii in 1748. Socially and politically, this was a time of great change, with the effects of the Industrial Revolution and colonization creating a larger middle class keen to become consumers of the arts. At the same time, the aristocracies of Europe, suffering from the ravages of the Napoleonic Wars, were less able to support musicians, and the old patronage system started to crumble.

PROFESSIONAL MUSICIANS

Traditionally, musicians employed by aristocratic courts were numbered among the servants – below the valets. However, as public concerts became more common, they were able to earn money from their performances, and publishing their compositions ensured a further income. Haydn, who was employed by the Esterházy family, was given frequent leave to travel, and towards the end of his life he had transcended his lowly position to become part of the court. Mozart, employed by the Archbishop of Salzburg, was not given the same freedoms and, resenting his servile position, moved to Vienna to become one of the very

VIENNESE COURT ORCHESTRA, MID-18TH CENTURY
The red-coated orchestra entertains the guests at a banquet in the Hofburg Palace, Vienna. In the Classical era, Vienna became the musical centre of Europe.

first freelance musicians. However, the music world could not yet support such an ambition, and he suffered considerable financial hardship. When Beethoven moved to Vienna in 1794, he succeeded in gaining the support of wealthy patrons and never had to hold an official appointment.

EVOLVING GENRES

As instrumental music became more popular than vocal music for the first time, composers had to develop ways of creating larger musical canvasses that could support more intense listening. The result was the "Sonata Principle" (sometimes known as Sonata Form), a musical structure consisting of three sections. Its use became almost synonymous with the first movements not only of sonatas, but also of symphonies and indeed most instrumental music of the era. It has remained in use until the present day.

THE SONATA PRINCIPLE

Music structured according to the "Sonata Principle" begins with an Exposition, which introduces the musical material and tends to be repeated. Two themes are usually presented, the second in a key a fifth higher than the original (tonic) key. The next section – the Development – alters the themes, frequently fragmenting them and playing them in different keys before leading the music to the third section, the Recapitulation. Here the opening themes are played again, but this time all in the tonic key. This structure allows a large span of music to be built from relatively little material with a minimum of repetition.

THE WALDSTEIN SONATA
Beethoven's Waldstein Sonata, Op. 53, is a brilliant example of the Classical sonata form.

The symphony evolved from the small-scale Baroque sinfonia into an iconic art form. Usually in four movements, the symphony would start with a gripping "sonata allegro" movement, followed by a slow movement. The third movement was usually an elegant minuet, but this evolved into the scherzo, which could be humorous, or express a more ironic, elemental passion. The finale was frequently a rondo, in which repetitions of a catchy, upbeat melody were interspersed with contrasting themes.

THE YOUNG MOZART AT THE PIANO
Between 1762 and 1767 the prodigious Mozart and his sister Nannerl toured all the main musical centres of Germany as well as Switzerland, Paris, and London.

TIMELINE: THE CLASSICAL ERA

1753
C P E Bach starts work on *The True Art of Keyboard Playing*

1762
First performance of Gluck's *Orfeo ed Euridice*; Mozart begins touring Europe aged 6

◁ **1774**
Start of reign of Louis XVI. Court life was one of elegant formality, expressed in dances such as the minuet

1750

◁ **1759**
Voltaire's *Candide* published

1760

1763 ▷
Pompeii excavations begin

1770

1775
Start of the American Revolution

1780

1781
Haydn composes 6 String Quartets, Op. 33

Other genres were also redefined. The three-movement concerto became a vehicle for just one soloist in which the ideals of balance and elegance were matched by instrumental virtuosity, while the sonata developed into a more formal composition for one or two instruments. The rise in domestic music-making created a market for new forms of chamber music, such as the string quartet – invented by Haydn – and the piano trio.

The symphony orchestra became a broadly standardized entity, smaller but not very different from the orchestra of today. With the orchestra's fuller sound, the role of the continuo gradually died out; instead, the first violin directed the orchestra until eventually displaced by a specialist conductor. Orchestras now had a far greater dynamic range. In the 1740s, the crescendos and diminuendos of the Mannheim Court orchestra, under Johann Stamitz, caused a sensation and were soon a staple of all symphonic writing.

THE OPERA

In opera, notably in the works of Gluck and Mozart, plots were now chosen for greater dramatic realism and music was written to serve the drama rather than decorate it. Gradually, Italian began to lose its dominance as important works were written in German and French.

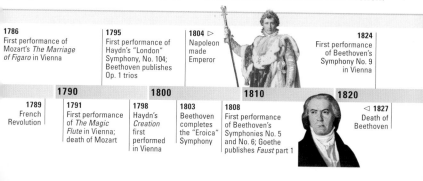

1786
First performance of Mozart's *The Marriage of Figaro* in Vienna

1795
First performance of Haydn's "London" Symphony, No. 104; Beethoven publishes Op. 1 trios

1804 ▷
Napoleon made Emperor

1824
First performance of Beethoven's Symphony No. 9 in Vienna

1790

1800

1810

1820

1789
French Revolution

1791
First performance of *The Magic Flute* in Vienna; death of Mozart

1798
Haydn's *Creation* first performed in Vienna

1803
Beethoven completes the "Eroica" Symphony

1808
First performance of Beethoven's Symphonies No. 5 and No. 6; Goethe publishes *Faust* part 1

◁ **1827**
Death of Beethoven

Christoph von Gluck

● 1714–1787   ⚑ German   ✍ 93

Although lacking the musical finesse of his rivals, Gluck earned himself a place in music history with the reforms he brought to opera. Espousing a more continuous texture in which music served the poetry and drama of the libretto rather than the singer's virtuosity, he employed vivid characterization, simple plots, and large-scale planning of music to bring universal human themes and emotions to life.

LIFE AND MUSIC

Largely self-taught, Gluck became an organist and cellist in Prague before moving to Vienna, and then Milan, where he joined an orchestra and studied composition with Sammartini, a leading symphonist. The success of Gluck's first opera ensured numerous commissions that took him all over Europe, but he returned to Vienna when appointed Kapellmeister of the Opera. He and poet Ranieri Calzabigi drew up a manifesto of operatic reform, eschewing stylized convention in favour of a symbiosis of music and drama. Starting with *Orfeo*, Gluck's work permanently changed operatic norms, whilst causing some controversy, particularly in conservative Paris.

MILESTONES	
1727	Leaves home to study in Prague
1735	Arrives in Vienna; meets Prince Melzi
1737	Accepts post in Melzi's Milan orchestra
1741	Debut opera *Artasere* is an instant success
1745	Presents two operas in London and befriends Handel
1748	Opera *Semiramide* is staged in Vienna
1750	Marries the heiress, Marianna Bergin
1754	Appointed Vienna Opera kapellmeister
1762	Writes opera *Orfeo ed Euridice* (in Italian)
1764	Writes opera *La rencontre imprévue*
1767	*Alceste* is premiered; it is later published with a preface on reforming opera
1774	Stages opera *Iphigénie en Aulide* in Paris
1778	Composes opera *Iphigénie en Tauride*
1779	Suffers a stroke and retires

KEY WORKS

LA RENCONTRE IMPRÉVUE

OPERA   ⏱ 110:00   📖 3   ♫♬♪

Also known as *Les pèlerins de la Mecque*, this was Gluck's last work in the opéra comique style, incorporating spoken dialogue. Set in Cairo, it features a

"harem escape", a plot much in vogue in 18th-century Vienna fascinated by

This fine score is of the Italian version of *Orfeo ed Euridice*. The 1774 French version includes the famous "Dance of the Blessed Spirits".

Islam and by Turkish music. It was performed extensively in Europe and revived in Vienna in 1780, when it influenced Mozart in his writing of *Die Entführung aus dem Serail*.

IPHIGÉNIE EN TAURIDE

OPERA   ⏱ 102:00   📖 4   ♫♬♪

Probably Gluck's finest work, this was written at the same time as Piccini's opera on the same theme, splitting Paris into Gluckists and Piccinists. Its first performance in 1779 was Gluck's greatest triumph, and much later, even inspired Berlioz to become a musician. The music is dramatic, expressive, and almost symphonic in its orchestration.

FOCUS

ORFEO ED EURIDICE

OPERA   120:00   3   ♆ ♨ ♂

In this, the first of Calzabigi and Gluck's "reform operas", their aim was to conjure a "beautiful serenity". Choosing a simple Greek tragedy in preference to the labyrinthine plots employed in opera seria, and using only three rather than six soloists, they created a work of unprecedented directness. The role of Orpheus was originally written for a castrato, but recast as a high tenor when the opera was extended and rewritten in French as *Orphée* for Paris in 1774. Later rearranged by Berlioz, it is now usually performed by a mezzo soprano.

ACT ONE (36:00) Lamenting Euridice's death, Orfeo sends away the mourning nymphs and shepherds and decides to bring her back from Hades. Cupid tells him he will succeed if he soothes the Furies with music and avoids looking at her until they are across the River Styx.

ACT TWO (44:00) At the gates of Hades Orpheus quells the Furies with his music and enters. In the Elysian Fields beyond, he finds Euridice and, with eyes averted, leads her back.

ACT THREE (40:00) Orpheus hurries on as Euridice pleads for reassurance. No longer able to refuse, he turns and she dies again. Overcome, he sings the aria "Che farò senza Euridice", vowing to kill himself, but Cupid restores her to life amidst rejoicing.

ALCESTE

OPERA   135:00   3   ♆ ♨ ♂

The second of the "reform operas", *Alceste* was published with a preface that declared Gluck's new principles of opera. The opera was altered considerably for Paris, but the original Italian plot is described below.

ACT ONE (50:00) King Admetus is dying while his Queen, Alceste, makes sacrifices at the temple. The oracle declares that he will live if someone will take his place. Alceste offers herself.

ACT TWO (60:00) In the Grove of Death the orchestra imitates the sounds of the night. Calling upon the Underworld, she insists on her sacrifice as long as she can bid her family farewell. Admetus discovers why he has returned to health and vows to die himself instead.

ACT THREE (25:00) About to take her farewell, Alceste is seized by the Furies and dies. Admetus issues threats and lamentations, but when he threatens suicide, Apollo restores Alceste to life.

Carl Philippe Emanuel Bach

● 1714–1788　🏴 German　✍ 875

Possibly the most important composer of his generation, C P E Bach bridged the gap between the Baroque style of his father, J S Bach, and the Classical style of Haydn and Mozart. The main exponent of the *empfindsamer Stil*, an expressive musical style, he also developed the sonata, and was renowned as a keyboard player whose *True Art of Keyboard Playing* is the major treatise on 18th-century music.

LIFE AND MUSIC

The second son of J S Bach, C P E Bach studied with his father until appointed court harpsichordist to Frederick II of Prussia. Although poorly paid, Bach composed, taught, and performed at the courts of Berlin and Potsdam for some 30 years before leaving to succeed his godfather, Georg-Philipp Telemann as Kantor and music director in Hamburg. Opportunity now abounded and Bach became responsible for 200 performances a year at five churches and started to write non-secular vocal music. The bulk of his works are, however, instrumental.

MILESTONES	
1731	Studies law at Leipzig university
1738	Becomes harpsichordist to Crown Prince Frederick of Prussia in Berlin
1744	Marries Johanna Danneman
1749	Writes Trio Sonata in C minor, "Sanguineus and Melancholicus", WQ161/1
1755	Composes Flute Concerto in G major, WQ169
1757	Writes Symphony in E flat major, WQ179
1768	Appointed Kantor and master of Church music at Hamburg

KEY WORKS

SIX PRUSSIAN SONATAS

SONATA　⏱ 90:00　📖 6　🎶

Bach's first published works, dedicated to Frederick II, were written not for the harpsichord, but for the much quieter and more sensitive clavichord, which could better express the subtle, but intensely emotional, nuances inherent in the *empfindsamer Stil*.

Among more than 150 of Bach's works in this form, each of these sonatas is written in three movements: fast, slow, and very fast.

SYMPHONY IN E FLAT MAJOR, WQ179

SYMPHONY　⏱ 11:15　📖 3　🎶

Among the last of the eight "Berlin" Symphonies, this piece clearly reflects the new Classical style, with its light homophonic (rather than complex polyphonic) effects. The symphony opens with an arresting movement, followed by a particularly sensitive Larghetto, and closing with a jaunty finale, showcasing the horns.

An autographed score from C P E Bach's notebook (1714–1788). Original scores can offer invaluable insights into his intentions and views on performance.

FOCUS

MAGNIFICAT IN D MAJOR, WQ215

MASS   ⏳ 45:00   📖 9   〰️ 🎻 🔔

Bach modelled his first major choral piece on his father's Magnificat (BWV 243). Although adapting the same key and text, he achieved rather more homophonic and melodious effects. Scored for trumpets, drums, flutes, oboes, horns, and strings, with four vocal soloists, it is one of the few major choral pieces to be written after J S Bach and before Haydn.

MAGNIFICAT (3:00) Opening with a full chorus, this spirited movement alternates choral and orchestral parts.

QUIA RESPEXIT (6:50) This lyrical soprano solo with string accompaniment encapsulates Bach's expressive style.

QUIA FECIT MIHI MAGNA (4:00) After a strong and direct opening, the tenor solo takes a virtuosic and agile role.

ET MISERICORDIA (7:00) With its lovely harmonies and quiet drama, this movement is very forward-looking.

FECIT POTENTIAM (4:00) For the first time since the start, the trumpets return to characterize this powerful bass solo.

DEPOSUIT POTENTES (7:50) A duet for tenor and alto, this movement is based on that of J S Bach's Magnificat.

SUSCEPIT ISRAEL (5:00) A haunting and slightly Baroque solo for alto.

GLORIA PATRI (3:00) With full orchestra and chorus, musical material from the first movement is repeated.

SICUT ERAT (5:00) The glorious closing fugue anticipates Mozart's Requiem.

FLUTE CONCERTO IN G MAJOR, WQ169

CONCERTO   ⏳ 24:00   📖 3   〰️ 🎺

One of five flute concertos adapted from keyboard compositions, this piece is perhaps the most virtuosic.

FIRST MOVEMENT (ALLEGRO DI MOLTO, 10:50) After a vigorous opening with some "sighing" motifs, the flute enters with music of a much gentler nature.

SECOND MOVEMENT (LARGO, 8:50) The strings set the scene for a pleading slow movement, while the flute responds with long, rhetorical phrases culminating in a tender cadenza.

THIRD MOVEMENT (PRESTO, 5:00) In this elegant finale of some rhythmic verve, the flautist has frequent opportunities to relish the highly virtuosic writing.

INFLUENCES

When Carl Czerny went to study with Beethoven, he was immediately required to purchase C P E Bach's *True Art of Keyboard Playing*. Perhaps now better known than any of his music, it codified contemporary musical style and established technical norms – including fingering – which underpinned most later keyboard playing.

Johann Adolph Hasse

● 1699–1783   ⚑ German   ♫ 1,600

In the mid-1700s, Hasse's operas – staged in high-quality productions, and tailored to individual singers – made him famous throughout Europe. His emphasis on beauty rather than complexity paved the way for the Classical style. Fêted by the nobility and royalty of Vienna, Naples, Paris, London, and Berlin, he was also admired by both J S Bach and Mozart. One of Alessandro Scarlatti's last pupils in Naples, he went on to serve for 30 years as musical director at the Dresden court, where music flourished. Hasse's vast output, very often composed at speed, includes 63 operas, 90 cantatas, and 80 flute concertos written for Frederick II of Prussia.

Hasse staged lavish productions at the Dresden Semperoper, often with the help of the librettist Pietro Metastasio.

MILESTONES	
1730	*Artaserse*, opera, performed in Venice
1730	Marries famous Italian mezzo--soprano, Faustino Bordoni
1731	*Cleofide*, opera, performed in Dresden; it impresses J S Bach
1742	*Lucio Papiro*, opera, staged in Dresden

Johann Joachim Quantz

● 1697–1773   ⚑ German   ♫ c.600

The son of a blacksmith, Quantz started learning music at the age of only 11. After training in Italy, France and England, he switched from the oboe to become one of the first professional flute players in Europe. A star member of the Dresden orchestra, he was spotted by the future Frederick II of Prussia, whom he went on to serve for over 30 years as a hard-worked but richly rewarded flute teacher, maker, composer and performer. Quantz's massive output, mostly for Frederick, includes 300 flute concertos and 235 flute sonatas, of variable quality, but all craftsmanlike. His book on the flute made him famous throughout Europe.

MILESTONES	
1718	Appointed court oboist in Dresden
1719	Specializes in the flute
1727	Adds a second key to the flute
1739	Begins making flutes
1741	Starts work for Frederick II of Prussia
1752	Publishes *On Playing the Tranverse Flute*

A keen flautist, Frederick II of Prussia performed for his courtiers under the expert guidance of his tutor, Johann Quantz.

Johann Wenzel Anton Stamitz

● 1717–1757   ♪ Czech   ✍ 150

The Classical symphony developed at intensely musical centres, such as the Electoral Court at Mannheim in Germany, where Stamitz served as violinist, composer and musical director. A star contributor, he brought international fame to the orchestra with its impeccable and dynamic renderings of his symphonies. Although he wrote countless concertos, he is famous for his 58 surviving symphonies, which established the four-movement pattern and the Classical style. Four other members of the Stamitz family, including his sons, Carl and Johann (Anton), became prominent musicians.

MILESTONES	
1741	Works at the court of Mannheim
1750	Serves as musical director at Mannheim
1754	Enjoys a season in Paris
1755	Publishes Orchestral Trios, Op. 1

Leopold Mozart

● 1719–1787   ♪ German   ✍ c.550

The father of Wolfgang Amadeus, Leopold was a noted court composer and violin teacher. Despite supporting his gifted son – as teacher, agent, and editor – he found time to pursue his own career. Haughty and hard to please, he was nevertheless a man of wit and wisdom who wrote copious concertos, symphonies, serenades, and Church music, but probably not the "Toy" Symphony often credited to him.

MILESTONES	
1743	Becomes court violinist at Salzburg
1756	Publishes popular violin tutor
1747	Marries Anna Maria Pertl
1757	Becomes court composer at Salzburg
1769	Writes Symphony in G major, G16, "*Neue Lambacher*" (*New Lambach*)
1778	Wife dies on tour with Wolfgang

François-Joseph Gossec

● 1734–1829   ♪ Belgian   ✍ 160

Gossec started his career as a court employee and ended up as the foremost musical representative of the French Revolution. A farmer's son, he had come to Paris as a protégé of Jean-Philippe Rameau, and worked for both private and court orchestras while composing comic operas, with mixed success. However, he became a key musician in Paris after founding the Concert des Amateurs, an independent orchestra, before directing the renowned Concert Spirituel and organizing the École de Chant. During the Revolution, he resigned his post at the Opéra and wrote pro-Revolutionary works. Though overshadowed by other composers, he stimulated a revival of instrumental music in dance-dominated France.

French rebels stormed the Bastille in Paris, in 1789, inspiring Gossec to create dramatic instrumental works celebrating the Revolutionary ideals.

MILESTONES	
1751	Becomes a chorister at Antwerp
1754	Composes Symphony No. 1
1766	*Les Pêcheurs* (*The Fishermen*), opera, first performed
1770	Founds the Concert des Amateurs
1773	Directs the Concert Spirituel
1795	Appointed Professor of Composition at the Paris Conservatoire

"My Prince was always satisfied…and I was in a position to improve, alter, and be as bold as I pleased."

FRANZ JOSEPH HAYDN, ON HIS EMPLOYER, PRINCE NICOLAUS

Franz Joseph Haydn

🕭 1732–1809   🏴 Austrian   ✍ 1,195

Born in the Baroque era, and still alive when Beethoven composed
his "Pastoral Symphony", Haydn was a key figure in the evolution of
the Classical style. Writing a vast oeuvre within the protective confines
of the Esterházy court, and establishing the standard forms of the
symphony, sonata, and string quartet, he emerged as an international
musical figure who both influenced
Mozart and taught Beethoven.

LIFE

Possessing a fine singing voice, Haydn
received elementary music training as a
choirboy, but when his voice broke he had
to earn a meagre living from performing
in ensembles and teaching children. He
continued his studies by reading treatises,
until the singer Nicola Porpora helped him
to hone his compositional skills. He was
introduced to a number of influential
people, and became Count Morzin's music
director in 1759. On the strength of his Symphony No. 1,
Haydn was appointed Vizekapellmeister at the court of
one of the richest and most influential Hungarian families,
the Esterházys, and by 1766 had taken full responsibility
for their music. Composing new instrumental works for the
twice-weekly concerts, as well as for festivities, church, and
theatre, he developed his skills unmolested by market forces.
When Prince Nicolaus died in 1790, Haydn's music had
already been published all over Europe. An invitation from
the impresario J P Salomon to present new works in England
swiftly followed, and during two extended stays Haydn
amassed a fortune, and was awarded a doctorate from
Oxford University. He was recalled to the Royal Court in
1795, following the accession of Prince Nicolaus's grandson,
and remained active as a composer in Vienna until 1803.

The music of Haydn
was full of bold effects,
but also had an intimate
lyricism, as can be seen
in his greatest work,
The Creation.

MUSICAL OUTPUT							Total: 1,195
SYMPHONIES (108)		2	42	27	24	13	
OTHER ORCHESTRAL (65)		2	26	10	11	15	1
CHAMBER (707)			105	104	43	206	249
SOLO INSTRUMENTAL (101)			31	35	18	17	
OPERA (25)		1	9	11	3	1	
CHORAL (88)		4	14	12	1	53	4
SONG (101)			2	4	36	49	10
	1732	1749	1760	1770	1780	1790	1800 1808

MUSIC

Mostly self-taught and largely cut off at court from mainstream music, Haydn later suggested that this very isolation had forced his originality upon him. While his oeuvre includes practically every genre of music, from folk-song arrangements to opera, it is through his innovations in instrumental music that Haydn had the greatest influence. Although frequently referred to as the "father of the symphony", he did not invent the form, but his 108 works in the genre pioneered its evolution, from a three-movement Baroque overture for fewer than 20 players to the dramatic four-movement form for as many as 60, which became the Classical period's finest legacy. Equally influential in the development of the instrumental sonata, he guided its transformation from the lightweight divertimento into a work of far greater gravitas which,

During his two 18-month sojourns in England between 1791 and 1795, Haydn composed 12 symphonies, known collectively as the London Symphonies. They include the "Surprise", "Drumroll", and "London".

modelled on the structure of the concerto, included a substantial slow movement. Haydn's finest achievement, however, was in the creation of a new medium: the string quartet. Whereas orchestral works had sometimes been performed by four players, and some pieces had been composed for the same combination with the accompaniment of a continuo part, Haydn established a genre in which each instrument was equal and independent.

MILESTONES

Year	Event	Year	Event
1740	Becomes a choirboy at St Stephen's Cathedral, Vienna	1772	First performance of "Farewell" Symphony, No. 45
1753	Starts to work as accompanist to singer Nicola Porpora	1791	First visit to England, where he remains for 18 months; composes six symphonies including "Surprise" Symphony, No. 94
1759	Composes Symphony No. 1		
1760	Marries Maria Keller, but they later separate after an unhappy marriage	1792	Meets and starts teaching Beethoven
		1794	Returns to England for a further 18 months; composes "English" Sonata, and is commissioned to write oratorio *The Creation*
1761	Becomes Vizekapellmeister at the court of Esterházy		
1762	Assumed date for String Quartet No. 1		
1765	Composes Cello Concerto No. 1	1795	Returns to the court of Esterházy, where he focuses on church music, writing six Masses in the following years
		1796	Composes Trumpet Concerto for Anton Weidinger's new keyed trumpet
		1798	First performance of *The Creation* is given in Vienna and is an immediate success; composes "Nelson" Mass

Hadyn composed many operas for the Italian opera company employed by Prince Nicolaus at his sumptuous pleasure palace at Esterháza.

KEY WORKS

TRUMPET CONCERTO

ORCHESTRAL   🕐 13:00   📖 3   ♫ 👁

In this, the first work written for the newly invented keyed trumpet, Haydn took full advantage of the instrument's ability to play all the notes within its compass by boldly presenting running passages and cantabile melodies in its lower range. Premiered in Vienna in 1800 by the instrument's inventor, Anton Weidinger, the concerto remains a cornerstone of every trumpet player's repertoire.

"ENGLISH" SONATA

PIANO SOLO   🕐 13:00   📖 3   👁

Numbering over 50, Haydn's piano sonatas have a staggering variety and originality. Featuring a rather whimsical first movement, the "English" Sonata (1794) is notable for its use of some of the first notated pedal effects, while the breadth of its Adagio was made possible by the mellow tone and resonating capacity of a new piano by John Broadwood. The amusing Finale takes great pleasure in sending the pianist down numerous wrong turns.

Renowned mezzo-soprano Cecilia Bartoli appears in Haydn's opera *L'anima del filosofo* at the Royal Opera House, London.

CELLO CONCERTO NO. 1

ORCHESTRAL   🕐 26:00   📖 3   ♫ 👁

Rediscovered in 1961, Haydn's Cello Concerto No. 1 immediately joined its brother, the Cello Concerto No. 2, in the standard repertoire. It shows Baroque tendencies in its reiteration of passages for full orchestra (ritornellos), while its mood is Rococo. On a grand scale throughout, the outer movements demand considerable agility and stamina, while the slow movement was composed to showcase the Esterházy cellist's beautiful tone.

"NELSON" MASS

MASS SETTING   🕐 42:00   📖 5   ♫ 👥 👁

Originally titled *Mass in Straitened Times*, the subsequent sobriquet was probably coined when Haydn met Lord Nelson in 1800. Lacking woodwind and horns, following their disbandment at court, the work has a unique sound for the period.

INFLUENCES

Although he was a musician's musician, after his death in 1809 Haydn's music was frequently dismissed as inferior to that of Mozart and a mere precursor to Beethoven's compositions. However, it has rightly been said that few music innovations in the century following Haydn's death could not be traced back to his works.

FOCUS

STRING QUARTET NO. 63, "SUNRISE", OP. 76, NO. 4

CHAMBER   ⏳ 22:00   🎵 4   ♟

Having decided not to move to England, Haydn returned to Esterháza in 1795, where his duties were now far lighter, and his international fame made him more of a trophy than a servant. No longer composing sonatas and symphonies, he turned once again to the more private medium of the string quartet, distilling the experiments of a long career into eight final works that demonstrate his total mastery over the genre which he had himself invented.

FIRST MOVEMENT (ALLEGRO CON SPIRITO 8:00) The spacious improvisatory violin ascending over a single chord that opens this piece led to comparisons with a sunrise, giving the work its nickname. The later passages have an expansiveness that is almost Romantic.

SECOND MOVEMENT (ADAGIO 6:00) A serene meditation with subtle interplay between the instruments, this movement, in the tradition of all the greatest chamber music, removes the listener from all that is mundane.

THIRD MOVEMENT (MENUETTO, ALLEGRO 4:00) Exuding charm and jovial good humour, the Minuet leads into a folk-like Trio, featuring a droning bass over a fragmented minor-key melody.

FINALE (ALLEGRO MA NON TROPPO 4:00) At first deceptively amiable and laconic, even perhaps reminiscent of English folk song, the pace of the finale

The string quartet, in which each instrument plays an equal part, was Haydn's greatest achievement.

SYMPHONY NO. 104 IN D MAJOR "LONDON"

ORCHESTRAL   ⏳ 26:30   🎵 4   🎶

Twelve of Haydn's later symphonies are known collectively as the "London" Symphonies. This was his final work in the series – and in the genre. Taking advantage of a far larger orchestra than he was used to in Vienna, this work features some of his most majestic music.

FIRST MOVEMENT (ADAGIO , ALLEGRO, 8:05) After a solemn introduction in the minor key, the main theme of the Allegro is surprisingly lyrical. This is swiftly usurped by faster, more exuberant music that makes frequent use of trumpets and drums.

SECOND MOVEMENT (ANDANTE, 7:45) After the charmingly poised opening melody, the sudden entry of the full orchestra is a real surprise. After this

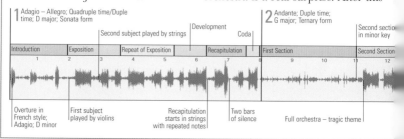

1 Adagio – Allegro; Quadruple time/Duple time; D major; Sonata form

		Second subject played by strings	Development	Coda		
Introduction	Exposition	Repeat of Exposition		Recapitulation		
1	2	3	4	5	6	7

Overture in French style; Adagio; D minor | First subject played by violins | | Recapitulation starts in strings with repeated notes | Two bars of silence |

2 Andante; Duple time; G major; Ternary form

	Second section in minor key
First Section	Second Section
9	10

Full orchestra – tragic theme

changes drastically towards the end,
concluding the quartet with an
effervescent flourish.

THE CREATION

ORATORIO ⏱ 99:00 📖 3 🎵🥁🎤

After hearing performances of
Handel's oratorios in London, Haydn
was inspired to write a similarly large-
scale biblical work. *The Creation* was
commissioned by Johann Salomon,
who presented an English libretto
based on the book of Genesis,
which Haydn had had translated
into German. The piece was an
immediate success in both England
and Germany, and became Haydn's
most performed work.

PART ONE (36:00) The opening
representation of chaos is possibly
the most extraordinary music of
the period. Conjuring timelessness,
Haydn juxtaposed seemingly
incongruous ideas, allowing
harmonies to meander until, with
a blaze of glory, the chorus sings,
"Let there be light." The music then
introduces each act of
the Creation with a
recitative, followed by one
or more lyrical commentaries
and concluded by the chorus
in a hymn of praise.

PART TWO (37:00) Continuing with
the "fifth day", Haydn achieves a
remarkable musical depiction of the
poetry of Genesis, most particularly
of the animals, from the roaring of
tigers to the gentle pastorality of
cows, and even the "sinuous worm".

PART THREE (26:00) The first humans,
Adam and Eve, praise God and the
act of Creation before a choral fugue
brings the work to a
glorious end.

disquieting display of
drama and passion,
the return to gentility
is never quite assured.

THIRD MOVEMENT

MENUETTO – ALLEGRO, 4:15)

Far faster than earlier minuets, the
third movement with its frequent
syncopations, surprises, and the
orchestral timbre of the Trio, point
firmly in the direction of Beethoven.

The Hungarian conductor
Antal Dorati has recorded
all of Haydn's symphonies.

FOURTH MOVEMENT

FINALE: SPIRITOSO (6:15)

Claimed both as
a traditional Croatian folk tune
and as a London street seller's cry,
the earthy melody used in the final
movement brings Haydn's career
as a symphonist to a joyful end.

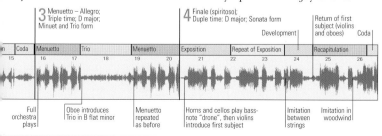

3 Menuetto – Allegro;
Triple time; D major;
Minuet and Trio form

4 Finale (spiritoso);
Duple time; D major; Sonata form

Development | Return of first subject (violins and oboes) | Coda

…n	Coda	Menuetto		Trio		Menuetto		Exposition		Repeat of Exposition		Recapitulation		
15		16	17	18		19	20	21	22	23	24	25	26	

| Full orchestra plays | Oboe introduces Trio in B flat minor | Menuetto repeated as before | Horns and cellos play bass-note "drone", then violins introduce first subject | Imitation between strings | Imitation in woodwind |

Johann Christian Bach

● 1735–1782   ▥ German   ♫ c.360

The most versatile and cosmopolitan of J S Bach's composing sons, "the London Bach" composed operas in Milan before moving to England and becoming music master to the royal family. He helped establish the Classical era, partly with music in the new lighter style – especially his symphonies and piano concertos – and also with the acclaimed public concerts he organized with the celebrated harpsichord player Carl Friedrich Abel, taking musical emphasis away from the church and into the concert hall. After enjoying financial success, fame, and respect, his reputation faded: his concerts lost money, he was defrauded, and he suffered a long and debilitating chest illness.

Concerts performed at the Hanover Square Rooms in London, featuring many fashionable musicians, were popular in the 18th century.

MILESTONES	
1760	Becomes cathedral organist in Milan
1762	Moves to London
1763	Writes variations on *God Save the King*
1764	First Bach–Abel concerts performed
1768	Plays first piano solo in public
c.1781	Composes Symphonies for Double Orchestra, Op.18

Johann Albrechtsberger

● 1736–1809   ▥ Austrian   ♫ 750

Many, including his friend Mozart, considered Albrechtsberger one of the world's greatest organists. He was also a prolific composer, writing keyboard pieces, church compositions with fine oratorios, and a range of other works, including a curious Concerto for Jew's Harp. As a composition teacher, known for his skill in counterpoint, he was in great demand. One of his pupils was Beethoven, whose later fugues reflect Albrechtsberger's enthusiasm for the form.

MILESTONES	
1772	Becomes court organist, Vienna
1790	Publishes popular textbook: *Fundamentals of Composition*
1793	Kapellmeister at St Stephen's, Vienna
1794	Tutors Beethoven

Karl Ditters von Dittersdorf

● 1739–1799   ▥ Austrian   ♫ c.200

A prolific composer of more than 100 symphonies, 40 concertos, as well as several comic operas, Karl Ditters (ennobled in 1773 with the title "von Dittersdorf") mainly wrote accessible, craftsmanlike music in the popular genres of the time, spanning the development of the Viennese Classical style. He held various court appointments and was a virtuoso violinist, gaining considerable celebrity through performing his own concertos.

MILESTONES	
1764	Writes Mass for Frankfurt coronation of Archduke Joseph
1786	*Doktor und apotheker*, opera, performed
1786	Composes twelve symphonies based on Ovid's *Metamorphoses*
1795	Sacked by Schaffgotsch, Prince of Breslau; awarded meagre pension

Giovanni Paisiello

🔵 1740–1816 🏴 Italian ✍ 180

The most popular opera composer of the late 1700s was not Mozart but Paisiello, a Neapolitan whose reputation  brought him lucrative posts with Catherine the Great, Napoleon, and the King of Naples. Over 30 of his operas were successes. His light, rhythmic style and melodic turns of phrase, as in his *The Barber of Seville* (the first opera setting of the story), influenced Mozart's *The Marriage of Figaro* and *Don Giovanni*, as well as Rossini, Bellini, and Donizetti.

MILESTONES	
1776	Works for Catherine III in St Petersburg
1783	Writes *The Barber of Seville*, opera
1789	Composes *Nina*, opera
1802	Works for Napoleon in Paris

Jean Paul Martini

🔵 1741–1816 🏴 French ✍ 150

Born in Germany, Martini established a successful career as a court musician in France. There he adapted shrewdly to the changing regimes throughout the Revolution, first directing concerts for the Queen, later writing music for Napoleon's marriage, and finally writing for the restored Royal Chapel. At best a minor innovator, Martini's melodic operas had mixed success, but *L'amoureux de quinze ans*, written in 1771, enjoyed considerable popularity, while his highly regarded church music combined old forms with modern theatricality, and his chansons, such as "Plaisir d'amour", were influential. In 1800 he became professor of composition at the Paris Conservatoire.

MILESTONES	
1783	Writes *Le droit du seigneur*, opera
1793	"Prière pour le Roi", political song
1814	Composes *Scene héroïque pour Napoléon*

Luigi Boccherini

🔵 1743–1805 🏴 Italian ✍ c.600

After studying in Rome and gaining acclaim as an outstanding cello virtuoso in Italy, Boccherini toured Europe to seek his fortune. Following success in Paris, he was invited to Madrid to be court chamber composer to the Infante Don Luis. There he wrote quintets – for his cello with Don Luis's existing quartet. Though still popular in Paris, Boccherini – who saw both wives and several of his children die – was dogged by illness and bad luck in his last years, and died in obscurity and poverty in a tiny apartment.

MILESTONES	
1757	Studies in Rome
1767	Success in Paris; publishes his first chamber music
1770	Starts work for Don Luis
1771	Writes String Quintet in E major
1786	Appointed court composer for Friedrich Wilhelm II of Prussia
1800	Lucien Bonaparte becomes patron

"There is perhaps no instrumental music more ingenious, elegant, and pleasing than his quintets", Charles Burney wrote of Boccherini in 1770.

Carl Stamitz

● 1745–1801   ♪ German   ✍ 250

Son of Johann, head of the renowned Mannheim orchestra, Carl Stamitz was born into music. First a violinist, he then became a prolific composer of lyrical, flowing orchestral music, writing 50 symphonies, 38 symphonies concertante, and 60 concertos. He went to Paris to work as a court composer, performing at the Concert Spirituel and publishing his music. He then worked around Europe, spending three years in London, where he worked with J C Bach. After a period at the court of William V, Prince of Orange, and more travelling, he ended up as music director and teacher at Jena university. But there was unhappiness: all his children died in infancy, his debts mounted, and his ambitious plans (even attempts at alchemy) came to nothing.

MILESTONES	
1762	Gains position as second violin in Elector of Mannheim's court orchestra
1770	Moves to Paris; begins concert career as virtuoso of violin and viola d'amore
1778	Holds own benefit concert in London
1780	Goes to work in The Hague
1790	Goes on working visit to Russia
1795	Moves to Jena

Born in Mannheim, Carl Stamitz's first appointment was as a violinist in the court orchestra. His father, its director, had built it up to being the best in Europe.

Domenico Cimarosa

● 1749–1801   ♪ Italian   ✍ 110

Shortly after leaving composition classes, Cimarosa burst onto the scene with his comic opera *Le stravaganze del conte* in Naples. After that, his 60 light, elegant operas, mostly comic, with witty and lively ensembles, were staged all over Europe. He also wrote chamber music in a Mozart-like style. When Napoleon occupied Naples in 1799, Cimarosa – then organist at the royal chapel – wrote a song of praise which was sung at the burning of the royal flag – only to see the king re-take the city and throw him in jail. His reputation saved his head, but he was exiled and died soon after in Venice.

MILESTONES	
1772	*Le stravaganze del conte*, opera, premiered
1780	*L'Italiana in Londra* staged at La Scala
1787	Visits court at St Petersburg
1792	*Il matrimonio segreto*, opera, staged while Kapellmeister in Vienna for two years
1793	Returns to Naples; accepts royal post

Cimarosa was probably the most successful Italian opera composer until Rossini. His biggest triumph was *Il matrimonio segreto (The Secret Marriage).*

Muzio Clementi

● 1752–1832　　🏳 English　　♫ 178

Largely forgotten today, Clementi was one of the first piano virtuosos. He codified his intimate knowledge of the new instrument in *Gradus ad Parnassum*, a seminal work of 19th-century piano teaching consisting of 100 piano studies. Also a successful publisher and piano manufacturer, he was much celebrated in his lifetime and was buried in Westminster Cathedral, where his epitaph reads, "The father of the pianoforte".

LIFE AND MUSIC

A child prodigy, Clementi was "bought" from his Italian father at the age of 13 and taken to a wealthy household in the southwest of England, where he occupied himself entirely with studying the harpsichord for seven years. Moving to London in 1774, he became England's pre-eminent keyboard player, but after two European tours and a piano "duel" with Mozart, he retired from the concert stage and concentrated on teaching. Clementi subsequently founded a music-publishing and piano-manufacturing firm, travelling extensively to establish it, and secured the publishing rights to several of Beethoven's compositions. However, it is for his virtuosic and dramatic piano sonatas, which certainly influenced Beethoven, that he is remembered.

MILESTONES

1752	Born in Rome
1766	Appointed organist in Damaso, Italy, but is brought to England by patron
1779	Publishes Piano Sonatas, Op. 2
1781	Piano contest with Mozart in Vienna
1787	Completes Two Symphonies Op. 18
1790	Retires from the concert stage; completes Six Piano Sonatas, Op. 25
1798	Establishes Longman, Clementi & Co.
1802	Begins eight-year tour of Europe on behalf of his firm
1807	Publishing contract with Beethoven
1816	Symphonies performed in Paris
1813	Becomes director of newly founded Philharmonic Society in London
1826	Completes *Gradus ad Parnassum*

KEY WORKS

PIANO SONATA IN F SHARP MINOR OP. 25, NO. 5

PIANO SOLO　⏱ 14:00　📖 3　🎵

Amongst the finest of Clementi's 64 piano sonatas, this dramatic work was certainly written for the concert stage rather than the drawing room. Although pianistically varied, its mood is unusually dark, and with all three movements in the minor mode, this is an intense and brooding work of considerable pathos.

Abandoning traditional two-movement sonatas, Clementi initiated three-movement forms.

GRADUS AD PARNASSUM

PIANO SOLO　📖 100　🎵

Published in three volumes between 1817 and 1826, this comprehensive collection of didactic pieces, ranging from finger exercises to fugues, studies, sonata movements, and character pieces, was the result of a long lifetime's experience playing the newly invented piano. Meaning "Steps to Parnassus" (the abode of the Muses), it was highly regarded and widely used throughout the 19th century, and was parodied by Debussy in his *Children's Corner* piano suite.

TROIS
SONATES
Pour Clavecin ou pianoforte
— AVEC —
Accompagnement de Violon et Violoncel
— DÉDIÉES —
A MISS BLAKE
Par Muzio Clementi
(Œuvre 28)
Prix :
A PARIS

Antonio Salieri

● 1750–1825   🏳 Italian   ✍ c.350

When the Viennese court composer F L Gassmann saw Salieri's talent in Venice, he took him to Vienna to complete his training. Once there Salieri blossomed, proved adept at making the right friends (such as Emperor Joseph II), and was a major contributor to Viennese musical life from 1770 to 1820. Many of his operas – rich, theatrical, and combining German power and Italian sweetness – enjoyed great success in Italy (the comedies), Paris (the tragedies), and across Europe. His later operas had a lukewarm reception and he devoted himself to teaching. Salieri's relationship with Mozart – contrary to myths created by Pushkin's play *Mozart and Salieri* (1831) and Peter Schaffer's film *Amadeus* (1984) – was no more than respectful rivalry.

MILESTONES

1779	Writes *La scuola de'gelosi*, comic opera
1781	*Der Rauchfangkehrer*, opera, published
1784	Composes *Les Danaïdes*, opera
1788	Writes *Axur re d'Ormus*, opera, with Lorenzo da Ponte
1788	Hofkapellmeister to Joseph II
c.1804	Concentrates on writing sacred music

Salieri wrote his opera *Europa riconosciuta* (*Europa Revealed*) for the grand opening of Theatre Alla Scala, Milan, in 1778. It includes several arias of great brilliance.

Luigi Cherubini

● 1760–1842   🏳 Italian   ✍ 300

After a modest early career in Italy and London, Cherubini moved to Paris, becoming a dominant figure in the music world as a conductor, publisher, composer, and teacher. His music – especially in his successful Revolution-era operas – could be self-expressive, dramatic, and dark. He adroitly rode changing circumstances, both stylistic (mixing comic and serious styles) and political (he wrote a piece celebrating Louis XVI's execution, then one praising his memory). After 1816 he wrote almost exclusively religious music.

Beethoven called Cherubini the greatest living composer, but his reputation faded after his death, possibly due to lack of a clear national identity.

MILESTONES

1780	Produces his first opera, *Quinto Fabio*
1786	Arrives in Paris
1791	Composes *Lodoïska*, opera, and achieves first international success
1797	*Medée*, opera, published
1815	Superintendent of French royal chapel
1822	Director of Paris Conservatoire
1836	Writes Requiem in D minor

Jean Auguste Dominique Ingres admired the music of Cherubini and, in recognition of his many talents, painted *Luigi Cherubini and the Lyric Muse* in 1842.

Jan Ladislav Dussek

● 1760–1812 ⚑ Czech ♫ c.280

Something of an early Romantic, Dussek was feted from London to St Petersburg as a touring piano virtuoso and composer. His accomplished concertos and sonatas sold very well, and in many ways are more harmonically adventurous than Mozart's, or even Beethoven's. However, they have been surprisingly neglected since his death. A piano innovator, he first placed the instrument sideways to improve the audience's view, and worked with a manufacturer to extend the keyboard. He flourished during a decade spent in London, but fled the city after a business failure. He then went on to lead a wild and reckless life, following the Prince of Prussia into battle, inspiring the piano work *Harmonic Elegy on the Death of Prince Louis Ferdinand of Prussia*.

MILESTONES	
1786	Moves to Paris; meets Marie Antoinette and Napoleon
1789	First known performance in London
1797	Piano works increase in complexity
1789	Flees London for Hamburg
1806	Writes *Elégie Harmonique sur la mort du Prince Louis Ferdinand de Prusse*, sonata

Dussek's villa near Prague was an important centre of musical activity, and visiting musicians, including Mozart, were always welcome.

Samuel Wesley

● 1766–1837 ⚑ English ♫ c.430

Wesley was a child prodigy who became something of a maverick celebrity in London music circles: he never held court appointments or official posts, but made a haphazard living as a teacher and writer, and as an organist known for his extraordinary improvisations. Most of his output is Latin church music, combining old and new styles. Attacks of depression, as well as a costly divorce, hindered his career.

MILESTONES	
1774	Composes *Ruth*, oratorio, aged eight
1799	Writes *The Death of Abel*, oratorio
1802	Symphony in B published
1813	Becomes regular organ soloist at Covent Garden, London
1817	Institutionalized after jumping out of a window

Franz Xaver Süssmayr

● 1766–1803 ⚑ Austrian ♫ 160

Known today as the composer who completed Mozart's Requiem, Franz Süssmayr – whose limitations are highlighted clearly next to Mozart's – was nevertheless a craftsmanlike composer who enjoyed considerable stage success in Vienna. Songs from his popular *Magic Flute*-like *Der Spiegel von Arkadien* were sung in cafés and taverns, and circulated in pirate copies. He held various institutional posts and wrote in many national styles – French and Italian comic idioms, Italian opera seria, and popular German forms – and his melodic gifts were at their best in his solos, duets, and trios. He was Kapellmeister of Vienna's National Theatre from 1794 until his death.

MILESTONES	
1791	Copyist and pupil of Mozart
1799	*Solimann II*, singspiel, published
1802	Writes *Il noce di Benevento*, ballet

"We cannot despair about mankind knowing that Mozart was a man."

ALBERT EINSTEIN

Wolfgang Amadeus Mozart

◐ 1756–1791   🏴 Austrian   ✍ 655

Probably the most prodigious musician ever born, Mozart's early tours around Europe not only made him famous, but familiarized him with many musical styles that he synthesized in his own cosmopolitan works. Unique in musical history for his accomplishment in all forms and genres and possessed of an astonishing compositional fluency, he was the first important composer to attempt to establish a "freelance" musical career.

LIFE

The son of a gifted musician, Mozart's first musical experiences were hearing his child-prodigy sister, Nannerl, at her lessons. His own gifts soon surpassed hers and, proud of their accomplishments, their father gave up his career to promote their talents before the astounded royalty and cognoscenti of Europe. Despite extensive tours, Mozart composed and studied continually, but, by 1772, no longer a child-prodigy, he had to settle for the realities of a court appointment, where his social status was between the valets and the cooks. Never happy at the small court of Salzburg and convinced of his own musical superiority, Mozart attempted to obtain other positions, but, failing so to do, left to become one of music's first "freelance" professionals. Arriving in Vienna in 1781, he married Constanze Weber and started to give concerts, publish music, and receive commissions, particularly for operas. Over the next ten years he wrote over 200 works and consolidated his reputation, but had to give piano lessons, take in boarders, and borrow money to maintain the lifestyle he desired. His death was probably from rheumatic fever. He was buried in a mass grave according to Viennese custom, without mourners, whilst obituary notices unanimously hailed his greatness.

Although his greatest love was opera, Mozart was the most brilliant pianist of his age. He took the piano concerto to new heights of richness and virtuosity.

MUSICAL OUTPUT

Total: 655

	1756	1765	1770	1775	1780	1785	1791
SYMPHONIES (59)			16	30	4	5	4
OTHER ORCHESTRAL (78)			7	9	28	20	14
CHAMBER (176)			15	40	33	29	59
OTHER INSTRUMENTAL (119)		22	14	6	17	35	25
OPERAS (23)			3	4	5	2	9
CHORAL (95)			13	19	17	16	30
SONGS (105)			9	4	16	22	54

MUSIC

The range of Mozart's musical output is extraordinary, and it has well been said that no other composer has been equally accomplished in so many different media, but it is his operas that hold the key to his essential style. Building on the operatic reforms of Gluck, Mozart combined vivid vocal characterization and supreme melodic gifts with an emphasis on orchestral expressivity and colour to achieve a far more dramatic

Leopold Mozart took his children on tour at early ages; in 1762, they played for the Bavarian elector in Munich and the imperial family in Vienna.

conception than had previously been encountered. The resulting depictions of character, psychology and human interaction evince a subtle complexity which blurred the lines between opera seria and opera buffa, particularly in the three operas written with Italian poet, Lorenzo Da Ponte, as librettist: *The Marriage of Figaro*, *Don Giovanni* and *Così fan tutte*. Mozart also wrote several operas in German, of which *The Magic Flute* has been the most enduringly popular. It combines joyous tunes with noble choruses and

includes the tour-de-force coloratura aria of the Queen of the Night.

Mozart also wrote a substantial amount of solo vocal and choral music, ranging from the short motet *Ave Verum Corpus*, a piece of utterly serene beauty, to the dazzlingly spirited *Exsultate, jubilate* for soprano and orchestra. Of his large-scale choral works, the *Missa solemnis* and the Requiem (both unfinished) show him in serious, darker mood, interleaved with sections of exultation or grandeur. Mozart's symphonies, concertos, and chamber works show a particular attention to instrumental colour. His peers were frequently amazed by the way he matched experimental combinations of instruments, such as those in the Quintet for Piano and Winds (oboe, clarinet, bassoon, and horn) and the *Kegelstatt Trio* (clarinet, viola, piano) with subtleties of orchestration,

Mozart wrote *Die Entführung aus dem Serail* in German for Leopold II's Imperial Court Burgtheater (below) in Vienna.

particularly in the use of wind instruments, the latter helping to establish the clarinet as a regular in the orchestra. His refinement of the concerto, especially the piano concerto, brought the genre to a new level of sophistication, establishing it as no less important than the symphony, which had far-reaching effects in the 19th century. In 1782, he began a period of concentrated piano concerto writing. The 15 (Nos. 11–25) he produced by the end of 1786 became ever more symphonically rich and pianistically virtuosic. Mozart had written most of his symphonies in his youth, but his last, the "Jupiter", was the summation of his symphonic development, ending with undiluted orchestral brilliance.

Composed in already well-established forms, Mozart's music is seldom regarded as revolutionary, but contemporaneous audiences certainly found some of his work difficult to appreciate, particularly in its startling contrasts, complexity, and sometimes dissonant harmony. Having assimilated the major European musical styles as a boy, his mature work allied a fusion of Italian lyricism, French brilliance and Middle-European compositional processes with a very natural sense of symmetry, which has come to be regarded as the epitome of Classical refinement.

Mozart fell in love with Constanze Weber in 1781 and married her in 1782. Of their six children, only two survived.

MILESTONES

1761	Composes Andante, K1a, Allegro, K1b
1764	Composes Symphony No. 1, K16
1767	Travels to Vienna and catches smallpox
1768	Opera *Bastien and Bastienne* is staged
1772	Appointed Konzertmeister at Salzburg
1773	Fails to gain post in Vienna; composes many string quartets, symphonies, and motet *Exsultate, Jubilate*
1778	"Paris" Symphony performed in Paris; his mother dies there; writes Concerto for Flute and Harp, Piano Sonata, K 310
1779	Becomes court organist; composes *Coronation Mass*, *Sinfonia Concertante*
1780	Receives commission from Munich for *Idomeneo*, opera; rehearses it there
1781	*Idomeneo* is a success; leaves his post to become freelance musician in Vienna
1782	Marries Constanze Weber; opera *Die Entführung aus dem Serail* is acclaimed
1784	Gives series of public concerts for which composes Piano Concertos Nos. 14–19
1785	Composes Piano Concerto No. 21
1786	Opera *The Marriage of Figaro*, produced; composes Piano Concertos Nos. 23–25, *Kegelstatt Trio*, "Prague" Symphony
1787	Visits Prague twice: "Prague" Symphony, opera *Don Giovanni* premiered there, *Figaro* is success; composes *Eine kleine Nachtmusik*

1788	Severe money problems: starts borrowing; composes his three greatest symphonies (Nos. 39, 40, 41), three piano trios, and "Coronation" Piano Concerto
1789	Travels to Dresden, Leipzig, Potsdam, and Berlin trying to obtain post or commissions; composes Clarinet Quintet
1790	Opera *Così fan tutte* premiered in Vienna; gives concerts in Germany
1791	Hears opera *La Clemenza di Tito* in Prague; opera *The Magic Flute* is success in Vienna; Clarinet Concerto; begins Requiem, which is left incomplete at his death

Mozart became a Freemason in Vienna (above) in 1784. The influence of their ideology is strongly felt in his sensationally successful comic opera *The Magic Flute*.

KEY WORKS

PIANO SONATA NO. 8, K310

| PIANO SOLO | 🕐 16:30 | 📖 3 | 🎵 |

Mozart wrote this sonata in Paris at the time of his mother's death. It is amongst the finest piano works of the early Classical period. One of only three minor key sonatas in his output, its drama is immediate in the orchestral textures of its opening. A restrained slow movement lulls the listener before the dark pathos of the finale.

SYMPHONY NO. 38, "PRAGUE", K504

| ORCHESTRAL | 🕐 30:00 | 📖 3 | 🎶 |

Following the success of *The Marriage of Figaro* in Prague, Mozart introduced this symphony there in 1787. Unusually formed of only three movements, it opens in a dark, majestic mood, which is immediately dispelled by the arrival of the faster main body of the music. An expressive slow movement balances the lively finale, in which, to the delight of the first audience, Mozart used a theme he borrowed from *The Marriage of Figaro*.

STRING QUARTET NO. 19, "DISSONANT", K465

| CHAMBER | 🕐 30:30 | 📖 4 | 🎵 |

This is one of six quartets that Mozart dedicated in 1785 to Haydn, whose recent Op. 33 quartets had brought the

Written in Italian, *The Marriage of Figaro* contains music of great beauty. The Countess's poignant aria, *Porgi amor* (Grant me love), is one of Mozart's greatest.

The Magic Flute is the beguiling story of the victory of love over adversity and light over darkness, set against the machinations of the Queen of the Night.

form to a new level of sophistication. Mozart's equally finely-wrought response seems effortless in its mastery of Haydn's innovations, but according to the composer was "the fruit of long and laborious endeavour". This, the last of the set, is named after its surprisingly dissonant introduction, which gives way to work of a graceful charm.

CLARINET CONCERTO, K622

| ORCHESTRAL | 🕐 28:00 | 📖 3 | 🎶 🎵 |

Mozart first met Anton Stadler in 1783 and, immediately taken by his virtuosity on the newly invented clarinet, they formed a friendship which inspired the Kegelstatt Trio, the Clarinet Quintet, and this lyrical concerto. Mozart capitalized on the clarinet's mellifluous tone quality, especially in the operatically inspired slow movement. Conducting the Viennese premiere was Mozart's final public appearance.

DON GIOVANNI, K527

OPERA ♟ 174:00 ▭ 5 ⚔ 🎭 ♂

Asked to write an opera for Prague after the success of *The Marriage of Figaro*, Mozart decided on the story of Don Juan. Notable for the vivid musical depiction of characters and emotions, and just as serious in emotion as it is comic in plot, it is still considered to be among the greatest operas ever composed.

OVERTURE AND ACT ONE (92:00) After the dramatic, brooding overture, Don Giovanni appears, masked and pursued by Donna Anna, whom he has been seducing. Her father, the Commendatore, insists on a duel, but is killed. She aks her betrothed, Don Ottavio, to swear vengeance. Don Giovanni now tries to seduce another woman, but has to escape when he recognizes her as Donna Elvira, a former mistress. Alone, Leperello lists Don Giovanni's "catalogue" of conquests. At wedding preparations in a village, Don Giovanni woos Zerlina, the bride, with the aria "Là ci darem mano". Elvira, Anna and Ottavio arrive, thus thwarting this and other seduction plans.

ACT TWO (82:00) Exchanging clothes with Leperello, Don Giovanni tries to seduce Elvira's maid while Leperello entices Elvira away. Zerlina's fiancé, Masetto, and some peasants appear, all after Don Giovanni's blood. They, together with the other protagonists, capture Leperello, who has to reveal his identity. Later, Don Giovanni finds him alone in a cemetery. The funerary statue of the Commendatore suddenly starts speaking and the Don flippantly invites it to supper. Meanwhile, Anna sings one of Mozart's most celebrated arias, "Non mi dir, bell'idol mio", to Octavio. Finally, at supper, Elvira begs Giovanni to mend his ways, but he refuses. The statue appears and drags him down to hell, leaving the others to ponder the moral of the tale.

PIANO CONCERTO NO. 21, K467

ORCHESTRAL ♟ 28:30 ▭ 3 ⚔ 🎵

This is one of Mozart's six 1785–86 concertos probably performed at his subscription concerts in Vienna. With some of the most complex piano writing of the time, even Mozart's father commented that "the new concerto is astonishingly difficult".

FIRST MOVEMENT (ALLEGRO MAESTOSO, 13:00) The martial quality inspired by the trumpets and drums at the opening is dispelled by the piano, which leads a rather independent life, even initiating its own musical material.

SECOND MOVEMENT (ANDANTE, 6:00) Silencing the brass and percussion, Mozart mutes the strings to give this songful movement its intimate colour.

THIRD MOVEMENT (ALLEGRO VIVACE ASSAI, 6:00) Ending in high spirits, this movement exudes a rustic charm, while requiring extreme virtuosity from the soloist.

INFLUENCES

While always noted for its formal beauty and elegance, Mozart's music was usually dismissed in the century after his death as an historically interesting precursor to Beethoven. Only more recently, as an antidote to Romanticism and Modernity, has he become a byword for musical perfection.

EINE KLEINE NACHTMUSIK, K525

ORCHESTRAL   🕭 16:30   📖 4   🎵

One of several divertimenti and serenades written for social occasions, *A Little Night Music* is scored only for strings and may even have been intended as a quintet. Originally in five movements, a second minuet was later removed from the manuscript.

FIRST MOVEMENT (ALLEGRO 5:45) With its two sharply contrasting themes, the opening of Mozart's most famous work is actually an extremely compact sonata principle movement.

SECOND MOVEMENT (ROMANZE 5:45) This effortlessly poised movement is given a mysterious quality by its darker middle section.

THIRD MOVEMENT (MENUETTO 2:00) The infectious rhythmic lilt of the minuet is here offset by the charmingly elegant Trio that follows it.

FOURTH MOVEMENT (RONDO 3:00) Heard five times in this brief movement, the joyfully appealing principal theme never outstays its welcome.

REQUIEM, K626

MASS SETTING   🕭 54:30   📖 8   🎵

The "grey messenger" who commissioned Mozart's final work was actually an emissary for Count Walsegg-Stuppach, who wished to perform the Requiem in memory of his wife and required anonymity because he wished to pass the work off as his own. Mozart started it in good spirits, but his health began to fail and he

SYMPHONY NO. 41, "JUPITER", K551

ORCHESTRAL   🕭 36:50   📖 4   🎵

Mozart wrote his last three symphonies without a commission, or any prospect of performance, in the summer of 1788. This, his last, probably received its nickname when Haydn showed it to his British impresario, Salomon, in 1791, and it was subsequently published with the title. As a tribute to Mozart after his death, Haydn quoted the theme from the slow movement in his Symphony No. 98.

FIRST MOVEMENT (ALLEGRO VIVACE 12:25) After a brief opening, there is a pause before Mozart starts again, adding far more subtle touches and varied moods.

SECOND MOVEMENT (ANDANTE CANTABILE 9:35) The peaceful string theme is interrupted by loud chords and

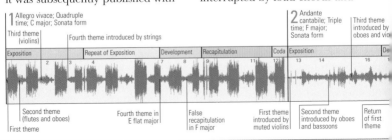

became obsessed with the idea that he was writing it for his own death. Death did indeed strike when the work was far from complete. His widow, needing the outstanding half of the fee to support their family, asked Mozart's assistant, Franz Xaver Süssmayr, to complete it.

INTROITUS (5:20) The only section which Mozart had fully scored dispenses with horns, flutes, and oboes in order to give the much darker orchestral sonorities which characterize the work's solemnity.

KYRIE (3:00) Reminiscent of Bach and Handel's religious music, the Kyrie is an inexorable fugue culminating in a unison chorus.

SEQUENZ (20:10) Divided into six sections, the music explores the terror of divine judgement in the gripping "Dies Irae", reassures as the solo trombone weaves gracefully around the "Tuba Mirum", and ends in the moving sadness of the "Lacrimosa".

OFFERTORIUM (8:50) The restless "Domine Jesu

When he died, Mozart had the score of the Requiem on his bed and had been explaining his ideas on how to finish it to Süssmayr.

Christe" is balanced by the otherworldly prayer of the "Hostias".

SANCTUS (1:50) This is a majestic setting, ending with a short fugue on "Hosanna". Here and in the next two movements, Süssmayr had no sketches by Mozart from which to work.

BENEDICTUS (5:20) Reminiscent of operatic quartets, the soloists join in this hymn of praise, which concludes with a fugue for full chorus.

AGNUS DEI (3:40) Using music from the Introitus, Süssmayr's reworking of it results in a most effective setting.

COMMUNIO (6:10) Once again using material from the opening, the music from the Kyrie brings the "Lux Aeterna" to its measured conclusion.

surprising harmonic changes, but, in spite of this, melody prevails throughout the movement.

THIRD MOVEMENT
(MENUETTO–ALLEGRETTO 5:50)
The rather courtly, serious Minuet contrasts with a quirky Trio which, from its very beginning, continually threatens to come to an end.

The "Jupiter" is now recognized as one of Mozart's greatest symphonies, but it was never played during his lifetime.

FOURTH MOVEMENT (FINALE 9:00)
In one of the most extraordinary symphonic movements ever written, Mozart presents and combines five different themes. In the brilliant, electrifying coda all five are reintroduced and heard together.

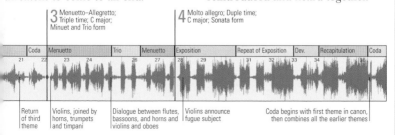

3 Menuetto–Allegretto; Triple time; C major; Minuet and Trio form

4 Molto allegro; Duple time; C major; Sonata form

Coda	Menuetto		Trio	Menuetto	Exposition		Repeat of Exposition	Dev.	Recapitulation		Coda
21	22	23	24	26	27	28	29	31	32	33	34	35

| Return of third theme | Violins, joined by horns, trumpets and timpani | Dialogue between flutes, bassoons, and horns and violins and oboes | Violins announce fugue subject | Coda begins with first theme in canon, then combines all the earlier themes |

"*Keep your eye on him; one day
he will make the world talk of him.*"

MOZART, ON HEARING THE 17-YEAR OLD BEETHOVEN

Ludwig van Beethoven

○ 1770–1827 ▯ German ✍ 398

The supreme iconic figure of Western music, Beethoven established the popular concept of the artist, who, separate from society, transcends personal tragedy to achieve his goal and becomes a hero. Calling himself a "Tondichter", or "poet in sound", his music mirrored his beliefs in the prevailing spirit of individualism by emphasizing personal expression over traditional form, and thus paved the way for musical Romanticism.

LIFE

Showing early musical talent, Beethoven was given a thorough music grounding by the Bonn court organist, Christian Gottlob Neefe, and was soon acting as his deputy. Aged 17, he left for Vienna to further his studies, but returned within weeks when he discovered his mother was dying. Impressed by his music, Haydn then invited him to study in Vienna. There, Beethoven was soon invited into aristocratic circles, where the beauty and virtuosity of his playing, and his compositional prowess won him many patrons who subsequently became dedicatees of his works. However, by 1802 he realized that his growing deafness would become total and, while staying in the village of Heiligenstadt, wrote a letter detailing his desperate unhappiness. Overcoming the crisis, he returned, determined to "seize Fate by the throat", and launched himself into an unprecedented period of creativity which bore many of his most famous works. By 1812, his deafness had engendered further depression and isolation and a lapse in creativity, but his final years, in a spirit of resignation, brought forth his most spiritual and exalted music. Suggestions that he died with a fist raised, though appropriate, are possibly apocryphal, but his death was mourned by the whole of Vienna.

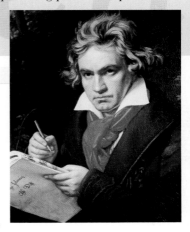

Beethoven's invariably intense music visits all points on the emotional scale, from the bleakest melancholy to the most joyful celebration.

MUSICAL OUTPUT

Total: 398

	1770	1780	1790	1800	1810	1820	1827
SYMPHONIES (9)					6	2	1
OTHER ORCHESTRAL (31)		2	8	12	7	2	
CHAMBER (92)		4	43	24	13	8	
OTHER INSTRUMENTAL (101)		7	46	30	7	11	
OPERAS (1)					1		
CHORAL (77)			9	9	26	33	
SONGS (87)		2	35	27	20	3	

MUSIC

Beethoven's compositional battles were hard fought, with certain works spending many years in laboured gestation. Once fully formed, however, the majority of them were instantly successful. The growing middle-class enjoyed their immediacy, power, and dramatic virtuosity, while the cultural elite was equally impressed by the thorough absorption and subsequent transcending of 18th-century musical styles.

Although Beethoven's output is usually divided into three periods, a fourth, before his arrival in Vienna, should also be considered, as by then he had already composed a number of vocal and chamber works, and a very accomplished set of variations for piano. These early works are all catalogued with "WoO" numbers (*Werke ohne Opus* – works without opus). His early reputation and fame rested on his phenomenal gifts of improvisation at the keyboard – some said even greater than Mozart's – and it is therefore natural that most of his early compositions are for piano.

Beethoven's usually-designated "early" period began after his arrival in Vienna in 1792 at the age of 22. Here he assimilated – and then began to transform – the sonata principle from a balanced, arch-like structure to a more dynamic, urgent form, where the recapitulation (the third section after the exposition and the development sections)

Beethoven preferred the new English piano – his own is shown here – as its heavier build suited his energetic playing better than the lighter Viennese ones.

was a culmination rather than a repetition. At first tending towards exploration and elaboration of the initial musical ideas – and preferring four movements to the customary three – Beethoven's solo piano works were highly successful. But, as his accomplishment grew, his compositions – including the Op. 18 string quartets, three piano concertos, two symphonies and the *Pathétique* and "Moonlight" piano sonatas – became more expressive and concentrated. The *Pathétique* sonata, with its French name meaning "passionate" or "emotional" (given to it by Beethoven himself) is regarded as his first masterpiece.

Beethoven's "middle" period dates from 1803 – the year after he realized the seriousness of his growing deafness and rejected suicide in favour of giving the world, he said, "all the music I felt was within me".

In 1808, Beethoven was granted an annuity for life by his pupil and friend, the Habsburg Archduke Rudolf of Austria.

His decision was of unimaginable significance. From this time, his music took on a new, "heroic" style whose dimensions, range, and power were a watershed in music history. Its first manifestation was the epic "Eroica" Symphony, a work of colossal energy and, at 50 minutes, the longest that had thus far been written, revealing new developments of the symphonic form. Beethoven's new "symphonic ideal" was applied to all genres and resulted in a torrent of productivity. From this period come four more symphonies, the Violin Concerto, Piano Concertos Nos. 4 and 5, and an opera, *Fidelio*. However, his increasing isolation through deafness marked the change into the "late" period. By 1813 Beethoven was exploring more intimate modes of expression, often emphasizing the lyrical and veiled. With an increasing fondness for variation and fugue (such as the *Diabelli Variations*), and further experimentation with sonata forms – which resulted in three, final piano sonatas of great intellectual and expressive depth – his music left the Classical world of Haydn and Mozart behind and entered the Romantic era. His *Missa solemnis* and Symphony No. 9 were also innovative, combining symphonic and choral writing "from the heart" as never before.

Beethoven tried many cures for deafness. This is one of the hearing aids he used late in his life.

MILESTONES

1778	First public performance in Cologne
1781	Takes lessons in organ and violin
1783	Composes Three Sonatas WoO. 47
1787	Studies briefly in Vienna with Mozart
1792	Goes to Vienna to study with Haydn
1795	First public concert in Vienna: performs Piano Concerto in B Flat, Op. 19 (his first)
1799	Publishes *Pathétique* Piano Sonata
1800	Symphony No. 1 and Septet performed in Vienna; composes Piano Concerto No. 3
1801	Ballet *Prometheus* is successfully staged; publishes "Moonlight" Piano Sonata
1802	Depressed by failing hearing, writes *Heiligenstadt Testament*; composes Symphony No. 2 and *Kreutzer* Violin Sonata
1804	Completes "Eroica" Symphony; composes "Waldstein" Piano Sonata

1805	Opera *Fidelio* premiered, but withdrawn after three performances owing to Austrian occupation of Vienna
1805	Composes "Appassionata" Piano Sonata
1806	Completes Violin Concerto, Symphony No. 4, *Razoumovsky Quartets*
1808	Symphonies Nos. 5 and 6, Piano Concerto No. 4, and *Choral Fantasy* premiered together in four-hour concert
1809	Writes "Emperor" Piano Concerto
1811	"Archduke" Trio written
1812	Completes Symphonies Nos. 7 and 8
1814	Revised *Fidelio* produced successfully; his final appearance as pianist in "Archduke" Trio is disastrous owing to his deafness
1816	Granted custody of his nephew, Karl – leads to legal battle with sister-in-law; writes song cycle, *An Die Ferne Geliebte*

1818	Is sent Broadwood piano from London; "Hammerklavier" Piano Sonata completed
1822	Finishes Piano Sonata No. 32
1823	Completes Mass in D (*Missa solemnis*; "Choral" Symphony"; and *Diabelli Variations*
1826	Writes String Quartet Op. 130

In 1827, Beethoven fell ill with dropsy and pneumonia. He died in March and some 10,000 people attended his funeral.

KEY WORKS

SONATA NO. 9 FOR VIOLIN AND PIANO, "KREUTZER", OP. 47

DUO   35:00   3

Beethoven dedicated this piece to Rudolphe Kreutzer, a famous violinist living in Paris, perhaps because he was considering a visit there even though he had composed it for British violinist, George Bridgetower. Avoiding the piano-centred style of his previous works in the genre, here there is a real equality in the virtuosity of the two instruments; indeed, the score bore the subtitle "written in a molto concertante style, as though a concerto".

TRIO NO. 6 FOR PIANO, VIOLIN, AND CELLO, "ARCHDUKE", OP. 97

CHAMBER   39:00   4

Beethoven dedicated more than 20 works to Archduke Rudolph, but, as one of the finest piano trios ever written and with its grand manner, this richly deserves its aristocratic sobriquet. It was the work he chose for his last public appearance as a pianist in 1814.

SYMPHONY NO. 6 "PASTORAL", OP. 68

ORCHESTRAL   40:00   5

Although the five country scenes, including a vivid storm, were inspired by Beethoven's love of nature, he emphasized that this was "more the expression of feeling

Beethoven dedicated his "Eroica" Symphony to Napoleon in admiration of his ideals, but removed the name in disgust when Napoleon made himself emperor.

than tone-painting". It was first given in December 1808 at an epic concert which included the premieres of the Symphony No. 5, Piano Concerto No. 4 and *Choral Fantasy*.

PIANO CONCERTO NO. 5, "EMPEROR", OP. 73

ORCHESTRAL   40:00   3

At the time, the most "symphonic" and longest piano concerto ever written, Beethoven's final work in this genre was nicknamed the "Emperor" by the composer J B Cramer in response to its grandeur. Unusually starting with flourishes for piano, it also broke with tradition by dispensing with an improvised cadenza in favour of an already written one. Too deaf to perform it himself, Beethoven had it premiered by his pupil, Carl Czerny. It was instantly hailed as a masterpiece.

The Heiligenstadt Testament is the letter Beethoven wrote to his brothers (but never sent) in the village of Heiligenstadt where he contemplated suicide at his deafness in 1802.

VIOLIN CONCERTO, OP. 61

ORCHESTRAL ⏱ 44:45 📖 3

The score for this concerto was finished only two days before the first performance, and was virtually read at sight. Not an immediate success, Beethoven arranged it for piano, but the original became popular after the 13-year-old Joseph Joachim performed it in London with Mendelssohn in 1844.

FIRST MOVEMENT (ALLEGRO MA NON TROPPO, 25:45) Beethoven developed Mozart's concerto style on an unprecedented scale in this movement, unusually giving prominent roles to the timpani and woodwind.

SECOND MOVEMENT (LARGHETTO, 10:00) Beginning with an ethereal set of variations accompanied by muted strings, the movement ends with a brief cadenza which leads directly into the finale.

THIRD MOVEMENT (RONDO, ALLEGRO, 9:30) A cheerful and traditional ending, with only a brief moment of Beethovian pathos in the minor key, concludes this eloquent work.

SYMPHONY NO. 9, "CHORAL", OP. 125

ORCHESTRAL ⏱ 69:00 📖 4

Possibly the most iconic work of Western music the "Choral" still stands as a colossus against which all subsequent symphonies have been judged. Having first wanted to set Schiller's *Ode to Joy* in 1793, Beethoven was eventually commissioned to write the work in 1822 by the London Philharmonic Society. It was first performed in Vienna in 1823.

FIRST MOVEMENT (ALLEGRO MA NON TROPPO, UN POCO MAESTOSO, 16:00) Opening mysteriously, this settles into a dark and forceful sonata style. Among many surprises is

Beethoven used several verses of poet and dramatist Friedrich Schiller's 1785 *Ode to Joy (An die Freude)* in his "Choral" Symphony.

a fortissimo repeat of the opening bars in the major key at the recapitulation.

SECOND MOVEMENT (MOLTO VIVACE, 16:00) Beethoven creates a large-scale movement from very economic and energetic material. After experimenting with timpani as a feature in the Violin and "Emperor" concertos, here he gives them a major role.

THIRD MOVEMENT (ADAGIO MOLTO E CANTABILE, 14:00) This sublime adagio is actually two sets of variations on two alternating themes. Two startling interruptions for the new valved horn come near the end.

FOURTH MOVEMENT (PRESTO, ALLEGRO, 23:00) Fragments of earlier movements are heard before instruments, then voices, settle on Schiller's *Ode to Joy* celebrating the universal brotherhood of mankind in a hitherto unprecedented choral addition to a symphony.

INFLUENCES

The first composer to establish a freelance career from the outset, Beethoven's refusal to be subservient to aristocratic patrons marked the change in the role of the musician from servant to autonomous cultural arbiter, and thus created a model of aspiration followed by almost every subsequent Classical musician.

STRING QUARTET, OP. 130
CHAMBER   ⏱ 42:00   📖 6   ♫

This work was commissioned by the Russian prince, Nicholas Galitzin. The finale was originally what is now known as Beethoven's *Grosse Fuge*, Op. 133, but he replaced it with the shorter present Allegro after the premiere.

FIRST MOVEMENT (ADAGIO MA NON TROPPO, ALLEGRO, 14:00) In this sonata-form movement, Beethoven explores aspects of both the adagio introduction and the subsequent allegro, only uniting the disparate elements in the short development and coda sections.

SECOND MOVEMENT (PRESTO, 2:00) In this very brief scherzo the first violin takes the lead in the humorous trio section.

It also includes a number of very surprising chromatic scales.

THIRD MOVEMENT (ANDANTE CON MOTO MA NON TROPPO, POCO SCHERZOSO, 6:00) Not quite a slow movement, this sunny music is more in the spirit of a "divertimento".

FOURTH MOVEMENT (ALLA DANZA TEDESCA, ALLEGRO ASSAI, 3:00) Although lyrical, with its rhythmic lilt and regular pulse, the rustic German origins of this music are never far away.

FIFTH MOVEMENT (CAVATINA, ADAGIO MOLTO ESPESSIVO, 8:00) A cavatina is an operatic song in simple style. Certainly the first violin retains the simple, operatic-style melody throughout, but Beethoven's almost too-intimate expression of feeling is far removed from the world of the stage. Perhaps most extraordinary is the unsettling middle section, marked "beklemmt" ("oppressed") in the score.

SIXTH MOVEMENT (ALLEGRO, 9:00) Having replaced the *Grosse Fuge* ending, Beethoven did not live to see this, his shorter, but very stark and gripping alternative performed.

In his final years, Beethoven concentrated on the intimate medium of the string quartet, redefining its boundaries and creating his most sublime works.

PIANO SONATA IN F MINOR, "APPASSIONATA", OP. 57
PIANO SOLO   ⏱ 23:00   📖 3   ♫

In this sonata, composed in 1804–05. Beethoven brought piano virtuosity to a new level of complexity, powerfully fusing it with his new, heroic style. Although the subtitle was not his own (it was added by the publisher), Beethoven seems to have approved of it. This violent,

impassioned piece was one of his favourite works in the medium.

FIRST MOVEMENT (ALLEGRO ASSAI, 9:00) Almost using the keyboard as an orchestra, Beethoven elicited a new kind of musical drama in this movement with its sudden changes in volume, register, and pace.

SECOND MOVEMENT (ANDANTE CON MOTO, 6:20) Starting with a chordal theme, this calm movement develops into a series

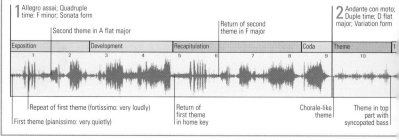

1 Allegro assai; Quadruple time: F minor; Sonata form

Second theme in A flat major

Return of second theme in F major

2 Andante con moto; Duple time; D flat major; Variation form

Exposition	Development	Recapitulation		Coda	Theme
1	2 3 4	5 6	7 8	9	10

First theme (pianissimo: very quietly)

Repeat of first theme (fortissimo: very loudly)

Return of first theme in home key

Chorale-like theme

Theme in top part with syncopated bass

over ten years and wrote three more overtures. The first three *Leonora* overtures are often performed alone. **OVERTURE AND ACT ONE** (78:00) Jaquino, a prison gatekeeper, wants to marry Marcellina, but she loves Fidelio, who works for the jailer, Rocco, her father. However, Fidelio is really Leonora – a woman in disguise looking for her husband, Florestan. The prison governor is indeed holding him illegally. His decision to murder Florestan to avoid ministerial criticism is overheard by Leonora, who decides to rescue her husband. **ACT TWO** (46:00) In his cell, Florestan muses on his fate. As Leonora and Rocco enter, he asks for food and she recognizes her husband. The governor then enters to kill Florestan, but she holds him off with a pistol. The minister's arrival ensures Florestan's freedom and the townspeople rejoice as the corrupt governor is arrested.

FIDELIO, OP. 72

OPERA　124:00　2

For his only opera, Beethoven set the story of an old French libretto, *Léonore, ou L'amour conjugal*, which reflected his belief in the triumph of free will, liberty, and human goodness. He revised *Fidelio*, as he renamed it, twice

of three variations, each higher and more decorative than the last. Its serenity provides a brief respite from the mood of tragic despair that dominates the rest of the work. It ends with a version of the opening interrupted by a mysterious arpeggio. **THIRD MOVEMENT** (ALLEGRO MA NON TROPPO, :40) Unusually, the third movement of the sonata flows directly from the second. The arpeggio gives way to a

The British pianist John Ogdon (1937–1989) gave many highly original and moving interpretations of Beethoven's piano music.

forceful outburst leading into a relentless finale, which the performer should keep reined in until the explosive coda and the abrupt and violent ending.

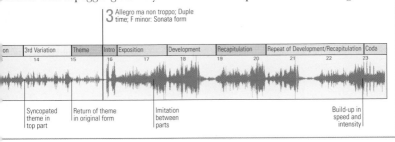

3 Allegro ma non troppo; Duple time; F minor: Sonata form

on	3rd Variation	Theme	Intro	Exposition	Development	Recapitulation	Repeat of Development/Recapitulation	Coda
	14	15	16	17	18	19　20	21　22	23

| | Syncopated theme in top part | Return of theme in original form | | Imitation between parts | | | Build-up in speed and intensity | |

Johann Nepomuk Hummel

🖝 1778–1837 🏳 Austrian ♫ c.450

A prodigy who, like Mozart, toured Europe as a boy, Hummel was idolized as a composer and fêted as Europe's greatest pianist. A warm person whose business acumen helped secure better copyright laws for composers and more financial security for his family, he wrote all types of music (except symphonies, deferring to Beethoven) in a polished late-Classical style. His best-selling folk songs for the Scottish publisher George Thomson show how well he wrote for the market.

MILESTONES	
1804	Becomes Konzertmeister at the court of Prince Nikolaus Esterházy
1810	*Mathilde von Guise*, opera, staged
1819	Kapellmeister at Weimar court
1828	Piano tutor sells out in days

Anton Reicha

🖝 1770–1836 🏳 Czech ♫ c.260

Though his operas never found success, Reicha's instrumental works, often exploring aspects of technique, were eventually published and widely performed. His good reputation as an author on music theory led to a professorship at the Paris Conservatoire, and it was as a teacher, rather than as a prolific composer, that he became best known. He befriended Haydn and Beethoven, and both Berlioz and Liszt admired his forward-looking ideas. Reicha's wind music was popular, and his colourful quintets proved models of the genre.

MILESTONES	
1794	Teaches music in Hamburg
1803	Composes 36 Fugues
1818	Professor at the Paris Conservatoire

John Field

🖝 1782–1837 🏳 Irish ♫ 70

By the age of 18, Field was an established piano virtuoso on the London concert scene. When he visited St Petersburg with his teacher, Muzio Clementi, he was so at home in the artistic and aristocratic milieu that he remained in Russia. There, he developed a distinctive style of piano playing (Chopinesque, but pre-Chopin), while also pioneering the nocturne, of which he wrote 16. Field's name spread across Europe, and as a teacher he was influential. By the 1830s, however, his music had fallen out of fashion. After an outrageous, Byronesque lifestyle of excess – quite unlike his serene music and delicate performing style – his health rapidly declined.

MILESTONES	
1792	First public performance in Dublin
1793	Field's family sets up home in London
1803	Visits St Petersburg, Russia
1811	Composes Piano Concertos, Nos. 1-3
1812	Writes Nocturnes, Nos. 1-3
1822	Settles in Moscow
1832	Visits London

The moonlit Thames, shrouded in mist, conveys the serene mood of Field's atmospheric nocturnes.

Louis Spohr

● 1784–1859   🏴 German   ✍ 208

One of the most celebrated musicians of his time, Spohr's instrumental compositions were favourably compared with those of Beethoven – and admired both by his peers – such as Mendelssohn, Schumann, and Chopin, and by the later Romantics Brahms and Tchaikovsky. A virtuoso violinist considered second only to Paganini, he also achieved great success as a teacher, his *Violin Tutor* being widely read.

LIFE AND MUSIC

From a musical family, Spohr started his career as a court chamber musician at Brunswick before touring throughout Germany as a virtuoso violinist. Appointed Konzertmeister at Gotha, he began to compose, and also became one of the first conductors to use a baton. After further touring with his harpist wife and public success with two operas, he finally settled in Kassel where, as Kapellmeister, he wrote more operas and symphonies for orchestra, presented works by Bach and Wagner, and taught violinists from all over Europe. Heavily influenced by Mozart, his music combines Classical forms with early Romantic modes of expression.

MILESTONES	
1799	Embarks on first concert tour to Hamburg; joins the Brunswick court
1805	Becomes Konzertmeister at Gotha
1806	Marries harpist Dorette Scheidler
1813	Directs Theatre an der Wien
1816	Writes Violin Concerto No. 8
1822	Appointed Kapellmeister at Kassel
1826	Composes Six Songs, Op. 72
1836	Marries pianist Marianne Pfeiffer
1840	Composes Symphony No. 6

Spohr, a consummate performer and natural showman, delighted his friends and family at his lively musical gatherings with his virtuoso technique and Romantic panache.

KEY WORKS

SYMPHONY NO. 6 IN G MAJOR, "HISTORIC", OP. 116

ORCHESTRAL   ⏱ 26:00   📖 4   🎶

Wishing to satirize grand opera, Spohr wrote each of the first three movements of this symphony as a pastiche of earlier musical styles and periods (1720, 1780, and 1810) whilst parodying the music of his contemporaries in the finale.

SIX SONGS, OP. 72

SONG CYCLE   ⏱ 14:00   📖 6   🎶♪

As a teacher, Spohr advocated a vocal approach to playing the violin, and he clearly loved writing songs, turning out more than 90. In the six songs here, Spohr sets a variety of Romantic poetry, and an "exotic" Persian love sonnet, with great passion and broad lyricism.

VIOLIN CONCERTO IN A MINOR, OP. 47

ORCHESTRAL   ⏱ 17:50   📖 1   🎶🎻

Of his 15 concertos and numerous solo works for the instrument, this is one of Spohr's few violin works still heard today. Written for performance in Italy, in the form of a vocal scene, its use of several operatic formulae in one instrumental movement made it an instant success.

The
ROMANTIC ERA
1810–1920

The Romantic movement emerged at the end of the 18th century in art and literature, and somewhat later in music. The Romantics rejected the confines of Classical convention; for them, originality was of paramount importance. They celebrated the emotional and the instinctive, and looked towards nature for inspiration.

B eethoven cast a long shadow over the 19th century. The emotional power of his music made him the chief precursor of what we now label Romanticism. His lifetime coincided with a watershed in history: the French Revolution of 1789 had been the most visible expression of the rights of the individual in the 18th century. Despite the oppressive regimes of the post-Napoleonic period, the Romantic cult of the individual flourished, along with an increasing awareness of the rights of nations to govern themselves and take pride in their own culture. In this climate of self-expression, women came nowhere near to winning equal rights, but a few were able to become composers and publish their works – Clara Schumann and Fanny Mendelssohn being the most celebrated examples.

Some music of the Romantic period was characterized by the virtuoso performer – for example, Liszt. A parallel trend was for intimate music intended for the salon – such as the shorter works, or "miniatures", of Chopin and Schumann. There lies a conflict here between the public character of many of the great Romantic solo and orchestral works and the solitude of such works as Schubert's song cycle *Winterreise*.

PAST AND FUTURE

The Romantic era was one of extremes, with composers not only looking back to the past but also abandoning classical conventions and experimenting with new and daring harmonic language and form. This progressive style is especially evident in Berlioz's *Symphonie fantastique*, with its extraordinary narrative of desire and destruction, or in Liszt's Sonata in B minor of 1852, with its snake-like one-movement form, or in the strange

SCHUBERT AT THE PIANO
The suffering so poignantly expressed in Schubert's greatest songs contrasts with the image of the cheerful evenings he apparently spent playing for his friends.

harmonies of the same composer's quasi-impressionistic late piano pieces, such as *Nuages gris*.

The Romantic period can claim to have "rediscovered" music from the past. When in 1840 Mendelssohn organised a performance of J S Bach's *St Matthew Passion*, he unlocked a great treasure trove of music which was revived in the next few decades. Not only did this alert musicians and audiences to the significance of Bach's own music, but it also encouraged musicians to perform music of the past and composers such as Brahms to use its materials and forms.

BERLIOZ CONDUCTING
The Romantics were often mocked for their style and excesses, in the case of Berlioz (pictured here in an 1846 cartoon) the vast orchestras required to perform his works.

themes, from the songs of Schubert to 20th-century works such as Richard Strauss's "Alpine" Symphony and Vaughan Williams' "Sea" Symphony.

With constant theorizing about the direction music should take, it is not surprising that the Romantic era was one of bitter disputes. One of the

CONNECTIONS

Whereas musicians of earlier periods had tended to concentrate on their craft alone, the Romantics blurred the lines between disciplines: Berlioz and Schumann both published criticism as well as music; Weber wrote a novel; Liszt wrote essays on a wide range of interests; and Wagner wrote his own libretti as well as the music for his operas. Romantic composers therefore frequently referred to ideas beyond music itself – for example, landscape and nature became important

THE SPIRIT OF ROMANTICISM
This painting of a solitary wanderer by Caspar David Friedrich (c.1818) embodies the mood evoked by many early Romantic composers.

TIMELINE: THE ROMANTIC ERA

◁ **1827**
Schubert composes great song cycle *Winterreise* in year before his death

1834
Schumann founds the review *Neue Zeitschrift für Musik*

1840 ▷
Marriage of Schumann to Clara Wieck

1853
Schumann champions music of the young Brahms

1830   **1840**   **1850**   **1860**

1824
Death of Byron at Missolonghi during Greek War of Independence

1832
Chopin gives first Paris concert

1839
Berlioz's dramatic symphony *Romeo and Juliet*

1840s ▷
Liszt tours the length and breadth of Europe to wild adulation

1848
Revolutions across Europe

most celebrated feuds was that between the followers of Brahms and those of Wagner. Brahms was seen by his partisans as a traditionalist, while Liszt and Wagner were believed by their supporters to represent the musical future. In fact, Brahms's musical language was at times highly adventurous, just as Wagner often looked to the past (most clearly in the music of *Die Meistersinger von Nürnberg*).

MUSIC IN THE HOME

If there is one instrument that symbolizes the Romantic period, it is the piano. Most Romantic composers composed not only concert music for the instrument but also music intended for amateur use. A measure of the political and social changes of the time was that far more homes now owned a piano. There was a consequent demand for music that could be played in the home, and many orchestral and operatic works were arranged for the piano.

A LIVING LEGACY

Music from the Romantic era has remained perennially popular with listeners. It continues to be enjoyed for its richness of melodic and harmonic invention, its poignancy and grandeur, as well as its extra-musical associations. Many late-20th-century composers have adopted certain characteristics of Romantic style – for example, in his score for the film *Star Wars*, the composer John Williams

LITERATURE AND ROMANTIC MUSIC

Literature substantially influenced music during the Romantic period, from Berlioz's use of Byron in *Harold in Italy* to Schubert's settings of the poets Heine and Goethe to Schumann's references to novels by Jean Paul and E T A Hoffman in his piano works. Hoffmann's strange stories also inspired Offenbach's *The Tales of Hoffmann* and Tchaikovsky's *Nutcracker Suite*, and he voiced the feelings of many Romantics when he asserted that "Music is the most Romantic of all the arts – in fact, it might be said to be the sole purely Romantic one."

HERO OF THE AGE
The English poet Byron inspired the Romantic movement across Europe.

used music in a Romantic symphonic style to represent the future. The American composer John Adams could likewise be called a neo-Romantic with regard to his great orchestral works, such as *Harmonielehre*. Romanticism survives in our time.

JOHANN STRAUSS THE YOUNGER
The lighter side of Romanticism was to be found in salons across Europe. Here Strauss provides the musical entertainment at an evening party in Vienna.

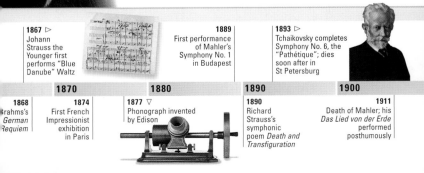

1867 ▷
Johann Strauss the Younger first performs "Blue Danube" Waltz

1889
First performance of Mahler's Symphony No. 1 in Budapest

1893 ▷
Tchaikovsky completes Symphony No. 6, the "Pathétique"; dies soon after in St Petersburg

1870 1880 1890 1900

1868
Brahms's *German Requiem*

1874
First French Impressionist exhibition in Paris

1877 ▽
Phonograph invented by Edison

1890
Richard Strauss's symphonic poem *Death and Transfiguration*

1911
Death of Mahler; his *Das Lied von der Erde* performed posthumously

Nicolò Paganini

◔ 1782–1840   ◗ Italian   ✎ c.250

Paganini's total mastery of the violin, demonic charisma, and personal mystique created the benchmark for the Romantic virtuoso. Most of his well-crafted and imaginative music, including a large body of chamber works, is now seldom heard. However he influenced a generation of composers – including Liszt, Chopin, and Schumann – to use instrumental virtuosity as an essential expressive element in their music.

LIFE AND MUSIC

Paganini's talent was rigorously nurtured by his father who forced him to practise obsessively, depriving him of food and water when he faltered. Thus acquiring an extraordinary facility, it was surprisingly not until 1809, after a long period as a court musician, that he became a travelling virtuoso. Even after a triumphant debut in Milan, he continued to tour Italy sporadically, only launching his career as an international artist at the age of 46 – mesmerizing audiences across Europe, and amassing great wealth. His spectacular music showcased an undreamed of virtuosity, giving rise to rumours that his playing relied on diabolical intervention.

MILESTONES	
1794	Gives first public performance
1795	Goes to Parma to study violin and composition
1796	Returns to Genoa to practise
1801	Leads an orchestra in Lucca
1805	Believed to have completed 24 Caprices
1809	Leaves Lucca to become a "free artist"
1813	Debut at La Scala, including *Le Streghe*; gives 11 more concerts in Milan
1817	Composes Violin Concerto No.1
1820	Six Sonatas for Violin and Guitar, Op. 3
1828	Gives 14 concerts in Vienna
1829	Tours throughout Germany
1831	Numerous concerts in Paris and UK
1833	Commissions *Harold in Italy* from Berlioz
1834	Settles in Parma, health deteriorates

KEY WORKS

VIOLIN CONCERTO NO.1

ORCHESTRAL   ⏲ 36:00   ▭ 3   ♫ ☉

Believed to have been written in 1817, this extremely popular work was premièred in 1819, and was always a show-stopper for Paganini. Opening with a theatrically expectant orchestral introduction, rather reminiscent of the Italian operas of Rossini, the violin entry is virtuosic, but ultimately vocally inspired, and frequently lyrical. The tragic and operatic slow movement reminds us that Paganini was equally renowned for his ability to move as to dazzle, which he does with high chords, brilliant runs, and "ricochet bowing" in the finale.

SIX SONATAS FOR VIOLIN AND GUITAR, OP. 3

CHAMBER   ▭ 6   ♟

Paganini's substantial output of chamber music frequently includes the guitar – upon which he was an accomplished performer – although in these six sonatas the guitar part is relatively simple, tending to accompany the more extrovert violin. Each work opens with a tender or passionate slow section before embarking on a spirited conclusion, often including a set of variations. Paganini dedicated these romantic sonatas to his first love, Eleanora Quilici.

FOCUS

24 CAPRICES
SOLO VIOLIN   24

Although Paganini had probably composed his caprices by 1805, he guarded their secrets closely, only publishing them in 1820, when he provocatively dedicated them "to the artists", knowing that few, if any, of his contemporaries would be able to play them. Each is a mini-masterpiece, exploring a different aspect of violin technique, and together they provide an almost complete compendium of the instrument's possibilities. Requiring a hand that is both large and flexible to encompass their technical difficulties, few performers have played them complete, but their influence goes well beyond the violin; Liszt and Schumann were inspired to write piano transcriptions of some of them, and the theme of the final caprice has been used for famous works by composers as diverse as Brahms, Rachmaninov, Lutoslawski, and Andrew Lloyd Webber.

Paganini amazed audiences in London with his extraordinary violin techniques and his showman's ability to astonish.

LE STREGHE
ORCHESTRAL   9:30   1

After four years as a travelling virtuoso, Paganini finally felt prepared to make his debut at La Scala in Milan. At the ballet, he heard the melody of Süssmayer's *Le streghe* (The Witches) and decided to capitalize on its immense popularity by writing a set of variations. After a majestic orchestral introduction, the violin enters, teasing the audience with a simple, gracious melody which is not the expected theme. Only after a repeat of this section does the actual witches' tune begin, but again performed quite unassumingly, raising expectation even further before the first variation where the fireworks finally begin. The listener is then subjected to a rollercoaster ride demonstrating Paganini's astounding techniques. Audiences were incredulous on hearing the work and rumours soon spread that its composer was in league with the devil.

Carl Czerny

● 1791–1857　　♩ German　　♫ c.1,800

A pupil of Beethoven and teacher of Liszt, Czerny is known to modern pianists for his technical exercises; though he wrote hundreds of works in all genres, few are played today. He was renowned as a performer of Beethoven's piano works (and knew them all by heart), but, put off by the prospect of long concert tours and unwilling to play to the gallery, he didn't pursue a career

MILESTONES	
1800	First public performance in Vienna
1801	Taught piano by Beethoven
1805	Cancels concert tour
1821	Teaches the young Liszt
1836	Retires from teaching
1839	Writes *Complete Theoretical and Practical Pianoforte School*, piano exercises

as a virtuoso. He concentrated instead on teaching – which he did for 12 hours a day for more than 20 years – and composing, with great financial success.

Thanks to Czerny, modern scholars know a great deal about performance practice of the early 19th century.

An only child who never married, Czerny devoted most of his time to teaching. His book of piano lessons is still in widespread use today.

Saverio Mercadante

● 1795–1870　　♩ Italian　　♫ c.350

Mercadante, born an illegitimate child, rose from poverty to be an opera composer of international fame by the 1830s, with successes in Italy, Spain, and Vienna. As director of the Naples Conservatory from 1840 he promoted the Neapolitan school of composition, and later turned towards writing instrumental music. He learned from other's successes (Meyerbeer's in Paris, for example) and his own mistakes, and rode turbulent changes in musical styles and international politics to enjoy great popularity and eventually financial comfort in his lifetime, only to slip into obscurity after his death.

MILESTONES	
1813	Composes Flute Concerto No. 2
1833	Becomes maestro di cappella at Novara Cathedral
1837	*Il giuramento*, opera, performed
1862	Becomes totally blind

Franz Adolf Berwald

● 1796–1868　　♩ Swedish　　♫ 80

The startling originality and modern-sounding harmonies of Berwald's music met with little enthusiasm in his lifetime; he had more success running a pioneering orthopaedic institute. Marriage, and small triumphs in Vienna, inspired him again, but back in Sweden he ended up running a glassworks. His music – bold, cheerful, and generous, like the man – has since established him as Sweden's first major composer.

MILESTONES	
1812	Violinist in court orchestra
1835	Abandons composing for orthopaedics
1845	Symphony No. 3 (unperformed)
1855	Piano Concerto (unperformed)
1862	*Estrella de Soria*, opera, finally performed

Carl Loewe

● 1796–1869   ♙ German   ✍ c.200

After studying theology and philology at Halle University, Loewe settled in the town of Stettin, Germany, in 1820. He established a reputation as a song composer and fine baritone singer and travelled widely, performing in England, Scandinavia, France, and Germany. Loewe's music was fairly conservative, though his accompaniments could be adventurous, and he frequently set music to folk myths, supernatural tales, and historical themes. He wrote operas, but with little success, and though reasonably popular in Germany after his death, he is now overshadowed by other composers – Loewe's setting of Goethe's ballad "Erlkönig", for example, was one of his early successes, but Schubert's more cohesive setting of the same text is far more often heard today.

MILESTONES

1824	*Balladen*, song collection, published
1834	First performance of *Die drei Wünsche*, opera
1837	Tours Germany
1847	Performs at court in London
1864	Falls into a coma for six weeks
1866	Asked to resign posts at Stettin due to health concerns

Loewe made Stettin in Germany his home town for more than 45 years, and he served there as professor, music director, and organist.

Fanny Mendelssohn

● 1805–1847   ♙ German   ✍ c.500

Fanny Mendelssohn was born into a liberal, talented, and cultured Jewish family, but her father, while encouraging her private musical activities, strongly discouraged publication or public performance. So she played the piano in a flourishing private salon in Berlin, for which she wrote her lyrical, traditional, and well-crafted pieces. She is also known to have played then-unfashionable composers such as J S Bach and Handel. Though she was a significant influence on her brother Felix, contributing musically to his oratorio *St Paul*, he still overshadows her; only two dozen of her pieces were published, and reviving her music is difficult as most of her manuscripts are in private collections. Her premature death from a stroke devastated Felix, who never really recovered.

MILESTONES

1829	Marries Prussian court painter Wilhelm Hensel
1838	Only public concert: her brother Felix's Piano Concerto No. 1
1840	*Das Jahr*, piano pieces, composed
1842	Mother dies; takes over the direction of the Mendelssohn family home
1846	Composes Piano Trio, Op. 11

Fanny Mendelssohn's piano cycle *Das Jahr* is a musical journal of an idyllic year spent travelling through Italy in 1839.

"Schubert's life was one of inner, spiritual thought, and was seldom expressed in words but almost entirely in music."

FRANZ ECKEL, SCHUBERT'S FRIEND FROM CHILDHOOD

Franz Schubert

♭ 1797–1828   ▣ Austrian   ✍ 1,009

One of music's greatest melodists, Schubert's tragically short life is constantly belied by his optimistic music. Achieving compositional maturity by the age of 17, his vast output evinces astounding fluency allied to an extraordinarily rich and varied musical imagination. The epitaph on his tombstone reads, "The art of music here entombed a rich possession, but even fairer hopes. Franz Schubert lies here."

LIFE

Born into a musical family, Schubert showed a precocious talent for the violin and piano. By the age of ten he was studying harmony and the following year became a chorister at the Court Chapel in Vienna, where he studied composition with Salieri, who had also taught Beethoven. Leaving in 1813, he was already an accomplished composer, having written numerous works, including a symphony, and even started an opera, but following his father's wishes he became a school teacher. Schubert continued to compose, however, and eventually he felt confident enough to give up school teaching, although he did become music teacher to the Esterházy family, who had formerly employed Haydn. Still not well known in Vienna, Schubert was in considerable financial difficulty, and when he caught syphilis in 1822 his unhappy situation threw him into despair. However, his creativity continued undiminished and by 1825 he was published and becoming known in Vienna – even the dying Beethoven requested a meeting. He gave his only public concert in 1828, but by the end of the year his health had deteriorated markedly, and he died on 19 November. His estate was valued at 63 gulden, while his unpaid bills amounted to nearly 1,000 gulden.

Many of Schubert's songs and solo works were first performed by the composer at evening parties hosted by his cultured and influential friends.

MUSICAL OUTPUT					Total: 1,009
SYMPHONIES (9)		1	5	2	1
CONCERTOS (1)			1		
PIANO MUSIC (147)		21	42	52	32
OTHER INSTRUMENTAL (77)		36	25	7	9
OPERA (10)		1	4	4	1
CHORAL (185)		41	81	28	35
SONGS (580)		50	372	81	77
	1797	1810	1815	1820	1825	1828

MUSIC

Whether to place Schubert's music within the context of the Classical or Romantic period has always been a topic of contention. Certainly subjective in its emotions, his work is far more dependent on the hedonism of melody for its own sake than that of Haydn, Mozart, or Beethoven, and is more adventurous. Sacrificing the Classical tenets of balance in favour of spontaneous imagination, his

Known for his love of the vine, Schubert enjoyed visiting the village of Grinzing near Vienna to sample the *heuriger*, the first wines of autumn.

music, however, invariably displays Classical forms and, with the exception of the songs, is almost entirely missing any external allusion or descriptive title. While formerly considered Romantic, perhaps influenced by the changing fortunes in his personal life, more recent commentators have placed his work alongside Beethoven's in historical

context. His huge output includes sacred and choral works, orchestral music including overtures and nine symphonies, over 70 chamber music works, and works for piano including 21 sonatas and some 60 works for piano duet. However, he was first known for his songs. Schubert was the central figure in the creation of the German art-song, or Lied. Frequently combining the very greatest poetry with accompaniments made possible by advances in piano design, his imagination was able to capture in music both the essential mood and the detail of the narrative. Furthermore, by setting narrative poetry cycles, he developed the genre to create the song cycle. It is therefore rather surprising that his many works for the stage are still almost unknown.

MILESTONES

1802	Studies violin with his schoolmaster father and piano with his brother
1808	Accepted as chorister at the Court Chapel, where he becomes a pupil of Antonio Salieri
1813	Completes Symphony No. 1, D82; starts work on an opera; commences teacher-training
1814	"Gretchen am Spinnrade", D118

1815	Becomes a schoolmaster; composes second and third symphonies, and the song "Erlkönig", D328, which in his lifetime becomes his best-known work
1816	Completes Symphony No. 5, D485, and more than 100 songs, including "Der Wanderer", D493
1818	Gives up school teaching and becomes music teacher to the Esterházy family
1819	Spends summer in Steyr; commissioned to write the "Trout" Quintet, D667
1822	Contracts syphilis; writes the "Unfinished" Symphony, No. 8, D759, and the "Wanderer" Fantasy, D760
1823	Admitted to Vienna hospital; composes song cycle *Die Schöne Mullerin*, D795
1827	Torch-bearer at Beethoven's funeral; composes first part of *Winterreise*, D911
1828	Public concert receives no press due to the arrival in Vienna of Paganini; completes "Great" Symphony No. 9, D944 and *Winterreise*, D911

The evening concerts where Schubert and his Bohemian friends performed their new music have since become known as "Schubertiads".

KEY WORKS

SYMPHONY NO. 9, THE "GREAT", D944

ORCHESTRAL	🕮 62:00	📖 4	♒

Visiting Schubert's brother in 1828, Schumann discovered this symphony, and sent it to Mendelssohn, who premiered it the following year. Nicknamed the "Great" for its size (Schumann wrote of its "heavenly length"), its Classical form and proportions encompass a Romantic lyricism and richness of harmonic and orchestral colour that bridge the gap between Beethoven and Bruckner.

"WANDERER" FANTASY, D760

PIANO SOLO	🕮 20:15	📖 1	🔊

The most outwardly virtuosic of Schubert's piano works, this one-movement fantasy consists of four distinct but dovetailed sections. Drawing on the theme of his own song "Der Wanderer", the outer sections explore its rhythm, while the melody inspires a series of variations in the second movement.

PIANO SONATA NO. 21, D960

PIANO SOLO	🕮 42:30	📖 4	🔊

Seldom performed in the 19th century, Schubert's last sonata has become an iconic work to post-war pianists. Its grand and spacious structure, leading the listener from resignation through contemplation to affirmation, is an optimistic journey which belies the fact that Schubert was to die only two months after its completion.

STRING QUARTET NO. 14, "DEATH AND THE MAIDEN", D810

CHAMBER	🕮 35:30	📖 4	♟

Schubert's earlier macabre song – where Death appears to a maiden disguised as her lover – gave this quartet both its title and the theme for its second movement. Written after the composer became aware of his ruined health, this sombre drama mirrors Schubert's despair.

DIE SCHÖNE MULLERIN, D795

SONG CYCLE	🕮 62:00	📖 20	🔊 🎤

Setting words by Wilhelm Müller, this song cycle tells the story of an apprentice miller who falls in love and, racked with infatuation and jealousy, drowns himself. The graphic depiction of his emotions is reflected by the flowing mill stream, which sings him a lullaby at the end of the work.

INFLUENCES

At his death, little of Schubert's music had been published, except for a number of songs and some mature works. Its slow dissemination in the 19th century limited its influence, as harmonic turns – surprisingly advanced for the 1820s – appeared commonplace at their first hearing 40 years later.

FOCUS

PIANO QUINTET, "DIE FORELLE" ("THE TROUT"), D667

CHAMBER   ⏱ 42:00   📖 5   ⚘

Schubert's early masterpiece adds a double bass, rather than the more usual second violin, to the piano-quartet ensemble. With its unquestioned joy and natural simplicity, this piece has an irresistible appeal.

FIRST MOVEMENT (ALLEGRO VIVACE, 13:20) With the double bass providing a sonorous foundation, the piano doesn't need to provide a bass line here, and so is frequently used as a purely melodic instrument.

SECOND MOVEMENT (ANDANTE, 7:00) A gentle dialogue between instruments which, threatening to come to an end in mid-movement, is immediately repeated in its entirety in a different key.

THIRD MOVEMENT (SCHERZO: PRESTO, 4:00) Brisk and vigorous, with a number of humorous silences as well as sudden

changes of dynamic and register, the Scherzo third movement is tempered by a wistful Trio section.

FOURTH MOVEMENT (ANDANTINO, 8:30) The "extra" movement which gives the work its name is a set of variations on Schubert's 1817 song "Die Forelle". In increasingly inventive variations, each instrument gets the melody in turn, and the movement ends with a fully collaborative reprise of the opening.

FIFTH MOVEMENT (ALLEGRO GIUSTO, 9:30) Surprising juxtapositions of elegance and rustic vitality, and the odd false ending, gives the work a mercurial if slightly unsatisfying conclusion.

WINTERREISE, D911

SONG CYCLE   ⏱ 73:00   📖 24   👁 ♨

Winterreise was written as Beethoven lay dying in Vienna. After he had been given nearly 60 of Schubert's songs to look over, Beethoven insisted on meeting the young composer. They met one week before his death, and Schubert subsequently became a torch-bearer at the great composer's funeral.

SYMPHONY NO. 8 IN B MINOR, "UNFINISHED", D759

ORCHESTRAL   ⏱ 24:00   📖 2   ⚞

The "Unfinished" Symphony, written in 1822, was not heard until the manuscript was rediscovered and performed in 1865. Sketches exist for a third movement, quashing theories that Schubert thought the work complete. It is actually the most complete of a number of unfinished

The Vienna Philharmonic Orchestra has recorded many of Schubert's works. Recommended recordings include Symphonies No. 3 and No. 8. Here Joseph Krips conducts the "Unfinished" in 1969.

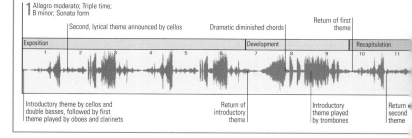

1 Allegro moderato; Triple time; B minor; Sonata form

| Exposition | | | Development | | Recapitulation |

Second, lyrical theme announced by cellos | Dramatic diminished chords | Return of first theme

Introductory theme by cellos and double basses, followed by first theme played by oboes and clarinets | Return of introductory theme | Introductory theme played by trombones | Return second theme

As with *Die Schöne Mullerin*, this song cycle is set to poetry by Wilhelm Müller, this time his *Posthumous Papers of a Travelling Horn Player*, where a traveller journeys out of town, dwelling on memories of an unfaithful lover. Poetically, the songs explore the psychological journey as much as the actual one, charting the loneliness of the protagonist through desolate winter scenery.

Musically, the hypnotic rhythms of the sparse accompaniments form a desolate background to the subdued melancholy of the vocals. Schubert's genius lay in providing infinite variety within this unity of mood – 24 vivid shades of grey.

Winterreise drew ambivalent responses at first. Schubert's friends recalled that "We were quite dumbfounded by the sombre mood of the songs. Schubert replied merely with the words 'I like these songs more than any, and they will come to please you too'; he was right, and we were soon thrilled by the impact of these melancholy songs."

symphonies by the composer.

FIRST MOVEMENT (ALLEGRO MODERATO, 14:00) It has been suggested that the dark turmoil of this movement mirrors Schubert's state of mind when he found out that he had contracted syphilis. Unlike the "Wanderer" Fantasy of the same period, this is introverted music, with each of the principal themes being introduced as quietly as possible. The movement is marked by passages of gentle lyricism interrupted by fierce outbursts.

SECOND MOVEMENT (ANDANTE CON MOTO, 10:30) The music of the second movement repeatedly tends towards agitation. Until the last few moments of the ethereal coda, it never quite recaptures the serenity of the opening. Even the beautiful clarinet melody is usurped by its syncopated string accompaniment.

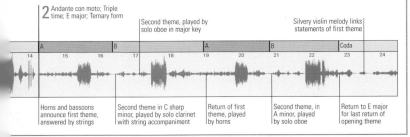

2 Andante con moto; Triple time; E major; Ternary form

A	B	A	B	Coda	
14	15	16	17	18	19	20	21	22	23	24

Second theme, played by solo oboe in major key

Silvery violin melody links statements of first theme

Horns and bassoons announce first theme, answered by strings

Second theme in C sharp minor, played by solo clarinet with string accompaniment

Return of first theme, played by horns

Second theme, in A minor, played by solo oboe

Return to E major for last return of opening theme

"Every composer knows the anguish and despair occasioned by forgetting ideas which one has no time to write down."

HECTOR BERLIOZ

Hector Berlioz

◗ 1803–1869   🏴 French   ♫ 124

Little appreciated in France during his lifetime, Berlioz's music and life embodied Romantic ideals perhaps more than any other composer, apart from Liszt. His startlingly original imagination, grandiose conceptions, and extraordinary skill in orchestration brought a new pictorialism to music. The first major composer who was not an instrumental performer, Berlioz became one of the first modern conductors, as well as a perceptive critic.

LIFE

Expected to become a doctor like his father, Berlioz received only a rudimentary early music training and, lacking a piano, had to study harmony in secret from treatises. In Paris, his medical studies succumbed to frequent visits to the Opéra and private musical study, and against his parents' wishes, he enrolled at the Conservatoire. There he heard Beethoven's symphonies and read Goethe's *Faust*, but his most formative experience was attending performances of Shakespeare, where his passion for the Bard was only eclipsed by his obsession for the leading lady, Harriet Smithson. Her initial rejection inspired the *Symphonie Fantastique*, but they were later married for nine disastrous years. Winning the Conservatoire's highest award, the Prix de Rome, did little to increase acceptance of his music, and in spite of a generous gift from Paganini, Berlioz turned to music journalism to support himself, where his erudite but acerbic wit did little to endear him to his peers. A third career beckoned when, unhappy with performances of his works, he started to conduct them himself, and then found himself in demand as an international conductor. For the following 20 years he toured extensively, and wrote some of his most important operatic and choral works.

Berlioz's final years saw the publication of his fascinating memoirs. On his deathbed he whispered "At last, they will now play my music.".

MUSICAL OUTPUT

Total: 124

	1803	1818	1830	1840	1850	1860	1869
SYMPHONIES (4)			3	1			
OTHER INSTRUMENTAL (20)		2	2	14	1		1
OPERAS (5)		1	1	1	1		1
CHORAL (42)		11	11	11	7		2
SONGS (53)		19	15	17	1		1

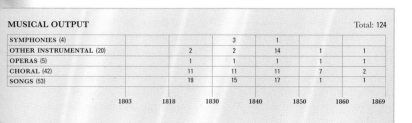

MUSIC

Unaccomplished as an instrumentalist, Berlioz instead made the orchestra his instrument. Eschewing the popularity of chamber and solo works, he expressed his intense personality in dramatic, and often epic orchestral, operatic, and choral forms. His works blurred formal boundaries by frequently incorporating programmatic elements, as in the operatic choral symphony, *Romeo and Juliet*, and the symphonic concerto, *Harold in Italy*. More revolutionary still was his use of orchestration. Not afraid to employ huge forces and newly-invented instruments, and to redistribute players around the hall, even off-stage, he was able to paint both subtler and more blazing colours than

MILESTONES	
1821	Enters medical school in Paris; makes first visits to the Opera
1824	Gives up medicine; composes *Messe solonnelle* (lost in 1835, found in 1991)
1826	Enrols at Paris Conservatoire
1827	Sees Harriet Smithson in *Hamlet*
1828	Hears Beethoven's symphonies and reads Goethe's *Faust*
1830	*Symphonie fantastique* wins Prix de Rome
1834	Composes *Harold in Italy*, viola concerto
1837	Writes *Grande messe des morts*
1841	*Les Nuits d'été*, vocal work, composed
1842	Begins first of many international tours
1849	Composes Te Deum
1858	Writes *The Trojans*, opera

Berlioz first saw Harriet Smithson in 1827 when she played Ophelia in *Hamlet* by Shakespeare. He finally met her in 1832. They married in 1833.

had previously been imagined. His melodies fall naturally, avoiding the regular beat and stylized ornamentation of Italianate music, while his harmony encompasses surprising dissonances for dramatic ends. As he wrote in his memoirs, "The ruling characteristics of my music are passionate expression, intense ardour, rhythmical animation, and unexpected turns".

KEY WORKS

THE TROJANS

OPERA   ⏱ 240:00   📖 5   🎻🥁🎤

Berlioz based his magnum opus, *Les Troyens*, on Virgil's *Aeneid*, completing both libretto and music in two years. The first two acts depict the story of the Trojan Horse, and the remainder, Dido and Aeneas in Carthage. He finished the work in 1858 and it was first performed in 1863 as two separate operas, as is often the case nowadays.

GRANDE MESSE DES MORTS (REQUIEM), OP. 5

MASS SETTING   ⏱ 76:00   📖 10   🎻🥁🎤

Berlioz's forceful and vivid setting of the Requiem, with its massive orchestra including 12 horns, 16 timpani and four brass ensembles, immerses the

listener in the drama of the text. Commissioned by the government for performance in the church of Les Invalides in Paris, Berlioz later said, "If I were threatened with the destruction of all my works but one, I would beg mercy for the *Grande messe des morts*".

LES NUITS D'ÉTÉ, OP. 7

VOCAL   ⏱ 31:00   📖 6   🎻🎤

Originally composed for single voice and piano, Berlioz orchestrated these settings of poems by Théophile Gautier in 1856 for multiple soloists. Varying from the joyful "Villanelle", to the despairing "L'île inconnue", the light but exquisitely coloured orchestration paved the way for similar works by Richard Strauss and Mahler.

SYMPHONIE FANTASTIQUE, OP. 14

ORCHESTRAL   56:00   5

Inspired by Beethoven, Berlioz decided to become a symphonist himself. This work became a Romantic auto-biography about his obsession with Harriet Smithson, who is musically portrayed by an *idée fixe*. His concert notes described a young musician of great sensibility and imagination, in despair because of hopeless love. Opium plunges him into a heavy sleep accompanied by weird visions.

DREAMS AND PASSIONS (16:00) Ranging from calm and melancholy to passion and despair, the artist recalls the time before love, then its delirious effect, and religious consolation.

A BALL (6:00) A brilliant and sumptuous waltz halts dramatically as the beloved's theme is heard once again.

SCENE IN THE COUNTRY (17:00) Off-stage players depict far-off shepherds piping. The melancholy artist almost achieves tranquillity, but the beloved is recalled and distant thunder sounds.

MARCH TO THE SCAFFOLD (7:00) To rasping brass and winds, he is condemned to death for his beloved's murder. We hear her plaintive theme, the blade drops and crowds cheer.

DREAM OF A SABBATH NIGHT (10:00) Grotesquely parodied, the beloved joins the devilish orgy while the ancient plainchant "Dies Irae" is intoned, surrounded by tolling bells.

TE DEUM, OP. 22

CHORAL   47:00   6

Written to be heard in church, Berlioz described this piece as being not only the ceremonial hymn of thanksgiving usual in a Te Deum, but also an offering of prayers whose humility and melancholy contrast with the majesty of the hymns. His placing of the orchestra and chorus (including a large children's choir) at the opposite end of the church to the organ, was essential to the musical effect. Berlioz also re-ordered the traditional text to control the overall tension of the work. As well as the six choral movements, there are two instrumental movements – originally designed for ceremonial purposes – which are not always included in modern performances.

> **INFLUENCES**
>
> Apart from the *Symphonie fantastique*, Berlioz's works were seldom heard until the 1880s, when they were revived in France as an antidote to Wagner. Only after the 1950s did his music become widely disseminated, although logistical difficulties still prevent regular performances of some of the works.

Johann Strauss Sr

● 1804–1849   ◪ Austrian   ✍ 251

Founder of the "Strauss Waltz Dynasty", Johann Strauss Sr helped to take the waltz – then a traditional Austrian folk dance – out of the village tavern and into Europe's finest ballrooms. He was famous for the rhythmic verve of his music and the finesse of his conducting, but his music has been eclipsed by the more memorable melodic gifts of his sons. He is now principally known for the stirring *Radetzky March*.

LIFE AND MUSIC

Of humble origins, Strauss learnt to play the violin in his teens whilst apprenticed to a bookbinder, spending the evenings performing traditional dances in local taverns. Following the lead of Carl Maria von Weber's 1819 piano piece *Invitation to the Dance*, he expanded the Viennese waltz into a chain of dances framed by an introduction and coda, and was soon presenting these works with his own orchestra. A six-year contract to play at the prestigious Sperl dance hall consolidated his fame, and he was soon in demand at ballrooms across Europe. In addition to some 150 waltzes, he composed a number of other fashionable dances.

MILESTONES	
1819	Joins Joseph Lanner's small band
1824	Becomes conductor of Lanner's second orchestra, attempts first waltzes
1825	Marries Maria Anna Streim; forms own orchestra; Johann Strauss Jr born
1829	Takes up residency at the Sperl
1837	Composes *Cachucha Galop*
1838	Plays for Queen Victoria of England
1842	Writes *Beliebte Annen Polka*, Op. 137; Maria Anna sues for divorce
1843	Composes *Loreley Rheinklänge*, Op. 154, and *Kunstlerball Tanze*, Op. 150
1846	Appointed first ever Royal and Imperial Hofballmusikdirektor
1848	Composes *Radetzky March*
1849	Dies of scarlet fever, aged 45

KEY WORKS

BELIEBTE ANNEN POLKA, OP. 137
DANCE   ⏱ 1:50   ▭ 1   ♫

Brought to Vienna from Bohemia in 1839, the lively polka was the newest dance craze. Strauss wrote the *Beloved Anna Polka* for his wife, a few months before she sued for divorce.

LORELEY RHEINKLÄNGE, OP. 154
DANCE   ⏱ 5:40   ▭ 1   ♫

The *Echoes of the Rhine Lorelei* was one of Strauss's most popular waltzes, and was performed to great acclaim in 1844 by his son Johann Strauss Jr, who went on to steal his father's crown.

KUNSTLERBALL TANZE, OP. 150
DANCE   ⏱ 6:20   ▭ 1   ♫

This archetypal waltz was performed at the 1843 Artists' Ball. Following a grand introduction, five linked waltzes are then briefly recalled in a coda.

The fruitful partnership between Strauss (violinist on left) and Joseph Lanner (violinist on right) began with a small band of Viennese musicians in 1819.

FOCUS

RADETZKY MARCH, OP. 228

DANCE   ▣ 3:00   ▭ 1   ✿

On 31 August 1848, to celebrate the Austrian army's victory over an Italian revolutionary uprising at Custozza, an open-air victory festival was held in Vienna. The concert was dedicated to the 82-year-old Commander-in-Chief of the Imperial Austrian army, Count Radetzky von Radetz, and a special march had been commissioned from Strauss to celebrate the occasion.

On the afternoon of the victory concert the piece had still not been composed. However, with the help of his colleague Philipp Farbach Sr, an eminent flautist who frequently assisted the composer with his orchestration, the *Radetzky March* was completed in around two hours and played to great acclaim that very evening. The march quickly became a Habsburg anthem, ensuring frequent performances and eventually bestowing immortality on a composer whose other works posterity has judged ephemeral.

The march actually incorporates two popular Viennese melodies which would have been very familiar to its first audiences. The outer, martial sections include a common street-song, while the more gentle trio section features one of the previous season's most popular dance melodies.

CACHUCHA GALOP, OP. 97

DANCE   ▣ 2:00   ▭ 1   ✿

In 1837, the Austrian ballerina Fanny Elssler performed "the cachucha" – a Spanish dance then very popular in Paris – for the audience of the Viennese Court Opera. After three performances of this "lascivious" dance, Vienna caught "cachucha fever".

Strauss was quick to realize the financial potential of the situation and promptly wrote this hair-raising galop to take advantage of the craze. An inscription by the composer Adolf Müller on the original manuscript shows the work had an even faster genesis than the *Radetzky March*: "This galop was composed by Johann Strauss one hour before the start of the ball, copied by the copyist, performed without rehearsal, received extraordinary applause, and was repeated three times."

The main section of the galop and the coda feature a castanet accompaniment to original melodies from the cachucha dance, while the central trio section is original Strauss.

INFLUENCES

Apart from fathering a musical dynasty, Johann Strauss's refinement of the waltz paved the way for composers such as Chopin, Brahms, and Ravel, who brought the dance into the concert hall. Strauss's best-known piece, the *Radetzky March*, is still featured in the annual telecast of the New Year's Day concert from Vienna.

"A Romantic who felt at ease within the mould of Classicism."

CELLIST AND CONDUCTOR PABLO CASALS

Felix Mendelssohn

1809–1847   **German**   **321**

One of the most naturally gifted and accomplished musicians in the history of music, Mendelssohn preserved Classical ideals of harmony and form. As such he was admired by conservative music lovers for his charm, craftsmanship, and picturesque imagination, particularly in staid Victorian drawing rooms, but his music was eclipsed as soon as the public fully embraced the ideals of Romanticism.

LIFE

Born into a wealthy, cultured family, Mendelssohn had the finest private education available. His musical training was so thorough that it included the hiring of orchestras to try out his compositions. Felix showed talents not only as a violinist, pianist, organist, composer, and conductor, but also in fine art and poetry, and in his teens he became a protégé of Goethe. One of the first musicians to be fully aware of musical history, at the age of 20 he conducted the second-ever performance of Bach's *St Matthew Passion*, leading to the 19th-century Bach revival. As he later recalled, "It was a Jew who restored this great Christian work to the people" (the Mendelssohns had actually converted to Christianity in 1816). There followed three years of travel and concert-giving. His love of all things British drew him back for ten lengthy visits to England and Scotland. He returned to conducting posts in Düsseldorf and then Leipzig, where he conducted the Gewandhaus orchestra. Here he established the now universal concept of programming both historical and modern works. Following the death of his sister Fanny, also a gifted pianist and composer, Mendelssohn suffered a series of strokes, and died at the age of 38.

Until his sister Fanny's death, Mendelssohn's life was relatively free of torment, struggle, or frustration, a fact which is mirrored in his sunny, cheerful music.

MUSICAL OUTPUT						Total: 321
SYMPHONIES (8)	5		1	1	1	
CONCERTOS (18)	14		2		2	
PIANO MUSIC (82)	27	13	6	17	17	2
OTHER INSTRUMENTAL (62)	13	11	5	8	10	15
OPERA (7)	5	2				
CHORAL (89)	21	10	12	13	19	14
SONGS (55)	12	3	11	12	11	6
1809 1820	1825	1830	1835	1840	1845	1847

MUSIC

Mendelssohn's style does not fit easily with other Romantic music, and it has been suggested that he could be called Neo-Classical. He drew on the fugal technique of Bach, the textures and clarity of Mozart, and the orchestration of Beethoven. By his mid-teens, his style, as evinced by the *A Midsummer Night's Dream* overture, had crystallized. Unlike his radical contemporaries, Mendelssohn used well-established forms, adapting them to his needs, but retaining their underlying principles. Neither sensuous nor flamboyant, his natural melodic gifts were always coupled with the very highest levels of craftsmanship. Where his music is specifically Romantic is in its use of extra-musical stimuli. Literary, artistic, and geographical inspiration drew forth the best from his picturesque imagination, and descriptive, rather than psychological, imagery informs much of his finest work.

MILESTONES	
1818	First public performance
1821	First visit to Goethe
1823	Grandmother gives him a score of J S Bach's *St Matthew Passion*
1825	*Octet*, Op. 20, is published
1826	Overture to *A Midsummer Night's Dream*, Op. 21; attends Hegel's course on aesthetics
1829	Conducts *St Matthew Passion*, first visit to England and Scotland
1832	First volume of *Lieder Ohne Worte* (*Songs Without Words*), Op. 19
1835	Director of Leipzig Gewandhaus
1837	Marries Cécile Jeanrenaud
1839	Conducts first performance of Schubert's "Great" Symphony No. 9
1841	Conducts first performance of Schumann's Symphony No. 1
1842	*Variations Sérieuses*, Op. 54; premiere of the "Scottish" Symphony
1844	Violin Concerto, Op. 64, is published
1846	First performance of *Elijah*, Op. 70

KEY WORKS

LIEDER OHNE WORTE
PIANO SOLO   □ 48   ◐

The elegant *Lieder Ohne Worte*, or *Songs Without Words*, were the province of the drawing-room before the concert hall. Played by almost every amateur, they greatly enhanced Mendelssohn's popularity in England.

VARIATIONS SÉRIEUSES, OP. 54
PIANO SOLO   ⏱ 11:00   □ 1   ◐

Composed for an album of works by various composers including Chopin, the proceeds of which were to go towards erecting a monument to Beethoven at Bonn in Germany, Mendelssohn's *Variations Sérieuses* is certainly the most substantial of the offerings.

Without doubt his finest piano work, the yearning theme can be heard in almost every one of the 17 variations, offset by the great variety of moods, textures and harmonies.

"SCOTTISH" SYMPHONY, OP. 56
ORCHESTRAL   ⏱ 38:30   □ 4   ◭

The last of Mendelssohn's symphonies, the "Scottish" Symphony was written 13 years after his first visit to Scotland in 1829, which also inspired his *Hebrides Overture* (also known as "Fingal's Cave"). The theme of the scherzo is akin to Scottish folk melodies; further Highland allusions are subjective.

Mendelssohn's Wedding March was first officially used at the wedding of the Princess Royal of Great Britain in 1858.

FOCUS

VIOLIN CONCERTO, OP. 64

ORCHESTRAL 25.00 📖 3

This famous and popular concerto in E minor was the last of Mendelssohn's orchestral works, and the last of his three violin concertos. The composer was too ill to conduct his friend Ferdinand David at the premiere, and was replaced by the Danish composer Niels Gade. The work was innovative in a number of ways, and the piece's three movements are played without interruption.

FIRST MOVEMENT

(ALLEGRO MOLTO APPASSIONATO, 11:00) Flying in the face of convention, Mendelssohn allowed the violin to present the memorable opening theme before the orchestra. This move influenced the majority of composers who followed him. He also moved the cadenza forward from the end of the movement, presumably to allow the tension to subside before the seamless entry of the second movement accompanied by the bassoon.

SECOND MOVEMENT (ANDANTE, 8:00) A

simple "song without words" with a more agitated central section, this slow movement gives the soloist nothing to hide behind but his own tone, intonation, and musical imagination.

THIRD MOVEMENT (ALLEGRO NON TROPPO, 6:00)

Opening with its own fanfare, here all our Mendelssohnian expectations of gossamer-light fantasy are fulfilled with effervescent virtuosity.

INFLUENCES
Numerous musicians over the past two centuries have been admirers of the work of Mendelssohn, but few, if any, can be said to have been influenced by it. However, Mendelssohn's part in the great 19th-century Bach revival turned a cult into a popular movement whose effect on subsequent generations is impossible to overestimate.

A MIDSUMMER NIGHT'S DREAM, OP. 21, 61

INCIDENTAL MUSIC 35:00 📖 9

This suite is Mendelssohn's most popular work. The overture and incidental music come from opposite ends of Mendelssohn's life, but use much of the same musical material.

OVERTURE (ALLEGRO DI MOTO, 12:00) Originally written at the age of 17 for piano duet, Mendelssohn orchestrated this precocious answer to the magic of Shakespeare's play the following year for a public performance. Opening with chords to depict the procession of Oberon and Titania, we are swiftly immersed in the scurrying fairy world. A touching melody describes the lovers, while a rustic dance for the "mechanicals" is interrupted by frequent donkey brays.

INCIDENTAL MUSIC (23:00) Commissioned by the King of Prussia in 1842, four of the eight pieces were conceived as entr'actes (music between acts), most famously the fleeting fairy scherzo. Also set are two songs, "You Spotted Snakes", and "Through This House Give Glimmering Light…" for soprano, mezzo, and chorus. Finally, the ubiquitous *Wedding March* first saw the light of day here.

"*After playing Chopin, I feel as if I had been weeping over sins that I had never committed, and mourning over tragedies that were not my own.*"

OSCAR WILDE, 1891

Frédéric Chopin

● 1810–1849   ▣ Polish   ✍ 219

Exiled by revolution, abandoned by his mistress, dying of consumption, but always elegantly dressed, the frail image of Chopin fulfils all the stereotypes of the Romantic artist. The first poet of the piano, his music was immediately popular and has always transcended the vagaries of fashion. A national hero, his music announced the liberation of his native Poland and still accompanies international statesmen to their graves.

LIFE

Exiled from Poland by the Russian capture of Warsaw in 1831, Chopin made his home and his name in the piano capital of the world – Paris. There his reputation was based as much on the finesse and poetry of his playing as on his extraordinary keyboard facility. An inveterate snob with exquisite manners, Chopin was soon the toast of aristocratic circles. Preferring private performances in the salons of Parisian nobility to the strain and artistic compromises of courting the general public, he also developed a very lucrative career teaching ladies of aristocratic birth. Fastidious about his dress, he was something of a dandy, noting to a friend "You think I am making a fortune? Carriages and white gloves cost more, and without them one would not be in good taste". In 1836 Liszt introduced him to George Sand, the novelist who had outraged Paris with her cigar-smoking and trouser-wearing. A nine-year relationship followed, during which Chopin wrote the majority of his most important works, starting with the Preludes, completed during the couple's stay in Majorca. However, his health began to wane, and following the couple's separation in 1847, it deteriorated rapidly and he wrote almost no more music. Following an extended visit to England and Scotland in 1848, he died the following year in Paris. 3,000 people attended his funeral.

Chopin's exquisitely crafted piano music is highly regarded for its lyricism, purity, and delicate charm.

MUSICAL OUTPUT

Total: 219

	1810	1815	1820	1825	1830	1835	1840	1845	1849
CONCERTOS (6)				4	2				
PIANO MUSIC (194)			3	3	36	54	49	31	18
OTHER INSTRUMENTAL (5)			1	3	1				
SONGS (14)					2	4	4	2	2

MUSIC

All of Chopin's music includes a piano, and most of it is for that instrument alone. His works seem to have sprung fully formed onto the page. Notation was simply the last stage of a process of improvization at the keyboard, and it was not unusual for a work to evolve further after publication.

His early music was written for his own concerts, and is fairly typical of the virtuoso material of the day, but after giving up the concert platform he found his unique voice, and every single work is a masterpiece. A simple, melodic style was refined and extended in numerous miniatures written primarily for his pupils, while virtuosity was sublimated into lofty drama in the more complex, large-scale concert works. Chopin was particularly drawn to dance forms – the waltz is evident in many works – but it was with the mazurka and the polonaise that he was able to assert his true, Polish identity.

MILESTONES	
1818	Gives first concert
1826	Becomes a student at Warsaw Conservatory
1829	Two concerts in Vienna; Variations, Op. 2, favourably reviewed by Robert Schumann
1830	First performance of Piano Concerto No. 2, Op. 21
1831	Arrives in Paris, meets Liszt
1832	First Paris concert, meets Mendelssohn and Berlioz
1835	Meets Robert Schumann, composes *Andante Spianato*
1836	Becomes engaged to Maria Wodzinska; meets George Sand
1837	Engagement broken; visits London; Etudes, Op. 25, published
1838	Goes to Majorca with George Sand
1839	Preludes, Op. 28, completed
1846	Composes *Barcarolle*, Op. 60
1847	Separates from Sand
1848	Last concert in Paris, tours Britain

KEY WORKS

SONATA IN B FLAT MINOR, "FUNERAL MARCH", OP. 35
SOLO PIANO   ⏱ 24:10   📖 4   ▣

Immediately plunging the listener into a maelstrom of desperation, even the more lyrical second theme exudes a hopeless pathos. The repeat is sometimes omitted by performers, rather shortening the passionate first movement. With its driving rhythms and chaste trio, the second movement is a very Beethovian scherzo. The third movement contains the most famous funeral march ever written. The focal point of this sonata, it predates the rest of the work by two years. The enigmatic fourth movement, with its stream of eerie, unharmonized notes, inspired Anton Rubinstein to imagine "night winds sweeping over churchyard graves".

PRELUDES, OP. 28
SOLO PIANO   ⏱ 35:00   📖 24   ▣

There is a breathtaking variety in these 24 pieces, perhaps the most forward-looking of all Chopin's music. Exploring every key, they are full of harmonic surprises and enigmatic melodies. Among the many later composers inspired by the Preludes were Debussy and Rachmaninov.

Chopin completed the Preludes in this cell in an abandoned monastery in Majorca in January, 1839.

BARCAROLLE, OP. 60

SOLO PIANO   🔊 8:40   📖 1   🔊

Originally named after the *barcarole* sung by Venetian gondoliers, the barcarolle was probably first popularized as a musical form outside its native city by travellers returning from the Grand Tour. Beloved by Romantic audiences for its gentle evocations of love, it was soon appropriated by composers for solo and operatic vocal works, perhaps most famously in Offenbach's *The Tales of Hoffmann*.

    The form also became associated with the piano, as Mendelssohn, Liszt, and Fauré penned a number of fine examples, but none is more celebrated than Chopin's. His last major work, it was premiered by the composer at his last recital in Paris in 1848. Although it was written not long before his final estrangement from George Sand, it shows no signs of melancholy. Featuring an almost continuous lilting rhythm, the bass conjures the ebb and flow of the water, while the rich harmony supplies the scene's shimmering, shifting colours. Two long alternating melodies evoke the vocal origins of the genre, evolving from beautiful simplicity to sublime radiance. Foreshadowing the music of Alexander Scriabin over 40 years later, the complex harmonies of the coda create one of the most extraordinary moments in the piano repertoire.

PIANO CONCERTO NO. 2 IN F MINOR, OP. 21

ORCHESTRAL   🔊 26:15   📖 3   🔊🔊 🔊

Chopin wrote his piano concertos to launch the virtuoso career that he later found so distasteful.

FIRST MOVEMENT (MAESTOSO, 11:00) After the first performance in 1830, Chopin wrote: "The first Allegro of my concerto, which relatively few could grasp, called forth applause, but it seems to me that people felt they had to show interest and pretend to be connoisseurs".

SECOND MOVEMENT (LARGHETTO, 8:00) Inspired by his feelings for Constantia Gladkowska, Chopin wrote that the slow movement "belonged" to her. With its distinctive harmony, poetic lyricism, and ornate decoration it stands in sharp relief to other concertos of the period.

THIRD MOVEMENT (ALLEGRO VIVACE, 7:15) Virtuosic yet always elegant, the finale pays tribute to the mazurka of Polish folk music. The horn call that ushers in the exciting coda was a great surprise to early audiences.

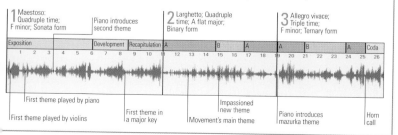

1 Maestoso: Quadruple time; F minor; Sonata form   Piano introduces second theme

2 Larghetto; Quadruple time; A flat major; Binary form

3 Allegro vivace; Triple time; F minor; Ternary form

Exposition	Development	Recapitulation	A	B	A	B	A	Coda
1 2 3	4 5 6 7 8	9 10 11	12 13 14	15 16 17 18	19 20	21 22 23	24 25	26

First theme played by piano

First theme played by violins   First theme in a major key   Movement's main theme   Impassioned new theme   Piano introduces mazurka theme   Horn call

"*I am affected by everything that goes on in the world… and then I long to express my feelings in music.*"

ROBERT SCHUMANN

Robert Schumann

● 1810–1856   ▶ German   ✍ 268

Schumann's deep and sensitive musicianship makes little attempt to play to the gallery, instead drawing the listener into the composer's remote and enigmatic inner world. Perhaps the most elusive composer of the Romantic period, his music is at turns fanciful, introspective, and bombastic. Daringly original, and frequently impractical, he captured, as no other did, the innocent spirit of early German Romantic literature.

LIFE

Obsessed equally by music and literature as a boy, though receiving no thorough education in either, Schumann was persuaded by his mother to become a lawyer. Whilst studying in Leipzig he heard Paganini play, and decided instead to become a musician. Enrolling with a local piano teacher, Friedrich Wieck, whose 11-year-old daughter, Clara, was already a piano prodigy, he gave up his law studies and moved into Wieck's home. When he injured his hand, allegedly in an attempt to strengthen his fingers, but probably as a result of a cure he was taking for syphilis, he gave up hope of a concert career and devoted himself to composition. In 1834, as editor of a new music journal, the *Neue Zeitschrift für Musik*, he brought the music of the young Chopin and Brahms to popular attention.

In spite of their age gap, Clara and Robert fell in love, exchanging their first kiss in 1835. Her father banned the liaison, but they took him to court, and were eventually married in 1840. They started a large family (seven children survived), but Schumann, in whose family mental illness ran, started to suffer badly from depression. In 1854 he attempted suicide by throwing himself into the River Rhine. Rescued, he entered an asylum where he died.

By turns whimsical, fantastic, and grotesque, Schumann's music is the apotheosis of Romanticism, rich in literary allusions.

MUSICAL OUTPUT								Total: 268
SYMPHONIES (6)				1		2	1	2
CONCERTOS (6)		2			1		1	2
PIANO MUSIC (90)		3	32	30	6		11	8
OTHER INSTRUMENTAL (40)		2	2	2	6		11	17
OPERA (2)						1	1	
CHORAL (38)	2				3		19	14
SONGS (86)		13		1	35		14	23
	1810	1820	1825	1830	1835	1840	1845	1850 1856

MUSIC

Between 1830 and 1840 Schumann published several piano masterpieces. Happiest when capturing moods and ideas in the white-heat of inspiration, he showed a love of miniatures, and grouping several together around a common musical or conceptual theme, he created the Romantic piano suite. He was less accomplished in the structuring of large-scale movements. Of his more expansive piano works, only the Fantasy in C makes a lasting impression. Following in the footsteps of Schubert, he then focused on the art song, completing 19 song cycles in one year alone. Chamber music, largely ignored by his contemporaries, was his next target. It drew forth some of his finest mature work, including three string quartets and works for piano and strings. He also penned four symphonies, which are among the most impassioned symphonic music of their time.

MILESTONES	
1828	Enters Leipzig University
1830	Hears Paganini, gives up law for music
1831	*Abegg Variations*, Op. 1, and *Papillons*, Op. 2 published
1832	Injures hand
1834	First edition of the music journal *Neue Zeitschrift für Musik*
1835	Completes *Carnaval*, Op. 9
1836	Is forced to break off all relations with Clara
1838	Composes *Kinderszenen*, Op. 15, and *Kreisleriana*, Op. 16
1839	Discovers Schubert's "Great" Symphony No. 9
1840	Marries Clara; composes songs
1842	Completes three string quartets, the Piano Quintet, Op. 44, and the Piano Quintet, Op. 47
1844	Suffers from depression and a nervous breakdown, moves to Dresden
1853	Meets Brahms
1854	Attempts suicide, enters asylum

KEY WORKS

SYMPHONY NO. 3, "RHENISCH", OP. 97

ORCHESTRAL   ⏱ 32:30   📖 5   🎼

In 1850 Schumann moved to the Rhineland and wrote this symphony as a tribute to its beauty. The work is unusually structured, and there is an extra, slow movement, powerfully inspired by the grandeur of a ceremony Schumann witnessed at Cologne Cathedral.

Schumann's workroom in Zwickau, where he lived until leaving for Leipzig to study law. While at school he read Schiller, Goethe, Byron, and Jean Paul Richter.

CARNAVAL, OP. 9

PIANO SOLO   ⏱ 24:00   📖 21   🎼

One of Schumann's most popular works, this suite suggests a ball, with fleeting movements describing the real and imaginary people in Schumann's life, as well as characters from the commedia dell'arte, such as Pierrot and Harlequin. It is richly diverse, even though many movements are based on the same four-note theme.

PIANO QUINTET, OP. 44

CHAMBER   ⏱ 31:00   📖 4   🎼

In 1842 Schumann took Liszt's advice and wrote a series of chamber works, a genre then unfashionable, ending with the Piano Quintet. It was the first important work for this medium, and blended a demanding piano part with quasi-orchestral string writing. It paved the way for the piano quintets of Brahms, Franck, and Dvořák.

FANTASY IN C, OP. 17

PIANO SOLO ⏱ 31:00 📖 3 🔊

Dedicated to Liszt, the superlative 1838 Fantasy in C was originally Schumann's tribute to Beethoven. At a time when he was forbidden to see his beloved Clara, the lines by the poet Friedrich von Schiller that preface the work were certainly intended for her eyes: "Through all the sounds of Earth's mingled dream, lies one quiet note for the secret listener".

RUINS (DURCHAUS PHANTASTISCH UND LEIDENSCHAFTLICH VORZUTRAGEN, 12:00)
This impassioned and kaleidoscopic outpouring finds little peace even in the earthbound central interlude. Only at the end do we achieve tranquillity, when Schumann quotes a song from Beethoven's *An die ferne Geliebte*. It is no coincidence that its opening words are "Take then these songs, my love".

TRIUMPHAL ARCH (MÄSSIG, 7:00) An overwhelmingly extrovert march whose infectious drive is produced by an almost constant stream of asymmetric rhythms even in the graceful middle section. In the maniacally exuberant leaps of the final pages, joy is unconfined. "It makes me hot and cold all over", Clara wrote.

WREATH OF STARS (LANGSAM GETRAGEN, 11:00)
Unusually ending with a calm, slow movement, Schumann's mercurial nature manifests itself in a vast musical landscape suggesting both serene peace and utter despair.

INFLUENCES

Schumann's most important music was too subtle and quirky to gain much popularity in his own lifetime, and he met with very little success as a conductor and teacher. It was mainly through performances by his widow, and by friends such as Joseph Joachim and Brahms, that his music eventually entered the musical canon.

DICHTERLIEBE, OP. 48

SONG CYCLE ⏱ 28:00 📖 16 🔊

For Schumann it was a small step from writing cycles of piano music such as *Carnaval*, where moods are swiftly captured, to distilling the essence of a poem in a song. Until 1840 he claimed that song was an inferior medium to instrumental music and ignored it, but once started, before the year was out he had written more than 150 individual songs.

The song cycle *Dichterliebe* (*A Poet's Love*), explores the journey from the joy of new love, through failure, to renunciation. The setting of Heinrich Heine's frequently bitter words is quietly compelling yet heart-rending in its lyrical pathos. Equally striking is his use of the piano; no longer an "accompanist", it is an equal partner, which sets the scene and then adds to and comments upon the narrative. In the majority of the songs, Schumann adds a piano postlude, in which he sums up the mood, most poignantly at the end of the cycle where he reflects on all that has passed. It is astounding that Schumann completed this entire masterpiece in only nine days.

*"My mind and fingers have worked
like two damned ones. Unless I go mad,
you will find an artist in me."*

THE 21-YEAR-OLD LISZT IN A LETTER TO A FRIEND, 1832

Franz Liszt

🏠 1811–1886   ◪ Hungarian   ✍ 749

Liszt can truly be said to have been the central figure of the Romantic movement. As a young man he set Europe on fire with his astonishing pianistic gifts. He slowly gained recognition as a composer, developing the potential of the piano and the role of the pianist. As famous for his life as for his music, he worked tirelessly to promote the work of his colleagues, and to teach subsequent generations of pianists and composers.

LIFE

By the age of 12, Liszt had already performed throughout Europe, but ill health and religious contemplation during his late teens saw him withdraw from public life. Only after hearing Paganini did he return to the piano, dazzling listeners with the unprecedented complexity of his music. Fame and fortune followed, but in 1835 he shocked Paris by eloping with the already married Countess Marie d'Agoult. Living in Switzerland and Italy they had three children, while Liszt concentrated on composition. Returning to the platform in 1838, he established the prototype of the modern concert pianist by performing from memory and giving the first solo recitals (indeed inventing the term). For eight years he toured extensively, but by 1847 he longed to settle and marry his new lover, Princess Carolyne Sayne-Wittgenstein. He became Kapellmeister at the court of Weimar, where until 1861 he wrote or revised most of his important works and taught the next generation of great pianists. However, when the Vatican stopped the annulment of the Princess's previous marriage, and following the deaths of two of his children, Liszt again sought solace in the Church. He became an abbé, but continued to compose, teach, and perform without income until his death.

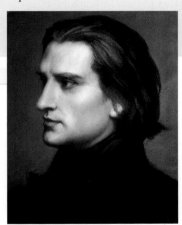

Liszt was one of the first in a long line of composer/musicians to gain celebrity as much for their stagecraft as for their music.

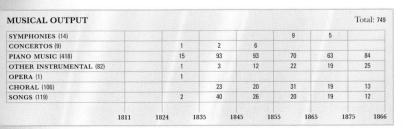

MUSICAL OUTPUT							Total: 749
SYMPHONIES (14)					9	5	
CONCERTOS (9)		1	2	6			
PIANO MUSIC (418)		15	93	93	70	63	84
OTHER INSTRUMENTAL (82)		1	3	12	22	19	25
OPERA (1)		1					
CHORAL (106)			23	20	31	19	13
SONGS (119)		2	40	26	20	19	12
	1811	1824	1835	1845	1855	1865	1875 1866

MUSIC

As a young virtuoso writing piano music to astound the public, Liszt's early works were showpieces that took piano technique to new heights of difficulty. Liszt incorporated virtuosity as an essential dramatic element of his music. However, his knowledge of the piano's evolving capabilities bore fruit in his transcriptions of operatic and symphonic music. Particularly in the symphonies of Beethoven and Berlioz, he found ways to transform the piano into a substitute orchestra. Following his retirement from concert life, he studied composition intensively. He became a true composer, whose harmonic language influenced Ravel and Wagner. This period produced his most important works, not only piano pieces, but also two symphonies and 12 symphonic poems, a genre he invented. In his final years Liszt's experiments foreshadowed the music of the 20th century in its unstable harmonies and sparse textures.

MILESTONES

1821	Studies with Beethoven's pupil, Carl Czerny
1822	First public concert in Vienna
1831	Hears Paganini play
1833	Transcribes Berlioz' *Symphonie fantastique*
1835	Elopes with Countess Marie d'Agoult
1839	Returns to concert platform, travelling extensively for 8 years
1847	Meets Princess Carolyne Sayn-Wittgenstein, retires to Weimar
1853	Composes Sonata in B Minor, S178
1857	Premiere of *Faust-Symphonie*, S108
1861	Moves to Rome, composes *Mephisto Waltz No. 1*, S110/514
1865	Takes minor orders of the Catholic Church, becoming an abbé

Long after retiring from public performance, Liszt would treat listeners to private recitals at his house in Weimar – now a museum devoted to the composer.

KEY WORKS

FAUST-SYMPHONIE, S108

ORCHESTRAL   ⏱ 71:00   📖 3

Liszt wrote this work in 1854, having been introduced to Goethe's play *Faust* by Berlioz in 1830. The three movements depict the main characters, Faust, Gretchen, and Mephistopheles. The work ends with the addition of a tenor soloist and male chorus, for a setting of Goethe's *Chorus Mysticus*.

TRANSCENDENTAL ÉTUDES, S139

PIANO SOLO   📖 12

Exploring the possibility of orchestral sounds at the piano, this monumental cycle opened new doors, requiring pianists to use not just their fingers, but arms, shoulders, and backs to master the necessary combination of speed and power.

SONATA IN B MINOR, S178

PIANO SOLO   ⏱ 27:00   📖 1

Hearing the Sonata in B minor for the first time, Wagner wrote to Liszt "The Sonata is beautiful beyond compare; great, loveable, deep, and noble, just as you are." The work's single movement encompasses the diverse movements of earlier sonatas. It is built on five themes, which are transformed and combined during the drama, in a way foreshadowing Wagner's technique of *leitmotif*. It remains a monolithic work of the piano repertoire.

FOCUS

PIANO CONCERTO NO. 1, S124

ORCHESTRAL   ⏱ 18:20   📖 4   🎵 🎼

Once one of the most popular works in the piano repertoire, the Piano Concerto No. 1 belongs to the unabashed virtuoso pianist. Now heard infrequently, suffering in part from its brevity, it was premiered in 1855 with Berlioz conducting and Liszt himself at the piano.

FIRST MOVEMENT (ALLEGRO MAESTOSO, 5:15) Pianist and orchestra vie for attention with abrupt musical interjections in this kaleidoscopic movement.

SECOND MOVEMENT (QUASI ADAGIO, 4:30) Simply the greatest nocturne Chopin never wrote. After presenting the exquisite melody, the piano destroys the mood, only to melt away as an accompaniment for the woodwinds.

THIRD MOVEMENT (ALLEGRETTO VIVACE, 4:20) Liszt's novel use of the triangle in this scherzo drew much derision. The soloist's role gradually changes from one of restrained virtuosity to that of unchallenged protagonist.

FOURTH MOVEMENT (ALLEGRO MARZIALE ANIMATO, 4:15) In a controlled series of gear changes, themes are brought back as pulses are inexorably raised.

MEPHISTO WALTZ NO. 1, S110/514

ORCHESTRAL   ⏱ 10:00   📖 1   🎵

Written first for orchestra and then arranged for piano, the programme for this work comes from Austrian poet Nikolaus Lenau's *Faust*, which differs from Goethe's play. In Lenau's version, Faust and Mephistopheles arrive at a tavern where, seeing a black-eyed beauty, Faust is overcome with reticence. Bored with the rustic music, Mephistopheles plays a diabolical waltz on the violin which inspires Faust and his inamorata to dance, and disappear into the woods…

A spectacular and daring concert piece, the devilish outer sections are tempered by a seductive core where the score explains that "they sink into the ocean of their own lust".

INFLUENCES

Whilst Liszt's codification of the possibilities of the piano influenced nearly every piano composer who followed him, only a few of his less important works were heard with any regularity after his death. Only in the 1960s was his music reassessed, and given its rightful place in the musical pantheon.

Michael William Balfe

● 1808–1870   ♫ Irish   ♪ c.300

A fine operatic baritone who impressed Rossini, Balfe found overnight success as a ballad opera composer in London with *The Siege of Rochelle* in 1835. His lasting fame as a composer rests on *The Bohemian Girl*, a huge box-office hit in London, and the only British opera of the 19th century to win an international reputation. In the 1850s Balfe toured Europe and was feted by Johann Strauss and, after further success in London, enjoyed a comfortable retirement at his country estate.

MILESTONES

1825	Sings at La Scala in Milan, Italy
1843	Opera *Le puits d'amour* succeeds in Paris; *The Bohemian Girl* performed
1827	Appears as Figaro in Rossini's *The Barber of Seville* in Paris

Adolf von Henselt

● 1814–1889   ♫ German   ♪ 65

Henselt made a rapid reputation as a composer of piano works; his studies, which were published regularly for more than 50 years across Europe, stretched technique on the instrument to new possibilities. He also found international fame as a Romantic-style virtuoso,

and was a friend of the Schumanns and Liszt. Henselt was, however, a reluctant performer, and instead became a highly respected music editor and teacher in Russia.

MILESTONES

1837	Piano works – 24 Studies, Op. 2 and Op. 5 – published
1838	Start of career in St Petersburg, where he teaches the royal family
1839	Composes Two Nocturnes, Op. 6
1847	Piano Concerto, Op. 16, published
1854	Ballade, Op. 31, composed for piano

Charles Valentin Alkan

● 1813–1888   ♫ French   ♪ c.100

Born Charles Henri Valentin Morhange, one of six Jewish children who all went on to become musicians, Alkan was a child prodigy, having his first compositions for piano published at age 14. During his youth he was a close friend of Chopin and Liszt, but over time he became reclusive and often disappeared for long spells. His concert appearances before 1873 were few, and although they established him as a virtuoso pianist, he preferred not to play his own compositions. His music is original, brilliant, and often hugely demanding – his Op. 39 includes a full "symphony" and "concerto", but scored for unaccompanied piano.

MILESTONES

1819	Enrolled in Paris Conservatoire
1838	*Le Chemin de Fer*, Op. 2, for piano
1847	25 Preludes, Op. 31, published
1857	Compiles 12 Études in all the Minor Keys, Op. 39
1860s	Disappears from public life
1873	Reappears to give concerts

Enrolled in the Paris Conservatoire at age six, Alkan won many prizes for his piano playing there, one of the most prestigious being the Conservatoire first prize for piano, which he won at age 11.

Henry Litolff

● 1818–1891 ♙ French ✍ 160

Primarily a performer and conductor, Litolff composed throughout his career. His four surviving piano concertos, No. 4 being the most popular, are grand and sweeping. His solo piano music – highly colourful, improvisatory, and ostentatious – reflected his life. Born in London to a French prisoner of war, from the age of 17 he toured Europe as a concert pianist. In 1851 he gave up performing and settled in Brunswick, Germany, where he bought a music publishing firm. He was soon travelling again, finally moving to Paris, where he spent the rest of his life.

MILESTONES

1849	Created Citizen of Brunswick
1852	Piano Concerto No. 4 published
1858	Finally settles in Paris

Charles François Gounod

● 1818–1893 ♙ French ✍ c.500

With his use of elegant harmonies and graceful melodies – such as in his enormously successful opera *Faust* – Gounod was a huge influence on Massenet, Bizet, and Saint-Saëns. A devout Catholic, he wrote 21 Masses, over 100 songs, and 12 operas. In the 1870s he sat out the Franco-Prussian War in England, where he began a relationship with a married woman, Georgina Weldon. Tiring of the public scandal which ensued, Gounod eventually returned to Paris alone.

MILESTONES

1852	Conducts Orphéon Choral Society
1858	Composes *Faust*, opera
1867	*Roméo et Juliette*, opera, performed
1886	*Mors et vita*, oratorio, performed for Queen Victoria in London

Henry Vieuxtemps

● 1820–1881 ♙ Belgian ✍ 80

Vieuxtemps was an eminent violin virtuoso and composer from an early age. He was adulated from America to Russia, and went on to write many brilliant chamber violin pieces and seven violin concertos. With up-to-date Romantic symphonic frameworks, these pieces filled a gap between the elegant, but old-fashioned, Classical works and the flashy showpieces of Paganini, and enjoyed great popularity in his lifetime.

MILESTONES

1828	First performs in Paris
1833	Tours Germany and Austria
1834	Meets Paganini in London
1840	Composes Violin Concerto No. 1
1846	Works for the Tsar in Russia
1861	Violin Concerto No. 5 composed
1871	Professor at Brussels Conservatory

Joachim Raff

● 1822–1882 ♙ Swiss ✍ c.250

Raff's career was set in motion in the 1840s with support from Mendelssohn and Liszt (who often helped him out of financial difficulties). Following an appointment at the Weimar court, he independently produced much of his

enormous output, which is extremely diverse. In the 1860s and 1870s, he was highly regarded as both a composer and a teacher – but accusations of quantity rather than quality, and arguments with employers, clouded his last years, and his reputation has since waned.

MILESTONES

1851	Composes *König Alfred*, opera
1856	Locates to Wiesbaden from Weimar
1864	Symphony No. 1
1871	Symphony No. 3, "Im Walde"
1878	Director of Frankfurt Conservatory

Clara Josephine Schumann

◗ 1819–1896   🏴 German   ✍ c.45

One of the great pianists of the 19th century, Clara Schumann (née Wieck) was among the first artists to present challenging programmes, of the highest musical quality, from memory. Both her husband, Robert, and close friend Brahms sought her music advice throughout their lives. Some of her own works were also highly regarded in her lifetime, but she believed that "a woman must not desire to compose".

LIFE AND MUSIC

Under her father's tuition, Clara Wieck became a great pianist, championing the music of Chopin, Schumann, and Brahms. She received widespread praise for her technique and bold repertoire, and for her thoughtful interpretations and pianistic singing tone, but marriage to Schumann, against her father's wishes, and numerous pregnancies curtailed her career. After Schumann's death she resumed touring and teaching, and also edited his music. Originally composing showpieces for her own concerts, her attitude to composition became increasingly ambivalent, and she wrote nothing after 1854. Clara's best work shows imagination and craftsmanship, but lacks melodic individuality. Her intimate friendship with Brahms is generally believed to have been platonic.

MILESTONES

1828	First public performance in Leipzig; meets Robert Schumann
1835	Composes *Piano Concerto*, Op. 7
1838	Appointed Kammervirtuosin to the Austrian court
1839	Writes *3 Romances*, Op. 11
1840	Marries Robert Schumann
1844	Tours Russia
1846	*Piano Trio*, Op. 17 published
1853	Writes *Songs from Jucunde*, Op. 23
1854	Schumann enters mental asylum,
1856	Schumann dies; first of 16 concert tours to England
1878	Appointed head of piano faculty, Hoch Conservatory, Frankfurt
1891	Last public performance

KEY WORKS

PIANO TRIO, OP. 17

CHAMBER	⏱ 29:00	📖 4	♟

Although she regularly played chamber music, this was Clara's first attempt at composing in the genre, and became her most frequently performed work. The instrumental writing encompasses a broad range of moods, from the rhythmically whimsical scherzo to the controlled tension of the Finale's fugato, which elicited the praise of Mendelssohn.

When Robert Schumann first heard Clara's charming *Romances* he wrote, "I can hear that we are destined to be man and wife. You complete me as a composer."

SONGS FROM JUCUNDE, OP. 23

POEM SETTINGS	⏱ 15:00	📖 6	🎵 ♟

Set to simple texts by the little-known Austrian poet Hermann Rollet, these vivid settings are probably Clara's finest work; the six songs, including "Geheimes Flüstern hier und dort" ("Secret Whisperings"), explore popular Romantic themes, such as love, melancholy, and mystery. Enjoying quite distinct roles, the piano and vocal lines frequently surprise the listener with quirky melodic and harmonic twists seldom heard in her output.

César Auguste Franck

● 1822–1890   ⚑ Belgian   ♫ 97

Franck's rejection of the frivolous and spectacular music of his contemporaries, in favour of symphonic and instrumental forms of high seriousness, strongly influenced successive generations of French composers. A late developer compositionally, his finest works – notable for their rich Wagner-inspired harmonies, innovative structures, and noble lyricism – were all written in his final years.

LIFE AND MUSIC

Franck toured Belgium as a pianist at the age of 11, but in maturity concentrated on composition. He later attracted considerable fame as an organist, and was subsequently appointed professor of the organ at the Paris Conservatoire, where his lofty music ideals inspired a group of young composers, including d'Indy and Dukas. A deeply religious man, he composed numerous sacred works, but his true legacy lies in the orchestral, keyboard, and

MILESTONES

1837	Enrols at the Paris Conservatoire
1846	First performance of a large-scale work, biblical oratorio *Ruth*
1848	Marries actress Félicité Desmousseaux
1861	Appointed organist at Sainte-Clothilde Church, Paris
1862	First important work, *6 Pièces*, organ
1880	First performance of Piano Quintet, and *Les Béatitudes*, oratorio
1884	*Prelude, Chorale, and Fugue* published
1885	Writes Variations Symphonique
1886	Composes Violin Sonata in A major

When Eugene Ysaÿe first performed Franck's Violin Sonata in Brussels, the room was so dark he had to play from memory.

chamber works written in the last years of his life. Harmonically rich, but based on traditional forms, these include some of the greatest French music of the Romantic period.

KEY WORKS

PRELUDE, CHORALE, AND FUGUE
SOLO PIANO   ⏱ 18:40   📖 3   🎵

Franck's organ-loft is never far away from this noble work. The improvisatory Prelude leads directly into a chaste Chorale, where the octave bass line imitates the organ's pedals. From this emerges the implacable Fugue, which climaxes with the return of the theme from the Chorale, before ending joyfully in the major key.

VIOLIN SONATA
VIOLIN/PIANO   ⏱ 27:00   📖 4   ⚏

Written as a wedding gift for Franck's countryman, the violinist Eugene Ysaÿe, this is one of the most popular Romantic violin sonatas. Arranged over four very different movements, Franck uses his own innovation, known as cyclic form, to unify the whole by bringing back the transformed opening theme in subsequent movements.

VARIATIONS SYMPHONIQUES
ORCHESTRAL   ⏱ 15:40   📖 1   🎼🎵

Often regarded as Franck's masterpiece, this set of six variations and a Finale form one of the most beautiful and compact piano concertos in the repertoire. Ranging from melancholy lyricism to glittering elegance, the solo part is sufficiently restrained to allow the piano and orchestra to be fully equal partners.

"Bruckner! He is my man!"

RICHARD WAGNER

Anton Bruckner

1824–1896 ♙ Austrian ✍ 36

Anton Bruckner was an important figure in the development of the symphony. Although a Romantic composer, he made use of, and expanded, Classical structures such as sonata form in his symphonies, and he was particularly influenced by the work of Wagner. Bruckner was also an organist, and in addition to the composition of nine symphonies, he produced a number of instrumental and sacred choral works.

LIFE

Born in Ansfelden, Austria, in 1824, Bruckner was largely self-taught as a composer. He was very dedicated and also worked as an organist, often practising for 12 hours a day. His first job as an organist was at St Florian's Monastery near Ansfelden in 1851, and he later went on to Linz Cathedral, where he worked from 1856 to 1868. He was a very religious man and his first surviving work is the *Requiem Mass*, written in 1849. Bruckner was from a peasant background and he had a strong provincial accent that was looked down upon in cosmopolitan Vienna. He was also a rather solitary figure and was reluctant to explain or discuss his music with others. However, his musical outlook was very modern for its time, and he took on many of the harmonic innovations of Wagner, a move that was held against him by many critics loyal to the more conservative figure of Brahms. His three Mass settings and Symphony No. 1 were all written during his tenure at Linz, and in 1868 he became court organist and a teacher at the Vienna Conservatory. He went on to write eight more symphonies, in addition to a number of other sacred works and substantial pieces for organ, piano, and choir. His Symphony No. 9 was left incomplete on his death in 1896.

A devout Catholic born in rural Austria, Bruckner produced works that were at once solemn and transcendent.

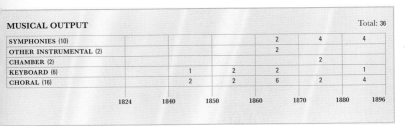

MUSICAL OUTPUT							Total: 36
SYMPHONIES (10)					2	4	4
OTHER INSTRUMENTAL (2)					2		
CHAMBER (2)						2	
KEYBOARD (6)			1	2	2		1
CHORAL (16)			2	2	6	2	4
	1824	1840	1850	1860	1870	1880	1896

MUSIC

Bruckner's music in many ways bridges the stylistic gap between early and late Romantic music, paving the way for major later figures such as Mahler and Sibelius. In his symphonies he relied on many Classical structures (including sonata form) and Baroque techniques, but he expanded the length and harmonic range of themes and the extent of their development. Bruckner's music is particularly unusual for the long durations of its sections and movements, although this allowed him to achieve a great subtlety in form, with many sections containing a number of related subsections. This, together with an often gradual rate of change, lends the music its famous transcendent or "otherworldly" quality. Bruckner's international reputation has grown enormously in recent decades and his works are particular favourites of many conductors and orchestras.

MILESTONES	
1837	Sent to St Florian's Monastery near Ansfelden; becomes choir boy
1849	*Requiem Mass*
1851	Organist at St Florian's Monastery
1856	Organist at Linz Cathedral, Austria
1861	Makes first concert appearance as composer at Linz
1864	Composes Mass No. 1 in D minor
1865	Hears *Tristan und Isolde* in Munich; becomes devoted Wagnerian
1866	Mass No. 2 in E minor
1866	Writes Symphony No. 1
1867	Mass No. 3 in F minor
1868	Becomes court organist and teacher at the Vienna Conservatory
1873	Symphony No. 3 first performed in Vienna
1887	Composes Symphony No. 8
1891	Receives honorary doctorate from the University of Vienna
1896	Dies while working on Symphony No. 9

KEY WORKS

MASS NO. 1 IN D MINOR

MASS   🔊 43:50   📖 6   🎵🎹

This Mass has quite symphonic proportions and the accompanying orchestra has a prominence reminiscent of Mozart and Haydn. Another principle that Bruckner took from the Classical era is that of cyclic form, and here themes from earlier movements are used in the Agnus

Bruckner studied at the Augustinian Abbey Church of St Florian, Austria as a boy and he went on to become organist in 1851.

Dei, the final movement. Inspired by Wagner's *Tannhäuser*, this work represents Bruckner's first piece as a fully mature composer.

SYMPHONY NO. 3

ORCHESTRAL   🔊 1:00:00   📖 4   🎵

This work is often known as Bruckner "Wagner" Symphony. The earliest version (of 1873) contained a number of quotations of Wagner's music and many remained in the published score of 1890. Two extra-musical ideas also appear in this piece. The first is the slow, dance-like theme in the Adagio that was written as an elegy for Bruckner's mother. The other concerns his view of the opposing factors of life. The humourous Polka and solemn Chorale recall an evening that he spent in Vienna when he heard dance music issuing from the house where the architect Schmidt lay in his coffin.

SYMPHONY NO. 9

ORCHESTRAL 🕮 60:30 📖 3 🎵

This piece, Bruckner's last, has a quality of isolation and intense spirituality that is not present in his other works. The chromaticism and dissonance are further heightened by the lack of an affirmative ending (the work is unfinished), which contributes to its dark and foreboding quality.

FIRST MOVEMENT (FEIERLICH, MISTERIOSO, 23:30) Literally meaning "ceremonious" or "dignified", the verbal direction of "Feierlich" captures the essence of the grand unfolding of this large-scale movement. It has an unusual ending, being in neither a major nor a minor key.

SECOND MOVEMENT (SCHERZO: BEWEGT, LEBHAFT; TRIO: SCHNELL, 10:15) The Scherzo reasserts the original key of D minor, but it has an unsettled, menacing quality. Its insistent, driving rhythm contrasts with sudden areas of light diversion. The Trio retains some of the mood of the Scherzo but has an additional sinister quality to it.

THIRD MOVEMENT (ADAGIO: LANGSAM, FEIERLICH, 26:45) Echoing Wagner and anticipating Mahler, this movement's opening theme has a searching quality, finally settling in the movement's key of E major, by way of unrelated keys such as D major. This expansive opening echoes the wide span of the first movement.

TE DEUM

CHORAL 🕮 23:15 📖 5 🎵 🎵 🎺 🎵

This work of 1884 shares many qualities with Bruckner's Masses of the 1860s and was one of his favourite pieces. The Latin title is taken from the first line of the text "Te Deum laudamus" ("We praise thee, o God"). The work is scored for the forces of solo soprano, contralto, tenor, and bass, a four-part choir, orchestra, and optional organ.

TE DEUM LAUDAMUS (6:30) The opening ostinato theme provides a driving motion also found in the Mass in F minor and the Symphony No. 9.

TE ERGO (3:00) This movement begins with a lyrical tenor solo, contrasting with the dynamic first movement.

AETERNA FAC (1:30) Scored for the full chorus, without soloists, this section ("Aeterna fac cum sanctis tuis in gloria numerai", or "Make us to be numbered with Thy saints in glory everlasting") re-establishes the opening drama.

SALVUM FAC (7:00) Here the composer once again establishes a calm, slow movement, accompanied by very sparing use of the orchestra, before launching into a forceful development section that uses the original motive from the beginning.

IN TE, DOMINE (5:15) This final movement opens with the four soloists together before the grand entrance of the chorus, which by way of a very inventive canonic section reminiscent of Mozart leads the work to its triumphal conclusion.

INFLUENCES

Bruckner's historical position is of great importance. Incorporating the thematic developments of Liszt and the harmonic boldness of Wagner with the Classical principles of Haydn and Mozart, he laid the groundwork for many later figures. Schoenberg's early style owes a lot to Bruckner via his teacher, Mahler.

"Without craftsmanship, inspiration is a mere reed shaken in the wind."

JOHANNES BRAHMS

ohannes Brahms

' 1833–1897   ♫ German   ✍ 135

rahms is a towering figure in 19th-century music, perhaps the last great
omposer in the Classical tradition. Once regarded as the unfashionable
ntithesis of Wagner and Liszt, his music has proven itself to be not
nly powerfully affecting, but also an important influence on the
evelopment of 20th-century music. A sometimes difficult,
ncompromising man, he composed
nasterpieces in all genres except opera.

LIFE

orn to a poor family in Hamburg, Brahms
nowed early promise as a musician. From
round the age of 13, however, he made
xtra income for the family by playing in
ars and houses of ill repute. Attempting
o make a career as a pianist, in 1853
rahms toured with the violinist Eduard
eményi and during the trip he made
ree of the most important acquaintances
f his life: the violinist Joseph Joachim, the
omposer Robert Schumann, and the latter's wife, Clara,
erself a renowned pianist. Schumann was so impressed
ith Brahms's compositions that he wrote a glowing article
roclaiming him to be Beethoven's heir. This gave Brahms's
areer an immediate boost, but heaped expectation upon
im. When Schumann suffered a breakdown the following
ear, Brahms went to Düsseldorf to help Clara and her
umily. He fell deeply in love with her, and the nature of their
elationship after Schumann died has been a source of great
peculation. They were undoubtedly intimate friends, and
rahms entrusted Clara with the first reading of many of
is greatest works. Brahms was famously abrasive and often
nade tactless remarks; however, this hid a sensitive and
noughtful character who could be very generous with his
me (and money), and inspired great loyalty from his friends.

Though the music of
Brahms was rooted in
the Classicism of past
masters, its expressive
and gigantic nature was
Romantic at its core.

MUSICAL OUTPUT					Total: 135
SYMPHONIES (4)				2	2
CONCERTOS (4)		1		2	1
CHAMBER (17)		4	5	4	4
PIANO MUSIC (24)		10	4	6	4
OTHER INSTRUMENTAL (15)		2	2	5	6
CHORAL (39)		17	6	9	7
SONGS (32)		5	9	9	9
	1833	1853	1863	1873	1883 1897

MUSIC

Brahms is often considered to be the last great composer in the Germanic Classical tradition, which stretches back through Beethoven, Mozart, and Haydn to Bach. At a time when the trend in composition was towards programmatic music, Brahms pointedly refused to see himself as a "modern" composer. Instead, he stuck to the Classical forms used by the masters and often spoke of the pressure he felt composing in their shadow. This dichotomy between Brahms's Classicism and the "progressive" music of Wagner, Liszt, and Bruckner has (for better or worse) become a key theme in 19th-century music history. But, as Schoenberg first showed in a now infamous essay titled "Brahms the progressive", Brahms's music was nonetheless extremely innovative. The key to his innovation is the so-called "developing variation", the constant reworking of small fragments of musical material as a composition progresses. This is epitomized in late

The influence of violinist Joseph Joachim led Brahms to include Hungarian folk rhythms in some of his work. Joachim also introduced Brahms to the Schumanns.

works such as the Clarinet Quintet, in which virtually every note can be seen as deriving from the opening bar. This style of writing paved the way for music in which every aspect of a composition arises from the same thematic cell. For all this, it is the *sound* of Brahms' music that has assured its place in history. Rarely rhetorical, it is frequently described as "autumnal" – passionate and romantic, yet controlled, refined, and infused with melancholy

MILESTONES

Brahms spent his adolescence in and around the docks of Hamburg, where he made money in taverns and brothels performing piano tricks for the locals.

1845	Studies piano with Otto Cossel and theory with Edward Marxsen
1853	Concert tour with Reményi; meets Joachim and the Schumanns; Robert Schumann writes a glowing review
1954	Schumann institutionalized; Brahms moves to Düsseldorf to help Clara
1857	Composes Piano Concerto No.1, Op. 15
1863	Director of the Vienna Singakademie
1867	Composes *Ein Deutches Requiem*, Op. 45
1868	Settles permanently in Vienna
1872	Conductor of the Vienna Gesellschaftskonzerte
1876	Writes Symphony No. 1, Op. 68
1877	Symphony No. 2, Op. 78
1878	Violin Concerto, Op. 77
1881	Piano Concerto No.2, Op. 83
1883	Symphony No. 3, Op. 90
1885	Symphony No. 4, Op. 98
1887	Writes Double Concerto for Violin and Cello, Op. 102
1889	Awarded freedom of the city of Hamburg
1890	String Quintet, Op. 111, which he vows will be his final work
1891	Hears clarinettist Richard Mühlfeld and writes Clarinet Quintet Op. 115 and Clarinet Trio Op. 114.
1896	Clara Schumann dies; composes *Vier Ernste Gesange*, Op. 121

KEY WORKS

SYMPHONY NO. 1, OP. 68

ORCHESTRAL   🕭 50:00   📖 4

Brahms had often spoken of hearing the "footsteps" of Beethoven behind him, and this self-imposed expectation is perhaps the reason it took him so long to write his first symphony (he began the work in 1862, but did not complete it until 1876). Immediately dubbed "Beethoven's Tenth", its lineage is plain to hear, but it is an epic and individual work.

VARIATIONS ON A THEME BY HANDEL, OP. 24

PIANO SOLO   🕭 27:00   📖 27

Like Beethoven before him, Brahms was attracted to the variation form and wrote several sets of variations on themes from other composers. The "Handel Variations", based on an air from one of Handel's keyboard suites, are perhaps his most appealing.

PIANO QUARTET NO. 1, OP. 25

CHAMBER   🕭 40:00   📖 4

Brahms appeared as pianist in the premiere of his first piano quartet, the first time he had presented himself as such to a Viennese audience. A stormy, passionate, and youthful work, it displays typical Brahmsian hallmarks, particularly in the way that material is derived from the opening 4-note figure.

INFLUENCES

In one sense, Brahms was the last "Classical" composer, even in his own time viewed by some as an anachronism. Composers such as Dvořák and Reger were directly influenced by his music, although his indirect influence on the development of 20th century music, through the advocacy of Schoenberg, is perhaps more significant.

VIOLIN CONCERTO, OP. 77

ORCHESTRAL   🕭 38:00   📖 3

Brahms wrote this concerto for his great friend Joseph Joachim. It is a large-scale work, ferociously difficult for the violin soloist.

SYMPHONY NO. 4, OP. 98

ORCHESTRAL   🕭 42:00   📖 4

Perhaps lacking the melodic appeal of his earlier symphonies, this work has a rugged charm that epitomizes Brahms's own character. A critic once described hearing the first movement as akin to "being beaten by two very clever men".

VIER ERNSTE GESANGE, OP. 121

SONGS   🕭 20:00   📖 4

Brahms's contribution to the Lieder tradition is often overlooked, if only because his legacy is so significant elsewhere. In fact Brahms wrote a great many songs, of which the *Four Serious Songs*, composed as a response to the death of Clara Schumann, are perhaps his most affecting.

Many of the piano works of Brahms, from the solo pieces to the concertos, have been performed or recorded by the young Russian pianist Evgeny Kissin.

FOCUS

CLARINET QUINTET, OP. 115

CHAMBER ♟ 36:00 📖 4 ♔

On completing the String Quintet No. 2 in 1890, Brahms resolved to retire from composition. However, inspired by the playing of clarinettist Richard Mühlfeld the following year, he wrote both the Clarinet Trio and the Clarinet Quintet. The Quintet has come to be seen as his very finest chamber work.

FIRST MOVEMENT (ALLEGRO, 12:00) All the melodic material in this sonata-form movement stems from the opening theme, presented by the two violins.

SECOND MOVEMENT (ADAGIO, 12:00) The Adagio begins with a peaceful clarinet melody. The central section is a remarkable imitation of Hungarian folk music, with wild arpeggios.

THIRD MOVEMENT
(ANDANTINO – PRESTO NON ASSAI, MA CON SENTIMENTO, 4:00) The third movement begins as an intermezzo, but quickly reveals itself to be a lively sonata-form movement based on a scurrying figure introduced by the violins.

FOURTH MOVEMENT (CON MOTO, 8:00) After the dark and unsettled theme is explored in five variations, the opening phrase from the first movement makes a dramatic and unexpected return, giving a sense of finality.

SYMPHONY NO. 3, OP. 90

ORCHESTRAL ♟ 33:00 📖 4 ♫

The most compact of his symphonies and perhaps the most immediately

accessible, in Brahms' lifetime the popularity of his Symphony No. 3 was such that the composer took to describing it as "unfortunately over-famous".

Although Brahms was seen as old-fashioned by admirers of Wagner and Liszt, he was highly regarded by many of his peers.

EIN DEUTCHES REQUIEM, OP. 45

BIBLICAL SETTING ♟ 70:00 📖 7 ♫♬♪

A German Requiem, first performed in its complete form in 1868, made Brahms's reputation in Vienna, and remains one of his most consistently popular works. Rather than use the standard Requiem texts, Brahms chose his own passages from the Lutheran bible, avoiding reference to Christianity and – notably – omitting the Last Judgement entirely. Although a believer, he was not overtly religious and later said that he would have liked to replace the word "German" with "Human" in the title. This has led some writers to suggest that the real motivation for the work was an expression of his pain at the deaths of his mother and of Robert Schumann.

PART SIX AND SEVEN

6 "Denn wir haben hie keine bleibende Statt" ("For here have we no continuing city"). Andante; Quadruple time; C minor: Quasi-fugal form

Second section (Vivace) starts with choir and full orchestra

Sopranos enter

First Section				Second Section				Third Section			
1	2	3	4	5	6	7	8	9	10	11	12

Choir accompanied by basses and cellos, playing pizzicato

Timpani roll followed by baritone solo

Timpani announce baritone solo

Third section (Allegro) is a fugue. Altos begin, accompanied by clarinets and followed by sopranos, basses, and finally tenors

RST MOVEMENT (ALLEGRO CON BRIO, :00) As is so common with rahms, the key to the whole novement is in the first few bars. he majestic first theme has been seen y some critics as a direct reference o Schumann's Symphony No. 3.

ECOND MOVEMENT (ANDANTE, 8:00) The mple folk-like theme of the second novement spoke to Clara Schumann f "worshippers neeling about heir little orest shrine".

THIRD MOVEMENT (POCO ALLEGRETTO, 6:00) One of Brahms's most beautiful creations, the heart-wrenching theme appears first on cello before returning after the sombre Trio section, now on the French horn.

FOURTH MOVEMENT (ALLEGRO, 9:00) The Finale begins in brooding fashion before more animated development leads eventually to a quiet, satisfying close, replete with ghostly hints of the first movement's opening theme.

he German equiem contains ome of the omposer's nost haunting and poignant music. he fourth part, "Wie schön sind eine Wohnungen" ("How Lovely are ny Dwellings Fair") is the emotional ore of the work, with the remaining x parts forming a huge arch ructure around it. The final part,

Brahms chose his own text for *Ein Deutsches Requiem*, which was scribbled on a page of manuscript.

"Selig sind die Toten" ("Blessed are the Dead") recalls material from the first to give a sense of closure. By making use of choral fugues (in the second and sixth parts), Brahms deliberately evokes the spirit of Bach's sacred choral works.

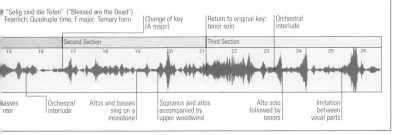

"Selig sind die Toten" ("Blessed are the Dead"). Feierlich; Quadruple time; F major: Ternary form

| Change of key (A major) | | Return to original key; tenor solo | | Orchestral interlude |

Second Section					Third Section					
15	16	17	18	19	20	21	22	23	24	25	26

| Basses nter | Orchestral interlude | Altos and basses sing on a monotone | Sopranos and altos accompanied by upper woodwind | Alto solo followed by tenors | Imitation between vocal parts |

"I am Russian in the completest possible sense of that word."

TCHAIKOVSKY IN A LETTER TO MME VON MECK, 1878

Pyotr Ilyich Tchaikovsky

 1840–1893   Russian   159

Tchaikovsky's intensely emotional music combines many influences in an individual style: Russian folk song with Western European technique; nationalism with a deeply personal agenda; the bombastic with the haunting and beautiful. The effects of the composer's homosexuality on his music and the mystery surrounding his death still cause speculation and controversy, but his music remains perennially popular.

LIFE

A sensitive and highly strung boy, Tchaikovsky was born into a large middle-class family in provincial Russia. After law school in St Petersburg, he became a civil servant, studying music privately but showing only average ability. However, he left his job to concentrate on music at St Petersburg Conservatory, and during five years under Anton Rubinstein his technique progressed rapidly. He moved to Moscow to teach and enjoyed celebrity in artistic and homosexual circles. At the age of 37 he entered into a platonic marriage of convenience with an infatuated student, Antonina Milyukova, but the effects that this had on his emotional state and his ability to compose were so destructive that they separated after two months. For the next 14 years Tchaikovsky corresponded with Nadezhda von Meck, a wealthy widow and lover of his music, who became his financial supporter (though by mutual agreement they intentionally never met). Nevertheless, by his early 50s Tchaikovsky was ill, depressed, and facing his own mortality. The official version of his death was that he absent-mindedly drank unboiled water and died of cholera, while a recent theory suggests he poisoned himself on pain of exposure for a homosexual scandal, but neither idea is very convincing.

Though a master of many forms of musical composition, Tchaikovsky is perhaps best known for his romantic ballets.

MUSICAL OUTPUT							Total: 159
ORCHESTRAL (47)		8	15	12	7	5	
CHAMBER (7)		1	3	2		1	
PIANO MUSIC (31)		5	12	6	2	6	
DRAMATIC (25)		1	11	4	4	5	
VOCAL (49)		7	14	11	8	9	
	1840	1850	1860	1870	1880	1890	1893

MUSIC

Critics were divided by Tchaikovsky's early work (his Violin Concerto and Piano Concerto No. 1 received very unfavourable reviews), but it was clear from the beginning that he could write "masterpieces" (such as his Symphony No. 6 and *The Queen of Spades*). Some of his music seems to reflect his life: in *Eugene Onegin*, the fifth of his ten operas, the "Letter scene" has Tatyana declaring her love to Onegin by letter,

Still displaying his piano and various personal effects, this is the house in Klin, near Moscow, where Tchaikovsky spent the final year of his life.

just as Antonina did to Tchaikovsky (though Onegin declines). Following on, the despair at Fate in his Symphony No. 4 is a commentary on his state of mind during the disastrous marriage that resulted, whereas his freewheeling orchestral suites evoke his sense of freedom during the travelling years after his separation. However, this idea is all too easy to overplay. The influence of Schumann and Beethoven, as well as Glinka, can be heard in Tchaikovsky's orchestral music, and there is often a strong sense of a psychological programme in which motto themes undergo transformation (as in the last three symphonies); he also made extensive use of folk tunes (especially in his Symphony No. 2, the "Little Russian"). His Violin Concerto and the first of his three concertos for piano are familiar showpieces that stretch the performer to the limit, while his three ballets – *Swan Lake*, *The Sleeping Beauty*, and *Nutcracker* – show off his trademark lusciously-scored melodies.

MILESTONES

1865	Appointed professor of harmony at new Moscow Conservatory
1866	Symphony No. 1, Op. 13, composed
1869	*Voyevoda*, Op. 3, opera, produced; *Fatum*, Op. 77, for orchestra, performed; begins *Romeo and Juliet* overture
1873	Symphony No. 2, Op. 17, performed in Moscow to great success
1874	*The Oprichnik*, opera, produced; String Quartet No. 2, Op. 22, and Piano Concerto No. 1, Op. 35, composed
1875	Piano Concerto No. 1, Op. 35, premiered in Boston, US; Symphony No. 3, Op. 29, premiered Moscow
1876	Begins correspondence with Nadezhda von Meck
1877	*Swan Lake* produced; begins Symphony No. 4 and *Eugene Onegin*; starts eight years of international travel
1878	Violin Concerto, Op. 35, composed; Symphony No. 4 and *Eugene Onegin*, Op. 24 completed

1880	*1812 Overture*, Op. 49 written
1881	Violin Concerto, Op. 35, premiered in Vienna, to terrible reviews
1890	*The Sleeping Beauty* produced in St Petersburg; *The Queen of Spades*, Op. 68 composed, premiered triumphantly; *Souvenir de Florence*, Op. 70 composed
1892	The ballet *Nutcracker*, Op. 71, produced

The Bolshoy Zal (Great Hall) in the Moscow Conservatory, where Tchaikovsky was made Professor of Harmony in 1865.

KEY WORKS

1812 OVERTURE, OP. 49

ORCHESTRAL 🎵 16:00 📖 1 ⚏

The "Solemn Overture" was composed in 1880 for the consecration of Moscow's Cathedral of Christ the Saviour, built in thanks for the Russian victory over Napoleon in 1812.

VIOLIN CONCERTO, OP. 35

CONCERTO 🎵 37:00 📖 3 ⚏ 🎵

Denounced as "unviolinistic" by early players and "stinking music" by critics, this noble, virtuosic showpiece injects Russian passion into the "Euro-style" concerto with hugely successful results.

PIANO CONCERTO NO. 1, OP. 23

CONCERTO 🎵 35:00 📖 3 ⚏ 🎵

Ukrainian folk themes, French song, a grand opening tune that promptly disappears, occasionally inexpert piano writing – it seemed an unsuccessful mix to potential performers, but proved another winner after its triumphant premiere.

SOUVENIR DE FLORENCE, OP. 70

CHAMBER 🎵 35:00 📖 4 ⚏

The unusual scoring – two violins, two violas, two cellos – gave Tchaikovsky problems, but he ended up producing a lyrical and warm masterpiece. Despite the title (recalling his Italian holidays), the work is richly Russian in character.

Rudolf Nureyev made his debut in the West performing *The Sleeping Beauty*. Written in 1889, it was Tchaikovsky's first successful ballet.

NUTCRACKER, OP. 71

BALLET 🎵 102:00 📖 2 ⚏

Tchaikovsky acknowledged that *Nutcracker* was twee compared to *The Sleeping Beauty*, but his setting of Hoffman's fairy tale has proved better box office, thanks to effects such as the Sugar Plum Fairy's celesta.

THE QUEEN OF SPADES, OP. 68

OPERA 🎵 170:00 📖 3 ⚏ ⚏ ⚏

Tragedy is literally on the cards in this rich, dense masterpiece, which hints at Mozart, Bizet, Orthodox music, Russian folk, French song, and more, yet remains a cohesive, powerful whole.

SYMPHONY NO. 6, OP. 74

ORCHESTRAL 🎵 45:00 📖 4 ⚏

Tchaikovsky's dark, despairing farewell – possibly an attempt to confront his demons – was prophetically named "Pathétique" by his brother Modest. The second movement's love "waltz" has an undanceable five beats.

INFLUENCES

Tchaikovsky greatly encouraged the young Rachmaninov, but his heartfelt style soon became old-fashioned outside Russia as composers looked for a more radical language. However, his popularity with audiences has remained consistent: many of his works are cornerstones of the Romantic repertoire, constantly performed and recorded.

FOCUS

EUGENE ONEGIN, OP. 24

OPERA ⏱ 140:00 📖 3 ♫ ♫ ♫ ♫

Completed in 1878, and based on a verse novel by Pushkin, this story of a bored, Byronic young aristocrat's desultory and damaging love affairs constantly reminds us that "real life is not like a novel"; yet its "Letter Scene" eerily reflects the composer's own personal struggles at the time.

Themes (including pre-Revolutionary Russia, town versus country, social convention, and death of inspiration) abound in this enduring opera, which in many ways is "about" Tatiana, the only character who grows, rather than the superficial, irredeemable Onegin. **ACT ONE** (65:00) Russia, c.1820. Eugene Onegin, having inherited his uncle's country estate outside St Petersburg,

SYMPHONY NO. 4 IN F MINOR, OP. 36

ORCHESTRAL ⏱ 46:00 📖 4 ♫ ♫

Begun in 1877 before his marriage and finished the following year after his separation, the symphony is an emotional diary in music.
FIRST MOVEMENT (ANDANTE, 18:00) An ominous brass fanfare, denoting fate, is followed by a string theme

reminiscent of decisive moments in Bizet's *Carmen*. The composer's comment on the recurrence of the fanfare was: "All life is an unbroken alternation of hard reality and swiftly passing dreams of happiness."
SECOND MOVEMENT (ANDANTINO, 12:00) A lament for oboe becomes a warmly nostalgic string theme, which passes through noble desperation to a quietly resigned conclusion.

FIRST MOVEMENT

1 Introduction: Andante sostenuto; Triple time; F minor; Sonata form

Moderato con anima (in movimento di valse)

Third subject introduced by violins in B major

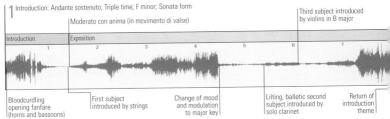

Introduction	Exposition					
1	2	3	4	5	6	7

Bloodcurdling opening fanfare (horns and bassoons)

First subject introduced by strings

Change of mood and modulation to major key

Lilting, balletic second subject introduced by solo clarinet

Return of introduction theme

is introduced by his poet friend Lensky to the Larin sisters: the flighty Olga, and the brooding, novel-reading Tatiana. Tatiana declares her love for Onegin by letter, but he brushes her off.

ACT TWO (40:00) Onegin, provoking his hot-headed friend takes Lensky's beloved Olga to a ball. A duel inevitably results, in which Onegin kills Lensky.

ACT THREE (35:00) Onegin falls in love with Tatiana, who is now married to his cousin Prince Gremin. She still loves him but stays with her husband, suspecting that her attraction is now only as a challenge.

SWAN LAKE, OP. 20

BALLET 🎵 140:00 📖 4

After its unsuccessful Moscow premiere in 1877, *Swan Lake* was revised in 1895, two years after Tchaikovsky's death. That version, with choreography by Petipa and

THIRD MOVEMENT (SCHERZO, 6:00) After the lament of the second movement recedes, the sprightly scherzo features pizzicato strings alternating with flocks of jaunty woodwind and brass in a good-natured jumble.

Ivanov, to a tighter libretto by Tchaikovsky's brother Modest (complete with happier ending), is the basis of the ballet we know today.

ACT ONE (50:00) At the royal palace, Prince Siegfried celebrates his coming-of-age. Various dances entertain the party to now-familiar themes, and a flight of swans appears, marked by the main oboe melody of the ballet.

ACT TWO (30:00) At a moonlit lakeside, Siegfried and friends are hunting swans, denoted by the oboe melody. However, one swan – Odette – tells him she is a woman, turned into a swan by the evil magician Rotbart.

ACT THREE (45:00) At the royal castle, Siegfried has to choose a wife at a ball, entertained by various dances. He thinks he sees Odette there, but she is actually Odile, Rotbart's daughter. Siegfried dances with her and nominates her as his bride, spelling doom for Odette.

ACT FOUR (15:00) Back at the lake, Odette is about to die – but Siegfried battles with Rotbart, breaks the spell and is reunited with her, as the swan theme triumphantly reappears.

This cartoon by Franklin McMahon shows Sir Georg Solti conducting Tchaikovsky's Symphony No. 4 with the Chicago Symphony Orchestra.

FOURTH MOVEMENT (ALLEGRO CON FUOCO, 10:00) A hectic, clattering theme is contrasted with variations on a Russian children's song about hopeful brides ("In the field a little birch tree stood"), evidently a reference to Antonina. The work ends in boisterous determination.

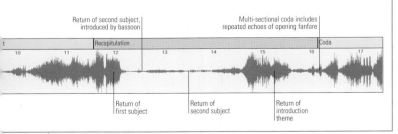

Return of second subject, introduced by bassoon

Multi-sectional coda includes repeated echoes of opening fanfare

Recapitulation

Coda

| 10 | 11 | 12 | 13 | 14 | 15 | 16 | 17 |

Return of first subject

Return of second subject

Return of introduction theme

"*The symphony must be like the world.
It must embrace everything.*"

GUSTAV MAHLER, 1907

Gustav Mahler

1860–1911 🏳 **Austrian** ✍ **18**

Known chiefly as a conductor in his short lifetime, (he directed the Vienna Opera for ten years), Mahler composed in his spare time. His large-scale songs with orchestra and nine epic, intense, emotionally exhausting symphonies, (plus beginnings of a tenth), are among the most recorded and performed of the repertoire. He is now seen as a link between the 19th-century Austro-German tradition and 20th-century Modernism.

LIFE

Mahler was born to a large German-speaking Jewish family in Bohemia, factors which made him feel a lifelong outsider. His father was a rough but successful man in the liquor trade. Mahler's musical talent showed early: he gave local recitals at ten and, at 15, he entered the Vienna Conservatory, soon winning prizes for piano and composition. Gradually he developed an international reputation as a conductor as he progressed – despite quarrels with authority en route – through Kassel, Prague, Leipzig, Budapest, and Hamburg, before ten years at the Vienna Opera and finally four in New York. An innovator in opera presentation, especially in Wagner, he was a demanding conductor, disliked by some musicians and respected by others. He suffered institutional anti-semitism, despite converting nominally to Catholicism in Vienna. At 41, he met 22-year-old Alma Schindler and married her four months later, ordering her to give up her composing ambitions to raise the two daughters she soon produced. However, one died aged six. That year, Mahler was diagnosed with a serious heart condition, drastically curtailing his beloved walking, swimming, and cycling. Alma's affair in 1910 with the the architect, Walter Gropius, (whom she eventually married), destroyed Mahler, who was now enjoying recognition as a composer. Six months later he contracted a serious blood infection of which he died.

Successful in his career because of his driving ambition, Mahler exacted the highest standards of music-making in both himself and others.

MUSICAL OUTPUT						Total: 18
SYMPHONIES (10)		1	2	5	2	
CANTATAS (1)		1				
SONGS (7)	1	2	1	2	1	
	1860	1880	1888	1897	1907	1911

MUSIC

Apart from lost student chamber works, Mahler's output is virtually all symphony and song; though an outstanding opera conductor, he completed none of the three he started. His style is late-Romantic, but he expanded the orchestra both in sound and size (his Symphony No. 8 requires 1,000 participants). However, what marks out a Mahler symphony is more theatrical: the feeling of many voices at work and a sequence of events. There is often an atmosphere of tension and fin-de-siècle angst contrasted with love and joy; Mahler consulted with Freud, and a strong psychoanalytical – some say self-pitying – aspect runs through much of his music. Sarcasm, parody, and irony abound in Mahler's mix of the sublime and the ridiculous, which may explain the popularity of his symphonies in the "knowing" era of the late 20th century.

MILESTONES	
1875	Enters Vienna Conservatory
1880	First conducting experience; completes cantata *Das klagende Lied*
1884	Starts Symphony No. 1
1888	Music director, Budapest opera; starts Symphony No. 2
1891	Starts conducting at Hamburg
1897	Starts at Vienna Hofoper
1901	Begins Symphony No. 5; meets Alma Schindler
1902	Marries Alma; finishes Symphony No. 5
1905	Song cycle *Kindertotenlieder* first performed
1906	Begins Symphony No. 8, the "Symphony of a Thousand"
1907	Daughter Maria dies; takes post at Metropolitan Opera, New York
1909	Completes song-symphony *Das Lied von der Erde*
1910	Finishes Symphony No. 9; learns of Alma's affair

KEY WORKS

SYMPHONY NO. 8

ORCHESTRAL ⏱ 75:00 📖 21

The "Symphony of a Thousand" (1,030 performers were needed to play in the 1910 premiere) is a tribute to enlightenment and divine love, orchestrated for eight solo singers, massive choir, and large orchestra. The first part is a setting of Latin religious texts, the second is set to the conclusion of Goethe's drama *Faust*.

SYMPHONY NO. 9

ORCHESTRAL ⏱ 70:00 📖 3

Like Beethoven and Bruckner, Mahler died jinxed on nine numbered symphonies; his last – in many ways an extension of *Das Lied von der Erde* – was finished in 1910 and not performed until after he died.

KINDERTOTENLIEDER

SONG CYCLE ⏱ 25:00 📖 5

Grimly prophetic of the death of Mahler's own daughter, *Songs for Dead Children* – possibly his finest song cycle – is a setting for baritone voice of poems by Friedrich Rückert, who lost two children, and is contemplative rather than dramatic.

Mahler was conductor at the Vienna Opera from 1897 to 1907, a significant achievement considering this appointment's reputation as a stressful and demanding position.

FOCUS

SYMPHONY NO. 5

ORCHESTRAL   🔊 80:00   📖 5   ♒

Mahler met Alma while composing this symphony. Its five movements progress from tragedy to triumph.

FIRST MOVEMENT (TRAUERMARSCH, 22:00) A funeral march, introduced by a baleful fanfare, is punctuated by two trios.

SECOND MOVEMENT (STÜRMISCH BEWEGT, 14:00) Marked "with utmost vehemence", this is a musical battleground which ends in inconclusive mystery.

THIRD MOVEMENT (SCHERZO, 18:00) Mahler wrote of "dancing stars" in this generally cheerful movement, with some poignant central passages of pizzicato strings and twilight mood.

FOURTH MOVEMENT (ADAGIETTO, 10:00) The Adagietto is Mahler's most popular work – often played as a stand-alone piece. As with much of his symphonic writing, it is related to his earlier songs. Mahler apparently sent the score of the Adagietto to Alma as a musical love letter.

FIFTH MOVEMENT (RONDO-FINALE, 16:00) The Adagietto theme is powered up in a brilliant finale that combines academic prowess with good spirits and zest for life.

DAS LIED VON DER ERDE

SONG-SYMPHONY   🔊 65:00   📖 6   ♒ 🎵

The Song of the Earth is a symphony-like work based on translations of ancient Chinese poems and set for two solo singers and orchestra. Filled with sadness and longing yet ultimately uplifting, simple yet profound, and achingly beautiful, it is possibly Mahler's greatest piece. It was premiered six months after his death.

DAS TRINKLIED VOM JAMMER DER ERDE (8:00) A powerful lament ("dark is life, dark is death"), challengingly high for the tenor, that seeks solace in wine.

DER EINSAME IM HERBST (10:00) Autumnal and despairing, the score is marked "ragging and weary", with small-scale and muted sounds.

VON DER JUGEND (3:00) A polished and miniature celebration of youth, with stylized "Chineseness".

VON DER SCHÖNHEIT (8:00) A delicate and poised portrayal of girls gathering flowers, longing for passing horsemen.

DER TRUNKENE IM FRÜHLING (5:00) "The Drunken Man in Spring" is woken from his post-binge sleep to find a bird announcing the new season.

DER ABSCHIED (31:00) "The Farewell" takes us from chilly funereal gloom to the world waking up again, as it always does, in renewal and ecstasy.

INFLUENCES

Mahler's works fell into obscurity after his death, partly because of opposition in Hitler's Germany to Jewish musicians, but became very popular in the last third of the 20th century. The dramatic and multi-layered nature of his symphonies can also be found in those of Dmitri Shostakovich.

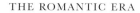

*"There is no such thing as Abstract music;
there is good music and bad music.
If it is good, it means something."*

RICHARD STRAUSS

Richard Strauss

◗ 1864–1949   🏳 German   ✍ 189

Richard Strauss began his career composing songs and symphonic poems, and ended it as the greatest opera composer of his day. His career, which rarely escaped controversy, spanned the last days of the Austrian Empire and the whole of Hitler's Nazi Germany, in which the composer allowed himself to become embroiled. His masterpieces are his orchestral tone poems, his songs, and his great operas.

LIFE

Richard Strauss was born in Munich, the son of a horn-player in the court orchestra. He began composing at six, and studied music privately, but did not attend a conservatory. He became assistant to Hans von Bülow in Meiningen, then travelled to Italy and later worked in Munich at the Opera. He married a general's daughter, the soprano Pauline de Ahna, who inspired many of his songs, which they performed together. His early operas, *Guntram* and *Feuersnot* (*Fire Emergency*) were not as successful as his tone poems, and *Salome* and *Elektra* caused an international scandal. The latter brought him together with the poet Hugo von Hofmannsthal: the two were to collaborate on five further operas. In 1908, the successful Strauss built himself a large villa at Garmisch in Germany. He conducted widely and also held a post as conductor of the Berlin Royal Opera, resigning from this in 1918 to become joint director of the Vienna Opera the next year. When the Nazi party came to power in 1933 Strauss was appointed president of the Reichsmusikkammer, though he lost the post two years later because of his collaboration with the Jewish librettist Stefan Zweig. Strauss spent much of World War II in Vienna, then returned to Garmisch, where he died in 1949.

The early tone poems of Strauss, such as *Also Sprach Zarathustra*, are works on a grand scale, full of flamboyant, dramatic gestures.

MUSICAL OUTPUT

Total: 189

	1864	1870	1880	1890	1900	1910	1920	1930	1940	1949
SYMPHONIES (4)			2				2			
CONCERTOS (10)		1	4				2		3	
OTHER ORCHESTRAL (38)		10	8	6	3	3	3	2	3	
OTHER INSTRUMENTAL (34)		12	17					1	4	
OPERAS (17)				1	4	2	2	5	3	
BALLETS (4)						1	1	1	1	
VOCAL (82)		28	17	13	8	5	3	4	4	

MUSIC

Strauss's early career as an orchestral conductor gave him enormous knowledge of the potential of the post-Wagnerian symphony orchestra, and he expanded this still further, using unusual timbres and combinations of instruments for the vivid and original characterizations of his great tone poems. The success of *Don Juan* established his reputation, and he built on it with *Till Eulenspiegel*, *Also Sprach Zarathustra*, *Don Quixote*, and *Ein Heldenleben*. His earliest attempts at opera were not successful, but *Salome* (and the scandal it caused with its New Testament subject and its libretto based on Oscar Wilde's play) gave him a new reputation as an opera composer. *Elektra* pushed the boundaries of operatic music, and many reacted against its dissonances and the huge, blatant waltz tune of its finale. Waltzes, too, run all through his next work, *Der Rosenkavalier*, in homage to his namesake and to the city of Vienna where it is set. His later collaborations with Hugo

The villa in Garmisch-Partenkirchen, Germany, where Strauss spent the final years of his life. He moved here after several years of exile in Switzerland.

von Hofmannsthal brought about philosophical works such as *Die Frau ohne Schatten*. After Hofmannsthal's death Strauss turned to Stefan Zweig and other librettists for his final operas, written first in the shadow of World War II, and then during the war itself. Strauss mourned the bombed-out theatres of Europe in *Metamorphosen*, but a chance meeting with an American soldier inspired one of his greatest instrumental works, the Oboe Concerto. The *Four Last Songs* were his last musical testament.

MILESTONES

Soprano Pauline de Ahna, Strauss's wife, as Elsa in Wagner's opera *Lohengrin*.

1875	Studies theory with Meyer
1881	Symphony No. 1 and String Quartet No. 1 performed in Munich
1884	Symphony No. 2 performed in New York
1885	Becomes assistant conductor to Hans von Bülow in Meiningen
1887	*Aus Italien* performed in Munich
1889	Becomes third conductor at Weimar Opera
1890s	Series of tone poems establishes his reputation as a composer; *Also Sprach Zarathustra*, Op. 30
1894	Marries soprano Pauline de Ahna
1898	Conductor of Berlin Opera
1904	Visits US and performs *Symphonia Domestica*, Op. 53
1905	Writes *Salome*, Op. 54
1909	*Elektra*, Op. 58, produced
1910	Writes Der Rosenkavalier, Op. 59, with von Hofmannsthal
1912	*Ariadne auf Naxos*, Op. 60, performed
1919	*Die Frau ohne Schatten*, Op. 65, produced in Vienna
1933	Nazi government appoints him director of the Reichsmusikkammer
1935	Removed from post due to his collaboration with Jewish librettist Stefan Zweig
1938	Operas *Friedenstag*, Op. 81, and *Daphne*, Op. 82, produced
1943	Writes *Metamorphosen*, a "poem for 23 strings"
1947	Visits London and conducts own works

KEY WORKS

ALSO SPRACH ZARATHUSTRA, OP. 30

TONE POEM   ⏳ 35:00   📖 1   ◥

Strauss based this piece, *Thus Spoke Zoroaster*, on Friedrich Nietzsche's philosophical prose poem of the same title. Zarathustra (Zoroaster) is Nietzsche's ideal thinker, a leader of humanity. Strauss wrote the piece between 1895 and 1896, and conducted its first performance in Frankfurt. The film *2001: A Space Odyssey* brought its majestic opening bars to many new listeners.

ARIADNE AUF NAXOS, OP. 60

OPERA   ⏳ 120:00   📖 2   ◥ ✋

Strauss collaborated with Hugo von Hofmannsthal on a reworking of Moliere's comedy *Le bourgeois gentilhomme*, to be performed with an operatic and vaudeville entertainment after the play. This six-hour show was not a success, but some years later Strauss and Hoffmannsthal rewrote the piece, adding a Prologue in which Moliere's comedy is hinted at and the situation is set up. Ariadne, lamenting the loss of Theseus on Naxos, is interrupted by Zerbinetta and her troupe of clowns, who try to cheer her up, before Bacchus arrives to take Ariadne with him to everlasting bliss.

Costume designs for *Elektra*, the opera which brought Strauss together with his librettist, the poet Hugo von Hofmannsthal.

SALOME, OP. 54

OPERA   ⏳ 105:00   📖 1   ◥ ✋

Strauss's *Salome* is a setting of Hedwig Lachmann's German translation of Oscar Wilde's play. The opera was first performed in Dresden in 1905, and was a great success throughout Europe. It tells the Biblical story of how Herodias's daughter Salome persuaded King Herod to give her the head of Jokanaan, John the Baptist.

The acclaimed African-American soprano Leontyne Price made her debut as Ariadne at the San Francisco Opera in October 1977.

INFLUENCES

Strauss outlived his age of late Romanticism, and though he had taken on much of what had been discovered by Stravinsky and other avant garde composers, his late work still remains tonal and late-19th century in its harmonic language. Only now is it becoming clear how much influence his work has had on post-war composers.

FOCUS

FOUR LAST SONGS

SONGS ⏱ 24:00 📖 4 🎵🔊

Strauss wrote his *Vier letzte Lieder* (*Four Last Songs*) in 1948, and although they were not his last songs, they were among his last major compositions. The first three poems are by Hermann Hesse, and the last is by Joseph von Eichendorff. All four poems have an atmosphere of elegy, as the composer bids farewell to the world. Hesse himself is said to have been surprised by the project, and when he first heard the songs he claimed that they were "virtuoso, refined, full of well-crafted beauty, but lacking in core, merely an end in themselves" – though he admitted to only having heard them on the radio.

BEIM SCHLAFENGEHEN (4:00) In the first song, "On Retiring to Rest", the poet, wearied by the day, is asking to be taken in by the starry night like a tired child. His hands and mind cease from working, and his five senses drift off into slumber. The soul hovers around the body, living on "in night's magic circle".

FRÜHLING (5:00) In "Spring", the poet dreams of springtime, with its trees, blue skies, and birdsong, then sees it unfold in all its beauty.

SEPTEMBER (6:00) At the other end of the year, the garden is in mourning, and summer comes to its end. The leaves fall as summer closes its eyes to rest.

IM ABENDROT (9:00) This, the most moving of the four songs, sets words by Eichendorff's "In the Evening Glow". Now it is clear that Strauss is once again addressing his wife Pauline, as they go hand in hand into the twilight, the larks still singing overhead as they go.

DER ROSENKAVALIER, OP. 59

OPERA ⏱ 195:00 📖 3 🎵🎭🔊

Strauss and his librettist Hugo von Hoffmansthal invented *Der Rosenkavalier* (*The Knight of the Rose*) as a fantasy of 18th-century Vienna at the time of the Empress Maria Theresa.

EIN HELDENLEBEN, OP. 40

ORCHESTRAL ⏱ 51:00 📖 6 🎵

The title of this tone poem translates as *A Hero's Life* and the hero is Strauss himself, portrayed as a man of high ideals, surrounded by enemies.

PART ONE: THE HERO (5:00) The first subject, the Hero's theme, makes it clear from the start that he is a noble character, a lively, confident individual but not without a gentle side.

Strauss always had a close relationship with the Vienna Philharmonic Orchestra, seen here playing in the hall of the Musikverein.

PARTS ONE AND SIX

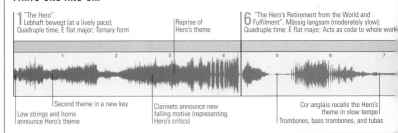

1 "The Hero".
Lebhaft bewegt (at a lively pace);
Quadruple time; E flat major; Ternary form

Reprise of Hero's theme

6 "The Hero's Retirement from the World and Fulfilment". Mässig langsam (moderately slow);
Quadruple time; E flat major; Acts as coda to whole work

Second theme in a new key

Low strings and horns announce Hero's theme

Clarinets announce new falling motive (representing Hero's critics)

Cor anglais recalls the Hero's theme in slow tempo

Trombones, bass trombones, and tubas

ACT ONE (75:00)
The heroine, the Marschallin – also called Marie Therese – is having an affair with young Octavian while her husband is away hunting. Her cousin, Baron Ochs von Lerchenau, interrupts their dalliance with a demand that she should provide a Knight of the Rose to present a silver rose to his fiancée, Sophie.

ACT TWO (60:00) Octavian is chosen for the task and delivers the rose to Sophie, who immediately falls in love with him, and vice versa. When Sophie then refuses to marry Baron Ochs, Sophie's snobbish father, von Faninal, tries to placate him, while Octavian fights the Baron and plots to have him disgraced.

ACT THREE (60:00) Octavian, dressed as Mariandl, seduces Baron Ochs in a tavern of ill repute. They are interrupted, and the Marschallin and Sophie come to break up the fracas. The Marschallin recognizes the depths of Sophie's feelings for Octavian, and gracefully gives up her lover to the younger woman.

PART TWO: THE HERO'S ADVERSARIES (4:00)
The Hero's enemies (Strauss's critics) are portrayed as dull and petty-minded. They are contrasted with the Hero and his lofty, high-minded ambitions.

PART THREE: THE HERO'S COMPANION (14:00)
This is a portrait of Strauss's loving, but capricious wife, Pauline.

PART FOUR: THE HERO'S DEEDS OF WAR (:00) The Hero does battle to overcome his rivals in art and love.

PART FIVE: THE HERO'S WORKS OF PEACE (7:00) In this section, Strauss quotes from a number of his own earlier musical works.

PART SIX: THE HERO'S RETIREMENT FROM THE WORLD AND FULFILMENT (13:00) The Hero retires from the world of action (something Strauss never did) and spends his time in contemplation. In the conclusion, his life-force asserts itself once more.

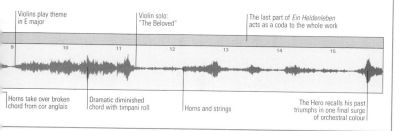

Violins play theme in E major

Violin solo: "The Beloved"

The last part of *Ein Heldenleben* acts as a coda to the whole work

| 9 | 10 | 11 | 12 | 13 | 14 | 15 |

Horns take over broken chord from cor anglais

Dramatic diminished chord with timpani roll

Horns and strings

The Hero recalls his past triumphs in one final surge of orchestral colour

ROMANTIC OPERA
1810–1920

The 19th century provided the most popular of all operas – Verdi's *La traviata*, *Rigoletto*, and *Aida*, Wagner's Ring Cycle, Bizet's *Carmen*, and Puccini's *La bohème*. The popularity of these works is based on their universal themes, the huge emotions they generate, and the mastery of their writing for voice and orchestra.

T he years between the death of Mozart in 1791 and the arrival of Rossini on the scene two decades later were comparatively barren for opera. Europe was too preoccupied with the Napoleonic Wars to have money to spare for this extravagant art form. 1813, when Rossini had his first great successes, was also the year in which two of the greatest Romantic opera composers, Verdi and Wagner, were born. Each revolutionized opera and polarized its enthusiasts into what even today can be – though should not be – two opposing camps.

Romantic opera covers over a century of composition. Up until World War I, Europe enjoyed a long period of relative peace, during which the revolutions of 1848 were a significant political upheaval. These involved Wagner directly (he was exiled for his participation in the Saxony riots) and several other composers indirectly.

INTERNATIONAL APPEAL
The other revolution to affect the century was the industrial one. By mid-century, railways criss-crossed Europe and steamships plied the Atlantic, allowing composers, singers, and conductors to embark on the international careers that all now accept as the norm. Verdi travelled to Russia, Dvořák to the USA, Tchaikovsky to England (to pick up a doctorate), and Puccini to his eventual death in a Brussels hospital. The soprano Adelina Patti, greatest of bel canto singers, retired to a castle in south Wales; the tenor Enrico Caruso made his greatest name in New York; and the Russian bass Chaliapin sang to audiences in Paris and London. In a century of nationalism, opera was a truly international art form.

BALLET SCENE FROM ROBERT LE DIABLE BY DEGAS
Giacomo Meyerbeer was the most successful exponent of French *grand opéra*. What his works lacked in musical inspiration they made up for in spectacle.

SET FOR VERDI'S *OTELLO*
Verdi drew on Shakespeare's plays for three of his operas: *Macbeth* (1847), *Otello* (1887), and his one comic masterpiece, *Falstaff* (1893).

Opera often springs from literary origins. Plays, epics, novels, and histories have always inspired librettists and composers, and 19th-century Romantic opera took its inspiration from a particular set of writers. Shakespeare's plays, Sir Walter Scott's novels, Goethe's *Faust*, and Schiller's historical tragedies all became sources for opera librettos.

Another great source of Romantic inspiration were the legends and poems of medieval Europe. Rossini took the old Swiss tale of William Tell for his last and possibly greatest opera, whereas Wagner drew on the great medieval German epics *Tristan und Isolde*, the *Nibelungenlied*, and *Parzifal*.

POWERFUL EMOTIONS

In Italy, Rossini's use of Romantic plots, often melodramatic and improbable, inspired his two immediate successors, Donizetti and Bellini, who took Romanticism still further. Donizetti drew on Sir Walter Scott for *Lucia di Lammermoor*, while Bellini told tales of Druid priestesses in *Norma* and of sleepwalking girls in *La sonnambula*. In each of these operas the central figure is that great Romantic icon, the damsel in distress.

TIMELINE: ROMANTIC OPERA

◁ **1813**
Rossini's *Tancredi* and *L'italiana in Algeri*, his first great successes

1829
Rossini's *William Tell*

1835
Donizetti's *Lucia di Lammermoor*, based on Walter Scott's novel

1851
Verdi's *Rigoletto*, based on Victor Hugo's play *Le Roi s'amuse*

1810   **1825**   **1840**   **1855**

1813
Verdi and Wagner born

1815
Battle of Waterloo; Congress of Vienna

1821 ▷
Weber's *Der Freischütz*

1858
Present Covent Garden Theatre opens in London

1848
Revolutions in Paris, Vienna, and other European capitals

Lucia in her bloodstained nightgown and Norma in her priestess's robes are among the most hauntingly dramatic heroines in all theatre, spoken or sung.

Verdi made further revolutions in the writing of opera. His earliest works told stirring tales of nationalism and heroism (*Macbeth, Ernani, Nabucco*), while in his middle period, in works such as *Rigoletto*, he examined the relationship between parent and child, portraying vulnerable heroines with uncomprehending, overbearing fathers.

Verdi's successors, Mascagni, Leoncavallo, and Puccini, added the new element of "verismo" or realism to their operas, telling stories in music that were none the less Romantic for being drawn from everyday life.

OPERA BEYOND ITALY

The great Russian composers, from Glinka to Tchaikovsky, all produced operas, usually on Russian themes. In France, Parisian *grand opéra* employed huge stage sets, vast orchestras and choruses, and prodigious solo voices, with Meyerbeer the dominant composer. Offenbach wrote in the rival form of *opéra comique*, concluding his career with a masterpiece of Romantic opera, *The Tales of Hoffmann*. Other French works that have lasted well include Bizet's *Carmen*, Gounod's *Faust*, and Massenet's *Cendrillon*.

In Germany the first great Romantic opera was Weber's *Der Freischütz*, based on a folk tale set in the forests of Bohemia. Weber had learned much from his studies of Beethoven, and brought a new richness of

SCORE OF *LA BOHÈME*
Puccini's account of the death of Mimi in Bohemian Paris remains one of the most popular of all Romantic operas.

orchestration to his score. *Der Freischütz* inspired Wagner, who decided that the German world needed its own form of music drama, and proceeded to invent it, writing both words and music. Richard Strauss followed the unfollowable Wagner, producing Romantic works until well into the 20th century. He was the last of the great Romantic composers.

BEL CANTO

The great vocal tradition of 19th-century Italian opera was bel canto, which simply means "beautiful singing". The three great bel canto composers were Rossini, Bellini, and Donizetti, and their works have been criticized by some for putting ornamented melodic line and florid coloratura embellishments before the job of telling a story. Two of the finest early exponents were Giulia Grisi (1811–69) and Giuditta Pasta (1797–1865). Later stars included Jenny Lind (1820–87) and Adelina Patti (1843–1919), who left a number of recordings, but these were made when she was past her vocal best.

JENNY LIND
The Swedish-born soprano won acclaim for the naturalness of her performances.

◁ **1871**
Verdi's *Aida* premiered in Cairo

1876
Wagner's Ring Cycle performed at Bayreuth Festspielhaus

◁ **1900**
Puccini's *Tosca* opens in Rome

1905
Franz Lehár's *The Merry Widow*

1911
Richard Strauss's *Der Rosenkavalier*

1870   **1885**   **1900**   **1915**

1864
Ludwig II of Bavaria becomes Wagner's patron

1875
Bizet's *Carmen* savaged by Parisian critics; Bizet dies three months after first performance

1883
Wagner dies in Venice; Metropolitan Opera House, New York, opens with Gounod's *Faust*

1901 ▷
Verdi dies in Milan; quarter of a million people follow his funeral cortège

Carl Maria von Weber

● 1786–1826   ▶ German   ✍ 306

Carl Maria von Weber was a composer, conductor, and pianist whose opera *Der Freischütz* marked the beginning of German Romantic opera. The huge success of *Der Freischütz* liberated German opera from the Italian influences that had bound it until then, and showed how a nationalist style of opera could be founded on folk tunes and folk tales. Weber was admired by Beethoven and influenced his disciple, Wagner.

LIFE AND MUSIC

Carl Maria von Weber was the son of a town musician who set up his own opera company, with which the young Weber spent much of his childhood on tour. He studied with Abbé Vogler, an eminent teacher and music director at several German Electors' courts, and worked under Joseph Haydn's brother Michael. At 17 Weber took up the post of Kapellmeister at the theatre in Breslau (Bratislava). Eventually appointed Kapellmeister in Dresden, Weber spent his life touring ceaselessly as a conductor to promote his own and other composers' music. He died in London at only 39, a few weeks after the premiere of his final opera, *Oberon*, succumbing to the tuberculosis that had undermined his health for years. Apart from his operas, he is noted for his brilliant clarinet works.

Weber's *Der Freischütz* is the ultimate distillation of German Romanticism in opera. It portrays the struggle of good and evil and evokes the beauty of nature.

MILESTONES	
1804	Appointed Kapellmeister at Breslau
1807	Composes his two symphonies
1811	Composes his two clarinet concertos
1813	Appointed director of Prague Opera
1817	Made court Kapellmeister, Dresden
1821	*Der Freischütz* a huge success in Berlin
1823	Completes *Euryanthe*, opera
1826	Completes *Oberon*, opera

KEY WORKS

OBERON

OPERA	⏱ 170:00	📖 3	🎵♨♙

Oberon, Weber's last opera, is a setting of an English libretto by James Robinson Planché and it was first performed in London in 1826 at Covent Garden. Weber overcame the difficulties of Planché's unpromising, convoluted text about the elf-king Oberon, the Caliph of Baghdad, his daughter Rieza, and Charlemagne, and wrote an opera that contains some of his best music, especially the inspired overture.

CLARINET CONCERTO NO. 1 IN F MINOR

ORCHESTRAL	⏱ 25:00	📖 3	🎵🎶

Weber wrote beautifully for the clarinet in *Der Freischütz*, but his knowledge and love of the instrument is shown in his two clarinet concertos and one concertino of 1811. The First Concerto has long been a favourite with concert goers and clarinettists alike, and illustrates Debussy's remark that Weber achieved his sound by "scrutinizing the soul of each instrument".

FOCUS

DER FREISCHÜTZ

OPERA　150:00　3

Weber set *Der Freischütz (The Freeshooter* or *The Marksman)* to a libretto by Johann Friedrich Kind based on a set of ghost stories. The overture opposes C major with C minor, setting up the world of goodness and light (major) against that of evil and darkness (minor). Hunting-horn calls are heard alongside Weber's favourite low clarinet, setting the atmosphere of Bohemian forest life and the black magic of the Wolf's Glen. The evocation of the glen is a superb example of tonal scene-painting.

ACT ONE (50:00) The opera is set in Bohemia in the 17th century. The forester Max wants to win Agathe's hand in a shooting match. Caspar, in league with the devil Samiel, persuades Max to accept his help in casting a magic bullet to ensure success.

ACT TWO (55:00) Agathe is full of dread about the shooting match. Max and Caspar go to the Wolf's Glen, summon up Samiel and cast seven bullets – but the last is dedicated to the devil.

ACT THREE (45:00) Agathe is shocked by a gift of a funeral wreath instead of her wedding wreath. Max, down to his last magic bullet, shoots at a dove, but hits Caspar, who falls dying. Max confesses his involvement with Samiel, is pardoned, and marries Agathe.

EURYANTHE

OPERA　165:00　3

Weber's "grand heroic-romantic opera in three acts" was commissioned by the Kärntnertortheater in Vienna as a result of the success of *Der Freischütz*. With one of the most ludicrously implausible plots in all opera (which is quite an achievement), it has not been performed as often as deserved by its superb music – a continuous flow without spoken word.

ACT ONE (60:00) The scene is 12th-century France. Lysiart has made a bet with Adolar that he can make his beloved Euryanthe unfaithful. Eglantine, also in love with Adolar, tells her rival Euryanthe to tell the tale of Adolar's murdered sister, Emma. Euryanthe welcomes Lysiart to the castle.

ACT TWO (45:00) Eglantine and Lysiart steal a poisoned ring from Emma's tomb and use it to prove that Euryanthe loves Lysiart, not Adolar, who loses his bet and forfeits his lands.

ACT THREE (60:00) Adolar takes Euryanthe to a mountain gorge, intending to kill her. He cannot bring himself to do so, and leaves her to die of exposure. King Louis VI and his huntsmen rescue her and bring her back to the castle, where Adolar learns of Lysiart's deception. Lysiart stabs Eglantine to death and is then led to the dungeons; Adolar and Euryanthe are reunited and marry.

Ferdinand Hérold

● 1791–1833   🏳 French   ✍ c.160

After lessons from his father, a pianist and composer, Hérold attended the Paris Conservatoire, performed his piano works in public, and won the Prix de Rome in 1812. But it was as a composer of masterful comic operas in the French style that he gained renown. His *La jeunesse de Henry V* was a success in Naples, where he served as pianist to Queen Caroline. A year after returning to Paris in 1816, he produced his opera *Les rosières*, the first of many resounding successes, punctuated by failures, mainly down to poor librettos. His ballets are also innovative in using new music, rather than old melodies. Shortly before the premiere of his last (and hugely successful) opera, *Le pré aux clercs*, he died prematurely from chronic tuberculosis.

The roguish pirate Zampa is flung to his death by the avenging spirits of his former bride, Alicia, in the final scene of Hérold's enormously popular *Zampa*.

MILESTONES	
1812	Wins the Prix de Rome
1813	Teaches royal princesses in Naples
1817	*Les rosières*, opera, premiered
1826	*Marie*, opera, staged
1827	Marries Adele Elise Rollet; becomes choirmaster at the Paris Opéra
1828	*La fille mal gardée*, ballet, premiered
1831	*Zampa*, opera, staged in Paris

Jules Massenet

● 1842–1892   🏳 French   ✍ c.450

Massenet's early career followed the regulation path for a French composer in the 19th century. After studies with Ambroise Thomas at the Paris Conservatoire, he won the Prix de Rome, then spent three years in Italy before returning home to break into the Paris opera scene in 1866. Success came gradually as Massenet honed his technical skills. Although he staged his first opera in 1867, a decade passed before he achieved his first real success with *Le roi de Lahore*. Lasting fame came in 1884 with *Manon,* an international hit that established him as France's leading opera composer. Now in control of his career, he continued producing successful, internationally staged operas, such as *Werther*, without needing to update his deft style. As a teacher at the Paris Conservatoire, he was admired for his meticulous, but kind, easy-going nature, apparently preferring family life to parties.

In the bleak finale to Massenet's blockbuster, *Werther*, Charlotte despairs at the suicide of her true love, Werther.

MILESTONES	
1863	Wins the Prix de Rome
1866	Returns to Rome and marries
1877	*Le Roi de Lahore*, opera, first success
1878	Becomes professor of composition at Paris Conservatoire
1884	*Manon*, opera, a huge success
1885	Writes *Le Cid*, opera, after Corneille
1892	*Werther*, opera, after Goethe, staged

Giacomo Meyerbeer

● 1791–1864   ⚑ German   ✍ c.285

A German composer who settled in France, Meyerbeer developed and dominated French Grand Opéra, the new epic and historic style that would influence the Romantics, from Verdi to Wagner. Although massively extravagant in scale, effects, casts and costs, Meyerbeer's lavish melodramas are now being revived and recorded, graphically illustrating their spectacular and fashionable appeal in his day.

LIFE AND MUSIC

Born Jakob Liebmann Beer to a Jewish family in Berlin, Giacomo Meyerbeer italianized his first name, and added "Meyer" to his second on receiving a legacy from a relative. A child prodigy on the piano, he performed in public from the age of seven. Nurturing a passion to compose, he turned out some disastrous oratorios until, inspired by Gioachino Rossini's operas in Italy, he produced *Il crociato in Egitto*, an instant hit in both Venice and Paris, where he settled. After a fallow patch during a spate of family tragedies in the 1820s, Meyerbeer experimented with the new style of Grand Opéra – epic in scale, drama, and effects – which he effectively invented with *Robert le Diable*. This and a run of similar box-office hits established him as a master of the genre.

MILESTONES

1810	Studies counterpoint with Abbé Vogler at Darmstadt in Germany
1815	Visits Italy to study vocal writing
1817	Produces his first Italian opera, *Romilda e Costanza*, in Padua
1826	*Il crociato in Egitto*, opera, staged
1831	*Robert le Diable*, opera, a huge hit
1836	*Les Huguenots*, opera, premiered
1837	Starts composing *L'Africaine*, opera
1842	Becomes Generalmusikdirektor (music director) in Berlin
1849	*Le prophète*, opera, premiered
1854	*L'étoile du nord*, opera, staged
1862	Represents German music at London's Great Exhibition
1863	Supervises *L'Africaine*, opera

KEY WORKS

ROBERT LE DIABLE

OPERA   ⏱ 240:00   📖 5   🎻🎵

Famous for its scandalous chorus of dancing nuns, its evocative orchestration, and brilliant writing for voice, *Robert le Diable* was the first product of a fruitful collaboration between Meyerbeer and the librettist Eugène Scribe. It tells the tale of the 13th-century Duke Robert of Normandy, whose love for Isabella saves his soul from the diabolic machinations of his demon father, Bertram.

Le prophète, one of Meyerbeer's most dramatic and bombastic operas, is famous for its stunning light effects and explosive finale.

LES HUGUENOTS

OPERA   ⏱ 240:00   📖 5   🎻🎵

Meyerbeer's moving opera explores the intense religious conflict that erupted in massacre on St Bartholomew's Day in 1572, when the Protestant minority of Huguenots were ruthlessly slaughtered by the Catholic majority. The historic drama is intensified by the fated love between a Protestant and Catholic, Raoul and Valentine, both doomed to die in the futile bloodbath. Tuneful, luscious, and inventive, it is probably Meyerbeer's finest opera for voices, displaying his melodic talents.

MUSIK-PERLEN.
AUSWAHL
der beliebtesten classischen u. modernen Musik

Nº 16

Krönungs-Marsch
aus der Oper
Der Prophet
von
GIACOMO MEYERBEER

FRITZ AUGUST'S NACHF. HAMBURG.

Gioachino Rossini

◯ 1792–1868   ▯ Italian   ✍ c. 240

Born a few months after Mozart's death, Rossini was the
greatest opera composer of the 1810s through to the 1830s,
when he took a premature retirement from opera
composition. His comic operas bubble with invention and fun, while his
serious operas have great melodic beauty and superb writing for both voice
and orchestra. An annual festival at his birthplace, Pesaro, celebrates his work.

LIFE AND MUSIC

Rossini was the son of Pesaro's town
horn player and his wife, a singer. He
entered Bologna Conservatory in 1806
and, by 1813, when he was 21, he had
written ten operas, which had all been
staged in northern Italy. In that year,
he wrote *Tancredi*, his first important
opera seria. He was the first composer
to write opera without recitative, so
creating an uninterrupted flow of
music. He went on to write for theatres
in Milan, Venice, Rome, and Naples,
and in 1824 moved to Paris where he
wrote five further operas, culminating
in *William Tell*. Then Rossini stopped

writing operas and composed only ve
occasionally for his remaining 38 year
His operatic Stabat mater dates from
1842 after a 12-year composing gap.

MILESTONES	
1813	Operas *Tancredi* and *L'italiana in Algeri* produced in Venice
1814	Engaged as music director for the two opera houses in Naples
1822	Marries Isabella Colbran, soprano
1823	Composes *Semiramide*, opera
1829	Made director of Théâtre Italien, Pari
1829	Writes *Guillaume Tell*, his last opera

KEY WORKS

TANCREDI

OPERA   ⏱ 165:00   📖 2   ♒ ♨ ♂

Tancredi is based on Voltaire's play of
the same name and on an episode in
Tarquino Tasso's epic poem of 1581,
Jerusalem Liberated. In Syracuse during
the Crusades, Tancredi returns from
exile to find that his beloved Amenaida
is about to marry Orbazzano.
Amenaida's letter to Tancredi is
intercepted, and she is accused of
colluding with the Saracens.
Tancredi fights to defend her name
and then defeats the Saracens.
Tancredi is a mezzo-soprano role
and *Tancredi* has some of Rossini's
finest writing for this voice.

A brilliant comic opera, Rossini's *La Cenerentola*,
seen here in performance in London, also has
some genuinely emotional scenes.

LA CENERENTOLA

OPERA   ⏱ 150:00   📖 2   ♒ ♨ ♂

Rossini's take on the Cinderella story
full of satire and wit. Cenerentola,
rejected by her stepfather and step-
sisters, is protected by Alidoro, a
philosopher, and falls in love with
Prince Ramiro, who arrives disguised
his valet Dandini. Dandini, disguised a
the Prince, wins over the family. The
real Prince can then marry his beloved

L BARBIERE DI SIVIGLIA

ERA 🎵 165:00 📖 2 🔀♿👁

ossini set Cesare Sterbini's libretto,
ased on the first of Beaumarchais's
garo plays *Le barbier de Séville (The
arber of Seville)* in 1816 and wrote the
usic, it is said, in 13 days. The play
ad been set to music before, and the
pporters of the most popular setting,
Paisiello, caused a riot at the first
ght of Rossini's rival version in Rome.
T ONE (90:00) Count Almaviva,
sguised as the student Lindoro, has
s heart set on Rosina, Dr Bartolo's
ard. The doctor wants to marry her
d keeps her under lock and key, but
lmaviva enlists
garo, barber
d factotum, to
sinuate himself
to the house.
artolo has heard
rumour from
osina's music teacher, Don Basilio,
out certain plots, but is not smart
ough to stop Almaviva entering first
a regimental horse doctor, and then
a music teacher for Rosina.
T TWO (75:00) After many confusions
d revelations, Figaro smuggles a
otary into the house and, before
Bartolo can do anything about it,
lmaviva and Rosina are married.

> **INFLUENCES**
>
> Rossini directly influenced Donizetti, Bellini, Verdi,
> Meyerbeer, Offenbach, and Sullivan, and indirectly
> influenced film scores and musicals well into the 20th
> century. His ornate vocal lines defined bel canto throughout
> his lifetime and his comic genius was never eclipsed. His
> serious operas are now making a comeback.

GUILLAUME TELL

OPERA 🎵 225:00 📖 4 🔀♿👁

The overture to *William Tell* is perhaps
Rossini's most famous work. Based on
Schiller's play about the Swiss patriot,
Wilhelm Tell, Rossini's opera was his
first – and last – work in the style of
French Grand Opéra with its grandiose
sets, huge choruses, and ballets, bound
together by Swiss alphorn melodies.
ACT ONE (60:00) Tell helps to rescue a
fugitive from the Austrian army of
occupation. Arnold, in love with the
Habsburg princess, Mathilde,
promises to join Tell's resistance army.
ACT TWO (60:00) Mathilde declares her
love to Arnold.
He learns that
the Austrians
have murdered
his father.
ACT THREE (60:00)
Mathilde and
Arnold part. The Austrian governor,
Gesler (bass), forces Tell to shoot an
apple from his son Jemmy's head. Tell
sings his great aria "Sois immobile",
and successfully fires the arrow, but he
is imprisoned and sentenced to death.
ACT FOUR (45:00) Tell escapes and kills
Gesler with an arrow. Arnold and his
army capture Gesler's stronghold and
restore Switzerland to freedom.

Gaetano Donizetti

◑ 1797–1848   ▥ Italian   ♫ c.550

In a life of extraordinary productivity, Gaetano Donizetti wrote 65 operas, a dozen of which are still an important part of the operatic repertory. Like his near-contemporary Bellini, Donizetti wrote bel canto operas that celebrated the beauty of the human voice in long, expressive melodies and vivid, elaborate coloratura ornamentation. He was equally successful with tragedy and comedy.

LIFE AND MUSIC

Donizetti was born into a poor family in Bergamo and studied with the great teachers Simon Mayr and Padre Mattei. He often produced four operas a year, writing in the widest variety of styles, though most of his works are based on historic or fictional figures. He made his name in Rome with *Zoraida di Granata*, and the success of *Anna Bolena* in Milan allowed him to concentrate on tragic opera, though he continued to write comedies. After working in Paris and Vienna, in 1844 he began to show symptoms of paralysis and insanity, brought on by syphilis, and returned to Bergamo, where he was nursed by his nephew and friends, dying there in 1848.

MILESTONES

1806	Begins studies with Mayr in Bergamo
1815	Studies with Padre Mattei in Bologna
1818	*Enrico di Borgogna* produced in Venice
1822	*Zoraida di Granata* successful in Rome
1830	*Anna Bolena* commissioned by La Scala opera house; first international success
1832	Composes *L'elisir d'amore*
1834	Composes *Maria Stuarda*
1835	Composes *Lucia di Lammermoor*
1840s	Composes for the Paris Opera
1840	*La fille du régiment* and *La favourite* written for Paris
1843	Composes *Don Pasquale*
1844	Begins to suffer symptoms of syphilis, paralysis and insanity
1846	Enters a sanatorium in Ivry

KEY WORKS

MARIA STUARDA

OPERA   ⏱ 150:00   📖 2   🎵 🎻 ♪

Based on Friedrich von Schiller's tragic play *Maria Stuart*, Donizetti's opera is set in England in 1567. Elizabeth has imprisoned Mary, Queen of Scots, but is jealous of Mary's love for her own favourite, the Earl of Leicester. Leicester persuades Elizabeth to meet Mary, who begs for mercy. Elizabeth rejects her plea, and Mary turns on Elizabeth. Elizabeth signs Mary's death warrant and makes Leicester witness her execution.

DON PASQUALE

OPERA   ⏱ 120:00   📖 3   🎵 🎻 ♪

Written for the four great bel canto singers of the Théâtre-Italien, this late opera tells the tangled tale of Don Pasquale's intrigue to disinherit his rebellious nephew Ernesto whom Dr Malatesta schemes to marry Ernesto to the widow Norina

The celebrated buffo bass Signor Lablache played the quack Doctor Dulcamara in 19th-century production of Donizetti's opera *L'elisir d'*

FOCUS

LUCIA DI LAMMERMOOR

OPERA   135:00   3

This opera is Donizetti's masterpiece. It is based on *The Bride of Lammermoor*, a novel by Sir Walter Scott. Donizetti used extraordinary orchestral effects (including a glass harmonica in the original scoring of Lucia's mad scene, later replaced by a flute), but the opera is most remarkable for his scoring for coloratura soprano in Lucia's scenes and arias. After years of neglect, the opera has returned to the repertoire in the last 50 years and is now as popular as it was when it was first composed.

ACT ONE (45:00) Scotland, the late 16th century. Lucia Ashton is in love with the family's enemy, Edgardo Ravenswood. Edgardo returns her love and, despite Lucia's fear of her brother Enrico's wrath, the couple exchange rings.

ACT TWO (40:00) Enrico forges a letter which persuades Lucia of Edgardo's unfaithfulness; in her distress, Lucia agrees to marry Arturo Bucklaw, an ally of her brother.

ACT THREE (50:00) Driven mad by her grief at losing Edgardo, Lucia murders Arturo and appears in a bloodstained nightgown in one of the most famous mad scenes in all opera. The music, evoking Lucia's wandering mind, returns to themes from earlier in the opera, highlighting her former happiness. Lucia kills herself, and Edgardo, heartbroken at the news, stabs himself to death.

L'ELISIR D'AMORE

OPERA   125:00   2

Ranking alongside the comedies of Rossini, *The Elixir of Love* is one of the most enduring comic creations of the bel canto era. Felice Romani wrote the libretto, based on a text by Eugene Scribe, itself based on Silvio Malaperta's play *Il filtro* (*The Philtre*). L'elisir d'amore was first performed at the Teatro Canobbiana, Milan, in 1832.

It is still one of Donizetti's most popular operas, and is regularly performed at opera houses all over the world.

ACT ONE (70:00) Nemorino is in love with the prosperous Adina, but vies for her attention with the gallant Sergeant Belcore, a recruiting officer stationed in their village. Doctor Dulcamara offers Nemorino a love potion that will make him irresistible, but it is in fact nothing more than red wine.

ACT TWO (55:00) Tipsy and emboldened, Nemorino tries to court Adina, but is rebuffed. However, she has noticed his kind-heartedness, and sheds a tear that prompts his beautiful aria, "Una furtiva lagrima", notorious among tenors for its high register and quiet opening phrase. As Adina comes to realize that she has loved Nemorino all along, the quack doctor mistakenly believes that his potion actually works.

INFLUENCES

Verdi learned much from Donizetti, and Puccini was also to benefit from the example of Donizetti's gift for melodic invention and the use of unusual instruments (such as the glass harmonica in *Lucia di Lammermoor*) to characterize scenes. Berlioz, too, admired Donizetti, in spite of the fact that his works monopolized opera in Paris for a decade.

Vincenzo Bellini

⬤ 1801–1835   🏳 Italian   ✍ c.60

Vincenzo Bellini, with Rossini and Donizetti, was one of the three great composers of Italian bel canto opera. In his short life he wrote ten operas, many of which have remained in the repertoire. His reputation rests on the long-breathed, beautifully lyrical lines he gave to his singers, as well as on the great vocal agility his music demanded. His masterpiece, *Norma*, contains the supreme bel canto aria in the repertoire.

LIFE AND MUSIC

Bellini was born in Catania, Sicily, and educated in Naples at the San Sebastiano Conservatory, where he studied under Zingarelli. His first opera, *Adelson e Salvini*, was given in concert in 1825. He was immediately commissioned to write an opera for the prestigious San Carlo opera house in Naples, and soon after won another commission – *Il pirata* – for the even greater La Scala in Milan. Bellini followed this success (in Paris as well as in Italy) with *I Capuleti e i Montecchi*, in which Romeo's part is written for female mezzo voice. *La sonnambula*, *Norma*, and *I puritani* followed, by which time Bellini had moved to Paris. He died there, tragically young.

MILESTONES	
1820s	Studies in Naples; meets Donizetti
1825	First opera, *Adelson e Salvini*, performed in concert
1826	Writes opera *Bianca e Gernando* (title changed to *Bianca e Fernando* in 1828)
1827	Opera *Il pirata* produced at La Scala, Milan; subsequent production in Paris makes him internationally famous
1830	Opera *I Capuleti e i Montecchi* is staged in Venice
1831	Writes operas *La sonnambula* and *Norma* for Milan with huge success
1833	Writes opera *Beatrice da Tenda*; goes to Paris; meets Rossini who advises him to write for Théâtre Italien there
1835	*I puritani* premiered in Paris

KEY WORKS

I CAPULETI E I MONTECCHI
OPERA   ⏱ 135:00   📖 2   🎵🎻🎤

The plot of *The Capulets and the Montagues* came not from Shakespeare, but from his source, a novel by Matteo Bandello. Bellini's libretto was by Felice Romani, who wrote seven in all for him. This opera displays several aspects of Bellini's style: dance-like rhythms in triple time, solo instrumental introductions to arias, and instrumenta[l] passages in parallel thirds.

LA SONNAMBULA
OPERA   ⏱ 180:00   📖 2   🎵🎻🎤

La sonnambula (The Sleepwalker) tells the story of Amina, who, accused of having an affair, is proved innocent when the villagers witness her walking in her sleep. The aria "Ah! non crede. mirarti" in the sleep-walking scene is one of Bellini's most beautiful long-phrased melodies.

Maria Callas's performances in the title role of *Norma* were a career highlight, showing her at her best, both as a singer and as an actress.

FOCUS

NORMA

OPERA | 160:00 | 2

The most famous aria in *Norma* is the
priestess heroine's great invocation to
the moon, "Casta Diva" ("Chaste
Goddess"). Long believed impossible
to perform as Bellini intended, it was
revived by soprano Joan Sutherland,
who did much to rediscover the great
bel canto roles of Bellini and Donizetti.
The opera, to a libretto by Romani,
was based on a tragedy of 1831 by
French playwright Alexandre Soumet.
ACT ONE (90:00) The setting is Gaul under
Roman occupation. Norma, daughter
of Oroveso, high priest of the Druids,
wants to avoid the war her father
desires against the Romans because she
is in love with the Roman proconsul,
Pollione. She already has two children
by him. However, he is having an affair
with her best friend, Adalgisa (also her
acolyte), who confesses this to Norma.
ACT TWO (70:00) Adalgisa wants Pollione
to go back to Norma. He refuses and is
sentenced to death, but Norma offers
herself, instead, as a sacrifice to her
tribe and gives up her children. She
mounts her own funeral pyre, where
she is joined by a repentant Pollione.
The role of Norma is one of the most
demanding in the whole soprano
repertoire, but it is now frequently
performed and *Norma* is acknowledged
as one the greatest bel canto operas.

I PURITANI

OPERA | 140:00 | 3

Bellini's last opera, *I puritani (The
Puritans)* is based, at some distance, on
Sir Walter Scott's novel *Old Mortality*.
It is set during the English Civil War.
ACT ONE (70:00) In Cromwellian
Plymouth, King Charles I's widow,
Enrichetta, is being held in a fortress,
whose Puritan governor, Gualtiero,
has promised his daughter Elvira in
marriage to Riccardo. But Elvira is
in love with a Royalist, Arturo. A plan
to allow Enrichetta to escape leads
Elvira to believe that she has a rival,
and she goes mad.
ACT TWO (40:00) Arturo, having played
a pivotal part in the royal escape plan,
is put under sentence of death if he
returns to the Royalist ranks.
ACT THREE (30:00) A Puritan victory
leads to a general amnesty. When
Arturo is released, Elvira regains her
sanity and is reunited with her lover.

Giulia Grisi, a great bel canto
soprano, first created the role of
Elvira. Bellini took his cue from the
military theme and setting to fill the
opera with marches and martial
music, in addition to some of his
sweetest melodic invention for Elvira
herself. *I puritani* was first performed
in Paris in January 1835 at the
Théâtre-Italien, only a few months
before Bellini's tragically early death.

*"Verdi... has bursts of marvellous passion.
His passion is brutal, it is true, but it is better
to be impassioned in this way than not at all."*

GEORGES BIZET IN A LETTER, 1859

Giuseppe Verdi

1813–1901   Italian   42

erdi composed opera throughout his long life, developing his art from
e influences of Rossini, Bellini, and Donizetti, through his use of
rench Grand Opera forms in operas written for Paris, and, eventually,
the creation of his great Shakespearian masterpieces, *Otello* and *Falstaff*,
which he began to use some of Wagner's innovations in operatic
rm. Throughout, his originality and
cundity remained unparalleled.

LIFE

iuseppe Verdi was born in the village of
e Roncole, Bussetto, near Parma, in 1813,
e same year as Richard Wagner. His
ther was an innkeeper, his first music
acher was the Church organist, and his
st patron a local grocer who was
epared to pay for him to study at the
ilan Conservatory. Unable to enter the
onservatory because of his inadequate
ano technique, he studied privately for
o years, then returned to Bussetto and married his

The operas of Verdi were generally based on historical or literary figures and settings; his love stories invariably ended in tragedy.

atron's daughter. His first opera, *Rocester*, has been lost,
t his next, *Oberto*, was performed at La Scala, Milan.
erdi lost his wife and his two children within two years
each other and, grief-stricken, was about to give up
omposing when he was commissioned to write *Nabucco*.
he opera's theme of national independence inspired him,
d its great chorus, "Hebrew Slaves", became an anthem
r the Italian Risorgimento movement for unification. After
ars of composing an opera a year, he achieved financial
dependence by the late 1840s, bought a farm, and
ttled down with the singer Giuseppina Strepponi, who
e eventually married. Verdi was elected to the first Italian
arliament after independence was declared in 1860. He
rote operas for St Petersburg, Paris, and Cairo, and then
aited 16 years before another composer, Boito, provided
m with librettos for his two final operas, *Otello* and *Falstaff*.

MUSICAL OUTPUT									Total: 42
OPERA (28)		1	14	8	2	1	1	1	
VOCAL (11)		1	1		2	1	2	4	
INSTRUMENTAL (3)			1		1	1			
	1813	1830	1840	1850	1860	1870	1880	1890	1901

MUSIC

Verdi's early operas, like *Macbeth*, *Ernani*, and *Nabucco*, took themes of national independence and used choruses as the "voice of the people", making powerful political statements. His soloists were given highly taxing roles, such as Lady Macbeth, Elvira, and Abigaille, which heightened the dramatic effect of arias and ensembles.

In his middle years, Verdi's dramatic skills developed and his orchestration grew increasingly subtle. *Rigoletto* and *La traviata* took realistic plots and set them with great lyrical beauty and emotional depth.

In his old age, after *Aïda*, Verdi returned to his beloved Shakespeare for his last two operas, in which his vocal writing, especially in *Otello*, shows power and expression beyond anything he had written before.

MILESTONES	
1839	*Oberto* produced at La Scala, Milan
1842	First great success, *Nabucco*
1847	*Macbeth*
1849	Buys a farm at Sant' Agata
1851	*Rigoletto* premiered in Venice
1852	*Il trovatore*
1853	*La traviata*
1858	*Un ballo in maschera*
1860	Elected deputy in the first Italian parliament
1869	Soprano Giuseppina Strepponi becomes his second wife
1871	*Aïda* performed in Cairo
1874	Composes Requiem in memory of the writer Alessandro Manzoni
1884	Arrigo Boito persuades him to resume writing operas
1887	*Otello* performed at La Scala, Milan
1892	Composes *Falstaff*

KEY WORKS

MACBETH

OPERA   ⏱ 150:00   📖 4   🎵 🎭 ♂

Verdi's librettist Piave took some liberties with Shakespeare's tragedy (the three witches become an entire female chorus), but Verdi's opera tells the story in a skilful, moving way. Lady Macbeth's sleepwalking scene is one of Verdi's finest, with its spectral orchestration for high strings, and its high-lying vocal line that disappears to a mere thread of voice. It was Maria Callas who helped to rediscover the role, and brought *Macbeth* back into the permanent repertoire.

LA TRAVIATA

OPERA   ⏱ 120:00   📖 3   🎵 🎭 ♂

Verdi courted the disapproval of the Venetian censors when he chose to set Alexandre Dumas's play, *La dame aux camélias*. The story is of the courtesan Violetta and her love for Alfredo, which is thwarted by Alfredo's father Germont, who tells Violetta to leave his son for the sake of his sister. Dying

Romanian soprano Angela Gheorghiu and French/Italia tenor Roberto Alagna sing a duet in a performance of Verdi's *La traviata* at London's Covent Garden.

of consumption, Violetta does as he asks, only to be reconciled with her lover and die in his arms.

REQUIEM

MASS SETTING   ⏱ 140:00   📖 15   🎵 🎭 ♂

Verdi wrote his Requiem in 1874 in memory of the great Italian novelist Manzoni. The setting of the Latin Mass for the dead includes many high operatic effects (like the trombone in "Tuba mirum"). The fiery "Dies irae" is one of his most dramatic choruses.

FOCUS

RIGOLETTO

OPERA ⏲ 120:00 📖 3 🔀🎭🔊

Verdi based *Rigoletto* on Victor Hugo's play *Le roi s'amuse*.

ACT ONE (55:00) Rigoletto, the hunchbacked jester to the libertine Duke of Mantua has a daughter, Gilda, whom he does not want to fall into the Duke's hands, but the Duke has been courting her in secret, disguised as a student. The Duke's men kidnap Gilda and take her to the palace.

ACT TWO (30:00) Rigoletto comes looking for Gilda, but when he finds her, she has already been disgraced.

ACT THREE (35:00) Rigoletto pays the assassin Sparafucile to murder the Duke, but Sparafucile's sister, Maddalena, who is in love with the Duke, persuades him to kill someone else instead. Gilda substitutes herself for the Duke, and is fatally wounded. Rigoletto takes the sack with the body, and finds, instead of the Duke, his dying daughter.

ACT THREE

Duke sings "La donna è mobile", while flirting with Maddalena, observed by Gilda and Rigoletto

Recitative. Rigoletto orders Gilda home. Thunder is heard in distance

Gilda is stabbed by Sparafucile

Duke heard singing offstage. Rigoletto realizes wrong person has been killed

Recitative. Gilda confesses she loves the Duke

Dukes sings of love for Maddalena; Gilda sobs

Quartet

Trio. Sparafucile tells Maddalena Duke is to be killed

Storm, then clock strikes

Final duet between Rigoletto and dying Gilda. She sings "Vi ho ingannato"

ÏDA

OPERA ⏲ 150:00 📖 4 🔀🎭🔊

When *Rigoletto* was performed in Cairo to celebrate the opening of the Suez Canal, the Khedive of Egypt was so impressed that he commissioned *Aïda* to stage in his newly completed opera house. The opera was given its first performance on 24 December, 1871.

ACT ONE (40:00) Aïda is an Ethiopian slave to Amneris, daughter of Ramphis the Pharaoh. She is in love with the Egyptian

general Radamès who is sent to lead the Egyptian army against Ethiopia.

ACT TWO (40:00) Amneris forces Aïda to admit that she loves Radamès, who returns victorious and is given Amneris as his bride.

ACT THREE (35:00) Amonasro, Aïda's father, has been captured. He convinces Aïda to find out from Radames the plan of his next campaign.

ACT FOUR (35:00) Ramphis discovers this betrayal. Radames is condemned to be walled up alive in a tomb, where Aïda joins him. They die together.

"*If one has not heard Wagner at Bayreuth,
one has heard nothing!*"

GABRIEL FAURÉ IN A LETTER, 1884

Richard Wagner

☙ 1813–1883   ♙ German   ✍ 43

Richard Wagner reinvented opera as music drama. His aim was to create a "Gesamtkunstwerk", a unified work of art combining poetry, drama, music, song and painting. In writing the music dramas of his maturity he wrote both text and music, and superintended staging and performance as his own director and conductor. He built the Festspielhaus in Bayreuth as a fitting home for his *Ring* cycle and his last great work, *Parsifal*.

LIFE

Wagner was born in Leipzig, and was educated in Dresden and at the Thomasschule, Leipzig, studying literature as intensively as he studied music. He was appointed choral conductor at Würzburg in 1833, and then took conducting posts at Lauchstädt and Magdeburg. He married an actress, Minna Planer, but their marriage was strained by Wagner's extravagance and infidelities. After working in Riga, he

One of the most influential composers of all time, Wagner changed the course of both opera an Classical music in general.

went to Paris, living from hand to mouth, then returned to Dresden where he was appointed court opera conductor. In Dresden he studied German epic poetry, gaining the subjects for the rest of his life's work. His participation in the Dresden uprising of 1849 led to his exile. In Switzerland he wrote several essays, including the important *Opera and Drama* and the anti-Semitic tract *Jewishness in Music*. Wagner visited London and Paris, and continued to travel until permitted to return to Saxony in 1862. The turning-point in his fortunes came when King Ludwig II of Bavaria invited him to Munich and became his patron, allowing Wagner to stage *Tristan und Isolde*, conducted by Hans von Bülow. Wagner fell in love with von Bülow's wife Cosima and fathered two children with her before Minna's death allowed them to marry. In Bayreuth, Wagner built a house and a theatre, the Festspielhaus, where he staged the *Ring* cycle. He completed his final opera, *Parsifal*, in 1882, and died in Venice in 1883.

MUSICAL OUTPUT							Total: 43
SYMPHONIES (1)	1						
OTHER ORCHESTRAL (15)	6	2		3	4		
OTHER INSTRUMENTAL (14)	6	2	3	3			
OPERAS (13)	3	3	3	1	2	1	
1813	1830	1840	1850	1860	1870	1880	1883

MUSIC

Wagner inherited an art of German opera that had been developed by Mozart, Beethoven, and Weber. He transformed it into his own definition of music drama, a unified work that combined poetry and music, the two being conceived together. Wagner's early operas, up to *Rienzi*, were influenced by the trends of the day, especially French Grand Opera. From *The Flying Dutchman* onwards, through *Lohengrin* and *Tannhäuser*, Wagner found his own unique musical language. Central to his new style of composition was the idea of the leitmotiv or leading motive, a musical theme linked to a specific character, symbol, or concept that recurred throughout the work. By the time he completed the *Ring* cycle, this had become a system of melody, harmony, and counterpoint that

The eccentric King Ludwig II of Bavaria (1845–1886) was Wagner's patron; he paid for the construction of the Bayreuth Opera House.

derived all its materials from a simple chord or opening phrase. At the same time, Wagner experimented with modulation and the key system, discovering ways of moving seamlessly to the remotest of keys with enormous emotional effect. Wagner's mastery of the orchestra (he invented the art of the modern conductor, invented new instruments such as the Wagner tuba, and discovered new timbres and combinations of instrumental sound) reached the height of its development in *Tristan und Isolde*. His understanding of the voice allowed him to write roles of huge length and complexity that were still singable and which were able to penetrate the heaviest of orchestral textures. With *Parsifal*, Wagner brought the art of his music drama to a point which, at the time, seemed likely to remain unsurpassable.

MILESTONES

1841	Completes *Der fliegende Holländer*
1842	Opera *Rienzi* produced in Dresden
1843	*Der fliegende Holländer* produced at Dresden
1845	*Tannhäuser* produced in Dresden
1849	Participates in revolution in Dresden; flees to Weimar, then Zurich

1854	Completes *Das Rheingold*
1856	Completes *Die Walküre*
1857	Completes first part of *Siegfried*
1959	Completes *Tristan und Isolde*
1863	Falls in love with Cosima, Liszt's daughter and Hans von Bülow's wife
1864	King Ludwig II of Bavaria, Wagner's passionate admirer, pays his debts and subsidizes his subsequent career
1865	*Tristan und Isolde* produced in Munich, conducted by Hans von Bülow
1866	Wife Minna dies
1867	Completes *Die Meistersinger von Nürnberg*
1871	Completes second part of *Siegfried*
1872	Building of Bayreuth Festspielhaus begins
1874	Builds villa, Wahnfried, in Bayreuth; completes *Götterdämmerung*
1876	Bayreuth theatre opens; *Ring* cycle first performed
1882	*Parsifal* performed at Bayreuth

Wagner's left-wing ideals led to his implication in the fighting of the Dresden Rebellion of 1849; a warrant was issued for his arrest, but he escaped to Zurich.

KEY WORKS

DER FLIEGENDE HOLLÄNDER
OPERA ⏱ 135:00 📖 3

The Flying Dutchman was Wagner's first attempt at reinventing opera. It has no distinct arias, and everything that happens, whether on the stage or in the pit, is there to enhance the drama. The Flying Dutchman himself is a man doomed to sail the seas alone until he finds the love of a true woman, which will save his soul.

TANNHÄUSER
OPERA ⏱ 180:00 📖 3

Based on a poem by Ludwig Tieck, *Tannhäuser* received its first, not very successful, performance at Dresden in 1845. Its hero, Tannhäuser, returns to Germany from the realms of the goddess Venus and competes in a song contest for the hand of Elisabeth, his old love. Singing of the joys of the flesh rather than the spirit, Tannhäuser is banished. The pair are eventually reunited in death.

LOHENGRIN
OPERA ⏱ 210:00 📖 3

Based on a German epic poem, and first performed in Weimar in 1850, *Lohengrin* tells of the rivalry between Telramund and Lohengrin over the succession to the dukedom of Brabant and the love of Elsa. Lohengrin's

Wagner's custom-built opera house the Festspielhaus in Bayreuth, Germany, has been used to host the Wagner Festival annually since its completion in 1876.

famous swan (on which he arrives to meet Elsa) turns out to be Gottfried, the missing heir to the dukedom.

PARSIFAL
OPERA ⏱ 250:00 📖 3

As usual, Wagner wrote his own libretto for *Parsifal*, based on the epic poem by Wolfram von Eschenbach. Set in Arthurian times, it tells the story of the Grail knights. Their wounded king can only be cured by a "pure fool, wise through compassion". Parsifal arrives, and proves to be both a fool and pure. He fights the evil Klingsor, restores the holy spear to the Grail castle, and leads the rite of the Holy Grail.

The operas of Wagner work best on a massive scale, such as in this production of Parsifal which, as is not unusual, makes use of massive sets and a large cast.

INFLUENCES

Wagner's influence on subsequent composers was incalculable. His innovations transformed the harmonic language of the 19th century and helped bring about the abandonment of the system of tonality. Poets and novelists, from Verlaine and T S Eliot to Thomas Mann and Marcel Proust, referred directly to his inspiration.

FOCUS

DER RING DES NIBELUNGEN

OPERA CYCLE　🏆 915:00　📖 4　⚔ ⚰ ☩

In its full form *Der Ring des Nibelungen*, Wagner's most ambitious masterpiece, is actually a complete opera festival in itself, taking place over three days and a preliminary evening.

DAS RHEINGOLD (1 ACT, 150:00) The dwarf Alberich steals the Rhinemaidens' gold to make a magic ring. The giants, Fafner and Fasolt, agree to exchange Freia – the goddess whose golden apples keep the gods young – for the gold Alberich has gained through the power of the Ring. They then demand the Ring in addition to the gold; Fafner kills Fasolt, taking the Ring.

DIE WALKÜRE (3 ACTS, 225:00) The two mortal children of the god Wotan, Siegmund and Sieglinde, fall in love. Sieglinde's husband kills Siegmund, although Brünnhilde the Valkyrie tries to protect him. Sieglinde is pregnant with Siegfried, the saviour of the gods. To punish Brünnhilde for trying to save Siegmund, Wotan puts her to sleep on a rock ringed with flames.

SIEGFRIED (3 ACTS, 255:00) Siegfried, the son of Siegmund and Sieglinde, succeeds in forging his father's shattered sword. He goes to Fafner's lair (the giant is now a dragon), and, killing Fafner, gains the Ring. Finding Brünnhilde on her rock, he wakes her with a kiss.

GÖTTERDÄMMERUNG (PROLOGUE AND 3 ACTS, 255:00) Siegfried, in love with Brünnhilde, gives her the Ring, but his enemies Günther and Hagen give him a drugged potion. He brings Brünnhilde, with the Ring, from her rock. Hagen

Fritz Lang's silent film of 1922–24 *Die Nibelungen* is split into two parts: *Siegfried* and *Kriemhild's Revenge*, which deal with the last two parts of the epic story.

TRISTAN UND ISOLDE

OPERA　🏆 255:00　📖 3　⚔ ⚰ ☩

Wagner's epic music drama of love and death, written in 1857–59, was first performed in Munich in 1865.

ACT ONE King Marke's henchman Tristan is returning to Cornwall with the Irish princess Isolde, Marke's betrothed. Isolde's first husband died at Tristan's hand, and although she nursed the wounded Tristan, she now hates him for what he did. She orders her servant Brangäne to prepare a poison, but Brangäne substitutes a love-potion. Each drink it, expecting death, but instead fall in love.

ACT TWO While Marke is away on a night-time hunt, arranged by the treacherous Melot, who is also in love with Isolde, the lovers meet for an extended tryst. Tristan and Isolde

PRELUDE AND LIEBESTOD (FROM ACT THREE)

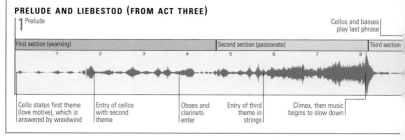

1 Prelude
Cellos and basses play last phrase

First section (yearning)　　Second section (passionate)　Third section

1　2　3　4　5　6　7　8

| Cello states first theme (love motive), which is answered by woodwind | Entry of cellos with second theme | Oboes and clarinets enter | Entry of third theme in strings | Climax, then music begins to slow down |

DIE MEISTERSINGER VON NÜRNBERG

OPERA   🖵 255:00   📖 3   ⚏ ⚌ ♦

When Wagner decided to write a comedy in 1861, he turned away from the high drama of the *Ring* cycle to focus on the small tale of a competition organized by the Meistersingers, societies of singers who guarded the integrity of the German song tradition.

ACT ONE (85:00) In 16th-century Nuremberg, the knight Walther von Stolzing is in love with Eva, Pogner's daughter. Pogner will give her in marriage to whoever wins the singing contest of the Meistersingers' guild.

ACT TWO (85:00) Walther does not know the rules of the contest, but the (real-life) cobbler and poet Hans Sachs coaches him, and helps him to fend off the town clerk Beckmesser, who also wants to marry Eva.

ACT THREE (85:00) Walther, singing a song composed by Hans Sachs, wins the contest and gains Eva's hand in marriage; he is then enrolled as a full member of the Meistersinger's guild.

kills Siegfried and Günther as he fights for the Ring. Brünnhilde builds a pyre for Siegfried, and burns herself and Valhalla. The Rhine overflows and the Rhinemaidens drown Hagen and take back the Ring.

express their passion in powerful, erotically charged music, but daylight comes, the hunting party returns, and Tristan is mortally wounded by Melot.

ACT THREE The dying Tristan, who has been taken back to Kareol, his castle in Brittany, by the faithful Kurwenal, waits for Isolde to come to him. She comes, followed by King Marke, but Tristan dies in her arms. As she sings the "Liebestod", an astonishing Wagnerian tour de force, in which eternal love is consummated by death, Isolde is transfigured, then dies herself.

Wagner's music makes it clear from the start that the doomed love of Tristan and Isolde can lead to no other end but death.

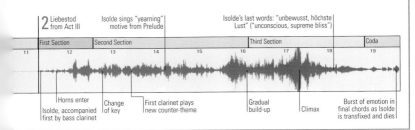

2 Liebestod from Act III	Isolde sings "yearning" motive from Prelude		Isolde's last words: "unbewusst, höchste Lust" ("unconscious, supreme bliss")		
First Section	Second Section		Third Section		Coda
11 12	13 14	15	16 17	18	19
Horns enter	Change of key	First clarinet plays new counter-theme	Gradual build-up	Climax	Burst of emotion in final chords as Isolde is transfixed and dies
Isolde, accompanied first by bass clarinet					

Léo Delibes

◉ 1836–1891   🏳 French   ✍ c.70

French composer and organist Léo Delibes achieved
considerable fame as a composer of enormously successful
operettas, operas, and ballets. His best-known work, the
ballet *Coppélia*, was one of the first to use "national" dances, such as the
Hungarian csárdás. *Lakmé*, written in the popular orientalizing style
fashionable in Paris, includes the beautiful "Flower Duet" for two sopranos.

LIFE AND MUSIC

Léo Delibes arrived in Paris from the
provincial town of Saint-Germain-du-
Val at the age of 12, after his father
had died. While still a boy, he sang in
the choir at La Madeleine and in the
Opéra chorus. He studied organ and
composition at the Paris Conservatoire
and, at 17, became organist at Saint
Pierre de Chaillot at the same time as
working as an accompanist at the
Théâtre Lyrique, where he began
composing operettas. In 1865 he
became chorus master at the Paris
Opéra, and was eventually appointed
professor of composition at the Paris
Conservatoire. His last opera, *Kassya*,
was unfinished at his death, and was
completed by Massenet.

MILESTONES	
1848	Begins to study organ and composition at the Paris Conservatoire; taught by Adolphe Adam, theatre composer
1853	Accompanist at Théâtre Lyrique
1855	Writes *Deux sous de charbon*, operetta
1865	Chorus master at the Paris Opéra
1866	Enjoys success with *Le source*, ballet, co-written with Louis Minkus
1870	Premiere of *Coppélia*, ballet
1873	Composes *Le roi l'a dit*, opera
1876	First performance of *Sylvia*, ballet
1880	Writes *Jean de Nivelle*, opera
1882	Composes *Le roi s'amuse*, suite of six dances: incidental music for play by Victor Hugo
1883	*Lakmé*, opera, first performed in Paris

KEY WORKS

LES FILLES DE CADIX
CHANSON   ⏱ 05:00   📖 1   👁 🎵

Delibes's most popular
song sets words by Alfred
de Musset. It has been
recorded by many of
the world's greatest
sopranos. Delibes uses
the popular Spanish
style in setting this
song about girls and
boys returning from
seeing the bullfight
and dancing the bolero.

Coppelia was the last ballet to be
performed at the Paris Opéra before the
Franco-Prussian War forced it to close.

SYLVIA
BALLET   ⏱ 90:00   📖 3   🎭

First performed in 1876, to a
libretto by Barbier and de Reinach,
and with choreography by
Mérante, *Sylvia* – the
story of a nymph
of Diana – is a
ballet on a pastoral
theme. Its dances
include "Fauns
and Dryads", an
Ethiopian dance,
a bacchanal,
and the march
and cortege
of Bacchus.

FOCUS

LAKMÉ

OPERA   ⏱ 155:00   📖 3   🔷🔷 🥁 👤

Lakmé's libretto was based on a novel by Pierre Loti. Set in 19th-century India, it describes the hatred of the Brahmin priests for the British soldiers who suppressed their religion. The elegance of Delibes's melodies, and the exoticism of the opera's setting, have made *Lakmé* a lasting favourite with singers and audiences alike. The role of Lakmé, with its coloratura display of the soprano voice, has drawn many great sopranos to interpret it. The "Flower Duet" in Act One, between Lakmé and her servant Mallika, is one of the most popular of all duets for soprano and mezzo.

ACT ONE (50:00) Two army officers, Gérald and Fréderic, are in a sacred Brahmin grove where they see Lakmé, the daughter of the Brahmin Nilakantha, and Gérald falls in love with her. Nilakantha swears vengeance on the trespassers.

ACT TWO (60:00) Nilakantha makes Lakmé sing the "Bell Song", to lure Gérald into his sight. Lakmé warns Gérald that her father wants to kill him, but he risks venturing into a procession, where he is wounded.

ACT THREE (45:00) Lakmé nurses Gérald, but Fréderic calls his comrade to return to his post. When Lakmé realizes Gérald is going to leave her, she takes poison and dies.

COPPÉLIA

BALLET   ⏱ 90:00   📖 2   🔷🔷

The German fantasy writer E T A Hoffmann wrote many stories that inspired operas and ballets. *Coppélia*, a ballet with a libretto by Nuittier, is one of these. Premiered at the Paris Opéra in 1870, it was one of the first operas to include national dances. Delibes visited Hungary and returned with the famous csárdás, the Hungarian national dance, which he wrote into the score.

ACT ONE (45:00) Dr Coppélius has made a mechanical doll, Coppélia, and passes her off as his daughter. Franz and Swanilda are engaged, but Swanilda thinks that Franz is captivated by Coppélia when he picks up a book the doll has dropped. When Swanilda finds Coppelius's door key, she leads her friends inside to talk to Coppélia. Franz also goes into the house to return Coppélia's book.

ACT TWO (45:00) Swanilda and her friends find Coppélia, and are shocked to discover that she is only a doll. There are other dolls in the house, and they play with them until Coppélius chases them away – all except Swanilda. Coppélius drugs Franz and attempts to transfer his life-force to the doll, but Swanilda, disguised as Coppélia, jumps up and runs off to marry Franz.

Georges Bizet

◗ 1838–1875   🏳 French   ✍ c.120

A precocious but short-lived talent, Bizet devoted the best part of his brief but creative life to opera, for which he wrote his greatest music. Although acclaimed at his death as a concert composer, it was for his avant-garde opera *Carmen* that he is now remembered. With *Carmen*, he changed the course of French opera, setting a style in lifelike drama and sensual music that reached its peak decades later.

LIFE AND MUSIC

The son of a singing teacher, Bizet was a child prodigy who read music at four, played the piano at six, entered the Paris Conservatoire at nine, and composed an accomplished symphony at 17. Although he produced some passable Italianate operas in the 1950s, real success did not come until 1863 with his sensual and melodic *Les pêcheurs de perles*. A fallow patch followed before Bizet turned out a string of instrumental successes, such as *Jeux d'enfants*, and started work on a new opera, *Carmen*. But, shocked by its raw realism, the first critics reacted coolly, disappointing Bizet, who died before it became a box-office hit.

MILESTONES	
1847	Studies at the Paris Conservatoire under Jacques Halévy
1855	Writes Symphony in C major
1856	Befriends Charles Gounod
1857	Wins the Grand Prix de Rome; *Le docteur miracle*, operetta, staged
1858	Studies in Rome
1860	Returns to Paris
1863	*Les pêcheurs de perles*, opera, premiered
1866	*La jolie fille de Perth*, opera, staged
1869	Marries Halévy's daughter, Geneviève
1871	*Djamileh*, one-act opera, premiered
1872	Commissioned to write *l'Arlésienne*, incidental music, staged at Vaudeville
1875	*Carmen*, opera, premiered in Paris

KEY WORKS

L'ARLÉSIENNE, SUITE NO. 1
ORCHESTRAL   ⏱ 17:00   📖 4   ♫

Bizet's enchanting orchestral suite, based on the incidental music that he wrote for Alphonse Daudet's play *L'Arlésienne* (*The Girl from Arles*), proved to be even more popular than the play.

The virgin priestess Leila in *Les pêcheurs de perles* captures the hearts of two friends who vie for her hand.

SYMPHONY IN C MAJOR
ORCHESTRAL   ⏱ 35:00   📖 4   ♫

Bizet's first and possibly finest orchestral score, produced while still in his teens, was based on Charles Gounod's Symphony in D. Although unoriginal, it is a fresh and delightful piece with beautiful melodies; but it could not be enjoyed until 1935, as the score disappeared for 80 years.

JEUX D'ENFANTS SUITE, OP. 22
PIANO DUET   ⏱ 30:00   📖 12   ♫

A brilliant pianist, Bizet wrote this charming suite, based on children's games, for piano duet, from which he later orchestrated five movements as the *Petite suite d'orchestra* in 1872.

FOCUS

LES PÊCHEURS DE PERLES

OPERA   🕐 100:00   📖 3   ♐♑♒

Bizet's first operatic hit, achieved in his 20s, never enjoyed *Carmen's* success, but still attracts audiences. Although written to an appalling libretto, its charm lies in its melodic music, sensual undertones, and exotic atmosphere, evoked by lively rhythms and spicy harmonies. The appealing vocal score, inspired by Bizet's mentor, Charles Gounod, also helps to enthrall listeners, with such sweet, memorable songs as "Au fond du temple saint".

ACT ONE (45:00) A fishing crew choose Zurga as their chief. He and his friend, Nadir, recall the time when they fell for the same woman, Leila, but avoided conflict by letting her go.

ACT TWO (30:00) Leila, now a priestess, arrives by boat to bless the fishermen. Nadir recognizes her as the woman he once loved, and reveals his passion. Learning of their love, the high priest Nourabad condemns them to death.

ACT THREE (25:00) Leila is led to her death, but Zurga relents and torches the camp, letting the lovers escape.

CARMEN

OPERA   🕐 160:00   📖 4   ♐♑♒

Bizet's *Carmen*, the first realistic opera, shocked the first audiences with its lifelike characters, sensual passions, and graphic on-stage murder. Set to a libretto by Henri Meilhac and Ludovic Halévy, the plot was inspired by Prosper Merimée's short novel about a passionate Spanish gypsy.

ACT ONE (60:00) Soldiers arrest Carmen for assaulting a fellow worker at the cigarette factory in Seville. She escapes by seducing Don José, one of the guards, who is then imprisoned.

ACT TWO (40:00) At Lillas Pastia's bar, Carmen attracts the bullfighter Escamillo. When Don José is released, she persuades him to desert the army and join a band of smugglers.

ACT THREE (40:00) Don José, Carmen, and the smugglers march through the night. Carmen foretells her own death. Escamillo follows, fights Don José, and just escapes with his life.

ACT FOUR (20:00) In Seville, Carmen goes to the bullfight to watch her new lover, but Don José confronts and kills her.

"I shall feel [the story] as an Italian, with desperate passion."

GIACOMO PUCCINI

Giacomo Puccini

1858–1924   Italian   38

Giacomo Puccini was the last in the great line of Italian composers of Romantic opera. With *Turandot*, his unfinished masterpiece, the tradition can be said to have ended, although in it Puccini had already begun to explore much of the new musical language of the 20th century. His most popular operas, *La bohème*, *Madama Butterfly* and *Tosca* demonstrate his gift for capturing an audience's attention with pure dramatic intensity.

LIFE

Puccini was born in Lucca, Tuscany, into the fifth generation of a family of Church musicians. His father died when Puccini was only five, but the position of organist at the church of San Martino was kept open for him until he was old enough to step into his father's shoes. However, a performance of Verdi's *Aïda*, which he saw in Pisa in 1876, convinced him that his true vocation was opera. He took up the position of church organist at the age of 19, but in 1880 went to study at the Milan Conservatory. When the publisher Sonzogno launched a competition for a one-act opera, Puccini entered *Le Villi*, which failed to win. Sonzogno's rival, Giulio Ricordi, commissioned another opera from Puccini, *Edgar*, and after its failure another, more successful: *Manon Lescaut*.

From now on Puccini devoted his life to writing opera, with country pursuits such as shooting and fishing as his recreations. In 1891, he bought a beautiful estate on a lake near Lucca. He was by now living with a married woman, Elvira Bonturi, whom he was unable to marry until the death of her husband. The relationship seems to have been a tempestuous one. In 1909, a servant killed herself after Elvira accused her of having an affair with Puccini.

During the writing of his last opera, *Turandot*, Puccini fell ill with throat cancer, and died while undergoing medical treatment in Brussels, leaving his masterpiece incomplete.

The operas of Puccini are based on passionate stories of love, revenge, and betrayal.

MUSICAL OUTPUT								Total: 38
ORCHESTRAL (4)			1	2	1			
INSTRUMENTAL (7)				5		2		
OPERA (12)				2	2	3	4	1
VOCAL (15)		3		10	2			
	1858	1870	1880	1890	1900	1910	1920	1924

MUSIC

Puccini's genius for melodic invention, his love for the pairing of soprano and tenor voices, and his gift for picking theatrically effective plots established him as the most popular of all opera composers. His Romantic lyricism is in the tradition of 19th-century Italian opera, but he took up 20th-century ideas of bitonalism and dissonance from Stravinsky and others.

Throughout his career, his taste for the exotic led him to incorporate music from the widest of sources, from the Roman matins bells in *Tosca*, the Japanese melodies in *Madama Butterfly* (supplied by a friend), and the Wild West tunes of *La fanciulla del West*. In *Turandot* he went even further, using pentatonic and whole-tone scales to evoke a mythical China, and adding tuned percussion to an already rich orchestral palette.

MILESTONES	
1880	Enters Milan Conservatory
1884	One-act opera *Le Villi* performed in Milan
1889	Second opera *Edgar* is a failure
1893	Third opera *Manon Lescaut* enjoys great success in Turin
1896	*La bohème* produced at Teatro Regio, Turin
1900	*Tosca* premiered at Teatro Costanzi, Rome
1904	Premiere of first version of *Madama Butterfly*
1906	Definitive version of Madama *Butterfly*
1910	*La fanciulla del West* premiered at Metropolitan Opera, New York
1917	*La rondine* performed in Monte Carlo
1918	*Il trittico* (three one-act operas)
1920	Starts work on *Turandot*, but work is left unfinished on his death in 1924

KEY WORKS

TURANDOT

OPERA   ⏲ 120:00   📖 3   🔊 🎭 👤

Turandot was Puccini's last opera. He fell ill while composing the last act, and died without completing it. In ancient China, Princess Turandot has declared that she will marry the prince who can answer her three riddles. Anyone who fails will be beheaded. Prince Calaf declares that he wants to face the test. He answers correctly, but she refuses to marry him. He proposes that she should guess his name by morning; if she does, she can behead him. Turandot orders her servants to torture the name from Calaf's servant, Liù, who is in love

with her master. Liù dies, and Turandot learns from her example what it means to love.

LA TOSCA

OPERA   ⏲ 140:00   📖 3   🔊 🎭 👤

Victorien Sardou wrote the melodram *Tosca* as a vehicle for the great actress Sarah Bernhardt. Puccini turned it into a spectacular opera, its title role a magnificent vehicle for singers like Maria Callas. Its three acts are set in Rome, in the Church of Sant'Andrea della Valle where th painter Cavaradoss helps the fugitive Angelotti, the Palazzo Farnese where the villainou Scarpia has his torture chamber, and the Castel San Angelo, where Tosca flings herself from the parapet.

Luciano Pavarotti enjoyed huge success in the 1990s with Calaf's aria "Nessun Dorma" from Turandot.

MADAMA BUTTERFLY

OPERA 140:00 3

Puccini saw David Belasco's play about a Nagasaki geisha and her American naval officer lover, *Madame Butterfly*, and decided to turn it into an opera. Belasco's play was based on a short story by John Luther Long, which was itself based on an incident witnessed by his sister, Jennie Correll, a US missionary working in Nagasaki.

ACT ONE (60:00) Pinkerton, an American naval officer, arranges to marry Madame Butterfly, a Nagasaki geisha. The marriage is attended by her family, the bride is deeply in love, but for Pinkerton his vows mean nothing.

ACT TWO (50:00) Pinkerton has sailed back to the USA, and Butterfly, who has had a son by him, awaits his return. When her servant Suzuki suggests Pinkerton may never come back, Butterfly sings the aria "Un bel di" ("One fine day"). She sees his ship entering Nagasaki bay. Butterfly, her son, and Suzuki wait all night for Pinkerton's arrival.

ACT THREE (30:00) The American consul tells Suzuki that Pinkerton has remarried. Pinkerton and his wife come to collect the child. On realizing the truth, Butterfly kills herself.

LA BOHÈME

OPERA 120:00 4

Puccini and his librettists, Illica and Giacosa, based *La bohème* on Henry Murger's *Scènes de la vie de Bohème*.

ACT ONE (40:00) Rodolfo the poet, Marcello the painter, and two other Bohemian friends share a Paris garret. It is Christmas Eve. They burn pages from Rodolfo's manuscript to keep warm. Mimì, a neighbour, knocks at the door. Rodolfo falls in love with her.

ACT TWO (20:00) The four friends and Mimì are at the Café Momus.

Marcello joins up with a former girlfriend Musetta, a singer, who tricks her current lover, the elderly Alcindoro, into paying the bill.

ACT THREE (30:00) Rodolfo is jealous of Mimì's infidelities, and at the same time feels they cannot continue living together in poverty, because she is dying of consumption.

ACT FOUR (30:00) The dying Mimì returns to the garret. The friends go off to buy her what comforts they can. They return to find Mimì dying in Rodolfo's arms.

ACT ONE

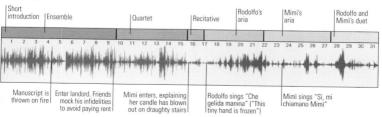

Otto Nicolai

● 1810–1849   ▶ German   ✍ 235

Surviving a traumatic childhood, during which he supported himself as an itinerant pianist, Nicolai studied in Berlin and made valuable contacts. His early career alternated between Italy (where his Italian-style operas *Enrico II* and *Il templario* made him an overnight sensation) and Vienna (where he eventually settled after fleeing a broken engagement in Italy). He gained respect as an innovative conductor at Vienna's Philharmonic Concerts and as a craftsmanlike, if eclectic, opera composer clearly influenced by Bellini, Weber, and others. But he found a distinctive voice in his enduring comic masterpiece *The Merry Wives of Windsor*, a new style of opera, in German, which was premiered to a quiet reception two months before his premature death.

Nicolai produced his comic opera *The Merry Wives of Windsor* in 1849 at the Berlin Opera, two years after becoming the chief conductor there.

MILESTONES

1834	Becomes an organist in Rome
1840	Writes *Il templario (The Templar)*, opera
1841	Appointed principal conductor of Hofoper, Vienna's opera house
1842	Appointed conductor of the Philharmonic Concerts in Vienna
1849	Premieres *Die lustigen Weiber von Windsor (The Merry Wives of Windsor)*, operetta

---

Louis James Alfred Lefébure-Wély

● 1817–1869   ▶ French   ✍ c.200

An extraordinary organist whose virtuosity with the pedals inspired César Franck and Charles Alkan, Lefébure-Wély is primarily remembered as an organ composer, though he also wrote symphonies, piano pieces, and stage and chamber works. He succeeded his father as church organist at 15 and, after studies at the Paris Conservatoire, held the major posts of organist at La Madeleine, and then St Sulpice. Always in demand as a harmonium recitalist in France and abroad, and for concerts inaugurating new organs, his popularity helped to establish wide appreciation of the French Romantic organ, especially the fabulous instruments built by Cavaillé-Coll.

MILESTONES

1833	Succeeds father as organist at St Roch
1835	Wins first prize for organ at Paris Conservatoire
1847	Appointed organist at La Madeleine
1850	Awarded the Légion d'Honneur
1861	Composes opera *Les recruteurs* and *L'office catholique*, Op.148, organ music

Lefébure-Wély built himself a successful career as the official organist at three of the most important churches in Paris, including that of Saint-Rochs, hown here in 1840, which was his first appointment.

Jacques Offenbach

● 1819–1880   ♙ French   ✍ c.100

Jacques Offenbach created the French operetta. Many of his works have never left the repertory, with *La belle Hélène* and *Orphée aux enfers (Orpheus in the Underworld)* among the most popular ever written. But he also wrote one masterpiece of grand opera, *The Tales of Hoffmann*, left unfinished at his death. Set in Germany and Venice, it includes a gondola scene with the famous Barcarolle.

LIFE AND MUSIC

Offenbach was born near Cologne in Germany, the son of the cantor at the city's synagogue. He studied in Paris, becoming a brilliant cellist and playing in the Opéra-Comique orchestra. In 1853 he began writing operettas. He then became theatre manager of the Théâtre Comte, which he renamed the Bouffes Parisiens. His light-hearted musical style, inventive in its melodies and enhanced by his choice of witty librettists as his collaborators, epitomized the style of the French Second Empire, while at the same time satirizing its excesses. He wrote more than 90 operettas, but also worked for many years on his grand opera, *Les contes d'Hoffmann (The Tales of Hoffmann)*. He died before finishing it, but it was completed and orchestrated from Offenbach's sketches by Ernest Guiraud.

MILESTONES	
1833	Begins studies at Paris Conservatoire
1849	Appointed conductor at Théâtre Français in Paris
1853	Begins composing operettas
1858	*Orphée aux enfers*, operetta, premiered
1855	Takes over Théâtre Compte
1864	Premieres of *Der Rheinnixen*, opera, in Vienna; *La belle Hélène*, operetta, Paris
1866	Writes *La vie parisienne*, operetta
1867	Writes *Robinson Crusoé*, operetta
1868	Writes *La Périchole*, operetta
1869	Writes *Princesse de Trébizonde*, operetta
1876	Moves to US; returns to Paris 1878
1880	Dies in Paris
1881	*Les contes d'Hoffmann*, opera, begun in 1877, given first performance

KEY WORKS

ORPHÉE AUX ENFERS
OPERETTA   ♬ 165:00   ▥ 2   ♫ ♨ ♂

This is a send-up of Greek mythology and a satire of French Second Empire society and its pretensions. Though openly caricatured in it, Napoleon III praised Offenbach for the piece. In the plot, Orpheus and Eurydice have each started affairs. Eurydice's new boyfriend, Pluto, takes her down to the Underworld, but Public Opinion forces Orpheus to get her back. The operetta ends with the *Galope infernal*, Offenbach's famous Cancan.

LES CONTES D'HOFFMANN
OPERETTA   ♬ 240:00   ▥ 5   ♫ ♨ ♂

Although Offenbach's last and greatest work is essentially quite dark and has much rich melody, it also offers moments of humour. Based on three tales by E T A Hoffmann, its prologue, three acts, and epilogue follow Hoffmann's love affairs with Olympia, Antonia, and Giulietta. The Giulietta act, set in Venice, begins with the celebrated Barcarolle.

Offenbach's Cancan is the most famous rendition of an Algerian dance popularized in the 1830s.

Johann Strauss Jr

🔵 1825–1899 🏳 Austrian ✍ c.250

Johann Strauss Jr, Vienna's "Waltz King", was the son of
Johann Strauss Sr, who had taught the Viennese to waltz
to the tunes of his famous band. His father forbade the
younger Strauss to follow his profession, but Johann started his own orchestra
and rivalled his father's success. When Offenbach's operettas were a hit in
Vienna, Strauss followed his example and wrote for the opera house.

LIFE AND MUSIC

Johann Strauss Jr studied the violin
against his father's wishes, and soon
gained a reputation as a fine violinist,
conductor, and composer. Throughout
his career his output was prolific; he
composed 15 operettas as well as
popular polkas and waltzes, such as *The
Blue Danube*. Strauss's superb operetta
Die Fledermaus premiered in 1874, and
within a year had been performed all
over the world. Admired by Brahms
and Liszt, he was considered to be the
master of light music and became the
most famous of the Strauss family.

MILESTONES	
1844	Forms his own orchestra
1855	Directs summer concerts in St Petersburg
1863	Conducts Austrian court balls
1867	Visits Paris and London, writes *The Blue Danube*
1868	Writes *Tales from the Vienna Woods*
1871	First operetta produced in Vienna
1874	*Die Fledermaus* first performed
1883	Composes *Eine Nacht in Venedig*, operetta
1885	*The Gypsy Baron*, operetta, performed
1888	Writes the *Emperor Waltz*

KEY WORKS

TALES FROM VIENNA WOODS

WALTZ   🕙 13:00   📖 1   ♒

Geschichten aus dem Wienerwald, written
a year after *The Blue Danube*, was one
of the most celebrated waltzes of
the 19th century. Strauss's waltzes
epitomized the essence of Viennese
high society during the twilight years
of the Austro-Hungarian Empire.

THE BLUE DANUBE

WALTZ   🕙 8:00   📖 1   ♒

The full title of Strauss's most famous
waltz is *An der schönen blauen Donau*
(*On the beautiful blue Danube*). Written
as a concert waltz in 1867, he later
included it in his operetta *Indigo and
the Forty Thieves*. Brahms admired the
waltz's elegance and vivacity so much
that he wished he had written
it himself. Strauss's waltzes
became so fashionable that
they soon spread from the
ballrooms of Vienna to the
rest of Europe, and *The Blue
Danube* is still one of the most
frequently performed works
in the Classical repertoire.

Although Strauss wrote such wonderful
dance music, he always maintained he
was unable to dance himself.

FOCUS

DIE FLEDERMAUS

OPERETTA 🎭 130:00 📖 3 ♒ ♨ ♂

The story of *Die Fledermaus* begins with a practical joke that took place three years before the opening scene. After a costume ball, Dr Falke is left by his friend Eisenstein to walk home through the city, drunk and alone, in his bat costume. Johann Strauss Jr wrote his three-act Komische Operette *Die Fledermaus* to a libretto by Carl Haffner and Richard Genée, who based their text on a French farce, *Le réveillon*, by Henri Meilhac and Ludovic Halévy. It was Strauss's third operetta, following *Indigo und die vierzig Räuber* and *Carneval in Rom*. Composed in a mere six weeks, it was first performed at the Theater an der Wien, Vienna, on 5 April 1874. Strauss was said to have composed this enjoyable comic operetta to take the minds of the Viennese off the Black Monday stock-market crash of 1873. The work soon entered the international repertory, and by the 1890s was treated as an opera and was produced in the world's major houses. In 1894, an especially celebrated production was staged at Vienna's Hofoper with the composer conducting.

ACT ONE (50:00) Falke invites Eisenstein, who is on his way to prison, to a ball at Prince Orlovsky's.

ACT TWO (50:00) At the ball, Eisenstein flirts first with his disguised housemaid, Adele, and then with his wife, Rosalinde (also in disguise, and herself having an affair with Alfred).

ACT THREE (30:00) When they all meet up in the prison the misunderstandings are resolved – it was all the fault of Orlovsky's champagne.

DER ZIGEUNERBARON

OPERETTA 🎭 120:00 📖 3 ♒ ♨ ♂

Written ten years after *Die Fledermaus*, *The Gypsy Baron* is Johann Strauss's other enduringly successful operetta.

It was written to a libretto by Ignatz Schitzer, and was first performed on 24 October 1885 in Vienna.

ACT ONE (40:00) In Banat, Hungary, in the 18th century, Baron Sándor Barinkay finds that his estates have been settled by gypsies. Zsupán, a wealthy pig-farmer, thinks Sándor would make an ideal son-in-law. However his daughter, Arsena, has her heart set on Ottokar, the son of her governess Mirabella.

ACT TWO (45:00) The gypsy Sáffi wins Sándor's love, and is revealed to be a wealthy princess descended from the last Pasha of Hungary.

ACT THREE (35:00) Sándor's fortunes are restored. Arsena marries Ottokar, and they are blessed by the Baron. They all live happily ever after.

Franz von Suppé

● 1819–1895   ◪ Austrian   ♫ c.200

Von Suppé drily insisted that his successful style came about by accident, when his poor knowledge of German misled him into setting a yodelling song sentimentally in the style of Donizetti. Nevertheless, his first theatre score in 1841 triumphed. During spells as Kapellmeister at the Theater an der Wien and the Carltheater, he conducted many historic performances of opera and wrote a succession of stage scores. He went on to become the first master of Viennese operetta – *Das Pensionat* was his first success, and *Boccaccio* was the work he considered his best. His light, fluent, and flexible music is most familiar now in overtures to operettas such as *Light Cavalry*.

MILESTONES	
1819	Born in Spalato (now Split, Croatia)
1834	Writes first comic opera, *Der Apfel*
1835	Moves to Vienna
1841	Score to the play *Jung lustig* triumphs
1846	*Poet and Peasant*, incidental music
1860	Composes *Das Pensionat*, operetta
1866	Writes *Light Cavalry*, operetta

Von Suppé studied in Vienna with Ignaz Xaver von Seyfried, and conducted at various Viennese and provincial theatres, including the Leopoldstadt, from 1841 until his death.

Sir Edward German

● 1862–1936   ◪ English   ♫ c.200

Edward Jones's promise as a gifted student of composition at the Royal Academy was amply fulfilled. Music for productions of Shakespeare at the Globe Theatre, where he was musical director, established his reputation, and he was soon besieged by commissions for concert works. He wrote operettas in the "Old English" style, such as *Merrie England*, though the appeal of Gilbert-and-Sullivan-esque music was diminishing. His elegant, warm, and romantic music – cosmopolitan yet always English – enjoyed both popularity and high regard (Elgar was an admirer). A meticulous conductor, German was also in demand to direct his own music.

MILESTONES	
1885	*Te Deum* wins a prize at the Royal Academy of Music, London
1888	Becomes music director of the Globe Theatre, London
1902	*Merrie England*, operetta, performed
1904	Writes *Welsh Rhapsody*, symphonic suite
1907	Composes *Tom Jones*, operetta
1928	Knighted for his services to music

Edward German's *Tom Jones*, based on Henry Fielding's novel, was a great success in 1907, although some were offended by the bawdiness of Tom's story.

Sir Arthur Sullivan

● 1842–1900   🏳 English   ✎ c.300

Sir Arthur Sullivan, together with W S Gilbert, invented the Savoy Opera, and their names became inseparable. Gilbert and Sullivan's operettas parodied operatic convention and ridiculed the pomposities of British officialdom (even in the guise of Japanese in *The Mikado*). But Sullivan longed for recognition as a serious composer, and wrote many instrumental, choral, and operatic works.

LIFE AND MUSIC

Arthur Sullivan was the son of an Irish bandmaster and an Italian mother. An enthusiastic chorister at the Chapel Royal, he published his first composition at the age of 13. After studying in London at the Royal Academy of Music, and then at the Leipzig Conservatory, he wrote cantatas and symphonies before writing his first comic operetta, *Cox and Box*. In 1871, Sullivan met the playwright, W S Gilbert, and began a collaboration that lasted until the pair famously quarrelled about a new carpet at the Savoy Theatre in 1889, only re-uniting to write two final operettas. In the meantime, Sullivan had written his one opera, *Ivanhoe*, which he hoped would establish his reputation. This, however, rests firmly with the comic operettas he wrote with Gilbert.

MILESTONES

1854	Chorister at the Chapel Royal
1856	Studies at the Royal Academy of Music, London
1862	Establishes reputation with incidental music for *The Tempest*
1866	Writes *Cox and Box*, operetta
1876	*Trial by Jury*, first successful collaboration with Gilbert
1878	Composes *HMS Pinafore*, operetta
1879	*The Pirates of Penzance* produced
1881	Richard D'Oyly Carte opens at the Savoy Theatre
1883	Receives a knighthood
1884	First performance of *The Mikado*
1889	Writes *The Gondoliers*
1890	Writes *Ivanhoe*, his only opera

KEY WORKS

HMS PINAFORE

OPERETTA   🕰 105:00   📖 2   🎻🥁🎵

Filled with sea-shanties and nautical airs, *HMS Pinafore* is a satire on the British class system and its embodiment in the Royal Navy. Sullivan rose to the challenge of Gilbert's intricate metres and patter-songs with a lively, bustling score, setting the story of *The Lass that Loved a Sailor*.

The Mikado, first produced in 1885, ran at the Savoy Theatre for 672 performances.

THE MIKADO

OPERETTA   🕰 135:00   📖 2   🎻🥁🎵

Gilbert and Sullivan were at their most imaginative in *The Mikado* – their longest-running show. Although making fun of British bureaucracy, the operetta is set in the mythical Japanese town of Titipu, where the strolling minstrel Nanki-Poo (the Mikado's son) is courting Yum-Yum, the ward of the Lord High Executioner. The wit of Sullivan's music is demonstrated by his ability to incorporate a genuine Japanese tune, an English madrigal, and a Bach fugue in his score.

Engelbert Humperdinck

🔵 1854–1921   🏳 German   ✍ c.230

Engelbert Humperdinck emerged from the shadow of
Wagner, his mentor and friend, to invent a new style of
German opera, based on fairy tales. Humperdinck assisted
Wagner on *Parsifal*, and learned a great deal from him about
orchestration and vocal writing, but he discovered his own original voice in his
use of simple children's songs, especially in his masterpiece *Hänsel und Gretel*.

LIFE AND MUSIC

Engelbert Humperdinck was born in
Siegburg in 1854 and studied architecture
in Cologne before being encouraged
to change his discipline to composition,
piano, and cello. He continued his studies
in Munich, winning prizes with his early
compositions, including the Mendelssohn
Prize, which took him to Naples. There
he befriended Wagner, who brought him
to Bayreuth as his assistant. Humperdinck
contributed a small section to *Parsifal*, but
this was later rejected. His sister then
encouraged him to write *Hänsel und Gretel*
as an entertainment for his children. This
and *Königskinder (Royal Children)* established
his reputation as an opera composer.

MILESTONES	
1876	Wins Mozart Scholarship, allowing him to study in Munich
1879	Writes *Humoreske* for orchestra
1880	Wins Mendelssohn Prize for *Die Wallfahrt nach Kevlaar*, choral work; meets Wagner in Naples.
1881	Wins Meyerbeer Prize of 7,600 marks. Goes to work for Wagner in Bayreuth
1893	Opera *Hänsel und Gretel* premiered
1897	Retires from teaching to devote himself to full-time composition
1910	Opera *Königskinder (Royal Children)* premiered in New York

KEY WORKS

HÄNSEL UND GRETEL

OPERETTA   ⏱ 105:00   📖 3   🎵 ♻ ♂

Humperdinck had been inhibited by his
close association with Wagner from
writing an opera until his sister, Adelhaid
Witte, suggested that he set the Grimm
brothers' fairy tale *Hansel and Gretel* as a
musical entertainment for her children.
First he set songs, then a *Singspiel* with
spoken dialogue, and finally in 1893 he
produced the full operatic score of his
first and most famous opera. It is also the
one most clearly influenced by the music
of Wagner, as heard in its complex
orchestration and repeating musical
themes. However, consistent with the
composer's choice of traditional fairy tale
as his subject matter, there is also fun and
lightness, with passages inspired by folk
dance and folk song, as well as musical
originality. The story is well known:
Hansel and Gretel, alone at home, play

Humperdinck's Hänsel und Gretel was premiered in
Weimar by Richard Strauss, who called it "original,
new, and authentically German". German audiences,
such as this one in Berlin in 1895, took it to their hearts.

games. Their mother returns, scolds
them, and sends them to pick strawberries
in the forest. They get lost and fall asleep.
They wake to find a gingerbread cottage.
Its owner, a witch, tries to fatten Hansel
for dinner, but Gretel bundles her into the
oven and frees the gingerbread children.

Franz Lehár

◗ 1870–1948　　🏳 Hungarian　　✍ c.260

Franz Lehár was for 20th-century Viennese operetta what Johann Strauss Jr had been for the 19th century. Lehár made his name as a composer of waltzes, then began writing operettas for the two leading Viennese theatres. *Die lustige Witwe (The Merry Widow)* made his fame in Europe and the US, as well as his fortune, and he went on to write many more operettas, operas, and film scores.

LIFE AND MUSIC

Franz Lehár was the son of a military bandmaster and studied at the Prague Conservatory. He then led army bands, while starting his career as a composer with an unsuccessful grand opera, *Kukuška*. His waltz *Gold and Silver* was popular enough to allow him to leave band life and compose more for the stage. In 1902 he had two operetta premieres in Vienna, followed by his greatest success, *The Merry Widow*. His operetta career then flourished, but declined during World War I. Working with the tenor Richard Tauber, he found new success with *Frasquita* and *Paganini*, culminating in *The Land of Smiles*. Under the Nazis, he was forced to retire (his wife was Jewish), but his work was still performed.

MILESTONES

1890	Conducts army bands for 12 years
1902	Writes concert waltz *Gold and Silver*; *Wiener Frauen*, operetta, is a success
1905	Has enormous, immediate success with operetta *The Merry Widow*
1920	Begins writing for Richard Tauber
1929	Writes operetta *The Land of Smiles*
1934	Writes a full-scale opera, *Giuditta*

The Merry Widow was so successful that it spawned a craze for "Merry Widow" corsets, hats, and cocktails. Lehár's income enabled him to buy this elegant villa in Bad Ischl in 1912.

KEY WORKS

DIE LUSTIGE WITWE

OPERETTA　⏱ 150:00　📖 3　🎻🥁🎵

The libretto for this still crowd-pulling operetta was adapted from *The Embassy Attaché*, a play by Henri Meilhac. Lehár used a larger orchestra than was until then usual for operettas. The music is a heady mix of Balkan folk dance, Parisian cabaret, and Viennese waltz. The operetta tells the story of a young "merry widow", Hanna, whose banker husband left her a fortune. To stop her marrying a foreigner, Count Danilo is sent by the Pontevedrian Ambassador to woo her. He does so. Her money thus stays in Pontevedro, rescuing her from bankruptcy.

DAS LAND DES LÄCHELNS

OPERETTA　⏱ 135:00　📖 3　🎻🥁🎵

The Land of Smiles is most famous for its aria "Dein ist mein ganzes Herz" ("You are my Heart's Delight"). The operetta tells how Viennese Lisa has to renounce her love for a Chinese prince because she cannot accustom herself to the smiling façade of the Chinese.

Lehár made his name as a composer of Viennese waltzes before finding success with operettas.

NATIONAL SCHOOLS
1830–1950

During the 19th and early 20th centuries, as modern nation states emerged, music for many composers became a means of asserting their national identity. Other composers included in this section were not actively nationalists, but their music nevertheless reflects their countries or regions of origin.

Much of the music of the Baroque and Classical periods has a style that cannot easily be pinned down to a single country; styles and forms were international. In the 19th century, however, musicians began to define themselves in terms of their nationalities as well as the styles or genres in which they worked.

European politics in the 19th century was dominated by nationalist movements. These were of two main kinds. There were peoples united by a common language, such as the Italians and Germans, whose aim was to form a single nation state, while other peoples – for example, the Hungarians, Czechs, and Irish – were subject to foreign rule and sought autonomy or independence. Music, along with language and literature, became a means of expressing their aspirations.

SPANISH GYPSY DANCERS (1898)
This painting by Ricardo Canals y Llambi expresses the fascination felt all over Europe in the late 19th century for vital folk traditions in music and dance.

The most clear-cut example of musical nationalism, however, did not emerge in a country ruled by an oppressive empire. Russia was itself great empire, but historically had been made to feel culturally inferior to Western Europe. European music had been imported into Russia by and for the aristocracy; the only truly Russian music was that of the folk tradition.

RUSSIAN NATIONALISM
The catalyst for change in Russia was Mikhail Glinka. His opera *A Life for the Tsar* was similar to Rossini in style, but recalled the Russian folk melodies he had heard in his childhood.

The so-called "group of five", who emerged in the middle of the 19th century, took Russian nationalism much further. Balakirev composed a symphonic poem *Russia* and Borodin wrote *In Central Asia*. A third member of the group, Mussorgsky, was not a formally trained musician; unfamiliar with Western harmonic progressions,

THE SPIRIT OF THE CZECH LANDS
Smetana was inspired both by
Czech history and his country's
landscapes, as in this piece, "From
Bohemia's Forests and Meadows",
part of *Má Vlast (My Country)*.

he composed music that
made full use of Russian
folk harmonies. Later
Russian composers, such
as Rimsky-Korsakov, also
made use of folk melodies
and influenced future
generations of composers,
including Glazunov and Stravinsky.

THE HABSBURG EMPIRE

Czech nationalist composers were
less virulently anti-Western than their
Russian counterparts. Their aim was
to affirm their cultural difference from
the Austrian Habsburg
Empire, which had ruled
Bohemia and Moravia
for centuries, suppressing
Czech language and
culture. Smetana,
Dvořák, and Janáček
all contributed to the
development of their
country's national
musical style. *Má Vlast*,
Smetana's cycle of
symphonic poems, is not only a
portrait of the Czech landscape, but
also an evocation of Czech culture and
history. The section *Tábor and Blaník*
includes a Czech Hussite chorale,
"Those who are Warriors of God".

Hungary's situation differed from
that of Czechoslovakia as its folk
music had been represented (or
misrepresented) by Romantic

TIMELINE: NATIONAL SCHOOLS

1836
Glinka's patriotic
opera *A Life for
the Tsar*

1848 ▷
Marx and
Engels publish
*The Communist
Manifesto*

1861
Unification of
most of Italy;
emancipation
of serfs in
Russia

1874
Mussorgsky's
Boris Godunov
performed in
St Petersburg

1876
Ibsen's *Peer
Gynt* performed
with Grieg's
incidental
music

1845   **1855**   **1865**   **1875**

◁ **1848**
Revolutions in Italy,
across the Habsburg
Empire, and in Paris

1850s
Balakirev and
other members of
the "Five" strive
to create Russian
style of music

1861–65 ▷
American
Civil War

1870
Franco-Prussian
War; unification
of Germany und
Kaiser Wilhelm

FRIDAY NIGHT AT THE HOUSE OF MITROFAN BELYAEV
Belyaev was a rich timber merchant who founded a Russian music publishing house in 1885. Among his guests pictured here are Rimsky-Korsakov and Lyadov.

composers, such as Liszt, Brahms, and Joachim. It was only in the 20th century that Bartók and Kodály began to collect Hungarian folk music more systematically and make use of it in a more authentic way.

FURTHER AFIELD

Political and cultural links between Germany and Scandinavian countries took some time to loosen; Denmark's Niels Gade, for example, spent much time studying and subsequently conducting in Leipzig. It was left to Nordraak and Grieg (who also studied in Leipzig) to create a distinctive Norwegian art music. Grieg's *Peer Gynt Suite* was written as incidental music for Ibsen's play about the eponymous adventurer. In Finland, the music of Sibelius has nationalist tendencies only in that it quotes Finnish folk music.

In North America, most art music of the 19th century ignored folk material, although MacDowell's *Indian Suite* uses American Indian

melodies. Charles Ives was a more distinctively American composer, and his quotations of music from his own environment provide a highly evocative if individual picture of his childhood in New England. Later on Aaron Copland would create a highly recognizable American music, partly by appropriating rustic styles such as the "hoedown" in *Appalachian Spring*.

A revival of folk music in Spain coincided with that in Britain in the early 20th century. Composers such as Granados and Albéniz in Spain and Vaughan Williams in England used the folk music of their respective countries in similar nostalgic ways.

FOLK MELODIES

Just as languages and dialects differ from each other, so folk melodies have distinctive and often immediately recognizable characteristics. Different cultures tend to use different kinds of intervals in their melodies, which give them a particular flavour. In the case of the Jewish Klezmer music of Central and Eastern Europe, for example, this is a particularly exotic flavour. The use of rhythm in folk music also differs greatly from one culture to another, just as it does in spoken language.

NORWEGIAN FOLK DANCING

In the late 19th century, musicians, painters, and social historians across Europe were enthusiastic recorders of vanishing regional folk traditions.

SET OF GLINKA'S *A LIFE FOR THE TSAR*
The plot of Glinka's groundbreaking opera revolved around the election of the first Romanov tsar in 1613 and included a lively depiction of Russian peasant life.

1883
Opening of Czech National Theatre with performance of Smetana's *Libuše*

1890
First of Danish composer Nielsen's six symphonies

◁ **1919**
Treaty of Versailles; Hungary, Czechoslovakia, Poland, and Finland gain independence

1885

1895

1905

1915

1878
Slavonic Dances make Dvořák's reputation

1888 ▷
Rimsky-Korsakov's *Sheherazade*

1900
Sibelius's tone poem *Finlandia*

1917
Russian Revolution

◁ **1919**
Pianist Paderewski becomes first prime minister of modern Poland

Mikhail Glinka

● 1804–1857   ⚑ Russian   ✍ c.195

Glinka is widely regarded as the father of Russian music and produced the first successful Russian national opera. Rejecting traditional German forms and harmony in favour of music developed from folk-like melodies, his works display rhythmic exuberance, quasi-oriental chromaticism, and vivid clarity of orchestral textures, which epitomize a Russian sound that inspired successive generations of composers.

LIFE AND MUSIC

From a wealthy family, Glinka only dabbled in music until his late 20s, when he established himself as a pianist in Milan. Subsequent musical studies in Berlin were cut short by the death of his father, and he returned home to start work on his opera *A Life for the Tsar*. Its success established him as Russia's pre-eminent composer. However, his next opera, *Ruslan and Lyudmilla*, was less well received, although musically more important. Travels to Paris and Madrid – including a meeting with Berlioz who conducted his music – inspired him to write the orchestral showpieces which now eclipse his many fine vocal and instrumental works.

MILESTONES

1824	Appointed under-secretary at Ministry of Communications until 1828
1830	Arrives in Milan; meets Mendelssohn, Bellini, and Donizetti
1833	Studies in Berlin for five months
1834	Returns to Russia; starts work on *A Life for the Tsar*, first successful Russian opera
1835	Marries Mariya Petrovna Ivanova; she remarries bigamously six years later
1836	First performance of *A Life for the Tsar*
1837	Appointed Kapellmeister of the Imperial Chapel
1844	First production of opera *Ruslan and Lyudmilla* arouses admiration of Liszt
1885	Composes *Kamarinskaya*, orchestral work

KEY WORKS

OVERTURE TO RUSLAN AND LYUDMILLA

ORCHESTRAL   ⏱ 4:50   📖 1   ✿

This arresting overture to Glinka's most important work vividly sets the scene for Pushkin's fantastical fairy-tale. Written during rehearsals for the first performance of the opera, its infectious rhythmic vitality has kept it in the repertoire even though the opera itself is seldom heard outside Russia.

VALSE FANTASIE

ORCHESTRAL   ⏱ 9:30   📖 1   ✿

Performed at Glinka's memorial concert, the *Valse Fantasie* started life in 1839 as a piano piece. The composer later created a sumptuous orchestration of this chain of waltzes, establishing a model for later Russian composers. *The Valse Fantasie* certainly influenced symphonic waltzes in the ballets of Tchaikovsky and Prokofiev.

CAPRICCIO BRILLIANTE

ORCHESTRAL   ⏱ 9:45   📖 1   ✿

After a slow, fanfare-like introduction, Glinka's effective *Capriccio* turns into an orchestral showpiece based on a traditional Spanish melody, also found in Liszt's *Rapsodie Espagnol* of the same year. The only product of Glinka's sojourn in Madrid, its extensive use of castanets amply justifies its alternative title, the "First Spanish Rhapsody".

FOCUS

A LIFE FOR THE TSAR
OPERA ⏱ 209:00 📖 5 🎭🎭🎭🎭

A celebration of nationalist fervour, this opera was originally titled *Ivor Susanin* after its tragic hero, but was renamed in honour of Tsar Nicholas I, to whom it was dedicated. When staged in Soviet times, the title reverted and the libretto was altered to expunge references to the Tsar.

OVERTURE AND ACT ONE (48:00) In a Russian village Ivan Susanin's daughter is about to marry Sobinin, who has returned from fighting the Poles and allays fears of a conquest of Moscow. Susanin approves the wedding only when he hears that a new Romanov Tsar has been crowned. **ACT TWO** (29:20) A messenger interrupts celebrations at the Polish court to tell the King that the Russians are fighting back under their newly crowned Tsar, whom the Poles decide to capture. **ACT THREE** (63:40) During the wedding Polish soldiers arrive and demand to know the Tsar's hiding place. Susanin leads them in the wrong direction and his stepson, Vanya, rides to warn the Tsar. Sobinin and a group of peasants follow Susanin to attempt his rescue.

Glinka's *Kamarinskaya* was the first important Russian work to have been based entirely on folk music.

ACT FOUR (48:00) Sobinin and his band are camped at night in the freezing forest, whilst Vanya warns the Tsar. In the morning the Poles realize they have been tricked and beat Susanin to death. **EPILOGUE** (20:40) The Russian people celebrate in Moscow whilst Susanin's family mourns. The opera ends with a hymn to the Tsar.

KAMARINSKAYA
ORCHESTRAL ⏱ 7:30 📖 1 🎭

Inspired by meeting Berlioz, Glinka started writing orchestral works with a nationalist character. The last of these, *Kamarinskaya*, proved highly influential – Tchaikovsky believed that the Russian symphonic school was "all in *Kamarinskaya*, just as the whole oak is in the acorn". Based entirely on two Russian melodies, the work begins, after a brief introduction, with a slow, traditional bridal-song repeated three times with different accompaniments. A lively dance tune (kamarinskaya) follows on the violin, and is repeated 13 times in increasingly complex orchestral combinations. Then the music slows to reintroduce the bridal song, but the kamarinskaya soon returns for 21 more variations.

Alexander Borodin

◓ 1833–1887   ⚑ Russian   ✍ 21+

One of the "mighty handful" of Russian nationalists, Borodin was perhaps the most overtly Romantic, turning out highly charged music, full of choral and orchestral colour. Essentially a "Sunday composer", with a full-time career as a chemist, he left a small but polished oeuvre. His Symphony No. 2 displays a peerless mastery of technique, while *Prince Igor* remains a landmark of Russian opera.

LIFE AND MUSIC

Born in St Petersburg, Borodin was the illegitimate son of a Georgian prince who registered the child under the name of a servant. Although Borodin excelled from childhood in both science and music, he chose a career in chemistry. While practising as a professor and researcher at the Academy of Medico-Surgery in St Petersburg, he composed in his spare time. Although he admired Schumann, it was his compatriot Mily Balakirev – with whom he studied in 1863 – who had the most dramatic influence on his style. Of the "mighty handful", Borodin was perhaps most able to assimilate Russian folk style with the European symphonic tradition. Due to professional commitments, his output was small but accomplished, including symphonies, songs, and chamber music.

MILESTONES

1850	Enters the Academy of Medico-Surgery in St Petersburg
1856	Qualifies in medicine
1859	Specializes in chemistry in Germany
1861	Joins the "mighty handful"
1863	Studies composition with Balakirev; marries Ekatarina Protopopova
1869	Symphony No. 1 premiered unsuccessfully
1872	Lectures at the School of Medicine for Women, St Petersburg
1876	Writes Symphony No. 2 in B minor
1880	*In the Steppes of Central Asia*, tone poem, staged
1890	*Prince Igor*, opera, premiered posthumously at St Petersburg

KEY WORKS

PRINCE IGOR

OPERA   ⏱ 240:00   ▣ 5   🎭 🎻 ♂

Eighteen years in composition, and only completed posthumously by Rimsky-Korsakov and Glazunov, *Prince Igor* is Borodin's best-known work. Set in 12th-century Russia, it depicts the imprisonment of a Russian prince by an invading Tartar tribe, the Polovetsians. A notable feature is Borodin's unusual handling of the chorus, which functions almost as a separate character in the

Prince Igor, imbued with Russian character, displays Borodin's flair for orchestral colour and exotic motifs.

drama. The thrilling Polovetsian dances that conclude the second act are often performed on their own in concert.

SYMPHONY NO. 2

SYMPHONY   ⏱ 26:00   ▣ 4   🎻

As Borodin worked concurrently on *Prince Igor* and his Symphony No. 2, the two share many musical parallels. This powerful, mature, and concise piece, full of Borodin's rhythmic drive and exuberance, is perhaps the best example of Russian nationalist music allied to Classical principles of form.

Mily Alexeyevich Balakirev

● 1837–1910   🏴 Russian   ✍ c.50

The driving force behind the Russian nationalist "school" of music, Balakirev formed, guided, and inspired the "mighty handful", a circle committed to the nationalist cause. His own career was punctuated by periods of inactivity, but he produced some striking works in an unmistakably Russian idiom. A complex, irascible character, he could inspire lasting loyalty in friends and pupils, but also made many enemies.

LIFE AND MUSIC

After receiving early musical training from his mother, Balakirev was spotted by the wealthy music patron Alexander Ulibishev, who sent him to St Petersburg to meet Mikhail Glinka. Enthusiastic about musical nationalism, Balakirev gathered a circle of kindred spirits, known as the "mighty handful", including Cui, Mussorgsky, Borodin, and Rimsky-Korsakov. A difficult and single-minded idealist, he brooked no opposition and antagonized many. Overwrought and overworked, he suffered a nervous breakdown in 1871, withdrew from public life, and turned to mysticism, before emerging again in 1883 when he was appointed to the Imperial Chapel.

MILESTONES	
1847	Studies music in Moscow
1855	Moves to St Petersburg
1861	Writes incidental music for *King Lear*
1862	Founds the Free School of Music
1869	*Islamey*, fantasy, composed
1871	Suffers breakdown; turns to mysticism
1872	Works for the Warsaw railway
1882	*Tamara*, symphonic poem, staged
1883	Director of the Imperial Chapel
1908	Writes Symphony No. 2 in D minor

The concerted force of the "mighty handful" changed the course of Russian music, creating a distinctive Russian style that successfully merged Classical forms with Russian folk idioms.

KEY WORKS

TAMARA

TONE POEM   🖥 20:00   📖 1   ♫

Regarded as Balakirev's greatest work, *Tamara* is based on a poem by Mikhail Lermontov, which relates the story of an alluring siren who entices a traveller into her lair with her seductive song. After a night of passion, all is silent in the morning as the traveller's corpse swirls past in the tide of the river. Although Balakirev is not overtly descriptive, the plot can be discerned in the music. A quiet timpani roll evokes the fairy-tale atmosphere, while Tamara's voice is heard in the sinuous woodwind figure.

ISLAMEY

SOLO PIANO   🖥 9:00   📖 1   ♫

Balakirev originally conceived *Islamey* as a study for his tone poem *Tamara*, but although the two are similar, *Islamey* has no dark undercurrents. Rather, it is an exuberant showpiece, good-humoured and entertaining, yet immaculately crafted. Typical of Balakirev's Russian style, it combines classical virtuosity with exotic modes, chromatic harmonies and oriental motifs. Russian Tartar folk style emerges in the opening obsessive ostinato figure, inspired by a Caucasian dance, which gave the work its name.

Modest Mussorgsky

● 1839–1881   🏳 Russian   ✍ c.50

A mercurial and brilliantly talented composer, Mussorgsky was also an incurable alcoholic who led a disordered and prematurely shortened life. As a member of Balakirev's circle, he strove to compose music that resonated with the Russian people. However, many of his works were left unfinished, or were completed by well-meaning friends in a manner that may not reflect the composer's true intentions.

LIFE AND MUSIC

Despite being a prodigy at the piano, Mussorgsky initially joined the army, but resigned his commission in 1858 for a life of "meaningful endeavour". Taking a job in the civil service he began to work on a symphony and an opera, but these came to nothing. For the rest of his life a combination of unsettled personal circumstances, a nervous temperament, and serious alcoholism contrived to limit his creative endeavours. Of the Russian "Mighty Handful", Mussorgsky's music is perhaps the most rough-hewn, earthy, and immediate.

MILESTONES

1852	Enters Imperial Guard Cadet School
1861	Forced to work family estate following emancipation of the serfs
1865	First serious alcoholic episode
1867	Writes *St John's Night on the Bare Mountain*
1872	Composes *The Nursery* (song cycle)
1874	Revised version of *Boris Godunov*; *Sunless* (song cycle); *Pictures at an Exhibition*
1875	*Songs and Dances of Death* (song cycle)

St John's Night on the Bare Mountain, is a dramatic musical portrait of the witches' Sabbath, held in the mountains near Kiev.

KEY WORKS

SALAMMBÔ

OPERA   UNFINISHED   🎻 🎺 ♂

Between 1863–66, Mussorgsky was living in an artists' commune with five other men. In these creative surroundings, Mussorgsky worked on the libretto and music for an opera, *Salammbô*, based on Flaubert's tale of the siege of Carthage. However by 1865 his drinking was beginning to get the better of him, and he never completed the work. Some of the music from *Salammbô* has survived and is still performed, including the fine choral piece, *Chorus of Priestesses*.

SUNLESS, AND SONGS AND DANCES OF DEATH

PIANO/VOICE   🔊 ♂

While they are not as well known as his instrumental works, for many commentators it is Mussorgsky's songs that are his true masterpieces. The musical language is direct and unadorned, emotional without being overwrought or melodramatic. But perhaps most striking are the protagonists in his songs – not the fanciful lovers and poets of the lieder tradition, but the old, insane, poverty-stricken, and desperate.

FOCUS

BORIS GODUNOV

OPERA ⏱ 210:00 📖 4 ♫ ♨ ☉

Identifying the "real" *Boris Godunov* is not straightforward. Mussorgsky produced two complete versions during his lifetime, the second in response to the opera's initial rejection from the Maryinsky Opera.

To compound the problem, Rimsky-Korsakov famously took upon himself the task of smoothing Mussorgsky's characteristically abrasive orchestration. His version is colourful and attractive, and was popular for many years. Nevertheless, it is now broadly agreed that Rimsky-Korsakov's alterations do little to enhance the work. Mussorgsky aimed

to portray life in its true colours, and this is reflected in his music. As a consequence, *Boris Godunov* is now usually performed in one or other of its original versions.

The opera is based on a story by Alexander Pushkin concerning the eponymous King's murderous accession to the throne. Musically, the most important innovation in the opera lies in Mussorgsky's use of the speech patterns of Russian language as the basis for his music. Rather than setting dialogue to pre-composed melodies, Mussorgsky's vocal lines follow the pitch and rhythm of spoken Russian. This gives the opera a sense of "reality", as characters appear to converse with each other in a manner that the Russian audience would immediately have recognized.

PICTURES AT AN EXHIBITION

PIANO ⏱ 35:00 📖 15 ☉

1873 saw the sudden death the artist Viktor Hartmann. The following year an exhibition of his works took place and Mussorgsky, who had been a close friend, saw an opportunity to write a musical tribute. This impressive work for piano opens with a *Promenade*, which recurs several times – with its steady pulse, but alternating tempo, it seems to suggest a viewer wandering around the gallery, pausing to inspect pictures more closely. The remaining 11 pieces are vivid interpretations of the individual paintings. The breadth of Mussorgsky's musical inspiration is unparalleled, conjuring images that range from playful to eerie or majestic. *Pictures at an Exhibition* is better known these days in Ravel's colourful orchestration from 1922 – although an impressive interpretation, it lacks something of the original's intensity and earthiness.

Nikolai Rimsky-Korsakov

🔴 1844–1908   🏴 Russian   ✍ c.130

Rimsky-Korsakov was a friend of Mily Balakirev and member of the "mighty handful", a group of five composers led by Balakirev who aimed to develop an authentically Russian art music. Rimsky-Korsakov's music, much of it based on themes from Russian folklore, is justly renowned for its brilliant, colourful orchestration. He was later important as a teacher and counted Prokofiev and Stravinsky among his pupils.

LIFE AND MUSIC

Following his elder brother into the navy, Rimsky-Korsakov began composing a symphony in his final year at naval college after making the acquaintance of Balakirev. This proved impossible to complete while at sea, and by the end of his three-year tour of duty, he had almost resolved to give up music altogether. On returning to shore, however, he was persuaded to finish the symphony and, after its successful premiere, decided on a switch of career. A committed nationalist, Rimsky-Korsakov wrote 15 operas on Russian themes and used folk melodies in many of his instrumental compositions. He had an instinctive mastery of the orchestra, although, arguably, his handling of large-scale form does not compare with that of contemporaries such as Borodin.

MILESTONES	
1861	Meets Balakirev; starts Symphony No. 1
1865	Symphony No. 1 premiered by Balakirev
1871	Leaves navy to study music full-time
1887	Composes *Capriccio Espagnol*
1888	Composes *Sheherazade* and *Russian Easter Festival Overture*
1889	Completes Borodin's opera *Prince Igor* with Glazunov
1896	Orchestrates Mussorgsky's opera *Boris Godunov*

KEY WORKS

SYMPHONY NO. 1

ORCHESTRAL   🕐 27:00   📖 4   🎼

César Cui described Rimsky-Korsakov's Symphony No. 1 as the first Russian symphony. Whilst not literally true, it was certainly the first to make explicit use of Russian folk themes – very clear in the slow movement.

RUSSIAN EASTER FESTIVAL OVERTURE

ORCHESTRAL   🕐 16:00   📖 1   🎼

This is based on three melodies from the *Obikhod*, the Eastern Orthodox

After his first opera, *Ivan the Terrible,* Rimsky-Korsakov wrote 14 others. They form his most important legacy.

Church hymnal. In the colourful music Rimsky-Korsakov tried to evoke images of ancient pagan rituals suggested by the Easter celebrations. Oddly, Tsar Alexander III disliked it and banned it from any concert he attended.

LE COQ D'OR

OPERA   🕐 120:00   📖 3   🎼🎭🎤

Rimsky-Korsakov's final opera, *The Golden Cockerel* is perhaps his finest. Based on a story by Pushkin, its fairytale setting belies a sharp political satire. As ever, the work brims with attractive melody and radiant scoring.

FOCUS

SHEHERAZADE

SYMPHONIC SUITE · 45:00 · 4 · ▨

Like many Russian composers and artists, Rimsky-Korsakov was fascinated by the Islamic cultures over Russia's borders, using them as a source of inspiration and an "exotic" reference. *Sheherazade* is a large-scale suite in four movements. It is based on the tale of *The Thousand and One Nights*, in which a young woman changes a cruel sultan's character by recounting stories.

Whilst Rimsky-Korsakov was especially drawn to four of the stories, to which the four movements of his work correspond, Sheherazade is not strictly descriptive. (He was initially persuaded to include programmatic titles for each of the movements, but later withdrew them). Neither is it symphonic, in the sense of containing extensive development of themes. Rather, Rimsky-Korsakov described it as a "kaleidoscope of fairy-tale images and designs of Oriental character", in which the music attempts to capture the mood of each story. Certain melodies recur throughout the work, however: notably the austere theme that opens the first movement – associated with

the Sultan – and the sinuous solo violin melody heard shortly afterwards, representing Sheherazade herself.

CAPRICCIO ESPAGNOL

ORCHESTRAL · 18:00 · 5 · ▨

Spanish music was popular with Russian composers as part of the general interest in the exotic, and Rimsky-Korsakov's enduringly popular *Capriccio Espagnol* is based on themes drawn from a volume of Spanish folk melodies. The main musical ideas are a morning, an evening, a Gypsy dance, and an Asturian song. In a sense, the work is Rimsky-Korsakov *par excellence* – limited musical argument, but brilliant orchestral colour. He emphasized that it should be thought of as a piece for orchestra rather than an orchestration of a piece that could otherwise stand alone.

INFLUENCES

Rimsky-Korsakov taught several important composers, including Prokofiev and Stravinsky. However, his major influence is in his mastery of orchestration – his treatise on the subject has become the standard reference work, and many composers have imitated, (but few bettered), his handling of musical colours.

Anton Rubinstein

◗ 1829–1894   ⚑ Russian   ✍ 200

One of the very few 19th-century pianists who could stand comparison with Liszt, Anton Rubinstein (brother of Nikolai) was also outstanding as a teacher and conductor. He toured Europe as a child virtuoso, and then as a mature artist known for his huge repertoire and remarkable stamina (in the US he played 215 recitals in under nine months). He was also twice director of the St Petersburg Conservatory. He composed prolifically – and lucratively, thanks to his fame – but many of the grandiloquent pieces he composed can feel glib and superficial. However, his opera *Demon* was a huge success, with the great Russian bass Fyodor Chaliapin often in the title role, and his *Melody in F*, Op. 3, No. 1, proved lastingly popular.

MILESTONES	
1848	Becomes chamber virtuoso to Grand Duchess Helena Pavlovna, Russia
1864	Composes Piano Concerto No. 4
1871	*Demon*, opera, published
1871	Conducts Philharmonic Concerts in Vienna
1872	Tours US with Henryk Wieniawski

The founding of St Petersburg Conservatory put the city on a par with Vienna, London, Paris, and Berlin, and soon attracted world-famous musicians to Russia.

Anatol Liadov

◗ 1855–1914   ⚑ Russian   ✍ 100

Born into a highly musical family, Liadov never completed any large-scale works. Talented but rather lazy, he was expelled from Rimsky-Korsakov's composition classes for non-attendance, idled his summers away at his wife's country house, and neglected Diaghilev's commission for *The Firebird*, which Stravinsky snapped up. Many of his pieces are arrangements of folk songs collected from various parts of Russia, and he brought vivid orchestral colour and characterization to these miniatures. He collaborated with Rimsky-Korsakov and Balakirev, and his student Prokofiev found him likeable, but pedantic.

MILESTONES	
1878	Starts teaching at St Petersburg Conservatory
1890	Composes *Pro starinu*, piano ballade
1897	Commissioned to collect folk songs by Imperial Geographical Society
1909	*The Enchanted Lake*, Op. 62, and *Kikimora*, Op. 63, tone poems, published

Liadov described *Baba Yaga* (1904) as a "tone picture after a Russian fairytale" and used a large orchestra, including a xylophone, to create sounds of the forest and other atmospheric effects.

Sergey Liapunov

● 1859–1924   Russian   ♫ 80

Liapunov's modest composing success didn't come until he was in his 40s, and then mainly thanks to encouragement and promotion from his friend Balakirev. In addition to conducting, Liapunov toured as a pianist and wrote with a complete understanding of the instrument. His best

pieces were the works for piano, such as the Liszt-influenced *12 Transcendental Studies*, and his piquant songs, such as "The Mountain Peaks".

MILESTONES	
1893	Commissioned to collect folk songs
1905	Finishes *12 Transcendental Studies*, Op. 11, for piano
1910	Professor at St Petersburg Conservatory
1913	Composes Prelude and Fugue in B minor, Op. 58, for piano

Mikhail Ippolitov-Ivanov

● 1859–1935   Russian   ♫ 80

A craftsman in the Russian academic vein rather than an original genius, Ippolitov-Ivanov's style and technique changed little throughout his career, taking the form of folk song-based nationalism with an Oriental twist and, after the Revolution, hints of Uzbek, Kazakh, Turkmen, or Arabic music. His popular *Caucasian Sketches* shows the influences of Georgia, where he lived for a few years, teaching and conducting.

MILESTONES	
1884	Conductor of Imperial Opera, Tiflis
1893	Professor at Moscow Conservatory
1894	*Caucasian Sketches*, orchestral suite
1895	Writes *Armenian Rhapsody*, symphony
1900	Composes *Assia*, opera
1934	Publishes memoirs: *Fifty Years of Russian Music*

Anton Stepanovich Arensky

● 1861–1906   Russian   ♫ c.80

Arensky was made a professor at the Moscow Conservatory immediately on graduating with a gold medal from St Petersburg, having studied composition under Rimsky-Korsakov. He went on to teach Rachmaninov and Scriabin. An eclectic composer, influenced by Chopin, Tchaikovsky, and Mendelssohn, among others, he worked unusual rhythms into his lyrical and sentimental music. As well as writing operas, he also composed Church music, songs, symphonies, and elegant piano pieces. Arensky's last years were spent successfully as a composer, pianist, and conductor, but were blighted by his addiction to alcohol and gambling.

MILESTONES	
1888	Directs Russian Choral Society
1894	Composes Piano Trio No. 1
1891	*A Dream on the Volga*, opera, published
1895	Becomes Director of Imperial Chapel, St Petersburg
1900	Composes *Egyptian Nights*, ballet

Arensky, seen here in his workroom, is best known for his charming, elegant, and melodically inventive Piano Trio No. 1 in D minor.

Alexander Scriabin

◉ 1872–1915   ⚑ Russian   ✍ c.200

Original to the point of eccentricity, Scriabin ranks among the 20th century's most important composers for the piano, and was one of its greatest musical innovators. In the later years of his short life, an all-consuming interest in mystical philosophy pervaded every aspect of his world. As his beliefs became ever more bizarre, so he pushed the boundaries of harmony and performance to their limits.

LIFE AND MUSIC

After setting out as a concert pianist, Scriabin injured his right hand, which put a temporary halt to his performing career but gave him more time to compose. Scriabin's early pieces, almost exclusively for the piano, show a clear affinity with the Romantics, with many works in characteristically Chopin-esque forms. In later years, however, Scriabin became increasingly interested in Helene Blavatsky's "theosophy". These beliefs came eventually to dominate his thinking about music, which in turn pushed his musical language in radically new directions. Nevertheless, he retained a curious reliance on classical formal principles.

MILESTONES	
1888	Studied at Moscow Conservatory
1896	Composes 24 Preludes, Op. 11; Piano Concerto, Op. 20
1898	Professor of Piano at the Moscow Conservatory
1903	Writes Piano Sonata No. 4, Op. 30
1907	*Poem of Ecstasy*, Op.54, symphonic poem
1909	Composes *Prometheus*, Op.60, symphony
1909	Moves to Brussels for two years
1911	Writes Piano Sonata No. 7, Op. 64 ("White Mass")
1913	Composes Piano Sonata No. 8, Op. 66
1913	Writes Piano Sonata No.9, Op. 68 ("Black Mass")
1915	Dies 27 April in Moscow, leaving *The Mysterium* unfinished

KEY WORKS

PIANO CONCERTO

ORCHESTRAL   ⏱ 28:00   📖 3   ♆ ☋

The Piano Concerto of 1896, Scriabin's first orchestral score, was well received by audiences and attracted him a degree of early fame. With distinct echoes of Chopin and Rachmaninov (a student friend of Scriabin's) it stands as a fascinating contrast with his more extraordinary later works.

SONATA NO. 9, "BLACK MASS"

SOLO PIANO   ⏱ 09:00   📖 1   ☋

After Scriabin described his Sonata No. 7 as the "White Mass", the ninth was soon dubbed the "Black Mass". Whereas the former work is radiant, even joyous, the latter is among his most dark, knotty works, emphasizing the dissonant minor ninth interval and ending with a grotesque march.

THE MYSTERIUM

MULTIMEDIA   ⏱ 7 DAYS

The Mysterium was left incomplete – Scriabin had barely begun work on it before his sudden death. Sketches indicate a seven-day long multimedia spectacle intended for performance in the Himalayas. Scriabin believed that this performance would act as a purification ritual, leading to the rebirth of the world.

FOCUS

PROMETHEUS – THE POEM OF FIRE

ORCHESTRAL 25:00 1

Prometheus – The Poem of Fire is the last of Scriabin's five symphonies, and one of the last pieces he composed before his death. It takes as its basis the Greek myth in which Prometheus defies Zeus to give mankind command of fire. For Scriabin, symbolism operated at every level in the work, from the so-called "mystic chord", on which much of the harmony is derived, to the specification of a wordless, white-robed chorus. Moreover, the work was intended to be an early – perhaps the first – example of multimedia performance. Scriabin wrote a complete part for "Tastiera per Luce" "keyboard of lights"), which would flood the performance space with different coloured light according to which combination of keys was pressed.

Considered for its purely musical merits, *Prometheus* is a striking work, and contains many moments of sensuous orchestration and bold, otherworldly harmony.

Scriabin was profoundly influenced by Helene Blavatsky's Theosophical Movement and, while in London, he visited the room in which she died in 1891.

PIANO SONATA NO. 4, OP. 30

SOLO PIANO 8:00 2

Scriabin's oeuvre consists in large part of piano works – he wrote many hundreds of preludes, études, and impromptus. Central to these is the series of ten sonatas, which began in 1892 in the sound world of Rachmaninov and Chopin and ended in 1913 with a work that is on the very verge of atonality. Sonata No. 4 was composed during a summer of extraordinary productivity for Scriabin, in which he completed some 40 piano pieces.

FIRST MOVEMENT (ANDANTE 3:50)
The first movement demonstrates some of Scriabin's most sensuous writing. It is based on one theme, introduced delicately and developed through a series of unexpected harmonic shifts.

SECOND MOVEMENT (PRESTISSIMO VOLANDO 4:50) The second movement explodes into life with a buoyant theme. A more lyrical second subject follows, then develops into a reintroduction of a theme from the first movement. After a recapitulation and coda, the sonata closes with a virtuosic flourish.

"Only one place is closed to me,
and that is my own country – Russia."

RACHMANINOV IN AN INTERVIEW FOR *THE MUSICAL TIMES*, 1930

Sergei Rachmaninov

● 1873–1943 ⚑ Russian ✍ 96

A highly-praised conductor and outstanding pianist whose many recordings show his crisp technique, unostentatious approach, and outstanding clarity, Rachmaninov was also the last major composer of the great Russian late-Romantic tradition. Most of his music was written before 1917, when he left Russia never to return; appropriately, some of his symphonies and piano concertos radiate passionate yearning or nostalgia.

LIFE

After his father squandered the family fortune, Rachmaninov's parents moved from a country estate to a crowded St Petersburg flat. His education was disrupted by their separation, so he was sent to Moscow Conservatory. He boarded with his piano teacher in a severe routine of all-day practice starting at 6:00 am, and graduated with the highest possible marks for his composition and playing. His career started well: the opera *Aleko* was successfully premiered, and he enjoyed Tchaikovsky's support. But a calamitous performance of his Symphony No. 1 (under an allegedly drunk Glazunov) drew savage reviews; for three years he could not face composing, and turned to conducting, with increasing success. However, a hypnotist doctor and musician, Nikolai Dahl, persuaded him to compose again. The Piano Concerto No. 2 was among the excellent works he now steadily produced. His reputation as composer, conductor and performer grew. By his 40s he had toured the US, Russia, England and Europe, but he lost his country estate in the Revolution, and fled to Scandinavia. He spent his last 25 years in the US and Europe, working, touring, recording, and publishing music. Growing ill-health made him cancel a concert tour, and he died of cancer aged 69.

To strangers
Rachmaninov could seem unsmiling and aloof, but with friends and family in their home-made Russian enclave he was warm, content, and generous.

MUSICAL OUTPUT

Total: 96

ORCHESTRAL (19)	7	5	3	4
CHAMBER (11)	5	5	1	
PIANO MUSIC (29)	8	9	11	1
DRAMATIC (8)	4	1	3	
CHORAL (10)	1	4	4	1
SONGS (19)	5	8	6	
	1873	1892	1901	1918	1943

MUSIC

The piano figures prominently in Rachmaninov's output, both solo and with orchestra. His orchestral works include three symphonies, and he wrote over 80 lyrical songs. There is little chamber music, and his three operas suffer from unpromising librettos. His choral work *Vespers* shows his liking for religious chant. His music up to the critically mauled Symphony No. 1 is energetic and highly competent, if sometimes derivative (the Tchaikovsky-ish opera *Aleko*, for instance). But when he started composing again after his years of self-doubt, Rachmaninov's style developed significantly into the now-familiar sweeping melodies, subtly and richly scored – for example, in the long seamless lines of the Piano Concerto No. 2 or Symphony No. 2. Among the few works he wrote after leaving Russia are the *Rhapsody on a Theme of Paganini*, Symphony No. 3 and Piano Concerto No. 4.

MILESTONES	
1891	Composes Piano Concerto No. 1
1892	Graduates as composer. Prelude in C sharp minor, Op. 3, No. 2 composed
1893	Successful premiere of *Aleko*
1897	Disastrous premiere of Symphony No. 1. Takes conducting post
1899	First international appearance, London
1900	Consults psychologist Dr Dahl; receives auto-suggestive therapy to deal with nervous breakdown
1901	Piano Concerto No. 2 composed, dedicated to Dr Dahl
1902	Marries cousin Natalia Satina
1908	Symphony No. 2 premiered
1910	Now an established composer-conductor-pianist. Tours US
1917	Flees Russia on outbreak of revolution
1918	Decides to live in US
1919	Makes his first recording; continues to record with Ampico for 10 years
1934	Writes *Rhapsody*
1936	Symphony No. 3 completed

KEY WORKS

VESPERS, OP. 37

ORCHESTRAL   ⏱ 50:00   📖 15

Also known as the *All-Night Vigil* or *Solemn Vespers*, this is Rachmaninov's setting of the service which takes place in Orthodox churches before important festivals. Nine of the pieces are based on traditional chants, with Rachmaninov's harmonies and variations. The central section is No. 9, the story of the Resurrection.

RHAPSODY ON A THEME OF PAGANINI, OP.43

CONCERTO   ⏱ 25:00   📖 26

After his troubled Fourth Concerto had a lukewarm reception, this – his final concerto-style work – proved a great success. Based on Paganini's familiar *Caprice*, it is a set of variations that ingeniously combines the lyrical with the brilliant, and spontaneity with organization.

PIANO CONCERTO NO. 3, OP. 30

CONCERTO   ⏱ 40:00   📖 3

The whole of this tightly-structured piece comes out of the bare, twisting opening theme. Large in scale and emotional range, it shows Rachmaninov's skill in writing long and beautifully phrased themes. It debuted in New York in 1909.

Rachmaninov's Piano Concerto No. 2 became famou when it was used to great effect in David Lean's 1946 film *Brief Encounter*.

FOCUS

PIANO CONCERTO NO. 2, OP. 18

CONCERTO   35:00   3

The endlessly flowing lyricism of Rachmaninov's first and most enduring success – the happy result of his confidence-building sessions with Dr Dahl – has inspired direct and indirect use in pop music and films.

FIRST MOVEMENT: (MODERATO, 11:00) Eight luminous piano chords introduce a sombre first theme, contrasted with the more optimistic second; a strident, martial short figure is repeated as a device to link the two.

SECOND MOVEMENT: (ADAGIO SOSTENUTO, 11:00) An aching theme, sparsely woven between piano, solo winds and strings, flows with a gentle sadness that seems to have no relief in sight.

THIRD MOVEMENT (ALLEGRO SCHERZANDO, 12:00) After a bustling start, two minutes or so in comes the nostalgic and sincere theme that brought Rachmaninov worldwide fame, played on oboe and violas and then taken up by piano. The theme reoccurs in more impassioned forms before the determined but unsettled finish.

SYMPHONY NO. 2, OP. 27

ORCHESTRAL   55:00   4

After the success of his Concerto No. 2, Rachmaninov produced this, possibly his greatest orchestral work,

> **INFLUENCES**
>
> Rachmaninov's music was considered outdated and emotionally clichéd after his death by some, and has had little influence on Western composers (though Shostakovich's Piano Concerto No. 2, for example, has a Rachmaninov-like slow movement). However, his reputation is now secure as the last of a great line.

to complete his comeback after the disasters of his first attempt at a symphony. Most of his works were composed in his idyllic country estate, Ivanovka, but the spacious No. 2 came from his time in Dresden.

FIRST MOVEMENT (LARGO, 19:00) A low, sombre motto theme opens this broad movement. It turns into flowing and resolute, but tragic, long melodies, with sunnier sections and some impassioned climaxes.

SECOND MOVEMENT (ALLEGRO MOLTO, 9:00) A vigorous and bright movement, sparklingly orchestrated, containing a trademark yearning theme, and with an unexpectedly subdued finish.

THIRD MOVEMENT (ADAGIO, 14:00) Sumptuous, classic Rachmaninov, that goes straight into a long-breathed, poignant clarinet melody against quietly intimate strings, and builds to some magnificently surging, almost triumphant, emotion with a tranquil finish.

FOURTH MOVEMENT (ALLEGRO VIVACE, 13:00) A bustling and vivacious rounding-off of a remarkable work.

Alexander Glazunov

◓ 1865–1936   ♟ Russian   ✍ c.150

Glazunov was an important figure in early-20th-century Russian music: he taught Shostakovich and helped Rimsky-Korsakov complete Borodin's opera *Prince Igor*, which had been unfinished on the latter's death. Glazunov's own compositions, whilst popular in their day, were conservative – a likeable but unchallenging blend of Germanic Classical with a somewhat outmoded Russian nationalism.

LIFE AND MUSIC

Glazunov studied with Rimsky-Korsakov, and his Symphony No. 1 was performed when he was just 16. Much of his adult life was spent as professor, and then director, of the St Petersburg Conservatory, and it was here that he had his most lasting influence as mentor to the "new" Russian school of composers. He was remembered as a strict teacher with a genuine concern for his students, but whose unabashed conservatism could jar with their progressive ideas; he famously walked out of the premiere of his student Sergei Prokofiev's Symphony No. 1.

Co-written with Rimsky-Korsakov, Glazunov's *Cleopatra* was performed by the Ballets Russes in typically exotic costumes.

MILESTONES	
1881	Composes *Stenka Razin*, symphonic poem, and Symphony No. 5
1884	Visits Liszt in Weimar
1897	Conducts Rachmaninov's Symphony No. 1 while drunk, causing it to fail
1899	Appointed professor at the St Petersburg Conservatory
1900	Composes *The Seasons*, ballet
1903	Writes Symphony No. 7 ("Pastorale")
1904	Composes Violin Concerto
1928	Leaves Russia for Paris
1934	Writes Saxophone Concerto

Glazunov's compositions were highly polished, if slightly backward-looking. He achieved the most successful balance of Russian and European elements of any composer of the nationalistic school, led by Balakirev. Many of Glazunov's works were premiered by Balakirev.

KEY WORKS

THE SEASONS
BALLET   ⏱ 60:00   📖 15   🎭

Written for the Russian Imperial Ballet, *The Seasons* is perhaps the last work in the Russian Classical ballet tradition before Stravinsky changed the genre forever. It is rarely danced, but has become Glazunov's most popular concert work: charming, inventive, and well scored.

VIOLIN CONCERTO
ORCHESTRAL   ⏱ 20:00   📖 2   🎭🎻

Glazunov's Violin Concerto was written for violinist Leopold Auer, and later taken up by the brilliant Jascha Heifetz

(a former pupil of Auer's), whose advocacy is chiefly responsible for its continued popularity. The first section develops a beautiful melody with strongly Russian overtones, before an extended cadenza links to the virtuosic finale.

SYMPHONY NO. 5
ORCHESTRAL   ⏱ 35:00   📖 4   🎭

This is the most popular of Glazunov's symphonies. Although clearly derivative, particularly of Mendelssohn in the Scherzo and of Tchaikovsky in general, it is a good example of his blending of Russian themes with Classical forms.

Henryk Wieniawski

🌑 1835–1880   🏳 Polish   🎵 c.50

A child violin prodigy with a concert career, Wieniawski became the great international violin virtuoso of his time after playing his own Concerto No. 1 in Leipzig. He went on to teach at the St

Petersburg Conservatory and composed many of his best works there. His music, like his playing, combined Paganini-like technique, Romantic expansiveness, and Slavonic emotion. His two concertos are often played.

MILESTONES

1843	Admitted to Paris Conservatoire
1853	Composes Violin Concerto No. 1
1860	Settles in St Petersburg
1862	Composes Violin Concerto No. 2
1872	Tours US with Anton Rubinstein; exhaustion and onset of heart trouble
1875	Goes to teach in Brussels for two years

Moritz Moszkowski

🌑 1854–1925   🏳 German   🎵 100

At age 17, Moszkowski, a piano prodigy, was teaching at the Berlin Conservatory. However, nerves cut short his early, glittering concert career, and he concentrated instead on composition. Sales of his melodic

piano works then made him wealthy. He settled in Paris, where he was in demand as a teacher, and married the composer Cécile Chaminade's sister. Later, his fortunes declined: his wife and daughter died, his music became unfashionable, and he lived and died alone in poverty.

MILESTONES

1873	Debut as pianist, Berlin
1897	Settles in Paris; height of fame
1898	Writes Piano Concerto, Op. 59
1914	Bankrupted during World War I
1921	Friends hold benefit concert in US

Josef Suk

🌑 1874–1935   🏳 Czech   🎵 c.90

Suk was Dvořák's favourite composition pupil at Prague Conservatory. At 18 he joined the renowned Czech Quartet as second violinist and played over 4,000 concerts with it. After his Serenade for Strings was published (on Brahms's recommendation), he became a leading Czech composer. Suk was most at home in instrumental music, but, unlike Dvořák, was un-influenced by folk. His style developed from lyrical Romanticism to a more complex, individual language with a masterful sense of colour. His *Asrael Symphony* is one of his finest works.

Suk's emotional *Asrael Symphony*, named after the Angel of Death, was written to express his grief at the death of his wife in 1905 and of Dvořák in 1904.

MILESTONES

1885	Begins study at Prague Conservatory
1892	Composes Serenade for Strings
1898	Marries Otilka, Dvořák's daughter
1906	Composes *Asrael Symphony*
1917	*Ripening*, tone poem, tells his life story
1922	Appointed professor of composition at Prague Conservatory
1933	Retires from Czech Quartet

Bedrich Smetana

🌑 1824–1884   📕 Czech   ✍ c.150

The music of Bedrich Smetana has become synonymous with Czech nationalism and greatly influenced later generations of composers, including Dvořák. A native of Bohemia, then controlled by Austria, Smetana wrote several operas and a magnificent cycle of symphonic poems depicting his homeland. His musical style, while clearly of the Romantic tradition, is attractively melodious and direct.

LIFE AND MUSIC

Smetana worked first in Prague and then Gothenburg, with moderate success, as a pianist and composer. By 1861, his nationalist sentiments compelled him to return to Prague. Unlike many "nationalist" composers, Smetana made comparatively little use of folk melodies. Rather, he wrote operas and programmatic pieces based explicitly on Czech stories and places – his own colourful and dramatic musical voice thus came to embody Czech music. Smetana led a difficult life – his first wife and three of four daughters died, and he contracted a syphilitic

MILESTONES	
1848	Writes *Six Characteristic Compositions*. Founds music school in Prague.
1856	Moves to Gothenburg, Sweden
1861	Returns to Prague
1863	*The Brandenburgers of Bohemia* performed
1866	Conducts Bohemian Provisional Theatre Orchestra.
1876	*String Quartet No. 1* "From my Life"
1882	*Má Vlast* (complete version) performed

infection that led to deafness and the acute tinnitus that drove him to his death in a mental asylum.

KEY WORKS

SIX CHARACTERISTIC COMPOSITIONS, OP. 1

SOLO PIANO   ⏲ 22:30   📖 6   🎙

Struggling to make ends meet, in desperation, Smetana sent his recently completed *Six Characteristic Compositions* to Franz Liszt, with a dedication and a plea for financial aid. While Liszt was unable to help financially, he was impressed with the work and sent it to his publisher. Although Smetana made no money, praise from such an esteemed figure gave him confidence.

STRING QUARTET NO. 1

CHAMBER   ⏲ 28:00   📖 4   ♊

Sub-titled "From my Life", this quartet ends dramatically on a piercing note held by the violin – a direct musical representation of Smetana's tinnitus.

THE BRANDENBURGERS OF BOHEMIA

OPERA   ⏲ 165:00   📖 3   🎻🥁🎶

First performed at the Prague Provisional Theatre in 1866, Smetana's first patriotic opera is notable not only because it made his name in Prague (winning the Prague opera competition), and marked the beginning of his most productive period, but also because it was his first extended composition to be based explicitly on Bohemian subject matter.

FOCUS

THE BARTERED BRIDE

OPERA   ⏲ 120:00   📖 3   🔱 ⚒ 🎵

The Bartered Bride was Smetana's second opera and his first attempt at a comedy, written – he later claimed – "to spite those who accused me of being Wagnerian" after the altogether more serious *Brandenburgers of Bohemia*.

First staged in 1866, hot on the heels of *Brandenburgers*, Smetana soon revised the work, adding a number of popular Czech numbers, such as drinking songs and polkas. It is

The Bartered Bride contains some of Smetana's most attractive music, full of colour and humour. The Overture has become a concert-hall favourite.

an engaging love story, and all the characters are given specific musical features, such as key signatures, which are maintained throughout the opera. The final version was staged in 1870.

MÁ VLAST

ORCHESTRAL   ⏲ 71:00   📖 6   🔱

Má Vlast (*My Country*) is an enormous cycle of six symphonic tone poems – with expansive melodies and dramatic rhythms – which Smetana wrote between 1872 and 1880. Dedicated to the city of Prague, it stands unmatched in the classical canon as a profound statement of nationalism.

VYSEHRAD (13:00) This first tone poem, cast in a more or less straightforward sonata form, refers to episodes from Czech history.

VLTAVA (11:00) *Vltava* traces the progress of the river from its source high in the Sumava mountains, through the forests and rural villages into Prague. Smetana makes reference here to folk songs as a means of depicting locations.

SÁRKA (10:00) Sárka is the name of a Bohemian warrior-woman who, in legend, led an army of maidens to claim vengeance against her unfaithful lover.

FROM BOHEMIAN FIELDS AND GROVES (12:00) This poem is a musical description of Smetana's beloved homeland, the countryside, and the rural people.

TÁBOR (12:00) Named after an ancient town in south Bohemia, this tone poem is based on a stirring choral, *Ye who are God's Warriors*.

BLANÍK (13:00) The final poem in the cycle tells of how the valiant Hussites marched to save their land. The choral melody from *Tábor* returns, but now transformed into a march interspersed with the sounds of shepherds piping.

"I should be glad if something occurred to me as a main idea that occurs to Dvořák only by the way."

JOHANNES BRAHMS

Antonín Dvořák

● 1841–1904   🏳 Czech   ✍ 189

Of all the 19th-century nationalists, Dvořák was perhaps the most successful in absorbing elements of national folk music into a sophisticated Classical idiom. Hailed as a champion of Slavic music, Dvořák also spent several years in America, where his ideas about national music had a profound impact on a generation of composers. His substantial output included ten operas, nine symphonies, and much chamber music.

LIFE

Dvořák's father was an innkeeper and butcher in a village outside Prague, and the young Dvořák was destined for the same trade. However, he showed promise as a viola player, and after studying at the Prague Organ School took a position with the Bohemian Provisional Theatre Orchestra. During this period he was also composing in a style increasingly influenced by the nationalist music of Smetana, who conducted the theatre orchestra for a time. Dvořák was awarded a Ministry of Education stipend for composition in 1875, by a panel that included Brahms. A couple of years later he won it again; Brahms was once more one of the judges, and was now sufficiently impressed with Dvořák's compositions to recommend them to his publisher. Through this connection his name became widely known across Europe over the next decade, and he achieved a strong following in England, where he conducted a series of concerts. His fame now firmly established, in 1891 he was invited to become Director of the National Conservatory of Music in New York. Dvořák attacked this new role with gusto, and composed a series of works betraying the more or less explicit influence of American folk music. He returned to Prague in 1895, and lived there until his death.

A quiet, deeply religious ruralist at heart, Dvořák was never happier than in the countryside of his native Bohemia.

MUSICAL OUTPUT	1841	1860	1870	1880	1890	1900	1904	Total: 189
SYMPHONIES (9)			2	3	3	1		
CONCERTOS (7)				3	1	3		
CHAMBER (42)			2	16	13	11		
PIANO MUSIC (24)				6	14	4		
OTHER INSTRUMENTAL (50)			3	21	12	12	2	
OPERAS (10)				5	2	1	2	
VOCAL (47)			2	20	17	6	2	

MUSIC

Dvořák is often compared with Brahms, no doubt in part because the two became good friends and were great admirers of each other's music. Dvořák wrote some of his greatest works in the Classical forms of the symphony, piano trio, and string quartet, of which Brahms is regarded as a master. Both had an interest in folk music, although in Brahms's case this was not the music of his native country but of the Hungarian gypsies he had heard as a boy.

Dvořák's musical temperament was rather different from that of Brahms. He never felt a weight of expectation composing in the shadow of Beethoven. Even so, some of Dvořák's symphonies, especially the

The Bohemian Polka was one of Dvořák's popular Slavonic Dances.

mighty No. 7, rank among the finest in the genre. Much has been made of Dvořák's capacity for incorporating Bohemian folk music into Classical models, in works such as the "Dumky" Piano Trio, Op. 90. By the standards of the time, he was not progressive in terms of harmony or form, but his lyrical melodies – Bohemian in style, but rarely, if ever, taken from actual folk music – are wholly distinctive.

MILESTONES	
1857	Attends organ school in Prague
1866	Joins Bohemian Provisional Theatre Orchestra
1873	Cantata Hymnus, Op. 30, performed
1874	Brahms recommends Dvořák to the publisher Simrock
1877	Stabat Mater, Op. 58, completed
1878	*Slavonic Dances, Book 1*, Op. 46
1885	Symphony No. 7, Op. 70
1892	Director of the National Conservatory of Music in New York
1893	Symphony No. 9, Op. 95, "From the New World"
1900	*Rusalka*, Op. 114
1901	Returns to Prague and becomes director of Conservatoire

KEY WORKS

SYMPHONY NO. 7, OP. 70
ORCHESTRAL   🕐 40:00   📖 4

If the No. 9 is Dvořák's best-known symphony, the No. 7 is in some ways perhaps the best. Written for the London Philharmonic Society, it is a sombre, even tragic work, less obviously influenced by folk music than the other late symphonies.

SLAVONIC DANCES, OP. 46, 72
ORCHESTRAL   🕐 38:00   📖 8

Dvořák composed his first set of Slavonic Dances at the instigation of Simrock, the publisher who had made such a commercial success of Brahms's *Hungarian Dances*. Perhaps to maximize the potential market,

versions for piano duet and for orchestra were written concurrently.

STABAT MATER, OP. 58
ORATORIO   🕐 85:00   📖 10

Based on the medieval Latin poem depicting Mary's grief at Christ's crucifixion, the mammoth Stabat Mater was begun in 1876 after the death of Dvořák's daughter Josefa. He then laid it aside, but was moved to complete it some years later after the death of two more daughters. This was the first of his works that Dvořák conducted in England, a country where he established a long-lasting reputation and great affection for his music.

FOCUS

SYMPHONY NO. 9 IN E MINOR, OP. 95, "FROM THE NEW WORLD"

ORCHESTRAL ⏱ 42:00 📖 4 🎵

Dvořák believed America's folk music could produce a distinctive national musical voice, yet, surprisingly, the "New World" does not contain any authentic American tunes.

FIRST MOVEMENT (ADAGIO, 9:30) Written in curiously strict sonata form, the movement builds to a rousing climax.

SECOND MOVEMENT (LARGO, 12:30) The Largo, with its famous cor anglais solo, is one of the most famous pieces of Classical music. Under the name "Going Home", the melody is often now mistaken for a genuine Negro spiritual.

THIRD MOVEMENT (SCHERZO, 8:30) The thrilling scherzo was based on material from Dvořák's abandoned opera *Hiawatha*.

FOURTH MOVEMENT (ALLEGRO CON FUOCO, 11:30) This combines themes from earlier in the work with march-like music to produce a thrilling climax.

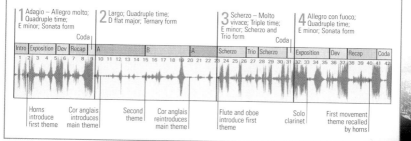

1 Adagio – Allegro molto; Quadruple time; E minor; Sonata form · Coda

2 Largo; Quadruple time; D flat major; Ternary form

3 Scherzo – Molto vivace; Triple time; E minor; Scherzo and Trio form · Coda

4 Allegro con fuoco; Quadruple time; E minor; Sonata form

| Intro | Exposition | Dev | Recap | | A | | B | | A | | Scherzo | | Trio | Scherzo | | Exposition | | Dev | | Recap | | Coda |

1 2 3 4 5 6 7 8 9 10 11 12 13 14 15 16 17 18 19 20 21 22 23 24 25 26 27 28 29 30 31 32 33 34 35 36 37 38 39 40 41 42

Horns introduce first theme

Cor anglais introduces main theme

Second theme

Cor anglais reintroduces main theme

Flute and oboe introduce first theme

Solo clarinet

First movement theme recalled by horns

CELLO CONCERTO, OP. 104

ORCHEATRAL ⏱ 33:00 📖 3 🎵 👁

This concerto has become a central work in the repertoire of the cello. Dvořák wrote it originally for his friend the cellist Hanus Wihan, but they fell out after Wihan made changes to the solo part and added two elaborate cadenzas, which Dvořák refused to include in the final version. Wihan eventually declined the premiere, which was given instead to Leo Stern.

FIRST MOVEMENT (ALLEGRO, 12:00) A lengthy orchestral introduction presents the main themes of the work before the soloist enters. Various development follows, before a radiant, full orchestra rendition of the lyrical second theme and a triumphant close in B major.

SECOND MOVEMENT (ADAGIO MA NON TROPPO, 10:30) The woodwind presents the expressive main theme before being joined by the soloist. A central section follows, quoting from a song Dvořák wrote in 1887. The main theme finally returns, this time led by the French horns.

SECOND MOVEMENT (ALLEGRO MODERATO, 10:30) The rondo form finale begins as a cheerful march, with plenty of opportunities for display from the soloist, before slowing to recall themes from earlier in the work.

Leos Janáček

● 1854–1928   🏳 Czech   ✍ c.150

Janáček is amongst the most significant opera composers of the 20th century. A late developer in composition, he was nearly 50 before he completed his first successful opera, *Jenufa*, and all of his best-known works date from after this time. Perhaps more than any other nationalist composer, aspects of his native folk music were a fully integrated part of his compositional voice.

LIFE AND MUSIC

After studying in Prague, Janáček moved to Brno, where he founded an organ school and made his living as a teacher. While dabbling in composition in a broadly late-Romantic idiom, he studied Moravian folk song and began to develop the idea that melodic lines should reflect the rhythms and pitch of Czech speech. This concept gave rise to the modal harmonies and seemingly disjointed, repetitive phrases of his mature style. In 1917, Janáček became infatuated with Kamila Stösslová and a copious correspondence followed. Their relationship remained unconsummated, but she inspired many of his late works, notably the opera *Káta Kabanová*.

MILESTONES	
1874	Attends Prague Organ School
1881	Becomes founding director of Brno Organ School (later Brno Conservatory)
1887	Writes first opera, *Sárka*, but rights to libretto are refused
1894	Begins work on *Jenufa*, opera
1894	*Jenufa* performed for the first time
1916	Revised version of *Jenufa* premiered in Prague to great acclaim
1917	Meets 25-year-old Kamila Stösslová
1921	Opera *Káta Kabanová* receives premiere
1923	Completes opera *The Cunning Little Vixen*
1926	Composes *Sinfonietta* and *Glagolitic Mass*
1928	Writes opera *From the House of the Dead*, staged 1930, two years after his death

KEY WORKS

JENUFA

| OPERA | ⏱ 120:00 | ▭ 3 | 🔀 ♣ |

This was Janáček's first full-blown attempt to write music according to his theory of "speech melody". First staged in Brno in 1904, it was later greatly reorchestrated (at the insistence of Karel Kovarovic, director of Prague Opera) and presented successfully in Prague. This was to prove a pivotal moment in Janáček's career.

Janáček's entertaining opera *The Cunning Little Vixen* was inspired by animal stories in a cartoon strip.

GLAGOLITIC MASS

| MASS | ⏱ 40:00 | ▭ 8 | 🔀 ◉ ♣ ♣ |

Janáček composed a large body of choral music, of which his masterpiece is the *Glagolitic Mass*. Almost certainly never intended for liturgical use (Janáček was a confirmed atheist) it can instead be seen as a statement of Slavic nationalism. The title refers to the alphabet used to write Old Church Slavonic. A thrilling, dramatic work, with outbursts of brass and strong rhythms, the Mass it contains a notably virtuosic organ solo before the orchestral close.

FROM THE HOUSE OF THE DEAD

OPERA ⏱ 90:00 📖 3 🎵🎙

With a long-standing interest in Russian literature and culture, Janáček based his last opera (to his own libretto) on Dostoevsky's novel, *The House of the Dead*, though the result is more a series of vignettes than a single story. After Janáček's death, parts of the score of Act III were found. Two of his pupils, believing the opera unfinished, "completed" it, adding a more uplifting finale and substantially changing the orchestration. It is now thought that Janáček's sparse orchestration and bleak ending were deliberate, and the opera is usually performed as originally written.

ACT ONE Goryanchikov is brought to a Siberian prison camp. He is interrogated and flogged. Other prisoners tease an eagle with a broken wing, then tell stories about their lives.

ACT TWO Goryanchikov teaches a Tatar boy, Alyeya, to read and a priest dispenses Easter blessings. The prisoners put on two plays. Alyeya is attacked and wounded by a prisoner.

ACT THREE In the prison hospital Alyeya recovers and a prisoner dies. Goryanchikov and the eagle – now recovered – are released to freedom.

SINFONIETTA

ORCHESTRAL ⏱ 22:00 📖 5 🎵

Janáček's last orchestral work, and probably his best known, grew out of an initial idea to write a series of fanfares for a gymnastic competition in Brno. However, it developed into an exuberant tribute to the town he had lived in since his student days, with each movement (after the initial fanfare) portraying a part of it.

FANFARE (ALLEGRETTO–ALLEGRO–MAESTOSO) The Sinfonietta is notable for its bold inclusion of 12 trumpets. Nine of the them are heard here in chorus.

THE CASTLE (ANDANTE–ALLEGRETTO) In reality a prison, this building is depicted by a sprightly, slightly sinister dance against a lyrical theme led by strings.

THE QUEEN'S MONASTERY (MODERATO) Beginning as a nocturne, the music builds to a dramatic climax, then disappears as quickly as it began.

THE STREET (ALLEGRETTO) The bustle of a Brno street is announced by a trumpet fanfare which is then taken up in complex counterpoint by the orchestra.

THE TOWN HALL (ANDANTE CON MOTO) The most developed movement builds towards a climax: the 12 trumpets are finally heard together in a thrilling recapitulation of the opening fanfare.

Carl Goldmark

● 1830–1915 ♘ Hungarian ♫ c.60

Largely self-taught, Goldmark established himself as a composer during his 30s, while conducting, teaching, and writing reviews in Vienna. His eclectic musical style incorporated elements of Hungarian folk and Jewish culture (his father was a cantor). His exotic opera *Die Königin von Saba (The Queen of Sheba)* was a triumph in Vienna and later staged worldwide. His later works were more modest successes, but he became a noted musical figure in Budapest and Vienna, and a good friend of Brahms.

MILESTONES

1858	Organizes concert of own works
1860	Composes String Quartet, Op. 8
1875	Opera *Die Königin von Saba* premiered
1876	New orchestral work *Rustic Wedding*, Op. 26, receives great popular acclaim

Ernö von Dohnányi

● 1877–1960 ♘ Hungarian ♫ c.120

Dohnányi was the most important Hungarian musical figure of the 20th century. By his mid-20s he was the greatest composer-pianist after Liszt. After 10 years teaching in Berlin he returned home and reformed Hungary's musical life through teaching, conducting, radio, and concerts. His lyrical, vibrant works often show humour (his *Variations on a Nursery Rhyme* are often played), and his chamber music is particularly successful.

MILESTONES

1920	Performs all Beethoven's piano works
1928	Head of piano and composition at Hungarian Academy in Budapest
1944	Composes Symphony No. 2
1930s	Struggles against Nazi influences
1949	Settles in US as composer-pianist at Florida State University

Bohuslav Martinu

● 1890–1959 ♘ Czech ♫ 383

Martinu was such a good violinist that his home town funded him at Prague Conservatory. Expelled for laziness, he moved to Paris, where he became recognized as a composer. Blacklisted by the Nazis for pro-Czech activities, he fled to the US, but later returned to Europe. His large output shows influences from Renaissance to jazz, using springy rhythms and generated themes from small fragments.

MILESTONES

1923	Studies in Paris with Albert Roussel
1934	Writes Piano Concerto No. 2
1938	Composes String Quartet No. 5
1941	Flees to US as refugee
1953	Composes Symphony No. 6
1957	Moves to Switzerland
1958	Writes *The Greek Passion*, opera

Viktor Ullmann

● 1898–1944 ♘ Czech ♫ 70

The career Ullmann was building in Prague as a freelance composer, teacher, journalist and broadcaster was cut short by Nazi anti-Jewish policies when he was sent to Terezin concentration camp. In two years of extraordinary musical life there, he directed the Studio for New Music, wrote reviews, performed, and composed satisfying and accessible music for concerts for prisoners, many being excellent musicians. Ullmann died at Auschwitz; his manuscripts were saved.

MILESTONES

1898	Born Teschen (now Cesky Tesin in the Czech Republic)
1933	Writes *Schönberg Variations* for orchestra
1942	Sent to Terezin by the Nazis
1943	String Quartet No. 3 composed
1943	Writes *Hölderlin-Lieder*, voice and piano
1943	Writes opera *Der Kaiser von Atlantis (The Emperor of Atlantis)* satirizing Hitler
1944	Dies at Auschwitz

Max Bruch

◑ 1838–1920 **🏳 German** **✍ c.200**

Bruch was an important figure in 19th-century German musical life, both as a composer and a conductor. He is chiefly remembered for his melodic Violin Concerto No. 1, although he also composed much choral music and several operas. Conservative by nature, Bruch believed music should be tuneful and accessible, and vehemently opposed the innovations of contemporaries such as Richard Strauss and Max Reger.

LIFE AND MUSIC

Bruch was born in Cologne and received his first music lessons from his mother. A musical prodigy, his Symphony No. 1 was premiered when he was just 14. After study in Frankfurt, he returned to teach in Cologne and began to establish himself as a composer and, chiefly, conductor. Various posts followed, including three years at the Liverpool Philharmonic Society, before he became professor of composition at the Berlin Academy in 1891. Bruch's straightforwardly Romantic idiom was essentially backward-looking, especially when compared with that of his later contemporaries. However, he had an undoubted gift for melody, and his best works, including the Symphony No. 3 and his famous Violin Concerto No. 1, make up for in beauty what they might seem to lack in depth.

MILESTONES

1863	Produces *Die Loreley*, the second and most enduring of his three operas
1866	Writes Violin Concerto No. 1
1867	Appointed director of court orchestra at Schwartzburg-Sonderhausen
1880	Appointed conductor of the Liverpool Philharmonic Orchestra
1881	Composes *Kol Nidrei*, orchestral work; marries the singer Clara Tuczek
1883	Conductor of the Breslau Orchesterverein; extensive US tour
1891	Becomes professor of composition at Berlin Academy; keeps post until 1910
1893	Honorary doctorate from Cambridge
1898	Begins two-years as conductor of Scottish Orchestra

KEY WORKS

VIOLIN CONCERTO NO. 1

ORCHESTRAL   ⏱ 22:00   ▥ 3   ♒ ▧

This concerto, in G minor, is Bruch's best-known work, and one of the most popular violin concertos in the repertoire. The first movement is an extended dialogue between soloist and orchestra which flows without pause into the second, an idea Bruch adapted from Mendelssohn. The famous Adagio shows Bruch's lyrical gift at its finest and has passages of quite exceptional beauty. The implications of the concerto's massive popularity were not lost on Bruch, who was known to muse (correctly, it transpired) that he would probably be remembered for this work alone.

Kol Nidrei, with its richly emotional cello part, was inspired by the Jewish prayer sung on the eve of Yom Kippur.

KOL NIDREI

ORCHESTRAL   ⏱ 11:00   ▥ 1   ♒ ▧

Written for solo cello and orchestra, this piece was written in Liverpool and premiered there by the cellist Robert Hausmann. Based on a Jewish prayer, Bruch's setting is remarkable for the cello's evocation of an anguished baritone human voice.

Joseph Rheinberger

● 1839–1901   ⚑ German   ✍ 200

Rheinberger's lavish talents as organist and composer, but primarily as a teacher, saw him progress quickly from student to professor at Munich Conservatory, and he received many honours through a long and successful career. His wife was a poet, and he set many of her works – amongst his large output of orchestral, chamber, and vocal music – which were masterfully crafted in traditional styles. His work is most familiar to organists and Catholic choirmasters, with the 20 organ sonatas among his finest achievements. He is also remembered for his fine Church music, which includes numerous Masses, and three Requiems.

As organist and choral conductor at St Michael's Church in Munich from 1860–66, Rheinberger composed many richly-textured sacred works.

MILESTONES	
1851	Moves to Munich to study
1859	After 100 unreleased pieces, publishes his Op. 1
1867	Becomes a professor; marries Franziska von Hoffnaass
1869	Writes *Der Tümers Töchterlein*, opera
1894	Ennobled
1898	Composes Mass in F, Op. 190

Alexander von Zemlinsky

● 1871–1942   ⚑ Austrian   ✍ c.70

Zemlinsky was known chiefly as an excellent conductor and as a champion of Czech music. He held various posts in Vienna, Prague, and Berlin, before fleeing from the Nazis to New York. As a composer, his relatively traditional music was more successful in his early career than later on, when it was eclipsed by his pupils' modernism – he taught Berg, Schoenberg (his brother-in-law) and Webern. The intense, emotional quality of much of his music (such as in *Die Seejungfrau*) reflects his rejection by Alma Schindler, another of his pupils, in favour of Mahler. In his last years Zemlinsky had to turn to composing hackwork to make ends meet. He suffered a series of strokes, and died almost forgotten.

MILESTONES	
1896	Opera *Sarema* wins major prize
1903	*Die Seejungfrau*, symphonic fantasy
1921	*Der Zwerg*, opera, performed
1923	Composes his *Lyric Symphony*
1924	Conducts premiere of Schoenberg's *Erwartung*
1938	Flees to New York

The rise of the Nazi Party in Germany, in 1933, forced Zemlinsky to move to Vienna; in 1938, after the Anschluss, he emigrated to the US along with many other Austrian Jews.

Hugo Wolf

● 1860–1903 ▥ Austrian ✍ c.350

One of the greatest masters of Lieder, Wolf composed some 300 songs, developing and extending the tradition of Schubert and Schumann. A committed disciple of Wagner, his use of *leitmotiv* – and his complete integration of music and text – transformed the Lied into a truly dramatic form. Wolf's music was very much affected by the depressive episodes from which his suffered throughout his life.

LIFE AND MUSIC

After briefly attending the Vienna Conservatory, Wolf scraped together an impecunious existence until he secured a job as music critic for the *Wiener Salonblatt* in 1884. Here he made a name for himself with caustic writing, an ardently pro-Wagnerian stance, and an implacable antipathy towards Brahms. From 1887 he resolved to compose full-time, and in the following nine years produced all of his most significant works. Eventually overcome by the mental illness that had dogged his adult life, he died in an asylum aged just 42. His musical significance rests on his songs, which are characterized by an unusual affinity with the poetic text, and an intensity of emotional expression redolent of large-scale dramatic forms, such as opera or symphony.

MILESTONES	
1875	Attends the Vienna Conservatory – dismissed in 1877
1870s	Contracts syphilis
1880	Composes *Italian Serenade* for string quartet
1883	Writes *Penthesilea*, symphonic poem
1884	Becomes critic for *Wiener Salonblatt*
1887	First songs published
1889	Writes settings of *Goethe* (51), *Mörike* (53), and *Eichendorff* (20)
1890	Writes *Spanisches Liederbuch*
1891	Composes *Italienisches Liederbuch* (vol. 1)
1895	*Der Corregidor*, opera, performed
1896	Writes *Italienisches Liederbuch* (vol. 2)
1897	Mental breakdown, leading to terminal illness; committed to asylum

KEY WORKS

GOETHE LIEDER

LIEDER 📖 51 🔊 👤

Schubert made extensive settings of Goethe, and by choosing to set the same poet, Wolf consciously aligned himself with the great lieder tradition. The Goethe songs date from Wolf's most productive period, and typify his mature style. The texts were given prominence, and were thus acknowledged as the inspiration for his music.

Wolf's admiration for literature is shown by his setting of texts by many great poets – from Shakespeare to Mörike.

SPANISCHES LIEDERBUCH

LIEDER 📖 44 🔊 👤

For the Spanish songs, Wolf chose German translations of Spanish texts from the 17th and 18th centuries. He allowed his musical imagination free reign to capture the Mediterranean character of the texts, and the resulting songs are filled with dance rhythms and pseudo-guitar figuration. Admired for this colourful, evocative, and inspiring Spanish collection, Wolf was perceived, in certain quarters, to be one of the finest songwriters of his time.

Max Reger

🌑 1873–1916   🏛 German   ✍ 500+

Despite being a prolific and wide-ranging composer, Reger's music has failed to capture audiences' imaginations. At its best, it has the authority of Brahms, allied with more progressive harmony; at its worst, it can seem dense, dry and harmonically wayward. Much admired by his professional colleagues, Reger was nonetheless a difficult character who made many enemies and aroused strong opinions.

LIFE AND MUSIC

Reger led an unremarkable life. After studying with the great musicologist Reimann, he gained a post at the Leipzig Conservatory, where he remained until his death. He was famously hard-living and hard-drinking, partaking of everything (some would say composition included) to excess. Reger's music can arguably be seen as the missing link between Brahms and Schoenberg as like them, he venerated Bachian counterpoint. Often, however, the density of his contrapuntal writing and incessant shifts of harmony make his music hard to follow. His orchestral music can often feel almost impenetrable but his large volume of chamber works is perhaps his most significant contribution to the concert repertory.

MILESTONES	
1886	Becomes church organist in Weiden
1890	Begins music studies with Heinrich Reimann in Munich and Wiesbaden
1899	Has mental and physical breakdown
1905	Appointed professor of composition at Munich Academy
1907	Appointed professor of composition at Leipzig; composes *Variations and Fugue on a Theme by J A Hiller*
1909	Has successful concert tour of UK
1911	Becomes conductor of ducal orchestra at Meiningen
1913	Composes *Introduction, Passacaglia and Fugue* in E minor
1915	Composes Clarinet Quintet

KEY WORKS

VARIATIONS AND FUGUE ON A THEME BY J A HILLER

ORCHESTRAL   🕐 40:00   📖 13   🎵

Among the more approachable of Reger's orchestral works, this set of 11 variations and a fugue is based on a theme from Johann Adam Hiller's stage work *Der Aernotekranz*. Somewhat akin to a longer, more austere version of Brahms's *Academic Festival Overture*, the work nonetheless bursts with invention and elaborate scoring.

Arnold Böcklin's The Isle of the Dead inspired Reger to compose his orchestral Four Böcklin Tone-Pictures in 1913 .

INTRODUCTION, PASSACAGLIA AND FUGUE IN E MINOR

ORGAN   🕐 30:00   📖 3   🎵

Of all Reger's output, the works he composed for organ, most of which were written before he was 25, have established the most secure position in the repertoire. Indeed, in some quarters he is regarded as the most significant organ composer since Bach. The organ was the perfect medium for Reger to indulge his passion for counter-point, as is well illustrated in this monumental work, commissioned by the city of Breslau.

Franz Schmidt

● 1874–1939 ⚑ Austrian ♪ 50

A highly regarded and much honoured pianist, cellist, conductor, and teacher in Vienna, Schmidt also found time to compose some impressive, large-scale works. These often show a Hungarian influence (he was from a Hungarian-speaking German family), as well as Classical-Romantic accomplishment and, in the fine works for organ, the influence of J S Bach. Schmidt's life was not easy: he battled against poor health all his life, his mentally ill first wife was murdered by the Nazis, and his daughter, commemorated in his Symphony No. 4 (his last), died shortly after birth. It was his symphonies that earned him most fame, although his opera, *Notre Dame*, from which he drew an orchestral gypsy-style intermezzo, was also an international success.

MILESTONES	
1901	Starts teaching at Vienna Conservatory
1904	Completes *Notre Dame*, opera
1930	Composes *Variationen über ein Husarenlied* (*Variations on a Hussar Song*), orchestral
1932	Composes Symphony No. 4
1937	Completes *Das Buch mit sieben Siegeln* (*The Book with Seven Seals*), oratorio; composes *Solemn Fugue*, for organ

Schmidt's oratorio, *The Book with Seven Seals,* composed between 1935 and 1937, was the only vocal work he completed apart from his two operas. It is inspired by biblical visions of the Last Judgement.

Sigfrid Karg-Elert

● 1877–1933 ⚑ German ♪ c.150

Karg-Elert's life was unusual – he married the daughter of the woman who had borne him an illegitimate son. His musical life was also unusual: despite being a talented pianist, he specialized in composing for the then popular art-harmonium, developed in France in the late-19th century. From 1924, he gave weekly radio harmonium recitals from his house in Leipzig. He also composed many works for organ, which were influenced by Impressionism and historical polyphonic styles. Popularity in England (a festival of his organ music was held in London) then made him unpopular in Germany. Short of money, he toured the US, but disastrously.

MILESTONES	
c1918	Destroys 20 works in an artistic crisis
1906	Composes *Konzertstücke*, harmonium
1910	Completes 66 Chorale Improvisations for organ
1912	Composes Sonata No. 2, harmonium
1919	Becomes professor at Leipzig
1930	Karg-Elert Festival held in London

An excellent organist, Karg-Elert also composed extensively for the harmonium. Among his best-known works are 33 stylistic studies inspired by the styles of composers as diverse as Palestrina and Schoenberg.

Fritz Kreisler

● 1875–1962   ⚑ Austrian   ✍ Unknown

A violin virtuoso of legendary sweet tone, expressiveness, and natural ability, Kreisler was a child prodigy who won the Paris Conservatoire's Gold Medal at 12. His virtuoso career – which lasted nearly 50 years – was disrupted by spells of fighting in World War I, fleeing the Nazis, and a traffic accident in 1941. Best known for his evocative, rich-toned performances of the Brahms and Beethoven violin concertos, he also gave the first recital of Elgar's Violin Concerto. An accomplished composer, too,

A virtuoso violinist of effortless flair, Kreisler was widely renowned for his rich, insightful performances.

he produced an operetta, a string quartet, and a variety of solos. More surprisingly, Kreisler proved also to be an imaginative hoaxer, admitting in 1935 that many of the 18th-century violin solos that he had "discovered", apparently by names such as Gaetano Pugnani or François Francoeur, had in fact been written by him. Not all critics were amused. But his dazzling, attractive forgeries continue to appeal to violinists and audiences, and they are frequently performed, though now are firmly attributed to Kreisler.

MILESTONES

1882	Enters Musikverein Konservatorium
1889	Tours the US before medical studies
1899	Starts his virtuoso career in Berlin
1910	Performs Elgar's Violin Concerto
1914	Fights for Austria in World War I
1919	Writes *Apple Blossoms*, operetta
1935	Admits to compositional hoaxes
1943	Becomes US citizen

Hanns Eisler

● 1898–1962   ⚑ German   ✍ Unknown

After receiving free lessons from Schoenberg in the 1920s, Eisler discovered Marx, and became a committed communist. Disaffected with new music, he wrote strongly political songs, theatre, and cabaret music, and film scores in an easily understood, yet clever style. In the 1930s, playwright

Bertolt Brecht became a lifelong friend and collaborator. When Hitler came to power, Eisler's work was banned and he was exiled. He fled to the US, where he wrote songs and film music, including the score for Fritz Lang's *Hangmen Also Die*. In the 1940s he fell foul of McCarthyism, and was deported to East Germany, where he wrote music for stage and film.

MILESTONES

1923	Composes Piano Sonata No. 1, Op. 1
1925	Teaches music in Berlin
1930	Writes *Die Massnahme*, music for stage
1937	Composes the "German Symphony"
1948	Deported from the US
1949	Writes *Auferstanden aus Ruinen*, East Germany's national anthem
1957	*Schweyk in zweiten Weltkrieg*, for stage

During America's "Red Scare", Eisler fell victim to the infamous witch-hunts spear-headed by Joe McCarthy (centre). Tried by the House Un-American Activities Committee, Eisler was found guilty and deported.

Carl Orff

◔ 1895–1982   ▥ German   ✍ 20

Despite composing countless large-scale stage works, Orff's fame rests almost entirely on just one, the hugely successful *Carmina Burana*. But perhaps his most lasting legacy lies in his innovative attitude to music education. Realizing the intrinsic relationship between music and movement, Orff stressed the value of playful participation, particularly through the use of voice and percussion.

LIFE AND MUSIC

Orff was born, raised, and educated in Munich, where in 1924 he co-founded a school for gymnastics, music, and dance. His hands-on approach emphasized direct experience and active participation, particularly through the use of voices and simple percussion instruments. Orff's own music reflects Stravinsky's influence and a passion for Classical texts. Striving for a musical language that would engage the listener's primitive impulses, Orff's sound-world is filled with pulsing rhythms, percussion, and direct vocal expression, achieving a powerfully visceral and sensual appeal.

MILESTONES	
1912	Attends Munich Academy of Music
1914	Leaves Academy to join army
1924	Co-founds the Günther School (with Dorothee Günther)
1930	Writes *Music for Children*, Vol. 1
1937	*Carmina Burana*, cantata, premiered
1943	*Antigone*, opera, performed
1950	Appointed Professor of Composition at Munich High School for Music
1961	Founds Orff Institute, in Salzburg, providing courses for music teachers

KEY WORKS

CARMINA BURANA

CANTATA   ⏱ 60:00   📖 25   ♊ ♨ ♂

Conceived for the stage, but more often performed as a concert oratorio, *Carmina Burana* is a setting of old German texts found at Benediktbeuern Monestery. However, its subject matter is rather less than holy, as the work's subtitle, *Cantiones profanae*, implies. For instance, *Bibunt Omnes*, which closes the central section, is a drinking song. The passage most often played on film is the evocative finale *O Fortuna*, now one of the best-known pieces of 20th-century Classical music.

MUSIC FOR CHILDREN

ORCHESTRAL   📖 5   ♊

Whilst not strictly part of his serious output, Orff's *Das Schulwerk, Musik für Kinder (Schoolwork, Music for Children)* ranks with *Carmina Burana* as his most significant and lasting contribution. Written for very young children to play, with simple percussion instruments, Orff's musical "schoolwork" shows his flair for and theory of teaching music.

The panoramic stage pageant *Carmina Burana*, famous for its infectious rhythms and arresting vocals, enjoyed instant and phenomenal success.

Edvard Grieg

● 1843–1907   🏴 Norwegian   ✒ c.80

Grieg is undoubtedly Norway's greatest composer and is responsible, together with Sibelius and Nielsen, for putting Scandinavia on the musical map. His exploration of Norway's folk music, and collaborations with Norwegian writers, helped him to develop a style that was unmistakably nationalist in spirit. Generally more comfortable with smaller-scale forms, he wrote many songs, piano pieces, and chamber works.

LIFE AND MUSIC

After studying in Leipzig, Grieg moved to Copenhagen to develop his career as a pianist. It was there that he met the young Norwegian composer Rikard Nordraak, who emphasized to him the need for a distinctive Norwegian music. On his return to Norway, Grieg began studying traditional folk music, and elements of this gradually pervaded his own romantic musical language. Sometimes derided as a miniaturist, it is nonetheless true – with the notable exception of the majestic Piano Concerto – that his best work is found in his lyrical songs, or his exquisitely crafted instrumental pieces.

MILESTONES

1858	Studies in Leipzig
1863	Moves to Copenhagen
1865	Composes Violin Sonata, No. 1, Op. 8
1866	Moves to Christiania (now Oslo)
1867	Marries Nina Hangerup, his first cousin
1868	Writes Piano Concerto in A minor
1874	Awarded a national artists' grant; moves back to Bergen
1875	Writes *Peer Gynt* suites No.1, Op.46, and No. 2, Op. 55
1880	Becomes conductor of the Harmonien Orchestra in Bergen
1884	*Holberg Suite*, Op. 40 (piano version)
1895	Composes *Haugtussa*, Op. 67

KEY WORKS

LYRIC PIECES

SOLO PIANO   📖 66   🎶

Grieg wrote ten volumes of "Lyric Pieces" for solo piano between 1867 and 1901. These delightful miniatures, full of references to traditional dance music, nature, and nationalist sentiment, show Grieg's art at its finest. They became a lucrative source of income for Grieg in his later years.

***Peer Gynt* tells the** story of a young rogue who travels the world in search of fortune and fantastical adventures.

HAUGTUSSA, OP. 67

SONG CYCLE   ⏲ 30:00   📖 8   🎶 👤

Haugtussa is a song cycle to poems by Arne Garborg, and one of many works that Grieg wrote for his wife Nina to sing. Telling the story of a simple shepherdess and her ill-fated love affair, Grieg's delightful settings evoke images of the Norwegian countryside.

HOLBERG SUITE

ORCHESTRAL   ⏲ 19:00   📖 5   🎻

Originally composed for piano, the *Holberg Suite* is now better known in its orchestrated version. Sometimes cited as an early example of musical Neo-Classicism, Grieg's charming score is a pastiche of a French dance suite that was popular in Ludvig Holberg's time.

FOCUS

PIANO CONCERTO, OP. 16

ORCHESTRAL   🕒 27:00   📖 3

As a student in Leipzig, Grieg heard Schumann's Piano Concerto, and his own concerto owes a clear debt to that work. Another influence was Liszt, who saw the work in manuscript and reportedly impressed the composer by playing it perfectly at sight. Premiered to great success in Copenhagen, the concerto is now among the most popular in the repertoire.

FIRST MOVEMENT (ALLEGRO MOLTO MODERATO 12:00) The opening bars of the Piano Concerto must be one of the most instantly recognizable in all Classical music – above a roll of timpani, the piano enters with a dramatic sequence of descending octaves. The remainder of the movement is a compressed sonata form, with a passionate cadenza appearing before the close.

SECOND MOVEMENT (ADAGIO 6:00) This lyrical movement is deceptive in its simplicity, disguising a sophisticated command of harmony.

THIRD MOVEMENT (ALLEGRO MODERATO MOLTO E MARCATO 9:00) Full of virtuosic writing for the soloist, the concerto's finale is its most distinctively Norwegian movement, with references to folk dances and even imitations of the hardanger (a Norwegian instrument).

PEER GYNT SUITES NO. 1, OP. 46, AND NO. 2, OP. 55

ORCHESTRAL   🕒 32:00   📖 8

Based loosely on Norwegian fairy tales, *Peer Gynt* was originally written as an extended prose-poem; however, its popularity led Ibsen to produce a stage version in 1876.

Grieg's two *Peer Gynt* suites were drawn from 23 short pieces he composed as incidental music for the play's first production. For Grieg, a master of the miniature, incidental theatre music was an ideal form – the perfect medium for his memorable short character pieces.

Among the eight pieces that comprise the two suites, three have become especially well known. *Morning Mood*, which opens the first suite, sets a beautiful rocking melody to a backdrop of woodwind bird calls. *In the Hall of the Mountain King* is a tongue-in-cheek depiction of the Troll King's lair, with a tentative theme gradually accelerating into grotesque dance. *Solveig's Song*, the final movement of the second suite, is based around a typically lyrical melody for strings with harp accompaniment.

INFLUENCES

Grieg has come to be somewhat marginalized in the history of Classical music. Nonetheless, his most important influence was surely on the French composers of the early 20th century. Ravel said that – besides Debussy – there was "no composer to whom I feel a closer affinity". Today, his work is returning to critical favour.

Carl Nielsen

● 1865–1931   ♙ Danish   ✍ c.120

Nielsen was one of the most important symphonic composers of the 20th century, and certainly the most famous Danish composer in history. He developed a highly individual compositional voice, at times romantic and passionate, at others aggressive and almost atonal, but always highly charged. In addition to six symphonies, he wrote three concertos, two operas, quartets, and a popular wind quintet.

LIFE AND MUSIC

Despite a rural upbringing as one of 14 children, Nielsen learned piano, violin, and trumpet. After studying at the Copenhagen Conservatory, he became a violinist in the Danish Royal Theatre Orchestra. Somewhat shielded from the European mainstream, and receiving little formal compositional training, his music developed along a highly individual path. His harmony, whilst essentially tonal, remains unique; he often created tension by using keys in opposing blocks, the work finishing in the "winning" key. The idea of struggle was central to his music, often explicitly so, as in his Symphony No. 5 where the drummer is instructed to improvise, as if to drown out the orchestra.

MILESTONES	
1884	Attends Copenhagen Conservatory
1889	Joins Royal Theatre Orchestra as second violinist
1894	Writes Symphony No. 1
1901	*Saul and David*, opera, performed
1902	Composes Symphony No. 2, "The Four Temperaments"
1908	Becomes conductor of the Royal Theatre Orchestra
1911	Symphony No. 3, "Sinfonia espansiva"
1916	Appointed professor at Royal Danish Conservatory; writes Symphony No. 4, "The Inextinguishable"
1922	Composes Symphony No. 5
1925	Writes Symphony No. 6, "Semplice"
1928	Clarinet Concerto premiered

KEY WORKS

SYMPHONY NO. 1

ORCHESTRAL   ⏱ 33:00   📖 4   ♫♫

This symphony gives the first example of Nielsen's "progressive tonality". A struggle between G minor and C major leads eventually to the work's conclusion in the latter key, despite opening in the former. One reviewer described the sound of the symphony as "a child playing

As a young violinist in the Royal Theatre Orchestra, Nielsen played in his own Symphony No. 1.

with dynamite" and the work now seen as an important forerunner to Nielsen's later musical development.

MASKARADE

OPERA   ⏱ 80:00   📖 3   ♫♫ ♪

Nielsen's comic opera shows a less familiar side of his music. Written extremely quickly, it is a glorious comedy of social conventions with an inspired, if somewhat chaotic, score. Still hugely popular in Denmark, it has been somewhat neglected elsewhere.

SYMPHONY NO. 4, "THE INEXTINGUISHABLE"

ORCHESTRAL   36:60   4

Probably Nielsen's most popular symphony, this work's curious title refers not to the symphony itself, but rather to the "elemental will of life", which, like music, is inextinguishable. Nielsen recognized his Symphony No. 4 as the beginning of a new, "organic" phase in his composition – the development of a direct musical language that was not programmatic, but which gave the appearance of growing naturally and spontaneously of its own volition (for the first time, the four movements are linked together). It was written at a difficult time for Nielsen: his marriage was on the rocks and he had resigned from the Copenhagen Opera. Also there is no doubt that World War I had an impact on the symphony, especially in the musical battle between two sets of timpani in the final movement.

FIRST MOVEMENT (ALLEGRO 12:00) The first movement pits an insistent triplet theme, introduced in counterpoint between wind and strings, against a radiant second subject in thirds.

SECOND MOVEMENT (POCO ALLEGRO 5:00) The second movement is a pastoral, led by the woodwind in a manner that is at once almost naively folk-like and yet oddly unsettled.

THIRD MOVEMENT (POCO ADAGIO QUASI ANDANTE 10:30) The slow movement begins with a brooding theme in unison violins, punctuated by timpani beats and joined in sparse counterpoint by the viols and cellos. A solo violin introduces a warmer theme before emphatic woodwind restatements of the opening material build to a stormy climax.

FOURTH MOVEMENT (ALLEGRO – GLORIOSO – TEMPO GUISTO 9:30) The finale is a dramatic duel between two timpanists, positioned at either side of the stage.

SAGA-DRØM

ORCHESTRAL   09:00   1

This delightful work – based on *Njal's Saga* – describes the passage in which Gunnar Hlidarende dreams of being pursued by wolves. Low strings open the work with a dreamy melody over a pedal bass. After a chorale on the brass, accompanied by ostinato figures on the strings, a slightly faster section is led by the woodwind. Technically the most remarkable, the central section is a sequence of overlapping cadenzas for six instruments that enter one at a time and are left to play at their own tempo before being brought to a halt by the entry of the strings. A final passage of muted trumpet fanfares brings the work to a gentle conclusion.

INFLUENCES

Whilst his earliest works show the clear influence of Beethoven and Brahms, Nielsen's unique mature style sets him apart. Few later composers have tackled the Classical symphony with such originality and vigour; along with Sibelius and Mahler, Nielsen may be thought to have had the last word on the subject.

Johan Svendsen

🌑 1840–1911   🏳 Norwegian   🎼 40

After an early career as a virtuoso violinist, Svendsen turned to composing. His music – which shows a natural mastery of large, traditional forms – complements that of his good friend and compatriot Grieg. However, he was also in such demand as a conductor that

he composed little of importance after moving to Copenhagen in 1883. Although his style is Romantic, it contains elements of Norwegian folk music. Only two of

his symphonies survive; in 1882 the manuscript of the third was burned in a jealous rage by his American wife, from whom he was later divorced.

MILESTONES	
1874	Composes Symphony No. 2, Op. 15
1876	*Norwegian Rhapsodies* published
1881	Writes *Romance* for violin and orchestra

Fredrik Pacius

🌑 1809–1891   🏳 Finnish   🎼 Unknown

After moving to Helsinki to lecture at the university, Pacius became a central figure in Finnish musical life. Whilst organizing concerts and conducting choirs, he wrote pieces in the style of Mendelssohn and Louis Spohr that include a string quartet, a violin concerto, songs, stage music, and the beginnings of a symphony. His singspiel *Kung Karls jakt* (*The Hunt of King Charles*) was his most important work, and his patriotic song "Vårt Land" ("Our Country") was adopted as Finland's national anthem.

MILESTONES	
1828	Violinist, court orchestra, Stockholm
1835	Settles in Helsinki
1848	Writes "Our Country", patriotic song
1852	*The Hunt of King Charles*, opera
1887	Composes *Loreley*, opera

Armas Järnefelt

🌑 1869–1958   🏳 Swedish   🎼 Unknown

Järnefelt's working life was spent in Finland and Sweden. After studies in Helsinki, Berlin, and Paris, he held various significant posts as opera and court conductor in Stockholm before returning to Finland. He was especially well known for his interpretations of Sibelius, who was his brother-in-law,

and gave the first Swedish performances of works by Mahler and Schoenberg. Järnefelt's main fame as a composer rests on two lyrical pieces for orchestra: *Praeludium* – from music for the drama *The Promised Land*, and *Berceuse*. He also wrote choral works, piano music, and film scores in a Romantic style, often with evocative Finnish titles.

MILESTONES	
1892	Sister Aino marries Sibelius
1903	Becomes director of Helsinki opera
1904	Writes *Berceuse* for small orchestra
1907	Conductor of Royal Opera, Sweden; composes *Praeludium* for small orchestra
1910	Takes Swedish nationality
1932	Returns to Finland

Situated in the heart of Stockholm, the Royal Opera House was where Järnefelt delighted Swedish audiences as composer and conductor from 1907 to 1932.

Christian August Sinding

● 1856–1941   ⚑ Norwegian   ✍ c.150

Though now a rather distant second to Grieg, Sinding was very much the "other" Norwegian Romantic composer in his lifetime. He went to Leipzig to study violin, but quickly proved to be an adept and prolific composer, writing rich, strong music clearly influenced by Wagner and Liszt.

He stayed in Germany for many years, financed by the Norwegian government, and was also professor of composition at the University of Rochester, New York, for two years. Perhaps because of the Romantic density and heaviness of his music, his work declined in popularity after his death; however, the well-known piano piece *The Rustle of Spring* is often heard in recitals and found on CD.

MILESTONES

1874	Studies at Leipzig Conservatory
1884	Composes Piano Quintet, Op. 5
1889	Piano Concerto, Op. 6, published
1890	Writes Symphony No. 1, Op. 21
1896	*The Rustle of Spring*, Op. 36, No. 6
1898	Writes Violin Concerto No. 1, Op. 45
1912	Composes *The Holy Mountain*, opera

Sinding wrote many lyrical songs, principally of Norwegian texts, and was honoured by the government in 1921 for his contribution to national music.

Rikard Nordraak

● 1842–1866   ⚑ Norwegian   ✍ 25

Sent to business school in Copenhagen at 15, the young Nordraak studied music instead and became an ardent member of the new national movement in art. He founded Euterpe – a society to promote Scandinavian composers – with his friend Grieg. His simple, economical music includes Norway's national anthem, "Ja, vi elsker dette landet" ("Yes, We Love This Land"). Nordraak was still developing as a composer when he met his premature death, but his influence on Grieg makes him a seminal figure in Norwegian music.

MILESTONES

1859	Joins New Norwegian Society
1860	Writes *Four Dances* for piano, Op. 1
1864	"Ja, vi elsker dette landet" first sung, 17 May
1865	*Maria Stuart i Skotland*, incidental music, published
1866	Contracts tuberculosis and dies

Selim Palmgren

● 1878–1951   ⚑ Finnish   ✍ c.500

Palmgren is best known for his evocative, wide-ranging, and graphic piano music: he wrote five concertos (No. 2 being an international success at the time) and more than 250 solo pieces. The works show a strong sense of mood and imagery: a fine pianist, Palmgren knew first-hand how to exploit the instrument's possibilities. After an early career conducting the Finnish Students' Choral Society, he concentrated on performing and toured widely across Europe and the US. For the last 15 years of his life he taught at the Sibelius Academy in Helsinki.

MILESTONES

1907	Composes 24 Preludes, piano
1913	Piano Concerto No. 2, "Virta" ("The River"), completed

"*I have more skill, but he is greater.*"

RICHARD STRAUSS ON SIBELIUS

Jean Sibelius

● 1865–1943 � Finnish ✍ 134

Sibelius ranks alongside Mahler and Carl Nielsen as one of the most important symphonists of the 20th century. His earlier, often fervently nationalist works were in a late-Romantic idiom, but in later years he developed a highly original musical language characterized by slow-moving harmony and distinctive, sometimes stark orchestration. Sibelius composed a number of tone poems based on Nordic subjects.

LIFE

Born into a Swedish-speaking family, Sibelius went to Helsinki to study law, but soon abandoned this in favour of full-time music study at the Helsinki Music Institute (now the Sibelius Academy). He befriended the composer Ferruccio Busoni, who encouraged him to seek further experience in Europe. After two years in Berlin and Vienna, Sibelius returned to Finland in 1892, taking a position at the Institute. Success came almost instantaneously with the vast symphonic poem *Kullervo*. Based on a character from Finnish mythology, it was a bald statement of nationalism at a time when Finland was itself a Grand Duchy under Russia's control. The Finnish cultural establishment took to Sibelius immediately, and his native fame was assured from that point on. However, it was not until his Symphony No. 1 (1899) that he began to achieve international recognition.

In 1904, unable to concentrate on composition in Helsinki, he built a house in the country and lived there for the rest of his life. Around this time his mature style began to emerge, less overtly patriotic and more concerned with "pure" music. The next 20 years were the most productive of Sibelius's life, although, after the bleak tone poem *Tapiola* in 1926, he wrote little in his final three decades.

An austere, unsmiling, yet good-natured and humorous man, Sibelius found inspiration in the nature and landscape of his native Finland.

MUSICAL OUTPUT
Total: 134

	1865	1875	1885	1895	1905	1915	1928	1943
SYMPHONIES (7)					2	2	3	
OTHER ORCHESTRAL (33)			1		7	15	10	
CHAMBER (13)				2	1	1	9	
PIANO (26)				2	4	8	12	
DRAMATIC (15)				1		6	8	
SONGS (15)				1	5	6	3	
CHORAL (25)				2	11	4	8	

MUSIC

Finland had no significant tradition of art music before Sibelius, and so it is no surprise that his major early influence was Tchaikovsky. Most of the works up to the Violin Concerto (1903) are conspicuously late Romantic and somewhat Russian in tone, their individuality coming more from their overtly nationalist programme than any unusual musical characteristics. Gradually, however, Sibelius's view of music – especially symphonic music – began to change. This is best illustrated by an oft-quoted conversation he had with Mahler, when the latter visited him in Helsinki in 1907. Discussing the most important aspects of a symphony, Sibelius admired "severity of style and the profound logic that creates an inner connection between all the motifs". Mahler countered to the contrary that "the symphony must be like the world. It must embrace everything." For Sibelius, the symphony was an organic

MILESTONES	
1886	Studies in Helsinki; befriends Busoni
1889	Begins studies in Europe
1892	Composes *Kullervo*, Op. 7, symphonic poem
1899	Composes Symphony No. 1, Op. 39
1900	*Finlandia*, Op. 26, first performed
1902	Symphony No. 2, Op. 43, composed
1904	Moves out of Helsinki
1907	Meets Mahler in Helsinki; composes Symphony No. 3, Op. 52
1909	Composes String Quartet Op. 56, "Voces intimae"
1914	Honorary doctorate from Yale
1923	Composes Symphony No. 6, Op. 104
1924	Symphony No. 7, Op. 105, composed
1926	Composes symphonic poem *Tapiola*, Op. 112

form, growing naturally from its opening bars. It is not fanciful to hear the increasing influence of Finnish natural life in the rugged, starkly beautiful music of his late works.

KEY WORKS

KULLERVO, OP. 7

TONE POEM   72:00   5

Kullervo is not normally counted as one of Sibelius's symphonies, but it is certainly symphonic in scope. A huge work, this tone poem takes as its text portions of the *Kalevala* – an epic poem compiled by the writer Elias Lönnrot from Finnish folk sources – which was itself a cornerstone of the burgeoning 19th-century Finnish nationalist movement.

Much of Sibelius's music refers to stories from Finnish mythology collected in the *Kalevala*, such as the story of Lemminkäinen's mother in his *Lemminkäinen Suite*.

SYMPHONY NO. 4, OP. 63

ORCHESTRAL   38:00   4

This piece was written in 1911, during a period of personal difficulty for Sibelius. Still convalescing from an operation to remove a throat tumour, he was under pressure to compose from his new publisher. The symphony contains some of his most difficult, stark music, and was described even by the composer himself as a "psychological" work.

TAPIOLA, OP. 112

TONE POEM   19:00   1

Tapio is the god of the forest in the *Kalevala*, and Sibelius's *Tapiola* is a symphonic poem depicting his dark, magical kingdom. This late work is a fine example of Sibelius's organic approach to composition; most of the material evolves directly from the murky opening theme.

FINLANDIA, OP. 26

TONE POEM   8:30   1

In 1899, Sibelius wrote music to accompany a series of patriotic tableaux depicting events in Finnish history, exhibited as part of the Press Celebrations and intended as a statement of Finnish nationalism. Parts of the work were performed in concert later in the year, and the stirring finale, originally titled "Finland Awakes", soon became popular with audiences. The following year Sibelius revised the work as a stand-alone concert version.

Finlandia opens with dramatic swells of brass and rumbling timpani, immediately conjuring images of the wild Finnish landscape. This music is developed by the strings and woodwind, before trumpet fanfares usher in a livelier section derived from the opening theme. This leads to the famous "Finlandia Hymn", sung first by the woodwind and then the strings, before the faster music returns to bring the work to a rousing conclusion.

SYMPHONY NO. 5, OP. 82

ORCHESTRAL   30:00   3

Originally written in 1915 and presented as part of his 50th birthday celebrations, Sibelius was unhappy with performances of this symphony and immediately set about revising it.

The now familiar version appeared in 1919, having been altered in significant respects, most especially in the collapsing together of the first two movements. This piece remains probably Sibelius's most popular and accessible symphony, a good-natured work that stands in total contrast to the stark, brooding Symphony No. 4.

FIRST MOVEMENT (TEMPO MOLTO MODERATO – LARGAMENTE – ALLEGRO MODERATO 13:00) An opening section scored for wind, horns, and drum presents the main theme, which is subsequently developed before a toccata-like section brings the movement to a grandiose close.

SECOND MOVEMENT (ANDANTE MOSSO, QUASI ALLEGRETTO 8:00) The Andante is a set of variations on a simple, pastoral theme presented after a short introduction.

THIRD MOVEMENT (ALLEGRO MOLTO 9:00) The finale is one of the most exciting movements in Sibelius's symphonic oeuvre. Its second main theme, played by the horn, was likened by one critic to Thor swinging his hammer.

INFLUENCES

In stylistic terms, Sibelius's influence on later composers is difficult to gauge since – along with the Danish composer Carl Nielsen – he represents the very end of a long tradition. However, his impact on Scandinavian music in general, and Finnish music in particular, was inestimable, as was his contribution to the development of the tone poem.

"There is music in the air. All you have to do is take as much as you require."

EDWARD ELGAR

Edward Elgar

● 1857–1934   ⚑ English   ✍ 79

For many, Elgar will always be associated with the imperial optimism of the late Victorian and Edwardian ages. Yet, his works – like the man himself – are more complex than their bluff exterior often suggests. His music encompasses not only the outwardly confident tone of his grand public works, but also the intimate, spiritual outpourings of a deeply sensitive musician; he wrote relatively little after the death of his wife in 1920.

LIFE

One of the constants of Elgar's life was his love for the countryside of his native Worcestershire and the Malvern Hills. He and his family returned many times to this part of England, where he had spent his early career as a freelance musician, regularly travelling the countryside to visit his piano pupils. It was one of these pupils, Caroline Alice Roberts, whom he later married and who gave him much of the encouragement he needed to concentrate more fully on composition. Despite initial difficulties in gaining national recognition as a composer, Elgar soon built up a solid reputation during the 1890s based on a series of choral works for festival performance. It was his *"Enigma" Variations* however, that truly cemented his national reputation as a composer. Following this success, his other works were hugely anticipated: the masterly oratorio *The Dream of Gerontius*, the two symphonies, and the concertos for violin and cello, all of which confirmed his place at the forefront of British music. He often cast himself as an outsider due to his lack of academic training, his social status as the son of a shop-keeper and his deep Roman Catholic faith in a largely Protestant society. Elgar was an extremely private man, never happier than when spending time with family or friends.

Elgar would often take music manuscripts from his father's music shop into the countryside to study them which forged his strong association between music and nature.

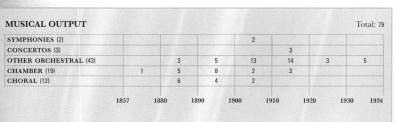

MUSICAL OUTPUT								Total: 79
SYMPHONIES (2)					2			
CONCERTOS (3)						3		
OTHER ORCHESTRAL (43)			3	5	13	14	3	5
CHAMBER (19)		1	5	8	2	3		
CHORAL (12)			6	4	2			
	1857	1880	1890	1900	1910	1920	1930	1934

MUSIC

A largely self-taught composer, Elgar absorbed elements of style from many different sources. There is a pervasive element of chromaticism in his music that adds colour and unexpected, yet innovative, turns of phrase. This fluid musical language allowed him, for example, to move easily between depictions of heaven and hell in *The Dream of Gerontius*, yet conversely also provided one of the biggest stumbling blocks for musicians attempting first performances of his works.

Elgar was also a consummate master of orchestration, having learnt his skills as a young man in his role as a jobbing musician. Many of his scores, such as the *Pomp and Circumstance Marches* and other public and ceremonial works, are full of the opulent, Edwardian textures for

MILESTONES	
1872	Leaves school, works as organist, piano teacher, conductor, and violinist
1889	Marries Caroline Alice Roberts
1890	Overture *Froissart*, Op. 19, performed at the Three Choirs Festival, Worcester
1899	"Enigma" Variations, Op. 36
1900	*The Dream of Gerontius*, Op. 38
1904	Knighted
1908	Symphony No. 1, Op. 35
1910	Violin Concerto, Op. 61
1911	Writes Symphony No. 2, Op. 63
1919	Cello Concerto, Op. 85, composed
1924	Appointed Master of the King's Music

which he is best known. Other works, however, like the poignant miniatures in the Serenade for Strings, demonstrate his subtle understanding of the intimate in music.

KEY WORKS

THE DREAM OF GERONTIUS, OP. 38

ORATORIO   95:00   2

Based on Cardinal Newman's 1861 poem, *Gerontius* portrays the death of an old man and his journey to rebirth in the next world. With its intensely moving operatic solos and imposing choruses depicting devils and angels, it has now become a regular fixture in the repertoire of British choirs.

English cellist Jacqueline du Pré (1945–87), won fame for her performances of Elgar's Cello Concerto. Her life was tragically cut short by multiple sclerosis.

POMP AND CIRCUMSTANCE MARCH, OP. 39, NO. 1

ORCHESTRAL   6:00   1

This ebullient and optimistic march (1901) was an immediate success . Its central section was later used by Elgar in his *Coronation Ode* of 1902 to the words of "Land of Hope and Glory".

SYMPHONY NO. 2, OP. 63

ORCHESTRAL   56:00   4

Elgar's joyous second symphony shows the composer in all his moods: noble, introverted, quixotic, and confident. The expansive second movement is particularly imposing.

VIOLIN CONCERTO, OP. 61

ORCHESTRAL   54:00   3

Composed at the same time as the Symphony No. 2, the Violin Concerto is itself symphonic in conception. Elgar's work demonstrates his subtle appreciation of the violin and develops a true musical partnership between soloist and orchestra.

FOCUS

VARIATIONS ON AN ORIGINAL THEME ("ENIGMA"), OP. 36

ORCHESTRAL   🕑 30:00   📖 15   🎼

Elgar brought an unusual personal touch to his Variations, using his original theme as a prism through which can be glimpsed his "friends pictured within". Over the course of 14 variations, Elgar provides musical character sketches of authors and poets (Richard Baxter Townshend in variation III, Richard Penrose Arnold, V), local dignitaries (William Meath Baker, IV, architect-pianist Troyte Griffith, VII), the characteristics of close friends (the calmness of Winifred Norbury, VIII, the delicate laugh of Dora Penny, X), and of course musicians (amateur pianist Hew David Steuart-Powell, II, violinist Isabel Fitton, VI, Hereford organist George Robertson Sinclair, XI, amateur cellist Basil Nevinson, XII).

In the case of Sinclair, the music is not a portrait of the man himself, but of the organist's bulldog, Dan. The most heartfelt variations describe Elgar's wife, Caroline Alice Elgar (I), his publisher, August Jaeger (IX) – whose majestic and brooding variation goes under the pseudonym of "Nimrod", the hunter – and himself (XIV), forming the finale.

CELLO CONCERTO, OP. 85

ORCHESTRAL   🕑 30:00   📖 4   🎼 🎧

FIRST MOVEMENT (ADAGIO – MODERATO, 7:15) The last major composition that Elgar completed opens with an anguished statement on the cello, momentarily soothed by the clarinet. A subtle, lilting melody gains in intensity to become the main theme, taken up by the soloist and orchestra in turn. Even the lighter moments in the second subject are haunted by the inevitable return of the opening.

SECOND MOVEMENT (LENTO – ALLEGRO MOLTO, 4:15) Querulous semiquavers and light, staccato orchestration mark the brief, elusive scherzo.

THIRD MOVEMENT (ADAGIO, 4:45) The cello takes centre stage in this almost continuous elegy.

FOURTH MOVEMENT (ALLEGRO – MODERATO – ALLEGRO, MA NON TROPPO, 10:45) The march-like main theme gives way to the cello's passionate ruminations. The anguished statement from the first movement reappears briefly.

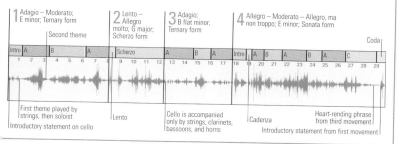

1 Adagio – Moderato; E minor; Ternary form
   Second theme
2 Lento – Allegro molto; G major; Scherzo form
3 Adagio; B flat minor; Ternary form
4 Allegro – Moderato – Allegro, ma non troppo; E minor; Sonata form
   Coda

| Intro | A | B | A | Scherzo | A | B | A | Intro | A | B | A | B | A | C |

1 2 3 4 5 6 7 8 9 10 11 12 13 14 15 16 17 18 19 20 21 22 23 24 25 26 27 28 29

First theme played by strings, then soloist
Introductory statement on cello
Lento
Cello is accompanied only by strings, clarinets, bassoons, and horns
Cadenza
Introductory statement from first movement
Heart-rending phrase from third movement

Sir Charles Stanford

◯ 1852–1924   ▶ Irish   ✍ c.300

At the Royal College of Music, in London Stanford taught many future English composers. His religious music is familiar to Anglican churchgoers, and he also enjoyed success in Europe and the US, particularly with his Irish Symphony, which Mahler conducted in New York. His style is light and lyrical and definitely "British" though his love of Ireland is revealed in his use of folk melodies. Stanford's beautiful setting of Mary Coleridge's *The Bluebird* is a well-known choir piece.

MILESTONES	
1879	Writes Service in B
1883	Professor of composition at RCM
1887	Composes *Symphony No. 3*, Irish
1897	*Shamus O'Brien*, opera, performed
1910	Writes *The Bluebird*, part-song

Sir Granville Bantock

◯ 1868–1946   ▶ English   ✍ 250

In between teaching at Birmingham University, travelling widely, and promoting the work of other composers, Bantock composed prodigiously himself: often works for large orchestra, but also brass band, choral, chamber, and piano pieces, and children's songs. Though popular in his lifetime, his music has since fallen out of favour. It is characterized by uncomplicated harmony and pseudo-Oriental or Celtic subjects. His tone poem *Fifine at the Fair* (1901) and overture *Pierrot of the Minute* are sometimes heard.

MILESTONES	
1908	Writes *Pierrot of the Minute* overture
1915	Composes *Hebridean Symphony*
1924	*The Seal Woman*, Celtic folk opera
1928	*Pagan Symphony* performed
1933	Writes *Prometheus* for brass band

Sir Hubert Parry

◯ 1848–1918   ▶ English   ✍ c.200

Parry's stirring Blake setting *Jerusalem*, written in 1916, is one of the most familiar pieces of music in England, and shows his imaginative, craftsmanlike style. Educated, in the upper-middle-class way, at Eton and Oxford, Parry was a musical amateur working in insurance until he was almost 30. However, he rose to become a major figure in the revitalizing of English music: as a scholar working on the new *Grove Dictionary of Music*; as a professor at the Royal College of Music (and later at Oxford University); and as a highly accomplished composer. His first major success was the cantata, *Blest Pair of Sirens*, which established him as one of England's leading composers, and resulted in a string of commissions – plus a knighthood and baronetcy. Although an avowed agnostic, he produced some of Britain's finest sacred choral music.

Parry's rousing and noble unison song *Jerusalem* – a setting of words from William Blake's Preface to *Milton* – became almost a second British national anthem during and after World War I.

MILESTONES	
1877	Leaves Lloyd's of London
1880	*Prometheus Unbound* performed
1883	Professor of Music History at RCM
1887	Composes *Blest Pair of Sirens*, cantata
1888	*Judith*, oratorio, performed
1898	Receives knighthood
1900	Becomes professor of Music at Oxford
1908	Created a Baronet
1916	Writes *Songs of Farewell*

Ethel Mary Smyth

● 1858–1944 🏳 English ✍ c.100

Born into a military family, Smyth was a battler: a persistent champion of women's causes, and of her own vigorous, idea-filled works. Against her parents' wishes, she studied music in Leipzig, where she gained private and public success with early pieces. Back in England, "E M Smyth's" orchestral works impressed critics, but she struggled to have her operas staged. Germany premiered many, but World War II closed that avenue. A prominent member of the suffrage movement, Smyth had intense love affairs with women of note. She gained official recognition in her 60s – as conductor, broadcaster, writer and, campaigner – as well as for her revived music, but sadly, deafness stopped her composing.

MILESTONES	
1877	Studies in Leipzig, Germany
1890	Debut of orchestral works, Crystal Palace, south London
1906	*The Wreckers*, opera, premiered in Leipzig
1911	Writes "The March of the Women", suffragette anthem
1922	Made a Dame

When jailed at London's Holloway Prison in 1912, Smyth led her fellow suffragettes in "The March of the Women", conducting with her Government-issue toothbrush.

Samuel Coleridge-Taylor

● 1875–1912 🏳 English ✍ c.160

The son of a black father, from Sierra Leone, and a white English mother, Coleridge-Taylor fought racial prejudice all his life, but musically enjoyed great respect – from Elgar among others – and popularity: his *Hiawatha's Wedding Feast* was England's most-performed choral work for ten years. His accomplished, sweetly Romantic style became unfashionable after his premature death from pneumonia, but is now enjoying a small revival.

MILESTONES	
1890	Studies violin at RCM
1899	Writes *Hiawatha's Wedding Feast*
1903	Becomes Professor of composition at Trinity College, London
1904	Compose *24 Negro Melodies*
1906	Tours US, meets President Roosevelt
1907	Writes *Thelma*, opera

Roger Quilter

● 1877–1953 🏳 English ✍ 125

 Trained in Germany, but English in style, Quilter was a shy, cultured, and well-travelled man from a moneyed family, with a wide circle of artistic friends. He was known in England as a songwriter – many of his works were performed by the major singers of the early 1900s. However, frequent illness meant composing was more difficult than seemingly effortless results suggest. His wealth may have diminished when he was blackmailed about his homosexuality, but he had used it generously to help Jewish friends flee Austria before World War II.

MILESTONES	
1905	Composes *To Julia*, song cycle
1922	*Children's Overture* included in first broadcasted BBC concert

Frederick Delius

🌑 1862–1934   🏴 English   ✍ c.120

Although Delius spent the majority of his life abroad, he is generally remembered as a quintessentially English composer who wrote evocative and timeless orchestral tone poems. The mountainous wilderness of Scandinavia, the tropical orange plantations of Florida, and the delicate beauty of rural France all find a place in the haunting and harmonious music of this truly cosmopolitan composer.

LIFE AND MUSIC

Enamoured of music from a very young age, it soon became clear that, despite the wishes of his family, Frederick Delius was not destined to become a businessman, but would make music his life's work. Studying in Leipzig, and eventually settling in France, Delius produced a succession of outstanding orchestral works – particularly in the first decade of the 20th century – which show the influence of Wagner and Grieg. In later years, Delius's music was championed by the conductor Sir Thomas Beecham, even as his debilitating illness made it necessary for him to dictate his final works through his amanuensis, Eric Fenby.

MILESTONES

1884	Takes on an orange plantation at Solano Grove, Florida
1887	Composes *Florida Suite*
1886	Studies at Leipzig Conservatory
1897	Moves to Grez-sur-Loing
1901	Writes *A Village Romeo and Juliet*, opera
1903	Marries German painter Jelka Rosen
1904	Composes *Sea Drift*, choral work
1908	Writes *In a Summer Garden* for orchestra
1912	*On Hearing the First Cuckoo in Spring*
1914	*Requiem* to text by Frederick Nietzsche

Delius and his wife, Jelka made their home in Grez-sur-Loing, near Fontainbleau, and received a steady stream of friends and admirers.

KEY WORKS

BRIGG FAIR – AN ENGLISH RHAPSODY

ORCHESTRAL   🕐 19:00   📖 1   🎵

Introduced to the Lincolnshire folk song "Brigg Fair" by his friend Percy Grainger, Delius used it as the basis of a series of orchestral variations.

IN A SUMMER GARDEN

ORCHESTRAL   🕐 15:00   📖 1   🎵

Inspired by Delius's own charming garden in Grez-sur-Loing, this evocative work even has a central episode to represent the gentle River Loing. The piece is dedicated to the composer's wife – painter and avid gardener Jelka Rosen.

VIOLIN SONATA NO. 3

DUO   📖 3   🎵

This was one of Delius's last works, and was completed with the assistance of Eric Fenby. It was first played to the composer by the celebrated British violinist May Harrison, accompanied by pianist and composer Arnold Bax.

FOCUS

A MASS OF LIFE

CHORAL　🎵 100:00　📖 2　♋️ 🎹

One of Delius's most ambitious works, this choral masterpiece was completed in 1905 and is a wholly secular affirmation of humanity – although even here there are moments of unease and despair. The text was carefully compiled by Delius and the German conductor Fritz Cassirer from Friedrich Nietzsche's *Also Sprach Zarathustra*. Together they selected a balanced sequence of 11 soliloquies that were particularly well suited to Delius's musical temperament. It is a huge and vigorous work with powerful choral writing and some imaginative orchestration, particularly in the evocative "Night Song".

THE WALK TO THE PARADISE GARDEN

INTERMEZZO　🎵 10:00　📖 1　♋️

This piece began life as an intermezzo in Delius's opera *A Village Romeo and Juliet*, which was based on a short story by the Swiss writer Gottfried Keller. Like the Shakespearean tragedy, the story tells of two families at odds over the rights to a piece of land between their farms. Despite the farmers' enmity, their children, Sali and Vreli, begin to meet in secret, and eventually fall in love. The purpose of the intermezzo was to smooth the transition between scenes for a Berlin production of the opera in 1907, and represented Sali and Vreli making their way to the Paradise Garden, a run-down inn that stood on the disputed piece of land. Delius's music captures the very essence of the opera as the two leading characters come to terms with their hopeless situation of forbidden love. Although the opera is seldom performed now, the intermezzo is a popular favourite of the concert hall.

ON HEARING THE FIRST CUCKOO IN SPRING

CHAMBER　🎵 8:00　📖 1　♋️

Written for small orchestra, this is one of two pieces composed by Delius between 1911 and 1912, the other being *Summer Night on the River*. In each work, the composer's colourful orchestration is strikingly suggestive of a pastoral idyll in France that appealed strongly to the English imagination; the subtle rhythms and instrumentation create a benign sense of rural tranquillity. As its title clearly implies, *On Hearing the First Cuckoo in Spring* is liberally interspersed with the call of the cuckoo, represented in the ensemble by the clarinet. The piece also introduces a Norwegian folk song, "In Ola valley, in Ola dale", which Delius found in a collection published by Grieg as *Norske Folkeviser*.

"*What we want in England is real music,
even if it be only a music-hall song.*"

RALPH VAUGHAN WILLIAMS IN *THE VOCALIST*, 1902

Ralph Vaughan Williams

1872–1958   **English**   **82**

A child of the late 19th century who received his training at the hands of the Victorian founders of the English musical renaissance, Ralph Vaughan Williams became one of the key British composers of the 20th century. Influenced by traditions as varied as English folk song and Tudor polyphony, he composed prolifically in many genres and continued to explore his own distinct musical style until well into his 80s.

LIFE

Although born into an affluent, professional family and educated both at Cambridge and London's Royal College of Music, Vaughan Williams firmly believed that music was for everyone. A socialist at heart, his dedication to music at all levels led him to devote his energies not only to the sophisticated high art of the symphony, but also to the simple beauty of everyday music like folk song and church hymns. He is often credited with leading the English "pastoral" school of composers and it is true that some of his works, such as *The Lark Ascending*, the *English Folksong Suite*, and *Fantasia on "Greensleeves"* are infused with this style. He was, however, a Londoner and an urbanite, and scores for his symphonies and film music are as challenging and sophisticated as those of any 20th-century European composer.

Despite his prolific output, Vaughan Williams' creativity matured slowly. He was highly critical of his works, revising them until he was absolutely satisfied, and often shared sketches with his great friend Holst, whom he trusted to give honest opinions on his current music projects. An acknowledged agnostic, he nevertheless used Christian themes and morality as the basis for many works including his opera, *The Pilgrim's Progress*, based on Bunyan's novel.

Vaughan Williams was of the great setters of English poetry, and vocal music comprises a large part of his output.

MUSICAL OUTPUT								Total: 82
SYMPHONIES (9)				1	2	1	2	3
CONCERTOS (9)				1	2	2	1	3
OTHER ORCHESTRAL (24)			3	1	4	3	8	5
CHAMBER (8)					4		3	1
OPERAS (11)					3	2		6
CHORAL (21)			2	1	3	9	1	5
	1872	1900	1910	1920	1930	1940	1950	1958

MUSIC

Vaughan Williams's study at the Royal College of Music (RCM) with Hubert Parry, Charles Villiers Stanford and Charles Wood provided him with a thorough foundation in contemporary German music. His own compositional voice, however, was also inspired by the music of earlier traditions, such as the simplicity and directness of English folk songs and the modal music he encountered editing *The English Hymnal* in 1904. He blended these elements with other styles and techniques – such as 16th-century polyphony and harmony, baroque counterpoint, and the delicacy of French orchestration learnt from Ravel – into his own musical language in his mid-thirties. During his long lifetime, Vaughan Williams composed in almost every genre and was active right into his 80s when the creativity of many similarly long-lived composers had long since dried up.

MILESTONES

1890	Studies at the RCM
1892	Trinity College, Cambridge
1895	Further study at the RCM; meets Gustav Holst
1897	Studies with Bruch in Berlin
1903	Collects first folk song, "Bushes and Briars"
1904	Music editor of *The English Hymnal*
1908	Studies with Ravel in Paris
1910	*A Sea Symphony* and *Fantasia on a Theme by Thomas Tallis* composed
1914	*A London Symphony; The Lark Ascending*
1922	Writes Mass in G minor
1923	*Fantasia on a Theme by Thomas Tallis* revised
1924	Writes *Hugh the Drover*
1940	Composes music for the film *49th Parallel*
1943	Symphony No. 5 composed
1951	Writes *The Pilgrim's Progress*
1953	*Symphonia Antartica* produced
1954	Tours US

KEY WORKS

THE LARK ASCENDING

ORCHESTRAL   🏊 15:00   📖 1   🎵 🎶

Taking George Meredith's poem as the inspiration for this one-movement work for violin and orchestra, Vaughan Williams creates exquisitely beautiful music that draws upon the contours of English folksong. Weightless cadenzas for the violin that disappear into the distance act as both prologue and epilogue. It was written in 1914, and revised in 1920.

MASS IN G MINOR

MASS   🏊 24:00   📖 5   🎵 🎶

This complete setting of the Mass for solo quartet and unaccompanied chorus makes use of the seamless, sinuous technique of 15th-century polyphony much admired by Vaughan Williams. It was first used liturgically by Sir Richard Terry and the choir of Westminster Cathedral.

SINFONIA ANTARTICA

ORCHESTRAL   🏊 39:00   📖 5   🎵 🎶 🎶

Based on material used for his score to the film *Scott of the Antarctic* (1949), this work shows Vaughan Williams the orchestrator at his best. Peppered with colourful percussion of all kinds, the Sinfonia portrays the stormy and changeable world of the Antarctic.

Vaughan Williams used a vibraphone in his Symphony No. 8. Invented in the US at the beginning of the 20th century, it was mainly used by jazz musicians.

FOCUS

FANTASIA ON A THEME BY THOMAS TALLIS

ORCHESTRAL 🏛 17:00 📖 1 ♐♐ ♔

There are few works in the repertoire that are so arresting and can match the depth of sonority found in Vaughan Williams's *Fantasia on a Theme by Thomas Tallis*. Composed for double string orchestra and solo quartet, it is based on the third tune in the Phrygian mode, "Why fum'th in fight?", that Thomas Tallis contributed to Archbishop Parker's Psalter of 1567. Vaughan Williams first encountered the melody when editing *The English Hymnal*.

Written in one continuous movement, the *Fantasia* begins quietly as Tallis's melody is picked out in pizzicato notes by the lower strings against an ethereal, sustained note in the violins. The theme is soon taken up by the larger ensemble with a fuller accompaniment before more intimate sections in which members of the solo quartet take elements of the theme, weaving independently against each other between interpolations from the larger ensemble in the manner of a concerto grosso.

SYMPHONY NO. 5

ORCHESTRAL 🏛 35:00 📖 4 ♐♐

FIRST MOVEMENT (PRELUDIO, MODERATO)
Scored for a smaller orchestra than Vaughan Williams had used previously, this symphony uses musical material the composer had earmarked for his (then incomplete) opera based on Bunyan's *The Pilgrim's Progress* that had occupied him for almost forty years.

SECOND MOVEMENT (SCHERZO, PRESTO)
The brief Scherzo passes quickly, yet demonstrates that Vaughan Williams's studies in orchestration with Ravel were hugely influential, with chorale-like moments for the brass and muted strings supporting a delicate and light texture peppered

with ubiquitous cross-rhythms.

THIRD MOVEMENT (ROMANZA, LENTO)
It is only in the Romanza that the composer allowed parallels to be drawn with the music for *The Pilgrim's Progress*, since it uses material destined for the scenes portraying "The House Beautiful" in the opera. As the true heart of the symphony, the music is heartfelt, expansive and wistful.

FOURTH MOVEMENT (PASSACAGLIA, MODERATO)
The final movement, a joyous ending to a meditative work, is cast in the mould of a passacaglia with its static, repeating ground bass while the other instruments provide rhythmic and melodic interest above.

Gustav Holst

● 1874–1934   ▶ English   ✍ c.120

Mainly remembered as the composer of *The Planets*, Gustav Holst was a true musical eclectic. He approached every composition from a fresh angle and drew his inspiration from sources as diverse as astrology, English folk song, Sanskrit poetry, Algerian melodies and the poetry of Thomas Hardy. He was also a natural teacher with an ability to inspire the minds of children and adults alike.

LIFE AND MUSIC

Like his lifelong friend Ralph Vaughan Williams, Holst studied composition at the Royal College of Music with Charles Stanford, a leading figure in the 19th-century renaissance of British music. After working as a trombonist and repetiteur, Holst became director of music at St Paul's Girls' School and also taught adults at Morley College, both in London. At the root of his music – mainly composed during the school holidays – is rhythm, and many of his works are based on ostinato patterns. His colourful harmonic style blends traditional tonality with inventive combinations of chords and spare, open intervals, giving his music a truly distinctive voice within his era.

MILESTONES	
1895	Meets Vaughan Williams
1896	Becomes conductor of the Hammersmith Socialist Choir
1905	Appointed director of music at St Paul's Girls' School, Hammersmith
1906	Composes *Somerset Rhapsody*
1907	Joins staff of Morley College
1908	Visits Algeria
1910	Writes *Beni Mora (Oriental Suite)*
1913	Composes *St Paul's Suite* for his pupils
1916	*The Planets* premiered
1917	Composes *The Hymn of Jesus*
1922	Completes *The Perfect Fool*, opera
1927	Composes *Egdon Heath*, tone poem
1932	Given a visiting lectureship at Harvard University

KEY WORKS

THE HYMN OF JESUS

CHORAL   ⏱ 21:00   📖 1   ♫♫

This joyous and popular work combines Latin plainsong chants with Holst's hallmark irregular rhythms, colourful harmony, and lush orchestration to portray the text from the Apocryphal Acts of St John, translated by the composer from the original.

BALLET MUSIC FROM THE PERFECT FOOL

BALLET SUITE   ⏱ 11:00   📖 4   ♫

The popular ballet music from Holst's one-act comic opera is now regularly featured in concert programmes. It is split into three dances, one each for the Spirits of Earth, Water and Fire. These are conjured by a wizard evoked by a trombone. Earth has a low bass tune, Water a stately dance, and Fire a lively caper.

Salisbury Plain was the inspiration for the Egdon Heath Thomas Hardy described in his novel *The Return of the Native*. In turn, this inspired Holst to write his austere tone poem *Egdon Heath*, considered one of his best works.

THE PLANETS

ORCHESTRAL SUITE   49:00   7

Not so much a portrayal of the planets as celestial bodies as of the human traits they embody, Holst's astrologically inspired orchestral suite has always enjoyed great popularity.

MARS, THE BRINGER OF WAR (ALLEGRO 7:00) Mars opens with a menacing five-beats-in-a-bar ostinato over which music surges in waves through the orchestra with rising intensity before a sudden and abrupt ending.

VENUS, THE BRINGER OF PEACE (ADAGIO :00) In stark contrast to Mars, the mood of Venus is one of sensuous longing. Harps and woodwind solos emphasize the goddess's gentleness.

MERCURY, THE WINGED MESSENGER (VIVACE 4:00) Quicksilver reactions and sparkling agility characterize Mercury, a brief and light scherzo movement.

JUPITER, THE BRINGER OF JOLLITY (ALLEGRO GIOCOSO 8:00) While depicting the majesty of this heavenly giant, the orchestra also emphasizes Jupiter's jovial spirit. The central, broad sweep of melody was later used for the popular hymn "I vow to thee, my country".

SATURN, THE BRINGER OF OLD AGE (ADAGIO 9:00) Beside the heartiness of Jupiter, the senility of Saturn is pulled into sharp focus. Tired, repeated patterns and heavy chords add weight to a solemn dirge on the brass.

URANUS, THE MAGICIAN (ALLEGRO 6:00) Beginning with four striking brass notes that act as Holst's musical calling card, this movement shows the quirky and changeable nature of the human spirit.

NEPTUNE, THE MYSTIC (ANDANTE 7:00) As he reaches the outer edges of the solar system and the human psyche (Pluto had not yet been discovered), Holst allows mysterious harmonies and a wordless, off-stage chorus of female voices to fade into nothingness.

ST PAUL'S SUITE

STRING ORCHESTRA   11:00   4

This joyful, four-movement work was composed for the young string players of the school at which Holst taught for most of his life.

JIG (VIVACE 3:00) The main theme is first played in unison by the upper strings.

OSTINATO (PRESTO 1:00) Based on a repeating pattern heard high in the violins, this movement is a light-footed scherzo.

INTERMEZZO (ANDANTE CON MOTO – VIVACE 4:00) A broad, lingering melody is interrupted twice by a frantic melody that Holst heard on a visit to Algeria.

FINALE: THE DARGASON (ALLEGRO 3:00) The finale takes us firmly back to London as two old English melodies, "The Dargason" (a dance tune) and "Greensleeves", are combined in the finale to the suite.

John Ireland

◉ 1879–1962   ◫ English   ✍ c.100

A pianist and composer in equal measure, Ireland originally trained as a performer, but gravitated towards composition in his teens. His mature musical voice is distinctive among British composers, reminiscent of the impressionistic style developed in France by Debussy and Ravel. Although he wrote for orchestral and chamber forces, Ireland's main compositional legacy is for his own instrument, the piano.

LIFE AND MUSIC

Having spent eight years studying at the Royal College of Music in London from his early adolescence, it is unsurprising that Ireland devoted most of his life to teaching, performance, and composition. His works often have a real sense of place that reflects the inspiration he found in the countryside and his enduring association with county of Sussex and the Channel Islands. Ireland was particularly drawn to the verse of English poets, such as Alfred Edward Housman and Thomas Hardy. Ireland's thorough compositional training under Charles Stanford is reflected in his detailed and disciplined craftsmanship and his ear for tonal colour.

MILESTONES	
1893	Studies piano at the Royal College of Music; loses both parents
1904	Becomes organist at St Luke's, London
1906	Composes Phantasie Trio
1909	Violin Sonata No. 1 wins the Cobbett Prize
1917	Writes *The Forgotten Rite* for orchestra
1920	Composes Piano Sonata
1927	Sonatina for piano premiered
1930	Writes Piano Concerto in E flat major
1936	Writes *A London Overture* in B flat major
1937	*These Things Shall Be*, for orchestra
c.1947	Film score for *The Overlanders* released

KEY WORKS

SONATINA

SOLO PIANO   ⏱ 10:00   ▥ 3   ◐

It is possible to hear Ireland himself as pianist in this delicate work. A masterly Moderato opening is followed by a deeply sombre Lento, culminating in a bubbling and rhythmic Rondo.

PIANO CONCERTO IN E FLAT MAJOR

ORCHESTRAL   ⏱ 26:00   ▥ 3   ◑ ◐

When Ireland heard the young pianist Helen Perkin play Prokofiev's Third Piano Concerto in 1930, he was so struck by her skill that he adapted his own Piano Concerto, making alterations to accommodate her small hands.

Ireland took great delight in the English countryside, absorbing its mellow colours, soft tones, and lyrical sounds, which emerged in his music.

Cast in the traditional three-movement concerto format, it still remains true to Ireland's characteristic, delicate style.

A LONDON OVERTURE IN B FLAT MAJOR

ORCHESTRAL   ⏱ 12:00   ▥ 1   ◑

Adapted from a comedy overture for brass, this orchestral version retains comic notes. A slow start leads to the main melody based on a bus conductor's cry of "Piccadilly!"

Arnold Bax

⬤ 1883–1953   🏴 English   ✍ c.300

Early in his studies, Bax's imagination was fired by the work of the Irish poet W B Yeats, whose Celtic verse and imagery provided the inspiration for some of the composer's most exquisite and atmospheric tone poems, such as *The Garden of Fand* and *Tintagel*. The breadth of his output, rivalling that of the recently acclaimed Vaughan Williams, has put Bax and his music back on the map.

LIFE AND MUSIC

Coming from an affluent family, Bax always had his own private income and never had to earn his living through teaching or performing. Once he had discovered his affinity for W B Yeats and his *Celtic Twilight*, Bax's music developed rapidly, and he also published his own novels under the pseudonym Dermot O'Byrne. His atmospheric tone poems, written during World War I, evoke the magic of nature, reflecting the Romantic mood of Richard Strauss and the impressionistic style of Debussy. By contrast, the lush, evocative music of his seven symphonies – each with three, rather than the more usual four, movements – incorporates the clarity and counterpoint he learned from Sibelius.

MILESTONES	
1893	Taken to concerts at the Crystal Palace, Sydenham, by his father
1900	Enrols at the Royal Academy of Music
1910	Visits Russia
1917	Writes *November Woods*, tone poem
1919	Composes *Tintagel*, tone poem
1922	Writes Symphony No. 1
1937	Receives knighthood
1939	Symphony No. 7 premiered

The otherworldly beauty of the Celtic landscape, with its luminous skies and ancient stones, inspired the rhapsodic effects in Bax's tone poems.

KEY WORKS

THIS WORLDES JOIE

CHORAL   ⏱ 10:00   📖 1   ♫

This piece for unaccompanied choir, from 1923, takes its words from a 14th-century English prayer. The music builds from wistful homophonic textures in the first verse to passionate counterpoint underpinned by an insistent ostinato that is only silenced by the final note.

TINTAGEL

ORCHESTRAL   ⏱ 15:00   📖 1   ♫

This confident, evocative orchestral tone poem captures the powerful, elemental nature of the rough sea off the coast of Tintagel in Cornwall, set against the Arthurian story of Tristram and Iseult. It quotes briefly from Wagner's staged version of the legend and also mirrors Bax's passion for the pianist Harriet Cohen, who he had met in 1912.

SYMPHONY NO. 6

ORCHESTRAL   ⏱ 40:00   📖 3   ♫

It is hard to choose just one of the seven symphonies that Bax wrote between 1922 and 1939, but No. 6, from 1934, and dedicated to the conductor Adrian Boult, is a model of focused musical thought showing Bax at his peak.

George Butterworth

🌐 1885–1916   📖 English   ✍ 15

In the English folk song revival of the early 1900s, no one set A E Housman's lyrical poetry to music better than Butterworth, depicting the English countryside with haunting simplicity. A popular man, Butterworth was also a renowned folk dancer and collected folk songs. In World War I he received a Military Cross for bravery in battle shortly before his death, and left a tiny output of high quality and unfulfilled promise.

MILESTONES

1912	Starts collecting folk songs
1911	Writes *A Shropshire Lad*, 6 songs
1912	Composes *Bredon Hill*, songs, and *Shropshire Lad*, rhapsody
1913	*Banks of Green Willow*, idyll, orchestra
1914	Joins Durham Light Infantry
1916	Killed in action, Somme, 5 August

Arthur Bliss

🌐 1891–1975   📖 English   ✍ 200

In some ways a natural successor to Elgar, whom he knew at Cambridge, Bliss wrote music that reflected his warm and outgoing personality. He served in World War I, and wrote his choral symphony, *Morning Heroes*, as a heartfelt tribute to those who died. Mixing modern and Romantic ideas, he skillfully matched his music to the purpose or the players: from brilliantly orchestrated, dramatic work for the ballet *Checkmate* to simple pieces suitable for amateur choirs or brass bands.

MILESTONES

1922	Composes *Colour Symphony*, orchestra
1935	Writes *Things to Come*, film score
1953	Master of the Queen's Musick
1969	Composes music for the investiture of Prince Charles

Gerald Finzi

🌐 1901–1956   📖 English   ✍ 50

Finzi lived simply with his artist wife in rural Hampshire, and an individual, but English, accent runs through much of his music. When setting words, such as Hardy's verse, he captured the essential atmosphere perfectly. His songs for piano and voice work beautifully, though he was neither a singer nor an accomplished pianist. Hospitable, yet introspective, Finzi was also a notable scholar and researcher, and his amateur orchestra promoted many new composers and performers.

MILESTONES

c.1926	Writes *Dies Natalis*, cantata
1930	Teaches at Royal Academy of Music
1938	*Intimations of Immortality*, choral work
1949	Writes Clarinet Concerto, Op. 31
1955	Composes Cello Concerto, Op. 40

Peter Warlock

🌐 1894–1930   📖 English   ✍ 125

Philip Heseltine was educated at Eton but only received an informal musical education. He enjoyed a lasting creative friendship with Delius, though his other relationships were often difficult, and he won public acclaim for the solo songs he wrote under the pseudonym Peter Warlock. A great admirer of early English music, he edited over 500 works, and set many songs in an idiosyncratic style, with influences from medieval music to Bartók.

MILESTONES

1911	Meets Delius
1918	Involved in occult in Dublin
1920	Edits *The Sackbut*, controversial music magazine
1922	Writes *The Curlew*, song cycle
c.1926	*Capriol Suite*, orchestra, published
1930	Dies in gas-filled flat, possibly suicide

Edouardo Lalo

● 1823–1892   French   ✍ c.70

Lalo's robust and inventive compositions impressed few people for most of his life.

He worked as a teacher and violinist – playing in a string quartet, and writing overlooked chamber music and an unperformed opera. But in his 50s, when his colleague Sarasate played Lalo's violin concerto and *Symphonie espagnole* (his most popular work today), his reputation grew, and other orchestral works were performed to great acclaim.

MILESTONES

1839	Abandons home to study in Paris
c.1850	Writes two piano trios
1874	Composes *Symphonie espagnole*, violin and orchestra
1882	*Namouna*, ballet, performed
1887	Symphony in G minor published
1888	*Le Roi d'Ys*, opera, triumphs at Opéra-Comique

In 1888 Lalo's opera, *Le Roi d'Ys*, was performed seven years after its composition. It was popular and brought him the success he had hoped for.

Félix-Alexandre Guilmant

● 1837–1911   French   ✍ 100

It was inevitable that an outstanding organist such as Guilmant would settle in Paris, with its magnificent Cavaillé-Coll organs. As an energetic organ recitalist across Europe and America, known for his precision and clarity as well as his versatility in managing unfamiliar organs,  he popularized and broadened the repertoire, exploring the work of both forgotten early composers and his gifted contemporaries. Guilmant succeeded Widor as organ professor at the Paris Conservatoire, and his compositional output includes eight attractive sonatas.

MILESTONES

1871	Becomes organist at La Trinité
1875	Composes Organ Sonata No. 1
1902	Organ Sonata No. 7 published

Cécile Chaminade

● 1857–1944   French   ✍ 400

Polished, colourful, witty, and typically French, Chaminade's music – much of it piano pieces or mélodies – was highly saleable. Popular in both England and the US, recognition in France was slower, and she often  had to battle against negative perceptions of female composers. A large proportion of her 400 works were published in her lifetime, but her late-Romantic style faded in popularity after her death.

MILESTONES

1880	Writes Piano Trio No. 1
1888	Composes *Callirhöe*, ballet
1892	Makes her London debut
1896	*Concertstück*, Op. 40, published
1908	Tours US to financial success
1913	First woman composer to be awarded the Légion d'Honneur

Camille Saint-Saëns

◉ 1835–1921   🏴 French   ✍ 420

A composer, pianist and organist, as well as being erudite in
other fields, Saint-Saëns was one of the most significant
French cultural figures of the 19th century. His long life and
music career encompassed the Romantic era and its transition into the modern
age. He acted as a vital bridge between the French light-opera tradition and the
new Romantic dawn of Wagner, while advocating a Classical renaissance.

LIFE AND MUSIC

As a child prodigy, Saint-Saëns was
hailed as the French Mozart. Classically
inclined, but an admirer of Liszt and
Wagner, he was influential in promoting
new French music, although he rejected
its later developments. His style was
admired for its technical fluency, clarity
of form, and sober elegance, but also
charged with superficiality. However,
there is much imagination, charm
and melodic inspiration in his vast
and versatile output, which includes
symphonies, concertos, chamber works
for often unusual combinations, organ
music, operas, secular and sacred
vocal music, and songs.

MILESTONES	
1846	Official debut as solo pianist
1851	Enters Paris Conservatoire
1857	Appointed organist at La Madeleine; retains prestigious post for 20 years
1867	Writes *Les noces de Prométhée*, cantata, his first success
1868	Composes Piano Concerto No. 2
1871	Co-founds National School of Music
1874	Composes *Danse macabre*
1877	Opera *Samson et Dalila* premiered
1880	Composes Violin Concerto No. 3
1886	Composes "Organ" Symphony and *Carnival of the Animals*
1915	Goes on triumphant American tour

KEY WORKS

DANSE MACABRE

SYMPHONIC POEM   ⏱ 7:30   📖 1   🎵

Saint-Saëns's most famous symphonic
poem is a quintessential blend of
fantastical imagination and Classical
rigour. At midnight, skeletons (depicted
by xylophones, used for
the first first time in
Classical music) emerge
from their graves to
dance in a churchyard.

SYMPHONY NO. 3, "ORGAN"

ORCHESTRAL ⏱36:00 📖2 🎵 🎹

Saint-Saëns's most
ambitious symphonic
work initiated a
renaissance of this

genre in France. Evolving rather than
transforming the traditional four-
movement form, it has two long
movements, each in two sections. The
organ appears in the second movement

VIOLIN CONCERTO NO. 3 IN B MINOR

ORCHESTRAL ⏱ 29:00 📖 3 🎵 🎻

This fine French violin
concerto deftly combines
heroic themes, lyrical
poetry, and swashbuckling
virtuosity – a masterly
fusion of varied influences

Saint-Saëns's lifelong interest in
lepidoptery began in childhood. His
musical talents were also evident
early on: he started composing at five

FOCUS

SAMSON ET DALILA

OPERA · 125:00 · 3

This opera was promoted by Liszt, who organized its 1877 premiere in Weimar, but its biblical subject was balked at by the French public until 1890. Its novel combination of a grand symphonic style and memorable set pieces drew criticism from reactionary quarters, but made it much loved by a wider public.

Samson exemplifies the dual tendencies of the composer's style, the oratorio-like first act suggesting the influence of Bach and Handel, while the more dramatic and lyrical second and third acts are in line with the tradition of Meyerbeer and Gounod.

ACT ONE (47:00) Refusing to worship the Philistines' deity, Dagon, Samson leads a Hebrew uprising. Despite warnings, he is seduced by the beguiling Dalila.

ACT TWO (42:00) The Philistine high priest orders Dalila to extract from Samson the secret of his strength. She appeals to Samson to put love above his god or people, and to confide his secret to her. He refuses at first, but is then persuaded to follow her into her house. Dalila allows the Philistine soldiers to enter.

ACT THREE, SCENE ONE (11:00) Samson turns a treadmill in prison, blinded and shorn.

The Hebrews lament the betrayal of his people and their God for a woman. **SCENE TWO** (25:00) At the bacchanalia in the temple, Samson is taunted by the high priest and Dalila. Samson pleads with God to restore his strength and brings the temple crashing down.

LE CARNAVAL DES ANIMAUX

INSTRUMENTAL · 22:30 · 14

Saint-Saëns did not design his "Grand Zoological Fantasy" for general performance. In fact, worried that it might compromise his reputation as a serious composer, he banned it from concerts altogether, excepting the 13th movement, "The Swan". The ban was only lifted by a provision in his will. A royal lion, hens and cocks, tortoises, an elephant, kangaroos, an aquarium, birds, donkeys, pianists (told to play like beginners), fossils, and a swan are all described in *The Carnival of the Animals* before a rousing finale. The work includes joking references to other composers' music and his own *Danse macabre*. "The Aquarium" and the finale are especially popular with the public, and the cello melody in "The Swan" is one of the most famous in all Classical music.

Gabriel Fauré

● 1845–1924   🏴 French   ✍ c.255

Unlike his mentor, Saint-Saëns, Fauré singularly succeeded in staying in tune with the artistic developments of his times, whilst retaining his own highly distinctive Romantic essence. Composer of a famous Requiem and widely regarded as master of the French song, he also created a very fine body of chamber and piano music. His gift for melody has tended to obscure the introspective, impassioned depth of his music.

LIFE AND MUSIC

The son of a country schoolmaster, Fauré was a protégé of Saint-Saëns's and took over from him as organist of the Church of La Madeleine in Paris. Prevented by financial struggles from composing regularly, his success was long in coming. While not obviously revolutionary, the stylistic independence that made him adaptable to the huge musical changes of his time also provoked the antagonism of reactionary peers. However, he was surprisingly made director of the Conservatoire and became venerated as the grand old man of French music. His musical spirit evolved from the sensuality of his youth to a darker, then a more forceful, and eventually a sparser style.

MILESTONES	
1861	Becomes Saint-Saëns's piano student
1871	Participates in foundation of the Société Nationale de Musique
1875	Composes Violin Sonata No. 1 and Piano Sonata, Op. 13
1877	Made choirmaster at La Madeleine
1887	"Clair de lune", Op. 46, No. 2, song
1900	Completes Requiem
1894	Completes *La bonne chanson*, song cycle
1896	Becomes composition teacher at Paris Conservatoire
1898	Composes *Pelléas et Mélisande*, suite
1903	Experiences early signs of deafness
1905	Made director of Paris Conservatoire
1913	*Pénélope*, opera, premiered
1921	Writes Nocturne No. 13, for piano

KEY WORKS

PELLÉAS ET MÉLISANDE
INCIDENTAL MUSIC   ⏱ 20:30   📖 5   🔊

Fauré was commissioned to set incidental music for the English premiere of Maeterlinck's Symbolist play of 1892, *Pelléas et Mélisande*, while Debussy was working on his own operatic version of it. The quasi-fairy tale concerns Princess Mélisande's doomed love for her husband's younger brother. Fauré's resulting suite is considered to be his orchestral masterpiece.

Fauré's lyric drama *Penelope* was a success in Monte Carlo in 1913, but is now little heard.

CLAIR DE LUNE
SONG   ⏱ 2:30   📖 1   🔊

This most celebrated of all Fauré's songs, initiating his association with Verlaine's poems, is imbued with the characteristic melancholy of his darkest period. The independence between voice and piano, and the importance given to the latter, were absolutely novel in their time.

REQUIEM

MASS   🎵 39:00   📖 7   🎶 🎻 ♦

Fauré's most famous work was composed in stages and has existed in slightly different versions. Initial elements of its composition may be traced back to 1877. Work on the *Requiem* itself started in 1887, "for no reason at all…for pleasure, if I dare say so," he commented. Its complete, seven-movement version was completed only in 1892, but just for a small, intimate orchestra. The full symphonic score was finally published in 1900.

Fauré's conception imbues the sober majesty of the Requiem form with a uniquely uplifting spirituality. Faced with criticism that, as a Mass for the dead, his work was not weighty enough, he responded, "It has been described as a lullaby of death. But that is how I perceive death: like a joyful deliverance, an aspiration to the bliss of the hereafter, rather than a painful experience."

The opening Introit et Kyrie and Offertoire movements are closer to the sombre mood one expects, but the Sanctus and Pie Jesu elevate the music towards ethereal realms. The great soprano solo of the Pie Jesu and the soprano voices in the choir were intended for children's voices. The Agnus Dei follows in a similar vein, but takes a dramatic turn that sets up the Libera Me, where the baritone solo imparts a darker and more tragic mood. These contrasts between light and gravity are resolved by the celestial In Paradisum, its extended, floating phrase one of the most spiritually blissful moments in music.

LA BONNE CHANSON, OP. 61

SONG CYCLE   📖 9   🎼 ♦

Fauré found his ideal poetic model for his melodies in the work of Paul Verlaine, setting nine of his poems in this song cycle. The free treatment of the poetic material, the expressive outpouring for the voice and the prominence of the piano, seemed alien to the mélodie genre and disconcerted many listeners. However, the cycle was soon recognized as the most open and richest expression of Fauré's bold and fiery nature.

Inspired by his liaison with Emma Bardac, later Debussy's second wife, Fauré organized the poems to chart the journey of this love, described in the second song, as "towards paradise". He also created a musical unity by organizing the cycle around five recurrent themes, often stated by the piano, four of which are rejoined in the last song. The first appears in the opening, setting the overall mood of rapt happiness. Occasional moods of anxiety, especially in the fourth and fifth songs, give way to the depiction of a summer's-day wedding. The motif of a singing lark in the last song heralds the return of spring.

Henri Duparc

● 1848–1933   ♙ French   ✍ 25

Perhaps no composer's place in history is assured by such a small output as Duparc's with his 14 remaining songs. His reputation as the finest representative of the French mélodie genre, along with Fauré, rests on just a few songs in a life plagued by illness. An obsessive perfectionist, he destroyed most of what little else he produced, and an extreme neurasthenic condition gradually left him blind and paralyzed.

LIFE AND MUSIC

Originally set for a career in law, Duparc was swayed towards music by César Franck, who considered him his most gifted pupil. Duparc was a friend and admirer of Saint-Saëns, who introduced him to Liszt and Wagner. His poetic intensity, in part inspired by Wagner (whom he nonetheless did not seek to copy) and encapsulated in his phrase "I wish to be moved", was tempered by a taste for simplicity. It found its ideal context in the setting of songs, to which Duparc largely devoted himself. He wrote most of these for voice and piano, but some he later orchestrated. He nurtured plans for theatrical works, but a strange neurasthenic condition left him unable to compose after 1884. Blind and paralyzed for many years, he immersed himself in an increasingly mystical existence.

MILESTONES	
1867	Produces his first composition
1868	Writes first songs, including "Chanson triste", "Soupir", and "Le galop"
1869	Writes "Au pays où se fait la guerre"
1871	Writes "La vague et la cloche", song; participates in the founding of the Société Nationale de Musique
1873	Composes *Poème nocturne* for orchestra
1874	Composes *Lénore*, symphonic poem
1879	Song "Le Manoir de Rosemonde"
1880	Song "Sérénade florentine"
1882	Composes "Phidylé", song, and *Benedicat vobis Domine*, motet
1883	Writes songs "Lamento", "Testament"
1884	Composes "La vie antérieure", song
c.1886	Begins work on an opera, *Roussalka*

KEY WORKS

CHANSON TRISTE

SONG   ⏱ 3:00   📖 1   🔊 ♂

This is one of three songs remaining from Duparc's first set of five, and was later orchestrated by the composer. Supported by a flowing accompaniment, the meltingly beautiful melody is shaped over a vast vocal range. It is one of his most passionate songs and shows complete maturity in its purity of design and characteristic delicacy.

Henry Duparc's song "Phidylé" is a setting of a poem by Leconte de Lisle. Its long-spun melody rises to a radiant climax.

LE MANOIR DE ROSEMONDE

SONG   ⏱ 2:45   📖 1   🔊 ♂

This most darkly dramatic song, reminiscent of Schubert in its obsessive rhythmic impulses, fully reveals the tortured undercurrents of Duparc's art.

LA VIE ANTÉRIEURE

SONG   ⏱ 4:40   📖 1   🔊 ♂

One of two settings of poems by Baudelaire, Duparc's last existing work seems eerily imbued with a sense of finality. Its majestic eloquence shifts to an elegiac mood that is intensified by the piano's fading close.

Vincent d'Indy

● 1851–1931   ♙ French   ✍ Unknown

D'Indy was a conservative figure whose music school, the Schola Cantorum, rivalled the Paris Conservatoire with considerable success. A pupil of César Franck, whom he idolized, d'Indy was not admired by modernists who wanted to re-establish a tradition of pure French music free from any hint of the academic. He had some success as a composer in his day, but his compositions are nowadays seldom played.

LIFE AND MUSIC

Born into a military family, d'Indy never shed his reputation as a conservative musician. Parental pressure forced him to study law, but he tenaciously continued musical activities during his 20s. In his 30s he began to achieve acclaim, first with the cantata *Le chant de la cloche (The Song of the Bell)* and then with the *Symphonie sur un chant montagnard français (Symphony on a French Mountain Air)* both reflecting his interest in French folk song and its revival. The re-editing of past French music was another passion, for example the operas of Rameau. His teaching was based on the study of music history, while his compositions centred on Teutonic musical structure.

MILESTONES	
1875	Graduates from Paris Conservatoire
1885	Wins Grand prix de la ville de Paris for cantata *Le chant de la cloche*
1885	Made secretary of Société Nationale de Musique promoting French music
1886	Writes *Symphonie cévenole*
1905	Writes *Jour d'été à la montagne*
1920	Marriage to much younger second wife inspires late-flowering creativity

D'Indy and his followers, Déodat de Sévérac and Joseph Canteloube, inspired a revival of folk song in France in parallel with a similar trend in Britain led by Vaughan Williams.

KEY WORKS

SYMPHONY ON A FRENCH MOUNTAIN AIR

ORCHESTRAL   ⏱ 24:30   ♫ ◉

This piece by d'Indy is also called *Symphonie cévenole*, reflecting its inspiration in the folk music of the Cévennes region of central France. It uses the device of colouristic change rather than thematic development for its effect.

L'ÉTRANGER

OPERA   ♫ ♨ ♦

D'Indy's most successful opera was first staged in 1903 in Brussels. He wrote his own libretto for it about a stranger arriving in a closed community. Though shot with modernism, the music still leans towards 19th-century techniques.

JOUR D'ÉTÉ À LA MONTAGNE

ORCHESTRAL   ▥ 3   ♫

Recalling *La Mer* by Debussy, *A Summer's Day in the Mountains* attempts to capture a whole day's experiences in the three movements of a quasi-symphony. It depicts the passage of time between dawn and nightfall and has brilliantly evocative orchestration. A late flowering of impressionism, it has been overshadowed by the works of Debussy and Ravel.

Emmanuel Chabrier

⬤ 1841–1894   🏴 French   ✍ Unknown

Chabrier could be considered an early Impressionist: he was admired by Debussy and Ravel, and was a friend of Manet. Gathering material for his most famous orchestral piece, *España*, he worked like a "plein-air" painter, noting down dance melodies and castanet rhythms from the streets of Andalucia, and subsequently transforming them through kaleidoscopic scoring for a large orchestra.

LIFE AND MUSIC

Chabrier came from the Auvergne, and was pressed into studying law by his father. Although he spent 20 years as a civil servant, he managed to produce several comic operas during this time. He also became notorious for his alcohol-inspired improvizations in the bars and cafés of Paris. An ardent Wagnerian, he was moved to tears when he heard the love theme of *Tristan und Isolde* in 1880. As a result of this experience, and of his growing success during the 1870s, he resigned from his administrative position to dedicate himself to music. There followed his most productive period during which he wrote music in all genres.

MILESTONES	
1858	Begins his studies in law.
1862	Composes nine melodies
1873	Publishes an Impromptu dedicated to Manet's wife.
1880	Composes the *Pièces pittoresques*
1883	*España* premiered and subsequently arranged as a piano duet
1888	Writes the *Marche Joyeuse*
1890	Begins work on *Briseïs*, an opera to a libretto after Goethe
1894	Dies as a result of syphilis, leaving collection of Impressionist paintings

KEY WORKS

ESPAÑA
ORCHESTRAL 🎵

España is a collage of Spanish dances collected in the streets of Andalucia. A precursor of Ravel's *Boléro*, it orchestrates the dances in a highly characteristic way. Chabrier described it as a "piece in F and nothing more". Stravinsky and Poulenc were particular fans.

PIÈCES PITTORESQUES
SOLO PIANO 🎵

Chabrier's longest set of piano pieces incorporates elements of popular music, some impressionistic pieces – for example "Sous bois" ("In the Woods") – and French regional folk dances that evoke his Auvergnat roots. They also contain some music in the "antique" style, reworking Baroque minuets, a technique that was later used by both Ravel and Debussy.

Chabrier had many friends among the writers and artists of Paris. An ebullient and colourful character, he wrote brilliant letters and many humorous songs.

MARCHE JOYEUSE
ORCHESTRAL 🎵

Originally written as a two-part piano work in 1883, Chabrier orchestrated the two as a pastorale and march in 1888. Further revision resulted in the version that is frequently performed today.

Charles-Marie Widor

● 1844–1937   ▶ French   ✎ c.100

Born in Lyon to a family of organ builders, Widor quickly gained a reputation as an organist in the French provinces. In his mid-20s, he replaced Lefebure-Wély at St Sulpice in Paris, where he remained for 64 years, he was still performing in his 90s. He also taught organ and composition at the Paris Conservatoire, but his thorough Germanic schooling (his own teacher had come from a line extending back to Bach) led to clashes with the more Gallic, contemporary Fauré. Widor wrote many ballets, operas, songs, and orchestral works, but his greatest compositional achievement were the magnificent ten Symphonies for Solo Organ, which vary from the austere and demanding No. 7 and No. 8 to the popular Toccata – the finale from No. 5 – a familiar component of wedding ceremonies.

MILESTONES	
1870	Becomes organist at St Sulpice, Paris
1872	Writes Organ Symphonies Nos. 1–4
1880	Composes *La korrigane*, ballet
1887	Writes Organ Symphonies Nos. 5–8
1891	Succeeds César Franck as organ professor at the Paris Conservatoire
1896	Succeeds Théodore Dubois as professor of composition

In his hour-long monumental Symphony for Organ No. 8, Widor pushed organ technique and artistic inventiveness to its absolute limit.

Ernest Chausson

● 1855–1899   ▶ France   ✎ c.75

Growing up amid salon culture and in financial comfort, Chausson dabbled at writing and drawing, and qualified as a barrister, but then decided to become a musician, inspired by hearing Wagner in Germany. His talents impressed his teacher Massenet, and his reputation as a composer grew in Parisian musical circles through his 30s as he abandoned Wagner for a more intimate, exotically flavoured personal style. After writing *Poème*, his most popular work today, he started to refine his style, but died in a cycling accident, aged 44. However, as secretary of the Société Nationale de Musique for ten years, he did much to encourage French contemporary music.

MILESTONES	
1877	Sworn in as barrister; writes first song
1879	Studies under Massenet
1882	Writes *Viviane*, symphonic poem
1883	Marries (five children)
1895	Finishes *Le roi Arthus*, opera, after ten years
1896	Writes *Poème* for violin and orchestra

Chausson led a quiet life shared between his family and his salon, which drew figures such as Ysaÿe and Debussy. Here Debussy plays a piano duet with Mme Chausson.

*"It is unnecessary for music to make people think…
it would be enough if it made them listen."*

CLAUDE DEBUSSY, 1900

Claude Debussy

1862–1918   **French**   **227**

Emerging as a radical innovator from within the conservative French music scene of the late 19th century, Debussy virtually single-handed changed the course of musical development. By dissolving traditional rules and conventions into a new language of unsuspected possibilities in harmony, rhythm, and form, texture, and colour, he created a rich body of works that would leave an indelible imprint on 20th-century music.

LIFE

Overcoming his simple background and his family's lack of affinity for music, Debussy entered the prestigious Paris Conservatoire at the age of 12. Early aspirations for a career as a concert pianist were unfulfilled, however, and his non-conformist tendencies were frowned upon. Although he was awarded the Grand Prix de Rome for composition in 1884, his earliest published works met with little success. Very much self-educated, Debussy travelled across Europe, absorbing the Oriental cultures that were being increasingly revealed to Westerners, and coming into contact with the leading artistic figures of the day. From 1892, his music started to attract wider attention, although it was not for another decade that the significance of his ground-breaking ideas became fully recognized. Debussy was also an outspoken music critic, writing under the pseudonym of Monsieur Croche (Mr Quaver). He had to endure trials in his private life, including financial struggles, the distancing of many friends after he left his first wife for the woman who would become his second, and a long battle with cancer. Debussy died just a few months prior to the end of the World War I, by then an internationally celebrated composer.

Debussy's works provoked sharply divided opinions and fierce controversies, but by the early 1900s, he was established as the figurehead of a new music movement.

MUSICAL OUTPUT

Total: 227

	1862–1880	1880–1890	1890–1900	1900–1910	1910–1918
ORCHESTRAL (16)		5	5	5	1
CHAMBER (10)		2	1	1	6
PIANO MUSIC (92)		6	16	24	46
OPERAS (1)			1		
BALLETS (5)				1	4
SONGS (83)		50	17	7	9
OTHER VOCAL (20)		9	2	4	5

MUSIC

It was apparent early on that Debussy conceived music in a novel way, but it took him time to assimilate and crystallize his ideas. *Prélude à l'après-midi d'un faune* marked the definitive spreading of his wings: thereafter, he took every genre (orchestral, vocal, piano, and chamber music) to new realms. His ability to perpetually build on his innovations and to renew himself creatively could leave even his most ardent followers confused. Though he has been called an Impressionist, Debussy's allusions to many idioms and movements, always masterfully integrated, are stamped with an individuality and inventiveness that defy all categorization. His interest in contemporary as well as ancient artistic currents, and of foreign, often exotic influences (including Spain and the Orient) reflected his insatiable curiosity and abhorrence of repetition.

MILESTONES	
1874	Begins studies at Paris Conservatoire
1880	Attends composition class of Ernest Guiraud
1884	Awarded the Grand Prix de Rome
1893	Composes String Quartet
1894	Writes *Prélude à l'après-midi d'un faune*
1899	Writes Nocturnes, for orchestra; marries Rosalie Texier
1902	*Pelléas et Mélisande* completed and premiered
1903	Has affair with singer Emma Bardac; writes *Estampes*
1905	Completes *La Mer*
1907	Completes Images, for piano (2 sets)
1912	Completes Images, for orchestra
1908	Success in England brings international fame
1913	Completes Preludes, for piano (2 sets); produces *Jeux*, a ballet
1915	Writes Cello Sonata and Sonata for Flute, Viola, and Harp
1917	Violin Sonata completed

KEY WORKS

ESTAMPES

SOLO PIANO   ⏲ 12:00   📖 3   ✆

Of these three works, "Pagodes" reflects the influence of Javanese gamelan music, "La soirée dans Grenade" evokes sultry Andalusia, while "Jardins sous la pluie" echoes the keyboard styles of Bach and Chopin. The three distinct pieces are united by their stylized clarity and economy, inspired by the prints, in particular from Japan, that the title refers to.

Debussy was influenced by the gamelan – an Indonesian music ensemble that typically plays gongs, chimes, metallophones, and cymbals.

VIOLIN AND PIANO SONATA

DUO   ⏲ 13:00   📖 3   ♬

Debussy's final composition, and the last piece he performed, is the third of a projected series of six chamber works. In a kaleidoscopic array of moods and idioms, these three brief movements display a broad variety of styles.

PRÉLUDE À L'APRÈS-MIDI D'UN FAUNE

ORCHESTRAL   ⏲ 9:30   📖 1   ♫

Debussy's first major orchestral experiment was, notwithstanding its striking novelty, immediately hailed as a masterpiece. Its escape from formal rigour and its highly imaginative orchestral colours heralded the dawn of a new age for Classical music. The seductive flute theme is contrasted by another melody that is the culminating expressive point of the work.

FOCUS

PELLÉAS ET MÉLISANDE

OPERA ⏱ 150:00 📖 5

Based on Maeterlinck's Symbolist play, Debussy's only opera has five acts, and its scenes are linked by orchestral interludes. Rejecting Italian conventions, it took opera beyond the sphere of Wagner's influence. The all but spoken style of the vocal parts and the delicacy of the orchestration lend the music an abstract quality that seemed almost scandalous at the time. However, the opera's originality and uniquely haunting beauty were quickly recognized and Debussy's stature was established.

ACT ONE (30:30) Golaud, grandson of King Arkel, finds a strange and alluring girl, Mélisande, lost in the woods. He persuades her to follow him home and we later learn that he has married her.

ACT TWO (27:00) While in the park with Pelléas, Golaud's younger half-brother, Mélisande drops her wedding ring in a fountain. At the same time Golaud is injured, and while Mélisande is tending to him he notices the ring is absent; he angrily sends her away to search for it, accompanied by Pelléas. In a grotto by the sea, where Mélisande claimed she lost the ring, she is scared away by three paupers.

ACT THREE (31:30) Golaud finds Pelléas embracing Mélisande's hair, cascading down onto him from her balcony; he chides them as children.

ACT FOUR (37:00) Golaud warns Pelléas to keep away from Mélisande and violently confronts her. When he surprises them again, he kills Pelléas.

ACT FIVE (24:30) Wracked with guilt, but still consumed by jealousy, Golaud pleads for Mélisande's forgiveness while seeking to find out the nature of her love for Pelléas. Having just given birth to a daughter, Mélisande dies without resolving the mystery.

LA MER

ORCHESTRAL ⏱ 24:30 📖 3

Debussy's largest purely orchestral work consists of three symphonic sketches of seascapes. It is the closest thing to a symphony he would ever compose.

DE L'AUBE À MIDI SUR LA MER (8:30) This charts the morning progression of the sun, from the first glimpses of light and rise to its zenith.

JEUX DE VAGUES (7:00) Part two explores the manifold perspectives of the sea through the play of light on the water (the rise and fall of waves, shimmering surfaces, the rush of the surf).

DIALOGUE DU VENT ET DE LA MER (9:00) Part three reiterates fragments of the first section, and depicts the dramatic interaction of wind and water.

Gabriel Pierné

◗ 1863–1937   🏴 French   ✍ c.150

After winning the Prix de Rome for his cantata *Edith*, Pierné spent three years in Italy before returning to Paris to teach. He succeeded César Franck as organist at St Clotilde, but from his 40s he built a career as a composer-conductor. Pierné absorbed the styles of the time

into his own balanced but individual language, and was always aware of his French cultural heritage. His charming, refined music covers all forms and genres.

MILESTONES	
1882	Wins the Prix de Rome in Paris
1890	Becomes organist at St Clotilde
1907	Writes *Les enfants à Bethléem*, oratorio
1910	Takes over as principal conductor at the Concerts Colonne in Paris
1917	Writes Piano Quintet
1923	*Cydalise et le chèvre-pied*, ballet, staged

Louis Vierne

◗ 1870–1937   🏴 French   ✍ c.70

Blind at birth, but given limited vision by an operation at six, Vierne became an outstanding organist and composer. A teaching assistant at the Paris Conservatoire, he was also organist at Notre-Dame for 37 years. Composed in enlarged symbols on huge sheets of paper, Vierne's six dazzling, wide-ranging symphonies for organ (inspired by the Cavaillé-Coll organs) are among the instrument's finest and most-played works. Vierne's later life was plagued by despair, illness, grief and hardship; he died of a heart attack in mid-recital at Notre-Dame.

MILESTONES	
1899	Writes Organ Symphony, No. 1
1900	Becomes organist at Notre-Dame
1926–7	Pieces de Fantaisie, Vols 1–4, organ

Reynaldo Hahn

◗ 1874–1947   🏴 French   ✍ c.150

Hahn's songs powerfully evoke the cultured Paris salon around 1900, a milieu the composer knew well. Born in Venezuela to a German father, he came to Paris as a child, and by 16, having found fame with his charming songs (set to poems by Paul Verlaine), was moving in the city's artistic circles, eventually working as critic, composer, and singer. Although he wrote much incidental music, as well as ballets, operas, and operettas, he is best remembered for his songs. Hahn was a lover, and lifelong friend of Marcel Proust and his music is often about memories, such as the operetta *Ciboulette*, set in 19th-century Paris. Hahn fought for France in World War I, but was banned by the Nazis in World War II. He returned after the occupation to direct the Paris Opéra.

MILESTONES	
1885	Enters the Paris Conservatoire
1890	Writes *Chansons grises*, songs
1909	Takes French nationality
1931	Writes Piano Concerto, No. 2
1934	Becomes music critic for *Le figaro*
1945	Directs the Paris Opèra
1955	*Le marchand de Venise*, opera, staged

The darling of the beau monde, Hahn delighted Parisian society with his lyrical songs. A friend of Sarah Bernhardt (right), he was a star guest at her Belle Ile parties.

Paul Dukas

● 1865–1935   ▣ French   ✍ 30

An intense perfectionist, Dukas composed scrupulously but slowly, turning out just a handful of choice, immaculately crafted pieces, much admired by Debussy. Among the most celebrated are the orchestral fantasy *The Sorcerer's Apprentice*, popularized by Disney's *Fantasia*; the widely acclaimed opera, *Ariane et Barbe-bleue*; and the ballet *La Péri*, which established Dukas as a major modern composer.

LIFE AND MUSIC

A Parisian, Dukas was born into a musical family and made a career not only as a composer but also as a major music critic on the *Gazette des Beaux Arts* and other journals. Although his first attempts at opera failed, his *Ariane et Barbe-bleue*, set to a text by the Belgian Symbolist Maurice Maeterlinck ranks among the most important French pieces of the early 20th century. Dukas's output was inhibited by his constant self-criticism: he destroyed much of his own work before dying. Piano pieces, such as the "Rameau Variations" and the Piano Sonata, still remain in the repertoire of specialists, as do many of the orchestral pieces. Dukas's broad-based teaching should not be forgotten, either, affecting such influential figures as Jean Alain, Maurice Duruflé, and Oliver Messiaen.

MILESTONES	
1871	Enrolls at the Paris Conservatoire
1888	Wins second prize in the Prix de Rome for his cantata, *Veléda*
1891	*Polyeucte*, overture, staged in Paris
1892	Reviews Wagner's *Ring* in London, embarking on a career as music critic
1896	Composes Symphony in C major
1897	*The Sorcerer's Apprentice*, tone poem for orchestra, premièred
c.1901	Writes Piano Sonata in E flat minor
1902	*Variations on a Theme by Rameau*, the "Rameau variations", premièred
1907	*Ariane et Barbe-bleue*, opera, staged
1910	Teaches at the Paris Conservatoire
1912	*Poème dansé La Péri*, ballet, premièred
1926	Teaches at the École Normale

KEY WORKS

ARIANE ET BARBE-BLEUE

OPERA   ⏱ 120.00   📖 3   ♙♛♙

Dukas's dramatic and spirited opera recounts the story of the serial polygamist Bluebeard who imprisoned his first five wives. It was an instant hit, due in part to the exotic orchestrations symbolizing the wives' bright jewels. Equally vivid is the driving, dynamic narrative, and choral folk song, evoking the actions and feelings of the busy townsfolk.

When the apprentice sorcerer asks an enchanted broom to fetch water in Dukas's most famous fantastical piece, he is overwhelmed by the response.

THE SORCERER'S APPRENTICE

ORCHESTRAL   📖 1   ♙

Based on Goethe's ballad about an enchanted broom, Dukas's tone poem can be ingenious, as he portrays the zealous antics of the broom sometimes amusingly but always tunefully, with jovial interjections from the woodwind.

Erik Satie

◉ 1866–1925   🏳 French   ✍ c.50

An eccentric figure of enormous importance in French music and admired by Debussy and John Cage, among others, Satie described himself as a "medieval musician who had wandered by mistake into the 20th century". His early piano pieces are now popular classics and his later ballets for the Ballets Russes and Swedish Ballet are masterful collaborations between choreographers, designers, and costumiers.

LIFE AND MUSIC

Satie never embraced tradition. Like Chabrier, his youthful idol, he played the piano in cabarets, and popular music was important in his often irreverent compositions. Many had unusual titles: there is a *Bureaucratic Sonata* and some *Pieces in the Form of a Pear*, written in response to an accusation that his music was formless. In the 1890s he founded the Metropolitan Church of Jesus Christ the Conductor, associated with a mystical movement known as the Rose+Croix. In 1905 he enrolled as a returning learner in Vincent d'Indy's Schola Cantorum and was a model pupil. He secured fame after World War I with his ballet commissions.

MILESTONES

1869	Enters Paris Conservatoire and hates it
1887	Takes up bohemian lifestyle in Montmartre; publishes *Sarabandes* for piano – first characteristic work
1888	Composes *Gymnopédies* for piano
1911	Ravel performs some of Satie's pieces at Société Musicale Indépendante.
1914	Publishes *Sports et divertissements*, piano pieces, in facsimile of own handwriting
1917	Collaborates with Cocteau, Massine, and Picasso on *Parade*, ballet
1918	Composes *Socrate*, symphonic drama

KEY WORKS

GYMNOPÉDIES

SOLO PIANO   ⏱ 7:45   🎵 3   🎼

These piano pieces have become Satie's most celebrated work. Orchestrated by Debussy and arranged by many others, the dreamy, dismembered waltzes are easy to play, and have a magic rarely matched.

SOCRATE

TEXT SETTING   ⏱ 30:15   🎵 1   🎼 👤

Considered to be the apex of his work, here extracts from Plato are set in a bare, simple style which inspired the modernist group known as Les Six, to which Satie was something of a father-figure.

PARADE

BALLET   ⏱ 14:30   🎵 1   🩰

Satie's fullest ballet score, the music contains a typewriter, the siren of the *Titanic*, and a *bouteillophone* – a set of bottles played by a Chinese conjuror.

In *Entr'acte* by film maker Réné Clair, Satie and French painter and designer Francis Picabia load a cannon in slow motion. The film was conceived by Picabia for showing during the interval of Satie's ballet *Relâche*.

FURNITURE MUSIC

SOLO PIANO   🎵 1   🎼

Satie's great statement, which would now be called conceptual art, is music for a concert interval: a short phrase played over and over again. It is surpassed only by his 24-hour-long, repetitious *Vexations*.

Albert Roussel

🔵 1869–1937   🏳 French   ✍ 100

After a stint in the navy, Roussel decided on a career in music at the unusually late age of 25. Despite not having enjoyed the widespread attention it deserves, his output is considered by many to be the finest French music to have been written between the wars. It shows Roussel's subtle and highly personal absorption of diverse styles, together with a great atmospheric sensitivity and rhythmic drive.

LIFE AND MUSIC

Having resigned his naval commission to devote himself to music, Roussel was still studying when his early compositions caught the music world's attention around 1906. His training with the conservatively inclined Vincent d'Indy, traces of Debussy's influence, and exotic musical ideas gained from travels to India and Southeast Asia in 1909 are reflected in the first period (1898–1913) of his creative output. After World War I, he gradually left these early influences behind. The works of his mature period (1926–37), which show an increasing interest in chamber music, are often described as Neo-Classical. They have a new, austere mood with strong Stravinsky-like rhythms and innovative harmonies.

MILESTONES	
1894	Leaves navy; begins music studies
1902	Begins 12 years' teaching at Schola Cantorum in Paris
1909	Travels to India and Indochina
1913	Writes *Le festin de l'araignée*, ballet
1918	Completes opera-ballet *Padmâvatî*
1930	Composes Symphony No. 3
1931	Composes *Bacchus et Ariane*, ballet
1935	Completes Symphony No. 4, his last

Roussel's opera-ballet *Padmâvatî* successfully combined his own style with Indian modes that he heard during his travels in India and Southeast Asia.

KEY WORKS

SYMPHONY NO. 3
ORCHESTRAL   ⏱ 22:15   📖 4   🎵

This bright and vigorous work, shaped in a conventional four-movement form, breathed new life into a genre that had seemed in decline.

BACCHUS ET ARIANE
BALLET   ⏱ 36:15   📖 2   🎵

Composed in 1930, this ballet has a rhythmic vitality and melodic inspiration that make it a worthy successor to Debussy's and Ravel's works in the genre. Roussel adapted each of the two acts into an orchestral suite, the second suite being one of his more popular works.

LE FESTIN DE L'ARAIGNÉE
BALLET   ⏱ 32:00   📖 2   🎵

The Spider's Banquet, Roussel's best-known work and his first masterpiece, shows traces of Debussy's influence. The plot of this ballet is set in a garden, where a spider, preparing to feast on insects caught in its web, is killed instead by a praying mantis.

These costumes were designed for one of the first performances of *Le festin de l'araignée*

Maurice Ravel

● 1875–1937   🏳 French   ✍ 88

Following in Debussy's path, Ravel established a distinctly
French style that broke away from Romantic conservatism.
A blend of sober refinement and luxuriant exoticism, his
work is characterized by exquisite craftsmanship: Stravinsky described him
as "the most perfect of Swiss clockmakers". This has sometimes obscured the
moving quality of his melodies and the troubled undercurrents of his music.

LIFE AND MUSIC

Faced at first with a reactionary
establishment, Ravel soon came to
be recognized as the most significant
French composer of the early 20th
century after Debussy. His attachment
to classicism was fused with eclectic
and adventurous tastes. While
preserving the integrity of his own
style, he drew inspiration from many
idioms, and boldly – often wittily –
blurred the boundaries between
serious and light music. Much of his
work plays on the contrast between
chiselled technical perfection and
fantastical imagination. A meticulous
perfectionist, his output was only
moderately sized, but of consistently

high quality, covering chamber music,
songs, an important body of piano
works, and orchestral and stage scores,
often originally written for piano.

MILESTONES	
1889	Enters Paris Conservatoire as a piano student
1898	Begins composition studies with Fauré; first published works.
1905	Writes *Miroirs* for piano
1907	Composes *Rapsodie espagnole*, orchestra
1911	*L'heure espagnole*, opera, produced
1912	*Daphnis et Chloé*, ballet, performed
1920	Completed *La Valse*
1925	*L'Enfant et les Sortilèges*, opera
1928	*Boléro* first produced

KEY WORKS

LE TOMBEAU DE COUPERIN

SOLO PIANO   ⏲ 25:00   📖 6   🎵

This suite for piano, written in homage
to the French 18th-century composer,
showcases Ravel's clarity, precision,
and grace. Each of the six movements
recreates past forms and is dedicated
to friends who fell in World War I.

LA VALSE

BALLET   ⏲ 12:30   📖 1   🎭

Composed in the years following
World War I, and originally intended
as commission by the ballet impressario,
Diaghilev, Ravel's satirical and haunting
evocation of the Viennese waltz reveals,
perhaps most clearly, the dark
undercurrents of his postwar music.

BOLÉRO

ORCHESTRAL   ⏲ 15:30   📖 1   🎭

In Ravel's best-known composition,
two melodic ideas build up in
an inexorable crescendo.
Boléro's brilliant
orchestration, and
the obsessively
repetitive
nature of its
music, generate
the tension for
which the piece
is famous.

Bright, imaginative costumes and
colourful orchestration were integral
parts of Diaghilev's Ballets Russes.

DAPHNIS ET CHLOÉ

BALLET · 49:00 · 📖 3 · 🎶 🎭

This ballet was commissioned in 1909 by Serge Diaghilev for his legendary Ballets Russes company. The reception of the first production, in 1912, was lukewarm. However, the work was soon hailed not only as one of Ravel's masterpieces, but also as one of the high points in a golden age for ballet. The plot is set in a fanciful pastoral setting of Greek antiquity.

FIRST PART: The lovers Daphnis and Chloé are separated by a lively dance of nymphs, shepherd lads and lasses. Chloé is seized by pirates. Daphnis implores the god Pan to rescue her.

SECOND PART: Chloé is made to dance for the pirates and tries to flee in vain. The god Pan arrives just in time to scatter the pirates.

THIRD PART: This section opens with a famous sunrise scene, one of the most intoxicatingly voluptuous musical passages ever written. The reunited lovers dance in Pan's honour, in a closing bacchanalia.

The opulent orchestration calls for large and varied instrumental forces, and an unseen, vocalizing choir. There are two concert suites of *Daphnis and Chloé*, of which the second, depicting the famous sunrise and bacchanalia, is the most often presented.

PIANO CONCERTO IN G MAJOR

ORCHESTRAL · 26:30 · 📖 3 · 🎶 👁

Composed in 1929, this much-loved piece proved to be Ravel's last large-scale work. The two exuberant outer movements frame a lyrical slow movement of haunting beauty.

FIRST MOVEMENT (ALLEGRAMENTE) Here, brilliant and bawdy exuberance, brimming with impish humour and surprising twists and turns, displays Ravel at his most carefree.

SECOND MOVEMENT (ADAGIO ASSAI) Inspired by the slow movement of Mozart's clarinet quintet, its extended theme is one of Ravel's most elaborate and moving melodic ideas, at once serene and elegiac. It is first presented by the piano in a long opening solo, and later reiterated by the cor anglais amidst the soloist's crystalline decorations.

THIRD MOVEMENT (PRESTO) Ravel was never more mercurial than in this chase between piano and orchestra, the dazzling virtuoso fireworks spiced up with jazzy inflections.

INFLUENCES

While Ravel's style is highly distinctive, his search for chiselled perfection was no doubt too personal and rarefied to be widely modelled upon. He did not have specific disciples, but his ability to remain relevant to 20th-century music, while embracing tonality and reworking past forms, anticipated Neo-Classicism.

Joseph Canteloube

● 1874–1947   ▶ French   ✍ c.150

Born into a musical family of the Auvergne, the young Canteloube was fascinated by the folk music he heard on country walks. Not until his early 20s – now married, having lost both parents – did he study music seriously (with d'Indy). He moved to Paris to further his studies and built a career, moving in circles passionately dedicated to rediscovering, preserving and popularizing folk music. He collected folk tunes and harmonized them, sometimes simply for amateur use, sometimes in a more elaborate, Impressionistic style. He also gave piano recitals, impressing Debussy, and lecture-recitals. Canteloube had limited success with his original compositions, but his very popular *Chants d'Auvergne*, while only "arrangements" of folk songs, are so exotically orchestrated that they are virtually original works.

MILESTONES	
1902	Meets composer Vincent d'Indy
1907	Studies at Schola Cantorum, Paris
1923	Writes *Chants d'Auvergne*, series 1 and 2
1933	His second opera, *Vercingétorix*, produced
1941	Writes article defending complex orchestrations
1954	Writes *Chants d'Auvergne*, series 5

Canteloube's most well-known works are arrangements of folk songs from the volcanic hills of the Auvergne.

Lili Boulanger

● 1893–1918   ▶ France   ✍ 54

Lili Boulanger's life was brief – in contrast with that of her sister Nadia, the renowned teacher of composition, who lived into her 90s. But Lili made history, aged only 19, as the first woman to win the prestigious Grand Prix de Rome, (her father had won it in 1835), with her cantata *Faust et Hélène*, which thereafter had great success in Paris. She wrote many of her finest works – mostly with mystical or biblical themes – in her gravely beautiful, clear, and dramatic style, during her stays in Rome, but these were cut short by World War I. After arriving home, she became terminally ill as a result of her immune system having been destroyed by childhood pneumonia. With remarkable serenity thanks to her strong faith, she dictated her intensely poignant Pie Jesu to Nadia on her deathbed in 1918.

MILESTONES	
1913	Composes *Faust et Hélène*, cantata
1913	Wins Grand Prix de Rome
1916	Visits Italy for second time
1914	Writes *Clairières dans le ciel*, song cycle
1917	Completes two symphonic poems
1918	Composes incidental music for Maeterlinck's play *La princesse Maleine*; dictates Pie Jesu on deathbed

Lili Boulanger's mother was a singer and her father taught at the Conservatoire. Her sister, Nadia (left, with fellow competitors), won a 2nd Prix de Rome.

Jacques-François Ibert

● 1890–1962   ♟ French   ✍ Unknown

Ibert was an important French composer of the first half of the 20th century. He was dedicated to the idea of continuing the French traditions of lightness, conciseness, and clarity, and adopted to this end a Neo-Classical style. His most celebrated works are a flute concerto and an orchestral Divertissement. Several operas, some remarkable chamber music, and songs complement these more celebrated works.

LIFE AND MUSIC

Ibert was a Parisian and played an important part in French musical life. He devoted himself to composition in his late teens, working as a piano teacher and accompanist to support himself. He also played for the silent cinema, an activity which was later to result in several film scores. His first major successes were in the 1920s, when several of his works were performed in Paris. Work at the Paris Opéra – for both ballet and opera – earned him further success. The latter part of his life was spent as director of the French Institute in Rome, where winners of the Prix de Rome, (a prize awarded to musicians which he himself had won), were awarded a subsidized year of working on their own projects. Works for the ballet, opera, radio, and film make up a considerable part of his output.

MILESTONES	
1910	Is admitted to Paris Conservatoire, and later studies with Paul Dukas.
1919	Wins Grand Prix de Rome at first attempt with *Le poète et la fée*, cantata.
1922	First public concert of his works given at Concerts Colonne in Paris.
1924	Impressionistic orchestral pieces, *Escales*, premiered with great success
1927	One-act opera, *Angélique*, is received well at the Paris Opéra.
1926	Composes *Divertissement*, for orchestra
1933	Composes Flute Concerto
1937	Appointed director of Académie de de France in Rome (until 1960)
1955	Begins two years as director of Paris Opéra-Comique

KEY WORKS

FLUTE CONCERTO
ORCHESTRAL 🎵 🎺

One of the challenges of the concerto repertoire, this piece builds on the French tradition of flute-playing, arguably the best-developed and most advanced in the European tradition.

ANGÉLIQUE
OPERA 🎵 🎭 🎶

This farcical opera tells of a woman who has been put up for sale by her husband. To portray the irony, Ibert claimed to have used "the minimum of instruments for the maximum of result".

Among the film scores that Ibert wrote is one for the 1951 film, *Macbeth*, starring Orson Welles.

DIVERTISSEMENT
ORCHESTRAL 📖 6 🎵

If Neo-Classicism means using modern harmonies and phrase-lengths within the frame of Classical forms, then Ibert's Divertissement is a masterpiece of the genre. It was written as incidental music for Eugène-Martin Lebiche's play, *The Italian Straw Hat*, and has a joyous mood typical of the 1920s.

ORSON WELLES
in
"MACBETH" Cast of
by
WILLIAM SHAKESPEARE
A RITZ FILM RELEASE

Frank Martin

● 1890–1974   ⚑ Swiss   ✍ 73

Although Martin lacked any formal musical training, he became one of the foremost teachers and composers of his generation. Initially drawn to theory, his early works, now mostly forgotton, were excessively theoretical. With maturity, he developed a personal language, based on the 12-tone system, and a personal style, delicate and expressive, reflected in such masterpieces as *Petite symphonie concertante*.

LIFE AND MUSIC

Born into an extended Swiss Calvinist family, Martin's music was initially suffused with craft and workmanship, quite the reverse of the more hedonist style adopted by his French peers. Martin's work for the Institut Jaques-Dalcroze (where the teaching method was based on rhythm) affected his compositions profoundly. Rhythmic innovation became one of his hallmarks. Although his music evolved through a variety of styles – sometimes tonal, and for a time 12-toned – all bear the composer's personal stamp, transcending his shifts in style. Martin's studies of Indian, Ancient, and Bulgarian music coloured his work throughout his life, particularly with regard to rhythm. While he composed profusely, his work remains largely undervalued.

MILESTONES	
1918	Shuttles between Zurich, Rome, Paris
1922	Starts work on his Mass for two choirs, eventually staged in 1962
1923	Settles in Paris
1926	Returns to Geneva to study; writes *Rhythmes*, symphonic suite
1928	Teaches at Institut Jaques-Dalcroze in Geneva, Switzerland
1933	Piano Concerto No. 1 premiered; founds and directs the Technicum Moderne de Musique in Geneva
1941	Writes *Le vin herbé*, secular oratorio
1945	*In terra pax*, cantata for Armistice Day, broadcast on Swiss radio
1946	Settles in Amsterdam
1950	Teaches at the Cologne Conservatoire

KEY WORKS

PETITE SYMPHONIE CONCERTANTE
ORCHESTRAL   📖 4   🔁 📀

A traditional symphony in the Teutonic four-movement framework, this piece reworks the elements of sonata, slow-movement, Scherzo and finale in a refreshingly modern way. Both solemn and witty, it is brilliantly orchestrated.

IN TERRA PAX
MASS   📖 12   🔁 ⛪ 👤

An intense, emotional choral work, premiered just after World War II, *In terra pax* is a quasi-Requiem. Martin associated the first part with the horrors of war, and the second with a return to peace and the need for forgiveness.

In Martin's *Le vin herbé*, Tristan and Isolde fall in love, provoking the jealousy of King Mark (far right), with tragic results, played out by a dark-toned chorus.

Pietro Mascagni

● 1863–1945   🏳 Italian   ✍ 60

One of the leading Italian composers and conductors of his time, Mascagni is renowned chiefly as an opera composer, although he also wrote songs, piano pieces, and orchestral music. He achieved sudden success with his opera *Cavalleria rusticana*, remembered today as the first verismo (realistic) opera, but which overshadowed the rest of his output, such as the lyrical comedy *L'amico Fritz*.

LIFE AND MUSIC

The son of a baker, Mascagni read law before moving to Milan to study at the Conservatorio, which he left after three years to pursue a career conducting opera. After some minor successes, his reputation was made overnight when *Cavalleria rusticana* won the prestigious Sonzogno competition. Although he wrote some 15 operas, all well received, none attained the lasting popularity of *Cavalleria rusticana*. Mascagni is often cited as the first composer of verismo opera, a term referring to the authentic depiction of everyday life in artworks; in fact, he wrote in a range of styles and forms, such as comedy, and some of his works were unashamedly populist in tone. Mascagni's reputation became somewhat tarnished through his close links with Mussolini's fascist regime.

MILESTONES

1881	*In Filanda*, cantata, wins first prize in a music competition in Milan
1882	Enters Conservatorio di Milano
1885	Leaves Conservatorio to conduct operetta season in Parma
1886	Becomes master of music at the Philharmony of Cerignola
1889	*Cavalleria rusticana*, opera, wins Sonzogno contest in Rome
1891	*L'amico Fritz*, comic opera, staged
1902	Incidental music for Hall Caine's *The Eternal City* premiered in London
1903	Becomes director of the Scuola Musicale Romana in Rome
1929	Directs La Scala in Milan
1940	50th tour of *Cavalleria rusticana*

KEY WORKS

CAVALLERIA RUSTICANA

OPERA   ⏱ 70:00   ☐ 1   ♫ ♨ ♂

Based on a short story by Giovanni Verga, *Cavalleria rusticana* is a powerful tale of forbidden love, betrayal, and revenge set in rural Sicily. The fast-paced plot revolves around Turridù, his conquests, and his betrayals. After seducing Santuzza, he revives an affair with an old flame, Lola, now married to Alfio.

A smash-hit at its premiere in Rome, Mascagni's tense, racy opera thrilled the audience and received 60 curtain calls.

On hearing of Lola's betrayal, Alfio challenges and kills Turiddù on Easter Sunday, heightening the pathos. While there is little formally innovative about the opera – Mascagni relied on the standard format of arias and recitatives – its originality lies in its inclusion of everyday reality in the world of opera. In an effort to create a sense of realism, Mascagni used much of the original play's coarse language and set it to earthy, folk-style music. As a result, *Cavalleria* is often hailed as the first verismo opera.

Ferruccio B Busoni

◖ 1866–1924   ♙ Italian   ✍ 325

A multi-talented musician best known in his own lifetime as a brilliant piano virtuoso, Busoni was also a leading avant-garde critic, theorist, and teacher at the forefront of the new microtonal and electronic music. Renowned also for his creative transcriptions of J S Bach for the piano, he was less well known as a composer in his own right, but his music is now highly acclaimed as both visionary and progressive.

LIFE AND MUSIC

Born to musical parents in Tuscany, Busoni showed early promise and toured widely as both performer and conductor. Espousing the "Young Classicism", based on the styles of J S Bach, Mozart, and Liszt, he promoted the music of young composers, such as Schoenberg, while also taking an active interest in ethnic folk music, such as the Native American melodies that surge through *Indianisches Tagebuch*. It is hard to distinguish his original music from his transcriptions, as he tended to quote existing music in his own works. Although he taught in many musical centres, his home for much of his adult life was Berlin.

MILESTONES	
1875	Concerto début; and enrols at the Vienna Conservatory
1880	Studies in Graz with Wilhelm Mayer
1891	Teaches at Helsinki Conservatory
1890	Wins the Rubinstein Prize for piano and composition; teaches in Moscow
1894	Settles in Berlin
1901	Gives masterclasses in Weimar; promotes new music concerts in Berlin
1902	Composes Piano Concerto in C major
1907	Writes *Sketch of a New Aesthetic of Music*
c.1911	*Die Brautwahl*, opera, staged
1915	Settles in Zürich during World War I
1916	Composes opera *Turandot*
1920	Writes *Sonatina super Carmen*

KEY WORKS

SONATINA SUPER CARMEN IN A MAJOR, K284

SOLO PIANO   ⏲ 9:00   ▯ 1   ✆

Although detesting verismo opera, Busoni recreates themes from Bizet's *Carmen* in his own style, achieving a subtle study of Carmen, rather than a medley of tunes. Opening with Bizet's Act 4 chorus, he follows with the "Flower Song", the "Habanera", and the finale motive.

Native American music inspired Busoni's radical *Indianisches Tagebuch*, with its sonorous Hopi tunes and flowing rhythms.

DOKTOR FAUST

OPERA   ⏲ 180:30   ▯ 6   ♬♬♨♪

Completed posthumously in 1925 by Philip Jarnach, Busoni's masterpiece is a powerful and mysterious opera that embraces the profundities of the Faustian legend more completely than any other. Although based in part on Marlowe's semi-farcical *Dr Faustus*, Busoni's drama reveals the innate beauty of human nature. Though Classical in form the music is lush, chromatic, and richly inventive.

PIANO CONCERTO IN C MAJOR

ORCHESTRA   70:35   5

A massive work, demanding stamina and skill from the pianist, Busoni's epic concerto, with its strong male chorus and huge orchestra, sounds more like a choral symphony than a concerto. A particularly unusual element is the inclusion of a choral setting of the "Hymn to Allah" from Adam Oehlenschläger's play *Aladdin*.

PROLOGO E INTROITO (15:40) The strings open with a long melody interrupted by a horn-call. The Introito follows with the entry of the soloist. A cadenza is heard before the second subject enters on the woodwind, then another cadenza and a recapitulation follow before the movement ends with a serene coda recalling the Prologo.

PEZZO GIOCOSO (9:45) The second movement opens with wild upward runs on the piano and a grotesque Turkish dance. After a short cadenza, the clarinet plays a traditional and lyrical Neapolitan song, "Fenesta che lucivi ("The light through the window"), interspersed with piano figuration. The lively dance is revived before the movement dies away.

PEZZO SERIOSO (23:00) After the Introito, the first section unfolds into a powerful, grand chorale with a variation. In the second section, the piano opens with a new theme, quickly followed by a resurgence of the opening music. The third section subsides into tranquillity.

ALL'ITALIANA (12:00) Italian songs, dances, and marches fuse with a dazzling piano cadenza, evoking "the crowded Roman street".

CANTICO (10:50) The uplifting finale opens in E minor, recalling earlier themes. The male chorus sings "Hebt zu der ewigen Kraft Eure Herzen ("Lift up your hearts to the Eternal Almighty") to the tune of the first movement's Introito, providing a glowing end to this grand concerto.

FANTASIA CONTRAPPUNTISTICA IN D MINOR

PIANO SOLO AND DUET   50:00   12

This impressive and influential piano music was composed in two versions, for both piano solo and duet, in 1910. Fascinated by both counterpoint and Bach, Busoni was inspired not only to complete Bach's unfinished *Art of Fugue*, but to build a keyboard work around it. Believing that Bach's *Contrapunctus XIV* would have consisted of four fugues, Busoni completed the fugue on the letters of Bach's name (in German the musical letter "B" is B flat, and "H" is B). Busoni composed a fourth fugue using a variety of elegant and polished contrapuntal techniques and variations, while also adding a chorale theme with variations.

Ottorino Respighi

◒ 1879–1936   🏛 Italian   ✍ c.35

Respighi is the first Italian composer after Scarlatti whose
fame does not rest on opera. He was a leading member
of the so-called "generation of 1880", which tried to revive
Italian music by going back to its roots in the Renaissance and Baroque eras.
At one time hugely popular, his star has fallen since World War II, though
there are now signs of a revival of interest in his music.

LIFE AND MUSIC

The son of a piano teacher, Respighi
grew into a man of wide culture in
many languages, as well as a gifted
violinist, pianist, and composer. A shy
man, he shrank from the controversies
between classicists and modernists in
Italian music in the 1920s and1930s,
though by temperament he sided with
the former. After an uncertain start as
a composer, he established the essential
elements of his style in *The Fountains
of Rome*. This showed an orchestral
mastery learned from studying under
Rimsky-Korsakov, and later from Ravel
and Strauss, as well as a passion for old
music, mostly Italian, which worked
its way into nearly everything he wrote.

MILESTONES

1891	Starts studying violin, viola, composition
1900	Visits Russia for first time and studies orchestration under Rimsky-Korsakov
1906	Begins lifelong research into old music
1913	Settles in Rome to teach composition
1916	*The Fountains of Rome* is a huge success
1923	Appointed director of Conservatorio di Santa Cecilia, but resigns in 1926
1924	Completes *The Pines of Rome*
1927	Composes *Trittico Botticelliano*
1931	Finishes third *Ancient Airs and Dances* suite
1932	Fascist government honours him with membership of Reale Accademia
1932	Signs petition condemning modernist trends in Italian music

KEY WORKS

THE PINES OF ROME
TONE POEM   ⏱ 21:00   📖 4   🎵

This was one of two sets of Roman
tone poems that Respighi wrote as
sequels to *The Fountains of Rome*. It
introduces new elements, such as the
recording of a nightingale's song in
"Pine Trees of the Janiculum" and a

memory of Ancient Roman triumphs
in the "Via Appia" finale – to some a
uncomfortable reminder of fascism.

THE BIRDS
ORCHESTRAL SUITE   ⏱ 25:00   📖 5   🎵

This charming orchestral suite of
1927 is entirely based on pre-existing
music: the Prelude and "The Cuckoo"
on pieces by Pasquini, "The Dove"
on music by French composer
de Gallot, "The Hen" (the most
famous) on a piece by Rameau,
and "The Nightingale" on
an anonymous English piece.

This set was designed for the premiere
in 1934 of *La fiamma (The Flame)*, one
of Respighi's eight rarely staged operas.

FOCUS

ANCIENT AIRS AND DANCES
ORCHESTRAL SUITES   48:00   4

Based on a collection of Renaissance-period lute music, this work consists of three suites for chamber orchestra, each in four movements. The first was so successful that Respighi wrote two more, in 1923 and 1928. The dances are based on dance forms popular at courtly entertainments and masques that Respighi found in ballets and dance manuals of the 16th and 17th centuries. The first suite consists of a balleto, a gagliarda, a villanella, and a "masquerade". Although each movement is based on the metre and rhythm of the dance, they are not historical reconstructions but charming and beautifully coloured evocations of the past.

THE FOUNTAINS OF ROME
TONE POEM   16:00   4

This was Respighi's first completely successful work, and perhaps his best. Here, the ponderous quality of his early work has been replaced by a new lightness of touch. The "silver rose" music from Richard Strauss's *Der Rosenkavalier* can be heard in the bright, celeste-coloured orchestral sound, but it is absorbed into something entirely personal. The four pieces portray various fountains in Rome at "the hour in which their character is most in harmony with the landscape". The final "Villa Medici Fountain at Sunset", for example, simply evokes the scene, painting tolling bells and rustling leaves, whereas "The Triton Fountain in the Morning", in which naiads and tritons join in a frenzied dance, depicts the myths associated with that fountain.

TRITTICO BOTTICELLIANO
TONE POEM   17:00   3

These orchestral evocations of paintings by the great Italian Renaissance painter Sandro Botticelli were dedicated to the American patroness of music Elizabeth Sprague Coolidge. Although Respighi's long study of early music, from medieval to Baroque, can be heard in every bar, the music is actually all his own. The first piece, "La primavera", is full of trilling birdsong and the rustling of new leaves, and evokes Vivaldi's "Spring" as much as Botticelli's. The second, "L'adorazione dei Magi", has an allusion to the Epiphany hymn "Veni, veni Emmanuel", while the last, "The Birth of Venus", is a beautiful example of Respighi's orchestral wizardry, here used to summon up waves and gentle sea breezes.

Ruggiero Leoncavallo

● 1857–1919   Italian   ♫ c.80

After a musical training in Naples, Leoncavallo led a bohemian existence in Paris, playing the piano in cafés and composing sporadically. He moved to Milan's artistic circles, earning money from writing. On seeing the success of Pietro Mascagni's *Cavalleria rusticana*, he composed his own short realist opera, *I Pagliacci*, a polished piece calculated to appeal. It was an instant hit in Milan, and the aria "Vesti la giubba" was the first recording to sell a million copies. But he found problems in Italy, partly due to his litigious nature and partly to bad luck. His *La bohème* was eclipsed by Puccini's, and Leoncavallo faded from public view.

The dramatic climax to the intense, verismo opera, *I Pagliacci* shocked its first audiences with the graphic, on-stage murder of Canio's faithless wife.

MILESTONES	
1876	Graduates from Naples Conservatory
1890	Collaborates on the libretto for Puccini's opera *Manon Lescaut*
1892	*I Pagliacci*, opera, successfully staged
1897	*La bohème*, opera, staged
1900	*Zazà*, opera, premiered successfully
1904	Enrico Caruso records arias, "Vesti la giubba" and "Mattinata"

Ermanno Wolf-Ferrari

● 1876–1948   Italian   ♫ c.50

Wolf was his German father's name, Ferrari his Italian mother's, and he always felt torn between the two cultures. He shuttled between Munich and Venice, and his operas combine German graveness with Italian lightness. Switching to music after first studying painting, Wolf-Ferrari won international fame fairly early with his cantata "La vita nuova" and opera *Le donne curiose*. For six years he headed the Liceo Benedetto Marcello in Venice, then left for Munich to compose in seclusion. During World War I he wrote little, but resumed with success in the 1920s, until war loomed again at the close of his life.

MILESTONES	
1901	*La vita nuova*, cantata, succeeds widely
1902	Directs the Liceo Benedetto Marcello
1906	*I quatro rusteghi*, comic opera, staged
1909	Writes *Il segreto di Susanna*, comic opera; moves to Munich to compose full-time
1927	Composes opera *Das Himmelskleid*
1939	Becomes professor of composition at the Salzburg Mozarteum in Austria

In the witty and fast-paced opera *I quatro rusteghi*, the rebellious beau Filipeto (left) balks at his arranged marriage, with unexpectedly comic consequences.

Pablo Martín de Sarasate

● 1844–1908   🏴 Spanish   ✍ 55

One of the most famous violin virtuosos of his time, Sarasate was the dedicatee of some of the best-loved works in the repertory. His own Spanish-flavoured compositions are almost all showpieces for the violin, written to display his dazzling technique and passionate playing. He made several famous arrangements of works by other composers, including the popular *Carmen Fantasy* (1883) based on Bizet's opera.

LIFE AND MUSIC

Born in Navarre, to an artillery bandmaster, Sarasate was an infant prodigy who gave his first public concert in Caruña at the age of eight and went on to play regularly at the court of Queen Isabel II in Madrid. At age 12, Sarasate's mother arranged for him to study with Jean Alard at the Paris Conservatoire. *En route* to Paris, his mother died of a heart attack, but the boy was rescued by the Spanish Consul. At 17, he won the coveted Premier Prix, establishing his career as a performer. Sarasate's compositions, mostly fantasies on Spanish melodies or themes from popular operas, were written primarily for his own performances. Renowned for his sweet tone and pure style, he was the dedicatee of many works, some of which have become repertory staples, including Edouard Lalo's *Symphonie espagnole* and Camille Saint-Saëns's Introduction and Rondo Capriccioso. Ever the *caballero* (cavalier), Sarasate reputedly received hundreds of propositions from admiring female fans, but remained a lifelong bachelor.

MILESTONES

1852	Public debut, aged eight, in Caruña
1856	Travels to the Paris Conservatoire to study with Jean Alard; mother dies of a heart attack *en route*; catches cholera
1859	Embarks on first major concert tour
1861	Wins the Conservatoire's prestigious Premier Prix; makes London debut
1874	Performs Lalo's *Symphonie espagnole*
1878	Composes *Zigeunerweisen* for orchestra
1883	*Carmen Fantasy*, Op. 25, composed

KEY WORKS

CARMEN FANTASY OP. 25

ORCHESTRAL   ⏱ 11:30   📖 5   🎻 🎵

Following the lead of many performer-composers before him, Sarasate wrote several concert fantasies on themes from popular operas, including Mozart's *Don Giovanni* and *The Magic Flute*, and Verdi's *Forza del destino*. Generally short and showy, such fantasies were popular with his audiences. The *Carmen Fantasy*, based on Bizet's hot-blooded opera

Carmen, is essentially a set of variations on five of the best-known melodies, such as the emotionally charged Habanera.

ZIGEUNERWEISEN

ORCHESTRAL   ⏱ 8:00   📖 3   🎻 🎵

Literally, "Gypsy Airs", *Zigeunerweisen* is a showpiece for violin and orchestra based on Spanish folk melodies arranged by Sarasate. After a lively start, full of technical trickery, a slow central section demands absolute control and tone, before closing with a breakneck finale.

A spectacular showcase for violin, *Zigeunerweisen* demands the utmost sensitivity and virtuosity.

Isaac Albéniz

1860–1909   Spanish   c.150

Albéniz is a key figure in the Spanish musical renaissance
of the late 19th and early 20th centuries. Through his
indefatigable efforts as impresario, conductor, pianist, and
composer, he became the first Spanish musician since Tomás Luis de Victoria to
enjoy an international reputation. His piano music, above all the masterly series
of tone poems *Iberia*, enlarged the domain of piano colour and expressivity.

LIFE AND MUSIC

Albéniz was pushed into the role of
travelling virtuoso at eight by his needy
family. His amazing facility as pianist
and improviser won him worldwide
fame, and by the 1880s he was pouring
out a stream of piano character pieces,
most hardly more than written-out
improvisations. But his ambition grew;
in the 1880s he wrote two piano
concertos and a symphonic piece and,
in the 1890s (by then living in London),
tried his hand at operetta. In 1894,
Francis Burdett Money-Coutts, the
banking heir, became his patron.
Albéniz then divided his time between
operatic projects based on Money-
Coutts's Arthurian libretti, works on
Spanish themes, and concert tours.

MILESTONES	
1865	Gives first public concert
1868	Begins life of travelling virtuoso
1882	Becomes conductor of a Spanish zarzuela company
1886	Writes *Suite española* No. 1 for piano
1887	Performs first concert of his own music
1890	Moves to London with family
1896	*Pepita Jiménez* premiered in Barcelona
1900	Returns to Spain; is discouraged by poor reception of his zarzuelas and moves back to Paris
1902	Completes opera *Merlin*; moves to Nice to ease symptoms of Bright's disease
1909	Completes *Iberia*, master piano work
1998	First-ever full concert performance of *Merlin* with orchestra

KEY WORKS

SUITE ESPAÑOLA NO. 1
SOLO PIANO   40:00   8

This suite of character pieces, written
in 1886, is like a foretaste of *Iberia*, but
without the latter's exuberant technical
difficulty. The common feature is the
evocation of Spanish folk idioms.
"Sevilla" is inspired
by flamenco forms
and "Asturias" is a
soleá (a rapid folk
dance) interrupted
by a song with

Composer Felipe Pedrell
taught Albéniz, inspiring
him with his own
enthusiasm for folk music.

Arab overtones (Albéniz liked to claim
that deep down he was a Moor).

PEPITA JIMÉNEZ
COMIC OPERA   120:00   2

Albéniz's most successful opera has a
Spanish theme but an English libretto
by Francis Money-
Coutts. Its constant
evocation of
thrumming guitars
makes it sound
familiar, partly
because of its
influence on better-
known works by
Manuel de Falla.

FOCUS

IBERIA

SOLO PIANO · 37:00 · 7

Worried about his declining health, friends persuaded Albéniz in 1905 to lay aside his operatic plans. Instead, he worked on these 12 character pieces (divided into three books), which turned out to be his masterpiece. Each is a portrait of a Spanish locale. Some, such as El Albaicín (an old quarter of Granada) or Málaga, are conventionally picturesque choices; others, such as Lavapiés (a poor district of Madrid), are surprising. All of them weave extraordinarily subtle webs of sound, in which a simple skeleton (such as an ostinato, or an accompaniment figure with typical guitar-inspired Spanish harmonies) is encrusted with layers of chromatic decoration. When he heard pianist Joaquín Malats perform "Triana" from Book 2, Albéniz was inspired to new heights in Books 3 and 4 in both technical difficulty and density of the inner parts. The influence of these works on later piano music was immense. No less a composer than Olivier Messiaen ranked *Iberia* alongside Bach's *The Art of Fugue* and the late sonatas of Beethoven.

MERLIN

OPERA · 137:00 · 3

Under the terms of his contract, Albéniz was obliged to set Francis Money-Coutts' three opera libretti about King Arthur to music. Though enthusiastic, he completed only *Merlin*. Like so many late 19th-century musicians, Albéniz was a passionate Wagnerian (he was a founder of Barcelona's Wagnerian Association). Wagner's influence can be heard in the grandeur of the first-act finale and the pervasive use of leitmotifs. There is even a direct quotation of the "peace motif" from *Siegfried*. All this will surprise anyone who knows Albéniz only through his "Spanish" piano music, but some of the *Merlin* music, notably the "Saracen Dances", recalls the more familiar Albéniz of *Iberia*.

INFLUENCES

Albéniz's worldwide fame gave Spanish music-making a confidence it had lacked for three centuries. His subtle use of folk-like idioms, and his amazingly refined use of the piano's resources of colour and chromatic decoration, inspired later Spanish composers such as Granados and de Falla, and were much admired by Debussy and Ravel.

Enrique Granados

◔ 1867–1916   ♊ Spanish   ✍ 25

Granados was one of a group of composers who were interested in developing a peculiarly Spanish form of art music by distilling the essence of Spanish indigenous folk music and blending it with the Romanticism of Schumann and Liszt. A virtuoso pianist as well as a composer, Granados died tragically at the peak of his career, before his potential had been completely fulfilled.

LIFE AND MUSIC

Granados studied in Barcelona with Felipe Pedrell, then in Paris, where he met the important French composers of the day, including d'Indy, Dukas, and Saint-Saëns. In 1890 he returned to Barcelona and began developing his career as a concert pianist. His music, much of it for piano and intended for his own performance, was strongly influenced by the Nationalist ideas of Pedrell, as shown by his use of folk themes. But it was also Romantic in nature, with an advanced appreciation of chromatic harmony. Granados died when the liner taking him home from the premiere of his opera *Goyescas* was sunk in the English Channel.

MILESTONES

1887	Goes to study with Charles Wilfrid de Bériot at Paris Conservatoire
1892	Gives Spanish premiere of Grieg's Piano Concerto.
1892	Three orchestrated pieces from *Danzas españolas* given premiere.
1901	Founds Granados Academy (later Marshall Academy) in Barcelona
1911	Composes *Goyescas*, suite for piano
1915	Completes opera, *Goyescas*
1916	Drowned with wife when English liner *Sussex* hit by German torpedo.

KEY WORKS

GOYESCAS

SOLO PIANO   ⏱ 55:00   📖 8   🔊

Perhaps Granados' greatest work is his piano suite *Goyescas*, a set of pieces inspired by the dramatic paintings and tapestries of Goya. Granados makes full use of the rich late-Romantic harmonic palette, whilst incorporating distinctively Spanish rhythms and melodic shapes.

GOYESCAS

OPERA   ⏱ 70:00   📖 1   🎭♿

Although Granados had already written several zarzuelas, he had long wanted to expand his piano work *Goyescas* into an opera. He finally began to arrange and extend the music with librettist Fernando Penquet, fitting the words around it. The resulting one-act opera was produced successfully in New York, although it has ultimately been felt to suffer from a thin plot and has not entered the repertoire.

Describing his piano suite *Goyescas*, Granados said that in his music he wanted to create "a palette of emotions such as appear in Goya's paintings".

DANZAS ESPANOLAS

SOLO PIANO   ⏱ 65:00   📖 12   🔊

The *Spanish Dances* are a set of 12 short pieces evoking the folk music of Spain, without being literal arrangements of folk tunes. In 1892, three of the pieces were performed in an orchestral version, bringing Granados' name to wider notice.

Manuel de Falla

◉ 1876–1946　🏳 Spanish　✍ 25

The greatest Spanish composer since the Golden Age of Cristóbal de Morales and Tomás Luis de Victoria, de Falla took the picturesque, Romantic Spanish style forged by Albéniz and Granados and imbued it with the modernism of Debussy and Stravinsky. In his later works, he turned his back on the gorgeous, Impressionist sound-world of his ballets to create a very Spanish form of Neo-Classicism.

LIFE AND MUSIC

Precocious as a pianist but slow to start as a composer, de Falla's real fame came with his ballets, particularly *The Three-Cornered Hat*. Composed for Diaghilev's Ballet Russes, it shows the strong influence of French Impressionism. An intensely religious man, de Falla retreated to the calm of Granada in the 1920s, where he developed a new, spare style, in which the influence of old Spanish music replaced picturesque "Spanishisms" (a trend begun in *The Three-Cornered Hat*). Distressed by the Spanish Civil War and murder of his friend, the poet Lorca, Falla accepted an invitation to Argentina, where he then remained. His last 20 years were spent writing the huge, unfinished *L'Atlántida*.

MILESTONES	
1905	*La vida breve* wins opera competition
1913	*La vida breve* finally premiered, in Nice
1919	*El sombrero de tres picos* premiered
1920	Moves from Madrid to Granada
1922	Manages flamenco festival with Lorca
1926	Finishes Harpsichord Concerto; begins *L'Altántida*, opera-oratorio
1939	Moves to Buenos Aires

The first work to result from de Falla's blending of French Impressionist and Spanish National styles was his luxurious *Midnight in the Gardens of Spain* of 1915.

KEY WORKS

LA VIDA BREVE

OPERA　⏱ 60:00　📖 2　🎭♂

Written as an entry for a competition (which it won), this passionate, fast-moving zarzuela, *A Short Life*, tells of a gypsy girl who dies of a broken heart after her fiancé marries another girl. Despite the influences of Wagner and contemporaries such as Puccini, the mature de Falla can already be heard.

EL SOMBRERO DE TRES PICOS

BALLET　⏱ 38:00　📖 2　🎭

The premiere of *The Three-Cornered Hat*, a story of mistaken identities, at the Alhambra Theatre in London in 1919 was one of the greatest triumphs of Diaghilev's Ballets Russes. The sets were by Picasso and choreography by Massine. Deriving its style from flamenco *cante jondo* (deep song), de Falla's music was praised for freeing itself from Debussy and Ravel.

HARPSICHORD CONCERTO

CHAMBER　⏱ 13:00　📖 3　🎹 🎻

Written for the great harpsichordist, Wanda Landowska, and much admired by Stravinsky, this ranks among the masterpieces of 1920s Neo-Classicism. The first movement quotes from a 15th-century Spanish song, and the second from Tomás de Victoria's Tantum Ergo.

Heitor Villa-Lobos

● 1887–1959   ⚑ Brazilian   ✍ c.1,000

Astonishingly prolific, the composer Villa-Lobos was a larger-than-life character who has attained legendary status in Brazil. He made an extensive study of the folk music of his native country, which he incorporated into an eclectic musical style. This knowledge later formed the basis for sweeping reforms in the Brazilian music education system under the nationalist government of the 1930s.

LIFE AND MUSIC

Villa-Lobos's influences were as diverse as his own musical style. As a young man he played as a café musician, toured Brazil exploring indigenous music, and studied in Paris. Almost inevitably, for a composer who wrote with such ease and fluency, the quality of his output is variable. His best works are perhaps those in which his reverence for the Baroque is most obvious, such as the *Bachianas Brasileiras* series. Rarely seen without a cigar and a broad smile, Villa Lobos was renowned for his rumbustious character and passionate advocacy of Brazilian music, an area in which he had an enormous impact as an educator.

MILESTONES	
1905	Visits north-east Brazil to collect folk music
1917	Writes *Amazonas*, tone poem
1918	Composes *A Prole do Bebê, No.1*, suite
1923	Moves to study in Paris, funded by government grant
1929	Completes *Chôros* series
1930	Returns to Brazil and becomes Director of Music Education for new nationalist government
1938	Writes *Bachianas Brasileiras No. 5*
1940	*Five Preludes for Guitar*, performed
1944	Composes *The Green Mansions*, film score
1945	Completes *Bachianas Brasileiras* series
1951	Writes *Concerto for Guitar*

KEY WORKS

CHÔROS NOS. 1–14

SUITE   📖 14   🎐

The *Chôros* date from the 1920s, and were Villa Lobos' own take on the "chorinho", a style of music that evolved in Rio de Janeiro in the late 19th century, blending European music with Afro-Brazilian rhythms. Scored for

In his tone poem *Amazonas*, Villa-Lobos uses an array of ethnic percussion instruments.

different instrumental ensembles, they present a kaleidoscope view of Brazilian music, as filtered through the young composer's active imagination. No. 5, for piano, is particularly fine.

CONCERTO FOR GUITAR

ORCHESTRAL   ⏱ 18:00   📖 3   🎶 🎧

The popular guitar concerto is one of comparatively few of Villa-Lobos' works to have taken a firm hold in the repertoire. An exciting piece, the finale in particular is full of syncopation and brilliant scoring. Villa-Lobos advocated the use of an amplifier to lift the volume of the guitar, but very few performers choose to use one.

FIVE PRELUDES FOR GUITAR

SOLO GUITAR 🕰 16:20 📖 5 🎵

Villa-Lobos' characterful guitar music has helped establish his international reputation, no doubt thanks to his idiomatic writing for the instrument (he was an excellent guitarist himself). Each of the *Five Preludes* is a portrait of a different aspect of Brazilian life, and – as ever with Villa-Lobos – they are quite stylistically diverse.

NUMBER ONE (4:30) A typically Brazilian-sounding melody is played in the mid-range of the guitar, accompanied by plucked chords.

NUMBER TWO (2:30) This Prelude depicts the *Capadocia*, a cocky native of the city of Rio. The first part is filled with light-hearted swagger, whilst the central section is a flurry of fast picking and parallel chords.

NUMBER THREE (3:00) Prelude No. 3 is a homage to Bach, opening with a figure in almost bitonal counterpoint, and leading to a middle section of Toccata-like figuration.

NUMBER FOUR (3:30) A haunting melody in the lower reaches of the instrument depicts the rainforest, returning – after a dramatic central section – in shadowy form using guitar harmonics.

NUMBER FIVE (3:30) The final Prelude, a homage to the lively and sophisticated social life of Rio, is a playful waltz that recalls themes from some of the earlier preludes.

BACHIANAS BRASILEIRAS NO. 5

SUITE 🕰 08:30 📖 2 🎻👤

The series of *Bachianas Brasileiras* are, like the *Chôros*, scored for a variety of different ensembles. Written as a homage to Bach, Villa Lobos makes a thoroughgoing attempt to fuse the composer's contrapuntal procedures with the spirit of Brazilian music. The fifth of the series is perhaps his best known work. Villa Lobos was a fine cellist, and it is surely his affinity for the instrument that enabled him to conjure a wide range of textures and sounds from this unusual ensemble of eight cellos and solo soprano.

ARIA (CANTILENA) The Aria begins with a pizzicato bassline accompanying a gentle counterpoint. The soprano enters with a wordless *vocalise*, shadowed by one of the cellos, intoning a vocal line with a distinctly Brazilian flavour. The central section is a setting of a poem in Portuguese, an impassioned paean to the moon. The opening material then returns, the soprano now humming the melody.

DANÇA (MARTELO) The second movement is a lively dance. The soprano sings a poem which describes a native Brazilian bird, and has to negotiate all manner of fast, repeated words and sudden leaps.

Joaquín Rodrigo

● 1901–1999　　♙ Spanish　　✍ c.200

Rodrigo is among the most significant Spanish composers of the 20th century. His approachable style, with its echoes of Spanish folk music, changed little throughout his long career. However, his influence has been significant and, while he wrote in many genres, he is remembered mainly for his guitar music. Blind from childhood, Rodrigo's prodigious output was composed using braille.

LIFE AND MUSIC

An attack of diphtheria rendered Rodrigo blind from the age of three. Nonetheless, as a child he showed great aptitude for music, studying firstly in Spain and then, following his fellow Spaniards, Granados, and Albeniz, in Paris. While hardly progressive, Rodrigo's music is an appealing blend of Spanish-inflected melody (although often without direct-reference folk sources) with a subtlety learned from his studies with Dukas and, at times, a certain Stravinskian coolness – characteristics epitomized in the celebrated *Concierto de Aranjuez*. Not a guitarist himself, it is notable that his large output contains many works for the instrument, and as such he played a significant role in establishing the guitar in the Classical mainstream.

MILESTONES

1918	Studied composition at Valencia
1927	Moves to Paris to study with composer Paul Dukas
1933	Marries the Turkish pianist Victoria Kamh
1935	Writes *Sonada de adios* for piano, in memory of Dukas
1939	Returns to Spain. Composes *Concierto de Aranjuez*
1942	Writes *Concierto Heroica* for piano and orchestra
1947	Appointed Manuel de Falla Professor of Music at Madrid University
1958	*Fantasia para un Gentilhombre* produced
1963	Awarded Légion d'Honneur by the French Government

KEY WORKS

CONCIERTO DE ARANJUEZ

ORCHESTRAL　⏱ 20:00　📖 3　🎵 🎧

Inspired by the beautiful Rococo palace at Aranjuez, this is certainly the most famous work in the guitar repertoire, and one of the best-known pieces of Classical music of the 20th century. The two outer movements are full of dance rhythms, while the gorgeous second is a masterpiece of subtle scoring – the evocative melody shared between the guitar and cor anglais.

The guitar is the instrument that Rodrigo is most associated with; but he never played it himself.

FANTASÍA PARA UN GENTILHOMBRE

ORCHESTRAL　⏱ 22:00　📖 4　🎵 🎧

Rodrigo's second best-known work for solo guitar and orchestra. Premiered in San Francisco by the renowned guitar virtuoso Andrés Segovia (the gentleman of the title), the work is a fantasy on themes from the 17th-century Spanish composer Gaspar Sanz.

SONADA DE ADIOS

PIANO　⏱ 4:00　📖 1　🎧

Rodrigo studied with the renowned composer Paul Dukas. His death in 1935 affected him deeply, and the touching *Sonada de adios* was written as a homage to his friend.

Carlos Chávez

● 1899–1978   🏳 Mexican   ✎ c.200

Composer, conductor, teacher, administrator, writer: Chávez was a prolific and major figure in the development of Mexican music in the 20th century. Trained as a pianist, but self-taught as a composer, he directed the Conservatory and Institute of Fine Arts, created and headed major national orchestras, and promoted both radical new music, and native Mexican music, to all social classes. Chávez's works cover traditional genres (for example his six symphonies) plus some of his own (such as the four "Solis"). They often show indigenous influences, sometimes using folk instruments – based on historical research, such as in the Aztec-influenced *Xochipilli*. His works are characterized by strong rhythms, a "Mexican accent", and spiky dissonance, but avoid repetition and cliché. He was also influenced by the music of Stravinsky and Schoenberg.

MILESTONES	
1921	Debut as composer: Piano Sextet
1922	Marries Otilia Ortiz, pianist
1925	Becomes head of OSM (Mexico Symphony Orchestra)
1928	Director of National Conservatory
1932	Composes *Caballos de vapor*, ballet
1947	Forms OSN (National Symphony Orchestra)

Xochipilli was written to commemorate an exhibition of Mexican Art in New York.

Alberto Ginastera

● 1916–1983   🏳 Argentina   ✎ c.100

Ginastera's *Panambi* made his name while still a student, and he went on to become the major Argentinian composer of the 20th century. He combined superb composing technique and eloquence with a strong sense of national identity: the virile rhythms and tough sounds of *Estancia* vividly suggest gauchos out on the ranch. However, his music also ranges from the charming (*Impresiones de la Puna*) to complex contemporary techniques (*String Quartet No. 1*). He directed the National Conservatory and taught – sometimes at loggerheads with the Perón government. In mid-career he wrote film music to support himself, but later commissions piled up: in his last 12 years, working in Switzerland, he composed prodigiously.

MILESTONES	
1941	Writes *Estancia*, ballet/orchestral suite
1948	Composes *String Quartet No. 1*
1954	*Pampeana No. 3*, orchestra, performed
1966	*Don Rodrigo*, opera, is a success in New York
1971	Remarries and moves to Switzerland

The atmospheric rhythms and meditative effects, in some of Ginastera's later works, suggest the wild landscape of the Argentinian Pampas.

Steven Collins Foster

◔ 1826–1864   ⚑ American   ✍ c.300

The American songwriter Stephen Foster has, curiously, become something of a cult figure. Perhaps because of his unrivalled ability to capture the essence of 19th-century American life and aspiration, he has come to be regarded as almost a folk hero, and his songs as authentic folk songs. In truth the bald facts of his life are rather mundane, rendering his achievements all the more remarkable.

LIFE AND MUSIC

Foster initially worked as a bookkeeper for his brother's steamboat business in Cincinnati, where he enjoyed his first major success with "Oh! Susanna". On returning to Pennsylvania in 1950, he decided to become a professional songwriter, a genuinely pioneering decision, as there was then no real "music business". Although almost wholly self-taught, Foster published his first song in his teens, and went on to write around 200 others. His songs were motivated by social purpose – both to capture the spirit of the American people, and to portray a world in which all were equal. At times, he deliberately adopted the musical and poetical style of immigrant groups, such as the cotton planters, which may be one reason why his works were mistaken for folk songs.

MILESTONES

1844	Publishes his first song, "Open Thy Lattice Love"
1846	Moves to Cincinnati to work as a bookkeeper for his brother
1948	Writes "Oh! Susanna", song
1950	Returns to Pennsylvania to become a professional songwriter; composes the song "Camptown Races"
1951	Writes "Old Folks at Home (Swanee River)" and "Laura Lee", songs
1953	Visits friends in Bardstown, Kentucky, inspiring him to write "My Old Kentucky Home", song
1954	Composes "Jeanie With the Light Brown Hair", song
1962	Writes "Beautiful Dreamer", song

KEY WORKS

OH! SUSANNA

SONG   ⏱ 3:00   📖 1   🔊 ♂

The song "Oh! Susanna" achieved huge popularity when it was taken up as the unofficial anthem of the "forty-niners", the families travelling to California in the American gold rush. Most would not have known that it was written just a year earlier; as such, it stands as a fine example of Foster's ability to write songs with the timeless appeal of folk standards.

A rhythmic minstrel song capturing the ebullient spirit of the gold rush, "Oh! Susanna" was Foster's first and most enduring success.

BEAUTIFUL DREAMER

SONG   ⏱ 3:00   📖 1   🔊 ♂

Foster's later songs rarely rivalled his earlier ones for popularity, bar the serenade "Beautiful Dreamer", made famous by Bing Crosby in the 1940s.

MY OLD KENTUCKY HOME

SONG   ⏱ 3:00   📖 1   🔊 ♂

Foster wrote many evocative songs about the American South. "My Old Kentucky Home", inspired by a visit to friends in the region, has since been adopted as the official state song.

OH, SUSANNA.

Written by S. C. Foster. Sung by Ward's Minstrels, 411 Broadway.

Louis Moreau Gottschalk

🌑 1829–1869   🏳 American   ✍ 130

Arguably the first American nationalist composer, Gottschalk was a virtuoso pianist and performer, whose flair won the praise of Chopin and Berlioz. Much of his life was spent touring outside his native country, yet the US remained his spiritual home and his music retained elements of the Afro-Creole qualities that shaped his early life. He composed much piano music, two symphonies, and two operas.

LIFE AND MUSIC

Gottschalk was born in New Orleans, of French-Creole descent. At the age of 13, apparently quite of his own accord, he determined to study in Paris. Although denied admittance to the Conservatoire, he studied privately, establishing himself as a pianist after a dazzling début in 1844. Indeed, his playing was greatly admired by both Chopin and Berlioz, who described his "irresistible prestige and…sovereign power" at the keyboard.

Gottschalk's composing, almost always secondary to his performing, has often been dismissed as mere light music, and his works have been largely forgotten today. However, his style can be seen as uniquely American in its exuberant integration of disparate influences.

MILESTONES	
1842	Travels to Paris; studies privately
1853	Returns to the US to tour widely
1856	New York concerts highly acclaimed
1854	Moves to West Indies for three years; composes *La Nuit des Tropiques*
1862	Returns to the US for the Civil War
1865	Forced to leave the US after scandal
c.1868	Composes *La Gallina: Cuban Dance*

A charismatic Creole virtuoso from French New Orleans, Gottschalk dazzled audiences with his heady mix of Romantic idioms and Afro-Creole folk music and rhythms.

KEY WORKS

THE LAST HOPE; THE DYING POET

SOLO PIANO   ⏱ 6:00   📖 1   🎵

The Last Hope and *The Dying Poet* are amongst the many overtly sentimental encore pieces that Gottschalk composed for use in his own performances. These two were particular favourites with his audiences, which were reported to have been largely made up of female admirers.

SYMPHONIE ROMANTIQUE: LA NUIT DES TROPIQUES

ORCHESTRAL   ⏱ 16:00   📖 2   🎵🎵

La nuit des Tropiques, written on the island of Guadaloupe during Gottschalk's three-year spell in the Caribbean, effectively fuses Romantic idioms with Afro-Creole folk music and Latin American dance rhythms, achieving striking colouristic effects. Whilst rarely performed nowadays, it has assumed a certain historical importance as the first genuine American symphony. That said, it bears little formal similarity to its European counterparts and is more akin to the freer form of symphonic poem. Its evocative mood and name probably derives from Félicien David's symphonic ode, *Christophe Colomb*, staged in 1847. A curious point of note is the fugue on a Cuban theme in the second movement.

Amy Marcy Cheney Beach

● 1867–1944 ♙ American ✍ 300

Amy Beach was one of the first US composers to gain a significant reputation outside her native country, and remains one of the foremost female composers of her time. Finding inspiration in Romanticism and the European folk music tradition of her New England ancestors, she composed copiously throughout her life, and in later years developed a significant performing career.

LIFE AND MUSIC

Amy Beach would almost certainly have made a career as a concert pianist, but her husband encouraged her to limit public appearances and concentrate instead on composition (she later returned to the platform following his death in 1910). In this she was immensely talented but largely self-taught, learning orchestration from a treatise by Berlioz and counterpoint by writing out fugues from Bach's *Well-Tempered Clavier*.

Whilst not especially innovative, her music is well constructed and shows a sophisticated grasp of harmony. In works such as the Piano Concerto she demonstrated an ability (and willingness) to tackle large-scale forms. Her output is large and covers all the major genres.

MILESTONES	
1885	Debut with Boston Symphony Orchestra; marries Dr Henry Beach
1896	Composes *Gaelic Symphony*, Op. 32
1898	Writes *Three Browning Songs*, Op. 44
1910	Death of husband
1911	Concert tour to Europe; remains in Germany until 1914
1914	Settles in New York

Beach composed music for the opening of the Women's Building at the World's Columbian Exhibition, held in Chicago in 1893.

KEY WORKS

GAELIC SYMPHONY, OP. 32

ORCHESTRAL ⏱ 43:00 📖 4 ♫

Rather than follow Dvořák's example of using Native American and Negro music to forge a national style, Beach turned instead to the Celtic folk tradition. Her *Gaelic Symphony* incorporates Irish melodies and was the first symphony by an American composer to gather significant attention in Europe.

PIANO CONCERTO, OP. 45

ORCHESTRAL ⏱ 36:00 📖 4 ♫ ♪

Beach's Piano Concerto is a large-scale, bravura masterpiece in the manner of contemporary late-Romantic concertos

such as those of Tchaikovsky and Grieg. Three of the four movements are based on material from Beach's own songs, including one to a poem by her husband. She premiered the work herself with the Boston Symphony Orchestra in 1900.

THREE BROWNING SONGS, OP. 44

SONGS ⏱ 7:00 📖 3 ♪ ♪

Beach composed over 100 songs, and it was for these that she was remembered until her revival in the mid-1970s in the wake of the US feminist movement. The *Three Browning Songs*, and in particular the delightful first song "The Year's at the Spring", have proven enduringly popular.

John Philip Sousa

● 1854–1932   ♙ American   ✍ 250

A composer, conductor, bandleader, and patriot, John Philip Sousa was known as the "March King". He composed many of the world's best-known military band pieces including *The Stars and Stripes Forever*, the official march of the United States. In addition to his band music, which remains immensely popular with bands today, his output included some 15 operettas and many songs.

LIFE AND MUSIC

After Sousa attempted to run away with the circus at age 13, his father – a military trombonist – apprenticed him to the Marines. Following his discharge in 1875, and a spell conducting theatre orchestras, he returned to the military to assume leadership of the US Marine Band. He went on to form his own hugely successful band in 1892, touring all over the world and setting new standards for the quality of marching band performance. From his first published composition in 1872 until the end of his life, Sousa wrote constantly, and his position as bandleader gave him ample opportunity to showcase his works. His 135 marches, many celebrating US places or events, are full of delightful melodies and possessed of a distinctive, good-natured swagger.

MILESTONES

1867	Father enlists Sousa in the Marines
1875	Discharged from Marines
1880	Returns to the military to lead the US Marine Band
1888	Composes march *Semper Fidelis*
1889	*The Washington Post*, march, first performed
1892	Forms the Sousa Band
1895	Composes *El Capitan*, his first successful operetta
1896	Composes *The Stars and Stripes Forever*
1899	Composes march *Hands across the Sea*
1900	Sousa Band tours Europe
1901	Second European tour
1905	Third European tour
1910	Sousa Band's world tour

KEY WORKS

THE STARS AND STRIPES FOREVER

MARCH   ♫ 3:30   ▭ 1   ♔

Sousa and his wife were on vacation in Europe when they heard of the death of his manager, David Blakely. Thinking over the news whilst onboard the ship returning to the US, Sousa began to hear "a rhythmic beat of a band playing within my brain". That melody was in his mind for the remainder of the voyage, and was to become *The Stars and Stripes Forever*, perhaps his most enduringly popular march.

John Philip Sousa is the inventor of the sousaphone, a now familiar instrument in the marching band ensemble.

THE LIBERTY BELL

MARCH   ♫ 3:30   ▭ 1   ♔

The Liberty Bell is well known as the theme tune to the classic British comedy series "Monty Python's Flying Circus". It is a fine example of Sousa's musical craft – a rousing march, with a memorable theme and a hint of humour.

Edward MacDowell

● 1860–1908   ♙ American   ✍ c.70

One of the first US composers to establish a reputation outside his country, MacDowell was held as the most important US composer of his day. As a pianist and teacher he founded the music department of Columbia University and, with his wife Marion, the MacDowell artists' colony, which still exists. His musical style owes much to the influence of his teacher, Joachim Raff, but became more individual in later years.

LIFE AND MUSIC

MacDowell studied first in New York, then Paris, but it was Germany where he settled, teaching the piano and establishing a career as a performer. Success as a composer followed his return to the US in 1888. After teaching at Columbia University, his final years were spent between New York and his house in Peterborough, New Hampshire. The artists' retreat he founded there with his wife in 1907 has flourished ever since. Inevitably, given his education, MacDowell's music was strongly influenced by the German Romantics, which may be the reason why it fell out of favour in the US between the two world wars.

MILESTONES	
1876	Moves to Paris to attend Conservatoire
1878	Dissatisfied with instruction in Paris, so moves to Weisbaden
1879	Studies composition at Frankfurt Conservatory with Joachim Raff
1881	Made piano professor at Darmstadt; composes *First Modern Suite*
1882	Composes Piano Concerto No. 1
1884	Becomes piano teacher at Wiesbaden
1886	Composes Piano Concerto No. 2
1888	Returns to US and settles in Boston
1892	Writes *Sonata Tragica* and "Indian" Suite
1896	Given first chair of music at Columbia University; writes *Woodland Sketches*
1907	Founds MacDowell Colony with wife

KEY WORKS

SONATA TRAGICA

PIANO SOLO   ⏲ 26:00   📖 4   ☞

MacDowell's four substantial piano sonatas are all inspired by European mythology except this, his first one. It is his most personal – a tribute to the death of his teacher and friend, Raff.

The MacDowell Colony at Peterborough, New Hampshire, is the oldest artists' colony in the US. Its oldest building was originally the composer's home.

SUITE NO. 2, "INDIAN"

ORCHESTRAL SUITE   ⏲ 30:00   📖 5   🎻

MacDowell felt that native Indian music held far more potential than Negro music as a source of inspiration for an "American" style. In this large-scale work for orchestra he employed material that has been traced to the Iroquois and Chippewa tribes.

FIRST MODERN SUITE

PIANO SOLO   ⏲ 30:00   📖 5   ☞

Despite its title, MacDowell's *First Modern Suite* for piano was resolutely in the European style he learned from his time studying with Raff. Nevertheless is it full of charming music and extremely idiomatic for the piano.

WOODLAND SKETCHES

PIANO SOLO 🕐 18:30 📖 10 🔊

Some of MacDowell's best-known music is contained in the late sets of short piano pieces, *Woodland Sketches* and *New England Idylls*. Influenced by the American landscape, particularly that of his country retreat in New Hampshire, the musical language is sparse, direct and even folksy compared with his earlier piano works. The individual pieces in *Woodland Sketches* are all evocatively titled.

The famous "To a Wild Rose", which opens *Woodland Sketches*, and the eighth piece, "A Deserted Farm", are perfect examples of pared-down piano writing – beautifully simple melodies arranged over poignant, mildly dissonant chords. "An Old Trysting Place" has richer harmony and the feel of an old choral setting, whilst "To a Water Lily" uses the full range of the piano to suggest a deep lake. "Will o' the Wisp" is full of gleeful, good humour. The most direct folk allusion is in "From an Old Indian Lodge", which imitates the rhythms of native Indian chant.

Although some of the pieces are now performed separately, MacDowell intended them to be played together: in fact, the final piece, "Told at Sunset", quotes from some of the earlier movements as if in reminiscence.

PIANO CONCERTO NO. 2

ORCHESTRAL 🕐 24:00 📖 3 🎵🎵 🔊

Received with success at its premiere in 1889, this work was described by one critic as sounding "a model of its kind – the kind that Johannes Brahms gave the world over 30 years ago in his D minor Concerto". If this is a little over-stated, there is no doubt that the work cemented MacDowell's position as the foremost composer in the US. The Concerto No. 2 is a distinctive and interesting work, made unusual by its adoption of a slow first movement and a scherzo second, and by the many dance rhythms that feature throughout. It has also remained popular, largely thanks to US pianist, Van Cliburn.

FIRST MOVEMENT (LARGHETTO CALMATO 10:00)
After a short introduction led by the brass, the soloist enters with an intense, passionate cadenza. Cellos and clarinets introduce the lyrical second theme.

SECOND MOVEMENT (PRESTO GIOCOSO 7:00)
This good-humoured section is a rondo, filled with quicksilver passages for the piano and almost jazz-like in its constant syncopation.

THIRD MOVEMENT (LARGO – MOLTO ALLEGRO 7:00)
Beginning darkly with cellos leading a slow introduction, the mood lightens into a lively waltz, in which the soloist recalls themes from the first movement.

MODERN MUSIC
1900–

Music since 1900 has developed in a wide variety of styles, many of them strongly influenced by ideological, social, and technological changes. Whereas composers of earlier times attempted to adopt and develop established styles, much music of the 20th century seems – at least on the surface – to break with the past.

T he first half of the 20th century was dominated by two very different composers who both established themselves in Europe before the First World War and who both ended their lives in California: the Austrian Arnold Schoenberg and the Russian Igor Stravinsky.

Schoenberg and his followers – raised on the high Romanticism of composers like Mahler and Wolf – saw themselves as building on the Austro-Germanic tradition. At the same time, Schoenberg's interest in painting indicates a close relationship between the expressionism of artists, such as Kokoschka and Kandinsky, and that of his own music and that of his followers, such as Berg.

Igor Stravinsky sprang to fame with his Russian ballets, such as *The Firebird* (1909) and *The Rite of Spring* (1913),

and reinvigorated music with the primitive force of his rhythmic language, mirrored in the angular lines of the paintings of Picasso from the same period.

NEO-CLASSICISM

Later Stravinsky looked back to the past by drawing on styles and actual materials of the 17th and 18th centuries, and this style or spirit of "Neo-Classicism" was embraced by many contemporary composers, especially in France. Stravinsky's *Pulcinella* (1918) was the seminal example of Neo-Classicism, and even as late as his *The Rake's Progress* (1948–51) there is a sense of reverting to the traditions (and plots) of the past.

In France, Ravel's music was sufficiently objective in its poise and clarity to adapt to the Neo-Classical ethos, as is shown in his *Le tombeau de Couperin* (1917–19), and even Debussy in his *Suite Bergamasque* succumbs to the charms of the past. In Britain,

CONCERT BY FELIX JOHANNNSEN-RANDEL (1924)
Movements and ideas in music in the 20th century tended to reflect – directly or indirectly – the major contemporary movements in art.

SCHOENBERG AND SERIALISM

Schoenberg devised the 12-note process of composition, whereby a pattern of all 12 semitones (known as a "series" or "row") should be used in a particular order before any one is repeated. The relationship between the notes of the row would always be maintained, though it was permissible to transpose the row (start on a different pitch), to reproduce it in "retrograde" (in reverse) or "inversion" (upside-down), and the notes could be combined simultaneously in chords.

The idea was to avoid any sense of key or tonality. This way of composing became known as "serialism" and dominated music in the mid-20th century.

INFLUENTIAL THEORY
Arnold Schoenberg's *Harmonielehre* (*Treatise on Harmony*) was published in 1911.

Walton and Constant Lambert took up the Neo-Classical style, while in Germany, Hindemith explored the forms of earlier periods, most notabl[y] in his series of duo sonatas for orchestral instruments and piano.

JAZZ

Just as many composers turned to th[e] past to react against Romanticism, others found in jazz a perfect foil to the music of the previous century. Virtually no composer in Paris was immune to the influence of jazz: Stravinsky composed a Rag-time (1918); Milhaud composed the first jazz fugue in his ballet *La création du monde* (1923); and Ravel's Violin Sonata (1923–27)

TIMELINE: MODERN MUSIC

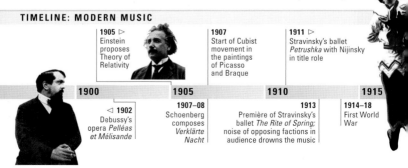

1905 ▷
Einstein proposes Theory of Relativity

1907
Start of Cubist movement in the paintings of Picasso and Braque

1911 ▷
Stravinsky's ballet *Petrushka* with Nijinsky in title role

| 1900 | 1905 | 1910 | 1915 |

◁ **1902**
Debussy's opera *Pelléas et Mélisande*

1907–08
Schoenberg composes *Verklärte Nacht*

1913
Première of Stravinsky's ballet *The Rite of Spring*; noise of opposing factions in audience drowns the music

1914–18
First World War

make settings of folk songs of their own countries, and other composers such as Ligeti, Reich, and Volans would be influenced (in very different ways) by the music of Africa.

MUSIC AND POLITICS

In Russia, several distinct and important voices emerged during the 20th century. Prokofiev spent some time in the West, and was influenced by the Neo-Classicism he found in Paris, whereas Shostakovich remained in the Soviet Union and was forced to pay lip-service to the Socialist Realism of the Soviet authorities.

Political interference also surfaced in Nazi Germany, where Jewish composers were banned during the 1930s and even the music of non-Jewish composers, such as Anton Webern and Alban Berg, was outlawed as "degenerate art". Among the potentially great composers who died or were killed in Nazi camps was the Moravian Gideon Klein and the Czech Viktor Ullmann.

contains a blues movement. At the same time, in the USA Gershwin was creating concert works, such as *Rhapsody in Blue*, that bridged the divide between popular and "serious" music.

FOLK INFLUENCES

Elsewhere, composers explored their musical folk heritage. In eastern Europe, Béla Bartók and Zoltán Kodály both travelled extensively to make recordings of folk songs and dances. The Australian composer and pianist Percy Grainger was equally industrious, collecting music from various parts of the world. In North America, Aaron Copland began to use cowboy songs, Quaker hymns, and Latin-American material in his own work, creating an immediately identifiable American style.

Later, European composers as diverse as Britten and Berio would

WRITER JEAN COCTEAU WITH "LES SIX" IN 1925
The group consists of (from left to right) Milhaud, a drawing of Auric, Cocteau at the piano, Honegger, Tailleferre, Poulenc, and Durey.

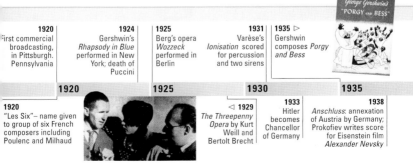

1920 First commercial broadcasting, in Pittsburgh, Pennsylvania	**1924** Gershwin's *Rhapsody in Blue* performed in New York; death of Puccini	**1925** Berg's opera *Wozzeck* performed in Berlin	**1931** Varèse's *Ionisation* scored for percussion and two sirens	**1935** ▷ Gershwin composes *Porgy and Bess*

1920   1925   1930   1935

1920 "Les Six"– name given to group of six French composers including Poulenc and Milhaud	◁ **1929** *The Threepenny Opera* by Kurt Weill and Bertolt Brecht	**1933** Hitler becomes Chancellor of Germany	**1938** *Anschluss*: annexation of Austria by Germany; Prokofiev writes score for Eisenstein film *Alexander Nevsky*

Some composers remained resolutely independent from other movements. Olivier Messiaen took religion as an important unifying factor for his music and at the same time used exotic scales and bird song. Pierre Boulez, meanwhile, was initially influenced by Messiaen, but later rejected his teacher and instead became a high priest of formalism, taking the principles of serialism to a new level.

MODERN TRENDS

In the USA, John Cage, who had studied with Schoenberg, turned his back on serialism and looked to the music and philosophy of the East for inspiration, while bizarre conceptual

GREAT FILM SCORES
Music plays a key role in cinema, whether Bernard Herrmann's score for Hitchcock's *Psycho* (right) or Ennio Morricone's for Sergio Leone's *Dollars* trilogy.

preoccupations inspired the work of Karlheinz Stockhausen, one of whose works involves a string quartet performing in mid-air in four helicopters. Technology impacted on all types of music, through recording and through the use of synthesized sound; Edgard Varèse, for example, created a tape-only piece, *Poème électronique*, for Le Corbusier's Philips Pavilion at the Brussels Expo of 1958.

A group of composers who emerged in the late 1960s were the minimalists. Terry Riley, Philip Glass, and Steve Reich composed music based on the repetition of simple motives that many found mesmerizing. Ultimately this style was taken up by composers who sought to reintroduce elements of development, such as John Adams, who has composed orchestral music and opera of romantic proportions both in scale and richness of expression. Just as the minimalists rebelled against the

MUSIC FOR STAGE AND SCREEN

The American stage musical has attracted composers from Gershwin *(Porgy and Bess)* to Bernstein *(West Side Story)* and Stephen Sondheim. Fugitives from Europe in the 1930s, including Erich Korngold and Miklós Rózsa, found work in Hollywood alongside American composers such as Bernard Herrmann *(Citizen Kane* and *Taxi Driver)*. Well-known classical composers who have also written film scores include Vaughan Williams, Milhaud, Prokofiev, Copland, Walton, and Philip Glass. An especially successful modern film composer is John Williams (of *Star Wars* fame).

WEST SIDE STORY
Bernstein's musical demonstrated the composer's surefire popular touch.

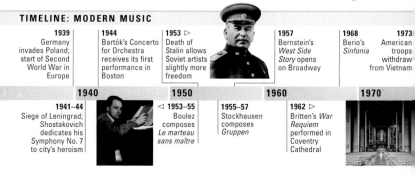

complexity of serialism, so a group of European composers, including John Tavener, Henryk Górecki, and Arvo Pärt, developed music that was equally simple in its construction, but emerged out of a spiritual calm.

CROSSOVER MUSIC

Popular music forms, such as jazz, rock, and folk music, inspired a great many modern classical composers, but musical cross-fertilization in the 20th century was by no means a one-way traffic. Jazz big band leaders such as Duke Ellington used an adapted orchestral format, with a wide instrumental range. In the 1950s and '60s, producers such as Frank Sinatra's collaborator Nelson Riddle and The Beatles' producer, George Martin, frequently aspired to full classical orchestral effects. In rock music, a number of bands such as Deep Purple and Pink Floyd dabbled with orchestral compositions. The impressive catalogue of over 1,200 compositions by the radical American musician Frank Zappa ranged from scatalogical heavy guitar rock to a ballet (*Lumpy Gravy*, 1968), an opera (*200 Motels*, 1971), and his final work, the *Yellow Shark* suite (1992), which saw him working with the Ensemble Moderne.

FRANK ZAPPA CONDUCTING
Zappa rehearses with the London Symphony Orchestra for a concert at the Barbican in 1984.

1976
Philip Glass's minimalist opera *Einstein on the Beach*; Górecki's Symphony No. 3

1985
First compact discs come on sale

1989 ▷
Fall of Berlin Wall; collapse of communism in Eastern Europe

1991
Breakup of the Soviet Union

2003
US-led invasion of Iraq

1980

1990

2000

2010

◁ **1987**
John Adams' opera *Nixon in China*

1990
Magnus Lindberg composes *Marea*

2000 ▷
Turnage's opera *The Silver Tassie*, based on the Sean O'Casey anti-war play, opens in London

"*My music is not modern,
it is merely badly played.*"

ARNOLD SCHOENBERG

Arnold Schoenberg

⬩ 1874–1951　🏳 Austrian　✍ 213

Schoenberg has probably inspired more misunderstanding and controversy than any other 20th-century composer. He remains a paradox: his music broke with the past and yet he saw himself as part of a tradition of Germanic music and his abandonment of tonality as an inevitable step in music progress. He was also a great, self-taught teacher. His music can seem unapproachable but he could also arrange Strauss waltzes.

LIFE

Schoenberg was born in Vienna where his father owned a small shoe shop. He began composing as a child, but met Alexander von Zemlinsky (his only teacher) when already a young adult, working in a bank. He converted from to Protestantism from Judaism in 1898 and three years later married Zemlinsky's daughter Mathilde. Their circle of friends included Berg and Webern (who had become pupils of

Schoenberg's death seemed to justify his superstitious belief in numerology: he died on Friday 13 July 1951, at 13 minutes before midnight.

Schoenberg), Mahler and the painter Richard Gerstl who gave art lessons first to Schoenberg – himself a talented artist – and later to Mathilde. In 1908, Mathilde briefly left her husband for Gerstl who committed suicide when she subsequently returned to Schoenberg. Mahler's death in 1911 was another blow to Schoenberg, and it was only when he moved to Berlin that he was able to regain some confidence. In 1933, horrified at the German anti-semitism of the time, Schoenberg rejoined the Jewish faith in a ceremony witnessed by the painter Marc Chagall. Later that year he left Europe permanently, moving first to Boston and then to Los Angeles where he took a teaching post at the University of California. Friends and near neighbours to his Hollywood home included George Gershwin and the writer Thomas Mann.

MUSICAL OUTPUT								Total: 213
CONCERTOS (4)						2	2	
OTHER ORCHESTRAL (13)		3	5			2	3	
PIANO MUSIC (20)		3	9	6		2		
OTHER INSTRUMENTAL (24)		4	11	2		3	2	2
OPERAS (4)			1			3		
CHORAL (62)		1	3	6		27	13	12
SONGS (86)	2	59	6	11		7	1	
	1874	1884	1894	1904	1914	1924	1934	1944　1951

MUSIC

After writing his early music in a late-Romantic style, Schoenberg developed a completely new musical language. Works such as the string sextet *Verklärte Nacht*, and the String Quartet No. 2 took dissonance to levels which audiences had not previously encountered. The last movement of String Quartet No. 2 appropriately quotes the German poet Stefan George: "I feel the air of other planets". The Three Pieces, Op. 11, for piano confirm this new and strange planet: they are effectively atonal and expressionist. This "free atonality" liberated Schoenberg from writing in any particular key, and

MILESTONES	
1898	Converts to Protestantism
1899	Writes *Verklärte Nacht*, Op. 4
1911	*Gurrelieder* produced
1904	Berg and Webern become pupils
1906	Chamber Symphony No. 1, Op. 9
1909	Three Pieces, Op. 11, for piano
1911	Meets Kandinsky
1912	*Pierrot lunaire*, Op. 21
1928	Variations, Op. 31, for orchestra
1933	Emigrates to US
1941	Becomes US citizen
1942	Writes *Ode to Napoleon Buonaparte*, Op. 41

traditional melodies were replaced by expressive gestures and extremes of pitch or dynamics. He later pared his music down in a way that reflected the Neo-Classicism of the day (for example the Six Little Pieces), and in his final years he strove towards some reparation with tonality.

The opera *Moses und Aron* – begun in 1932– was one of Schoenberg's unfinished works. Ever superstitious, he spelt "Aron" with one "r" to avoid a title with thirteen letters.

KEY WORKS

SUITE, OP. 25

SOLO PIANO   24:30   5

Schoenberg wrote little music for solo piano and tended to treat the instrument as a laboratory, experimenting with new compositional ideas on the instrument. As a result, the piano yielded many of Schoenberg's most interesting ideas, and the wonderfully fresh Suite for piano is no exception. It was the first work to be created in its entirety from a single note row – the first use of the 12-note technique that became known as "serialism". Nevertheless, the novelty of the compositional method is offset by the traditional dance forms used: there is a prelude, gavotte, musette, minuet, and trio, and an energetic gigue.

ODE TO NAPOLEON BUONAPARTE, OP. 41

CHAMBER   15:32   1

The *Ode to Napoleon Buonaparte* is a setting of a poem by Lord Byron for a most unusual ensemble – speaker, string quartet, and piano. Schoenberg uses the 12-note procedure, but in fact much of the work sounds tonal and indeed the final cadence reaches the key of E flat – one of Beethoven's favourite keys, and appropriately the same key in which the "Eroica" was written (a symphony also originally dedicated to Napoleon). Like Beethoven, Schoenberg despised dictators, and this work is aimed at Hitler and the fascism which had enveloped Europe at the time of its composition (1942).

FOCUS

PIERROT LUNAIRE, OP. 21

CHAMBER   🕮 32:00   📖 3   ♟♂

Pierrot lunaire has gained a certain notoriety as one of Schoenberg's most radical works despite the composer's intention that it should be "light, ironic, and satirical". It is a setting of poems by Albert Giraud about the traditional commedia dell'arte character Pierrot. The work is scored for a female reciter and a chamber ensemble of eight instruments (flute, piccolo, clarinet, bass clarinet, violin, viola, cello, and piano) played by five performers, who play together for the first time in the very last song. The work's surreal quality is enhanced by the *sprechgesang* (speech-song) of the reciter, which appears to presage madness.

PART ONE Pierrot fantasizes on the nature of love, sex and God. It is mostly calm, as in No. 5, the "Valse de Chopin" and No. 7, "Der kranke Mond" ("The Sick Moon"). In No. 2 however, Columbine's violin solo is neurotically active.

PART TWO This is where the expressionist nightmare world truly makes itself felt in grotesque and sometimes violent music; No. 13, "Enthauptung" ("Beheading"). No. 8, "Night", ("Nacht") is a passacaglia (a set of variations on a ground bass).

PART THREE Pierrot begins his journey home to Bergamo and a sense of calm returns in songs that verge on the sentimental, such as "Heimfahrt" ("Homeward journey"). There are also moments of great contrapuntal ingenuity such as No. 18, "Der Mondfleck" ("The Moon-spot") where Pierrot turns round to look at himself – this is represented by a palindromic canon between violin and cello, which reverse their lines from the middle of the piece onwards. The final piece almost resolves tonally in the key of E major, as if Schoenberg had begun to come to terms with his personal and artistic crises of the previous years.

GURRELIEDER

CANTATA   🕮 120:00   📖 3   ♫♨♂

This epic cantata was originally conceived as a song cycle based on a text by Jens Peter Jacobsen. It is the story of Waldemar, a medieval king of Denmark, and charts his doomed love for Tove, his blasphemy, penance, and the summer winds which sweep him and his ghostly retinue away in the dawn. The work is immersed in romantic symbolism and calls for a gigantic orchestra, choruses, soloists, and narrator. Significantly, it opens with an ethereal sunset, evoked by shimmering woodwind chords, and ends with a sunrise, symbolizing hope for the future.

> **INFLUENCES**
>
> Schoenberg was influenced by composers as diverse as Bach and Mahler. His own influence was immense, partly through his teaching (such composers as Berg, Webern, and John Cage were among his pupils), but also through the wide adoption of serialism on both sides of the Atlantic after 1950.

Anton Webern

◓ 1883–1945　　📖 Austrian　　✍ c.31

Webern's legacy was relatively small in terms of works, but substantial in terms of subsequent influence. All his music is immaculately crafted and he developed Schoenberg's 12-note procedures in distinctive ways. Most of Webern's compositions are extremely concise – he was able to compress a range of emotions into a few bars of music – yet they are among the most important works of the 20th century.

LIFE AND MUSIC

Webern was born into the middle class in Vienna (his father was a mining engineer). Although he studied musicology under Guido Adler at the University of Vienna, it was Schoenberg who was to be the decisive influence on his music. Webern enjoyed some success as a conductor in the 1920s but gradually withdrew from public life. His music was banned by the Nazis and his teaching activities were restricted after the Anschluss. During the Second World War he moved outside Vienna to escape the bombing of the city; ironically, he was shot one night (just after the war had ended) while smoking a cigar outside his daughter's house.

MILESTONES	
1904	Becomes a pupil of Schoenberg
1906	Graduates with a doctorate from the University of Vienna
1908	Composes Passacaglia, Op. 1
1911	Six Bagatelles for String Quartet, Op. 9; moves to Berlin with Schoenberg; marries Wilhelmine Mörtl
1913	Five Pieces, chamber orchestra, Op. 10 Undergoes psychoanalysis with Albert Adler
1925	Teaches at the Israelisches Blindeninstitute in Vienna
1928	Writes Symphony, Op. 21
1936	Variations for Piano, Op. 27 published
1938	Composes String Quartet, Op. 28
1940	Writes Variations, for Orchestra, Op. 30

KEY WORKS

PASSACAGLIA, OP. 1

ORCHESTRAL　　⏱ 10:20　　📖 1　　🎻

This is an early work, written whilst Webern was still a pupil of Schoenberg. It is Romantic in style and is one of the last works he wrote to have a key signature (D minor).

SYMPHONY, OP. 21

CHAMBER　　⏱ 8:00　　📖 2　　🎺

Although titled "Symphony", this work is for a small chamber orchestra (clarinets, horns, harps, and strings) and avoids the development principles to be found in traditional symphonies. The texture is transparent, mostly consisting of single notes with occasional chords. The quality of tone changes continually – Webern entirely avoids long Romantic phrases – and the entire work is based on complex principles of symmetry.

PIANO VARIATIONS, OP. 27

SOLO PIANO　　⏱ 7:00　　📖 3　　🎹

These variations contain symmetries which cannot be detected by the listener, but were clearly important to Webern. For example, the note row used for all three movements, when turned around on itself and upside down, is identical to the original form.

FOCUS

FOUR SONGS FOR VOICE AND INSTRUMENTS, OP. 13

SONG ⏲ 07:00 📖 4 ♊ ♪

These four songs – which were composed during World War I – draw together poems of four different poets. That Webern composed so many songs at this time shows not only that he was interested in literature, but also how important it was for composers of free atonal music to have a structure in which to work. Each song is accompanied by a chamber ensemble (including woodwind, brass, percussion, and string instruments), and the different combinations of instruments reveal Webern's fascination for variations in timbre.

WIESE IM PARK (LAWN IN THE PARK) is a setting of a poem by Karl Krause. The delicate vocal part consists of short motives with numerous dissonant intervals. Webern draws attention to important words – such as the word "Wunder" (wonder) – by means of expressive leaps, or through sudden changes in instrumental colouring.

DIE EINSAME (THE LONELY GIRL) is a setting of a poem by Wang-Seng-Yu. As in the first song, there is much word-painting, including a climax on the word "sehnsucht" (longing) in the middle of the song. Appropriately for the theme of solitude, the song finishes with the voice alone.

IN DER FREMDE (IN A FOREIGN LAND) is another setting of a Chinese poem – this one written by Li-Tai-Po. The use of the celesta is particularly exotic, and the emphasis given to the word "Mond" (moon) is reminiscent of Schoenberg's *Pierrot lunaire*.

EIN WINTERABEND (A WINTER EVENING) is a setting of words by Georg Trakl, and further pursues the idea of dislocation and solitude, by contrasting the warmth and cheerfulness of a brightly-lit house with the loneliness of the wanderer. The wide and dissonant intervals of the vocal part are highly suggestive of the wanderer's pain and suffering. Webern's acute awareness of timbre is present in the very last note – a ghostly harp harmonic.

Alban Berg

◯ 1885–1935   ▥ Austrian   ✍ 83

Although he composed relatively few works, Berg is one of the most distinctive voices of the early 20th century. Much of his music employs the new 12-tone principles of his teacher Schoenberg, but still retains a Romantic generosity and the emotional intensity of Expressionism. His music is inherently dramatic: many of Berg's later works are linked to programmes and some are autobiographical.

LIFE AND MUSIC

Berg was born into a middle class Viennese family, but his first formal training in music came from Schoenberg at the relatively advanced age of 19. The relationship with Schoenberg was always to be strained, as Berg attempted to please his teacher, but rarely succeeded in doing so. Although his Piano Sonata, Op. 1, marked a new artistic confidence, it was not until the 1920s that his reputation became firmly established, particularly with the success of his opera *Wozzeck*. After completing his Violin Concerto, Berg spent time in the countryside and an insect bite brought about the infection that was to result in his death.

MILESTONES	
1901	Takes job as a civil servant
1904	Begins studies with Schoenberg
1908	Composes Piano Sonata, Op. 1
1910	Marries Helene Nahowski
1912	Composes *Five Altenberglieder* for voice and orchestra
1915	Called up for service in the Austrian army
1923	Works performed in ISCM Festival in Salzburg
1925	Composes Chamber Concerto; *Wozzeck* receives its première in Berlin
1926	Arranges the *Lyric Suite*
1929	Begins opera *Lulu*, which remains unfinished
1935	Composes Violin Concerto

KEY WORKS

CHAMBER CONCERTO

CHAMBER   ⏱ 30:00   📖 3   ⚘ ⚲

The *Chamber Concerto*, scored for piano and 13 wind instruments, reveals Berg's fascination for anagrams: its themes contain musical equivalents of letters in his own name and in those of Arnold Schoenberg and Anton Webern, the other members of the Second Viennese School. Despite complex counterpoint and structural symmetries, Berg described the work is "full of friendship, love and a world of human and spiritual references".

LYRIC SUITE

ORCHESTRAL   ⏱ 27:00   📖 5   ♫

Originally composed as a work for string quartet, Berg arranged the three central movements for orchestra. The first and last movements are written according to the principles of Schoenberg's 12-tone system, but the slow movement contains a quote from Wagner's *Tristan und Isolde*.

Georg Büchner's 1914 play *Wozzeck* gave Berg the plot for his opera of the same name, one of his most successful works.

VIOLIN CONCERTO

ORCHESTRAL   🔊 25:00   📖 2   🎵 🎙

Soon after he began composing this 12-tone work, Berg was made known of the death of Manon, the daughter of the architect Walter Gropius and Alma Mahler. She had suffered from poliomyelitis, and was only seventeen years old when she died. Berg decided to dedicate the Violin Concerto to her memory – the work is inscribed "To the memory of an angel".

FIRST MOVEMENT The first movement consists of two sections, a dreamy and quasi-improvisational Andante and a dance-like Allegretto. Berg used some existing melodies, such as a Carinthian folksong in the Allegretto – this is played by the horn.

SECOND MOVEMENT This also consists of two sections, Allegro and Adagio. The Allegro is the most tortured and expressionist part of the concerto and represents the suffering of Manon. This culminates in a flourish for the violin, which gives way to another quotation, this time from Bach's harmonization of the Lutheran chorale "Es ist genug" ("It is enough"). This chorale enters very quietly, played by clarinets, and this must surely be one of the most poignant moments in any concerto. The soloist soars above the orchestral parts (representing the soul of Manon rising to heaven). Symbolically, the folk-tune from the first movement makes a return appearance as a flicker of life before the violin plays the entire note-row to end the work.

WOZZECK

OPERA   🔊 105:00   📖 3   🎵 🎭 👤

Berg saw Büchner's play *Wozzeck* in Vienna in 1914 and knew immediately that he should set it to music. However, World War I intervened and this atonal, expressionist opera was only completed in 1921.

ACT ONE Wozzeck, an infantry soldier, is ridiculed by his Captain. His lover Marie flirts with a passing Drum-Major, inviting him into her home.

ACT TWO Hearing of Marie's infidelity, Wozzeck confronts her, but she denies any wrongdoing. Wozzeck spies on her as she dances with the Drum-Major. Back at the barracks, he starts a fight with the Drum-Major; Wozzeck is knocked unconscious to the ground.

ACT THREE The next day, when out walking, Wozzeck stabs Marie in the throat. Later, drinking at a nearby tavern, Wozzeck notices the blood on his hands. Rushing to a pond, he throws in his knife, but frightened by the blood-red moon he tries to retrieve it to throw it in deeper, but accidentally drowns.

INFLUENCES

Berg was greatly influenced by his teacher, Schoenberg, but also by late Romantic composers such as Wagner and Richard Strauss. Always the most popular of the Second Viennese School with audiences, his own influence on composers has continued to grow since his death, particularly towards the end of the 20th century.

"*Bartok's name… stands for the principle and the demand for regeneration stemming from the people, both in art and in politics.*"

ZOLTÁN KODÁLY

Béla Bartók

⬤ 1881–1945   🏴 Hungarian   ✍ 695

Hungary's most important composer of the 20th century and a major exponent of modern music, Bartók was also an outstanding specialist in musical folklore and a teacher of wide repute. His music was invigorated by the themes, modes, and rhythmic patterns of the Hungarian and other folk music traditions he studied, which he synthesized with influences from his contemporaries into his own distinctive style.

LIFE

Bartók was born in southern Hungary to parents who were both teachers and amateur musicians. His idyllic childhood was disrupted in 1888 by the death of his father, and his mother was compelled to move between different towns in the region. The young Bartók composed enthusiastically, but suffered from various childhood illnesses. He entered the Academy of Music in Budapest in 1899, and shone as a pianist: he was soon invited to perform in Vienna, Berlin, and Manchester among other cities. In 1904 Bartók met his contemporary Kodály and discovered that they shared a mutual interest in folk music. Eventually they collected music from all over Eastern Europe. Bartók's first wife was Márta Ziegler, who assisted him in his field trips to collect folk music; the couple divorced in 1922 and Bartók subsequently married the pianist Ditta Pásztory; a son Péter was born in 1924. Bartók left Hungary after the German invasion of Austria and settled in New York in 1940. Life in the US proved precarious, although some financial security was provided by the intervention of friends such as Serge Koussevitsky, who commissioned new works from him. After a long period of ill-health Bartók died in New York while completing his Third Piano Concerto.

In 1907 Bartók was made Professor of Piano at the Royal Academy of Music in Budapest and in 1911 he and Kodály founded the New Hungarian Music Society

MUSICAL OUTPUT							Total: 695
CONCERTOS (6)			1		1	1	3
OTHER ORCHESTRAL (31)		1	9	4	8	8	1
PIANO MUSIC (436)		47	140	68	31	149	1
OTHER INSTRUMENTAL (65)		7	5	1	5	47	
DRAMATIC (3)				3			
CHORAL (36)			2	4		30	
SONG (118)		3	55	30	25	1	4
	1881	1890	1900	1910	1920	1930	1940 1945

MUSIC

Bartók's early music clearly shows the influence of German Romantics such as Richard Strauss. However, his interest in folk music exerted a strong pull and, even when he refrained from using actual folk tunes, his melodic and rhythmic language showed the folk character. Much of the music Bartók wrote around 1910 (such as the *Allegro Barbaro* for piano) was percussive in style, mirroring the primitivism of Stravinsky's music of the same period.

Bartók's music is meticulously crafted with remarkably clear proportions: different parts often mirror each other and the three sections of the ballet *The Wooden Prince*, for example, are arranged symmetrically. Bartók's most expressionistic phase was after World War I in such compositions as the pantomime *The Miraculous Mandarin*. His later music powerfully evokes the night noises of the Eastern European countryside in its slow sections.

In 1917, Bartók (centre) travelled through Romania with his fellow Hungarian composer Zoltan Kodály (right) and Joan Busitia to collect native folk songs.

MILESTONES	
1889	Enters Academy of Music, Budapest
1904	Meets Kodály; plans folk song collection
1906	Joins staff of Academy of Music
1909	Marries Márta Ziegler
1911	*Bluebeard's Castle*, Op. 11
1914	Begins *The Wooden Prince*, Op. 13
1923	Divorces Ziegler; marries Ditta Pásztory
1928	First concert tour of the US
1936	Music for Strings, Percussion, and Celeste
1937	Begins Violin Concerto No. 2
1938	*Contrasts* written for Benny Goodman
1940	Leaves Hungary for the US
1943	Concerto for Orchestra

KEY WORKS

MUSIC FOR STRINGS, PERCUSSION, AND CELESTE
ORCHESTRAL   ⏱ 34:00   📖 4

This piece was written for Paul Sacher and the Basle Chamber Orchestra in 1936. As with many of Bartók's works, percussion features strongly, not only as a means of rhythmic organization, but also as colour. He integrates folk music and original material highly successfully in this work.

BLUEBEARD'S CASTLE, OP. 11
OPERA   ⏱ 32:00   📖 1

Bluebeard's Castle is a one-act opera of 1911, based on a libretto by Béla Balázs. The work is a dark and expressionistic examination of the human soul, involving just Duke

Bluebeard and his new wife, Judith. The two characters are represented by different kinds of music: Bluebeard by pentatonic melody and Judith by tortured chromatic lines.

MIKROKOSMOS
SOLO PIANO   📖 150+

Between 1932 and 1939, Bartók composed over 150 short piano pieces as part of a set called the *Mikrokosmos*. Ranging from easy to concert-standard, they reflected his wish to introduce Eastern European and Arabic folk tunes to a wider audience, as well as to create piano pieces for his young son Péter to learn. Many of these pieces show Bartók's interest in mirror images between left- and right-hand patterns.

FOCUS

CONCERTO FOR ORCHESTRA

ORCHESTRAL 🕙 37:30 📖 5 ♫

The conductor Serge Koussevitsky commissioned the Concerto for Orchestra in memory of his late wife, Nathalie. The title reflects Bartók's admiration for the virtuosity of Koussevitsky's orchestra.

INTRODUCTION (ALLEGRO NON TROPPO – ALLEGRO VIVACE) The first movement begins mysteriously with a theme in the low strings accompanied by whispering violin tremolandi. Instrumental groups are gradually added until the bright and energetic Allegro vivace begins with a theme from the violins. A second theme is introduced by solo trombone in regular metre.

GAME OF THE PAIRS (ALLEGRETTO SCHERZANDO) The second movement features pairs of instruments, which move at all times in parallel: the bassoons (a sixth apart) are followed by oboes (a third apart), clarinets (a seventh apart), flutes (a fifth apart), and, finally, trumpets (a second apart). The chorale-like middle section is given to the brass.

ELEGY (ANDANTE, NON TROPPO) Bartók called the third movement a "lugubrious death song". The opening theme on

low strings recalls the beginning of the first movement. The misty section for flutes and clarinets that follows is accompanied by string tremolandi and harp glissandi. The music becomes more and more agitated until the passionate material from the first movement reappears.

INTERMEZZO INTERROTTO (ALLEGRETTO) This movement was apparently influenced by a broadcast of Shostakovich's Symphony No. 7. Bartók thought that Shostakovich's patriotism was misguided and quoted a theme of that work in raucous parody. There is then an outrageous response from muted trumpets, clarinets, and trombones.

FINALE (PRESTO) The finale is announced by a horn fanfare and athletic strings. The flurry of movement never lets up, and the coda is a brilliant and exciting culmination to one of the great orchestral works of the century.

> **INFLUENCES**
>
> Bartók was greatly influenced by the folk music of Eastern Europe. In his youth he admired the music of Richard Strauss and later in his career developed an interest in Baroque music as well as the compositions of contemporaries such as Stravinsky. He influenced the composers Lutoslawski and Britten.

George Enescu

1881–1955   **Romanian**   c.300

Despite his astounding memory for music – he knew every note of Wagner's *The Ring of the Nibelung* – and his prodigious ability as a violinist, Romania's greatest composer was a modest man. Perhaps too modest: he wrote prolifically, but published only 33 works with opus numbers. When he conducted his folk-inspired *Poème roumain* in Bucharest at 17, he instantly became a figure of national importance. Enescu spent his long career moving between France and Romania, performing internationally, composing (his main love), and developing Romanian musical life. His music reflects the variety of stylistic changes he saw in his lifetime, and his chamber works are especially fine. A perfectionist, he spent ten years writing his opera, *Oedipus*.

MILESTONES	
1889	First public performance, aged eight
1893	Studies at Paris Conservatoire
1898	*Poème roumain* for orchestra triumphs
1926	Composes Violin Sonata No. 3
1936	*Oedipus*, opera, premiered, Paris
1946	Exiled from Romania, falls ill
1954	Writes Chamber Symphony

Although Enescu's work transcended nationalism, he never abandoned his beloved native country.

Zoltán Kodály

1882–1967   **Hungarian**   c.250

An all-round, practical musician who needed little formal tuition, Kodály did his doctoral thesis on Hungarian folk song, which he collected in rural tours over many decades. Like his friend Bartók, he used it to inspire his own melodic, inventive work, much of it choral. His flourishing career – as academy teacher, critic, scholar, and composer – was affected by the war, but was revived internationally by *Psalmus Hungaricus*. To the end of his life he toured worldwide, both lecturing and conducting his own works. Composing for 70 years, and constantly promoting Hungarian music, Kodály was lavishly honoured at home and abroad. His logical step-by-step teaching methods are still highly influential today.

As a keen educator, Kodály devoted much of his time to visiting Hungarian schools and was actively involved in the development of music for children.

MILESTONES	
1915	Solo Cello Sonata Op 8
1926	Composes *Háry János*, Singspiel
1927	*Psalmus Hungaricus* premiered in London
1933	Composes *Dances of Galánta*, orchestra
1939	Writes *The Peacock* variations, orchestra
1945	Becomes president of the Hungarian Arts Council

Percy Grainger

⬤ 1882–1961 🏳 Australian ✍ 186

Grainger was a virtuoso pianist, a collector, and arranger of folk songs, and a highly original composer. With an unusual breadth of creative vision, his interests spanned the ages – from medieval music to the latest developments by his contemporaries Delius and Grieg. He was a pioneer of what he called "free music" and was particularly keen that music should be available for all.

LIFE AND MUSIC

Grainger studied for a short time with Ferruccio Busoni in Germany, but despite a mutual admiration for each other's abilities, their temperaments were too different to remain on close terms. When he moved to London in 1901, Grainger began to establish himself a reputation as a concert pianist. During his 20s he became friendly with Edvard Grieg, who encouraged him to collect English folk songs; these form the basis for many of his inspired settings, such as *Country Gardens* and *Molly on the Shore*. Often experimental in his approach, Grainger's interest in "free music" led him to come up with the new idea of "elastic scoring" – meaning that a work could be played by whatever instruments happened to be available, rather than by a prescribed instrumentation.

MILESTONES

1894	Makes his début in Melbourne
1895	Studies in Frankfurt
1901	Moves to London; composes *Hill Song No. 1*
1903	Tours Australia, New Zealand, and South Africa
1907	Writes *Molly on the Shore*, orchestra
1913	Composes *The Warriors*, orchestra
1914	*Tribute to Foster* published; moves to US
1917	Serves in US Army
1918	Composes *Country Gardens*, folk song setting
1922	Mother commits suicide
1928	Marries Ella Ström at première of *To a Nordic Princess*, Hollywood Bowl

KEY WORKS

HILL SONG NO. 1

CHAMBER ⏱ 27:00 📖 1 ♆

Grainger considered this to be his finest work, and it was originally scored for a highly unusual ensemble of wind instruments: with the exception of the piccolos, the group comprised double-reed instruments which produce a nasal sound quality (he asked for oboes, cor anglais, bassoons, and contra-bassoon). He later felt that this was not realistic and rescored the work in 1923

Grainger's close bond with his mother was only broken when she committed suicide by jumping off a New York skyscraper.

for an even more diverse group. There are five main sections, and the "fast walking pace" is somewhat obscured by the frequently changing metre.

TRIBUTE TO FOSTER

CHORAL ⏱ 21:00 📖 1 🎵🎵🎵🎵

Late in life, Grainger recalled his mother having sung him to sleep with the tune of Stephen Foster's "Camptown Races". His *Tribute to Foster* uses an up-tempo version of the tune in its outer sections and a slow lullaby version in the middle section, in which the choir play "musical glasses".

"*Music is given to us with the sole purpose of establishing an order in things, including, and particularly, the coordination between man and time.*"

IGOR STRAVINSKY

Igor Stravinsky

● 1882–1971   ⚑ Russian   ✍ 127

Generally considered to be the greatest composer of the previous century, Stravinsky's long life spanned continents, cultures, and eras. As an iconic figure in the modern arts, he was perhaps equalled only by Pablo Picasso, whose early innovations created the same shock and excitement. He also resembled Picasso in his gift for radical artistic transformations, yet, despite this quality, Stravinsky always remained ineffably himself.

LIFE

Stravinsky was born near St Petersburg, where his father was principal bass singer with the Imperial Opera at the Mariinsky Theatre. Borodin, Dostoyevsky, and Stravinsky's future teacher, Rimsky-Korsakov, were family friends. Stravinsky's talent was not obvious at first, and he was forced to study law at St Petersburg University, applying himself to music in his free time. Success came in 1910, with the commission of *The Firebird* from Serge Diaghilev, director of the Ballets Russes. The ballet's Paris premiere also launched the career of another Diaghilev protégé, the dancer Vaslav Nijinsky, and was hugely successful. Diaghilev encouraged Stravinsky to develop his "Russian" vein, commissioning further ballets such as *The Rite of Spring*, whose premiere prompted part of the audience to riot. Stravinsky joined Europe's artistic elite, with many of whom (Picasso, Gide, Cocteau) he went on to collaborate in further ballets. Settling in Switzerland, then France, Stravinsky was never to live in Russia again. In mid-career, he fell increasingly under the influence of the European "Classical" heritage. Having fought off tuberculosis, he fled World War II, moving to the United States and spending his final years in the company of other notable émigrés in Hollywood.

Despite its "shocking" modernity, Stravinsky's music is also very structured, precise, and controlled, full of artifice and theatricality.

MUSICAL OUTPUT

Total: 127

	1882	1910	1930	1950	1971
CONCERTOS (2)		1	1		
OTHER ORCHESTRAL (22)	3	7	8	4	
OTHER INSTRUMENTAL (47)	4	22	16	5	
OPERAS (3)		2		1	
BALLETS (12)	1	6	4	1	
SOLO VOCAL (25)	7	9	3	6	
CHORAL (16)	1	3	5	7	

MUSIC

Stravinsky's musical output falls into three main periods: "Russian", "Neo-Classical", and "serial" (or "12-tone"). From his teacher, Rimsky-Korsakov, Stravinsky had learnt to orchestrate in the exquisite, iridescent colours that characterize *The Firebird*. As Serge Diaghilev challenged him to find an ever-more Russian style, Stravinsky began to incorporate Russian folk tunes (something the touchy composer played down in later years) and to invent new sounds based on pounding, irregular rhythms and pungent harmonies. The result was an entirely original kind of music beyond simple tonality and which (especially in *The Rite of Spring*) could not be written in a constant time signature. Such

Serge Diaghilev, Russian impresario and founder of the Ballets Russes, gave Stravinsky his first ballet commission.

music shocked and excited, flying in the face of the accepted rules of music composition. However, in time (and to the displeasure of those who had admired him for his uncompromising originality), his music returned to the tonal idiom. Stravinsky created the "Neo-Classical style", which its detractors called "classicism with wrong notes". Arnold Schoenberg, inventor of the 12-tone system, was particularly disdainful of such backsliding, and the mutual recriminations which often marked relations between Neo-Classicists and serialists (not excluding Schoenberg's and Stravinsky's own somewhat inflammatory statements) made it all the more astonishing to many when, in the US, Stravinsky underwent his final metamorphosis, and himself took up the 12-tone method.

MILESTONES

1902	Studies law at university, and composition with Rimsky-Korsakov
1909	Premiere of *Scherzo fantastique*; Diaghilev commissions *The Firebird*
1910	Debussy expresses his admiration; he and Stravinsky become friends
1913	Premiere of *The Rite of Spring*
1920	At Diaghilev's suggestion, arranges music by Pergolesi for *Pulcinella*
1921	Writes *Les Noces* and embarks on love affair with Vera Sudeykina
1926	Returns to the Russian Orthodox Church after experiencing a "miracle" in Venice
1927	Première of *Oedipus Rex*; the work is poorly received
1928	US premiere of Apollo
1937	Adopts French citizenship; writes last piece in Europe, Dumbarton Oaks
1939	Sails for the US after the deaths of his eldest daughter and first wife

1940	*The Rite of Spring* features in Walt Disney's animated film, *Fantasia*
1945	Writes "Ebony" Concerto for Woody Hermann's jazz band.
1951	Premiere of *The Rake's Progress*, opera
1962	Revisits Russia; composes *Elegy* on the death of John F Kennedy.
1964	Completion of *Requiem Canticles*, his last major work

In 1913, with choreography by Vaslav Nijinsky, Stravinsky's *The Rite of Spring* received its troubled premiere at the Théâtre de Champs Elysées, Paris, a theatre which is still in existence today.

KEYWORKS

THE FIREBIRD

BALLET 45:00 1

The ballet tells the story of the battle between the magical Firebird and the demon Kashchey. Dancers who missed their cues at the premiere blamed their confusion on the unusualness of the orchestration.

LES NOCES ("THE WEDDINGS")

BALLET 25:00 4

The most startlingly scored of all Stravinsky's works, *Les noces* evokes both the earthiness of peasant life and the hieratic splendour of Russian Orthodox ritual.

PULCINELLA

BALLET 38:00 1

Inspired by the Italian commedia dell'arte, this work arranges music by Pergolesi and his 18th-century contemporaries. However, by slight changes of harmony and idiosyncratic orchestration, Stravinsky makes the music entirely his own.

APOLLO

BALLET 30:00 2

A ballet of Classical poise and restraint, scored for strings alone, *Apollo* began Stravinsky's connection with the inspired choreographer of so many of his later works, George Balanchine.

AGON

BALLET 24:00 12

An ingenious conflation of styles and periods, *Agon* takes inspiration from Renaissance dance and works by his contemporaries Boulez and Stockhausen.

OEDIPUS REX

CHORAL 48:00 2

Stravinsky's collaborator Jean Cocteau based the text of this "opera-oratorio" on Greek tragedy, yet Stravinsky chose to set the text in Latin. Between movements, a spoken narration keeps the audience abreast of the story.

THE RAKE'S PROGRESS

OPERA 135:00 3

This work, with a libretto by W H Auden and Chester Kallman, was based on the series of engravings of the same name by English 18th-century painter and moralist William Hogarth. A "number opera" with arias and recitatives, it marked the end-point of Stravinsky's Neo-Classical phase. It was Stravinsky's largest work, and premiered in Venice in 1951.

> **INFLUENCES**
>
> Stravinsky's impact on other composers was immediate. Edgard Varèse's *Amèriques* is full of reminiscences of *The Rite of Spring*. In fact, most music of recent times could not have been written without Stravinsky's innovations. Villa-Lobos, Hindemith, Messiaen, Britten, Poulenc, Bernstein, Pärt – all these composers owe him a profound debt.

The Firebird premiered in Paris in 1910. Its success transformed Stravinsky's career and strengthened his friendship with Diaghilev, with whom he produced two more balletic works: *Petrushka* (1911) and *The Rite of Spring* (1913).

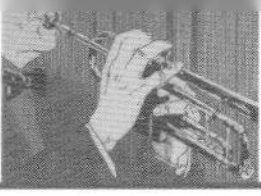

FOCUS

DUMBARTON OAKS

CONCERTO 11:00 3

Written at a time of many crises in Stravinsky's life, *Dunbarton Oaks* is a reminder of his assertion that music "expresses nothing but itself". The work met with a mixed reaction on its premiere, being deplored by those who thought serious composers should be in the vanguard of a continuous musical revolution.

FIRST MOVEMENT (TEMPO GIUSTO, 4:00) The opening movement is reminiscent of J S Bach's "Brandenburg" Concertos. The modest instrumental forces and the regularity of the metre all hark back to Baroque practice.

SECOND MOVEMENT (ALLEGRETTO, 3:00) This has a sly, jazzy insouciance. It features flute and violin as solo instruments – plus the clarinet, an instrument that was unknown in Baroque times.

THIRD MOVEMENT (CON MOTO, 4:00) A movement with a pronounced "finale", returning to the Baroque model. Yet Stravinsky abandons counterpoint in favour of his characteristic games of deft chordal interplay, shifting accents and sprightly syncopation.

PETRUSHKA

BALLET 32:00 4

Stravinsky first intended *Petrushka* to be a concert work for piano and orchestra, but he became possessed by the idea of the piano representing "a puppet suddenly endowed with life, exasperating the patience of the orchestra with diabolical cascades of arpeggios". Diaghilev soon persuaded him that the work was destined to be a new ballet.

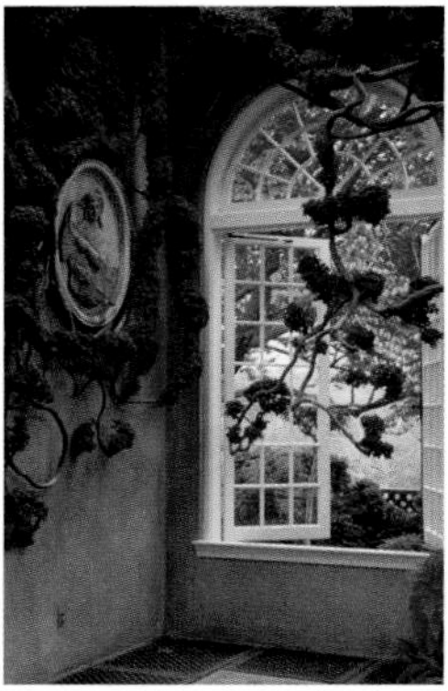

Dumbarton Oaks takes its name from the estate of Roberts Woods Bliss, who commissioned the piece for his 30th wedding anniversary in 1938.

THE RITE OF SPRING

BALLET 32:00 2

The Rite of Spring, set in primeval Russia, portrays a ritual in which a young girl dances herself to death to win the favour of the god of Spring. The ballet is a work of savage ecstasy, driven forward by its powerful, primitive rhythms.

PART ONE (15:30) After the mysterious Introduction comes the "Dance of the Adolescents", in which young girls dance to the insistent stamping of a single chord repeated continuously with changing accents, while off-beat horn chords punch the air. After further ritual dancing, the first part of the ballet breaks off in mid-air like a terrifying cliff-hanger.

PART TWO (16:30) Both parts of the ballet begin quietly and end in pulsing violence. In the dawn-like introduction

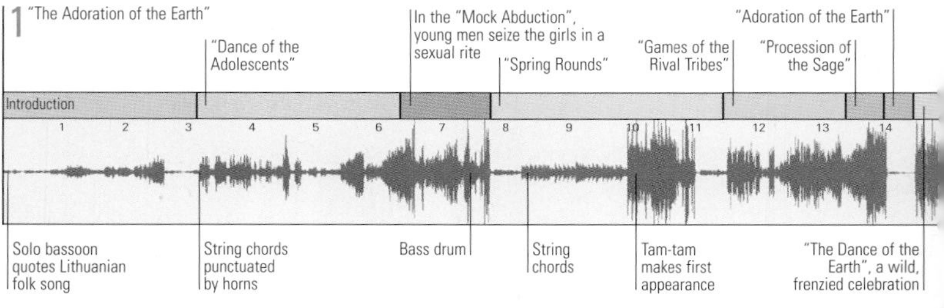
1
"The Adoration of the Earth"
"Dance of the Adolescents"
In the "Mock Abduction", young men seize the girls in a sexual rite
"Spring Rounds"
"Games of the Rival Tribes"
"Adoration of the Earth"
"Procession of the Sage"
Introduction
1
2
3
4
5
6
7
8
9
10
11
12
13
14
Solo bassoon quotes Lithuanian folk song
String chords punctuated by horns
Bass drum
String chords
Tam-tam makes first appearance
"The Dance of the Earth", a wild, frenzied celebration

FIRST PART (10:00) *Petrushka* is set in St Petersburg during the Shrovetide Fair. Superimposing a number of characterful instrumental lines and harmonies, the music evokes the ebb and flow of the crowd, interspersed with the antics of street entertainers.

SECOND PART (4:00) Petrushka is in his cell. Hiccups of melody suggest the jerking puppet, whilst melancholy, discordant reveries of piano and clarinet evoke Petrushka's hopeless love for the heartless Ballerina.

THIRD PART (5:00) Petrushka's rival in love, a handsome, scimitar-wielding Blackamoor, dances with the Ballerina. He is portrayed by a trumpet, she by a coy flute; mechanically tender, the music stutters and preens, evoking the reedy sonorities of a fairground organ.

FOURTH PART (13:00) Suddenly Petrushka is chased from a tent and cut down by the Blackamoor's scimitar. The crowd disperses, and in the eerie twilight Petrushka (or his ghost) returns to haunt the terrified showman – and to taunt anyone in the audience who might have been moved by the tale.

to the second part, some of the strings play delicate harmonics while others sound shudders of fearful anticipation.

Stravinsky keeps several dramatic orchestral effects in reserve for the final climax. As the girl chosen for the sacrifice dances herself to death, the horns play "with bells up", projecting their exultant high notes straight over the heads of the orchestra and out into the auditorium.

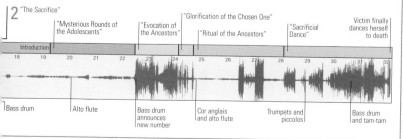

The ecstatic rhythms of *The Rite of Spring* have ensured its continuing popularity, both as a ballet and as a concert piece. This performance at Avignon in 1995 was choreographed by Pina Bausch.

2 "The Sacrifice"

"Mysterious Rounds of the Adolescents"

"Evocation of the Ancestors"

"Glorification of the Chosen One"

"Ritual of the Ancestors"

"Sacrificial Dance"

Victim finally dances herself to death

Introduction

18 19 20 21 22 23 24 25 26 27 28 29 30 31 32

Bass drum | Alto flute | Bass drum announces new number | Cor anglais and alto flute | Trumpets and piccolos | Bass drum and tam-tam

Darius Milhaud

● 1892–1974   🏳 French   ✍ 426

Milhaud was incredibly prolific and it is unavoidable that his output should be uneven in quality, but it is studded with brilliant little jewels as well as works of vast ambition. Much of his work is saturated with the colour and warmth of his native Provence and an optimistic spirit, which, in later life, survived critical disfavour and decades in which severe arthritis confined him to a wheelchair.

LIFE AND MUSIC

Milhaud entered the Paris Conservatoire at 17 and then, in 1917, was taken to Rio de Janeiro by poet and diplomat, Paul Claudel, so that they might work on music theatre projects together. The music of Brazil made a lasting impression on Milhaud. Despite deep-seated differences, (he was unshakeably Jewish in his faith, Claudel a proselytizing Catholic), they collaborated for many years. In later life, Milhaud's career as a teacher alternated between the Paris Conservatoire and the US. His pupils covered the spectrum of 20th-century music and included Iannis Xenakis, Stockhausen and Dave Brubeck.

MILESTONES

1909	Studies violin at Paris Conservatoire, then composition there
1917	Composes *Les Choëphores* for stage; travels to Brazil with Claudel
1920s	Is member of "Les Six" radical young French composers' group
1919	Writes ballet *Le bœuf sur le toit* in collaboration with Jean Cocteau
1921	Ballet *L'homme et son désir* premiered
1930	Opera *Christophe Colomb* is acclaimed
1932	Leaves Nazi-occupied France for US

KEY WORKS

LES CHOËPHORES

MUSIC THEATRE   🔊 33:00   📖 7   ♒♒ ♨ ♁

Some of Milhaud's first and finest music was for Claudel's translation of Aeschylus' *Oresteia*. Devising a way of setting texts of elemental force, Milhaud had passages spoken by the chorus or narrator to a purely percussion backing. The "Incantation" section is stern, bracing, rich, and atmospheric.

Milhaud wrote *Saudados do Brazil* in 1920–21 as a dance suite for piano, but later orchestrated it.

LE BŒUF SUR LE TOIT

BALLET   🔊 15:30   📖 1   ♒♒

This was Milhaud's most popular work right from the start, even though it includes bi-tonal passages (music in two keys at once): one of his favourite devices. He was dismayed that people thought of him as a prankster, largely because of this witty and joyous tribute to the music of Brazil. But, however uproarious it sounds in his hands, he said that he sensed the dark side of this gaiety.

Paul Hindemith

◔ 1895–1963   ⚑ German   ✍ 415

A prolific composer and amazingly gifted all-round musician, Hindemith wrote significant pieces for almost every known instrument in Classical music, many of which he could play himself. His early works, often mixing jazz with Neo-Classicism, labelled him a mischief-maker – a far cry from the pedant detractors accused him of becoming later on. His best works, such as *Mathis der Maler*, resound with a timeless nobility.

LIFE AND MUSIC

Always a composer first and foremost, Hindemith nonetheless spent the first half of his life making his living as a full-time performer. He became first violinist at the Frankfurt opera house while still a student at the city's conservatory and was soon playing viola in professional quartets. Hearing of the death of King George V the night before appearing as a soloist in England, he wrote his *Trauermusik* for violin and string orchestra at one sitting – allegedly on the train. During the Nazi era, he lived in the US, teaching composition at Yale. His youthful exuberance sometimes surfaced even in later works such as his *Concerto for Orchestra* and *Symphonic Metamorphoses on a Theme of Weber*, but his style is generally characterized by his love of Baroque counterpoint and Classical forms.

MILESTONES

1918	Serves as a military bandsman
1921	Opera *Murderer, Hope of Women*, to a libretto by Expressionist painter Oskar Kokoschka, causes outrage
1922	Completes Kammermusik No. 1
1923	Programmes the Donaueschingen Music Festival, where his song cycle, *The Life of Mary*, is premiered
1929	Plays in string trio with cellist Emmuel Feuermann
1934	Fürtwangler premieres *Mathis der Maler* in Berlin, and defends Hindemith against Nazis in a newspaper article
1940	Takes US citizenship
1953	Returns to Europe
1957	Conducts premiere of his opera *The Harmony of the World* in Munich

KEY WORKS

KAMMERMUSIK NO. 1, OP. 24 NO. 1.

CHAMBER   ⏲ 15:00   ▭ 4   ♫

Hindemith modelled his early "Chamber Music" series on Bach's *Brandenburg Concertos*. Most feature a solo instrument, but this work is for a band of equals, playing – among other instruments – xylophone, accordion, trumpet, and siren. The music is inventive and uproarious in equal measure. It was written to inaugurate the Donaueschingen Festivals in 1921 with a minimum of pomposity.

Kammermusik No. 6 is scored for the viola d'amore, a Baroque instrument favoured by Hindemith.

MATHIS DER MALER – SYMPHONIE

ORCHESTRAL   ⏲ 27:00   ▭ 3   ✿

This symphony consists of preludes and studies for an opera Hindemith later wrote on the life of the German painter, Matthias Grünewald. It portrays panels from the Isenheim altarpiece: the *Concert of the Angels*, *Entombment of Christ*, and *Torments of St Anthony*. The last movement is an instrumental version of the opera's climactic scene, when the anguished painter identifies himself with the tormented saint – surely an echo of Hindemith's own predicament in the troubled 1930s.

Francis Poulenc

⬤ 1899–1963   🏳 French   ✍ 185

Poulenc was well aware that he was not a musical innovator, but believed there was still a place for new music that used familiar means. As a master of natural, unpretentious melody, Poulenc has few rivals; his manner of blending Neo-Classical harmonies with the bittersweet touches of French popular song gives his music a distinct and subtle charm, even when it touches on tragedy.

LIFE AND MUSIC

Poulenc was born into a cultured and wealthy Parisian family (the pharmaceutical giant Rhône-Poulenc still carries its name). Although he studied piano from childhood, he was 22 years old before he went to Charles Koechlin for composition lessons. He joined the group of young French composers known as "Les Six" and, in 1923, Diaghilev commissioned a ballet from him *Les biches* which achieved popular and critical success. From the 1930s, Poulenc gave concerts of his own songs with the baritone Pierre Bernac. By turns joyous and melancholy, sacred and profane, Poulenc's music faithfully reflects its composer – a manic depressive, a devout Catholic, and one of the few public figures of his time to be openly (and often turbulently) gay.

MILESTONES

1913	Studies piano with Ricardo Viñes
1917	First piece *La Rhapsodie Negre* performed in public. Stravinsky helps him find a publisher
1924	*Les biches* performed by the Ballet Russes in Monte Carlo.
1934	Forms duo with Pierre Bernac
1936	Makes pilgrimage to Notre-Dame de Rocamadour, and writes *Litanies à la vierge noire*
1938	Concerto for organ, strings and timpani
1948	First tours America with Bernac
1957	Composes his great opera, *Dialogues des Carmelites*
1958	*La Voix Humaine* to text by Cocteau

KEY WORKS

SONATA FOR OBOE AND PIANO

CHAMBER   ⏱ 13:00   📖 3   ♉

Poulenc had a gift for chamber music and a special understanding of wind instruments. Towards the end of his life, he wrote a number of sonatas for piano and wind, and this proved to be the last. Dedicated to the memory of Prokofiev, it is a plangent, elegiac piece – all the more haunting for being the composer's own swansong.

Perhaps Poulenc's greatest success was his surrealist comic opera, *Les Mamelles de Tirésias*, based on a farce by Apollinaire.

CONCERTO FOR ORGAN, STRINGS, AND TIMPANI

ORCHESTRAL   ⏱ 22:00   📖 7   ♫

In middle life, after the death of a close friend, Poulenc was increasingly drawn to religion. In 1938, when he wrote this piece, he joked that it showed a "Poulenc who was on his way to joining a monastery". Yet the work's seven sections cover the gamut of his style, ranging from irreverent burlesque to gothic majesty. The key (G minor) is perhaps an indication of its debt to Bach's G minor Fantasia.

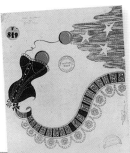

William Walton

● 1902–1983   ▥ English   ✍ 121

A largely self-taught composer, Walton was one of the great traditionalists of the 20th century. In time, he became the pre-eminent British "establishment" composer, inheriting the mantle of Elgar, both for his mastery of the English choral style and for his celebrated ceremonial music. A man of fastidious musical taste, his major works are relatively few, but of magisterial quality.

LIFE AND MUSIC

Walton owed much to his fortunate early connections. A boy chorister at Christ Church Cathedral, Oxford, he stayed at the university to study music, and was befriended by the Sitwells, an aristocratic family of writers who supported Walton whilst he established his career. His first famous work was *Façade* – an "entertainment" much influenced by the jazz of the "flapper" era – to which Edith Sitwell recited her melodious bohemian poetry. Walton's finest pieces were all written early in his career – the expressive Viola Concerto, the stupendous oratorio *Belshazzar's Feast*, and his renowned Symphony No. 1. His war-time film scores won him great popular acclaim. In later years, he lived with his Argentinian wife on the picturesque island of Ischia, near Naples.

MILESTONES	
1912	Becomes a chorister in Oxford
1920	Moves in with the Sitwells
1922	Premiere of *Façade*
1931	*Belshazzar's Feast*, oratorio, premiered to great acclaim
1935	Leaves the Sitwells, who disapprove of his liaison with Lady Alice Wimborne
1936	Writes *Crown Imperial* for George VI's coronation
1939	Violin Concerto for Jascha Heifetz
1943	Writes film score for *Henry V*
1951	Receives knighthood
1956	Composes music for the coronation of Elizabeth II
1954	*Troilus and Cressida*, opera, performed

KEY WORKS

SYMPHONY NO. 1

ORCHESTRAL   ⏱ 40:00   ▥ 4

Most of this symphony was composed between 1932 and 1933, and the white heat of its intensity owes much to a turbulent love affair with Imma von Dörnberg, a baroness with whom Walton had been living in Switzerland. The four movement work was premiered late in 1935 by the conductor Sir Hamilton Harty; its rapturous reception proved to be the zenith of Walton's life and achievements.

BELSHAZZAR'S FEAST

ORATORIO   ⏱ 35:00   ▥ 10

This is a work of harsh splendour for orchestra, baritone soloist, and choir (for which, as a former boy chorister, Walton always wrote magnificently). Walton treats Belshazzar's story not as sacred scripture, but as a lurid tale of the supernatural, and the work crams all the drama of an opera or film score into just half an hour.

Walton's magnificent film score for Laurence Olivier's *Henry V* was one of his most outstanding achievements.

Constant Lambert

● 1905–1951   ◪ English   ✍ 30

Lambert composed his first orchestral work at the precocious age of 13, but in later life could never dedicate himself to composition with the energy his talent deserved. He was not helped by poor health and alcoholism. His most successful work, the ebullient *The Rio Grande*, made such an impression on public and critics alike that it overshadowed his less extrovert pieces – a situation which perhaps persists even today.

LIFE AND MUSIC

Lambert's father was a painter who left his family for Australia when Constant was only 15. After studying composition with Vaughan Williams at the Royal College of Music and conducting with Malcom Sargent, Lambert became friends with William Walton, Peter Warlock, and painter Charles Ricketts. He then met Serge Diaghilev, who commissioned the 22-year-old composer to write a ballet, *Romeo and Juliet*, but it was *The Rio Grande* in 1927 that made Lambert's name. Always short of money, he pursued a busy career as a conductor, eventually becoming the founding music director of the Royal Ballet. He was also a gifted writer and in his final decade, he achieved notoriety as an eloquent, and sometimes merciless, critic.

MILESTONES	
1920	Father deserts family
1920s	Wins a scholarship at Royal College of Music in London
1923	Encounters jazz – a lifelong influence
1926	Co-recites with Edith Sitwell at premiere of Walton's *Façade*
1926	*Romeo and Juliet*, ballet, premiered in Monte Carlo by Ballets Russes
1927	*The Rio Grande*, acclaimed choral work
1931	Made music director at Sadler's Wells
1934	Publishes *Music Ho!*, a well-written, richly personal view of recent music
1935	Finishes *Summer's Last Will and Testament*
1938	Writes ballet, *Horoscope*, for Margot Fonteyn and Vic-Wells company

KEY WORKS

THE RIO GRANDE

CHORAL   ⏱ 15:00   📖 3   🎵 🔊 🎶

Setting a poem by Lambert's friend, Sacheverell Sitwell, this is an Englishman's fantasy portrait of Brazil. It provides a heady cocktail of languid exoticism, jazz, and rousing choral writing.

SUMMER'S LAST WILL AND TESTAMENT

CHORAL   ⏱ 50:00   📖 7   🎵 🎶 🎵

Lambert valued this haunting, valedictory piece as his best work, not only, perhaps, for its quality, but also because it was true to his melancholic nature. The sombre mood creates tensions which are finally released in the sixth movement's frenetic dance of death. The last part sets words by the Elizabethan poet Thomas Nashe.

HOROSCOPE

ORCHESTRAL   ⏱ 25:00   📖 5   🎵

Lambert's one-act ballet *Horoscope* was a tribute to his close friendship with Margot Fonteyn and choreographer Frederick Ashton. The glittering orchestral suite that Lambert drew from it consists of five contrasting dances.

Dame Margot Fonteyn (seen here in *Horoscope*) and Lambert were both leading figures in the birth of English national ballet.

Carl Ruggles

🔵 1876–1971   🏴 American   ✍ 40

Ruggles had only eight works published, but was held in high regard by his experimentalist colleagues Charles Ives and Henry Cowell. Like them, he looked for radical new approaches to writing in his own independent style, creating largely atonal, dissonant music.

He frequently revised his works and heard his longest and best-known piece, *Sun-Treader*, only from a recording. He turned increasingly to painting in later life.

MILESTONES

1920s	Work published in Cowell's New Music Edition and is noticed by Ives
1924	Publishes *Men and Mountains*, orchestral
1929	Befriends Charles Ives
1931	Completes *Sun-Treader*, orchestral
1950	Finishes *Evocations*, piano, begun 1937
1965	First hears *Men and Mountains*

Walter Piston

🔵 1894–1976   🏴 American   ✍ 80

Largely self-taught as a musician (he trained as an engineer and painter) Piston learned various instruments in dance bands and ended up as a respected, meticulous, yet unpedantic teacher at Harvard. An expert in orchestration and theory, he wrote a set of highly esteemed textbooks and received many honours. His music is Neo-Classical in style and often notable for its strong rhythms. He had popular success with pieces such as *The Incredible Flutist*, his only stage work, and his even-numbered symphonies.

MILESTONES

1926	Starts teaching at Harvard University
1938	Completes *The Incredible Flutist*, ballet
1943	Writes Symphony No. 2
1955	*Orchestration*, textbook, published
1959	Composes *Three New England Sketches*

Edgard Varèse

🔵 1883–1965   🏴 French   ✍ c.50

Varèse's driving ambition was to find radical new directions in music. After studying at the Paris Conservatoire, he spent much time in Berlin, befriending Busoni and Debussy (whom he introduced to Schoenberg's atonality). It was in New York, however, that he pioneered new sounds, treading the border between organization and noise. *Hyperprism* provoked audience outrage, but it, and pieces such as his percussion-plus-siren *Ionisation*, established his modernist credentials. His output was erratic, with many unfinished projects, and he suffered depression in the 1930s when refused research funds; but after World War II his advances in tape-based sound art proved revolutionary.

Varese said "I refuse to limit myself to sounds that have already been heard". In the 1940s he adopted the ondes Martenot, (here played by Maurice Martenot).

MILESTONES

1915	Leaves Europe to settle in New York
1923	Composes *Hyperprism*, for wind and percussion
1931	Composes *Ionisation*, percussion
1936	Composes *Density 21.5* for solo flute
1953	Starts experimenting with electronics
1954	Completes *Déserts*, instruments and tape

"*When you hear strong, masculine music like this, stand up and use your ears like a man!*"

CHARLES IVES, TO AN AUDIENCE MEMBER WHO WAS HECKLING
A NEW PIECE BY HIS FRIEND CARL RUGGLES

Charles Ives

⚫ 1874–1954   📕 American   ✍ 313

Charles Ives was a great pioneer modernist, who experimented with polytonality and multiple tempos and many-layered textures decades before the famous European modernists. However, in many ways he was a conservative, and a religious, hymn-singing vein runs through even his most radical pieces. The combination of experiment and sturdy affirmation gives his music a strenuous aspirational quality.

LIFE

Ives was the son of a provincial bandmaster with adventurous musical tastes. George Ives's fondness for getting his children to sing a hymn in one key while accompanying them in another left an indelible mark on his son's music. Ives was a precocious child: by the age of 14 he'd become the youngest salaried organist in Connecticut and had composed dozens of works. He studied music for four years at Yale University with Horatio Parker, who succeeded in instilling some academic discipline into his unruly student. In 1898 he got a job as an actuary, and ten years later married Harmony Twichell after a long courtship. Later he founded his own insurance firm with his old friend Julian Meyrick, and his high-minded principles and hard work made it one of the most respected firms in New York. In 1912 the Ives's bought a farm, to which they invited poor families to stay. One of these agreed to have their daughter adopted; she became Edith Osborne Ives. Declining health forced Ives to give up composing in 1926, and in 1930 he retired from the business. During the 1930s and 40s his music, which had been ignored, was rediscovered by younger admirers. During the 60s and 70s his music was championed by Stokowski, Bernstein and others, and his key pieces are now firmly in the repertoire.

The employees at Ives's insurance firm pretended not to know about the "old man's" weekend composing, which continued at breakneck pace up to and beyond World War I.

MUSICAL OUTPUT					Total: 313
ORCHESTRAL (43)	4	14	20	4	1
CHAMBER (23)		7	14	2	
KEYBOARD (23)	9	4	6	4	
CHORAL (42)	12	17	7	5	1
SONGS (182)	22	76	31	51	2
	1874	1894	1905	1915	1926	1954

MUSIC

Ives's style is made of many disparate things, but the elements aren't welded together; they keep their separateness. A typical Ives piece might have a sturdy hymn tune harmonized with sturdy chords (but in the wrong key), followed by a wildly rhapsodic line with tumbling piano chords. Or it might feature a quick all-American Stephen Collins Foster melody, next to slow, massive chordal clusters and Debussyan shimmers. However, Ives doesn't just put these ideas side by side, he puts them on top of each other, so they sound simultaneously. Ives was the first composer to have radically different sorts of music going on at once, an effect apparently inspired by childhood memories of hearing brass bands approaching Danbury town square, each playing in a different key and at a different speed. The effect is joyously anarchic. Ives has none of the anxiety of European modernists like Schoenberg. But, despite its democratic appearances, in the end the music affirms conservative values. Chaos is typically subsumed into a hymn tune and a sense of mystical affirmation.

The *Fourth of July* from *A Symphony: New England Holidays* (1913), which celebrates life in small-town America was one of Ives's most popular works.

MILESTONES	
1888	Becomes youngest salaried church organist in Connecticut
1894	Begins 4-year course at Yale
1907	Sets up own insurance business (Ives and Co) with Julian Myrick
1908	Marries Harmony Twichell
1915	Begins the mystical *Universe* Symphony; never completed
1916	Completes Fouth Symphony
1918	Heart attack persuades Ives to put his vast collection of sketches and manuscripts in order
1947	Receives Pulitzer Prize

KEY WORKS

STRING QUARTET NO. 2

CHAMBER   ⏱ 29:00   📖 3   ⚓

Ives described this quartet as an argument between four men who "converse, discuss, argue, fight, shake hands, shut up – then walk up the mountainside to view the firmament." Lowell Mason's hymn "Bethany" occurs in all three movements, and in the middle movement the second violin is cast as "Rollo", a character in a well-known children's book.

THE UNANSWERED QUESTION

ORCHESTRAL   ⏱ 6:00   📖 1   🎶

The first piece of *Two Contemplations* for chamber orchestra, this is a masterly example of Ives's ability to pile up different kinds of music moving at different speeds into a meaningful near-chaos. There is a slow-moving string background, a series of woodwind phrases which become ever more dissonant, and an enigmatic repeated trumpet "question".

CONCORD SONATA

SOLO PIANO   ⏱ 48:00   📖 4   🎧

This vast work was described by Ives as "one person's impression of the spirit of the literature, the philosophy, and the men of Concord, Massachussetts of over a half-century ago." As always with Ives, the music is peppered with quotations from marches and parlour songs.

FOCUS

THREE PLACES IN NEW ENGLAND
ORCHESTRAL   18:00   3

Composed between 1903 and 1914, this much-played orchestral piece follows the typical Ives progression from bracing co-existence of different elements, through riotous complexity, to a radiant vision of eternity.

THE "ST GAUDENS" IN BOSTON COMMON (8:00) Subtitled "Col. Shaw and his Colored Regiment", this section is an assemblage of marching tunes and songs, sounding as if overheard from a great distance.

PUTNAM'S CAMP, REDDING, CONNECTICUT (6:00) An amalgam of two pre-existing pieces, *Overture 1776* and *Country Band March*, this part is a perfect example of Ives's layering of two tempi, one above the other.

THE HOUSATONIC AT STOCKBRIDGE (4:00) Inspired by the memory of a morning walk that Ives and his wife took along the misty banks of the Housatonic, this is a modern chorale prelude, the hymn tune heard through a beautifully woven orchestral mist.

SYMPHONY NO. 4
ORCHESTRAL   31:00   4

This is the quintessential Ives work. The symphony is stuffed with quotations from hymns, marches, and songs. It absorbs many earlier and unfinished works, and the palette conjured by its vast orchestra ranges from the noisiest piled-up complexity to the ethereal delicacy of harp and violins.

FIRST MOVEMENT (PRELUDE, MAESTOSO, (3:00) According to Ives, this asks the question "Why?", to which the following movements offer three diverse answers. Stern fanfares are responded to by a beatific choir, with memories of "Bethany" and "Watchman, tell us of the Night".

SECOND MOVEMENT (ALLEGRETTO, 12:00) This is the most extreme movement Ives ever wrote. Crammed into this "comedy" is a riotous piled-up assemblage of melodies, quotations, polyrhythms, and quarter-tones, which summon up the chaos of life itself.

THIRD MOVEMENT (FUGUE, ANDANTE MODERATO, 8:00) A calm and correct fugue which, as Ives says, expresses "the reaction of life into formalism and ritualism."

FOURTH MOVEMENT (VERY SLOWLY, LARGO MAESTOSO, 8:00) Gathering everything heard so far into an affirmative apotheosis, a military-sounding dirge introduces memories of Ives's childhood, a chorus singing "Bethany" leads to a climax, and then the music fades into an evocation of eternity.

> **INFLUENCES**
>
> In the 1950s, John Cage gave Ives's American-sounding experiments a Zen Buddhist tinge, governed by chance. Elliott Carter went the other way, making Ives's complexity much more ordered. Since the 1960s, Ives's influence on composers as diverse as Luciano Berio, Frederic Rzewski, and Peter Maxwell Davies has been immense.

Roger Sessions

● 1896–1985 ♙ American ♬ 42

Born in Brooklyn, New York, Sessions was an intellectual prodigy – he wrote an opera at 13, graduated from Harvard at 18, and spoke French, Italian, German, and Russian. An able symphonist, he wrote nine symphonies as well as four concertos, three piano sonatas and many vocal pieces, and much of his work was written after he was 60. His technically difficult music has generally proved more popular with students and musicians than the public. However, this did not trouble the idealistic, good-humoured composer, who inspired many important American composers during his long and distinguished teaching career.

MILESTONES

1925	Moves to Europe for eight years
1923	The Black Maskers, incidental music, first performed
1957	Composes Symphony No. 3
1963	Montezuma, opera, produced
1965	Begins teaching at the Juilliard School of Music
1971	Writes Concerto for Orchestra

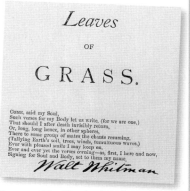

Leaves

OF

GRASS.

Come, said my Soul,
Such verses for my Body let us write, (for we are one,)
That should I after death invisibly return,
Or, long, long hence, in other spheres,
There to some group of mates the chants resuming,
(Tallying Earth's soil, trees, winds, tumultuous waves,)
Ever with pleased smile I may keep on,
Ever and ever yet the verses owning—as, first, I here and now,
Signing for Soul and Body, set to them my name,

Walt Whitman

The cantata *When Lilacs Last in the Dooryard Bloom'd* (1970) was an imaginative setting of verse from *Leaves of Grass* by Walt Whitman, Sessions' favourite poet.

Virgil Thomson

● 1896–1989 ♙ American ♬ c.300

Educated at Harvard, Thomson continued his studies in Paris, where he met Satie, who became a major influence on his work. There he also collaborated with fellow expatriate Gertrude Stein on his most famous work, the opera *Four Saints in Three Acts*, setting Stein's wordplay and random remarks (tidied up by Thomson's close friend, the painter Maurice Grosser) to a mosaic of hymn tunes, chant, and straightforward harmony. Back in the US he wrote film scores (often using American ingredients, such as cowboy tunes and spirituals) and orchestral pieces in various styles, and collaborated again with Stein. A fearless but respected critic, he lectured throughout the US and Europe; he also continued to compose, and received many honours.

In his score for *Louisiana Story* – a documentary about life in the bayou seen through the eyes of a Cajun boy – Thomson included many folk melodies.

MILESTONES

1928	Writes *Four Saints in Three Acts*, opera
1940	Returns to New York; becomes music critic for the *Herald Tribune*
1936	*The Plow that Broke the Plains*, film score
1947	Writes *The Mother of Us All*, opera
1948	*Louisiana Story*, film score, wins Pulitzer Prize
1968	Composes *Lord Byron*, opera

Henry Dixon Cowell

◔ 1897–1965   ᴾᵁ American   ◢ 996

Henry Cowell was one of America's rugged "can-do" modernist spirits, in the same mould as Nancarrow, Charles Ives, and John Cage. However, a vein of traditional religiosity can be heard beneath the modern surface of his work, in his allusions to hymns and chorales. Cowell had a tremendously liberating effect on later composers; as Cage put it, he was "the 'Open Sesame' for new music in America".

LIFE AND MUSIC

An unorthodox upbringing by parents who were "philosophical anarchists" left its mark on the young Cowell, and he found himself on the margins of musical life. In 1914, this talented "wild child" met his greatest mentor, ethnomusicologist Charles Seeger, who taught him much about modern music and what we now call "world music". Cowell's early works explore the modernist devices described in his pioneering book *New Musical Resources* and include tone clusters, graphic notation, the use of several simultaneous tempi and proto-electronic instruments, such as the rhythmicon. In later works an interest in Irish mythology comes to the fore, as part of a general move towards a startlingly eclectic sound-world combining modernism, "world music", and naively simple diatonic melodies.

MILESTONES

1914	Cowell's debut concert, includes *Adventures in Harmony*
1917	Composes *Quartet Romantic*
1923	European tour performing his ultra-modernist piano works
1927	Creates *New Music* – concert series, magazine, and record label
1928	Concerto for piano and orchestra
1930	His vision of music of the future: published
1933	Writes article *Towards Neo-Primitivism* about his interest ethnomusicology
1936	Homosexual encounter leads to arrest and four-year imprisonment
1949	Works for Columbia University
1957	Composes *Persian Set*, chamber music

KEY WORKS

EIGHT SIMULTANEOUS MOSAICS

EXPERIMENTAL   ☷ 9:00   ▭ 1   ⚐

Despite its late date (1963), this piece is amazingly experimental in form. There is no full score, only a series of instrumental parts whose combination in time is left deliberately free.

PERSIAN SET

CHAMBER   ☷ 20:00   ▭ 4   ⚐ ☍

Cowell intended this work to be "a simple record of musical contagion, written at the end of a three-month stay in Iran". Written for the Iranian lute (the tar) accompanied by a chamber orchestra, it is one of Cowell's successful evocations of distant music cultures.

Cowell was a pioneer of innovative piano effects, such as playing groups of keys together in "tone-clusters", and strumming the strings directly.

"I don't think there has been such an inspired melodist on this earth since Tchaikovsky..."

LEONARD BERNSTEIN

George Gershwin

● 1898–1937   ⚐ American   ✎ 369

George Gershwin was one of the most exuberantly talented and successful composers of the 20th century, and its most tragically short-lived. He had his first Broadway success in 1919, and his first "Classical" success in 1924, and thereafter remained dominant in both fields, winning the respect of such severe "Classical" masters as Rachmaninov and – amazingly – Arnold Schoenberg.

LIFE

Gershwin's parents were Russian Jews who emigrated to the US in the 1890s. From 1910 Gershwin studied piano seriously and soon progressed to Chopin, Liszt, and Debussy. In 1914 he abandoned Classical music in favour of Tin Pan Alley (though he returned to it later in life), by dropping out of High School to work for Jerome Remick and Co. In 1920 he had his first hit with *Swanee*, recorded by Al Jolson. Over the next four years he wrote five Broadway reviews, two London shows, and three Broadway ones, one of which, *Lady be Good*, was the first of many with lyrics by his brother Ira. In 1924 he gave the premiere of his *Rhapsody in Blue*. His new wealth allowed him to move into a smart townhouse on the Upper West Side, and to seduce innumerable women. During the late 1920s he followed up the success of *Rhapsody* with other "Classical" pieces including the Concerto in F and the Preludes. In 1928 he travelled in Europe and met Prokofiev, Milhaud, Ravel, and Berg. Through the 30s he divided his time between concert tours as a pianist and composing musicals, including *Strike up the Band* and *Girl Crazy*. In 1936 he and Ira signed a contract with RKO film studios, which led to *Shall we Dance?*, *A Damsel in Distress* and *The Goldwyn Follies*. Gershwin died at the height of his fame in 1937.

A true crossover artist, Gershwin's serious compositions remain highly popular in the Classical repertoire, and his stage and film songs continue to be jazz and vocal standards.

MUSICAL OUTPUT				Total: 369
ORCHESTRAL (6)		2	1	3
CHAMBER (9)	1	5		3
MUSICAL THEATRE (28)		13	11	4
FILM MUSICALS (7)		1		6
OPERAS (1)				1
SONGS (318)	3	122	96	97
1898	1919	1925	1931	1937

MUSIC

Gershwin's importance in the history of American "Classical" music should not obscure the fact that he was in essence a song writer. His genius needed no more than the four-minute frame of the popular song, with its predictable verse and chorus structure. They fall into a number of types: the sturdy march song such as "Swanee", "Strike up the Band"; fast, syncopated songs, such as "Fascinating Rhythm" and "I got Rhythm"; the slow romantic ballad, of which the best-known are "Someone to Watch over Me" and "Embraceable You"; and the medium-tempo song with an irresistible swinging beat, like "Nice Work if You can Get It". Though formally simple, these songs were enriched by startlingly original modulations.

The regular 2- and 4-bar phrases of his songs recur in Gershwin's concert works, and in his opera *Porgy and Bess*, as do the characteristic

MILESTONES	
1914	Starts work in Tin Pan Alley
1918	Has three songs accepted by Broadway shows
1919	First full Broadway show La La Lucille opens
1924	Lady be Good opens on Broadway; premiere of Rhapsody in Blue with Gershwin himself at the piano
1925	Concerto in F major premiered
1928	An American in Paris premiered
1930	*Girl Crazy* opens on Broadway
1932	*Cuban Overture*
1935	*Porgy and Bess* opens on Broadway
1936	Signs contract with RKO film studios and moves with his brother, Ira, to Hollywood, but dies the following year

"blue-note" harmonies of African-American music. The concert works achieve their effect by their melodic appeal and accumulation of contrasts, although the Concerto in F major shows a remarkable subtlety of form.

KEY WORKS

CONCERTO IN F MAJOR

ORCHESTRAL   33:00   3

Unlike the earlier *Rhapsody in Blue*, which was scored by an assistant, this concerto was scored by Gershwin himself. In the four years since composing *Rhapsody in Blue*, Gershwin had made a close study of European modernist composers, so it is not surprising that, whereas the earlier

rhapsody had relied on simple alternations of soloist and orchestra, the concerto makes use of thematic transformation (the recurrence of a main theme in different guises to lend unity to the piece). The result was the pinnacle of Gershwin's achievement as a concert composer.

AN AMERICAN IN PARIS

ORCHESTRAL   22:00   1

Gershwin said of this piece "my intention here is to portray the impressions of an American visitor in Paris as he strolls about the city, listens to various street noises and absorbs the French atmosphere". An opening section of infectious gaiety leads to a slow reflective blues, showing perhaps an attack of homesickness. But cheerfulness returns, and at the end "the street noises and French atmosphere are triumphant".

The film *An American in Paris* (1951), starring Gene Kelly and Leslie Caron, had a score by George Gershwin, lyrics by his brother Ira, and a book by Alan Jay Lerner.

PORGY AND BESS

OPERA   ⏱ 190:00   📖 3   ♫ ♙ ♟

Given Gershwin's love of African-American idioms, it is not surprising that his one "serious" music-drama should be on an African-American theme. The piece is criticized today for its clichéd, folksy image of African-Americans, but Gershwin can hardly be blamed for accepting the mindset of his time. The opera remains a riveting and profoundly moving work.

ACT ONE The action opens in Catfish Row, a poor fishing community. The drunken, brutal Crown kills a man during a craps game, then flees. The drug-dealer Sportin' Life offers to take Bess, Crown's woman, to New York with him. Instead Bess goes to stay with the crippled Porgy.

ACT TWO Porgy and Bess sing the love duet "Bess, you is my Woman now,", then Bess leaves for a picnic on an island. Crown appears at the picnic to reclaim Bess and she stays on the island with him. Two days later she is found, delirious. She wants to stay with Porgy, but is afraid that Crown still has a fatal hold over her. The act ends with a hurricane starting to blow.

ACT THREE Porgy kills Crown, but nobody gives him away. However, he is jailed for a week and, while he is away, Bess is drugged by Sportin' Life, who takes her to New York. When Porgy is freed, he vows to find her and prepares to leave on his quest.

RHAPSODY IN BLUE

ORCHESTRAL   ⏱ 13:45   📖 1   ♫ 🎷

The premiere of this piece in 1924 propelled Gershwin into the history books as the man "who first brought jazz into the concert hall". In many people's eyes the idea that the "low", socially disreputable popular music of African-Americans could fuse with Classical music was too shocking to contemplate.

Gershwin advertised the work as "an experiment in modern music". The combined frisson of being fashionably new and risqué drew a glittering audience to the premiere. The work has a sectional form, with a big slow central melody. The obvious jazzy elements in the score have obscured the distinctly Jewish tinge in the melodies, some of which recall synagogue chants.

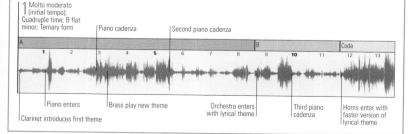

1 Molto moderato (initial tempo); Quadruple time; B flat minor; Ternary form | Piano cadenza | Second piano cadenza

A   1   2   3   4   5   6   7   8   9   B   10   11   Coda   12   13

Piano enters | Brass play new theme | Orchestra enters with lyrical theme | Third piano cadenza | Horns enter with faster version of lyrical theme

Clarinet introduces first theme

"I do not compose, I assemble materials."

AARON COPLAND

Aaron Copland

🔵 1900–1990   📕 American   ✍ 135

Aaron Copland is probably the best-known, and certainly one of the most profoundly gifted, Classical composers that America has ever produced. In the 1930s and 40s he synthesized jazz, Neo-Classical, and folk elements into a style that for many people summons up the spirit of his native country. This, combined with his energetic entrepreneurial and organizational gifts, make him the key figure in 20th-century American music.

Though best known to the public for his "Americana", Copland was also a composer of jazz, avant garde, and serialist works.

LIFE

Copland was born in New York into a prosperous family of Polish–Lithuanian Jews. During his teens he studied music privately, scoured libraries for scores of new music, took an interest in jazz, and from 1921, spent three years in Paris. While there he acquired a cast-iron technique and a Neo-Classical aesthetic from music teacher Nadia Boulanger, and was dazzled by Parisian artistic life. Back home, early works such as the Piano Concerto earned him the reputation of a hot-headed modernist. Lacking commissions, he staved off destitution by teaching and writing, and threw himself into the cause of new music. He was co-director of the Copland–Sessions concerts, and co-founder of the Yaddo Festival, the Arrow Music Press, and the American Composers' Alliance. In 1934 he wrote workers choruses and an article on proletarian music, which got him into trouble with Senator McCarthy's House Committee on Un-American Activities in the 1940s. However, by then he had become the musical voice of America with populist works such as *El salón México* and the ballet *Appalachian Spring*, which won a Pulitzer Prize. In the 1960s he became American music's wise, urbane father figure, dispensing advice and friendship to younger musicians like Bernstein.

MUSICAL OUTPUT					Total: 135
ORCHESTRAL (33)	2	6	11	3	11
FILM SCORES/INCIDENTAL (14)		1	8	4	1
CHAMBER (19)	7	4	2	1	5
PIANO MUSIC (26)	9	6	2	4	5
DRAMATIC (8)	1	2	3	1	1
CHORAL (13)	3	2	4	4	
SONGS (22)	13	2	2	5	
	1900	1926	1937	1947	1958 1990

MUSIC

At first Copland behaved like a true avant-garde composer, shocking audiences with sharp dissonance and jazzy irreverence. But he was never an ivory-tower composer; he wanted his music to relate to contemporary issues, and to appeal to public taste.

In the 1930s, under the impact of the Depression and a wave of left-wing sentiment among artists, he found a new awareness of himself as an American and as a citizen. In a series of ballets, *Billy the Kid*, *Rodeo*, and *Appalachian Spring*, he crystallized

the style that made him famous. It was a style rooted in the forms of Stravinskian Neo-Classicism, but this was united with a specifically American lyricism and feeling for landscape, both rural and urban. In the later years of his career, in the 1960s, he even succeeded in marrying Schoenberg's 12-tone technique with his own personal sound-world.

MILESTONES	
1925	Completes first major work, the ballet *Grohg*
1938	*Billy the Kid*, first of his three great ballets, premiered by Lincoln Kirstein's Ballet Caravan
1944	*Appalachian Spring* performed by Martha Graham Touring Company
1954	Elected to American Academy of Arts and Letters
1958	Debut with New York Philharmonic launches 20-year conducting career
1961	Moves to Peerskill NY, where he lives until his death
1964	Presidential Medal of Freedom
1972	Ceases composing

Copland wrote extensively for films in the 1940s. His score for William Wyler's 1948 film *The Heiress*, starring Olivia de Havilland, won an Academy Award.

KEY WORKS

PIANO VARIATIONS
SOLO PIANO   ⏱ 11:00   🎧

Copland said "this was the first of my works where I felt very sure of myself". It is generally regarded as the most impressive product of Copland's "abstract" period in the early 1930s. The piece has an unusual combination of rhythmic propulsion derived from jazz and a very strict compositional logic, influenced by Schoenberg's 12-tone system.

SYMPHONY NO. 3
ORCHESTRAL   ⏱ 42:00   📖 4   🎶

Copland was aiming for a big statement in this work, appropriate to a time of national stress (he began writing the symphony during World War II). The "public" manner

culminates in the grandeur of the finale, which begins by quoting Copland's earlier *Fanfare for the Common Man*.

CLARINET CONCERTO
ORCHESTRAL   ⏱ 17:00   📖 2   🎶 🎧

Like Copland's earlier piano concerto, this consists of two movements separated by a cadenza. The first movement is one of his most inspired pastoral melodies, which unfolds over a stately slow-motion waltz accompaniment. The second explodes in jazzy fireworks, inspired by jazz clarinettist Benny Goodman, for whom the piece was written.

FOCUS

APPALACHIAN SPRING

BALLET ⏳ 35:30 📖 8 ⚘

The third and most perfect of Copland's "American" ballets, the work was commissioned in 1943 for the choreographer Martha Graham. It was originally scored for only 13 players, though it's more often heard today in the arrangement Copland made for full orchestra. The ballet portrays a "pioneer celebration of Spring in a newly built farmhouse in Pennsylvania in the early 1800s".

The young farmer and his bride-to-be act out their feelings of hope, excitement, and trepidation. Copland said he was inspired by Graham's choreography, which he described as "prim and restrained, simple yet strong… the music reflects, I hope, the unique quality of a human being, an American landscape and a way of feeling". Towards the end, the traditional Shaker tune "Simple Gifts" is first quoted and then subtly varied.

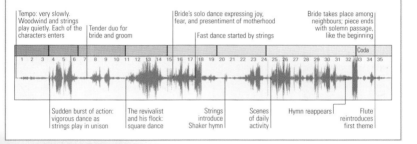

Tempo: very slowly. Woodwind and strings play quietly. Each of the characters enters | Tender duo for bride and groom | Bride's solo dance expressing joy, fear, and presentiment of motherhood | Fast dance started by strings | Bride takes place among neighbours; piece ends with solemn passage, like the beginning

Coda

1 2 3 4 5 6 7 8 9 10 11 12 13 14 15 16 17 18 19 20 21 22 23 24 25 26 27 28 29 30 31 32 33 34 35

Sudden burst of action: vigorous dance as strings play in unison | The revivalist and his flock: square dance | Strings introduce Shaker hymn | Scenes of daily activity | Hymn reappears | Flute reintroduces first theme

12 POEMS OF EMILY DICKINSON

SONG-CYCLE ⏳ 28:00 📖 12 ♿ 🎧

This setting of poems by the visionary, reclusive poet Emily Dickinson is one of the great song-cycles of the 20th century. They are set in Copland's lean mature style, the piano part often confined to single notes in each hand, a style perfectly suited to the poems, which deal with the grandest subjects in the simplest language. The wide-open sounds of the music match Dickinson's rural imagery, and the unfussy rhythms of the songs accords with the Biblical plainness of Dickinson's verse. Within these limits the range of moods is vast: homely simplicity in "Nature, the gentlest mother", a funereal tread in "I felt a funeral in my brain", bugle-calls and rushing scales in "There came a wind like a bugle".

Samuel Barber

◉ 1910–1981   🏳 American   ✍ c.50

Barber's music defies easy classification. Effortlessly lyrical, Romantic, and yet unmistakably contemporary, he achieved huge popularity without aligning himself to any school of composition or appearing concerned with modernist trends. His comparatively small output covered all genres, although he is best remembered for his vocal works and the *Adagio for Strings*, made famous by the conductor Toscanini.

LIFE AND MUSIC

Barber trained both as a composer and singer at the renowned Curtis Academy. At a time when music was dominated by European modernists such as Schoenberg and Stravinsky, Barber's easy Romanticism struck a chord with audiences. His gift for flowing,

memorable melody lines served to mask over the more contemporary aspects of his composition, notably an acute

Barber's *Adagio for Strings* owes its fame to Toscanini, who performed it with the NBC Orchestra in 1937.

handling of dissonance and highly inventive orchestration. His output, already less than prodigious, declined sharply after the failure of his opera *Antony and Cleopatra* at the New York Metropolitan in 1966.

MILESTONES	
1924	Enrolled at Curtis Institute
1931	Composes vocal work *Dover Beach*
1935	Fellow of American Academy in Rome
1936	Composes Symphony No. 1
1939	Composes Violin Concerto
1938	Arranges *Adagio for Strings*
1942	Serves in US Air Corp
1947	Composes *Knoxville, Summer of 1915*
1949	Piano Sonata premiered by Horovitz
1958	Opera *Vanessa* wins Pulitzer Prize
1962	Composes Piano Concerto

KEY WORKS

SYMPHONY NO. 1

ORCHESTRAL   ⏱ 22:00   📖 4   🎼

Barber's Symphony No. 1 must be ranked as one of the great American orchestral pieces of the 20th century. It is a work of great power, at once traditional in form and yet original in the treatment of its theme.

KNOXVILLE, SUMMER OF 1915

SONG   ⏱ 16:00   📖 1   🎼♪

Knoxville, Summer of 1915 was a short piece of prose by the American poet James Agee, recalling his feelings of wonder and confusion as a child

growing up in the deep South. Barber's setting is extraordinary not only for its lyrical beauty, but the delicacy with which it captures the shifting moods of the text. As the soprano Leontyne Price later said, "you can smell the South in it".

HERMIT SONGS, OP.29

SONGS   ⏱ 16:00   📖 10   🎧♪

The beautifully crafted *Hermit Songs* are settings of Irish monastic texts from the 8th to 13th centuries, and are a wonderful illustration of Barber's mastery of the voice.

FOCUS

ADAGIO FOR STRINGS

ORCHESTRAL 🔊 8:30 📖 1 ❀

The poignant *Adagio for Strings* is Barber's most popular work. Composed in 1936, the *Adagio* originally formed the central movement of his String Quartet, Op. 11. The following year Barber rescored it for a full orchestra of strings, taking advantage of the extra resources to add weight and sonority.

The form of the *Adagio* has been likened to a long arch, based on the gradual expansion of a single, simple theme. This is heard first in hushed tones on the violins, before a more strident presentation by the cellos. After a process of ascending development an impassioned climax is reached, before the music breaks off abruptly, almost as if overcome by emotion. The work then concludes quietly, recalling fragments of the theme.

Perhaps because of its profoundly melancholic, contemplative tone, the *Adagio* has found wide resonance with the public and has been played at many funerals including those of Kennedy, Roosevelt, and Einstein. In 1967, Barber re-scored it for chorus, setting the Agnus Dei text. Arguably less successful than previous incarnations, it was nevertheless popularized further in this guise in the film *Platoon*.

VIOLIN CONCERTO

ORCHESTRAL 🔊 21:00 📖 2 ❀ ☺

Commissioned for a child prodigy, the first two movements of the Violin Concerto were – according to the young violinist – insufficiently taxing to showcase his talent. In response, Barber wrote a finale so difficult that the young violinist couldn't play it.

FIRST MOVEMENT (ALLEGRO, 10:00) Rich melody abounds in this movement. Unusually, Barber elected to dispense with an introduction, the soloist launching immediately into the lyrical main theme of this sonata movement.

SECOND MOVEMENT (ANDANTE, 8:00) A haunting oboe solo introduces the first theme, which is developed by the strings before the soloist enters after nearly three minutes and leads into a darker and more impassioned section.

THIRD MOVEMENT (PRESTO IN MOTO PERPETUOSO, 3:00) An astonishing tour de force for the soloist against a background of wild rhythms from the orchestra, this finale could hardly cut a greater contrast with the first two movements.

John Cage

● 1912–1992   🏴 American   ✍ 229

John Cage may well be the most original composer in the history of Western music. His life's project was to repudiate the entire Western tradition, but not in a spirit of anger or negativity. Even at its most chaotic, his music comes across as exuberant and life-affirming. He used chance procedures to free sounds from the "bullying" effects of human intentions and rules, so that they could "be themselves".

LIFE AND MUSIC

Born in Los Angeles, John Cage became interested in classical Indian music and Oriental philosophies. He formed a percussion orchestra before settling in New York in 1942 and beginning a lifelong collaboration with dancer Merce Cunningham's dance company. His life-project began with a ruthless process of stripping away, starting with harmony and melody. (Cage's earliest pieces are built out of pure rhythm, played on percussion or the "prepared piano".) Then he stripped away intention and form by introducing chance operations into music, ending up with pure silence in his famous piece *4′ 33″*. This led to a welcoming in, when any chance noises could become part of a "piece". This is why Cage's later music ranges from the simplicity of *Two* to the riotous complication of *Roaratorio*.

MILESTONES

1934	Meets Arnold Schoenberg and decides to dedicate his life to music
1938	Invents the "prepared piano"
1940s	Studies Zen Buddhism
1948	Completes *Sonatas and Interludes* for prepared piano.
1950	Creates first "chance pieces" after reading Chinese book of *I Ching*
1952	Creates silent piece *4′ 33″*
1961	*Variations II* premiered. *Silence* (collected writings) brings him world fame
1978	Starts to "write" music as graphic designs at Crown Point Press
1979	*Roaratorio*, with tape, premiered
1987	Employing randomness, writes *Two*, first of his late "time bracket" pieces

KEY WORKS

SONATAS AND INTERLUDES

SOLO PIANO   🎚 64:00   📖 16   🎶

This sequence of 16 sonatas, interleaved with four interludes, attempts to represent the eight "permanent emotions" of ancient Indian thought, "and their common tendency towards tranquillity". It is scored for "prepared piano", Cage's invention whereby metal and rubber objects are placed inside a piano to alter the sound.

In *4′ 33″* the pianist sits reading the score, shown here, for four minutes 33 seconds, but does not play.

I

TACET

II

TACET

III

TACET

VARIATIONS II

CHAMBER   📖 1   🎷

This is perhaps Cage's most extreme experiment in notation. The "score" consists of 11 transparent sheets bearing lines or dots. These are tossed down and the resulting patterns used to determine the basic characteristics of the sounds.

ROARATORIO

TAPE & VOCAL   🎚 75:00   📖 1   🎷🎤

This exuberant work – a joyous cacophony – for electronic tape and live performers is an attempt to translate James Joyce's vast novel *Finnegans Wake* into sound.

Roy Harris

● 1898–1979   ♙ American   ✍ c.200

Harris's broad, sweeping melodies, robustly based on hymns and American folk tunes and with vigorous but unusual rhythms, suggest the Midwest landscapes he knew well (he grew up on a farm in Oklahoma and drove a truck during his college days).

After winning a music competition, he went to New York, where he befriended Aaron Copland, and then to Paris to study under Nadia Boulanger. There, his Concerto for Piano, Clarinet, and String Quartet received acclaim. Back in the US, he established his "American" style with great success in his orchestral works. He taught at several institutes and was widely honoured. His Symphony No. 3 is often called the greatest American symphony.

MILESTONES	
1925	Andante for Strings wins competition
1926	Goes to study in Paris
1929	Injured in a fall; returns to US
1933	Conductor Sergei Koussevitsky commissions symphony from him
1934	Completes first of his 13 symphonies
1938	Composes Symphony No. 3

The rugged landscape of the American West is reflected in a distinctly rugged quality in many of Harris's works.

Conlon Nancarrow

● 1912–1997   ♙ American   ✍ c.75

Turning his back on an engineering career, Nancarrow studied music privately, fought in the Spanish Civil War, and – escaping anti-communist feeling in America – moved to Mexico City permanently. There he composed in isolation an extraordinary series of studies for the player piano, which could be "programmed" to automatically play

music punched into piano rolls. The 50 or so works use an astounding variety of techniques, such as inhumanly fast tempos, relentless accelerations, and unimaginably mathematical cross-rhythms. In the late 1970s Nancarrow's music was discovered and recorded, and he found fame: he was given commissions, he was invited to international music festivals, and received a $300,000 award.

In his early career, Nancarrow notated all his mature compositions on player-piano rolls. Most of them are impossible for human hands to play.

MILESTONES	
1930	Starts composing conventionally
1939	Refused US passport after having fought in Spanish Civil War
1940	Moves to Mexico City
1947	Buys player piano
1948	Writes Study No. 1 for player piano
1992	Writes Study No. 52 for player piano

Leonard Bernstein

● 1918–1990   ♙ American   ✍ 90

Bernstein was one of the most dazzlingly gifted musicians of the 20th century. He was also an immense personality, with huge intellectual curiosity. He achieved pre-eminence in two fields: conducting, and composing for Broadway musicals and dance shows. He was also an eminent composer of concert music, though here his achievement is more uneven and controversial.

LIFE AND MUSIC

Bernstein was the son of a family of rabbis, and Jewish themes remained prominent in his music. By the end of his student years, it was clear his talents would be divided between "serious" music and Broadway. His greatest successes as a composer came before he was 40, both in the musical theatre (*West Side Story, Candide*) and in concert music (Symphonies Nos. 1 and 2, and *Serenade*). After becoming chief conductor of the New

Bernstein became a "giant of the podium", the only rival to Herbert von Karajan.

York Philharmonic, conducting took up more of his time. However, he strove to compose at the same pace, while leading a complicated love-life, and showing support for unpopular causes such as the Black Panthers. "I'm over-committed on all fronts" he once said.

MILESTONES	
1939	Writes thesis "race elements in music"; graduates from Harvard University
1943	Wins fame conducting New York Philharmonic when Bruno Walter is ill
1944	Symphony No. 1, ballet *Fancy Free*, and musical *On the Town* are big successes
1949	Composes Symphony No. 2
1953	Is first American to conduct at La Scala
1956	Completes operetta, *Candide*
1973	Lectures at Harvard televised in US and abroad as *The Unanswered Question*
1983	Opera, *A Quiet Place*, premiered

KEY WORKS

CANDIDE

OPERETTA   ⏱ 140:00   📖 2   🎷♂

Based on Voltaire's brilliant satire of human folly written in 1759, this is one of Bernstein's greatest creations. It reflects the 1950s trend for cross-fertilization between the Broadway musical on one hand, and "straight" theatre and opera on the other. Much of *Candide*'s verve springs from its joyous parodies of different styles: Baroque "moto perpetuo", the "waltz aria" of French operetta, and even 12-tone music in the duet "Quiet".

A QUIET PLACE

OPERA   ⏱ 150:00   📖 3   🎷♂

Bernstein considered this the summation of his work. It takes *Trouble in Tahiti*, his early (1951) "operetta" about social malaise – which portrays the failing marriage of Sam and Dinah – and inserts it, unchanged, into a contemporary soap opera that opens 30 years later at Dinah's funeral. The use of flashback, the mix of musical styles, and the treatment of difficult themes, including homosexuality, make this a challenging work.

FOCUS

WEST SIDE STORY

MUSICAL　⏱ 90:00　📖 2　🎵🎭♪

Bernstein's masterpiece, and one of the great musicals of all time, takes the idea of Shakespeare's *Romeo and Juliet* and transfers it to 1950s New York. Choreographer Jerome Robbins, Leonard Bernstein, and writer Arthur Laurents together elaborated the story of a native-born Polish boy and a Puerto Rican girl newly arrived in America, describing how their love is thwarted by the constant warfare between rival gangs on the city's West Side. Bernstein offered the job of lyricist to the then unknown Stephen Sondheim, who proved to be a brilliant choice. The show's debt to Rodgers and Hammerstein's *South Pacific* can be seen in its mix of opera and Broadway idioms, the dramatic integration of dance, and the use of song to highlight social tensions. However, the hard-edged gang music, and the sheer range of Bernstein's invention, takes this work far beyond its model. Bernstein later created a suite of orchestral Symphonic Dances from the musical.

Bernstein was a noted conductor of Mahler, Brahms, and Copland.

SYMPHONY NO. 2, "THE AGE OF ANXIETY"

ORCHESTRAL　⏱ 36:00　📖 2　🎵🎶

This symphony takes its scenario of three men and a woman who meet in a New York bar during the Second World War from W H Auden's ingenious long poem, *The Age of Anxiety*. For its relatively short length, the symphony has a very complicated form: it is a combination of piano concerto, and theme and variations. In addition, it is also divided into two parts. The first closely follows the poem's portrayal of "seven ages and seven stages" – hence the 14 variations. The second portrays the goings-on back at the girl's apartment and begins with a dirge (this includes a 12-note row) followed by a strange masque in Bernstein's most brilliant jazz idiom, and a final affirmative chorale. The combination of influences – Brahms, Hindemith, Berg, and jazz – makes for a fascinating, if only partially successful, mix.

INFLUENCES

Bernstein's blending of classical "Americana" with jazz elements and his concern to address big metaphysical and social issues, certainly find an echo in contemporary American music. However, his sources – jazz, Jewish music, and "classic" American composers such as Copland – still remain more influential than Bernstein himself.

Elliott Carter

◗ 1908–   ℙ American   ✍ 100

Elliott Carter is the oldest of that vanishing breed of modernists born before World War II. Since the late 1940s Carter has clung to the unfashionable view that music has to be many-layered and full of complex cross-currents, because only then can it be true to the complexity of modern life. In his music of the 1980s and 90s the textures thinned out, but the thought was as quick and subtle as ever.

LIFE AND MUSIC

Carter was born in New York into a prosperous lace-importing family, which spent much of its time in Europe. Having got acquainted with new music through Charles Ives he joined the long line of American composers who studied with the great Paris-based advocate of Neo-Classicism, Nadia Boulanger. In the late 1940s Carter had a creative crisis which led him to abandon his populist American Neo-Classical stance in favour of an uncompromising modernism. Until the 1980s and 90s this made him better known in Europe than America, but recently the American establishment has woken up to the fact it has a great modernist master in its midst.

MILESTONES	
1924	Meets Charles Ives
1926	Enters Harvard to study literature, Greek, and philosophy; studies music on the side at the Longy School
1932	Begins three-year stay in Paris
1939	Marries sculptress Helen Frost; begins teaching in Annapolis, US
1948	Composes "breakthrough" piece, the Cello Sonata
1960	String Quartet No. 2 wins Pulitzer Prize, New York Music Critics Award, and UNESCO First Prize
1976	Composes Symphony of Three Orchestras; premiere of vocal work *A Mirror on Which to Dwell*
1999	Premiere of opera *What Next?*

KEY WORKS

STRING QUARTET NO. 2
CHAMBER   ⏱ 12:30   ▦ 4   ♇

This quartet followed a three-year gap in composing while Carter explored chord types and a new method of changing smoothly from one tempo to another, which he called "metric modulation". Both these ideas can be seen in the String Quartet No. 2. The third guiding idea was that of music conceived as a drama played out by musical "characters". Here the violin is virtuosic and fantastic, the second violin is "laconic and orderly, sometimes humorous", the viola is theatrically doleful, while the cello is played as impetuous.

WHAT NEXT?
OPERA   ⏱ 50:00   ▦ 1   🎻🥁🎵

Carter's first opera, premiered at Berlin Staatsoper under Daniel Barenboim, is a sparkling 50-minute comedy about a group of people marooned on a freeway after a car crash, trying to remember who and where they are.

SYMPHONIA
ORCHESTRAL   ⏱ 45:00   ▦ 3   🎻

In 1992, Carter embarked on his biggest project to date; a three movement piece for large orchestra lasting 45 minutes. Carter gave it the subtitle "sum Fluxae Pretium Spei" ("I am the prize of flowing hope").

FOCUS

SYMPHONY OF THREE ORCHESTRAS

ORCHESTRAL　⏱ 15:45　📖 1　♣

This single-movement orchestral work was Carter's response to Hart Crane's magnificent poem *The Bridge*, a mystical evocation of Brooklyn Bridge and the city of New York. In Hart's poem the bridge becomes a symbol which spans a river and a continent, and which unites an ancient past and a technological future. To capture this visionary quality Carter created a dense, glistening soundscape for three orchestras, the first consisting of brass, timpani, and strings, the second of percussion, clarinets, and solo strings, the third of winds, horns, and upper strings. Each orchestra has its own repertoire of chords and melodic shapes, and its own independent succession of tempi. These are unfolded simultaneously, creating Carter's most extreme experiment in collage. The piece begins with a high trumpet solo, which has been described as the definitive portrait in sound of New York, and ends with a "factory-noise" coda which tumbles down to the depths of the orchestra.

CELLO SONATA

ORCHESTRAL　⏱ 21:45　📖 4　♔

In the 1940s Carter had become dissatisfied with the populist style of his early works, and over the next decade he began to grope his way towards a new style. The second movement of the Cello Sonata, originally intended as the first, is in a jazz-tinged style, but the next two movements introduce musical ideas moving at different speeds. He then composed a new first movement, which instead of starting with a "theme" presents chords and intervals which will be a "quarry" for everything that follows. This movement picks up from the ending, which means the work is in the shape of an endless loop, with the "beginning" in the middle.

Milton Babbitt

● 1916– ◉ American ✍ c.110

After playing jazz, Babbitt was a music graduate by 19 and carried on studying privately. An early proponent of 12-tone music, he worked in music and mathematics university faculties, developing advanced theories of musical systems. He taught at Princeton and the Juilliard School among others and became a significant writer and lecturer – and though a major intellectual, he is also a sports fan and raconteur. Babbitt's highly structured and complex works makes them unlikely to gain popular success but they, and his teachings, have proved very influential. Frequently honoured, he was still composing and working well into his 80s.

Babbitt's exploratory compositions have involved at various times tape, synthesiser (including the 1960s model shown left), and conventional instruments.

MILESTONES	
1940	Composition for String Orchestra, 12-tone work
1960	Professor of Music at Princeton
1963	Philomel, soprano and synthesiser
1970	String Quartet No 3
1973	Composition faculty at Juilliard
1982	Pulitzer Prize citation for life's work

Lou Harrison

● 1917–2003 ◉ American ✍ c.220

Harrison was a US West-Coast experimenter, synthesising world native and Western styles, working in different tuning systems, and creating novel percussive sounds. With his partner William Colvig he developed 'American gamelan', from items such as garbage cans, tins, and baseball bats. He also wrote for standard Western instruments, usually with a lyrical flavour, and collaborated with Ives and Cage. His opera *Young Caesar* shows his advocacy of gay rights. .

MILESTONES	
1946	Conducts premiere of Ives's Symphony No 3
1974	Suite for Violin and American gamelan
1988	*Young Caesar*, opera

Leon Kirchner

● 1919– ◉ American ✍ 50

Alongside a distinguished teaching career Kirchner has served as pianist and conductor. His music – sometimes agonised, sometimes driving and energetic – is firmly in the tradition of his mentor, Schoenberg, flowing and unfolding, but always governed by some underlying idea, and resistant to temporary musical fashions. He received a Pulitzer Prize for his Third Quartet.

MILESTONES	
1958	String Quartet No 2
1963	Piano Concerto No 2
1966	Professor of Music at Harvard
1973	*Lily*, chamber ensemble and tape (arrangement of opera)
1997	*Of things exactly as they are*, two singers, chorus, orchestra

Ned Rorem

● 1923– 🎹 American ♫ c.450

Rorem studied with Thomson (for whom he was secretary and copyist) and Copland, at the Juilliard School. After winning prizes with the Lordly Hudson (best published song of 1948) and his Overture in C (Gershwin Prize) he went to Paris, where he lived for several years and became part of the artistic circles of Cocteau and Poulenc, one of his inspirations. Back in New York, where the success of his songs drew him, he taught at various institutes and increasingly developed his reputation as an excellent song composer (he has written nearly 400, with naturalness of word-setting and advanced but never impossible harmonies), and as a writer (such as for his elegant and frank diaries).

During his time in Paris, Rorem wrote his entertaining journal the *Paris Diary of Ned Rorem* (1950–55)

MILESTONES	
1949	Goes to Paris
1958	Returns to New York
1965	*Miss Julie*, opera
1966	*Paris Diary of Ned Rorem*, book
1976	*Air Music*, orchestra, wins Pulitzer Prize
1997	*Evidence of Things Not Seen*, song cycle

Morton Feldman

● 1926–1987 🎹 American ♫ c.150

Spurning conventional academic training – he worked in the family business – Feldman was influenced by both the new sounds of Varèse, the pioneering work of Cage, and especially by New York's 1950s abstract expressionist school of painters and their faith in directness and instinct. His modernist pieces can involve non-standard notation (his series of pieces *Projections and Intersections* are written on graphical scores, with general directions rather than individual notes on a stave), and can be of immense length – his String Quartet II lasts almost six hours. One of his last works, *Palais de Mari*, is unusual for a late composition in that it is only 20 minutes long. It came about from a request for Feldman to sum up everything he was doing in his very long pieces and to condense that into a smaller piece. After some time in Berlin, where he gained several commissions, he returned to the US to teach composition in Buffalo.

Blue Penumbra, 1957 (oil on canvas) by painter Mark Rothko, a friend of Feldman's and one who helped shape his sound world.

MILESTONES	
1951	*Projections*
1971	Residency in Berlin
1971	Rothko Chapel, singers and ensemble
1973	Professor at SUNY, Buffalo
1984	*For Philip Guston*, ensemble
1986	*Pallais de Maris*
1987	Marries composer Barbara Monk

George Crumb

● 1929–   ♫ American   🎵 c.60

Raised in a musical family accustomed to the classics, trained in the conventional way rounded off at Berlin's Hochschule, and having made a career in teaching mostly at Pennsylvania, Crumb was at home in the standard repertoire. After initially being influenced by Webern, he has become almost notorious for requiring unusual sounds and innovative techniques in his relatively small but refined output. *Black Angels*, for example, evokes the horrors of Vietnam by asking the string quartet players to shout and bow wine glasses, while *Vox Balanae* (*The Voice of the Whale*) requires its musicians to wear masks and perform under a blue light (the latter also features an electric flute, an electric cello, and an amplified piano). Many of his works set texts by Lorca, and the theatrical nature of his music – sometimes trance-like, other times explosive – has made it popular with dance companies.

MILESTONES	
1965	Begins association with Pennsylvania University
1968	Wins Pulitzer Prize for *Echoes of Time and the River*
1970	Writes *Ancient Voices of Children*; *Black Angels* string quartet produced
1973	Writes *Makrokosmos* for piano
2002	Joint residency at Arizona University

Poem of the Deep Song, one of several poems by Federico Garcia Lorca set to music by Crumb.

POEM OF THE DEEP SON
POEMA DEL CANTE JONDO

Federico Garcia Lorca

Frederic Rzewski

● 1938-   ♫ American   🎵 c.70

A prodigiously talented pianist and composer, Rzewski went from Harvard and Princeton to Europe, where he performed and taught through the 1960s. He worked on radical jazz-based improvisation, and live electronic projects, some with a socialist theme. He has been based in Rome and Liège since 1976 and teaches widely. His popular *The People United* is a 50-minute set of virtuoso variations in an astonishing array of styles on a worker's revolutionary song; later works were more experimental, before a recent freer phase. Miles 49–56 of his mammoth seven-hour-long piano solo *The Road* involve playing the floor and stool, whistling, humming, screwed-up paper and a radio, plus sections for each hand alone.

MILESTONES	
1960	Studies under Dallapiccola in Florence
1962	Premiere of Stockhausen's *Klavierstück X*
1975	Writes *The People United Will Never Be Defeated* for piano
1983	Professor of composition at Liège
1988	Writes *Triumph of Death* oratorio
1998	*The Road* written for piano

Rzewski's magnum opus, *The Road*, is a musical "novel" composed of 64 parts, each marking a "mile" in the work's journey.

John Corigliano

⚲ 1938–   ▥ American   ✍ c.50

John Corigliano belongs to the same generation as the minimalists Reich, Glass, and Riley. But whereas they took a long and winding route to Romantic expressivity, via the severities of minimalism, Corigliano knew from the beginning that expressivity was his true home. His eclectic language, which calls on the evocative power of musical memory, has won him a wide audience.

LIFE AND MUSIC

Corigliano was a somewhat slow starter as a composer, and after studying at Columbia University worked in Classical music radio and as a concert programmer. Corigliano describes his early works, such as the Violin Sonata and the earlier movements of the *Dylan Thomas Trilogy*, as "a tense, histrionic outgrowth of the 'clean' American sound of Barber, Copland, Harris and Schuman". The later works, beginning with the Clarinet Concerto, present a very different musical palette, less driven and with many more layers. But it is not Elliott Carter's intellectual complication that Corigliano is aiming at. Memory, nostalgia, and the evocation of different emotional worlds are what interest him, which is why he is a truly post-modern composer.

MILESTONES	
1959	Graduates from Columbia University
1960	Works as music programmer at New York music station WXQR
1961	Starts work with Leonard Bernstein on the *Young People's Concert* series
1971	Starts teaching at Manhattan School of Music
1977	Clarinet Concerto premiered by Bernstein in New York
1991	*The Ghost of Versailles* premiered in New York
1992	Teaches composition at Juillard School in New York
1997	Feature film *The Red Violin* opens with score by Corigliano
2000	Premiere of Symphony No. 2

KEY WORKS

A DYLAN THOMAS TRILOGY

ORATORIO   ⏱ 90:00   📖 3   ♆ ♅ 🥁

It took Corigliano around 40 years to complete this large-scale "memory play in the form of an oratorio", as he calls it. It consists of setting three poems by Dylan Thomas particularly dear to Corigliano: "Fern Hill", "Poem in October", and the darker "Poem on his Birthday". As Thomas himself wrote, in his *Poetic Manifesto* (1951); "What the words stood for, symbolized, or meant was of very secondary importance; what matters was the sound of them".

SYMPHONY NO. 1

ORCHESTRAL   ⏱ 43:00   📖 3   ♆

"During the past decade I have lost many friends and colleagues to the AIDS epidemic... My first symphony was generated by feelings of loss, anger, and frustration". Each movement is a memorial to a different friend; the moment in the first when a memory of Albéniz's "Tango" floats through the orchestra is typical of Corigliano's directness.

A still from *The Red Violin*, which featured a haunting, complex, and lyrical score by Corigliano.

Steve Reich

◔ 1936–   ⚑ American   ✍ 46

One of the best-known American composers, Steve Reich is generally acknowledged as the most sophisticated of the four pioneer minimalists (the others being Terry Riley, Philip Glass, and La Monte Young). Like Glass, Reich has gone on to broaden the range of his work, embracing his Jewish heritage and musically tackling political and ethical issues. Of the four, however, it is he who has stayed closest to his musical roots.

LIFE AND MUSIC

Although Reich reacted against the serial orthodoxy taught in the US, his early music was no less rigorous in the way it took a few simple ideas and pursued them relentlessly. In the 1960s, he found that, when started together, identical tape loops in old-style tape recorders would soon move out of synchronization. He began to transfer these phasing effects to conventional instruments, elaborating on them in ingenious ways. By the mid-1970s, his technique of making music from repeating, slowly changing patterns was established. In the 1980s, he returned to speech recordings for inspiration.

MILESTONES	
1962	Studies with Milhaud and Berio
1966	Creates *Come Out*, first loop-phase piece; starts concerts with own ensemble
1967	Composes Violin *Phase*
1970	Studies in Ghana with Ewe tribe
1971	Composes *Drumming*, first appearance in big concert venue with orchestra
1973	Studies Balinese music in America
1976	Studies traditional Jewish chant
1984	*Desert Music* premiered
1988	*Different Trains* introduces speech samples into his music
2002	*Three Tales* premiered: dark multi-media exploration of new technologies

KEY WORKS

DRUMMING

CHAMBER   ⏱ 90:00   📖 1   ♬

Written after his study of Ghanaian drumming, this piece sums up Reich's discoveries in phase accumulation and gap-fill. It is his first big public statement and the first appearance of his rippling, multi-keyboard sound.

VIOLIN PHASE

VIOLIN & TAPE   ⏱ 15:00   📖 1   🎻

This piece asks a live performer to mimic the phase-shifting Reich had already achieved with tape recorders, but in a more complicated way, with the violinist playing against one, then two, and finally three pre-recorded tape tracks of himself/herself. The final refinement is that the violinist sometimes bows out of the phasing process in order to tease out and reinforce the new patterns formed in the mind by the phasing process. This has a fascinating effect, as if an aural illusion were to become suddenly real.

Profoundly influenced by African drumming, Reich's music consists of "pattern games" which are concerned not with melody, but with changes in time.

MUSIC FOR 18 MUSICIANS
CHAMBER 🔊 55:00 📖 1 ⚇

This big, single-movement piece, created in 1974 and 1975 for an enlarged form of Reich's own ensemble, has a good claim to be his masterpiece. What makes it so irresistible is the way the moment-to-moment unfolding of Reich's familiar "pattern games" is embedded in a convincing architectural frame.

The frame consists of a cycle of 11 chords, announced at the beginning, which is then repeated, in hugely expanded form, across the remainder of the piece. Each chord becomes the basis of a "movement" lasting several minutes, which may be in an arch form (ABCDCBA) or cast in one of Reich's typical processes, such as substituting beats for rests.

The division of the ensemble into "breathing" wind instruments and voice and "pulsing" instruments gives rise to a layered texture, with slow-moving phrases set against pattering activity – a texture that has become so characteristic of his work.

THE CAVE
MULTI-MEDIA 🔊 142:00 📖 1 ⚇ ♻

In this ambitious work created between 1989 and 1993 with his wife, video artist Beryl Korot, several of Reich's interests come together: the use of speech rhythms in recordings –

an idea revived after a lapse of more than 20 years; a concern with Jewish themes; and a desire to create a new kind of multi-media experience involving music, voices, and images. What is striking about this piece (and the subsequent *Three Tales*, also created with his wife) is the way speech, music, and images are strictly co-ordinated in time.

The work concerns the Cave of Hebron, the burial place of both Abraham and Sarah and thus sacred to both Muslims and Jews. Recorded in Israel and in the US, the work explores the troubled legacy of the cave through interviews seen on screens and heard over speakers. The key phrases are teased out and repeated, and their rhythms and speech melodies caught and amplified by live instruments and voices.

INFLUENCES
Reich's effect on general musical culture is perhaps not as great as Philip Glass's, although within classical circles his influence may be greater, owing to the continuing modernist rigour of his music. Nonetheless, his characteristic pattering, marimba-and-winds sound has managed to spread further, appearing on pop remix albums.

Philip Glass

◔ 1937–   🏳 American   ✍ 170

Glass is one of the founding fathers of minimalism, along with Steve Reich, Terry Riley, and La Monte Young. He shares with Riley and Young a respect for Indian music, and with Reich an interest in repetitive patterns. Today, he is most famous of them all, because of his vast productivity, his eagerness to collaborate with artists in different media, and the increasing emotional range and lyricism of his music.

LIFE AND MUSIC

Glass said, "Taboos – the things we're not supposed to do – are often the most interesting. In my case, musical materials are found among the ordinary things, such as sequences and cadences." Those ordinary things were indeed taboo in Glass's formative years, when the strict serial techniques of Stockhausen held sway. Through meeting Ravi Shankar and, later, the great percussionist Alla Rakha, he liberated himself from modernism and forged a hypnotic, repetitive style that was exactly suited to the rhythmic sax-and-keyboard sound of his own ensemble. After a difficult start playing New York lofts and galleries, Glass gained a cult following.

MILESTONES

1949	Starts composition lessons, also works in his father's record shop
1957	Enrols at Juilliard School of Music
1963	Studies in Paris with Nadia Boulanger
1967	Takes lessons in Indian rhythm
1976	Premiere of *Einstein on the Beach*, the first of Glass's "character operas"
1980	*Satyagraha*, opera, performed
1983	Composes *Akhnaten*, opera
1984	Composes music to inaugurate Los Angeles Olympics
1992	*The Voyage*, opera, for 500th anniversary of Columbus's arrival in America
1998	Composes Symphony No. 5
2002	Writes score for Stephen Daldry's film *The Hours*

KEY WORKS

VIOLIN CONCERTO

ORCHESTRAL   ⏱ 25:00   📖 3   🎵 ◉

Written in 1987, this was the piece through which Glass discovered a liking for the conventional symphony orchestra. Here he treats it like a vastly enlarged Philip Glass Ensemble (his own performing group), with all the colours merged in gentle arpeggiated undulations (in the slow movement) or hectic motor rhythms (in the fast ones). Above this unceasing rhythmic activity the haunting violin dances and floats.

Philip Glass's soundtrack of atmospheric simplicity for *The Hours* is based on common chords and arpeggios, and is played in strange, circulating patterns by piano and strings.

SYMPHONY NO. 5

CHORAL   ⏱ 98:00   📖 12   🎵 ⚙ ♀

This ambitious work brings together texts from many different "wisdom traditions", as Glass calls them. The 12 movements describe a journey through Death to Enlightenment, in music of statuesque simplicity.

EINSTEIN ON THE BEACH

OPERA   ⏳ 300:00   📖 4   ♇ ♿

Glass's first major collaboration, was the one that brought him fame (or notoriety). His collaborator was Robert Wilson, known for creating a multimedia "theatre of visions" which avoided conventional narratives in favour of a dream-like strangeness. Although it is based on the life of the great physicist Albert Einstein, the piece avoids plot, presenting instead a series of tableaux based on key images or ideas. These include Einstein's violin, and the image of the train used in the theory of relativity. The text consists of numbers and solfèges, which are set to insistently repetitive music. When you add the choreographed movement, the bizarre costumes, the five-hour duration, and the invitation to the audience to wander in and out of the auditorium at will, you have the most extreme work Glass ever created.

MUSIC IN 12 PARTS

CHAMBER   ⏳ 205:00   📖 12   ♇

The longest and most ambitious piece Glass ever wrote for the Philip Glass Ensemble, this work is the summit of his early minimalist style. It began in 1971 as a single piece in 12 horizontal parts (six on keyboards, three on woodwind, and three vocal parts). Glass played it to a friend, who remarked, "Very beautiful. What will the other 11 parts be like?" Glass took this misunderstanding as a cue to compose 11 more pieces. Each projects a texture of rigorously patterned stasis, with single harmonies sustained for minutes at a stretch. What supplies the interest is the way the repeating patterns gradually change, one step at a time. When the harmony eventually alters, "it's as if a wall of a room has collapsed to reveal a new view," as one critic put it.

AKHNATEN

OPERA   ⏳ 150:00   📖 3   ♆ ♫ ♿

Glass's "character operas" deal respectively with a brilliant scientist (Einstein), a great politician (Gandhi), and an influential religious reformer (Akhnaten). The last of the three works is the closest to a conventional opera. The characters sing in what is known, or imagined, of the languages of Ancient Egypt, while a narrator explains and interprets in English. The music has a majestic slowness, in keeping with the vast timescale of the Egyptian world.

INFLUENCES

Glass's influence has been immense, entering the general consciousness in a way no other living composer can match. The most telling evidence of this is the countless TV soundtracks and commercials which imitate his style. However, his reputation in the classical world is much less secure, and his influence there has been minimal.

John Adams

🔘 1947–   🏳 American   ✍ 55

John Adams has become the most frequently performed living classical composer in the US, and quite possibly the world, due to his brilliant transformation of the minimal language he inherited from Glass and Reich. He retains the relentless forward momentum of minimalism, but vastly expands its expressive resources, and imports an exuberant range of cultural references, both "high" and "low".

LIFE AND MUSIC

Adams' name evokes the US of the Founding Fathers, and his birth in Massachusetts seems to confirm this East Coast orientation. But his music evokes a very different West Coast mindset, symbolized by his move to California and it is shown by an openness both to high-flown culture and Americana. These elements are held together in an idiom that grew out of the continuities of minimalism, and which, in its quieter moods, has a laid-back "Californian" feel. However, this mood is increasingly inflected by other elements – from dark European Romanticism to bright US pop.

MILESTONES	
1965	Music course at Harvard University
1971	Moves to Bay Area, California
1977	Writes the piano pieces *Phrygian Gates* and *China Gates*
1982	Becomes San Francisco Symphony Orchestra's composer in residence
1987	Premiere of *Nixon in China*
1991	*Death of Klinghoffer* premiered
1995	Wins Grawemeyer Award for his Violin Concerto
2000	Nativity oratorio, *El Niño*, produced
2002	Writes *On the Transmigration of Souls* to commemorate 9/11
2005	Premiere of *Doctor Atomic*

KEY WORKS

THE DHARMA AT BIG SUR

ORCHESTRAL   ⏱ 30:00   📖 2   ♫ 🎻

Completed in 2003, this is an exuberant concerto for electric violin and orchestra. "Big Sur" refers to a famous scenic spot on the San Francisco–Los Angeles freeway, while "Dharma" is a Sanskrit word meaning "universal truth". The Californian

reference is bolstered by subtle evocations of three Californian composers: Terry Riley, LaMonte Young, and Lou Harrison.

DEATH OF KLINGHOFFER

OPERA   ⏱ 160:00   📖 2   ♫ 🎻 🥁

This dark opera is based on the hijacking of the cruise liner *Achille Lauro* by Palestinian terrorists, and their subsequent murder of an elderly disabled Jewish passenger, Leon Klinghoffer. The model behind this work were the Passions of J S Bach. Adams was attacked for portraying the terrorists in a sympathetic light.

Adam's conducting his nativity oratorio, *El Niño* – an impressive reworking of the Christmas story, based on texts from religious and multi-cultural sources.

FOCUS

GRAND PIANOLA MUSIC

ENSEMBLE   🎵 30:00   📖 3   🎐 🎷 ♂

Adams has often spoken of the folly of ignoring popular culture and the necessity of embracing his US heritage. Some of his works revel in that heritage to an exuberant, irreverent degree; this is one of them. As he put it, "Beethoven and Rachmaninoff soak in the same warm bath with Liberace, Wagner, the Supremes, Charles Ives, and John Philip Sousa." Much of the writing is delicate, with the two pianos playing slightly out-of-phase. The loud, bombastic finale, entitled "The Dominant Divide", applies minimalist techniques to the simplest possible chord progression.

HARMONIELEHRE

ORCHESTRAL   🎵 40:00   📖 3   🎐

This work marked the decisive shift in Adams' work from the minimalist purity of his early works to his mature, more expressive style. The title comes from Schoenberg's harmony textbook of 1911, but the first inspiration for the piece came from a dream in which Adams saw a huge tanker rise out of San Francisco bay and take off like a rocket. The music mirrors this "take off" in a series of hammered E minor chords which speed up and disintegrate. The surprise comes later, when a long-breathed melody of a distinctly late-Romantic cast rises out of the cellos. The second movement, "The Amfortas Wound", is the darkest of the three, while the third, "Meister Eckhardt and Quackie", begins in radiance and ends in E flat major triumph.

NIXON IN CHINA

OPERA   🎵 160:00   📖 3   🎐 🎭 ♂

In Adams' first opera, the music is scored for only 34 players, including saxophones and synthesizers. The narrative is based on the visit by US president Richard Nixon to China in 1972, and much of the action consists of big public set-pieces. There are also intimate scenes in which the characters reveal their hopes and fears. Adams shows great sensitivity to Alice Goodman's text, notably in the aria "The News", sung by Nixon at the foot of the steps to his aircraft, *Spirit of '76*. The gasping rhythm and obsessive repetitions reveal the anxiety, the hunger for greatness, and perhaps the shallowness of the leading character.

Terry Riley

● 1935–　　🏳 American　　✍ 80

Terry Riley is one of the founding fathers of minimalism.
His 60s piece *In C* is acknowledged as a key moment in
the emergence of a driving repetitive style that was picked up
by composers who are now better-known than Riley, such as Reich and Glass.
The success of this piece has obscured the great variety of Riley's music,
which ranges from tape-delay montages to Indian-inspired lyricism.

LIFE AND MUSIC

Terry Riley's life has been as unorthodox as his music. After study at the University of California, he led a rootless life playing piano in bars in Europe and America. In the early 60s he was a co-founder of the San Francisco Tape Music Centre, where he created highly innovative pieces using montage and tape-echo techniques, some in collaboration with underground composer La Monte Young.

Riley's main influence has been Indian Classical music – a form he now teaches at the Christi Sabri School in New Delhi.

His 1964 piece *In C* defines the 60s like no other Classical piece, but Riley would say that the meeting with Kirana vocal master Pandit Pran Nath in 1970 was the real watershed in his life. Since then his music has reflected the profound influence of Indian Classical music, in its incorporation of improvisation, its use of unorthodox tuning systems, and in its yearning for mystical transcendence.

MILESTONES

1960	Collaborates with La Monte Young
1962	Begins two-year stay in Europe
1964	Premiere of *In C*
1970	Meets Pandit Pran Nath
1980	Starts writing for the Kronos Quartet
1989	Leads Khayal group until 1993
1993	Starts teaching at Christi Sabri School of Indian Classical Music

KEY WORKS

IN C

EXPERIMENTAL

To be played "by any instruments", this is a joyous affirmation of the chord of C major. The entire score consists of a single page of melodic fragments, through which the players move at their own pace. The fixed element is a hammered octave C, which holds the key and the rhythm.

THE SAINT ADOLF RING

OPERA　🎭 🎻 🎵

Like several other contemporary composers, Riley has become fascinated by the strange visions of the Swiss schizophrenic artist Adolf Wöfli. In

1992 he founded the Travelling Avant-Garde Theatre Company to perform his multi-media chamber opera *The Saint Adolf Ring*, in which he performed as player, singer and actor.

CONCERT FOR TWO PIANOS AND FIVE TAPE RECORDERS

EXPERIMENTAL　🎭

Much inspired by the chance works of John Cage, this work was premiered by Riley himself and La Monte Young. It is a joyously anarchic collage of keyboard sounds (both live and on tape-loops) and recorded sounds such as explosions, screams and laughter.

Aram Khachaturian

● 1903–1978   ⚑ Armenian   ✍ 76

Khachaturian was the first, and so far the only, Armenian composer to achieve world renown. This was due to his two Romantic ballets *Gayaneh* and *Spartacus*, and his attractively melodious concertos. Like many Soviet ballets, his recall the exotic romanticism of Rimsky-Korsakov and early Stravinsky. The extra ingredient is an Armenian folk flavour, which can be heard in nearly all Khachaturian's works.

LIFE AND MUSIC

Khachaturian had a generous, optimistic nature. Throughout the horrors of Stalin's Terror in the 1930s and the denunciations of the cultural commissar Zhdanov, he conducted himself with dignity, refusing to point the finger at fellow composers. His music has a similar straightforward cheerfulness; even the tragic moments in the ballets are picturesque rather than moving. The influence of Armenian folk music can be seen in the frequent hectic ostinati, in chords based on fourths and fifths (inspired by the open strings of the Armenian *saz*) and a rhapsodic improvisational form of melody.

MILESTONES

1929	Enters Moscow Conservatory
1932	Joins Composers' Union
1933	Marries fellow Conservatory student Nina Makarova
1936	Premiere of Piano Concerto,
1939	Awarded Order of Lenin
1940	Premiere of Violin Concerto
1942	Premiere of *Gayaneh*
1948	Denounced as a formalist by Zhdanov, alongside Shostakovich and others
1956	Premiere of *Spartacus*
1973	Appointed Hero of Socialist Labour

KEY WORKS

GAYANEH

BALLET   ⏱ 150   📖 4   🎵

The first of Khachaturian's two balletic masterpieces, Gayaneh contains the famous "Sabre Dance", which soon became a hit for, among others, the Andrews Sisters (a fact which, along with Khachaturian's risky habit of wearing double-breasted "American" suits may have led to his problems with Zhdanov in 1948).
Almost as famous is the "Adagio", used by Stanley Kubrick in *2001: A Space Odyssey*.

Spartacus tells the tale of a group of gladiators who defeat the Roman Army in the 1st century BC.

SPARTACUS

BALLET   ⏱ 140:00   📖 4   🎵

This ballet portrays the heroic efforts of the slave Spartacus to free himself and his comrades from captivity. Given the date of the piece (1956) the conservatism of the musical language is astonishing. But so is the music's sheer Hollywood-ish orchestral bravura.

"*I abhor imitation and I abhor the familiar.*"

SERGEI PROKOFIEV

Sergei Prokofiev

◗ 1891–1953   ⚐ Russian   ✍ 102

Prokofiev had an immense natural gift as a composer and pianist and a determinedly optimistic character. His pre-Revolutionary music is vivid, sarcastic, sometimes brutal; the later music is more measured and lyrical, and after his return to the Soviet Union, more conventional. Throughout his life Prokofiev kept his strong pictorial and dramatic sense, revealed as much in his "abstract" symphonies and sonatas as in his famous ballets.

LIFE

An adored only child with a highly musical mother, Prokofiev had composed two operas by his 11th birthday. From 1905 he studied at the St Petersburg Conservatory, where he quickly became known as an arrogant, rebellious composer of brashly modernist music. After the upheavals of the Bolshevik Revolution, in 1918 Prokofiev left for what he thought would be a short trip abroad. It turned out to be an 18-year sojourn, of which the first two were spent in the US. He scored an instant hit as a pianist, and received a commission for *The Love for Three Oranges*, the only one of his operas to win international fame in his lifetime. In 1921 his ballet *Chout* was a great success in Paris, and the following year he resettled, firstly in Bavaria, then Paris. The 1920s brought two further successes with the Ballets Russes: *Le Pas d'Acier (The Steel Step)* and *The Prodigal Son*. In between composing, Prokofiev made many successful tours as a pianist, to the US, Europe, and the Soviet Union. But he missed home. He started to accept Soviet commissions, and in 1935 returned to the Soviet Union, then in the grip of the Stalinist Terror. In the late 1940s he was criticized for "formalist tendencies" by the authorities. He died of a brain haemorrhage on the same day as Stalin.

Though Prokoviev wrote several "official pieces" for state occasions, his music was also criticized by the Soviet regime.

MUSICAL OUTPUT						Total: 102
SYMPHONIES (7)		1	1	2		3
CONCERTOS (9)		3	1	3	1	1
CHAMBER (46)		10	9	11	13	3
FILM SCORES (11)				3	7	1
OPERAS (9)		2	3		3	1
BALLETS (10)		2	2	3	1	2
OFFICIAL PIECES (10)					6	4
	1891	1909	1917	1926	1936	1945 1953

MUSIC

Up to the time of World War I there were two distinct strands in Prokofiev's music. There was a rich, post-Romantic mood, derived from Scriabin and Rachmaninov, evident in works like the opera *The Fiery Angel*. Then there was a mood of biting sarcasm, revealed in such hectically rhythmic and dissonant pieces as the *Scythian Suite* and the piano work *Sarcasms*. Here the model was Stravinsky, with whom Prokofiev kept up a not always friendly rivalry. Prokofiev also had a quality all his own: this was a childlike playfulness, shown in a fondness for primary-colour orchestration, and a tendency for the harmony to jump unexpectedly to distant chords, often within a single melodic phrase. But the chords themselves are not dissonant, and they always find their way back to their starting point. In the music

MILESTONES	
1913	Sensational premiere of Piano Concerto No. 2, Op. 16
1918	Travels to US via Siberia and Japan
1923	Settles in Paris after a year in Bavaria
1929	*The Prodigal Son*, Op. 46, premiered in Monte Carlo and Paris; *The Gambler*, Op. 24, premiered in Brussels
1935	Returns to Soviet Union in December
1936	*Peter and the Wolf*, based on a Russian folk tale written for chidren
1943	Completes draft of *War and Peace*, Op. 91, while evacuated to Alma-Ata
1945	Has serious concussion after a fall, which permanently weakens him

of the Soviet period the dissonance and sarcasm withdraw, and the lyrical Prokofiev is revealed ever more clearly. The result in some people's eyes is disappointingly conventional, but the later works have their admirers too.

KEY WORKS

SYMPHONY NO. 5, OP. 100

ORCHESTRAL   ⏱ 42:00   📖 4   🎵

Composed in the darkest days of World War II, the premiere of this symphony in 1945 was heard against the thunderous background of an artillery salute. Prokofiev wrote that the piece portrayed "the grandeur of the human spirit". The affirmative final movement ends in jubilation, reflecting Soviet victories in the war.

VISIONS FUGITIVES, OP. 22

SOLO PIANO   📖 20   🎵

These 20 piano miniatures, by turns grotesque, tender, and sardonic, were written in 1915–17. The title comes from a line by the symbolist poet Balmont: "In every fugitive vision I see whole worlds: they change endlessly, flashing in playful rainbow colours".

ALEXANDER NEVSKY

ORCHESTRAL   📖 7   🎵

In 1937 the great Russian director Sergei Eisenstein asked Prokofiev to provide the score for his film *Alexander Nevsky*. Eisenstein had great respect for the composer's work, and at times cut or shortened sequences to fit in with Prokofiev's music.

In this 1930s production of Prokofiev's *Romeo and Juliet* by the Bolshoi Ballet, Galina Ulanova, creator of the role of Juliet, dances with Yuri Zhadonov.

VIOLIN CONCERTO NO. 1, OP. 19

ORCHESTRAL ⏱ 20:00 📖 3 🎶 🎧

Composed in 1917, in the same period as *Visions Fugitives*, the concerto was not premiered until 1923 in Paris. It has an unconventional form, with two slow movements framing a quicksilver, acid scherzo.

FIRST MOVEMENT (ANDANTINO, ANDANTE ASSAI, 9:00) This begins with a radiantly lyrical theme, but soon the tempo quickens and the mood becomes brittle and strange, with a high-stepping balletic second theme. The reprise of the opening theme carries the music aloft to a shimmering, pianissimo ending.

SECOND MOVEMENT (SCHERZO, VIVACISSIMO, 4:00) The light-footed scherzo is brilliantly orchestrated. The contrasting second theme is a galumphing march, like a dance for trolls, whereas the ending is pure glittering colour, the violin playing a stream of high harmonics.

THIRD MOVEMENT (MODERATO, 7:00) A dry bassoon theme provides a neutral background for the lyrical violin. The bassoon theme's more emphatic return later on takes on a fugal texture. This leads to the climax, after which there is an exact reprise of the ending of the first movement.

ROMEO AND JULIET, OP. 64

BALLET ⏱ 135:00 📖 3 🎶

Composed in 1934, this is a classic example of the Soviet taste for full-length, traditional ballets.

ACT ONE The Prince of Verona's command that no one break the peace is portrayed in unusually sharp dissonance. Prokofiev lavishes three tender themes on Juliet, and portrays with great subtlety the moment when she sees herself in the mirror and realises she's no longer a girl. The ensuing "Masked Ball" where Juliet meets Romeo has some of Prokofiev's finest dance music.

ACT TWO Juliet and Romeo are married in secret by Friar Lawrence in a marvellously tender and intimate scene. The fight scenes are full of restless, "cinematic" music.

ACT THREE Prokofiev at first contrived a happy ending (this may have been a concession to the Soviet demand for optimism in art), but the original tragic ending was reinstated.

SUITE NO.2 (OP. 64b)

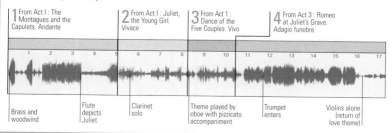

1 From Act I : The Montagues and the Capulets. Andante

2 From Act I : Juliet, the Young Girl. Vivace

3 From Act 1 : Dance of the Five Couples. Vivo

4 From Act 3 : Romeo at Juliet's Grave. Adagio funebre

| 1 | 2 | 3 | 4 | 5 | 6 | 7 | 8 | 9 | 10 | 11 | 12 | 13 | 14 | 15 | 16 | 17 |

Brass and woodwind

Flute depicts Juliet

Clarinet solo

Theme played by oboe with pizzicato accompaniment

Trumpet enters

Violins alone (return of love theme)

"To me he seemed like a trapped man, whose only wish was to be left alone, to the peace of his own art and to the tragic destiny to which he had been forced to resign himself."

NICHOLAS NABOKOV ON MEETING SHOSTAKOVICH IN 1949 IN NEW YORK

Dmitri Shostakovich

● 1906–1975   Ⓟ Russian   ✍ 110

Alongside Benjamin Britten, Shostakovich is the most popular composer of the mid-20th century. His 15 symphonies are acknowledged as the greatest since Mahler's his 15 string quartets the most significant since Bartók's. But he's also a controversial figure. Modernists dismissed him as a reactionary, or a lackey of the Soviet regime, and recent attempts to find anti-Stalinist messages in his music have aroused fierce debate.

LIFE

Until the age of 11 Shostakovich lived a comfortable life in a well-off bourgeois Russian household. However, in October 1917 the Bolsheviks came to power, sweeping away the privileges of the middle class. After study at the St Petersburg Conservatory, Shostakovich's first big success came with his Symphony No. 1, premiered in 1925, when he was only 19. He spent much of the 1920s and 30s writing film and theatre scores to earn money, but, despite the frantic pace of work, he found time for a complicated love life. He married the physics student Nina Varzar in 1932, but had several affairs thereafter. Along with all creative artists in Russia at that time, Shostakovich's life was overshadowed by Stalin's repressive policies. In 1936 his opera *Lady Macbeth of the Mtsensk District* was attacked in the official newspaper *Pravda*. He eventually rehabilitated himself with his Symphony No. 5, but in 1948 he was attacked again for formalism. From the 1930s onwards he was obliged to write optimistic "official" pieces alongside his "pure" symphonies and quartets. After Nina's death in 1954, Shostakovich remarried twice, latterly to Irina Supinskaya, who outlived him. In the 1960s his health, which had never been strong, declined further, and much of his last years were spent in hospital.

Though a controversial figure, Shostakovich was the pre-eminent Russian composer of the Soviet era.

MUSICAL OUTPUT					Total: 110
SYMPHONIES (15)	1	3	5	2	4
CONCERTOS (6)		1		3	2
FILM/THEATRE SCORES (48)		16	19	7	6
CHAMBER MUSIC (21)	1	2	4	5	9
OPERAS (4)		2		1	1
BALLETS (4)		3			1
OFFICIAL PIECES (12)			5	4	3
	1906	1925	1936	1948	1960	1975

MUSIC

Shostakovich's early works, such as the Symphony No. 1, have the exuberant balletic energy of Tchaikovsky and Stravinsky, and often a sarcastic spirit learned from Prokofiev. In the late 1920s and 30s two more ingredients entered the mix: the combination of grotesque parody and tragedy of Mahler, and the fierce expressionism and social satire of Alban Berg's opera *Wozzeck*. At first the result was gleeful and exuberant, as in the opera *The Nose* and his 1936 hit *Lady Macbeth of the Mtsensk District* an opera that proved to be the watershed in Shostakovich's life. After it was attacked, and he was disgraced, his music lost its high spirits. The parody was still there, but it had become anguished, and the general tone became angular, lean, and serious. In the Symphony No. 5, Shostakovich strikes a delicate balance between satisfying the communist regime's demand for simplicity and optimism (ie "representing contemporary reality

in a musical language comprehensible to The People") and expressing his own views on the regime. What those views were is still a matter of debate, but there are many signs that in later life he hated it, as witnessed by the overblown fake triumphalism of Symphony No. 10's finale, the use of Jewish melodies (anti-semitism was rife in Stalinist Russia) and his attraction to dissident poets, like Yevtushenko, whose verses appear in Shostakovich's late, bleak Symphony No. 13.

It was at the Composers' Union at no.s 10–11 Bryusov Pereulok that Shostakovich was forced to read an apology for works that deviated from Socialist Realism.

MILESTONES

1917	Bolshevik Revolution
1919	Enters St Petersburg Conservatory
1925	Symphony No. 1, Op. 10, wins acclaim
1934	Composers' Union promulgates official aesthetic of Socialist Realism
1936	*Lady Macbeth* condemned in *Pravda*
1937	Premiere of Symphony No. 5, Op. 47
1941	Hitler invades Soviet Union
1942	Premiere of Symphony No. 7 in Moscow; American premiere conducted by Toscanini; symphony becomes symbol of resistance to fascism
1948	Accused of "anti-democratic tendencies" by cultural commissar
1949	Visits US as part of Soviet-sponsored "Peace Conference"; forced to declare allegiance to Stalinist aesthetics
1953	Death of Stalin brings relaxation of controls on expression
1953	Premiere of Symphony No. 10
1954	Wife Nina Varzar dies; his mother dies the following year
1960	Joins Communist Party
1962	Premiere of "Babi Yar"
1966	Suffers heart attack; is made Hero of Socialist Labour and receives second Order of Lenin
1972	Travels to East and West Germany, and England to meet his friend Benjamin Britten

Shostakovich (right) worked as a fireman during the Siege of Leningrad. In 1941, the first year of the siege, he composed his Symphony No. 7.

KEY WORKS

CONCERTO FOR PIANO, TRUMPET, AND STRINGS, OP. 35

CONCERTO 🎵 22:00 📖 4 ♫ ◐

This concerto is heavily influenced by the clean-cut Neo-Classicism of composers such as Paul Hindemith. The first movement pits a nostalgic piano theme against a Baroque-sounding military fanfare on trumpet, while the second is an elegiac waltz. The third is full of busy Neo-Classical counterpoint, and the last is one of Shostakovich's most effervescent finales.

Shostakovich wrote several film scores, including this one for *The New Babylon*, directed by Grigori Kozintsev and Leonid Trauberg.

SYMPHONY NO. 13, OP. 113

ORCHESTRAL 🎵 45:00 📖 5 ♫ 🥁 ♪

This piece, consisting of settings of poetry by dissident poet Yevgeny Yevtushenko, begins with "Babi Yar", which describes a massacre of Jews in Russia by the Nazis in 1943. The music has the bare, hollow style typical of Shostakovich's late music. After the symphony's premiere, Yevtushenko was forced to add a stanza to his poem claiming that Russians and Ukrainians had died alongside the Jews at Babi Yar.

SYMPHONY NO. 5, OP. 47

ORCHESTRAL 🎵 50:00 📖 4 ♫

The most played and discussed of all Shostakovich's works, this symphony encapsulates the agonies of his creative life. Subtitled "A Soviet Artist's Practical Creative Reply to Just Criticism", it begins with a great despairing outcry, followed by a long, numb lament. Of the apparently optimistic finale, Shostakovich said, "It's as if someone was beating you with a stick and saying, 'Your business is rejoicing, your business is rejoicing.'"

INFLUENCES

Because of his isolation from the West, Shostakovich's influence on the wider world of Classical music has been minimal. However, his influence on Russian composers, particularly Sofia Gubaidulina, Galina Ustvolskaya, and Alfred Schnittke, has been immense.

The famous Russian violinist Maxim Vengerov (below, left) performs Shostakovich's Piano Trio No. 2 at the Barbican Theatre in London.

FOCUS

LADY MACBETH OF THE MTSENSK DISTRICT, OP. 29

OPERA   🕑 155:00   📖 4

Shostakovich's second opera was based on a brutal tale about a woman who murders her father-in-law and husband. He composed a brilliant score mingling tragedy, comedy, and satire. The seamless, symphonic texture incorporates tension-building orchestral interludes between scenes, inspired perhaps by Berg's *Wozzeck*. The erotic scenes shocked Prokofiev and the author of "Muddle Instead of Music" (in *Pravda*) who complained that "...'love' is smeared all over the opera in the most 'vulgar' manner".

ACT ONE Katerina is bored in her marriage to Zinovy. The new labourer, Sergei, arrives, tries to molest the cook, Aksinka, and is wrestled to the ground by the outraged Katerina.

However, by the end of the act Sergei and Katerina become lovers.

ACT TWO Katerina's father-in-law catches Sergei leaving Katerina's room and thrashes him. He orders Katerina to make a meal for him, which she poisons. Later Zinovy returns and is beaten to death by Katerina and Sergei.

ACT THREE Katerina and Sergei are about to marry. An old peasant finds Zinovy's corpse and runs off to tell the police. At the wedding reception the police arrive and the couple give themselves up.

ACT FOUR Katerina and Sergei are now convicts in Siberia. Sergei rejects Katerina and makes advances to Sonyetka. At the end, the infuriated Katerina throws Sonyetka and herself into the river.

Lady Macbeth, staged here by the English National Opera, was originally suppressed for being "too divorced from the proletariat".

SYMPHONY NO. 10 IN E MINOR, OP. 95

ORCHESTRAL   🕑 51:00   📖 4

This symphony was written in 1953, the year of Stalin's death. Some see its second movement as a menacing portrayal of one of Stalin's military parades. As is so often the case with Shostakovich, the work's apparently triumphal ending is deceptive.

FIRST MOVEMENT

FIRST MOVEMENT (MODERATO, 22:00) This immense sonata-form movement has a dark, uncertain first subject, and an anxious, wavering second subject like a distorted waltz.

SECOND MOVEMENT (ALLEGRO, 4:00) The ruthlessly aggressive scherzo is played at breakneck speed.

THIRD MOVEMENT (ALLEGRETTO, 11:00) In the first part a forthright woodwind theme is framed by a quiet, enigmatic theme

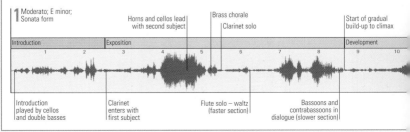

Moderato; E minor; Sonata form		Horns and cellos lead with second subject	Brass chorale		Start of gradual build-up to climax
Introduction	Exposition				Development
1	2	3	4	5	6	7	8	9	10
Introduction played by cellos and double basses		Clarinet enters with first subject	Flute solo – waltz (faster section)	Bassoons and contrabassoons in dialogue (slower section)	

STRING QUARTET NO. 8, OP. 110

CHAMBER   🎧 19:00   📖 5   ♁

In 1960 Shostakovich witnessed the devastation wrought on Dresden by the Allies during World War II, and in a mere three days wrote this piece.

FIRST MOVEMENT (LARGO, 5:00) This begins with Shostakovich's personal musical "cipher", DSCH (the notes D, E flat, C, and B) in the cello, which slowly ascends through the parts in a canon. The bleak mood is sustained by a quotation of the first symphony.

SECOND MOVEMENT (ALLEGRO MOLTO, 2:00) This scherzo has a driving rhythm taken from the fifth symphony combined with DSCH in a canon. This builds to a climax in which the Jewish theme from Shostakovich's Piano Trio is played fortissimo.

THIRD MOVEMENT (ALLEGRETTO, 4:00) A varied reprise of the previous movement, refracted through the rhythm of a diabolical waltz.

FOURTH MOVEMENT (LARGO, 5:00) A high note on the first violin is accompanied by three terrifying chords followed by various themes from the Cello Concerto, Symphonies Nos. 10 and 11, DSCH, the revolutionary song "Tormented by grievous bondage", and *Lady Macbeth*.

FIFTH MOVEMENT (LARGO, 3:0) This reprise of the opening fugue combines with a new lullaby-like countersubject, which descends to C minor and the DSCH motive.

in the violins. Hidden in the woodwind theme is Shostakovich's personal music cipher DSCH (D, E flat, C, B), which is more prominent later in the movement, and in the quiet wistful coda.

FOURTH MOVEMENT (ANDANTE – ALLEGRO, 14:00) After an Andante introduction with a plaintive melody for woodwind, the

Yevgeny Mravinsky unveiled the Symphony No. 10 with the Leningrad Philharmonic Orchestra.

Allegro bursts into life with a cheekily trivial theme. But the cheeriness is constantly undercut by memories of the Andante opening, and of Shostakovich's cipher, which entwines in majestic counterpoint with the main theme at the end.

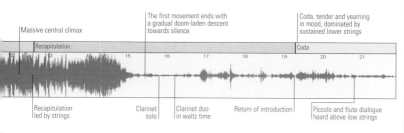

	The first movement ends with a gradual doom-laden descent towards silence		Coda, tender and yearning in mood, dominated by sustained lower strings
Massive central climax			
Recapitulation			Coda

| Recapitulation led by strings | Clarinet solo | Clarinet duo in waltz time | Return of introduction | Piccolo and flute dialogue heard above low strings |

Sofia Gubaidulina

● 1931–   Ⓝ Russian   ✍ c.120

With a Tatar father and Russian mother, Gubaidulina mixes East and West in her deep, spiritual music. It found disfavour at times during the Soviet era, when she made a living from film scores. In 1990, however, she was invited onto the State prize-awarding committee and has received numerous prizes herself. Her affecting, mystic music mixes unusual textures and instruments in techniques ranging from microtones to mathematically generated rhythmic structures. Her violin concerto *Offertorium* helped establish her in the West.

MILESTONES	
1961	Graduates from Moscow Conservatory
1978	Composes *De profundis* for accordion
1980	Composes *Offertorium*, violin concerto made famous by Gidon Kramer
1982	*Seven Last Words* for cello, bayan, strings
1992	Moves to village outside Hamburg
2000	Writes *The Passion According to St John*

The Kronos Quartet, renowned for its love of the new, commissions work from Gubaidulina.

Rodion Shchedrin

● 1932–   Ⓝ Russian   ✍ c.110

A virtuoso pianist, Shchedrin became professor of composition at the Moscow Conservatory in 1964 and stayed in official favour in the USSR, despite his refusal to endorse the Czech Invasion in 1968. Since 1990 he has received many commissions and spends a lot of time in Germany. His compositions mix cultured music references with humour in styles from jazz to folk music and atonality. He has impeccable academic credentials, but his music (such as his ballet *Carmen Suite*) also enjoys popular appeal, both within Russia and increasingly outside. He has recorded his own vibrant, witty piano music, including five concertos and the 1972 *Polyphonic Notebook*. His output also includes ballets and operas, as well as orchestral, choral, and chamber works, and even a Japanese musical.

MILESTONES	
1967	Composes *Carmen Suite*, after Bizet
1969	Turns freelance
1970	Writes *24 Preludes and Fugues*, piano
1973	Succeeds Shostakovich as president of Composers' Union of USSR
1999	Composes Piano Concerto No. 5

Shchedrin is married to ballerina Maya Plisetskaya, for whom he created the ballet *Carmen Suite*, an affectionately joking tribute to Bizet's opera.

Alfred Schnittke

● 1934–1998   ⚑ Russian   ✍ 246

Alfred Schnittke is easily the best-known Russian composer since Shostakovich. He achieved that eminence through the shocking emotional rawness of his music, which to some people is the authentic voice of modern spiritual deracination. However, his critics say that this bleakness is only a reflection of the conditions peculiar to Soviet Russia, and that his hyper-intensity veers close to musical chaos.

LIFE AND MUSIC

Schnittke grew up – and lived – torn between different cultural roots: Russian, Jewish, and Austro-German. He also had to live with the Soviet hostility to anything that smacked of experimentation. The result is a music of spiritual torment that veers between Mahlerian irony and the bleakness of late Shostakovich. However, Schnittke goes much further than these, creating tension from the co-existence within single pieces of many stylistic references, a technique he dubbed "polystylism". In his music, as exemplified in his Concerto Grosso No. 1, a phrase of Mozartian sweetness can turn into a dissonant scream and a Vivaldi concerto Allegro can become a danse macabre.

MILESTONES	
1953	Enters Moscow Conservatory
1958	Union of Composers condemns his oratorio *Nagasaki*
1962	Begins successful career as freelance composer for film and theatre
1974	Composers' Union chief condemns his emblematic Symphony No. 1
1977	Writes Concerto Grosso No. 1
1990	Moves permanently to Hamburg

Schnittke's *Requiem* of 1975 expressed spiritual deracination at its most extreme. The fall of communism has allowed his music to be more widely heard in Russia.

KEY WORKS

CONCERTO GROSSO NO. 1

CHAMBER   ⏱ 32:00   📖 6   ♟

Like many of Schnittke's works, this piece reworks material from a film score. He achieves an alienating effect by sampling Baroque music, by mixing micro-intervals and chromaticism, and by quoting "banal popular music which enters as if from the outside with a disruptive effect".

SYMPHONY NO. 1

ORCHESTRAL   ⏱ 66:00   📖 4   🎻

One of Schnittke's most extreme works, his first symphony exemplifies, as he once said, all the ingredients of his life's music.

It begins with the players arriving one by one and improvising chaotically until a signal from the conductor brings silence. Towards the end they leave, only to return and begin the work all over again.

VIOLA CONCERTO

ORCHESTRAL   ⏱ 35:00   📖 3   🎻 🎧

Written for the Russian violist Yuri Bashmet, this piece has a moment which starkly illustrates Schnittke's way of making familiar things seem strange. The violist launches a conventional-sounding phrase, which mounts higher and higher until it becomes a deranged scream.

Kurt Weill

⬤ 1900–1950　　🏳 German　　✍ c.100

Weill is one of few composers to make the transition successfully from modernist art music to the Broadway stage. With Bertold Brecht, he developed a sophisticated form of political theatre that satirized contemporary life and incorporated popular music. After emigrating to the US, he adapted these ideas to the stage, writing several hit works and having a huge influence on the development of the musical.

LIFE AND MUSIC

During his early career in Weimar Germany, Weill embraced the *neue Sachlichkeit* (new objectivity) of Paul Hindemith and Ernst Krenek – music of cool modernism, consciously detached from the "excesses" of the Romantic era. Weill's interests became increasingly political, and he began a collaboration with left-wing playwright Bertold Brecht that revolutionized music theatre by openly satirizing the establishment. After condemnation by the Nazis in 1935, he emigrated to the US and turned to composing for Broadway. His style, always deliberately referential and incorporating elements of popular music and jazz, proved ideally suited to this new medium.

MILESTONES	
1918	Attends Berlin's Hochschule für Musik; taught by Humperdinck and Busoni
1924	Composes Violin Concerto
1926	Writes *Der Protagonist*, opera; marries singer Lotte Lenya
1927	First collaboration with Brecht: result is *Mahagonny*, a Singspiel for radio
1928	Composes *The Threepenny Opera* and *The Tsar Has His Photograph Taken*, operas
1930	Transforms his Singspiel *The Rise and Fall of the City of Mahagonny* into a full opera
1933	Moves to Paris, then US two years later
1936	*Johnny Johnson* is his first Broadway work
1946	Writes *Street Scene*, opera; elected as only composer-member of the US Playwrights' Producing Company

KEY WORKS

CONCERTO FOR VIOLIN AND WIND ORCHESTRA

ORCHESTRAL　⏱ 28:00　📖 3　🎼 🎵

As well as stage works, Weill also wrote instrumental music, including two symphonies, and this violin concerto, composed in 1924 in the *neue Sachlichkeit* style. The influence of Stravinsky can be heard, particularly in the wind scoring.

The world of 1920s Berlin lowlife and the theatre were both inspirational to Weill.

THE THREEPENNY OPERA

OPERA　⏱ 90:00　📖 3　🎭🎵🎶🎵

Based loosely on John Gay's *Beggar's Opera* of 1728, *The Threepenny Opera* was Weill's first collaboration with Brecht on a piece for the stage, and remains Weill's best-known work. Brecht's sardonic libretto is a damning critique of capitalism, depicting a world of beggars, prostitutes, thieves, and corrupt officials, where money and personal gain are all-important. "Mack the Knife", perhaps Weill's most famous song, is from this opera.

FOCUS

THE RISE AND FALL OF THE CITY OF MAHAGONNY

OPERA ⏱ 120:00 📖 3 ♒ ⚒ ♿

The premiere of this full-length opera, based on a radio Singspiel that was Weill's first collaboration with Brecht, was delayed for a year, owing to both the publisher's misgivings about the frank sexual references, and the hostile reception of other new satirical operas, such as Hindemith's *Neues von Tage*.

Mahagonny is a biting satire on capitalist society. It tells the story of three escaped convicts, who, stranded in the US during the gold rush, decide to establish a city, Mahagonny, devoted to the hedonistic pleasures of drink, women, and gambling. Business booms and so do prices. Jim, a gold prospector, is unable to pay his debts and is executed by electric chair when his prostitute girlfriend refuses to assist. The people demonstrate, while the city collapses in flames.

Musically, *Mahagonny* is a curious blend of abrasive Neo-Classicism in the mould of Hindemith, pastiche of grand opera, and popular jazz and cabaret. By juxtaposing these styles, Weill adds bite to the satirical libretto.

STREET SCENE

OPERA ⏱ 130:00 📖 2 ♒ ⚒ ♿

After success with stage musicals, Weill began to harbour a desire to write what he called an "American opera". This would be in the mould of a verismo opera, with most of the dialogue sung rather than acted, but still based on the musical virtues of Broadway.

The story Weill chose was *Street Scene*, a Pulitzer Prize-winning play by Elmer Rice. Set over 24 hours in a run-down New York tenement, it tells of a tragic murder among the immigrant community. A bullying husband catches his wife in flagrante with her lover, shoots them both dead, and, after briefly escaping, is caught.

The musical styles are diverse, from Anna's touching aria "Still I could never believe", reminiscent of Puccini, to the pure 1940s jive of "Moon-faced, starry-eyed", and all manner of blues and jazz in between. Although this multiplicity of reference has led some critics to question whether Weill's vision of an American opera was truly fulfilled, *Street Scene* is certainly immaculately crafted and enjoyable to see in production.

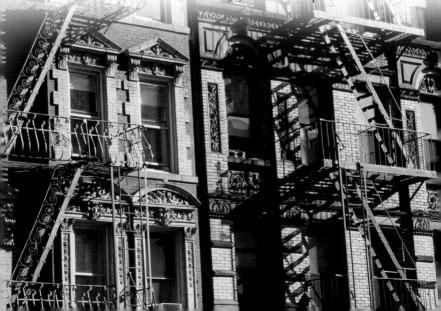

Olivier Messiaen

● 1908–1992   🏴 French   ✍ 74

Olivier Messiaen is one of the most paradoxical figures
in music. A great radical of the 20th century, on a par with
Debussy or John Cage, he was also a deeply traditional
figure, serenely convinced of the truths of the Catholic faith. Messiaen saw no
contradiction between these attitudes. He felt he had to develop his radically new
language in order to give his fervently held beliefs the most vivid expression.

LIFE AND MUSIC

Messiaen's early influences were
Wagner, Debussy, and Mussorgsky, and
later, while at the Paris Conservatoire,
Christian chant and folk music. His
early piece "Le banquet céleste"
already has the essential elements of
Messiaen: it was scored for his own
instrument, the organ; it has a Catholic
subject; and it seems to bring time to a
halt, through its incredibly slow tempo.
Over the next 64 years Messiaen
invented many other ways of loosening
the grip of measured time on music,
to give a foretaste of the eternity of
heaven. Among these were rhythmic
modes learned from ancient Indian
sources, the use of patterned, repetitive
forms, and imitation of birdsong.

MILESTONES	
1923	Enters Paris Conservatoire
1931	Becomes organist at La Trinité
1932	Marries violinist Claire Delbos
1936	Founds "La Jeune France" (with others) in opposition to Neo-Classicism
1940	Interned in a prisoner-of-war camp in Poland
1947	Begins teaching at Conservatoire
1949	*Turangalîla Symphony* produced
1951	Begins systematic study of birdsong
1956	Composes *Réveil des Oiseaux*
1961	Marries Yvonne Loriod
1965	Begins work on *La transfiguration de notre seigneur Jésus-Christ*, choral
1978	Retires from teaching
1984	Premiere of *St François d'Assise*, opera

KEY WORKS

TURANGALÎLA SYMPHONY
ORCHESTRAL   ⏱ 70:00   📖 10   🎵 🎧

One of a cycle of three pieces based
on the Tristan legend and its theme of
boundless love, this piece includes a
prominent part for ondes martenot,
whose tremulous, swooping
melodiousness is an
essential ingredient of
its fascination. The ten
movements alternate
passionate love-music with
austere rhythmic games.

Organist at the church of La Trinité in
Paris for 60 years, Messiaen's work was
both an expression of his Catholicism
and a joyful celebration of earthly life.

ST FRANÇOIS D'ASSISE
OPERA   ⏱ 180:00   📖 3   🎵 🥁 🎻

Messiaen spent nearly a decade writing
this, his longest work and only opera.
It's an ambitious piece, uniting the
"old" Messiaen of long, ecstatic melody
and the "new" Messiaen
of fast, glittering birdsong.
It avoids drama in the
normal sense and includes
blocks of almost static
sound. The characters
involved are all monks,
apart from the Angel and
the Leper, and the aim is
to show "the progress of
grace in St Francis's soul".

FOCUS

QUARTET FOR THE END OF TIME

CHAMBER 🕐 50:00 📖 8 ⊕

Messiaen composed this quartet for violin, cello, clarinet, and piano while being held in a German prisoner-of-war camp in Silesia in Poland during World War II. The premiere took place one freezing night, on a piano with faulty keys and a cello with only three strings. Years later, Messiaen said, "Never have I been listened to with such concentration and understanding." The piece is full of Messiaen's apocalyptic imagery of angels, rainbows, and birds (for Messiaen, birds were God's true musicians). The opening "Liturgie de cristal" has repeating harmonic and rhythmic cycles of different lengths for cello and piano, outlining a pattern that, if completed, would take aeons to come back to its starting point (an image of the "end of time"). Later, there is a gentle monody, "Abyss of birds"; a savage "Dance of fury for the seven trumpets"; and finally an ecstatic "Louange a l'immortalité de Jésus" ("Praise to the Immortality of Jesus").

VISIONS DE L'AMEN

DUO 🕐 50:00 📖 7 ⊕

A vast, tumultuous cycle of pieces for two pianos, first performed in 1943 by Messiaen and his wife-to-be, Yvonne Loriod, whose amazing virtuosity inspired the piece. It began a new era in Messiaen's creative life in which the piano became central. The titles "Amen of Creation" and "Amen of the Agony of Jesus" give a flavour of the apocalyptic imagery of the piece.

DES CANYONS AUX ÉTOILES

ORCHESTRAL 🕐 75:00 📖 3 🐦

This immense orchestral piece was described by Messiaen as "an ascending from the canyons to the stars – and higher still, to the resurrected in Paradise – in order to glorify God in his creation... a work of sound-colour, where all the colours of the rainbow rotate around the blue of the Stellar's Jay and the red of Bryce Canyon." The work is scored for a late-Messiaen orchestra, designed to produce his favourite effect of "dazzlement" – serried ranks of brass, woodwind, and exotic percussion, a solo piano, and only a modest complement of strings.

"*I like to think of composing as a physical business. I compose at the piano and like to feel involved in my work with my hands.*"

MICHAEL TIPPETT

Michael Tippett

⬤ 1905–1998   🏳 British   ✍ 73

Tippett is the only rival to Benjamin Britten for the title of Britain's most significant composer since World War II, though he has only recently found a place in the hearts of music-lovers. In his determination to articulate an all-embracing world-view in his music, he is almost unique; the only comparable figure is the Catholic composer Olivier Messiaen. But unlike Messiaen, Tippett had to work out his own salvation.

LIFE

The two important factors in Tippett's childhood were his rural surroundings (he spent almost his whole life in the English countryside) and his freethinking parents, who gave him a stubborn independence of mind. He was slow to develop, spending five years at London's Royal College of Music, returning for a further two years from 1928–1930. During the 30s he taught French to earn a living, and composed on the side. His socialist sympathies led him to found the South London Orchestra, composed of unemployed musicians. But in the mid-1930s he withdrew from politics, and after a personal crisis following the break-up of his first serious gay relationship, he began an intense engagement with Jungian analysis. By the late-1930s he'd formed his deeply spiritual and yet agnostic beliefs. For him life was a never-ending process of uncovering the dark and light aspects of the personality, and reconciling them into wholeness. From *A Child of our Time* onwards, all his art was dedicated to articulating this world view. In the 1960s and 70s his delighted discovery of America and its music brought on an Indian summer of creativity. In his old age he gained the reputation of a sage, particularly among a new, young audience.

Many of Tippett's works explore a world illuminated by Jungian theories of psychology.

MUSICAL OUTPUT
Total: 73

	1905	1939	1953	1963	1972	1983	1998
ORCHESTRAL (22)			6	5	2	3	6
CHAMBER (15)		2	3	3	1	2	4
BRASS BAND (6)			1	2		1	2
DRAMATIC (6)				3	1	1	1
CHORAL (16)			4	9	2	1	
SOLO VOCAL (8)			2	3	1		2

MUSIC

Tippett once declared that in an age of "shattered dreams" it was the duty of an artist to create images of "generous, abounding beauty". He achieved this many times, but not without an immense struggle, first to work out a world view, and then to forge a personal musical language. At first this language took the form of a rich, very English Romanticism with a folk-like flavour.

In the early 1960s, Tippett's music underwent a dramatic change. The new style consisted of accumulations of short, contrasted fragments and used a much more astringent harmonic language. But the urge to ecstasy and transcendence was still there. The works of the 1980s and 1990s incorporated American pop influences into his earlier styles. The results were exuberant, if not always coherent.

MILESTONES	
1923	Enters Royal College of Music in London
1928	Settles in Oxted, Surrey
1935	Joins British Communist Party, but leaves within a few months
1939	Undergoes Jungian analysis after personal crisis
1940	Becomes music director of Morley College, London
1943	Imprisoned for refusing to join armed forces during World War II
1955	*Midsummer Marriage* premiered
1962	Premiere of second opera *King Priam* at Coventry Cathedral
1965	Visits Aspen Summer School in Colorado, the beginning of his love affair with America
1970	Moves to rural Wiltshire; third opera *The Knot Garden* premiered
1983	Appointed to the Order of Merit

KEY WORKS

SYMPHONY NO. 3

ORCHESTRAL   🔊 55:00   📖 4   ♫♫ ♙

This is a bleak, questioning piece, cast in four sections. In the finale Tippett parodies the vision of universal brotherhood expressed in Beethoven's Symphony No. 9, setting it off against the blues. The soprano sings Tippett's own text, which embraces both humanism and the horrors of Auschwitz, and at the end offers

King Priam, first performed at the Coventry Cathedral Festival in 1962, has had several successful revivals. This is the English National Opera production of 1995.

a small ray of hope ("What though the dream crack, we shall remake it").

CONCERTO FOR DOUBLE STRING ORCHESTRA

ORCHESTRAL   🔊 23:00   📖 3   ♫♫

Tippett's first undoubted masterpiece, the concerto belongs to the tradition of English string music established by Elgar, Vaughan Williams, and Britten. Further English traits are the "sprung" rhythms of the first movement, and the use of the folk song "Ca' the yowes".

KING PRIAM

OPERA   🔊 125:00   📖 3   ♫ ♙ ♫♫

The theatre director Peter Brook advised Tippett to base his second opera on a public myth, avoiding the private mythology of *The Midsummer Marriage*. It marked a startling new departure in Tippett's style. The music is made of short, hard-edged, contrasting blocks – a "mosaic of musical gestures" as Tippett put it.

FOCUS

THE MIDSUMMER MARRIAGE
OPERA   ⏱ 150:00   📖 3   👤👤👥

Tippett's first opera was six years in the making. Written in his early lyrical style, it encapsulates his vision of life as a struggle to reconcile warring elements within the individual and between peoples. The protagonists of the opera, Mark and Jenifer, refuse to accept aspects of each other. Mark feels Jenifer is too emotional and intuitive; she feels he is too rational.

ACT ONE The action begins at dawn on Midsummer's Day. Jenifer, daughter of the manipulative and powerful King Fisher, has decided to elope with Mark. But at Jenifer's insistence their marriage is delayed by a spiritual quest, involving journeys to Heaven and Hell.

ACT TWO The focus shifts to a second couple, Jack and Bella, and to the dance rituals of the supernatural beings who are the shadowy counterparts of the human characters.

ACT THREE King Fisher's attempts to manipulate his daughter and Bella fail. Jack and Bella go off happily together. King Fisher tries to unveil the mysterious soothsayer Sosostris, but this causes his death. Mark and Jenifer reappear and are engulfed in the flames of an ecstatic ritual fire dance. Dawn then rises and they can celebrate their union.

A CHILD OF OUR TIME
ORATORIO   ⏱ 60:00   📖 3   👤👤👥

This piece established Tippett's reputation at the age of 39. It was prompted by the shooting of a German official by the Polish Jewish agitator in 1938, which became the pretext for a pogrom. In Tippett's piece this event becomes a symbol for the oppression of the individual by dark collective forces. But the libretto suggests that these forces are in fact our own faults, projected onto other groups who are then perceived as hostile. Tippett followed the advice of T S Eliot to write his own libretto, a practice he always followed thereafter. The piece is a kind of modern Passion along the lines of J S Bach's *St Matthew Passion*, with the Lutheran chorales replaced by negro spirituals. The closing ensemble sums up Tippett's philosophy: "I would know my shadow and my light, So shall I at last be whole".

PART THREE

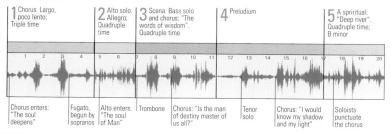

1 Chorus. Largo, poco lento; Triple time	2 Alto solo. Allegro; Quadruple time	3 Scena. Bass solo and chorus: "The words of wisdom". Quadruple time	4 Preludium		5 A spriritual: "Deep river". Quadruple time; B minor
1 2 3 4	5 6	7 8 9 10 11	12 13 14 15 16 17		18 19 20
Chorus enters: "The soul deepens"	Fugato, begun by sopranos	Alto enters: "The soul of Man"	Trombone	Chorus: "Is the man of destiny master of us all?"	Tenor solo	Chorus: "I would know my shadow and my light"	Soloists punctuate the chorus

"*It is cruel, you know, that music should be so beautiful. It has the beauty of loneliness and of pain... The beauty of disappointment and never-satisfied love.*"

BENJAMIN BRITTEN

Benjamin Britten

🌑 1913–1976   🏴 British   ✍ 267

Benjamin Britten is the only British composer since Elgar to have achieved worldwide renown. He single-handedly created a school of British opera, and left a large body of instrumental and vocal music which gives fresh new life to the familiar forms and harmonies of Western music. By the 1950s he had become a national institution, and today his popularity and musical influence seem more secure than ever.

LIFE

A precociously gifted child, Britten began several years of study with Frank Bridge at the age of 11. They proved to be far more fruitful than his later years at the Royal College of Music. His plans to study in Vienna with Alban Berg were quashed on the grounds that Berg would be a bad influence, but in 1935 Britten found an equally bad influence at home, in the shape of the poet W H Auden. He collaborated with Auden on films for the GPO film unit, and on several mordant satires, including *Our Hunting Fathers*. In 1939 he met the love of his life, the tenor Peter Pears. They set up home in 1945 in the Suffolk coastal village of Aldeburgh, where Britten would remain for the rest of his life. Many of Britten's greatest roles were created for Pears, including the lead in *Peter Grimes*, which reopened Sadlers Wells Opera in 1945. From 1947 the newly formed English Opera Group would be the centre of Britten's operatic endeavours, though there were big commissions from Covent Garden (*Billy Budd*, *Gloriana*), BBC television (*Owen Wingrave*) and, most prestigious of all, the Anglican Church (the *War Requiem*, written for the reopening of Coventry Cathedral). His last decade was clouded by ill-health, though his very last works are among his greatest.

Born in Lowestoft, Britten was inspired by his native county of Suffolk, where he also began the institution of the Aldeburgh Festival at the Snape Maltings.

MUSICAL OUTPUT					Total: 267
ORCHESTRAL (33)	1	14	9	5	4
OTHER INSTRUMENTAL (54)	9	17	8	6	14
FILM SCORES/INCIDENTAL (11)		5	6		
OPERAS AND BALLET (20)			5	10	5
SOLO VOCAL (96)	7	25	31	21	12
CHORAL (37)	3	10	8	10	6
MUSIC FOR CHILDREN (16)		2	2	8	4
	1913	1930	1939	1948	1962 1976

MUSIC

The numerous works of Britten's childhood reveal one of the great prodigies of all time, with an amazing variety of styles ranging from Viennese expressionism to modal lyricism. The stylistic uncertainty persisted into his 20s, though certain traits emerged that would be lifelong. There's a fondness for parody and stark funereal tragedy akin to Mahler, and a debt to the clear, clean textures of Stravinsky's Neo-Classicism. In *Peter Grimes* all these things come together in a brilliant, miraculous synthesis. By this date nearly all of Britten's vocabulary was in place, the only major additions being the sound-world of Balinese music, as revealed in the ballet *The Prince of the Pagodas*, and in the 1960s a Japanese spareness and economy, expressed most directly in the *Three Church Parables*. These opened the final phase in Britten's music, in which he refined his style to its essence.

MILESTONES

1924	Meets adventurous composer Frank Bridge, who becomes his mentor
1930	Enters Royal College of Music, London
1935	Meets W H Auden
1939	Leaves war-time England for the US with the tenor Sir Peter Pears
1942	Reading Suffolk poet George Crabbe, especially *Peter Grimes*, brings on Britten's decision to return home
1945	7 June premiere of *Peter Grimes*, Op. 33, makes Britten world famous
1948	Aldeburgh Festival founded: this soon becomes the centre of Britten's musical life
1951	Premiere of *Billy Budd*, Op. 50 at Covent Garden
1962	Premiere of *War Requiem*, Op. 66
1964	Premiere of church parable Curlew River, Op. 71, the first of his late, lean works
1973	Premiere of Britten's last opera *Death in Venice*, Op 88, with Pears in main role of Aschenbach

KEY WORKS

SERENADE FOR TENOR, HORN, AND STRINGS, OP. 31

ORCHESTRAL   🕐 25:00   📖 6   🎵 🎧 🎼

Of Britten's five song cycles for voice and instruments, this is probably the greatest. It consists of six songs in a predominantly meditative or nocturnal mood, framed by a prologue and epilogue for solo horn.

BILLY BUDD, OP. 50

OPERA   🕐 150:00   📖 4   🎵 🎭 🎼

This is one of Britten's most profound explorations of his favourite theme; the helplessness of innocence and goodness in the face of evil. It contains some of Britten's most gripping inventions, including the desperately sad chorus of seamen and Billy's lullaby sung the night before his execution – a perfect example of Britten's ability to plumb emotional depths with the most hackneyed materials.

Benjamin Britten's opera for children *Let's Make an Opera!* in rehearsal at Aldeburgh in Suffolk, the composer's home town.

YOUNG PERSON'S GUIDE TO THE ORCHESTRA, OP. 34

ORCHESTRAL   🕐 16:00   📖 1   🎵 🎧

One of Britten's most irresistibly ebullient works, this piece leads the listener through each section of the orchestra. It ends with a brilliant fugue, out of which the original theme majestically emerges.

PETER GRIMES, OP. 33

OPERA ⏱ 150:00 📖 3

Britten's first opera has an anti-hero: Peter Grimes, an outcast from the Borough, a fishing village not unlike the Aldeburgh Britten had recently settled in. He's a sadistic bully, who wants to get rich and marry; but in Britten's opera he also has a poetic side. The wonderful orchestral interludes (known as the *Four Sea Interludes*) may have been suggested by Alban Berg's opera *Wozzeck*, while the saucy tavern music shows the influence of Gershwin's *Porgy and Bess*.

ACT ONE The opening courtroom scene shows Britten's gift for comedy (later expressed more fully in *Albert Herring*). The following scene where Grimes recruits a new apprentice is a brilliant portrayal of village small-mindedness.

ACT TWO Grimes's mistreatment of the boy becomes clear in Scene 1, and in Scene 2 the boy falls to his death (notice this appearance, early in Britten's career, of the theme of innocence abused). In the intervening interlude comes Britten's brilliant reinvention of an old form, the passacaglia.

ACT THREE After a jolly dancing scene with a brilliant evocation of rustic bands, a posse is organised to hunt for Grimes. But his suicide (set to music which is brilliantly understated for some, and a disappointment to others) thwarts their revenge.

TURN OF THE SCREW, OP. 54

OPERA ⏱ 103:00 📖 2

Again the theme is innocence corrupted, but here it has an extra twist: is the boy Miles willing to be corrupted by the ghost of the evil Quint? And is the Governess, who wants to protect him, herself corrupted? With his small chamber orchestra Britten invents a fascinating sound-world that takes familiar symbols of innocence – the high tinkly sound of the celesta, children's voices, simple folk songs – and gives them a subtle twist which makes them appear sinister.

ACT ONE (53:00) The Governess's arrival at the house to look after Miles and his sister Flora starts well, but soon the ghosts of the dead Quint and Miss Jessel appear, and the Governess is horrified to discover that the children are unafraid of them. The act climaxes in a sensuously uncanny duet between Jessel and Quint, one of the great moments in Britten's operas.

ACT TWO (50:00) The Governess challenges the children to reveal their knowledge, but is rebuffed. At the end she wrests Miles away from Quint's evil influence, but he dies, and the opera ends with her heartbroken rendition of Miles's song "Malo".

INFLUENCES

Britten's influence has been most marked in Britain, where his interest in arranging Early Music and folk song has been as important as his own music. However, he is revered by composers who share his concern for reinvigorating simple tonal devices, and even younger composers who are less respectful cannot entirely escape his influence.

Yrjö Kilpinen

● 1892–1959   ♫ Finnish   ✎ c.750

Kilpinen was almost exclusively a composer of songs, writing over 750, but only half were published. After training in Helsinki, he travelled throughout Scandinavia and central Europe, and, in the 1930s, he was particularly popular in Nazi Germany, where he was seen as a Lieder composer in the tradition of Schubert or Wolf. However, his austere and bare style was neither modernist nor Romantic. Many of the poems he set were Finnish or Swedish, although he wrote 75 songs to German texts by Morgenstern.

MILESTONES	
1920	Writes Leino songs; reputation grows
1922	Concentrates on Swedish poets
1923	First concerts of his works, Helsinki
1928	Composes Tunturilauluja; Writes Lieder der Liebe, Lieder um den Tod
1954	Hochgebirgswinter published
1955	Starts Savonlinna Music Days

Elisabeth Lutyens

● 1906–1983   ♫ English   ✎ 190

Daughter of the architect Sir Edwin, Lutyens had a turbulent personal and professional life. She was a radical innovator and wrote uncompromisingly modern expressionist works, but also had to produce film and radio music to support her four children. Notorious for her dismissal of English pastoral music (such as that of Vaughan Williams) as "the cowpat school", she often felt isolated and met with incomprehension from the music establishment, whose recognition of her consistent achievement came late.

MILESTONES	
1939	Composes Chamber Concerto No. 1
1952	Writes String Quartet No. 6
1957	De amore, cantata, produced
1967	Time Off? Not a Ghost of a Chance!, opera, performed

Elizabeth Maconchy

● 1907–1994   ♫ English   ✎ c.200

The only musician in her family, Maconchy studied at Prague Conservatory and was influenced by the urgent energy of Janáček and Bartók. Her suite The Land triumphed in a London Proms concert and launched a highly successful composing career, briefly interrupted by tuberculosis. Though a placid person, her music can be immensely passionate. Her ten string quartets – rhythmic and profoundly argued works – are a major achievement. She also wrote effective music for amateurs and children.

MILESTONES	
1930	The Land, suite, performed
1933	Composes String Quartet No. 1
1957	Writes The Sofa, first of three operas
1981	My Dark Heart, song cycle, performed
1984	Composes String Quartet No. 13

Gian Carlo Menotti

● 1911–   ♫ American   ✎ 70

Born and brought up in Italy, where he wrote two operas before entering the Milan Conservatory at 13, Menotti settled in the US, becoming a versatile director, librettist, and composer of stage works. He has directed many film versions of his works, whose popular success is due to their light and open orchestral textures and memorable melodies. His TV opera Amahl and the Night Visitors has been broadcast annually since 1951.

MILESTONES	
1946	Writes The Telephone, one-act opera
1950	The Consul, first full-length opera
1951	Amahl and the Night Visitors, first opera for TV, broadcast
1958	Founds Festival of Two Worlds, Italy
1976	Composes The Halcyon, symphony
1986	Goya, opera, performed

Roberto Gerhard

● 1896–1970 🏴 Spanish ✍ 130

From a multicultural European background, Gerhard considered himself firmly Catalan, but settled in England to escape the Spanish Civil War. His music combines Spanish nationalism with modernism (he studied with both Pedrell and Schoenberg), and he wrote everything from innovative TV and radio incidental music to pioneering works for tape. All his work has imaginative genius and colour – his Symphony No. 3 reflects the feeling of a transatlantic flight. After a precarious career, serious recognition eventually came in the 1960s, and his music was widely performed.

MILESTONES	
1915	Teaches music in Barcelona
1939	Settles in Cambridge, England
1941	*Don Quixote*, ballet, performed
1947	Writes *The Duenna*, opera
1952	Composes Symphony No. 1
1959	*Lament on the Death of a Bullfighter*, speaker and tape

In Barcelona, Gerhard studied piano with Granados and composition with Carlos Pedrell who aroused his interest in Catalan folk music.

Henri Dutilleux

● 1916– 🏴 French ✍ 46

Henri Dutilleux, one of France's most distinguished post-war composers, has led a quiet, reclusive life away from the public eye. Since he retired as head of music commissions at French Radio in 1963 he has focused all his energies on composition. His works have the typical French virtues of a subtle and sensuous palette of instrumental colour and an ornamented form of melody. They are like a series of subtle half-hints, where nothing is ever stated definitively – no sooner does a melodic or harmonic shape emerge than it is transformed into something new. Even though he has an international reputation, his ruthless self-criticism means that his work list has remained relatively small.

MILESTONES	
1933	Studies at the Paris Conservatoire
1938	Wins Prix de Rome with cantata, *L'anneau du roi*
1940	Conducts choir at the Paris Opéra
1946	Composes Piano Sonata, Op. 1
1951	Symphony No. 1 premiered
1985	Premiere of *L'arbre des songes*, concerto

After a year's service as a stretcher-bearer in the French Army, Dutilleux returned to Paris in 1940 to work as a pianist, arranger, and teacher.

Robert Simpson

● 1921–1997   🏳 English   ✍ 65

As a writer and broadcaster, Simpson related complex ideas in an accessible way. He did the same with his music, especially his 11 symphonies and 16 string quartets, whose feel of cosmic energy released from small, nuclear reactions reflects his passion for astronomy. He wrote significant books on Bruckner and Nielsen, and worked for the BBC Music Division for 30 years before resigning to compose more. His music is tonal and rigorously structured, makes great use of dissonance, and is noted for its power, energy, and drive.

MILESTONES	
1951	Completes Symphony No. 1
1952	Composes String Quartet No. 1
1965	Second book on Danish composer Carl Nielsen published
1986	Moves to live in Ireland
1989	Composes *Vortex* for brass band
1991	Composes Symphony No. 11

George Lloyd

● 1913–1998   🏳 English   ✍ 55

After modest, early success with his lyrical, traditionally tuneful music – and a period of less popularity in rural Dorset as a market gardener, composing in his spare time – Lloyd's heyday came in the last 20 years of his life. A 1977 broadcast of his Symphony No. 8 re-established his reputation and many listeners disaffected by modernism eagerly discovered his music on CD. His substantial output includes 12 symphonies, four piano concertos, two violin concertos and three operas.

MILESTONES	
1932	Composes Symphony No. 1
1938	Covent Garden stages *The Serf*, opera
1963	Composes Piano Concerto No. 1
1965	Composes Symphony No. 8
1998	Composes Cello Concerto

Einojuhani Rautavaara

● 1928–   🏳 Finnish   ✍ 220

Rautavaara has found popularity with sombre, beautiful, and imaginative orchestral pieces such as *Cantus arcticus* (for taped bird-song and orchestra), the mystical Symphony No. 7 "Angel of Light" and his lyrical Piano Concerto No. 3. His *Serenades of the Unicorn* for guitar uses a teaspoon to suggest giggling nymphs, while his eerie Symphony No. 6 (based on his opera *Vincent*) portrays van Gogh's troubled mind with a synthesizer.

MILESTONES	
1952	Writes Pelimannit (Fiddlers) for piano
1972	Composes *Cantus arcticus*
1976	Begins 14 years as professor at Sibelius Academy in Helsinki
1987	Completes *Vincent*, opera
1994	Composes Symphony No. 7
1999	Composes Piano Concerto No. 3

Malcolm Arnold

● 1921–   🏳 English   ✍ 265

For 20 years, the gregarious Arnold composed direct, melodic, and colourful music with astonishing energy, including over 100 film scores (his Oscar-winning music for *Bridge on The River Kwai* being written in just ten days in 1957), plus extraordinary amounts of lively concert music – his 20-odd concertos were written for friends such as Dennis Brain, Julian Bream, and Yehudi Menuhin. The strain told, however, with descent into drink and depression, and his story is told in nine wide-ranging symphonies that span his creative life.

MILESTONES	
1953	Composes Symphony No. 2
1956	Writes *A Grand, Grand Overture*, vacuum cleaners, floor polisher, and orchestra
1959	Composes Guitar Concerto
1973	Composes Symphony No. 7

Krzysztof Penderecki

● 1933– ♙ Polish ✍ c.110

At a time when avant garde experimental music mainly avoided emotion, the harrowing directness of *Threnody to the Victims of Hiroshima* – scored for 52 strings and using innovative notation and a shocking range of sounds – made Penderecki's name. (The original title was *8′ 37″*; the Hiroshima connection came after he first heard it played.) His *St Luke Passion* resulted in invitations to work abroad and regular commissions. In the mid-1970s, his radical language softened and became more lyrical (his Symphony No. 3 of 1995 is mainly traditional-sounding) but the passion and anger at human injustice remains. His oratorios, in particular, reflect the struggle between Church and State in 1980s Poland.

MILESTONES	
1959	Wins the top three prizes in Warsaw composing competition
1960	Composes *Threnody to the Victims of Hiroshima* for 52 strings
1966	Composes *St Luke Passion*
1972	Becomes rector at Kraków Academy
1980	Writes *Lacrimosa*, choral, for Solidarity

Often conducting his own music, Penderecki was one of the pioneers of microtones and the use of whistles, hissing, shouting, and mechanical noise in music.

Hans Werner Henze

● 1926– ♙ German ✍ c.260

Henze escaped from a pro-Nazi family upbringing into music. He gained a wide stylistic knowledge and soon found himself in demand to write for musical theatre. From 1950–53 he was music director of Wiesbaden Ballet, but then moved to Italy. After 1968, disillusioned with European capitalist society, he spent some time in Cuba and began writing works reflecting his socialist ideals. He has since become a major international composer, with a prolific output of operas, choral, and large and small instrumental works, in complex but expressive style.

MILESTONES	
1958	Writes *Kammermusik*, tenor and guitar
1964	Composes *Der junge Lord*, opera
1992	Composes Symphony No. 8

John Rutter

● 1945– ♙ English ✍ 100+

Known throughout Britain and the US for his lively choral pieces – easily sung, memorable and written with great craft, drawing from the English tradition of partsong – Rutter is probably the most widely performed British composer of his generation. His *Shepherd's Pipe Carol* and *Star Carol* are regular features of amateur and professional Christmas concerts. His three volumes of *Carols for Choirs*, as editor with Sir David Willcocks, have made his work familiar to many singers and listeners. Usually joyful, with an interest in writing for young people, he can also be sombre, as in his *Requiem* and *Te Deum*.

MILESTONES	
1974	Writes *Gloria* for chorus and orchestra
1979	Founds Cambridge Singers
1984	Performing edition of Fauré *Requiem*
1988	Writes *Te Deum*, choral work
1990	Writes *Requiem*, choral work

Witold Lutoslawski

● 1913–1994   ♙ Polish   ✍ 86

Lutoslawski lived in difficult times. His early works had to please the communist authorities and were largely inspired by Polish folk music. Later he was able to experiment publicly, expanding his harmony and incorporating passages in which performers were given some degree of rhythmic autonomy. In his last period, he strove to incorporate both worlds in his music, blending modernism with nostalgia.

LIFE AND MUSIC

Lutoslawski's early years were darkened by the death of his father in Russia (where he had fought the Bolsheviks) and the loss of the family estate. Despite privations, he studied violin and piano, and entered the Warsaw Conservatory in 1927. By 1938 his music had been championed by Poland's leading conductor, Grzegorz Fitelberg, but World War II brought mobilization and capture by the Germans. Lutoslawski escaped and returned to Warsaw, where he survived by playing dance music and piano duets with fellow composer Andrzej Panufnik. In later life, Lutoslawski became Poland's pre-eminent composer, honoured both for his music and his political integrity during the struggles against communism. His work was greatly influential both in his homeland and internationally.

MILESTONES

c.1914	Witnesses Bolshevik Revolution in Moscow; father and uncle executed
1927	Enters the Warsaw Conservatory, later studies with Maliszewski
1939	*Symphonic Variations* broadcast by Polish radio; mobilized
1940	Escapes enemy capture; returns to Warsaw; forms piano duo with Panufnik
1949	Symphony No. 1 denounced by the communist authorities
1954	Success of *Concerto for Orchestra*
c.1958	*Musique funèbre* and *Jeux vénitiens* win international acclaim.
1994	Awarded Poland's rare Order of the White Eagle weeks before his death

KEY WORKS

LES ESPACES DU SOMMEIL

ORCHESTRA & VOICE	🕐 15:30	📖 1	🎵👤

Some of Lutoslawski's most sensuously beautiful music was inspired by the French poetry of Robert Desnos. This sensitive vocal work, written for the acclaimed baritone Dietrich Fischer-Dieskau, evokes the mysterious world of sleep. The night is full of half-understood, hallucinatory images, but always "there is also you" – the beloved woman who haunts the poet's dreams.

The artistry of violinist Anne-Sophie Mutter inspired many of Lutoslawski later pieces.

MI-PARTI

ORCHESTRAL	🕐 15:00	📖 1	🎵

A compact work of great lucidity and visceral excitement, *Mi-Parti* moves from dreaming hesitancy towards a climactic tumult, peaking on a *sforzando* chord. The music then settles on a distant "icy" harmony, before melting away into a meditative coda. In archetypal Lutoslawskian fashion, the piece alternates strictly conducted passages with *ad libitum* sections in which individual players repeat melodic motifs in free time.

Iannis Xenakis

● 1922–2001　　♙ Greek　　✍ c.160

World War II disrupted Xenakis's education; he fought for the Greek resistance, fled a death sentence, and ended up penniless in Paris. He then worked in the great architect Le Corbusier's studio for 12 years, as an engineer and architect, whilst studying music privately. His ideas on electro-acoustic music established him as a pioneer, and he taught at many institutions. His rigorous works are often intricately computer-generated by detailed mathematical processes, and generally written for combinations of conventional instruments, sometimes played unconventionally. Xenakis's explorations of the fundamentals of music continue to fascinate and influence advanced performers and listeners.

MILESTONES	
1947	Arrives in France as illegal immigrant
1953	Writes *Metastasis* for orchestra
1957	Works with Schaeffer's electro-acoustic group
1962	Starts composing with a computer
1967	Teaches at Bloomington, Indiana
1991	Writes computer program, GENDYN

An architect with an understanding of advanced mathematics, Xenakis designed the Philips Pavilion for the Brussels World Fair in 1958.

Luigi Nono

● 1924–1990　　♙ Italian　　✍ c.60

Born into a family of artists, Nono was strongly influenced by painting, philosophy, and poetry. He established himself at the renowned Darmstadt summer school and became a key figure in the postwar avant-garde. His 1950s theatrical pieces, often with a strongly socialist theme, use innovative sounds and textures. Having rejected Darmstadt, he turned to electronics and amplification in the 1960s, creating political works based on vocal material and centred around his performers. Through the 1980s, his experimentation in music theatre – and with new technical resources – continued, moving occasionally from the political to the more private, and his concentration on the nature of music and communication made his work widely influential.

MILESTONES	
1946	Meets Maderna
1955	Marries Schoenberg's daughter, Nuria
1956	Writes *Il canto sospeso* for soloists, chorus, and orchestra
1959	Gives controversial lecture criticizing Darmstadt
1984	*Prometeo*, "azione scenica", produced

The premiere of Nono's opera *Intolleranza,* in 1960, with electronic sound, visual projections, and a political message, caused uproar in Venice.

György Ligeti

● 1923–   ♙ Hungarian   ✍ 117

One of the few great modernists to have reached a wider
audience, Ligeti's own work bears the traces of a bewildering
variety of styles and techniques, from late medieval Europe
to the music of the pygmies of Central Africa. Other inspirations reflect the
range of his intellectual curiosity, embracing the philosophy of Karl Popper, the
paradoxes of Escher's art, and the intricacies of Mandelbrot's fractal geometry.

LIFE AND MUSIC

Ligeti was born in a small Hungarian-
speaking enclave in Romanian
Transylvania. At first intent on a career
in science, his education was disrupted
by anti-Jewish legislation, and he turned
to composition. After World War II,
Ligeti found his progress as a composer
frustrated by communism, and in 1956
he fled to the West. Befriended by
Stockhausen, Ligeti experimented with
electronic music, but resisted pressures
to adopt systematic methods of
composition. The use of Ligeti's music
in the film *2001: A Space Odyssey* won
him a world-wide following.

MILESTONES

1944	Deaths of his father and brother at the hands of the Nazis
1956	Flees Hungary; works in Stockhausen's electronics studio in Cologne
1960	Premiere of *Apparitions*, orchestra
1961	Premiere of *Atmosphères*
1966	Survives a critical illness
1968	Stanley Kubrick uses Ligeti's *Requiem* in *2001: A Space Odyssey*
1970	Granted a political "amnesty", Ligeti revisits Hungary.
1978	Premiere *La Grand Macabre*, opera
1985	Meets Benoit Mandelbrot

KEY WORKS

REQUIEM

CHORAL   ⏱ 25:00   📖 4   🎻 🎹 🎤

Ligeti's Requiem is a work of
apocalyptic power, influenced by
Renaissance polyphony and the choral
works of Bach, but dividing orchestra
and choir into so many individual parts
that the intricate counterpoint dissolves
into spectacular clouds of sound.

ATMOSPHÈRES

ORCHESTRAL   ⏱ 09:00   📖 1   🎻

His first great success, Ligeti's
Atmosphères is entirely concerned
with subtly evolving textures, and is
strongly influenced by his experience
of working with tape and electronics.

LA GRANDE MACABRE

OPERA   ⏱ 120:00   📖 2   🎻 🎹 🎤

Ligeti's only opera to date is set in
an imaginary country inspired by
the paintings of Pieter Breughel
and Hieronymus Bosch. The score
teems with grotesque invention,
shot through with moments of
poignant beauty.

Ligeti's atmospheric *Requiem* (1965) was used on the
soundtrack of *2001: A Space Odyssey* for scenes with
strange visual effects and dreamlike sequences.

LONTANO

ORCHESTRAL   ⏱ 11:30   📖 1   ⚓

Like *Atmosphères* and other early masterpieces, *Lontano* is composed of countless barely audible canons. Great control is needed by orchestra and conductor to sustain the hushed flow of mysteriously shifting, infinitely delicate sound. A study in subdued restlessness, *Lontano* consists of quiet murmuring until a point two-thirds of the way through. A climax for a group of solo strings is followed by a second crescendo for the entire string section (except the double basses). The final climax is suddenly cut off, movement almost ceases, and the music moves into catatonic retreat.

SAN FRANCISO POLYPHONY

ORCHESTRAL   ⏱ 13:00   📖 1   ⚓

Ligeti's career charts a gradual recovery of the musical language of the past. Each new piece reclaims techniques which other modernists judged to have outlived their usefulness. He has always liked polyphony (the overlaying of many voices in independent lines), but before *San Francisco Polyphony*, permitted himself to use it only on the microscopic level. Here the counterpoint comes to the surface in bold, characterful gestures, whose virtuosity once led orchestras to regard the piece as unplayable; moments such as the frantic conclusion, in which ostinato figures spin like tops as the horns yelp in excited syncopation, still test performers to the limit.

VIOLIN CONCERTO

ORCHESTRAL   ⏱ 27:00   📖 5   ⚓ 🎶

Ligeti's late works achieve a magical synthesis between direct – even naive – music reminiscent of his Hungarian roots and innovative techniques honed through a lifetime of experimentation.

PRAELUDIUM (VIVACISSIMO LUMINOSO 4:00) Inspired by the music of French-Canadian Claude Vivier, and instruments like the sacred flutes of Papua New Guinea, Ligeti brings strange "natural" tunings into his orchestra. An orchestral violin and viola play with their strings tuned to slightly different pitches, while the solo violin plays normally.

ARIA, HOQUETUS, CHORAL (ANDANTE CON MOTO 8:00) The soloist plays a sad folk-like melody borrowed from an early work, but Ligeti takes the strange tunings to the brink of absurdity by adding incorrigibly out-of-tune ocarinas – almost toy whistles – to the orchestra.

INTERMEZZO (PRESTO FLUIDO 2:00) The violin soars aloft as descending scales cascade all around like falling stars.

PASSACAGLIA (LENTO INTENSO 6:00) Tragedy is in the air, brusque interjections attempt to silence a lament, but the soloist ignores them, climbing to a distraught climax.

APPASSIONATO (AGITATO MOLTO 7:00) Materials from the previous movements are thrown into a volatile mix, ending in violinistic fireworks and another feature of the traditional concerto: a solo cadenza.

Pierre Boulez

◔ 1925–   ⚑ French   ♫ 36

For almost 40 years, Boulez has been the dominant force in contemporary music, not only as a composer, but also as a conductor, theorist, broadcaster, and as the founder of IRCAM, a Paris-based centre for research into music and technology. In his middle years, his composing seemed dangerously close to being stifled by other activities, but recent years have seen a steady succession of large-scale works.

LIFE AND MUSIC

Noting Boulez's youthful talent for maths, his father sent him to study engineering. Boulez, however, defected to the Paris Conservatoire, where he was taught by Messiaen and gained a fearsome reputation for heckling at concerts of contemporary works that he judged insufficiently radical. He

made his name as a composer in 1955 with *Le marteau sans maître*. With Stockhausen, he dominated the Darmstadt summer schools,

Boulez was appointed director of the French government-sponsored IRCAM studio in 1977.

the centre of new music in the 1950s. Having taken to the podium as an advocate of new music, Boulez began an international career as a conductor. His interest in technology resurfaced in the 1970s, when he founded IRCAM to find ways of extending music's frontiers.

MILESTONES	
1944	Studies with Messiaen
1955	Premiere of *Le marteau sans maître*
1960	*Pli selon pli* premiered
1969	Becomes chief conductor of BBC Symphony Orchestra
1971	Succeeds Bernstein as music director of New York Philharmonic Orchestra
1976	Founds Ensemble Intercontemporain
1977	Opens IRCAM at Pompidou Centre
1976	Conducts Wagner's *Ring* at Bayreuth
1982	Premiere of *Répons* at London Proms
2000	Wins Grammy award for *Répons*

KEY WORKS

PIANO SONATA NO. 2

SOLO PIANO   ⏲ 30:00   📖 4   ✐

This fiercely demanding work has become a pillar of the modern piano repertoire – especially thanks to the advocacy of pianist Maurizio Pollini.

LE MARTEAU SANS MAÎTRE

CHAMBER   ⏲ 30:00   📖 8   ♫ ♪

A sequence of songs and instrumental cadenzas ("commentaries"), this piece was influenced by Schoenberg's *Pierrot lunaire* and, in its use of percussion, by African, Japanese, and Javanese music.

To Stravinsky, *Le marteau*'s fascinating but cerebral sound suggested "ice-cubes clinking in a cocktail glass".

PLI SELON PLI

ORCHESTRA & VOICE   ⏲ 68:00   📖 5   ♫♫ ♪

Boulez based this cycle of movements on words by Mallarmé, and on the poet's idea of an open-ended book – a potent image for Boulez, who revises works such as this every few years. The work ends with the same hammer-blow chord with which it began, as if to start the cycle all over again.

FOCUS

ÉCLATS/MULTIPLES

CHAMBER   🎬 37:00   📖 2   ♗

This diptych actually consists of a "complete" piece *(Éclats)* and its open-ended sequel *(Multiples)*. *Éclats* was intended to give its 15 players some freedom in choosing when and what they wished to play, in response to the rhythmic complexity of much contemporary music reducing musicians to the level of virtuosic machines. However, in performance Boulez did not always like the results of *Éclat*'s freedoms and soon began to eliminate them, giving all the decisions about the order in which sections would be performed to the conductor (usually Boulez himself). *Multiples* is one of the first works which pointed to the use of what were to become more straightforward rhythms in his music – rhythms which audiences find easier to "hear", just as musicians find them easier to play.

ÉCLATS (10:00) Fifteen instruments are divided into two groups: strings and wind, which can hold notes almost indefinitely; and piano and tuned percussion instruments, which cannot. The sustaining instruments (strings and wind) hold background harmonies, which the soloists' group peppers with "fragments" of melody.

MULTIPLES (17:00) To the previous ensemble, Boulez adds a basset horn and nine violas, which often play in warm unison. Towards the end, they divide, rhapsodizing in voluptuous chords. At the end, the piece dissolves in flurries of sustained trills.

RÉPONS

ELECTRONIC   🎬 43:00   📖 10   ♗

Boulez's first major work to come out of IRCAM uses computers to produce real-time transformations of music played by two pianos, a harp, and bell-like instruments; background music provided by 24 string, brass, and wind players is unaffected.

The arrival of IRCAM's glittering new technology is announced majestically after six minutes or so, at the beginning of the second section; the group of soloists surrounding the pianos peals out a chord which is then seized on by the computer and is then electronically treated and projected through six loudspeakers.

For music of such kaleidoscopic modernity, Boulez chose a dryly archaic title. *Répons (Responses)* refers to early Church music in which a soloist's music alternates with that of the choir. Though the separation of the soloists and their attendant electronics is clear enough at the beginning and end, most of the piece overlays "questions" and "responses" within a shape which Boulez himself compares to the spiral ramp of the Guggenheim Museum's interior in New York. At every stage of the ascent, snatches can be heard of things which have just occurred, or which are just around the corner.

Luciano Berio

◉ 1925–2003   🏳 Italian   ✍ 29

The leading Italian composer of the second half of the 20th century, Berio was a composer of formidable intellect and technique. He numbered among the pioneers of the avant-garde, yet even his most exuberant music had an undertone of Mediterranean melancholy. His ear for sonority, feeling for context, and knowledge of tradition helped to give whatever he wrote the rich hues of an old master.

LIFE AND MUSIC

Berio came from a family of musicians, and was taught piano and harmony by his father. In 1944, a hand injury sustained on his first day in the army put an end to his soldiering as well as his hopes of becoming a pianist. While studying composition in Milan, Berio met his first wife, American soprano Cathy Berberian. He spent the 1960s teaching across the US. After the break-up of a second marriage, he returned to Italy, developing an interest in Sicilian folk music and working with writers and personal friends such as Umberto Eco, Edoardo Sanguinetti, and Italo Calvino. His final marriage to Israeli musicologist Talia Packer is reflected in his works on Jewish themes.

Berio often worked, as here, with his first wife, Cathy Berberian. In 1958 he created *Thema* for electronics based on her reading from James Joyce's *Ulysses*.

MILESTONES

1955	Co-founds Italy's first studio for electro-acoustic music
1958	Begins solo-instrumental *Sequenza* series
1969	*Sinfonia* confirms his global reputation
1973	Begins *Points on a Curve to Find*
1974	Directs research at IRCAM electronics studio in Paris until 1980
1975	Joins Israel Chamber Orchestra
1980	Starts work on operas with Italo Calvino
1984	Composes *Voci: Folksongs II*

KEY WORKS

FOLKSONGS

SONG   ⏱ 23:00   📖 11   ♫ ♦

Berio was the great arranger of recent times. These transparent, affecting, unsentimental versions of traditional songs from the US, France, Armenia, Azerbaijan, and Italy were made for his first wife, Cathy Berberian, in 1964.

LABORINTUS II

VOICE   ⏱ 33:0   📖 2   ♫ ♦

Many of Berio's best works involve the human voice. In this piece for voice and orchestra, it is featured speaking, singing, scatting in jazz style, and reciting the poetry of Sanguinetti and Dante. *Laborintus II* was written in 1965 for Dante's 700th anniversary.

POINTS ON A CURVE TO FIND

ORCHESTRAL   ⏱ 13:30   📖 1   ♫ ◉

Berio liked to base his pieces on the simplest music devices. Here the piano ducks and dives, tracing a single chromatic line. It often hovers on adjacent notes, pursued and worried by other instruments like a hare chased by hounds.

FOCUS

VOCI: FOLKSONGS II

SONG ⏱ 28:00 📖 1 ⚏ ⦿

In this piece there are work songs, lullabies, love songs, and *abbagnate* (street-vendors' cries), all originating from Sicily. They play continuously, so, like *Points on a Curve to Find*, the work is essentially an elaborated monody (solo line). With *Voci*, Berio wished to draw attention to Sicilian folk music, which is among the "richest, hottest, and most complex" of the Mediterranean. At times, the viola imitates folk singers, reminiscing, lamenting, and sliding between notes against a tremulous backdrop provided by two instrumental ensembles. Elsewhere, the other players encourage, nudge the soloist's memory, or even take over entirely.

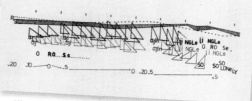

Luciano Berio often used graphic notation in his scores, which give performers scope for exercising personal choice in performance.

The music flickers with forest noises, summoning up a torrential river of orchestral sound.

SECOND MOVEMENT: O KING (5:00) The singers intone syllables from the name "Martin Luther King" while trumpets and a snare drum salute his memory.

THIRD MOVEMENT (12:00) This dazzling montage of quotes from the Romantic and modern repertoires is carried along on the "river" of the third movement of Mahler's Symphony No. 2.

FOURTH MOVEMENT (2:00) A subdued interlude, in which the singers mull over fragments of their texts so far.

FIFTH MOVEMENT (7:00) The inspired finale samples music that has already been sampled from other music.

SINFONIA

ORCHESTRAL ⏱ 32:00 📖 5 ⚏⚏ ⦿

Berio's most celebrated work caught the mood of its time (the late 1960s) to perfection, and still crackles today with undiminished electricity. Eight voices supply a montage of fragmentary texts, acting like a section of the orchestra.

FIRST MOVEMENT (6:00) This evokes Brazilian myths on the origin of water.

INFLUENCES

In postmodern style, Berio boldly advertised his influences: Mahler, Stravinsky, Berg, Stockhausen are all detectable in the third movement of *Sinfonia*. However, Berio above all thought of music as a kind of speech. By analyzing speech and applying the post-structuralist ideas of thinkers like Eco and Calvino to music, Berio found his own musical voice.

Karlheinz Stockhausen

◉ 1928–   **🏴 German**   **✍ 313**

Stockhausen has won cult status, thanks to a genius for music and publicity. Yet his stunts often have a serious point; even his recent *Helicopter Quartet*, in which a string quartet performs whilst airborne in four different helicopters, develops his long-standing fascination for music which moves in space, and which has led him to dream of concert halls in which the sound assails the listener from every direction.

LIFE AND MUSIC

Stockhausen was the first composer of the avant garde to devote himself fully to electronic music. His teenage years were scarred by the deaths of his mother and father during World War II, leaving him to pay for his music studies in Cologne by playing in piano bars and accompanying a stage magician. He then studied with Messiaen in Paris and became involved in the birth of electronic music, producing seminal works such as *Gesang der Jünglinge*. Stockhausen became a leading figure at the Darmstadt summer schools, where John Cage introduced him to the use of chance processes in music. In recent years he has concentrated on completing the "seven days" of a week-long opera, *Licht*.

MILESTONES

1945	Serves in military hospital; father dies.
1947	Begins music studies
1952	Studies with Messiaen; produces first electronic pieces
1956	Starts teaching at Darmstadt; writes *Gesang der Jüngling*, boy's voice and tape
1957	*Gruppen* for three orchestras
1958	Hears John Cage lecture at Darmstadt
1960s	Forms his own ensemble; tours world
1968	Composes *Stimmung*, 70-minute work for six singers based on a single chord
1970	Complete works performed in Osaka
2003	Completes his 29-hour opera, *Licht*

KEY WORKS

GRUPPEN

ORCHESTRAL   🕐 22:00   📖 1   ⚶

This early work remains truly epoch-making. It requires three orchestras and conductors, and is composed according to arcane rules linking pitch and rhythm, but the impact is spatial and, indeed, visceral. Few venues can place the musicians around an audience, but even so, to hear three massed orchestras in intricate, three-way converse is still unforgettable.

GESANG DER JÜNGLINGE

ELECTRONIC   🕐 13:00   📖 1   🎧 ♁

The power of this piece (which even influenced the Beatles, causing them to include a photo of Stockhausen on the cover of their *Sgt Pepper* album) lies not only in the use of early tape technology, but also in the emotional effect of a boy's voice singing the Benedictus among a welter of alien sounds. Stockhausen envisaged it as walking unharmed through a "fiery furnace", an image which surely has autobiographical wartime resonances.

Stockhausen's scores are the result of tireless and highly disciplined scientific study into sound of any type and sound technology.

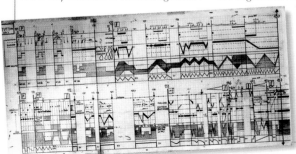

György Kurtág

● 1926–   ♩ Hungarian   🎼 c.80

After graduating from the Liszt Academy in Budapest and winning state prizes, Kurtág gained a name as a pianist, especially of Bartók, a major influence. In 1958–59 he encountered Western music in Paris, especially admiring Schoenberg, Webern, and their serial music. He then produced his String Quartet No. 1 – a new starting point for his music. He returned to Hungary, becoming a renowned piano teacher, vocal coach, and repetiteur. In his mid-40s, he was commissioned to write children's piano music and the results inspired new creativity. Success with his *Troussova* songs in France made his name abroad, and since 1985 (having reached only Op. 23) he has composed more frequently.

MILESTONES	
1973	Writes *Games*, children's piano works
1980	Completes song cycle *Messages of the Late Miss R V Troussova*
1987	Writes *Kafka Fragments*, voice and violin
1990	*Samuel Beckett Sends Word Through Ildikó Monyók...*, for soprano and piano
1993	Moves to Berlin
1994	*Stele*, for orchestra, premiered in Berlin

Many of Kurtág works are small scale, such as his 1980 *Messages of the Late Miss R V Troussova* for soprano and chamber ensemble with cimbalom.

Jonathan Harvey

● 1939–   ♩ English   🎼 c.95

After receiving doctorates from Cambridge and Glasgow universities and a fellowship at Princeton, Harvey's visionary experiments with electronic music impressed Boulez, who invited him to work at IRCAM in Paris. Harvey's innovative works, which include chamber, orchestral, and many choral pieces, have a meditative, spiritual, and ecstatic character (he has found the writings of Rudolf Steiner particular inspirational) and have been widely recorded and performed across Europe. He is especially successful at combining conventional instruments with electronic or electronically modified sounds. Harvey has received honours in both the UK and US, and continues to fulfil constant new commissions, including some from the BBC Scottish Symphony Orchestra.

MILESTONES	
1977	Composes String Quartet No. 1
1980	Writes *Mortuos plango, vivos voco*, tape
1981	Writes *Passion and Resurrection*, church opera; staged at Winchester Cathedral
1982	Composes *Bhakti*, 15 players and tape
1986	Composes *Madonna of Winter and Spring*, live electronics
1992	Composes *Scena*, violin concerto

Jonathan Harvey's *Hymn*, a piece for chorus and orchestra, was composed for the 900th-anniversary celebrations of Winchester Cathedral.

Peter Maxwell Davies

● 1934–   ▣ British   ✍ 273

Intense energy is as apparent in Davies's charismatic personality as it is in his prolific output. Davies has dominated British music since the appearance of his explosive works of the 1960s, which gave exemplary expression to the anarchic spirit of the times. Responsible since then for works of the grandest integrity, his musical voice can be heard clearly, even in the many works he has written for children or film.

LIFE AND MUSIC

Davies's earliest memory of music is of being taken to see a local performance of Gilbert and Sullivan's *The Gondoliers*. He encountered very different musical experiences at the Royal Manchester College, however, where his friends included fellow composers Alexander Goehr and Harrison Birtwistle. Davies studied in Italy and America before returning to England to teach at a grammar school. He soon became known for eclectic music-theatre works, like *Eight Songs for a Mad King*, but the direction of his work changed when he moved to Orkney and fell under the spell of its majestic seascapes.

MILESTONES	
1957	Studies with composer Goffredo Petrassi in Rome
1959	Teaches music at Cirencester Grammar School
1969	Writes *Eight Songs for a Mad King*
1972	Premiere of *Taverner*, opera
1971	Moves to Orkney
1976	Premiere of Symphony No. 1
1977	*Black Pentecost* performed; founds the St Magnus Festival
1987	Receives knighthood
1997	Visits Antarctica prior to writing his *Antarctic Symphony*
2004	Becomes Master of the Queen's Music

KEY WORKS

EIGHT SONGS FOR A MAD KING

MUSIC THEATRE   ⏱ 30:00   ▥ 8   ♟ ♂

Variously shocking tour de force and high camp, this portrait of the "madness" of George III made Davies widely famous. The work is expressionistic and relies on parody and distortion to represent an extreme mental state. Davies places the musicians in cages, like King George's own pet bullfinches.

St Magnus Cathedral on Orkney offers perfect acoustics for players at Davies's summer festival.

TAVERNER

OPERA   ⏱ 130:00   ▥ 2   ♒ ♨ ♂

Davies's largest work is based around the life and legend of the Tudor composer John Taverner and his conversion to Protestantism, for which cause he destroyed the churches that had once inspired him to create his own choral masterpieces. Davies uses much of Taverner's own music – in various transformations – in this musically complex and violently theatrical opera about a character who betrays his true vocation to save his skin.

FOCUS

IMAGE, REFLECTION, SHADOW

CHAMBER 36:00 3

This chamber masterpiece is written for six instruments, including piano and cimbalom (a Hungarian dulcimer whose strings are struck with mallets). It might seem an odd choice for a tribute to the Orkney landscape, but – as the title suggests – the music teems with echoes and doublings, and the cimbalom is the pungent, brackish double of the scintillating piano. The title comes from a poem by Charles Senior, which describes the flight of gulls and the dance of their shadows over rocks and waves.

FIRST MOVEMENT (ADAGIO 13:00) A brooding, lyrical nocturne, evoking an earlier work, Davies's *Ave maris stella*. Alto flute and bass clarinet drift hauntingly, like shadows, through the pre-dawn stillness.

SECOND MOVEMENT (ALLEGRO 8:00) A buoyant, contrapuntal scherzo. In the first part, the piano effervesces in mad, upward-rushing arpeggios, only for them to cascade down again in the second, like waves dashed against rocks. After a hushed cimbalom solo comes a rush of swirling radiance, fading into mist.

THIRD MOVEMENT (LENTO; ALLEGRO 15:00) A subdued opening with a keening lament for the cimbalom. But soon the gulls catch the updraught, and the clarinet spins aloft in jaunty pirouettes. A flighty cadenza for the cimbalom precedes a whirling free-for-all, before the music freezes once more on dark chords, over which the piccolo sighs like a final, solitary bird.

SYMPHONY NO. 3

ORCHESTRAL 56:40 4

In pursuit of their compelling logic, Davies bases his pieces on numeric "magic squares". Here, the square contains the proportions of an Italian cathedral on which the great medieval composer Dufay also based a famous motet over five centuries earlier.

FIRST MOVEMENT (LENTO 18:00) This majestic movement establishes D as the symphony's starting point, and quotes a medieval chant in praise of the Archangel Michael.

SECOND MOVEMENT (ALLEGRO 9:00) The first of two scherzos centered on the vanishing point which, in the Italian architect Brunelleschi's church nave, marked the position of the altar. The movement also expresses Davies's wonderment at a precipitous Orkney cliff-face thronged with a cloud of spiralling seabirds.

THIRD MOVEMENT (ALLEGRO VIVACE 7:40) Davies alters the angle at which the same nave is viewed: some elements are foreshortened, others magnified. Through side arches, the dark expanses of the final movement can be glimpsed.

FOURTH MOVEMENT (LENTO; ADAGIO FLESSIBILE 22:00) Davies pays tribute to the last movement of Mahler's ninth symphony, and ends his impressive work with intimations of eternity.

Sir Harrison Birtwistle

◔ 1934–   🏴 English   ✍ 112

A few bars are all you need to hear to know that a piece is by Birtwistle. The quirky rhythms, the layered textures, and the immediate sense of theatre are unmistakable fingerprints. His music sounds idiosyncratically English, and often there is a dominant part for his favourite instrument – the clarinet. However, in recent years, Birtwistle has become known above all for his vocal music and his majestic, ritualistic operas.

LIFE AND MUSIC

Birtwistle studied clarinet at the Royal Northern College of Music, where he formed the New Music Manchester Group with fellow students, including Peter Maxwell Davies and trumpeter and conductor Elgar Howarth. After graduating, Birtwistle worked briefly as a professional clarinettist, but dedicated himself to composing on hearing that his first acknowledged piece had been selected for the Cheltenham Festival in 1959. Landmarks since that time have included his orchestral piece *The Triumph of Time* (inspired by Breughel), the parody opera *Punch and Judy*, and the mighty *Masque of Orpheus* with its elaborate stage spectacle and haunting electronics.

MILESTONES	
1952	Studies clarinet
1955	Plays in the Royal Artillery band
1959	*Refrains and Choruses*, wind quintet, performed at Cheltenham Festival
1965	Composes *Tragoedia*; the music reappears in *Punch and Judy*, opera
1972	Writes *The Triumph of Time*, orchestra
1981	Composes music for Peter Halls' production of the *Oresteia*
1986	*The Mask of Orpheus* premieres at the English National Opera.
1988	Receives knighthood
1991	*Gawain* performed at Covent Garden

KEY WORKS

GAWAIN'S JOURNEY

OPERA SUITE   ⏱ 25:00   📖 1   🎶

This impressive piece is derived from Birtwistle's second epic opera, depicting Gawain's quest for the mysterious Green Knight. The earthy and evocative music draws on his rite-of-passage journey, the three attempts by the Green Knight's beautiful wife to seduce Gawain (each marked by a cockcrow), and the clopping horse hooves and whirling figures which characterize the encounters with her terrifying, if finally beneficent, husband.

Each character in *Orpheus* appears in three guises: as a singer, a dancer, and a mime.

THE MASK OF ORPHEUS

OPERA   ⏱ 210:00   📖 3   🎶🥁🔔

This remarkably complicated work retells three conflicting Greek legends about the death of Orpheus, enacted by singers and giant puppets. It is also a wonderfully baffling reconstruction of the rites once associated with the worship of Orpheus. Each act focuses on a specific ritual serving as a fixed point around which the opera revolves. Electronics are used to imitate the voice of Apollo and to create "auras" suggesting the sounds of tides and bees, both of which have rich symbolic connotations.

Toru Takemitsu

● 1930–1996   ♙ Japanese   ♬ 104

Takemitsu first heard Western music when he was 14. After the World War II, he listened to Classical music on US-forces radio, and it was mainly by listening to the works of composers like Debussy and Messiaen that he taught himself compositional technique. In 1959, Stravinsky heard Takemitsu's *Requiem* for strings, and declared it a masterpiece. It was only after talking to John Cage in 1964 that Takemitsu began to pay any attention to Japanese music, producing works like *November Steps* for orchestra and Japanese instruments. His most famous piece is probably *A Flock Descends into the Pentagonal Garden*. Takemitsu also wrote music for films, including Oshima's *The Empire of the Senses* and Akira Kurosawa's *Ran*.

MILESTONES	
1944	Military service
1951	Founds an experimental workshop
1957	*Requiem* for strings wins acclaim
1967	Composes *November Steps*
1977	*A Flock Descends into the Pentagonal Garden*
1994	Wins prestigious Grawemeyer Award for Music Composition

A love of nature and Japanese traditional culture are constant themes in Takemitsu's music.

Tan Dun

● 1957–   ♙ Chinese-American   ♬ 63

Tan Dun grew up during the Chinese Cultural Revolution, receiving no regular education and working as a rice planter. Later he was employed as a violinist and arranger at the Beijing Opera theatre, only encountering Western music when he entered the newly re-opened Central Conservatory of Music in 1976.

His music began to show avant-garde influences and was even denounced as "spiritual pollution" by the Chinese government in 1983. Three years later he moved to New York, and has since taken American nationality and has begun to write film scores. His music shows a wide range of influences, from jazz to Chinese opera, and often features unusual sounds, such as ancient Chinese bells or splashing water. As a conductor, Dun has created programmes which reach a new and diverse audience.

MILESTONES	
1976	Enters Beijing Music Conservatory
1983	Moves to the US
1998	Composes *Peony Pavilion*, opera
1999	Writes *Orchestral Theatre IV, The Gate*, for a Peking Opera actress, Japanese puppeteer, and string orchestra
2001	Wins awards for his score for Ang Lee's film *Crouching Tiger, Hidden Dragon*

Dun's *Heaven Earth Mankind*, written to celebrate the reunification of Hong Kong with China, featured 65 ancient tuned bronze bells (excavated in 1978).

Arvo Pärt

◗ 1935–   ⚑ Estonian   ✍ 93

Pärt has a following like few others in contemporary music. Starting out as a "progressive" composer, frequently in an atonal idiom, he stopped composing in the 1970s and emerged – after a period of creative silence – with an entirely new musical voice – imbued with simplicity and devotional humility. Inspired by the sound of bells, and the music of the distant past, his works seem to exist outside time.

LIFE AND MUSIC

As a child, Pärt attended evening music school. His early compositional experimentation was encouraged by necessity – only the lowest and highest notes on the piano at home worked properly. Having survived a serious illness, he entered the Central Tallinn Conservatory, and by the time he graduated he was already a successful film composer. His early serious music used a "collage" technique, mixing various styles. Although he achieved a national reputation, both his progressive and religious works were often banned by the authorities. In the early 1970s, Pärt joined the Russian Orthodox Church. He left Estonia in 1980 and settled in Germany.

MILESTONES	
1957	Enters Central Tallinn Conservatory
1957	Begins working for Estonian radio; writes film and television scores.
1960	Composes *Nekrolog* for orchestra – the first piece of Estonian 12-tone music. It earns official disfavour.
1962	Starts writing "collage" pieces, juxtaposing various styles. The final piece in this period being *Credo*
1969	Seven-year period of silence and self-renewal; joins the Russian Orthodox Church; breaks silence with his first tintinnabuli piece, *Für Alina*, for piano
1977	Composes *Arbos*, *Cantus in memoriam Benjamin Britten*, *Fratres*, and *Tabula Rasa*
1980	Leaves Estonia for the West

KEY WORKS

CANTUS IN MEMORIAM BENJAMIN BRITTEN

ORCHESTRAL   ⏱ 5:00   📖 1   ⚡

One of the first of Pärt's "little bell" pieces does indeed feature a bell, tolling for the death of a composer that he had recently come to admire. Overlapping scales in the strings, ever more drawn out, pay homage to Britten's own love of scalic melodies. In the final bar, a bell is struck inaudibly and resonates – once the strings have stopped playing – as if sounding from nowhere.

TABULA RASA

ORCHESTRAL   ⏱ 26:00   📖 2   ⚡ ◉

The title means "clean slate" and reflects Pärts desire to return to the basics of sound in order to create music of innocence and purity. Like many of Pärt's mature pieces, it is largely "white note" music, built on a tonic chord, arpeggiated, and overlaid with simple scales. Bell-like "chimes" are provided by a prepared piano.

Für Alina, **for piano,** is based on a simple tonic triad; Pärt may have been influenced by St Gregory of Palamas' book, *Triads*.

FOCUS

CREDO

ORCHESTRAL   ⏱ 12:00   📖 3   🎶 👁 🥁

Audiences enthused over this work – the last written in Pärt's earlier "collage" style – but the communist authorities vilified it on account of its religious text. The music in Parts 1 and 3 is derived from the first C major prelude in J S Bach's *Well-tempered Clavier* – for, as in all the collage pieces, Pärt "borrows" the tonal material from older composers. The piece dramatizes the conflict between good and evil, with good being represented by pure C major and evil by dissonant note clusters (represented in the score by thick black lines, rather than actual notes). However, the transitions between these two extremes are gradual. The final resolution on a quiet C major chord (which now, as in later works, seems to evoke the presence of God) is like an echo from the dawn of time.

FRATRES

CHAMBER   ⏱ 12:00   📖 1   ♆

The fact that *Fratres* can be heard in seven versions – for different instrumental combinations – reflects the fact that it is one of Pärt's most loved works. One of the early so-called "tintinnabuli" pieces, it sets the notes of an A minor tonic chord against overlapping scales in subtly shifting patterns – a technique which has some similarity to the compositional techniques of late medieval composers. That Pärt originally left the choice of instruments open to the performers also reflects the aesthetics of an earlier time; the notes themselves were presumed to suggest a divine order, which could be communicated in any medium. Fratres means "brethren", perhaps suggesting a vision of society in which conflict and egotism has been supplanted by the "brotherly love" of communities living according to the Christian gospel.

MISERERE

CHORAL   ⏱ 35:00   📖 4   ♆ 🥁 🔔

A piece that can be appreciated even by those who dislike minimalism, *Miserere* sets two ancient hymns: the *Miserere* itself and the Dies Irae sequence, depicting the Last Judgment. After repeated pleas for mercy, interspersed with fateful pauses, the day of wrath itself is ushered in by a thunderous drum-roll. The drum initiates each new verse, as the choir sings the most terrifying words in the Christian liturgy. Pärt here applies a medieval technique to descending A minor scales; the music is in five parts, each successive part singing at half the speed of its predecessors, the slowest voice taking 16 times longer to finish the scale. Two electric guitars colour the ensemble, but it is the climax on trombone and trumpet that sets the spine tingling. Having confronted catastrophe, the choir ascends to radiant heights over the deep-throated resonance of the organ, tam-tam, and bell.

Henryk Górecki

◔ 1933–   🏳 Polish   ✍ 83

There is more to Górecki than the meditative minimal music which has made him famous in recent years. In the earlier part of his career he was an aggressively experimental composer of the avant garde, but – as with Arvo Pärt – Górecki's search in later decades for a pure, transparent style has been inspired by a religious sensibility. He is a devout Catholic for whom music is often a form of prayer.

LIFE AND MUSIC

Górecki was born in Silesia, a part of Poland in which Polish, German and Czech cultures exist side by side in a mix that has coloured his musical interests. His studies at Katowice Academy of Music, where he embraced the radical "Polish School" (which also included Krzysztof Penderecki) resulted in his Symphony No. 1 and *Scontri*, both aggressively dissonant. He later taught at the Academy and became its rector, but resigned for political reasons in 1979. By the mid-1970s, influences such as a growing love of Polish folk music and medieval Polish chants caused him to adopt a far less astringent style. His Symphony No. 3 shot him to huge international fame.

MILESTONES

1959	Writes Symphony No. 1
1960	Writes *Scontri (Collisions)*, orchestral.
1961	Meets Boulez on study tour to Paris; wins first prize at Youth Biennale
1973	Wins UNESCO first prize in Paris for *Ad Matrem*, choral work
1976	Composes Symphony No. 3
1979	*Beatus Vir*, choral work, premiered at Kraków for visit of Pope John Paul II
1987	Completes *Miserere*, choral work
1988	*Already it is Dusk* for string quartet
1992	Soprano Dawn Upshaw's recording of Symphony No. 3 creates huge interest

KEY WORKS

SYMPHONY NO. 3, "SORROWFUL SONGS"

ORCHESTRAL   ⏱ 45:00   📖 3   🎻♪

This symphony is a daring conception: it is unusual for a symphony to be uniformly slow and meditative. It could also be thought risky to quote such famous works as Beethoven's "Eroica" Symphony and a famous Chopin mazurka as Górecki does in his last movement, but these quotations are both expressive and symbolic:

the two chords he takes from the fourth of Chopin's Op. 17 mazurkas alternate like the rocking refrain of a lullaby for the souls of the Silesian freedom-fighters of both world wars, whilst the Eroica quote surely pays tribute to their heroism.

MISERERE

CHORAL   ⏱ 37:00   📖 1   🎵

Górecki composed this piece for unaccompanied chorus as a protest against the brutal treatment of peaceful Solidarity members in 1981. This political "programme" ensured that the work was not performed for another six years. As with the Symphony No. 3, the mood is rapt and poignant.

In Górecki's spiritual and meditative Symphony No. 3, a soprano sings poignant words written by a girl on a wall in a concentration camp.

John Tavener

⬤ 1944–   🏴 English   ✍ 209

For Tavener – who has had several brushes with death – music is a way of communing with God. His pieces resemble the sacred images of the Christian Orthodox faith with which he surrounds himself in both his Greek and English homes. He is influenced by Orthodox chant, as well as by mystical Islamic and Indian music; one of his favourite musicians, soprano Patricia Rozario, is herself Indian.

LIFE AND MUSIC

Tavener's first success came in 1968 with an avant-garde piece titled *The Whale*. In the following year a simpler work, the *Celtic Requiem*, appeared on the Apple label, thanks to contacts made by his brother, a builder, who was then working for Ringo Starr. Despite the religious nature of many early pieces, it took two events in the late 1970s to confirm Tavener in his pursuit of the harmonious simplicity for which he is now renowned: the failure of a musically and technically taxing opera at Covent Garden, and his reception into the Russian Orthodox Church. Since that time, Tavener has concentrated on writing devotional choral music – what he calls "icons in sound". By this, he means music that is "non-developmental" – that is, simple in texture and form, in the same way that religious icons are limited in their colour palette and three-dimensionality, but yet inspire calm, spiritual illumination.

Tavener's work includes a dance-opera, *Mary in Egypt*, with a libretto by Orthodox abbess Mother Thekla.

MILESTONES

1968	*The Whale*, cantata, and *In Alium*, tape, soprano and orchestra, are premiered
1969	Music is released on Apple label
1977	Joins the Orthodox faith.
1979	Opera, *Thérèse*, attracts hostile reviews
1980	Writes *Akhmatova: Rekviem*. Has a stroke
1989	*The Protecting Veil* premiered
1991	Almost dies during in heart surgery
2000	Knighted for "services to music".

KEY WORKS

AKHMATOVA: REKVIEM

CHORAL   ⏱ 120:00   📖 4   ♫♫ 🎭 ♪

This is a spare, searing work based on Byzantine chant. Premiered in 1981, it played to scanty audiences and met with little sympathy from critics. It sets poems written in secret by the great Russian poet Anna Akhmatova during the Stalinist years. Between her words are funeral texts from the Orthodox liturgy.

THE PROTECTING VEIL

ORCHESTRAL   ⏱ 43:00   📖 1   ♫♫ 🎼

Tavener had written nothing but vocal music for several years when leading cellist Steven Isserlis asked him for a piece. Yet in a way, this piece is "vocal" too: throughout, the solo cello soars in a tender, continuous "song" representing the voice of the Mother of God. Isserlis has suggested that people who find this music monotonous might understand its aims better if they attended an Orthodox service. The Feast of the Protecting Veil is an annual service commemorating a tenth-century Byzantine mystic's vision of the Virgin Mary. The string orchestra that supports the cello acts like an echo chamber and represents the vast resonant spaces of an Orthodox church. Like *Akhmatova: Rekviem*, the work is based on Byzantine chant.

Poul Ruders

◔ 1949–   ♙ Danish   ✍ 100

Ruders decided to be a composer at 16, when he heard Penderecki's *Threnody for the Victims of Hiroshima*. A Royal Danish Academy graduate in piano and organ, he became an acclaimed freelance composer, despite being mostly self-taught. He spent four years in London, after the Proms success of his Symphony No. 1, and then returned to live and work in Copenhagen. The success of his opera based on

MILESTONES

1967	Publishes first music
1980	*Four Compositions*, chamber concerto
1989	Composes Symphony No. 1
1994	Returns to Copenhagen
1998	*The Handmaid's Tale*, opera, produced
2005	Premiere of *The Trial*, opera

Atwood's novel *The Handmaid's Tale* established his reputation internationally. His music can be gloriously joyful and exuberant one moment and then change suddenly to introspection and despair. Using an expressive and flexible musical language – with passages of parody, quotation, and – Ruders has produced an impressive body of work.

Ruder's most recent opera, *The Trial*, was commissioned for the opening of the new opera house in Copenhagen (2005).

Wolfgang Rihm

◔ 1952–   ♙ German   ✍ c.240

Rihm's encyclopedic knowledge of Western music, and his affinity for the great Germans, has informed his enormous output of vocal and instrumental music. He studied under Stockhausen in 1972 and attended Darmstadt, where he is now a regular instructor. He is also professor of composition at Karlsruhe, where he was a student. Rihm started composing at 11, but his reputation was established in the 1970s with his cerebral but expressive music – particularly with the

frequently staged *Jakob Lenz*, an opera on the descent of the poet into madness. He has frequently set texts by Nietzsche, and many of his works have historical allusions. Subjective in nature and emotionally powerful, yet retaining intellectual weight, Rihm's music enjoys high esteem with many serious listeners.

Rihm's *Oedipus*, seen here in performance with Andreas Schmidt in the title role, was written as a series of ten vignettes, two of which are pantomimes.

MILESTONES

1972	Studies with Stockhausen
1978	Composes *Jakob Lenz*, chamber opera
1985	Professor of composition, Karlsruhe
1987	*Oedipus*, opera, performed
1992	*Gesungene Zeit*, for violin and orchestra
1994	Premiere of *Séraphin*, music-theatre
1999	Writes *Jagden und Formen*, orchestra

Kaija Saariaho

● 1952–   ▣ Finnish   ♫ 87

After studying at the Sibelius Academy, and in Freiburg, Germany, under the English composer Brian Ferneyhough, Saariaho moved to Paris where she has worked regularly at the IRCAM electronics studio. After writing melodious vocal works in the late 1970s, she started working with computers – exploiting techniques such

Saairiaho's opera, *L'amour de loin* was first performed at the Salzburg Festival in 2000, and featured Vienna's acclaimed Arnold Schoenberg Choir.

as transforming synthesized sounds slowly into others. In recent years she has written for more conventional instrumentation, often in a dramatic and extrovert style, and occasionally using experimental effects like selective amplification. Saariaho has been involved in various multimedia projects, including a full-length ballet, *Maa*. In 2003, her lyric opera *L'amour de loin* won the Grawemeyer Prize, one of many awards that her works have received, and she continues to fulfil regular commissions across Europe.

MILESTONES	
1982	Moves to Paris
1986	Composes *Lichtbogen*, instruments and live electronics
1987	Records *Stilleben*, tape
1991	*Maa*, ballet, performed
1994	Writes *Graal théâtre*, violin concerto
2000	Premiere of *L'amour de loin*, opera

Anne Boyd

● 1946–   ▣ Australian   ♫ c.50

On graduating from Sydney, having studied under Peter Sculthorpe, Boyd spent several years in England (at York, under Mellers, then teaching at Sussex), and here she achieved success with her imaginative but disciplined, uncluttered music. Back at home she spent a period as a freelance composer, often setting Australian and Asian themes, as in her oratorio *The Death of Captain Cook*. Her interest in Asian music took her to Hong Kong for ten years, before returning to Sydney. As her academic career flourished, there was not always time for composing. However, she continues to produce works, such as the orchestral *Black Sun* and *Grathawai*, and lectures internationally.

Anne Boyd explores the music and tone worlds of a wide range of styles and cultures in her colourful works.

MILESTONES	
1969	Moves to England
1974	Composes *Angklung*, for piano
1975	Writes *As I Crossed the Bridge of Dreams*, for 12 voices
1977	Returns to Australia
1981	Becomes head of music at Hong Kong University
1990	Head of music, Sydney University

Judith Weir

◔ 1954– ▥ Scottish ✍ 75

Judith Weir's music is accessible, unpretentious, and beautifully crafted. She is a tireless advocate of the "middle way" in contemporary music, rejecting both the extremes of simplicity (attributing much of the success of Górecki, Pärt, and Nyman to commercial forces) and intellectualism. She is best known for her operas, although theatrical wit and a strong gift for narrative inform all her work.

LIFE AND MUSIC

Whilst still at school, Judith Weir studied with John Tavener, and later at Cambridge University with Robin Holloway. Since then, she has held teaching positions at universities in Britain and the US, but these have not deflected her from composing works of broad appeal, working with children and amateurs, and striving to build "wider musical communities". Whilst director of London's Spitalfields Festival, she regularly programmed Indian music alongside contemporary pieces and community music-making events. Her own works draw inspiration from Chinese and Indian traditions (recently she has collaborated on projects with the Indian storyteller Vaiyu Naidu), as well as from her own Scottish roots. Her interest in medieval culture also shows in her music.

MILESTONES

1985	Composes *The Consolations of Scholarship* for ensemble and soprano, based on a Chinese drama of the Yuan period
1987	*A Night at the Chinese Opera* premiered by Kent Opera
1988	Completes choral work *Missa del Cid*; it is televized by the BBC
1995	Takes over as artistic director of Spitalfields Festival for five years
1999	*Natural History* (setting of Taoist texts) for soprano and orchestra premiered
2000	*woman.life.song* commissioned by Jessye Norman to words by Clarissa Estés, Maya Angelou, Toni Morrison
2002	Collaborates with storyteller Vayu Naidu on *Future Perfect*, a blend of music and narrative

KEY WORKS

MISSA DEL CID

CHORAL   ⏱ 25:00   📖 6   ♫ ⚒ ♂

This work for chorus and narrator is full of dark truths. It blends the Latin Mass with extracts from a Spanish medieval epic recounting the exploits of the Cid – the fanatical slayer of the Moors. The brutality of his era is satirized by its absorption into the liturgy, but the work ends in desolation, portraying the aftermath of battle.

Simon Rattle commissioned Weir's *We Are Shadows* for the City of Birmingham Symphony Orchestra in 1999.

A NIGHT AT THE CHINESE OPERA

OPERA   ⏱ 90:00   📖 3   ♫ ♂

Judith Weir's first full-length opera is an expansion of her earlier *The Consolations of Scholarship*, which forms the central act as a play within a play. The plot concerns the revenge of an orphan who has been unwittingly reared by a despot who killed his family. Act II echoes Chinese opera in providing music whose task is to support drama and stage gestures.

Magnus Lindberg

◔ 1958   🏳 Finnish   ✍ 52

In recent years, Finland has produced a throng of outstanding musical talents. Amongst its composers, Lindberg has one of the highest international profiles. The reasons are not hard to find: his music is dramatic, harmonically clear, colourful, ebullient (one of his major pieces is called *Joy*), and he uses the orchestra with prodigious skill to produce works of powerful immediacy.

LIFE AND MUSIC

Lindberg studied at the Sibelius Academy with composers Einojuhani Rautavaara and Paavo Heininen. Rautavaara would have encouraged Lindberg to see himself as a descendant of the founding father of Finnish music, Sibelius, but Heininen was interested above all in the works of the European avant-garde. Lindberg's early works such as *Kraft* and *Action-Situation-Signification*, are bracingly modernist, in keeping with the exploratory aesthetics of Toimii, the performance group he helped found with the conductor Esa-Pekka Salonen in 1981. Lindberg's debt to Sibelius and other symphonic composers has become become more audible, albeit with no dilution of his own musical voice.

MILESTONES	
1970s	Works with Swedish electronics studio
1977	Co-founds the modernist "Korvat auki" (Ears Open Society)
1981	Goes to study in Paris
1982	Difficulties of performing *Action-Situation-Signification* lead to founding of Toimii ensemble
1985	*Kraft* is first successful orchestral work
1994	*Aura* premiered in Tokyo
1996	Directs Meltdown Festival at London's South Bank
1997	Writes *Related Rocks* for IRCAM studio
2001	*Related Rocks* Lindberg Festival tours

KEY WORKS

AURA (IN MEMORIAM WITOLD LUTOSLAWSKI)

ORCHESTRAL   ⏲ 40:00   📖 4   🎺

Lindberg considered this massive work to be a cross between a symphony and a concerto for orchestra – both forms at which the modern Polish composer, Lutoslawski, excelled. The four movements play continuously, the last building hypnotically to a climax based on repeating figurations, giving way to a strongly melodic epilogue for strings.

RELATED ROCKS

CHAMBER   ⏲ 18:00   📖 1   ♟

Related Rocks, for two percussionists, two pianos, and electronics, was inspired by a geological exhibition at which Lindberg was impressed both by the variety and the ordered unity of the exhibits. The electronics provide a sonic "exhibition space" in which the instruments are presented. The work also develops an idea Lindberg had nurtured for some years: using electronically sampled recordings made during the demolition of a grand piano. The resultant sounds seem to have a symbolic power, perhaps the violence of events that formed the crystalline rocks.

In the 1970s, Lindberg was impressed by the energy of the English punk band The Clash, and the destruction performances of Germany's Einstürzende Neubauten.

James MacMillan

● 1959–   🏳 Scottish   ✍ 103

Macmillan is one of the diplomats of contemporary music. His music can be challenging, but attracts a broad audience. He is Scottish and proud of it, but without fanaticism. A practising Roman Catholic, his theology is liberal and, though his music reflects his faith, it does not offer serenity by ignoring the "conflict and ambiguity" which is typical of most people's lives and on which, indeed, he believes music thrives.

LIFE AND MUSIC

Macmillan started composing while learning to play the trumpet as a child. He studied at Edinburgh and Durham universities, but only began to find his personal voice as a composer in his late 20s as he identified his national and religious sources of inspiration. His first success was *Búsqueda (Search)*, a music-theatre piece that combined the Catholic liturgy with poems written by the mothers of the disappeared in Argentina during the military dictatorship there in the 1970s. *Búsqueda* and *The Confessions of Isobel Gowdie* set the course for his development: his works expressing religious conviction, while still engaging with the "real world".

MILESTONES

1988	Writes *Búsqueda*, ensemble and actors
1990	*The Confessions of Isobel Gowdie*, orchestral, premiered at the Proms
1992	Completes *Veni, Veni Emmanuel*
1994	Writes Symphony No. 1 and *Vigil*
1996	Cello Concerto is performed by Mstislav Rostropovich
1999	*Quickening* premiered at Proms

MacMillan has a strong interest in Scottish and Irish folk music. In 1989 he was composer-in-residence at the St Magnus Festival in Orkney.

KEY WORKS

VENI, VENI EMMANUEL

ORCHESTRAL   ⏱ 26:00   📖 1   🎶 🎷

Veni, Veni Emmanuel (Come, O Come, Emmanuel) was written for leading percussionist, Evelyn Glennie, who is also Scottish. As a percussion concerto, it allows a performer to demonstrate mastery of a vast array of instruments, but this presents a problem for the composer, because the number of sounds the soloist produces risks producing a fragmentary effect. MacMillan avoids this by turning the concerto into a set of clearly audible variations on one of the most glorious and familiar of all the liturgical chants for Advent.

VIGIL

ORCHESTRAL   ⏱ 40:00   📖 3   🎶

This large work is part of an epic triptych called *Triduum*. It was commissioned by Mstislav Rostropovich, who had come to know and admire *Veni, Veni Emmanuel*. Rostropovich premiered *Vigil* at the Barbican in London with the London Symphony Orchestra in 1997. *Vigil* was inspired by the Easter service, when Catholics anticipate Christ's Resurrection, and uses plainsong associated with the service. MacMillan describes *Vigil* simply, but graphically, as a journey from "despair to joy, from darkness to light, from death to life".

Mark-Anthony Turnage

● 1960–ㅤㅤ🏳 English ㅤ✍ 60

Mark-Anthony Turnage has a gift for crossing boundaries. Many of his most striking works are infused with the spirit, harmonies, and rhythms of jazz. The energy this imparts to much of his music, together with his sense of drama and his commitment to contemporary social issues commands attention from listeners of all persuasions – not only from those with "Classical" tastes.

LIFE AND MUSIC

Turnage began to win major composition prizes soon after completing his studies with John Lambert and Oliver Knussen. Important conductors and composers began to take note. Hans Werner Henze commissioned an opera for the Munich Biennale in 1988, and the hard-hitting result, *Greek*, to a libretto by playwright Steven Berkoff, became an international success. In 1989, Simon Rattle invited Turnage to become composer-in-association with the City of Birmingham Orchestra. The first result of the partnership was *Three Screaming Popes*, a work which proved that Turnage could be as aggressive and compelling in the concert hall as on the opera stage. Successes since then have come thick and fast, his greatest achievement so far perhaps being his opera, *The Silver Tassie*.

MILESTONES

1978	Attends Royal College of Music
1981	Wins Guinness Prize for *Night Dances*
1988	*Greek* composed for Munich Biennale
1989	Made composer-in-association at City of Birmingham Symphony Orchestra
1993	Composes *Your Rockaby*, concerto; for saxophone, a favourite instrument
1996	Collaborates with John Scofield and other jazz musicians on *Blood on the Floor*, for large ensemble and jazz trio
1998	Turnage retrospective festival, *Fractured Lines*, is held in London
2000	*The Silver Tassie* is premiered at English National Opera; later wins awards
2002	*Blood on the Floor* performed by Berlin Philharmonic under Simon Rattle

KEY WORKS

THE SILVER TASSIE

OPERAㅤ⏱120:00ㅤ📖 4ㅤ🎻🥁🎹

The Silver Tassie takes its text from Sean O'Casey's pacifist play about a young Dubliner who wins a coveted football trophy before leaving to fight in World War I. The opera does not shy away from depicting the horrors of the trenches; but, yet more disturbing, are the consequences for the young man who returns home to face betrayal and rejection because of his injuries.

Turnage is a great admirer of the trumpeter, Miles Davis) and jazz guitarist, John Scofield.

BLOOD ON THE FLOOR

ORCHESTRALㅤ⏱70:00ㅤ📖 9ㅤ🎻🎺

Commissioned as a ten-minute piece for an evening of jazz-inspired works by Gershwin, Bernstein, and others, *Blood on the Floor* outgrew the original brief. Like *Three Screaming Popes*, it takes its title from a haunted, visceral painting by Francis Bacon. With movements such as "Junior Addict" and "Needles", its subject is very personal as Turnage's brother died from a drug overdose. Yet the work is an absorbing experience, a compelling blend of composed music and jazz improvisation.

George Benjamin

● 1960–　　📖 English　　🎼 c.30

After studies with Olivier Messiaen in Paris and Alexander Goehr in Cambridge, Benjamin quickly emerged as a mature and confident composer. An early piece, *Ringed by the Flat Horizon* – written for an orchestra of 93 – was played at the London Proms, making Benjamin, at 20, the youngest composer to have a piece performed at the Proms. His serious yet colourful, direct, even flamboyant style – compared by some to the mood of J M W Turner's late paintings – led to frequent high-profile commissions through the 1980s. *Antara*, for Pierre Boulez, celebrated the 10th anniversary of IRCAM (the electronic music studios in Paris) and won a major recording award. Benjamin has also been active as both pianist and festival organizer, and regularly conducts leading international orchestras. He has won several prizes and awards, and has recently enjoyed a close association with the Tanglewood label, while also holding teaching posts at the Royal Academy and London university.

MILESTONES

1974	Studies with Olivier Messiaen
1980	Composes *Ringed by the Flat Horizon* for large orchestra
1984	Researches music at IRCAM
1987	Writes *Antara* for small orchestra
2001	Becomes Professor of Composition at King's College, London university

The evocative sound of Peruvian pan pipes (*antara*), manipulated electronically, gives the innovative composition *Antara*, its futuristic and cosmic quality.

Thomas Adès

● 1971–　　📖 English　　🎼 c.40

Winning "only" second prize as a pianist at the BBC Young Musician of the Year in 1989 proved a blessing in disguise for Thomas Adès. He concentrated instead on composing, becoming composer-in-residence for the Hallé Orchestra, shortly after leaving Cambridge university, and has since risen rapidly to prominence. His vivid, detailed, mightily assured style brought commissions from major orchestras, and his opera *Powder her Face* established his name worldwide. The orchestral piece *Asyla* was commissioned by Sir Simon Rattle, who conducted it at two seminal concerts, at Birmingham in 1998 and at Berlin in 2000 and the piece also won the coveted Grawemeyer Award, the largest international prize for composition. Adès is also active as a gifted conductor, teacher, and outstanding performer of his own and others' piano works.

The acclaimed production of *The Tempest*, conducted by Adès and premiered at London's Royal Opera House in 2004, starred Cyndia Sieden as Ariel.

MILESTONES

1992	Double-starred first from Cambridge
1993	Performs first public recital in London
1995	*Powder her Face*, chamber opera, achieves international recognition
1997	*Asyla*, for orchestra, highly acclaimed
1999	Becomes artistic director of Aldeburgh Festival
2004	*The Tempest*, opera, premiered

Kevin Volans

● 1949– ♙ South African ✍ c.70

Volans became popularly known in 1986 with the Kronos Quartet's best-selling CD of his work, *White Man Sleeps*. After university in Johannesburg, he studied in Cologne in Germany, became Karlheinz Stockhausen's teaching assistant, and was commissioned to write for IRCAM. Associated with the New Simplicity school in the late 1970s, he became increasingly influenced by African music, incorporating its techniques into his original style, which established him in the 1980s. After further success with Kronos, Volans turned to dance in the 1990s, collaborating with British dancers, such as Siobhan Davies, Jonathan Burrows and Shobana Jeyasingh.

MILESTONES	
1975	Teaching assistant to Stockhausen
1986	Moves to Ireland
1986	Writes *White Man Sleeps*, string quartet
1987	*Hunting: Gathering*, string quartet
1993	*The Man with Footsoles of Wind*, opera
2001	Writes *Zeno at 4am*, for puppets, actors, bass, string quartet, and chorus

African drummers perform at a dance on the Ivory Coast. African music inspired much of Volans's output, shaping his style and technique.

Carl Vine

● 1954– ♙ Australian ✍ c.50

Vine completed an electronic commission for West Australian Ballet while still at school, and won various music prizes while majoring in Physics at university. Now one of Australia's most performed and eminent composers, he has produced 20 vibrant, witty, and very danceable scores, as well as six symphonies, music for film and theatre, and several other works. After winning many prizes in Australia, Vine worked as a freelance composer and pianist before embarking on a variety of composing residencies. He has appeared as a conductor and pianist in Europe, and has lectured widely on electronic music. Vine lives in Sydney, where he is again composing after a four-year sabbatical.

MILESTONES	
1978	Composes *Poppy*, dance music
1979	Co-founds contemporary music ensemble Flederman
1984	Writes *Café Concertino*, chamber music
1985	Made resident composer at the New South Wales State Conservatorium
2000	Becomes artistic director at Musica

Vine's stirring score for the closing ceremony of the 1996 Olympics invoked the heroic spirit of the Games.

Peter Sculthorpe

● 1929–   ᵽ Australian   ✍ 184

Despite his love and respect for the classical, Sculthorpe has
deliberately distanced himself from it, creating instead an
Australian sound world by reflecting the continent's landscape
and by frequently basing his works on Aboriginal chants. He also incorporates
elements from Japanese and Balinese music, reasoning that Australian art should
link to a wider Pacific Rim culture, just as British music relates to Europe's.

LIFE AND MUSIC

Sculthorpe wrote music under the
bedclothes by torchlight as a boy, after
being rebuked by his piano teacher for
composing rather than practising. He
was only 16 when he began studying
music at Melbourne University. In 1955,
his Piano Sonatina was selected to
represent Australia at the International
Society for Contemporary Music
Festival in Germany and in 1958 he won
a scholarship to study in England. On
returning home, he wrote the desolate
Irkanda 1 for solo violin – a farewell to
Europe as well as to his recently
deceased father. It established the basis
for a vivid new "Australian" soundscape,
which he has explored ever more
resourcefully in all his subsequent work.

MILESTONES	
1955	Piano Sonatina played at ISCM
1961	Writes *Irkanda 1*
1963	Joins Sydney University staff (to 1999)
1965	Begins *Sun Music* series for orchestra
1986	Composes *Earthcry* for orchestra
1998	Elected one of Australia's 100 Living National Treasures by popular vote
2004	Premiers *Requiem*, large work for choir, soloists, orchestra, four didgeridoos.

Evoking the blazing heat of
the Outback, Sculthorpe's
typically rhythmic works
sharing the title *Sun Music*
include a ballet and chamber,
orchestral, and vocal pieces.

KEY WORKS

PORT ESSINGTON
ORCHESTRAL   ⏱ 15:00   📖 6   ◓

Port Essington is an unsettling, powerfully
atmospheric piece that draws on music
Sculthorpe wrote for a film about the
history of a doomed, 19th-century
British settlement in northern Australia.
A string trio plays gracious, romantic,
"civilized" music to represent the ill-
fated settlers, while the string orchestra
constantly encroaches with the wilder,
eerier sounds of the Bush. Both kinds of
music comprise a series of variations on
an aboriginal tune, *Djilili*, which occurs
in many of Sculthorpe's works.

EARTHCRY
ORCHESTRAL   ⏱ 11:00   📖 1   ◓

Earthcry brings together two of
Sculthorpe's abiding concerns: the
horror he feels at modern civilization's
abuse of the environment, and its
dispossession of native peoples. The
work recasts an earlier piece, *The Song
of Tailitnama*, which was based on an
Aboriginal chant for greeting the Earth
at dawn. *Earthcry*, however, takes the
material in new directions, working the
music up into a fierce, mesmeric dance
before reaching a final plateau of
spectacular grandeur.

Glossary of music terms

A CAPPELLA Literally "in the style of the chapel" (Italian), the term describes a piece written for unaccompanied voice(s).

ATONAL Describes any music without a recognizable tonality (key), such as serial music.

ARIA Literally "air" (Italian), a vocal piece for one or more voices in an opera or oratorio, more formally organized than a song. Arias written in the 17th and 18th centuries usually take the form of "da capo arias", with a three-part structure, the third part being a reiteration of the first.

ARS NOVA Literally "the new art" (Latin), a term coined in c.1322 to refer to a new style of music incorporating a wider range of note values than that of earlier music (of the "ars antiqua").

BASSO CONTINUO Harmonic, quasi-improvisatory accompaniment to a melodic piece used extensively in the Baroque period. The continuo usually comprised a harpsichord and strings, but could also include woodwind and brass instruments.

BARCAROLLE Song or piece of music associated with Venetian gondoliers, characterized by a lilting 6/8 or 12/8 rhythm. Well-known examples include Offenbach's Barcarolle from his *Tales of Hoffman* and Chopin's piano Barcarolle in F sharp.

CADENZA Literally "cadence" (Italian). Originally an improvised solo passage by the solo performer within a concerto, from the 19th century onwards cadenzas became more formalized and less spontaneous.

CANON Piece in which each line is split into phrases of equal length. The entries of the voices or instruments are staggered to produce a layered, imitative effect. If a canon is strict, the melody line is repeated exactly by all parts.

CANTATA Literally "a thing to sing" (Italian), a cantata is in many respects similar to opera, being a programmatic piece generally for voice and orchestra that is designed to tell a story. The 17th and 18th centuries saw the rise of both the cantata da camera (a secular chamber piece) and the cantata da chiesa (its sacred equivalent). Writers of these types of cantata include J S Bach and Heinrich Schütz, whereas the modern, freer version of the cantata has enjoyed treatments by Britten, Stravinsky and Britten, among others.

CANTUS FIRMUS Literally a "fixed song" (Latin) – usually comprising very long notes and often based on a fragment of Gregorian chant – that served as the structural basis for polyphonic composition, particularly during the Renaissance.

CANZONA Short, polyphonic part song popular in the 16th and 17th centuries. In many ways a canzona is similar to a madrigal, although the writing is lighter.

CAPRICCIO Short piece in a generally free style. Capriccios written in the 17th century tend to be fugal in structure and rather more formalised than their Romantic equivalents – written by the likes of Brahms and Paganini, for example – which tend to be solo rhapsodic pieces.

CATCH Part song popular in the 17th century that is canonic in form, which causes the words often often to take on new and bizarre meanings.

CHACONNE 17th-century instrumental or vocal piece composed above a ground and characterized by a slow, stately triple-time beat.

CHAMBER MUSIC Music composed for small groups of two or more instruments such as duet, trios and quartets. Chamber music was originally designed to be performed at home for the entertainment of small gatherings, but is now more often performed in concert environments. Similarly, chamber orchestras and operas are pieces written for small numbers of instruments, although all orchestral instruments are represented.

CHANSON Old French part song similar to the canzona and often arranged for voice and lute.

CHITARONNE Literally "big guitar" (Italian), a very large double-necked lute.

CHROMATIC Literally "of colour" (Latin), the term refers to a progression of notes that move in semitone steps.

CLAVICHORD Early stringed keyboard instrument whose strings are sounded by being struck at a tangent, rather than being struck (like a piano's) or plucked (like a harpsichord's).

CODA Literally "tail" (Italian), a final section of a piece of music that is distinct from the overall structure yet is based on the piece's thematic elements.

CONCERTO Today, the term "concerto" – derived from terms meaning both "performing together" and "struggling" – is given to describe a large piece for a solo instrument and orchestra, designed to be a vehicle for the solo performer's virtuosity on his instrument. In the earlier Baroque concerto grossos, however, there was a more equal interplay between the much smaller orchestra ("ripieno") and a group of soloists ("concertino").

CONCERTO GROSSO See *Concerto*.

CONTINUO See *Basso Continuo*.

CONTRAPUNTAL Describes a styles of music writing whereby single, interweaving lines of music are played simultaneously to create a complex, continually shifting texture, as typified by the writing of J S Bach.

COUNTERPOINT See *Contrapuntal*.

CRESCENDO Literally "growing" (Italian), a musical direction to play or sing gradually louder. The opposite is diminuendo.

DA CAPO ARIA See *Aria*.

DANCE SUITE See *Suite*.

DIMINUENDO Literally "waning, lessening" (Italian), a musical direction to play or sing gradually more quietly. The opposite is crescendo.

DISSONANCE Sounding together of notes to produce discord (ie sounds unpleasing to the ear). The opposite of these terms are "concordance" and "concord". Much 20th-century music is dissonant.

DIVERTIMENTO Classical instrumental genre for chamber ensemble or soloist, often performed as light entertainment. Mozart wrote many divertimentos.

DYNAMICS Differences in volume of a piece or section of music.

EMBELLISHMENT See *Ornamentation*.

ENLIGHTENMENT Social move towards rational scientific reasoning and rational thinking that occurred towards the end of the 18th century, and found its musical expression in the writing of composers such as Haydn.

EQUAL TEMPERAMENT System of tuning whereby each note of the chromatic scale is separated from its neighbours by exactly the same degree. Equal temperament was introduced in the 18th century, before which the intervals varied slightly and the sharps and flats in a scale were all at slightly different pitches.

FUGATO Passage written in the manner of a fugue.

FUGUE Traditionally, a complex, highly structured contrapuntal piece, in two or more parts, popular in the Baroque period. Each line comprises a subject, counter-subject and free part, in that order, which are then performed by the other parts or voices to produce a highly imitative sound.

GALANT SOUND Special musical style of the 18th century characterized by elegance, formality and profuse ornamentation.

GRAND OPÉRA French development of opera, Grand Opéra is characterized by historic plots, large choruses, crowd scenes, ornate costumes and spectacular sets.

GROUND Composition developed on a ground bass (a constantly repeated bass figure, often melodic). Can also refers to the bass part itself.

HARMONIC The harmonic series consists of a fundamental (ie the note played) and a logarithmic, ascending progression of partials (ie overtones) determining the individual tone colour of an instrument.

HOMOPHONIC Describes a style of writing popularized in the Classical period whereby a lyrical melody line is supported by a dense chordal harmony and a solid bass.

INTERMEDI Short musical dramas performed between the acts of spoken plays.

IRCAM Institut de Recherche et Coordination Acoustique/Musique, a France-based research centre for electronic music, founded in 1969 by Georges Pompidou and Pierre Boulez.

KAPELLMEISTER/HOFKAPELLMEISTER Choirmaster/music director. The term Kapellmeister later came to be synonymous with the English term "conductor".

LIBRETTO Text of an opera or other vocal dramatic work

LIED Traditional German song, popularized by the Lieder of Schubert.

LUTE Early precursor of the modern guitar, of Eastern origin, with five pairs of strings, two tuned to each note, which were plucked.

MADRIGAL Secular a cappella song popular in the Renaissance period – particularly in England and Italy – often set to a lyric love poem.

MASQUE Elaborate English stage entertainment chiefly cultivated in the 17th century and involving poetry, dancing, scenery, costumes, instrumental and vocal music. The masque was related to opera and ballet.

MASS Main service of the Roman Catholic Church, highly formalized in structure, comprising specific sections – known as the "Ordinary" – performed in the following order: Kyrie, Gloria, Credo, Sanctus with Hosanna and Benedictus, and Agnus Dei and Dona nobis pacem. The Baroque period was a fertile time for the Mass as most composers were employed by the churches of Europe.

MÉLODIE French equivalent of the German Lied and English song.

MINUET AND TRIO A graceful dance in 3/4 time, normally in three sections: the Minuet section (either binary or ternary form), then the Trio (originally intended for three musicians to play, and consisting of unrelated material), and finally a reprise of the Minuet. The piece appears as a movement of Baroque suites and Classical sonatas and symphonies, but was replaced with the faster Scherzo by Beethoven.

MODES Eight-note scales inherited fromAncient Greece via the Middle Ages in which they wwere most prevalent, although they still survive today in folk music and plainsong.

MODULATION In a passage of music, a shift from one key (tonality) to another – for example, C major to A minor.

MONODY Vocal style developed in the Baroque period whereby the musical intent is conveyed by a single melodic line, either accompanied or not.

MONOPHONIC Describes music written in a single-line texture, or melody without an accompaniment.

MOTET Originally, in medieval times, a vocal composition elaborating on the melody and text of plainsong. In the 15th century, the motet became a more independent religious choral composition, set to any Latin words not included in the Mass.

MOTIVE Short but recognisable melodic or rhythmic figure that recurs throughout a piece, often used programmatically to refer to a character, object, or idea, as with Wagner's Leitmotiv and Berlioz's idée fixe.

NATURAL INSTRUMENT Usually refers to a woodwind or brass instrument consisting of a basic tube with no extra mechanisms for modifying the sound, other than breath control and embouchure.

NOCTURNE Night piece. As a solo, one-movement piano piece, the nocturne originated with John Field, but was developed to a great degree by Chopin, who made the form his own.

OPERA Drama in which all or most characters sing and in which music is an important element. Traditionally, the writing is for full orchestra, soloists, and chorus, although examples exist that include fewer or more than these elements.

OPÉRA COMIQUE Exclusively French type of opera which, despite its name, is not always comic, nor particularly light. It is always based on original material, however, and always includes spoken dialogue.

OPERA BUFFA Type of comic opera that was especially popular in the 18th century (eg Mozart's *The Marriage of Figaro*, Rossini's *The Barber of Seville*).

OPERA SERIA Literally "serious opera", and the direct opposite of opera buffa. The style is characterized by the use of castrato singers, heroic or mythological plots, Italian libretti, and formality in music and action, and was popularized in the writings of Rossini.

OPERETTA Literally "little opera", and sometimes known as "light opera", this term refers to a lighter style of 19th-century opera involving dialogue.

ORATORIO Work for vocal soloists and choir with instrumental accompaniment originating in the congregation of Oratorians, founded by St Philip Neri in the 16th century. Oratorios traditionally take biblical text as their subject matter and are usually performed "straight", although they originally involved sets, costumes, and action.

ORNAMENT Also known as an "embellishment", an ornament is a modification of a note by alternating it rapidly with its neighbour either above, below, or both.

OSTINATO Repeated musical figure, usually in the bass part, than can provide a foundation for harmonic and melodic variation above. Similar to a ground bass.

OVERTURE Literally "opening" (French), an instrumental part of an opera played at the beginning of the work to present the important thematic material therein. In the Romantic period, stand-alone overtures were written – ie Brahms' *Tragic Overture* and Mendelssohn's *Hebrides Overture* – and performed in their own right. These pieces are usually in sonata form.

PASSACAGLIA Originally a slow and stately dance in moderately slow triple metre appearing in 17th-century keyboard music. These pieces are based on a short, repeated bass-line melody that serves as the basis for continuous variation in the other voices. With later passacaglias, the repeated theme did not necessarily appear in the bass.

PEDAL (POINT) A held note that usually occurs in the bass, above which harmonies change, sometimes even becoming discordant. A pedal point will often occur at the climax of a fugue.

PIZZICATO Literally "pinched" (It.), a style of playing stringed instruments, such as the violin or cello, by plucking the string with a finger of the bowing hand, or occasionally with the fretting hand between bowed notes.

PLAINSONG Also known as plainchant (from the Latin *cantus planus*), plainsong is medieval church music which still survives today in the Roman Catholic Church. It consists of a unison, unaccompanied vocal line in free rhythm, like speech, with no regular bar lengths. Gregorian chant is a well-known type of plainsong.

POLYPHONY Literally "many sounds", in Classical music this refers to a style of writing in which all parts are independent and of equal importance, unlike homophonic music, and therefore implies contrapuntal music. Music forms that typify this style include the canon, fugue, and motet.

PROGRAMME MUSIC Any music written to describe a non-musical theme, such as an event, landscape, or literary work.

RECITATIVE Style of singing in opera and oratorio that is closely related to the delivery of dramatic speech in pitch and rhythm. The notes of the recitative are fixed, but there is no fixed time.

REPETITEUR Someone who plays a piano reduction of a work for voice and orchestra so that the singers can practise their lines to an accompaniment.

RICERCARE Literally "to seek out" (It.), an instrumental fugal work played on keyboard instruments or by a consort of string or wind instruments. Can be seen as the instrumental counterpart of the madrigal or motet.

RONDO Piece (or movement) of music based on a recurring theme with interspersed material, often written in rondo sonata form.

RONDO SONATA FORM See *Sonata Principle/Form*.

SCHERZO Lively dance piece (or movement) in triple time. During the Classical and Romantic periods, the third movement of a symphony one of a sonata's middle movements was a Scherzo, usually paired with a Trio. The Scherzo and Trio replaced the Baroque Minuet and Trio.

SERENATA A kind of 18th-century secular cantata, often of an occasional or congratulatory nature, and performed either as a small quasi-opera or as a concert piece.

SERIAL MUSIC System of atonal composition developed by Arnold Schoenberg and others of the Second Viennese School, in which fixed sequences of musical elements are used as a foundation for more complex structures. Most commonly these sequences comprise arrangements of each degree of the chromatic scale – known as a "tone row" – although shorter sequences may also be used. This tone row, or series, can then appear in four different ways: forwards, backwards (retrograde), upside-down (inversion), and upside-down and backwards (retrograde inversion). Pieces composed to this method include Schoenberg's Serenade, Op. 24, and Webern's String Trio, Op. 20.

SINGSPIEL Literally "song play" (German), Singspiel generally refers to a comic opera with spoken dialogue in lieu of recitative, as typified in Mozart's *The Magic Flute.*

SONATA Popular instrumental piece for one or more players. Appearing first in the Baroque period, when it was a short piece for a solo or small group of instruments accompanied by a continuo, the Classical sonata adhered to a three- or four-movement structure for one or two instruments (although the three-instrument trio sonata was often popular), comprising usually three or four movements: an opening movement (in what later became known as "first movement" or "sonata" form), a slow second movement, a lively Scherzo, and finally a Rondo.

SONATA DA CAMERA Literally "chamber sonata" (Italian), a multi-instrumental piece (usually for two violins with basso continuo) of the late 17th and early 18th centuries that often took the form of a collection of dance movements, usually with a quick first movement.

SONATA DA CHIESA Literally "church sonata", a multi-instrumental piece similar in many respects to the secular sonata da camera, usually comprising four movements: a slow introduction, a fugal movement, a slow movement, and a quick finale.

SONATA PRINCIPLE/FORM Structural form popularized in the Classical period, and from this period onwards the first movements of sonatas, symphonies, and concertos were written mainly in this form.
1. A piece written in sonata form traditionally comprises an exposition, comprising a subject followed by a second subject (linked by a bridge section and modulated to a different key), after which the initial material is expounded on in the development section, and finally the recapitulation restates the exposition, although remaining in the tonic (main key).
2. A variation on sonata form is "rondo sonata form", in which the restated rondo theme is constructed around a similar developmental format, with a refrain (ie a section which returns regularly) alternating with contrasting sections called "episodes". If the refrain is labelled as A and the episodes as B and C, a typical rondo form will be as follows: ABACAD (with D being the coda).

STACCATO Literally "detached" (Italian), a performance technique whereby each note is articulated separately, without slurring.

SUBJECT In musical terms, a group of notes forming a basic element or idea in a composition by repetition and development, particularly in a fugue or rondo. Pieces composed in sonata form contain first and second subjects, but these are thematic groups rather than individual themes.

SUITE Multi-movement work (generally instrumental) made up of a series of contrasting dance movements, usually all in the same key.

SYMPHONY Large-scale work for full orchestra. The Classical and Romantic symphony, popularized by Haydn and Mozart, contains four movements – traditionally an Allegro, a slower second movement, a Scherzo, and a lively Finale – but later symphonies can contain more or fewer. The first movement is often in sonata form, and the slow movement and Finale may follow a similar structure.

SYMPHONIC POEM Extended single-movement symphonic work, usually of a programmatic nature, often describing landscape or literary works. Also known as a tone poem.

TEMPERAMENT See *Equal Temperament.*

TOCCATA Literally "a thing to touch (ie play)" (Italian.), and thus distinguished from a "cantata". The term came to be associated with touching a keyboard to test it, and so toccatas came to include rapid ornamentation and brilliant passages, a trend that continued into later Classical and Romantic toccatas.

12-TONE MUSIC System of composition on which the later works of Schoenberg and his followers are based, whereby each degree of the chromatic scale is ascribed exactly the same degree of importance, thus eliminating any concept of key or tonality. (See also *Serial Music.*)

VERISMO Style of opera with thematic material and presentation rooted firmly in reality.

VOLUNTARY Traditionally, an organ piece written for performance before and after an Anglican church service. The term also applies generally to a free-style keyboard piece.

ZARZUELA Light Spanish one- or two-act musical stage play or comic opera, usually strongly nationalistic with spoken dialogue and, sometimes, audience participation.

Index

Page numbers in **bold** refer to main entries.

Picture Credits

LEB; 269b,t AKG; 270b,t AKG; 271t AKG; 271c AKG/Jerome de Cunha; 271b Co/Archivo Iconografico,S.A; 272 Petit Palais, Geneva, Switzerland/BAL; 273 Co/Royalty Free; 274t AKG; 274bl Co/Archivo Iconografico,S.A; 274bc Co/Bettmann; 274br Co/Medford Historical Society Collection; 274c LEB; 275bc Co/Bettmann; 275crb ART/Edward Grieg House, Nordas Lake, Bergen, Norway/ Dagli Orti (A); 275bl,br,tl LEB; 276t Co/Michael Nicholson; 277b Co/Michael S.Yamashita; 277t ART/Bibliotheque des Arts Decoratifs, Paris / Dagli Orti; 278b,t LEB; 279t LEB; 279c TOP; 280c Hamburg Kunsthalle, Hamburg, Germany/BAL; 280t Co/Michael Nicholson; 281 Co/Charles O'Rear; 282b,t LEB; 283 AL/Michael Juno; 284b Archives Charmet/BAL; 284ca DK/Demitrio Carrasco; 284cb,t LEB; 285b,tl AKG; 285tr LEB; 286Co/ Bettmann; 287t MEPL; 287b GI/Photographer's Choice; 288AL/PhatSheep; 289 LEB/Royal Academy of Music Collection; 290 RGA / Courtsey of Rank/ITV; 291 GI/Stone; 292t AKG; 292c ART/Private Collection/Marc Charmet; 293br The De Morgan Centre, London/BAL; 293l,tr LEB; 293cl LEB/Interfoto, Munich; 294t LEB; 295b Co/Liba Taylor; 295t LEB/Donald Cooper; 296 GI/Image Bank; 297 LEB; 298 LEB; 299 AL/A.Parada; 300t LEB; 300b LEB/Donald Cooper; 301 Co/Sanford/Agliolo; 302b,tl LEB; 302tr LEB/Laurie Lewis; 303t AKG; 303b Private Collection/BAL; 304b,cl AKG; 304cr Co/Michael Nicholson; 304tl LEB/Interfoto,Munich; 305b,t AKG; 306t AKG; 306b Peter Willi / Kunstmuseum, Basel, Switzerland/BAL; 307cr Musee des Tapisseries, Angers, France/BAL/Lauros/Giraudon; 307b DK; 307cl,t LEB; 308c AKG; 308b Co/Bettmann; 308t LEB; 309b AKG/Gert Schutz; 309t LEB; 310t Co/Michael Nicholson; 310b LEB; 311 AL/ImageState; 312t AKG; 312b Co/Ludovic Malsant; 313 GI/Photographer's Choice; 314tl AKG; 314b Co/Underwood & Underwood; 314cl,tr LEB; 315t AKG; 315c Co/Freelance Consulting Services Pty Ltd; 315br LEB; 316 AL/Frank Chmura; 317 Co/Hulton-Deutsch Collection; 318 Co/Archivo Iconografico, S.A; 319 Co/Chris Lisle; 320 AL/Peter Adams Photography; 321 Co/Hulton-Deutsch Collection; 322 GI; 323 AL/ImageState; 324bl AKG; 324cl Co/Hulton-Deutsch Collection; 324tl,tr LEB; 325bl Co/Bettmann; 325cl Co/Hulton-Deutsch Collection; 325tl LEB/C. Lambton; 325br LEB/ Royal Academy of Music Collection; 326t Co/Michael Nicholson; 326c LEB; 327 AL/The Garden Picture Library; 328 GI/Hulton Archive; 329 Co/Bettmann; 330 DK/Dave King; 331 AL/Steven May; 332t Co/Bettmann; 332b Co/John Heseltine; 333 NASA/SPL; 334b Co/Jon Sparks; 334t LEB; 335c AL/Chromepix.com; 335t LEB/Royal Academy of Music Collection; 336tr Co/Hulton-Deutsch Collection; 336br,cl,tl LEB; 337bl,tl,tr AKG; 337br Co/Hulton-Deutsch Collection; 338t Co/Bettmann; 338b Co/Michael Freeman; 339 AL/Agripicture Images; 340t Co/Michael Nicholson; 340b LEB; 341t AL/Robert Llewellyn; 341t bg Co/Craig Aurness; 342b,t LEB; 343t AKG; 343c Co/Michael Busselle; 344t AKG; 344b Musee des Beaux-Arts, Reims, France/BAL/Lauros/Giraudon; 345c AKG; 345b,t LEB; 346 Co/Keren Su; 347 Co/Bettmann; 348 Co/Michael Freeman; 349 AL/Stephen Bond; 350tl Co/Bettmann; 350b Co/Musee Citadelle Vauban/Sygma; 350tr LEB; 351b AKG; 351t LEB; 352t AKG; 352b 'Les BalletsSuedois' Cinematheque francaise, Paris; 353b,t AKG; 353c Co/Steve Raymer; 354t Co/Bettmann; 354b ART/Bibliotheque des Arts Decoratifs Paris/Dagli Orti; 355 AL/thislife pictures; 356cr Co/Sylvian Saustier; 356b,cl,t LEB; 357t Roger-Viollet, Paris/BAL; 357 RGA/Courtesy Literary Classic Productions; 358t Co; 358b TOP; 359b AKG; 359t Co/Pietro Mascagni; 360b,t Co/Bettmann; 361 GI/Taxi; 362t Co/Bettmann; 362b LEB; 363 Co/Vittoriano Rastelli; 364cl,cr,t AKG; 364b LEB/Sabine Toepffer/Deutsches Theater; 365t LEB; 365b LEB/Manchester Art Gallery; 366t Co/Archivo Iconografico,S.A; 366b LEB; 367 Co/Reuters; 368b Real Academia de Bellas Artes de San Fernando, Madrid, Spain/BAL/ Giraudon; 368tl LEB; 369t Co/Bettmann; 369c Co/O. Alamany & E.Vicens; 370b Co/Jeremy Horner; 370t Co/John Springer Collection; 371 AL/Sue Cunningham/Worldwide Picture Library; 372t Co/Bettmann; 372b DK; 373cl,tl Co; 373b Co/Craig Lovell; 373cr DK/conaculta-inah-mex - Authorised reproduction by the Instituto Nacional de Anthropologia e Historia; 374t AKG; 374b LEB; 375b Co/Alan Schein Photography; 375t Co/Bettmann; 376c Christie's Images/BAL; 376t LEB; 377t Co; 377b DK; 378 t LEB; 378b Courtesy of The MacDowell Colony/Joanna Eldredge Morrissey; 379 Co/John Sohm; ChromoSohm Inc.; 380 The Art Museum of Estonia, Tallinn Estonia/BAL; 382cb Co/Bettmann; 382c ART/Society of The Friends of Music Vienna / Dagli Orti (A); 382bl,br LEB; 382-383t LEB/Laurie Lewis; 383br,cr LEB; 383cb LEB/Kurt Weill Foundation; 384bl AKG/Daniel Frasney; 384cl AKG/Mirisch-7 Arts/United Artists/ Album; 384t AKG/United Artists/Album; 384br Co/Angelo Hornak; 384bc Co/Bettmann; 385cb Co/Reuters; 385tl Co/Sunset Boulevard/Sygma; 385br LEB/Alastair Muir; 385bl LEB/Laurie Lewis; 385c Retna Pictures Ltd/Michael Putland; 386 AL/Pedro Lobo; 387 LEB; 388 LEB/Private Collection; 389 Co; 390 Co/Bettmann; 391 Co/Craig Tuttle; 392t Co/Bettmann; 392b LEB; 393 AL/Images Etc.Ltd.; 394 GI/Stone; 395 Co/BBC; 396 AKG; 397 GI/Taxi; 398clb AKG; 398cla Co/Bogdan Cristel/Reuters; 398br Co/Hulton-Deutsch Collection; 398tl LEB; 399b,t LEB; 400 Co/David Cumming/Eye Ubiquitous; 401 Co/Hulton-Deutsch Collection; 402t AKG; 402b Co/Phillippa Lewis/Edifice; 403 LEB/Laurie Lewis; 404c Co/Kelly-Mooney Photography; 405c AKG/Niklaus Strauss; 405t Co/Tim Hawkins/Eye Ubiquitous; 406b AKG; 406t AKG/Paul Almasy; 407t AKG; 407b DK/Dave King; 408b AKG/©Sevenarts Ltd 2005. All Rights Reserved, DACS; 408t AKG; 409b Co/Hulton-Deutsch Collection; 409t LEB/G. Salter; 410t Co/Hulton-Deutsch Collection; 410b LEB; 411cl,tl Co/Bettmann; 411br GI/Hulton-Deutsch Collection; 411tr LEB; 412 AL/Tomas del Amo; 413 LEB; 414 LEB/(c) 1932 renewed by Associated Music Publishers BMI. International copyright secured. All rights reserved. Reprinted by permission; 415 GI/Taxi; 416cr Private Collection/BAL; 416cl,t Co/Bettmann; 416b KOB/Flaherty Prods.; 417b Co/Bettmann; 417t LEB; 418 GI/Taxi; 419 Co/Underwood & Underwood; 420 RGA/ Courtesy MGM; 421 Co/David Muench; 422 GI/Image Bank; 423 Co/Bettmann; 424 KOB/Paramount; 425 Co/Wolfgang Kaehler; 426t Co/Bettmann; 426c Co/ David Lees; 427 GI/Stone; 428 AKG/Binder; 429cr Co/Joseph Sohm; Visions of America; 429tl LEB; 429cl LEB/Betty Freeman; 429b LEB/ R. Booth; 430b,t Co/Ted Spiegel; 431 Co/Jon Hicks; 432 Co/Jacques M Chenet; 433 Co/G.E.Kidder Smith; 434br Co/Bettmann; 434bl Co/Christher Felver; 434t LEB/Betty Freeman; 434cl LEB/Susurrea; 435cr AKG/Gert Schutz; 435tl AKG/photo by Georgette Chadbourne/ © ADAGP, Paris and DACS, London 2005; 435bl James Goodman Gallery, New York, USA / BAL/ © 1998 Kate Rothko Prizel & Christopher Rothko/DACS 2005; 435cl LEB; 436b AL/IMAGINA The Image Maker; 436cr City Lights Bookstore; 436tl Co/Bettmann; 436cl LEB/Betty Freeman; 437t Co/Reuters; 437b Kobal Collection/New Line/Ch 4/Telefilm; 438b Co/Tony Wilson-Bligh/Papillio; 438t LEB/Betty Freeman; 439 DK/Alastair Duncan; 440t Co/Piotr Redlinski; 440b KOB/Paramount/ Miramax/Clive Coote;441 Co/Julia Waterlow/Eye Ubiquitous; 442t LEB/Betty Freeman; 442b LEB/ Laurie Lewis; 443 Co/Reuters; 444t LEB/Betty Freeman;

444c TOP/HIP/The British Library; 445t Co/Dean Conger; 445b Co/Robbie Jack; 446 Co/Marc Garanger; 447 LEB; 448 LEB; 449 Co/Robert Yin; 450 AL/Bryan & Cherry Alexander Photography; 451 GI; 452cr DK/Demetrio Carrasco; 452b LEB; 453t RGA /Courtesy Mosfilm; 453b LEB/Richard H Smith; 454 LEB/B.Rafferty; 455tr Co/Bettmann; 455c LEB; 456tl AKG/Marion Kalter; 456b Co/Galeb Garanich/Reuters; 456cr LEB/Zdenek Chrapek; 457t AKG/Marion Kalter; 457c Co/Peter Turnley; 458b The Stapelton Collection/ BAL/© DACS 2005; 458t LEB/Kurt Weill Foundation; 459 Co/Lawrence Manning; 460t Co/Hulton-Deutsch Collection; 461 AL/FogStock; 462 GI/Stone+; 463 Co/Hulton-Deutsch Collection; 464 LEB/B. Rafferty; 465 Co/Clay Perry; 466 GI/Image Bank; 467 Co/Hulton-Deutsch Collection; 468 GI/Time Life Pictures; 469 AL/The National Trust Photolibrary; 470br Co/Bettmann; 470tr Co/Hulton-Deutsch Collection; 470bl LEB/Suzy Maeder; 471cl AKG/Marion Kalter; 471cr AL/Andrew Bargery; 471b Co/Bettmann; 471t Co/Hulton-Deutsch Collection; 472b,t Co/Hulton-Deutsch Collection; 472c LEB/Matti Kolho; 473b AKG; 473t LEB/Forum; 474t AKG/Horst Maack; 474b LEB/Laurie Lewis; 475bl AKG/Bianconero; 475cr AKG/Paul Almasy; 475tl Co/Hulton-Deutsch Collection; 475cl LEB/Betty Freeman; 476b KOB/MGM; 476t LEB/Betty Freeman; 477 SPL/Gregory Sams; 478c Co/Catherine Panchoot; 478t Co/Philippe Caron/Sygma; 479 Co/Ted Horowitz;

480c GI/Erich Auerbach; 480t LEB/Robin Del Mar; 481b AL/Pat Behnke; 481t Universal Music/LEB; 482t AKG/Horst Maack; 482b Karlheinz Stockhausen – Stockhausen scores, CDs, books & videos may be ordered directly from the Stockhausen-Verlag, Kürten, Germany, stockhausen-verlag@stockhausen.org /LEB; 483cr DK; 483br John Crook; 483t LEB/Betty Freeman; 483cl LEB/George Newson; 484b Co/Lawson Wood; 484t LEB/Richard H Smith; 485 AL/Doug Houghton; 486t AKG/Ullstein; 486b LEB/B.Rafferty; 487t AKG/Marion Kalter ; 487b Co/Liu Liqun; 487cl Co/Reuters; 487cr DK/Demetrio Carrasco; 488b Richardson and Kailas Icons, London, UK/BAL; 488t LEB/Nigel Luckhurst; 489 Co/Craig Tuttle; 490b AL/lookGaleria; 490t Co/Van Parys /Sygma; 491c Kremlin Museums, Moscow, Russia/BAL; 491t LEB/Richard H Smith; 492br AKG/Horst Maack; 492clb LEB/Betty Freeman; 492t LEB/Nigel Luckhurst; 492cla TOP/copyright 2004 Polfoto; 493cl AKG/Marion Kalter; 493b Co/Penny Tweedle; 493tl LEB/Betty Freeman; 494b Co/Catherine Panchout; 494t LEB/Kate Mount; 495b Co/Roger Ressmeyer; 495t LEB/Riichard Haughton; 496c DK/Paul Harris; 496t LEB/Jim Four; 497b Co/Bettmann; 497t LEB/Betty Freeman; 498tr DK/Andy Crawford; 498b LEB/Alastair Muir; 498cl,tl LEB/Betty Freeman; 499b Co/Ales Fevzer; 499c Co/Cardinale Stephane/Sygma; 499t Co/Fulvio Roiter; 500c Co/Charles & Josette Lenars; 500t LEB/Betty Freeman

Recording information for works featured in the waveform graphics:

67 Palestrina: Missa Benedicta Es
Peter Phillips, The Tallis Scholars, Gimmell CDGIM001

115 Handel: Water Music
Jane Glover, London Mozart Players, Sanctuary Classics CD CDRSN3024

115 J S Bach: Brandenburg Concerto No. 5 in D, BWV1050
Gustav Leonhardt, Bruggen, Kuijken, Bylsma et al., BMG SB2K 62946

136–37 Haydn: Symphony No. 104 in D, "London"
Christopher Hogwood, The Academy of Ancient Music, Decca 411833-2

154–55 Mozart: Symphony No. 41 in D, K551, "Jupiter"
Jeffrey Tate, English Chamber Orchestra, EMI CDC 7471472

162–63 Beethoven: Sonata, Op. 57, "Appassionata"
Rudolf Serkin (Philips Classics 456 964-2)

178–79 Schubert: Symphony No. 8, "Unfinished", D 759
Sandor Vegh, Camerata Academica des Mozarteums Salzburg (Capriccio 10503)

193 Chopin: Piano Concerto No. 2 in F minor
William Steinberg, NBC Symphony, Arthur Rubinstein, Red Seal 09026630172

214–15 Brahms: Ein Deutsches Requiem
Klaus Tennstedt, London Philharmonic Orchestra and Choir, Jessye Norman (soprano) and Jorma Hynninen (baritone) EMI 077776781921

254–55 Wagner: Tristan und Isolde
Klaus Tennstedt, London Philharmonic Orchestra, Jessye Norman (soprano), HMV 5740432

220–21 Tchaikovsky: Symphony No. 4 in F minor, Op. 36
Mariss Jansons, Oslo Philharmonic Orchestra, Chandos 8672/8

230–31 Richard Strauss: Ein Heldenleben
Bernard Haitink, Concertgebouw Orchestra, Philips 464 743-2

249 Verdi: Rigoletto, Act 3
Bonynge, LSO, Sutherland, Pavarotti, Milnes, London 414269

263 Puccini: La Bohème (Act 1)
Karajan, Berlin Philharmonic, Freni, Pavarotti, Decca 5562952

299 Dvor˘ák: "New World"' Symphony No. 9 in E minor, Op. 95
Klauss Tennstedt, Berlin Philharmonic Orchestra, HMV Classics 5721362

323 Elgar: Cello Concerto
Sir John Barbirolli, London Symphony Orchestra, Jacqueline du Pré, EMI 23849

404–05 Stravinsky: The Rite of Spring
Riccardo Chailly, The Cleveland Orchestra, (Decca 430 709-2

421 Gershwin: Rhapsody in Blue
Richard Hickox, City of London Sinfonia, Wayne Marshall, HMV 5721232

425 Copland: Appalachian Spring
Leonard Slatkin, St Louis Symphony Orchestra, HMV 572308

449 Prokofiev: Romeo and Juliet, Suite no. 2 (Op. 64b)
Koussevitzky, Boston Symphony Orchestra, BMG/RCA Victor 61657

454–55 Shostakovich: Symphony No. 10
Herbert von Karajan, Berlin Philharmonic Orchestra, Deutsche Grammophon 429716-2

465 Tippett: Child of our Time (Part 3 only)
Sir Colin Davies, BBC Symphony Orchestra, Jessye Norman, John Shirley Quirk, Decca 4734212